D0765413

BIBLE WISDOM FOR MODERN LIVING

ARRANGED BY SUBJECT

BIBLE WISDOM FOR MODERN LIVING

ARRANGED BY SUBJECT

Edited by

DAVID BROWN

Chaplain, Oriel College, Oxford

SIMON AND SCHUSTER
New York

Published by Simon and Schuster
A Division of Simon & Schuster, Inc.
Simon & Schuster Building
Rockefeller Center
1230 Avenue of the Americas
New York, New York 10020

Published in Great Britain as *The Dictionary of Life*
by Sidgwick & Jackson

Typeset by Florencetype Limited, Bristol
Printed and bound in Great Britain by
Richard Clay (The Chaucer Press)
Bungay, Suffolk

1 3 5 7 9 10 8 6 4 2

Library of Congress Cataloging in Publication Data

Bible. English. Revised Standard. Selections. 1986.
Bible Wisdom for Modern Living.

1. Bible—Indexes. I. Brown, David, date.
BS391.2.B75 1986   220.5′2   86−11922
ISBN 0 − 671 − 62545 − 4

PUBLISHER'S NOTE

This new concept in biblical reference books lists quotations
from the Revised Standard Version of the Bible under headings
of contemporary interest. The headings are arranged in
alphabetical order and have been chosen because they represent
topics of current concern, whether political, commercial,
domestic, personal or spiritual. The quotations have been
chosen for the directness with which they speak to the modern
reader, and those have been favoured which describe universal
truths or which advise on different aspects of the human
condition, telling us how we should behave.

ACKNOWLEDGEMENTS

The publishers would like to thank the Editor,
the Reverend Dr David Brown, Chaplain of Oriel College, Oxford.
In addition, they are also grateful to Deirdre Watts,
Nicholas Jones, Jane Rogers and Ian Henderson for their help
with this volume.

Yet among the mature we do impart wisdom, although it is not a wisdom of this age or of the rulers of this age, who are doomed to pass away. But we impart a secret and hidden wisdom of God, which God decreed before the ages for our glorification. None of the rulers of this age understood this; for if they had, they would not have crucified the Lord of glory.

1 Corinthians 2.6—8

A

Abandonment

The Lord our God be with us, as he was
with our fathers; may he not leave us or
forsake us.

1 Kings 8.57

My God, my God, why hast thou forsaken
  me?
Why art thou so far from helping me, from
  the words of my groaning?
O my God, I cry by day, but thou dost not
  answer;
and by night, but find no rest.

Psalms 22.1

Ability

See also **Aptitude, Gifts, Strength, Talent**

Every man shall give as he is able, according to the blessing of the Lord your God
which he has given you.

Deuteronomy 16.17

Yea, by thee I can crush a troop;
  and by my God I can leap over a wall.

Psalms 18.29

For truly, I say to you, if you have faith as
a grain of mustard seed, you will say to this
mountain, 'Move from here to there,' and it
will move; and nothing will be impossible to
you.

Matthew 17.20

To one he gave five talents, to another
two, to another one, to each according to
his ability.

Matthew 25.15

All things are possible to him who
believes.

Mark 9.23

And the Lord said, 'If you had faith as a
grain of mustard seed, you could say to this
sycamine tree, "Be rooted up, and be
planted in the sea," and it would obey you.'

Luke 17.6

Having gifts that differ according to the
grace given to us, let us use them.

Romans 12.6

Not that we are competent of ourselves to
claim anything as coming from us; our
competence is from God.

2 Corinthians 3.5

I can do all things in him who strengthens
me.

Philippians 4.13

As each has received a gift, employ it for
one another, as good stewards of God's
varied grace.

1 Peter 4.10

Abortion

When men strive together, and hurt a
woman with child, so that there is a mis-
carriage, and yet no harm follows, the one
who hurt her shall be fined, according as
the woman's husband shall lay upon him;
and he shall pay as the judges determine.

Exodus 21.22

I call heaven and earth to witness against
you this day, that I have set before you life
and death, blessing and curse; therefore
choose life, that you and your descendants
may live, loving the Lord your God.

Deuteronomy 30.19

Before I formed you in the womb I knew
  you,
and before you were born I consecrated you;
I appointed you a prophet to the nations.

Jeremiah 1.5

Let the children come to me, do not hinder them; for to such belongs the kingdom of God.

Mark 10.14

Abstinence

See also **Celibacy, Fasting, Moderation, Temperance**

Let us then cast off the works of darkness and put on the armour of light.

Romans 13.12

Hold fast what is good, abstain from every form of evil.

1 Thessalonians 5.21—22

Beloved, I beseech you as aliens and exiles to abstain from the passions of the flesh that wage war against your soul.

1 Peter 2.11

Absurdity (of Life)

Surely every man stands as a mere breath!
Surely man goes about as a shadow!
Surely for naught are they in turmoil;
   man heaps up, and knows not who will
      gather!

Psalms 39.5—6

Vanity of vanities, says the Preacher,
   vanity of vanities! All is vanity.

Ecclesiastes 1.2

Again I saw that under the sun the race is not to the swift, nor the battle to the strong, nor bread to the wise, nor riches to the intelligent, nor favour to the men of skill; but time and chance happen to them all.

Ecclesiastes 9.11

The creation was subjected to futility, not of its own will but by the will of him who subjected it in hope; because the creation itself will be set free from its bondage to decay and obtain the glorious liberty of the children of God.

Romans 8.20—21

Abuse

See also **Gossip, Insult, Slander**

Blessed are you when men revile you and persecute you and utter all kinds of evil against you falsely on my account.

Matthew 5.11

He who speaks evil of father or mother, let him surely die.

Matthew 15.4

You shall not speak evil of a ruler of your people.

Acts 23.5

The reproaches of those who reproached thee fell on me.

Romans 15.3

Let all bitterness and wrath and anger and clamour and slander be put away from you, with all malice, and be kind to one another.

Ephesians 4.31—32

But now put them all away: anger, wrath, malice, slander, and foul talk from your mouth.

Colossians 3.8

Do not return evil for evil or reviling for reviling.

1 Peter 3.9

And keep your conscience clear, so that, when you are abused, those who revile your good behaviour in Christ may be put to shame.

1 Peter 3.16

If you are reproached for the name of Christ, you are blessed.

1 Peter 4.14

Academe

See also **Education, Knowledge, Learning, Wisdom**

The price of wisdom is above pearls.

Job 28.18

Apply your mind to instruction
and your ear to words of knowledge.

Proverbs 23.12

Of making many books there is no end,
and much study is a weariness of the flesh.

Ecclesiastes 12.12

Woe to those who are wise in their own
eyes,
and shrewd in their own sight!

Isaiah 5.21

About the middle of the feast Jesus went
up into the temple and taught. The Jews
marvelled at it, saying, 'How is it that this
man has learning, when he has never
studied?'

John 7.14–15

Acceptance (of God)

See also **Calling, Discipleship, Welcome**

The beloved of the Lord . . .
dwells in safety by him;
he encompasses him all the day long.

Deuteronomy 33.12

To all who received him, who believed in
his name, he gave power to become children of God.

John 1.12

Abide in me, and I in you. As the branch
cannot bear fruit by itself, unless it abides
in the vine, neither can you, unless you
abide in me.

John 15.4

Receive the Holy Spirit.

John 20.22

If, because of one man's trespass, death
reigned through that one man, much more
will those who receive the abundance of
grace and the free gift of righteousness
reign in life through the one man Jesus
Christ.

Romans 5.17

Let the word of Christ dwell in you richly.

Colossians 3.16

Put away all filthiness and rank growth of
wickedness and receive with meekness the
implanted word, which is able to save your
souls.

James 1.21

Acceptance (of Lot)

You shall not covet your neighbour's
house; you shall not covet your neighbour's
wife, or his manservant, or his maidservant,
or his ox, or his ass, or anything that is your
neighbour's.

Exodus 29.17

Better is a little with righteousness
than great revenues with injustice.

Proverbs 16.8

Do not toil to acquire wealth;
be wise enough to desist.

Proverbs 23.4

Again, I saw vanity under the sun: a
person who has no one, either son or
brother, yet there is no end to all his toil,
and his eyes are never satisfied with riches,
so that he never asks, 'For whom am I
toiling and depriving myself of pleasure?'

Ecclesiastes 4.7–8

Every man . . . to whom God has given
wealth and possessions and power to enjoy
them, and to accept his lot and find enjoyment in his toil — this is the gift of God.
For he will not much remember the days of
his life because God keeps him occupied
with joy in his heart.

Ecclesiastes 5.19–20

I am oppressed . . . but what can I say?
For he has spoken to me,
and he himself has done it.
All my sleep has fled
because of the bitterness of my soul

Isaiah 38.14–15

Therefore I tell you, do not be anxious
about your life, what you shall eat or what
you shall drink, nor about your body, what

you shall put on. Is not life more than food, and the body more than clothing?

Matthew 6.25

Be content with your wages.

Luke 3.14

There is great gain in godliness with contentment; for we brought nothing into the world, and we cannot take anything out of the world; but if we have food and clothing, with these we shall be content.

1 Timothy 6.6−8

Keep your life free from love of money, and be content with what you have; for he has said, 'I will never fail you nor forsake you.' Hence we can confidently say,
'The Lord is my helper,
I will not be afraid;
what can man do to me?'

Hebrews 13.5−6

Access (to God)

What great nation is there that has a god so near to it as the Lord our God is to us, whenever we call upon him?

Deuteronomy 4.7

Who shall ascend the hill of the Lord?
And who shall stand in his holy place?
He who has clean hands and a pure heart,
who does not lift up his soul to what is
false,
and does not swear deceitfully.

Psalms 24.3−4

Jesus said to him, 'I am the way, and the truth, and the life; no one comes to the Father, but by me.'

John 14.6

And when they arrived, they gathered the church together and declared all that God had done with them, and how he had opened a door of faith to the Gentiles.

Acts 14.27

Through him we have obtained access to this grace in which we stand, and we rejoice in our hope of sharing the glory of God.

Romans 5.2

Through him we both have access in one Spirit to the Father.

Ephesians 2.18

And you, who once were estranged and hostile in mind, doing evil deeds, he has now reconciled in his body of flesh by his death, in order to present you holy and blameless and irreproachable before him, provided that you continue in the faith, stable and steadfast, not shifting from the hope of the gospel which you heard.

Colossians 1.21−23

Therefore, brethren, since we have confidence to enter the sanctuary by the blood of Jesus, by the new and living way which he opened for us through the curtain, that is, through his flesh, and since we have a great priest over the house of God, let us draw near with a true heart in full assurance of faith, with our hearts sprinkled clean from an evil conscience and our bodies washed with pure water.

Hebrews 10.19−22

Accessory

The partner of a thief hates his own life.

Proverbs 29.24

Do not be hasty in the laying on of hands, nor participate in another man's sins.

1 Timothy 5.22

Accident

See also **Misfortune**

'Today or tomorrow we will go into such and such a town and spend a year there and trade and get gain'; whereas you do not know about tomorrow. What is your life? For you are a mist that appears for a little time and then vanishes.

James 4.13−14

Accountability

See also **Judgment, Responsibility, Reward**

For God will bring every deed into judgment, with every secret thing, whether good or evil.

Ecclesiastes 12.14

I tell you, on the day of judgment men will render account for every careless word they utter.

Matthew 12.36

Obey your leaders and submit to them; for they are keeping watch over your souls, as men who will have to give account.

Hebrews 13.17

As each has received a gift, employ it for one another, as good stewards of God's varied grace.

1 Peter 4.10

Achievement

See also **Advancement, Ambition, Promotion, Success**

This book of the law shall not depart out of your mouth, but you shall meditate on it day and night, that you may be careful to do according to all that is written in it; for then you shall make your way prosperous, and then you shall have good success.

Joshua 1.8

But they who wait for the Lord shall renew
    their strength,
they shall mount up with wings like
        eagles,
they shall run and not be weary,
    they shall walk and not faint.

Isaiah 40.31

But the people who know their God shall stand firm and take action.

Daniel 11.32

For what will it profit a man, if he gains the whole world and forfeits his life?

Matthew 16.26

I have fought the good fight, I have finished the race, I have kept the faith. Henceforth there is laid up for me the crown of righteousness, which the Lord, the righteous judge, will award to me on that Day, and not only to me but also to all who have loved his appearing.

2 Timothy 4.7–8

Acknowledgement

Turn to me and be saved,
    all the ends of the earth!

Isaiah 45.22

So every one who acknowledges me before men, I also will acknowledge before my Father who is in heaven.

Matthew 10.32

Action

See also **Practicality**

Talk no more so very proudly,
    let not arrogance come from your mouth;
for the Lord is a God of knowledge,
    and by him actions are weighed.

1 Samuel 2.3

Arise and be doing! The Lord be with you!

1 Chronicles 22.16

For John came neither eating nor drinking, and they say, 'He has a demon'; the Son of man came eating and drinking, and they say, 'Behold, a glutton and a drunkard, a friend of tax collectors and sinners!' Yet wisdom is justified by her deeds.

Matthew 11.18–19

For it is not the hearers of the law who are righteous before God, but the doers of the law who will be justified.

Romans 2.13

And let us not grow weary in well-doing, for in due season we shall reap, if we do not lose heart.

Galatians 6.9

And whatever you do, in word or deed, do everything in the name of the Lord

Jesus, giving thanks to God the Father through him.

Colossians 3.17

Good deeds; these are excellent and profitable to men.

Titus 3.8

But be doers of the word, and not hearers only, deceiving yourselves. For if any one is a hearer of the word and not a doer, he is like a man who observes his natural face in a mirror; for he observes himself and goes away and at once forgets what he was like. But he who looks into the perfect law, the law of liberty, and perseveres, being no hearer that forgets but a doer that acts, he shall be blessed in his doing.

James 1.22–25

Religion that is pure and undefiled before God and the Father is this: to visit orphans and widows in their affliction, and to keep oneself unstained from the world.

James 1.27

So faith by itself, if it has no works, is dead.

James 2.17

You see that a man is justified by works and not by faith alone.

James 2.24

Little children, let us not love in word or speech but in deed and in truth.

1 John 3.18

Adaptability

For everything there is a season, and a time for every matter under heaven:
  a time to be born, and a time to die;
  a time to plant, and a time to pluck up
    what is planted;
  a time to kill, and a time to heal;
  a time to break down, and a time to build
    up;
  a time to weep, and a time to laugh;
  a time to mourn, and a time to dance;
  a time to cast away stones, and a time to
    gather stones together;
  a time to embrace, and a time to refrain
    from embracing;
  a time to seek, and a time to lose;
  a time to keep, and a time to cast away;
  a time to rend, and a time to sew;
  a time to keep silence, and a time to
    speak;
  a time to love, and a time to hate;
  a time for war, and a time for peace.

Ecclesiastes 3.1–8

Rejoice with those who rejoice, weep with those who weep. Live in harmony with one another.

Romans 12.15–16

If possible, so far as it depends upon you, live peaceably with all.

Romans 12.18

I have become all things to all men, that I might by all means save some.

1 Corinthians 9.22

I know how to be abased, and I know how to abound; in any and all circumstances I have learned the secret of facing plenty and hunger, abundance and want. I can do all things in him who strengthens me.

Philippians 4.12–13

Addiction

See also **Alcohol, Lust**

Be not among winebibbers . . .
for the drunkard and the glutton will
come to poverty.

Proverbs 23.20–21

If you have found honey, eat only enough
  for you,
  lest you be sated with it and vomit it.

Proverbs 25.16

Therefore God gave them up in the lusts of their hearts to impurity, to the dishonouring of their bodies among themselves, because they exchanged the truth about God for a lie and worshipped and served the creature rather than the Creator, who is blessed for ever!

Romans 1.24–25

I consider that the sufferings of this present time are not worth comparing with the glory that is to be revealed to us. For the creation waits with eager longing for the revealing of the sons of God; for the creation was subjected to futility, not of its own will but by the will of him who subjected it in hope; because the creation itself will be set free from its bondage to decay and obtain the glorious liberty of the children of God. We know that the whole creation has been groaning in travail together until now; and not only the creation, but we ourselves, who have the first fruits of the Spirit, groan inwardly as we wait for adoption as sons, the redemption of our bodies. For in this hope we were saved. Now hope that is seen is not hope. For who hopes for what he sees? But if we hope for what we do not see, we wait for it with patience.

Romans 8.18−25

No temptation has overtaken you that is not common to man. God is faithful, and he will not let you be tempted beyond your strength, but with the temptation will also provide the way of escape, that you may be able to endure it.

1 Corinthians 10.13

Administration

See also **Authority, Leadership, Power**

Moreover choose able men from all the people, such as fear God, men who are trustworthy and who hate a bribe; and place such men over the people as rulers of thousands, of hundreds, of fifties, and of tens.

Exodus 18.21

When one rules justly over men,
   ruling in the fear of God,
he dawns on them like the morning light,
   like the sun shining forth upon a
      cloudless morning,
   like rain that makes grass to sprout from
      the earth.

2 Samuel 23.3−4

Thus says the Lord: Set your house in order.

Isaiah 38.1

The rulers of the Gentiles lord it over them ... It shall not be so among you ... whoever would be first among you must be your slave; even as the Son of man came not to be served but to serve, and to give his life as a ransom for many.

Matthew 20.25−28

And there are varieties of service, but the same Lord; and there are varieties of working, but it is the same God who inspires them all in every one.

1 Corinthians 12.5−6

But all things should be done decently and in order.

1 Corinthians 14.40

Adolescence

See also **Children, Youth**

Honour your father and your mother, that your days may be long in the land which the Lord your God gives you.

Exodus 20.12

How can a young man keep his way pure?
   By guarding it according to thy word.

Psalms 119.9

Rejoice, O young man, in your youth, and let your heart cheer you in the days of your youth; walk in the ways of your heart and the sight of your eyes. But know that for all these things God will bring you into judgment.
   Remove vexation from your mind, and put away pain from your body; for youth and the dawn of life are vanity.

Ecclesiastes 11.9−10

Remember also your Creator in the days of your youth, before the evil days come, and the years draw nigh, when you will say, 'I have no pleasure in them'.

Ecclesiastes 12.1

It is good for a man that he bear
   the yoke in his youth.

Lamentations 3.27

And your sons and your daughters shall
    prophesy,
    and your young men shall see visions.

Acts 2.17

Let no one despise your youth, but set the
believers an example in speech and conduct, in love, in faith, in purity.

1 Timothy 4.12

Do not rebuke an older man but exhort
him as you would a father; treat younger
men like brothers, older women like
mothers, younger women like sisters, in all
purity.

1 Timothy 5.1

Likewise urge the younger men to control
themselves.

Titus 2.6

Likewise you that are younger be subject
to the elders. Clothe yourselves, all of you,
with humility toward one another, for 'God
opposes the proud, but gives grace to the
humble.'

1 Peter 5.5

Adoration

See also **Glory, Praise, Thankfulness, Worship**

O come, let us worship and bow down,
    let us kneel before the Lord, our Maker!

Psalms 95.6

Not to us, O Lord, not to us,
    but to thy name give glory,
for the sake of thy steadfast love
    and thy faithfulness!

Psalms 115.1

Holy, holy, holy is the Lord of hosts;
    the whole earth is full of his glory.

Isaiah 6.3

Through him then let us continually offer
up a sacrifice of praise to God, that is, the
fruit of lips that acknowledge his name.

Hebrews 13.15

To the only God, our Saviour through
Jesus Christ our Lord, be glory, majesty,
dominion, and authority, before all time
and now and for ever. Amen.

Jude 25

Holy, holy, holy, is the Lord God
    Almighty,
    who was and is and is to come!

Revelation 4.8

Adornment

See also **Clothes**

In that day the Lord will take away the
finery of the anklets, the headbands, and
the crescents; the pendants, the bracelets,
and the scarfs; the headdresses, the armlets,
the sashes, the perfume boxes, and the
amulets; the signet rings and nose rings; the
festal robes, the mantles, the cloaks, and
the handbags; the garments of gauze, the
linen garments, the turbans, and the veils.
    Instead of perfume there will be
        rottenness;
        and instead of a girdle, a rope;
    and instead of well-set hair, baldness;
        and instead of a rich robe, a girding of
        sackcloth;
    instead of beauty, shame.

Isaiah 3.18−24

And when I passed by you, and saw you
weltering in your blood, I said to you in
your blood, 'Live, and grow up like a plant
of the field.' And you grew up and became
tall and arrived at full maidenhood; your
breasts were formed, and your hair had
grown; yet you were naked and bare.
    When I passed by you again and looked
upon you, behold, you were at the age for
love; and I spread my skirt over you, and
covered your nakedness: yea, I plighted my
troth to you and entered into a covenant
with you, says the Lord God, and you
became mine. Then I bathed you with
water and washed off your blood from you,
and anointed you with oil. I clothed you
also with embroidered cloth and shod you
with leather, I swathed you in fine linen and

covered you with silk. And I decked you with ornaments, and put bracelets on your arms, and a chain on your neck.

Ezekiel 16.6—11

Women should adorn themselves modestly and sensibly in seemly apparel, not with braided hair or gold or pearls or costly attire but by good deeds, as befits women who profess religion.

1 Timothy 2.9—10

Let not yours be the outward adorning with braiding of hair, decoration of gold, and wearing of fine clothing, but let it be the hidden person of the heart with the imperishable jewel of a gentle and quiet spirit, which in God's sight is very precious.

1 Peter 3.3—4

Adultery

See also **Fornication, Lust**

You shall not commit adultery.

Exodus 20.14

And you shall not lie carnally with your neighbour's wife, and defile yourself with her.

Leviticus 18.20

If a man commits adultery with the wife of his neighbour, both the adulterer and the adulteress shall be put to death.

Leviticus 20.10

If there is a betrothed virgin, and a man meets her in the city and lies with her, then you shall bring them both out to the gate of that city, and you shall stone them to death with stones, the young woman because she did not cry for help though she was in the city, and the man because he violated his neighbour's wife; so you shall purge the evil from the midst of you.

Deuteronomy 22.23—24

The eye of the adulterer also waits for the twilight,
  saying, 'No eye will see me';
  and he disguises his face.

In the dark they dig through houses;
  by day they shut themselves up;
  they do not know the light.
For deep darkness is morning to all of them;
  for they are friends with the terrors of deep darkness.

Job 24.15—17

For the lips of a loose woman drip honey,
  and her speech is smoother than oil;
but in the end she is bitter as wormwood,
  sharp as a two-edged sword.

Proverbs 5.3—4

For a harlot may be hired for a loaf of bread,
  but an adulteress stalks a man's very life.

Proverbs 6.26

He who commits adultery has no sense;
  he who does it destroys himself.
Wounds and dishonour will he get,
  and his disgrace will not be wiped away.

Proverbs 6.32—33

This is the way of an adulteress:
  she eats, and wipes her mouth,
  and says, 'I have done no wrong.'

Proverbs 30.20

Woe to those who devise wickedness
  and work evil upon their beds!

Micah 2.1

And this again you do. You cover the Lord's altar with tears, with weeping and groaning because he no longer regards the offering or accepts it with favour at your hand. You ask, 'Why does he not?' Because the Lord was witness to the covenant between you and the wife of your youth, to whom you have been faithless, though she is your companion and your wife by covenant. Has not the one God made and sustained for us the spirit of life? And what does he desire? Godly offspring. So take heed to yourselves, and let none be faithless to the wife of his youth.

Malachi 2.13—15

But I say to you that every one who looks at a woman lustfully has already committed adultery with her in his heart.

Matthew 5.28

Jesus . . . said to her, 'Woman, where are they? Has no one condemned you?' . . . 'Neither do I condemn you; go, and do not sin again.'

John 8.10–11

Let marriage be held in honour among all, and let the marriage bed be undefiled; for God will judge the immoral and adulterous.

Hebrews 13.4

I gave her time to repent, but she refuses to repent of her immorality. Behold, I will throw her on a sickbed, and those who commit adultery with her I will throw into great tribulation, unless they repent of her doings; and I will strike her children dead. And all the churches shall know that I am he who searches mind and heart, and I will give to each of you as your works deserve.

Revelation 2.21–23

Advancement

See also **Promotion**

Therefore you shall keep his statutes and his commandments, which I command you this day, that it may go well with you, and with your children after you, and that you may prolong your days in the land which the Lord your God gives you for ever.

Deuteronomy 4.40

For not from the east or from the west
  and not from the wilderness comes lifting
    up;
but it is God who executes judgment,
  putting down one and lifting up another.

Psalms 75.6–7

Thus says the Lord,
  your Redeemer, the Holy One of Israel:
'I am the Lord your God,
  who teaches you to profit,
  who leads you in the way you should go.'

Isaiah 48.17

But when you are invited, go and sit in the lowest place, so that when your host comes he may say to you, 'Friend, go up higher';

then you will be honoured in the presence of all who sit at table with you. For every one who exalts himself will be humbled, and he who humbles himself will be exalted.

Luke 14.10–11

Train yourself in godliness; for while bodily training is of some value, godliness is of value in every way, as it holds promise for the present life and also for the life to come.

1 Timothy 4.7–8

Adventure

When you pass through the waters I will
    be with you;
  and through the rivers, they shall not
    overwhelm you;
when you walk through fire you shall not be
    burned,
  and the flame shall not consume you.
For I am the Lord your God,
  the Holy One of Israel, your Saviour.

Isaiah 43.2–3

Adversity

See also **Affliction, Suffering, Trouble**

Behold, happy is the man whom God
    reproves;
  therefore despise not the chastening of
    the Almighty.
For he wounds, but he binds up;
  he smites, but his hands heal.

Job 5.17–18

The Lord is a stronghold for the
    oppressed,
  a stronghold in times of trouble.
And those who know thy name put their
    trust in thee,
  for thou, O Lord, hast not forsaken those
    who seek thee.

Psalms 9.9–10

Even though I walk through the valley of
    the shadow of death,
  I fear no evil;
for thou are with me;
  thy rod and thy staff,
  they comfort me.

Psalms 23.4

For his anger is but for a moment,
  and his favour is for a lifetime.
Weeping may tarry for the night,
  but joy comes with the morning.
Psalms 30.5

Many are the afflictions of the righteous;
  but the Lord delivers him out of them all.
He keeps all his bones;
  not one of them is broken.
Psalms 34.19−20

God is our refuge and strength,
  a very present help in trouble.
Psalms 46.1

And call upon me in the day of trouble;
  I will deliver you, and you shall glorify
    me.
Psalms 50.15

Cast your burden on the Lord,
  and he will sustain you;
he will never permit
  the righteous to be moved.
Psalms 55.22

It is good for me that I was afflicted,
  that I might learn thy statutes.
Psalms 119.71

He that goes forth weeping,
  bearing the seed for sowing,
shall come home with shouts of joy,
  bringing his sheaves with him.
Psalms 126.6

A friend loves at all times,
  and a brother is born for adversity.
Proverbs 17.17

If you faint in the day of adversity,
  your strength is small.
Proverbs 24.10

Sorrow is better than laughter,
  for by sadness of countenance the heart is
    made glad.
Ecclesiastes 7.3

In the day of prosperity be joyful, and in
the day of adversity consider; God has
made the one as well as the other, so that
man may not find out anything that will be
after him.
Ecclesiastes 7.14

And though the Lord give you the bread
of adversity and the water of affliction, yet
your Teacher will not hide himself any
more, but your eyes shall see your Teacher.
Isaiah 30.20

A bruised reed he will not break,
  and a dimly burning wick he will not
    quench;
he will faithfully bring forth justice.
Isaiah 42.3

Behold, I have refined you, but not like
  silver;
  I have tried you in the furnace of
    affliction.
Isaiah 48.10

Are not two sparrows sold for a penny?
And not one of them will fall to the ground
without your Father's will. But even the
hairs of your head are all numbered. Fear
not, therefore; you are of more value than
many sparrows.
Matthew 10.29−31

In the world you have tribulation; but be of
good cheer, I have overcome the world.
John 16.33

More than that, we rejoice in our sufferings, knowing that suffering produces
endurance, and endurance produces character, and character produces hope.
Romans 5.3−4

Who shall separate us from the love of
Christ? Shall tribulation, or distress, or
persecution, or famine, or nakedness, or
peril, or sword? As it is written,
  'For thy sake we are being killed all the
    day long;
  we are regarded as sheep to be
    slaughtered.'
No, in all these things we are more than
conquerors through him who loved us. For
I am sure that neither death, nor life, nor
angels, nor principalities, nor things present, nor things to come, nor powers, nor

height, nor depth, nor anything else in all creation, will be able to separate us from the love of God in Christ Jesus our Lord.

Romans 8.35–39

Rejoice in your hope, be patient in tribulation, be constant in prayer.

Romans 12.12

Blessed be the God and Father of our Lord Jesus Christ, the Father of mercies and God of all comfort, who comforts us in all our affliction, so that we may be able to comfort those who are in any affliction, with the comfort with which we ourselves are comforted by God.

2 Corinthians 1.3–4

We are afflicted in every way, but not crushed; perplexed, but not driven to despair; persecuted, but not forsaken; struck down, but not destroyed; always carrying in the body the death of Jesus, so that the life of Jesus may also be manifested in our bodies.

2 Corinthians 4.8–10

I will all the more gladly boast of my weaknesses, that the power of Christ may rest upon me. For the sake of Christ, then, I am content with weaknesses, insults, hardships, persecutions, and calamities; for when I am weak, then I am strong.

2 Corinthians 12.9–10

Bear one another's burdens, and so fulfil the law of Christ.

Galatians 6.2

Since indeed God deems it just to repay with affliction those who afflict you, and to grant rest with us to you who are afflicted, when the Lord Jesus is revealed from heaven with his mighty angels in flaming fire.

2 Thessalonians 1.6–7

Share in suffering as a good soldier of Christ Jesus.

2 Timothy 2.3

Remember those who are in prison, as though in prison with them; and those who are ill-treated, since you also are in the body.

Hebrews 13.3

Count it all joy, my brethren, when you meet various trials, for you know that the testing of your faith produces steadfastness.

James 1.2–3

In this you rejoice, though now for a little while you may have to suffer various trials, so that the genuineness of your faith, more precious than gold which though perishable is tested by fire, may redound to praise and glory and honour at the revelation of Jesus Christ.

1 Peter 1.6–7

Do not be surprised at the fiery ordeal which comes upon you . . . But rejoice in so far as you share Christ's sufferings, that you may also rejoice and be glad when his glory is revealed.

1 Peter 4.12–13

Resist him, firm in your faith, knowing that the same experience of suffering is required of your brotherhood throughout the world.

1 Peter 5.9

Advice

The way of a fool is right in his own eyes, but a wise man listens to advice.

Proverbs 12.15

Without counsel plans go wrong, but with many advisers they succeed.

Proverbs 15.22

'Woe to the rebellious children,' says the Lord,
'who carry out a plan, but not mine; and who make a league, but not of my spirit.'

Isaiah 30.

Therefore hear the plan which the Lord has made.

Jeremiah 49.2

Aestheticism

See also **Beauty**

He has made everything beautiful.

Ecclesiastes 3.11

Whatever is lovely, whatever is gracious, if there is any excellence, if there is anything worthy of praise, think about these things.

Philippians 4.8

Affectation

See also **Hypocrisy, Pretension**

The Lord said:
Because the daughters of Zion are
    haughty
    and walk with outstretched necks,
    glancing wantonly with their eyes,
mincing along as they go,
    tinkling with their feet;
the Lord will smite with a scab
    the heads of the daughters of Zion,
    and the Lord will lay bare their secret
        parts.

Isaiah 3.16—17

The pride of your heart has deceived you,
    you who live in the clefts of the rock,
    whose dwelling is high,
who say in your heart,
    'Who will bring me down to the ground?'
Though you soar aloft like the eagle,
    though your nest is set among the stars,
    thence I will bring you down, says the
        Lord.

Obadiah 3—4

And when you fast, do not look dismal, like the hypocrites, for they disfigure their faces that their fasting may be seen by men. Truly, I say to you, they have received their reward. But when you fast, anoint your head and wash your face, that your fasting may not be seen by men but by your Father who is in secret; and your Father who sees in secret will reward you.

Matthew 6.16—18

Affliction

See also **Adversity, Suffering, Trouble**

For affliction does not come from the dust,
    nor does trouble sprout from the ground;
but man is born to trouble
    as the sparks fly upward.

Job 5.6—7

Many are the afflictions of the righteous;
    but the Lord delivers him out of them all.

Psalms 34.19

Thus says your Lord, the Lord,
    your God who pleads the cause of his
        people:
'Behold, I have taken from your hand
    the cup of staggering;
the bowl of my wrath
    you shall drink no more;
and I will put it into the hand of your
        tormentors.'

Isaiah 51.22—23

For a brief moment I forsook you,
    but with great compassion I will gather
        you.

Isaiah 54.7

For the Lord will not
    cast off for ever,
but, though he cause grief, he will have
        compassion
    according to the abundance of his
        steadfast love;
for he does not willingly afflict
    or grieve the sons of men.

Lamentations 3.31—33

For this slight momentary affliction is preparing for us an eternal weight of glory beyond all comparison, because we look not to the things that are seen but to the things that are unseen; for the things that are seen are transient, but the things that are unseen are eternal.

2 Corinthians 4.17—18

MONKS OF MT. TABOR

Affluence

See also **Money, Prosperity, Riches, Wealth**

And you shall eat and be full, and you shall bless the Lord your God for the good land he has given you.

Deuteronomy 8.10

Take heed . . . lest, when you have eaten and are full, and have built goodly houses and live in them, and when your herds and flocks multiply, and your silver and gold is multiplied, and all that you have is multiplied, then your heart be lifted up, and you forget the Lord your God.

Deuteronomy 8.11—14

If you keep the commandments of the Lord your God, and walk in his ways . . . the Lord will make you abound in prosperity, in the fruit of your body, and in the fruit of your cattle, and in the fruit of your ground, within the land which the Lord swore to your fathers to give you. The Lord will open to you his good treasury the heavens, to give the rain of your land in its season and to bless all the work of your hands; and you shall lend to many nations, but you shall not borrow. And the Lord will make you the head, and not the tail; and you shall tend upward only, and not downward; if you obey the commandments of the Lord your God.

Deuteronomy 28.9—13

Honour the Lord with your substance
and with the first fruits of all your
produce;
then your barns will be filled with plenty,
and your vats will be bursting with wine.

Proverbs 3.9—10

A slack hand causes poverty,
but the hand of the diligent makes rich.

Proverbs 10.4

The righteous has enough to satisfy his
appetite,
but the belly of the wicked suffers want.

Proverbs 13.25

Behold, what I have seen to be good and to be fitting is to eat and drink and find enjoyment in all the toil with which one toils under the sun the few days of his life which God has given him, for this is his lot. Every man also to whom God has given wealth and possessions and power to enjoy them, and to accept his lot and find enjoyment in his toil — this is the gift of God.

Ecclesiastes 5.18—19

The more they increased,
the more they sinned against me;
I will change their glory into shame.
They feed on the sin of my people;
they are greedy for their iniquity.
And it shall be like people, like priest;
I will punish them for their ways,
and requite them for their deeds.
They shall eat, but not be satisfied;
they shall play the harlot, but not
multiply;
because they have forsaken the Lord to
cherish harlotry.

Hosea 4.7—10

If you would be perfect, go, sell what you possess and give to the poor, and you will have treasure in heaven.

Matthew 19.21

Afraid

See **Fear**

Afterlife

See **Heaven, Hell, Resurrection**

Age

See also **Maturity**

You shall rise up before the hoary head, and honour the face of an old man, and you shall fear your God.

Leviticus 19.32

I said, 'Let days speak,
and many years teach wisdom.'
But it is the spirit in a man,
the breath of the Almighty,
that makes him understand.

It is not the old that are wise,
nor the aged that understand what is
right.

Job 32.7–9

Do not cast me off in the time of old age;
forsake me not when my strength is
spent.

Psalms 71.9

The years of our life are threescore and
ten,
or even by reason of strength fourscore;
yet their span is but toil and trouble;
they are soon gone, and we fly away.

Psalms 90.10

So teach us to number our days
that we may get a heart of wisdom.

Psalms 90.12

The righteous flourish like the palm tree,
and grow like a cedar in Lebanon.
They are planted in the house of the Lord,
they flourish in the courts of our God.
They still bring forth fruit in old age,
they are ever full of sap and green.

Psalms 92.12–14

My son, do not forget my teaching,
but let your heart keep my
commandments;
for length of days and years of life
and abundant welfare will they give you.

Proverbs 3.1–2

A hoary head is a crown of glory;
it is gained in a righteous life.

Proverbs 16.31

The glory of young men is their strength,
but the beauty of old men is their grey
hair.

Proverbs 20.29

Hearken to your father who begot you,
and do not despise your mother when she
is old.

Proverbs 23.22

For if a man lives many years, let him
rejoice in them all; but let him remember
that the days of darkness will be many.

Ecclesiastes 11.8

Remember also your Creator in the days
of your youth, before the evil days come,
and the years draw nigh, when you will say,
'I have no pleasure in them'; before the sun
and the light and the moon and the stars
are darkened and the clouds return after
the rain; in the day when the keepers
of the house tremble, and the strong men
are bent, and the grinders cease because
they are few, and those that look through
the windows are dimmed, and the doors
on the street are shut; when the sound of
the grinding is low, and one rises up at the
voice of a bird, and all the daughters of
song are brought low; they are afraid also
of what is high, and terrors are in the
way; the almond tree blossoms, the grass-
hopper drags itself along and desire fails;
because man goes to his eternal home, and
the mourners go about the streets; before
the silver cord is snapped, or the golden
bowl is broken, or the pitcher is broken at
the fountain, or the wheel broken at the
cistern, and the dust returns to the earth as
it was, and the spirit returns to God who
gave it. Vanity of vanities, says the Preacher; all is vanity.

Ecclesiastes 12.1–8

Even to your old age I am He,
and to grey hairs I will carry you.
I have made, and I will bear;
I will carry and will save.

Isaiah 46.4

And your old men shall dream dreams.

Acts 2.17

Do not rebuke an older man but exhort
him as you would a father.

1 Timothy 5.1

But as for you, teach what befits sound
doctrine. Bid the older men be temperate,
serious, sensible, sound in faith, in love,
and in steadfastness. Bid the older women
likewise to be reverent in behaviour, not to
be slanderers or slaves to drink.

Titus 2.1–3

So I exhort the elders among you, as a
fellow elder and a witness of the sufferings
of Christ as well as a partaker in the glory
that is to be revealed. Tend the flock of
God that is your charge, not by constraint

but willingly, not for shameful gain but eagerly, not as domineering over those in your charge but being examples to the flock. And when the chief Shepherd is manifested you will obtain the unfading crown of glory.

1 Peter 5.1–4

Ages

To him be glory in the church and in Christ Jesus to all generations, for ever and ever. Amen.

Ephesians 3.21

Aggravation

See also **Anger**

You shall not wrong a stranger or oppress him.

Exodus 22.21

Let us have no self-conceit, no provoking of one another, no envy of one another.

Galatians 5.26

See to it that no one fail to obtain the grace of God; that no 'root of bitterness' spring up and cause trouble.

Hebrews 12.15

Agnosticism

See also **Atheism, Doubt, Scepticism**

He who is not with me is against me.

Matthew 12.30

Help my unbelief!

Mark 9.25

He that is not against us is for us.

Mark 9.40

But he who has doubts is condemned, if he eats, because he does not act from faith; for whatever does not proceed from faith is sin.

Romans 14.23

Do not be mismated with unbelievers. For what partnership have righteousness and iniquity? Or what fellowship has light with darkness? What accord has Christ with Be'lial? Or what has a believer in common with an unbeliever?

2 Corinthians 6.14–15

Agony

See **Anguish, Distress, Suffering**

Aimlessness

See also **Confusion**

Let them be turned back and confounded
   who devise evil against me!
Let them be like chaff before the wind,
   with the angel of the Lord driving them
      on!

Psalms 35.4–5

I have gone astray like a lost sheep; seek thy servant.

Psalms 119.176

A man who wanders from the way of
      understanding
will rest in the assembly of the dead.

Proverbs 21.16

The city was filled with the confusion; and they rushed together into the theatre . . . some cried one thing, some another; For . . . in confusion . . . most of them did not know why they had come together.

Acts 19.29,32

Besides that, they [young widows] learn to be idlers, gadding about from house to house, and not only idlers but gossips and busybodies, saying what they should not.

1 Timothy 5.13

For he who doubts is like a wave of the sea that is driven and tossed by the wind. For that person must not suppose that a double-minded man, unstable in all his ways, will receive anything from the Lord.

James 1.6–8

Alcohol

See also **Drunkenness, Temperance, Wine**

You have not eaten bread, and you have not drunk wine or strong drink; that you may know that I am the Lord your God.

Deuteronomy 29.6

Thou dost cause the grass to grow for the
    cattle,
    and plants for man to cultivate,
that he may bring forth food from the
    earth,
    and wine to gladden the heart of man,
oil to make his face shine,
    and bread to strengthen man's heart.

Psalms 104.14–15

Wine is a mocker, strong drink a brawler;
    and whoever is led astray by it is not
    wise.

Proverbs 20.1

Hear, my son, and be wise,
    and direct your mind in the way.
Be not among winebibbers,
    or among gluttonous eaters of meat;
for the drunkard and the glutton will come
    to poverty,
    and drowsiness will clothe a man with
    rags.

Proverbs 23.19–21

Who has woe? Who has sorrow?
    Who has strife? Who has complaining?
Who has wounds without cause?
    Who has redness of eyes?
Those who tarry long over wine,
    those who go to try mixed wine.
Do not look at wine when it is red,
    when it sparkles in the cup
    and goes down smoothly.
At the last it bites like a serpent,
    and stings like an adder.
Your eyes will see strange things,
    and your mind utter perverse things.
You will be like one who lies down in the
    midst of the sea,
    like one who lies on the top of a mast.
'They struck me,' you will say,
    'but I was not hurt;
    they beat me, but I did not feel it.
When shall I awake?
    I will seek another drink.'

Proverbs 23.29–35

Give strong drink to him who is perishing,
    and wine to those in bitter distress;
let them drink and forget their poverty,
    and remember their misery no more.

Proverbs 31.6–7

And I commend enjoyment, for man has
no good thing under the sun but to eat, and
drink, and enjoy himself.

Ecclesiastes 8.15

Go, eat your bread with enjoyment, and
drink your wine with a merry heart.

Ecclesiastes 9.7

Woe to those who rise early in the
    morning,
    that they may run after strong drink,
who tarry late into the evening
             till wine inflames them!

Isaiah 5.11

Woe to those who are heroes at drinking
    wine,
    and valiant men in mixing strong drink.

Isaiah 5.22

Woe to the proud crown of the drunkards
    of E'phraim,
    and to the fading flower of its glorious
    beauty,
which is on the head of the rich valley of
    those overcome with wine!

Isaiah 28.1

These also reel with wine
    and stagger with strong drink;
the priest and the prophet reel with strong
    drink,
    they are confused with wine,
    they stagger with strong drink;
they err in vision,
    they stumble in giving judgment.
For all tables are full of vomit,
    no place is without filthiness.

Isaiah 28.7–8

Wine and new wine
    take away the understanding.

Hosea 4.11

The Son of man came eating and drinking,
and they say, 'Behold, a glutton and a
drunkard, a friend of tax collectors and
sinners!' Yet wisdom is justified by her
deeds.

Matthew 11.18–19

Let us conduct ourselves becomingly as in the day, not in revelling and drunkenness, not in debauchery and licentiousness.

Romans 13.13

And do not get drunk with wine, for that is debauchery; but be filled with the Spirit.

Ephesians 5.18

For those who sleep sleep at night, and those who get drunk are drunk at night. But, since we belong to the day, let us be sober.

1 Thessalonians 5.7—8

No longer drink only water, but use a little wine for the sake of your stomach and your frequent ailments.

1 Timothy 5.23

Alertness

My soul waits for the Lord
  more than watchmen for the morning.

Psalms 130.6

For in vain is a net spread
  in the sight of any bird.

Proverbs 1.17

Happy is the man who listens to me,
  watching daily at my gates,
  waiting beside my doors.

Proverbs 8.34

Watch therefore, for you do not know on what day your Lord is coming.

Matthew 24.42

Watch and pray that you may not enter into temptation; the spirit indeed is willing, but the flesh is weak.

Matthew 26.41

Take heed, watch; for you do not know when the time will come.

Mark 13.33

Blessed are those servants whom the master finds awake when he comes.

Luke 12.37

But take heed to yourselves lest your hearts be weighed down with dissipation and drunkenness and cares of this life, and that day come upon you suddenly like a snare; for it will come upon all who dwell upon the face of the whole earth. But watch at all times, praying that you may have strength to escape all these things that will take place, and to stand before the Son of man.

Luke 21.34—36

Besides this you know what hour it is, how it is full time now for you to wake from sleep. For salvation is nearer to us now than when we first believed.

Romans 13.11

Be watchful, stand firm in your faith, be courageous, be strong.

1 Corinthians 16.13

Pray at all times in the Spirit, with all prayer and supplication. To that end keep alert with all perseverance, making supplication for all the saints.

Ephesians 6.18

As for you, always be steady, endure suffering, do the work of an evangelist, fulfil your ministry.

2 Timothy 4.5

Remind them to be submissive to rulers and authorities, to be obedient, to be ready for any honest work.

Titus 3.1

Be sober, be watchful. Your adversary the devil prowls around like a roaring lion.

1 Peter 5.8

Awake, and strengthen what remains and is on the point of death, for I have not found your works perfect in the sight of my God. Remember then what you received and heard; keep that, and repent. If you will not awake, I will come like a thief, and you will not know at what hour I will come upon you.

Revelation 3.2—3

Alienation

See **Exile**

Alms

See also **Charity, Generosity**

And if your brother becomes poor, and cannot maintain himself with you, you shall maintain him; as a stranger and a sojourner he shall live with you.

Leviticus 25.35

He who gives to the poor will not want,
but he who hides his eyes will get many a curse.

Proverbs 28.27

Beware of practising your piety before men in order to be seen by them; for then you will have no reward from your Father who is in heaven.

Thus, when you give alms, sound no trumpet before you, as the hypocrites do in the synagogues and in the streets, that they may be praised by men. Truly, I say to you, they have received their reward. But when you give alms, do not let your left hand know what your right hand is doing, so that your alms may be in secret; and your Father who sees in secret will reward you.

Matthew 6.1–4

But give for alms those things which are within; and behold, everything is clean for you.

Luke 11.41

Sell your possessions, and give alms; provide yourselves with purses that do not grow old, with a treasure in the heavens that does not fail, where no thief approaches and no moth destroys. For where your treasure is, there will your heart be also.

Luke 12.33–34

Your prayers and your alms have ascended as a memorial before God.

Acts 10.4

If I give away all I have, and if I deliver my body to be burned, but have not love, I gain nothing.

1 Corinthians 13.3

Alone

See **Loneliness, Solitude**

Altruism

See also **Goodness, Usefulness**

Love the sojourner therefore; for you were sojourners in the land of Egypt.

Deuteronomy 10.19

And the Lord restored the fortunes of Job, when he had prayed for his friends.

Job 42.10

Give to him who begs from you, and do not refuse him who would borrow from you.

Matthew 5.42

You have heard that it was said, 'You shall love your neighbour and hate your enemy.' But I say to you, Love your enemies and pray for those who persecute you.

Matthew 5.43 (Leviticus 19.18)

So whatever you wish that men would do to you, do so to them.

Matthew 7.12

But I say to you that hear, Love your enemies, do good to those who hate you, bless those who curse you, pray for those who abuse you.

Luke 6.27–28

But love your enemies, and do good, and lend, expecting nothing in return.

Luke 6.35

We who are strong ought to bear with the failings of the weak, and not to please ourselves; let each of us please his neighbour for his good, to edify him.

Romans 15.1–2

Let no one seek his own good, but the good of his neighbour.

1 Corinthians 10.24

Give no offence to Jews or to Greeks or to the church of God, just as I try to please all men in everything I do, not seeking my own advantage, but that of many, that they may be saved. Be imitators of me, as I am of Christ.

1 Corinthians 10.32−11.1

Bear one another's burdens.

Galatians 6.2

So then, as we have opportunity, let us do good to all men, and especially to those who are of the household of faith.

Galatians 6.10

Ambition

See also **Achievement, Success**

'Come, let us build ourselves a city, and a tower with its top in the heavens, and let us make a name for ourselves, lest we be scattered abroad upon the face of the whole earth' . . . So the Lord scattered them abroad from there over the face of all the earth.

Genesis 11.4,8−9

A man's mind plans his way,
  but the Lord directs his steps.

Proverbs 16.9

A faithful man will abound with blessings,
  but he who hastens to be rich will not go
    unpunished.

Proverbs 28.20

Therefore thus says the Lord God: Because it towered high and set its top among the clouds, and its heart was proud of its height, I will give it into the hand of a mighty one of the nations; he shall surely deal with it as its wickedness deserves. I have cast it out.

Ezekiel 31.10−11

So the last will be first, and the first last.

Matthew 20.16

But whoever would be great among you must be your servant.

Matthew 20.26

For every one who exalts himself will be humbled, and he who humbles himself will be exalted.

Luke 14.11

Do you not know that in a race all the runners compete, but only one receives the prize? So run that you may obtain it.

1 Corinthians 9.24

But earnestly desire the higher gifts.

1 Corinthians 12.31

So, my brethren, earnestly desire to prophesy.

1 Corinthians 14.39

Christ . . . gave himself for us to redeem us from all iniquity and to purify for himself a people of his own who are zealous for good deeds.

Titus 2.14

But if you have bitter jealousy and selfish ambition in your hearts, do not boast and be false to the truth.

James 3.14

For where jealousy and selfish ambition exist, there will be disorder and every vile practice.

James 3.16

Ambivalence

See also **Doubt**

Jesus said to him, 'No one who puts his hand to the plough and looks back is fit for the kingdom of God.'

Luke 9.62

As for the man who is weak in faith, welcome him, but not for disputes over opinions.

Romans 14.1

But he who has doubts is condemned, if he eats, because he does not act from faith; for whatever does not proceed from faith is sin.

Romans 14.23

If any of you lacks wisdom, let him ask God, who gives to all men generously and without reproaching, and it will be given him. But let him ask in faith, with no doubting, for he who doubts is like a wave of the sea that is driven and tossed by the wind. For that person must not suppose that a double-minded man, unstable in all his ways, will receive anything from the Lord.

James 1.5–8

Draw near to God and he will draw near to you. Cleanse your hands, you sinners, and purify your hearts, you men of double mind.

James 4.8

Anarchy

See also **Disorder**

In those days there was no king in Israel; every man did what was right in his own eyes.

Judges 21.25

If a kingdom is divided against itself, that kingdom cannot stand. And if a house is divided against itself, that house will not be able to stand.

Mark 3.24–25

And brother will deliver up brother to death, and the father his child, and children will rise against parents and have them put to death.

Mark 13.12

For the mystery of lawlessness is already at work.

2 Thessalonians 2.7

Anathema

See **Damnation**

Ancestors

See also **History**

For inquire, I pray you, of bygone ages,
   and consider what the fathers have
      found;
for we are but of yesterday, and know
   nothing,
   for our days on earth are a shadow.

Job 8.8–9

Angels

When I look at thy heavens, the work of
   thy fingers,
   the moon and the stars which thou hast
      established;
what is man that thou art mindful of him,
   and the son of man that thou dost care
      for him?
Yet thou hast made him little less than
   God,
   and dost crown him with glory and
      honour.

Psalms 8.3–5

For he will give his angels charge of you
   to guard you in all your ways.
On their hands they will bear you up.

Psalms 91.11–12

The field is the world, and the good seed means the sons of the kingdom; the weeds are the sons of the evil one, and the enemy who sowed them is the devil; the harvest is the close of the age, and the reapers are angels.

Matthew 13.38–39

The Son of man will send his angels, and they will gather out of his kingdom all causes of sin and all evildoers.

Matthew 13.41

Truly, truly, I say to you, you will see heaven opened, and the angels of God ascending and descending upon the Son of man.

John 1.51

God deems it just to repay with affliction those who afflict you, and to grant rest with us to you who are afflicted, when the Lord Jesus is revealed from heaven with his mighty angels in flaming fire.

2 Thessalonians 1.7–8

Let brotherly love continue. Do not neglect to show hospitality to strangers, for thereby some have entertained angels unawares.

Hebrews 13.1–2

And the angels that did not keep their own position but left their proper dwelling have been kept by him in eternal chains in the nether gloom until the judgment of the great day.

Jude 1.6

Then I looked, and I heard around the throne and the living creatures and the elders the voice of many angels.

Revelation 5.11

Anger

See also **Aggravation, Frustration, Impatience**

Surely vexation kills the fool, and jealousy slays the simple.

Job 5.2

Refrain from anger, and forsake wrath! Fret not yourself; it tends only to evil.

Psalms 37.8

He who is slow to anger has great understanding, but he who has a hasty temper exalts folly.

Proverbs 14.29

A soft answer turns away wrath, but a harsh word stirs up anger.

Proverbs 15.1

A hot-tempered man stirs up strife, but he who is slow to anger quiets contention.

Proverbs 15.18

He who is slow to anger is better than the mighty, and he who rules his spirit than he who takes a city.

Proverbs 16.32

Good sense makes a man slow to anger, and it is his glory to overlook an offence.

Proverbs 19.11

Make no friendship with a man given to anger, nor go with a wrathful man.

Proverbs 22.24

If you have been foolish, exalting yourself, or if you have been devising evil, put your hand on your mouth. For pressing milk produces curds, pressing the nose produces blood, and pressing anger produces strife.

Proverbs 30.32–33

Be not quick to anger, for anger lodges in the bosom of fools.

Ecclesiastes 7.9

But I say to you that every one who is angry with his brother shall be liable to judgment.

Matthew 5.22

He who believes in the Son has eternal life; he who does not obey the Son shall not see life, but the wrath of God rests upon him.

John 3.36

Be angry but do not sin; do not let the sun go down on your anger.

Ephesians 4.26

Let all bitterness and wrath and anger and clamour and slander be put away from you, with all malice, and be kind to one another, tenderhearted, forgiving one another, as God in Christ forgave you.

Ephesians 4.31–32

I desire then that in every place the men should pray, lifting holy hands without anger or quarrelling.

1 Timothy 2.8

Know this, my beloved brethren. Let every man be quick to hear, slow to speak, slow to anger, for the anger of man does not work the righteousness of God.

James 1.19−20

Anguish

See also **Distress, Suffering**

When the righteous cry for help, the Lord hears,
  and delivers them out of all their troubles.
The Lord is near to the brokenhearted,
  and saves the crushed in spirit.

Psalms 34.17−18

The sacrifice acceptable to God is a broken spirit;
  a broken and contrite heart, O God, thou wilt not despise.

Psalms 51.17

Animal

Six days you shall do your work, but on the seventh day you shall rest; that your ox and your ass may have rest, and the son of your bondmaid, and the alien, may be refreshed.

Exodus 23.12

Thou hast given him dominion over the works of thy hands;
  thou past put all things under his feet,
all sheep and oxen,
  and also the beasts of the field,
the birds of the air, and the fish of the sea,
  whatever passes along the paths of the sea.

Psalms 8.6−8

Man and beast thou savest, O Lord.

Psalms 36.6

A righteous man has regard for the life of his beast,
  but the mercy of the wicked is cruel.

Proverbs 12.10

The wolf shall dwell with the lamb,
  and the leopard shall lie down with the kid,
and the calf and the lion and the fatling together,
  and a little child shall lead them.
The cow and the bear shall feed;
  their young shall lie down together;
  and the lion shall eat straw like the ox.
The suckling child shall play over the hole of the asp,
  and the weaned child shall put his hand on the adder's den.
They shall not hurt or destroy in all my holy mountain;
  for the earth shall be full of the knowledge of the Lord
as the waters cover the sea.

Isaiah 11.6−9

Even the wild beasts cry to thee.

Joel 1.20

Are not five sparrows sold for two pennies? And not one of them is forgotten before God. Why, even the hairs of your head are all numbered. Fear not; you are of more value than many sparrows.

Luke 12.6−7

Answer

See also **Petition, Prayer**

He will surely be gracious to you at the sound of your cry; when he hears it, he will answer you.

Isaiah 30.19

If any of you lacks wisdom, let him ask God, who gives to all men generously and without reproaching, and it will be given him. But let him ask in faith, with no doubting, for he who doubts is like a wave of the sea that is driven and tossed by the wind.

James 1.5−6

Have no fear of them, nor be troubled, but in your hearts reverence Christ as Lord. Always be prepared to make a defence to any one who calls you to account for the hope that is in you, yet do it with gentleness and reverence.

1 Peter 3.14−15

Anxiety

Anxiety in a man's heart weighs him
   down,
   but a good word makes him glad.

Proverbs 12.25

Fear not, for I am with you,
   be not dismayed, for I am your God;
I will strengthen you, I will help you.

Isaiah 41.10

Therefore I tell you, do not be anxious
about your life, what you shall eat or what
you shall drink, nor about your body, what
you shall put on. Is not life more than food,
and the body more than clothing? Look at
the birds of the air: they neither sow nor
reap nor gather into barns, and yet your
heavenly Father feeds them. Are you not of
more value than they? And which of you by
being anxious can add one cubit to his span
of life? And why are you anxious about
clothing? Consider the lilies of the field,
how they grow; they neither toil nor spin;
yet I tell you, even Solomon in all his glory
was not arrayed like one of these. But if
God so clothes the grass of the field, which
today is alive and tomorrow is thrown into
the oven, will he not much more clothe
you, O men of little faith?

Matthew 6.25–30

Let the day's own trouble be sufficient for
the day.

Matthew 6.34

But the cares of the world, and the delight
in riches, and the desire for other things,
enter in and choke the word, and it proves
unfruitful.

Mark 4.19

Let not your hearts be troubled.

John 14.1

Peace I leave with you; my peace I give to
you; not as the world gives do I give to you.
Let not your hearts be troubled, neither let
them be afraid.

John 14.27

Have no anxiety about anything, but in
everything by prayer and supplication with
thanksgiving let your requests be made
known to God.

Philippans 4.6

Cast all your anxieties on him, for he cares
about you.

1 Peter 5.7

Apartheid

See also **Discrimination, Racism**

Behold, how good and pleasant it is
   when brothers dwell in unity!

Psalms 133.1

And I have other sheep, that are not of
this fold; I must bring them also, and they
will heed my voice. So there shall be one
flock, one shepherd.

John 10.16

And he made from one every nation of
men to live on all the face of the earth,
having determined allotted periods and the
boundaries of their habitation . . . 'For we
are indeed his offspring.'

Acts 17.26,28

For in Christ Jesus you are all sons of God,
through faith.

Galatians 3.26

There is neither Jew nor Greek, there is
neither slave nor free, there is neither male
nor female; for you are all one in Christ
Jesus.

Galatians 3.28

For he is our peace, who has made us both
one, and has broken down the dividing wall
of hostility, by abolishing in his flesh the
law of commandments and ordinances, that
he might create in himself one new man in
place of the two . . . So then you are no
longer strangers and sojourners, but you
are fellow citizens with the saints and
members of the household of God.

Ephesians 2.14–15,19

Apathy

See also **Boredom, Indifference, Laziness**

How long will you be slack to go in and take possession of the land, which the Lord, the God of your fathers, has given you?

Joshua 18.3—4

Go to the ant, O sluggard;
consider her ways, and be wise.

Proverbs 6.6

When will you arise from your sleep?
A little sleep, a little slumber,
a little folding of the hands to rest,
and poverty will come upon you like a
vagabond,
and want like an armed man.

Proverbs 6.9—11

His watchmen are blind,
they are all without knowledge;
they are all dumb dogs,
they cannot bark;
dreaming, lying down,
loving to slumber.

Isaiah 56.10

Let not your hands grow weak.

Zephaniah 3.16

Awake, O sleeper, and arise from the
dead,
and Christ shall give you light.

Ephesians 5.14

Now we command you, brethren, in the name of our Lord Jesus Christ, that you keep away from any brother who is living in idleness and not in accord with the tradition that you received from us.

2 Thessalonians 3.6

Faith apart from works is barren.

James 2.20

Apocalypse

See also **Armaged'don, Judgment**

And I will give portents in the heavens and on the earth, blood and fire and columns of smoke. The sun shall be turned to darkness, and the moon to blood, before the great and terrible day of the Lord comes.

Joel 2.30—31

For nothing is covered that will not be revealed, or hidden that will not be known.

Matthew 10.26

For nation will rise against nation, and kingdom against kingdom, and there will be famines and earthquakes in various places: all this is but the beginning of the birth-pangs . . . But he who endures to the end will be saved.

Matthew 24.7—8, 13

For then there will be great tribulation, such as has not been from the beginning of the world until now, no, and never will be.

Matthew 24.21

For false Christs and false prophets will arise and show great signs and wonders, so as to lead astray, if possible, even the elect . . . For as the lightning comes from the east and shines as far as the west, so will be the coming of the Son of man.

Matthew 24.24,27

Immediately after the tribulation of those days the sun will be darkened, and the moon will not give its light, and the stars will fall from heaven, and the powers of the heavens will be shaken; then will appear the sign of the Son of man in heaven, and then all the tribes of the earth will mourn, and they will see the Son of man coming on the clouds of heaven with power and great glory; and he will send out his angels with a loud trumpet call, and they will gather his elect from the four winds, from one end of heaven to the other.

Matthew 24.29—31

But on the day when Lot went out from Sodom fire and sulphur rained from heaven and destroyed them all — so will it be on the day when the Son of man is revealed.

Luke 17.29—30

I consider that the sufferings of this present time are not worth comparing with the glory that is to be revealed to us. For the creation waits with eager longing for the revealing of the sons of God.

Romans 8.18–19

Now if any one builds on the foundation with gold, silver, precious stones, wood, hay, straw — each man's work will become manifest; for the Day will disclose it, because it will be revealed with fire, and the fire will test what sort of work each one has done.

1 Corinthians 3.12–13

Therefore do not pronounce judgment before the time, before the Lord comes, who will bring to light the things now hidden in darkness and will disclose the purposes of the heart. Then every man will receive his commendation from God.

1 Corinthians 4.5

When the Lord Jesus is revealed from heaven with his mighty angels in flaming fire, inflicting vengeance upon those who do not know God and upon those who do not obey the gospel of our Lord Jesus.

2 Thessalonians 1.7–8

For that day will not come, unless the rebellion comes first, and the man of law-lessness is revealed. . . And the Lord Jesus will slay him with the breath of his mouth and destroy him by his appearing and his coming.

2 Thessalonians 2.3,8

Therefore gird up your minds, be sober, set your hope fully upon the grace that is coming to you at the revelation of Jesus Christ.

1 Peter 1.13

Behold, he is coming with the clouds, and every eye will see him, every one who pierced him; and all tribes of the earth will wail on account of him.

Revelation 1.7

Then I saw heaven opened, and behold, a white horse! He who sat upon it is called Faithful and True, and in righteousness he judges and makes war. His eyes are like a flame of fire, and on his head are many diadems; and he has a name inscribed which no one knows but himself. He is clad in a robe dipped in blood, and the name by which he is called is The Word of God. And the armies of heaven, arrayed in fine linen, white and pure, followed him on white horses. From his mouth issues a sharp sword with which to smite the nations, and he will rule them with a rod of iron; he will tread the wine press of the fury of the wrath of God the Almighty. On his robe and on his thigh he has a name inscribed, King of kings and Lord of lords.

Revelation 19.11–16

Apology

See also **Reconciliation**

If your brother sins, rebuke him, and if he repents, forgive him; and if he sins against you seven times in the day, and turns to you seven times, and says, 'I repent,' you must forgive him.

Luke 17.3–4

Apostasy

See also **Betrayal, Disobedience, Idolatry**

Then if you walk contrary to me, and will not hearken to me, I will bring more plagues upon you, sevenfold as many as your sins.

Leviticus 26.21

The hand of our God is for good upon all that seek him, and the power of his wrath is against all that forsake him.

Ezra 8.22

Blessed is the man who makes
    the Lord his trust,
who does not turn to the proud,
    to those who go astray after false gods!

Psalms 40.4

Your wickedness will chasten you,
    and your apostasy will reprove you.
Know and see that it is evil and bitter
    for you to forsake the Lord your God.

Jeremiah 2.19

If a man divorces his wife
  and she goes from him
and becomes another man's wife,
  will he return to her?
Would not that land be greatly polluted?
You have played the harlot with many
    lovers;
  and would you return to me? says the
    Lord.

Jeremiah 3.1

For our backslidings are many,
  we have sinned against thee.

Jeremiah 14.7

Therefore thus says the Lord God: Because you have forgotten me and cast me behind your back, therefore bear the consequences of your lewdness and harlotry.

Ezekiel 23.35

Jesus said to the twelve, 'Do you also wish to go away?'

John 6.67

Appearance

See also **Beauty, Hypocrisy, Superficiality**

But the Lord said to Samuel, 'Do not look on his appearance or on the height of his stature, because I have rejected him; for the Lord sees not as man sees; man looks on the outward appearance, but the Lord looks on the heart.'

1 Samuel 16.7

He shall not judge by what his eyes see,
  or decide by what his ears hear;
but with righteousness he shall judge the
    poor,
  and decide with equity for the meek of
    the earth.

Isaiah 11.3—4

Woe to you, scribes and Pharisees, hypocrites! for you are like whitewashed tombs, which outwardly appear beautiful, but within they are full of dead men's bones and all uncleanness. So you also outwardly appear righteous to men, but within you are full of hypocrisy and iniquity.

Matthew 23.27—28

Do not judge by appearances, but judge with right judgment.

John 7.24

Let not yours be the outward adorning with braiding of hair, decoration of gold, and wearing of fine clothing, but let it be the hidden person of the heart with the imperishable jewel of a gentle and quiet spirit, which in God's sight is very precious.

1 Peter 3.3—4

Approach

Draw near to God and he will draw near to you.

James 4.8

Approval

Let the words of my mouth and the
    meditation of my heart
  be acceptable in thy sight,
  O Lord, my rock and my redeemer.

Psalms 19.14

His master said to him, 'Well done, good and faithful servant; you have been faithful over a little, I will set you over much; enter into the joy of your master.'

Matthew 25.23

Do your best to present yourself to God as one approved, a workman who has no need to be ashamed, rightly handling the word of truth.

2 Timothy 2.15

Aptitude

See also **Ability, Capacity, Talent**

Having gifts that differ according to the grace given to us, let us use them: if prophecy, in proportion to our faith; if service, in our serving; he who teaches, in his teaching; he who exhorts, in his exhortation.

Romans 12.6—8

But each has his own special gift from God, one of one kind and one of another.

1 Corinthians 7.7

Now there are varieties of gifts, but the same Spirit; and there are varieties of service, but the same Lord; and there are varieties of working, but it is the same God who inspires them all in every one. To each is given the manifestation of the Spirit for the common good. To one is given through the Spirit the utterance of wisdom, and to another the utterance of knowledge according to the same Spirit, to another faith by the same Spirit, to another gifts of healing by the one Spirit, to another the working of miracles, to another prophecy, to another the ability to distinguish between spirits, to another various kinds of tongues, to another the interpretation of tongues. All these are inspired by one and the same Spirit, who apportions to each one individually as he wills.

1 Corinthians 12.4—11

But grace was given to each of us according to the measure of Christ's gift . . . And his gifts were that some should be apostles, some prophets, some evangelists, some pastors and teachers, to equip the saints for the work of ministry, for building up the body of Christ.

Ephesians 4.7, 11—12

Do not neglect the gift you have, which was given you by prophetic utterance when the council of elders laid their hands upon you.

1 Timothy 4.14

Every good endowment and every perfect gift is from above, coming down from the Father of lights.

James 1.17

As each has received a gift, employ it for one another, as good stewards of God's

varied grace . . . in order that God may be glorified through Jesus Christ.

1 Peter 4.10—11

Argument

See also **Quarrelling**

Teach me, and I will be silent;
 make me understand how I have erred.

Job 6.24

Should a wise man answer with windy
  knowledge,
 and fill himself with the east wind?
Should he argue in unprofitable talk . . . ?

Job 15.2

By insolence the heedless make strife.

Proverbs 13.10

A fool's lips bring strife.

Proverbs 18.6

Argue your case with your neighbour
  himself,
 and do not disclose another's secret.

Proverbs 25.9

There must be factions among you in order that those who are genuine among you may be recognised.

1 Corinthians 11.19

Forbearing one another and, if one has a complaint against another, forgiving each other; as the Lord has forgiven you, so you also must forgive.

Colossians 3.13

Have nothing to do with stupid, senseless controversies; you know that they breed quarrels. And the Lord's servant must not be quarrelsome.

2 Timothy 2.23—24

Argumentativeness

If any one teaches otherwise and does not agree with the sound words of our Lord Jesus Christ and the teaching which accords with godliness, he is puffed up with conceit, he knows nothing; he has a morbid craving for controversy and for disputes about words, which produce envy, dissension, slander, base suspicions, and wrangling among men who are depraved in mind.

1 Timothy 6.3–5

Remind them of this, and charge them before the Lord to avoid disputing about words, which does no good, but only ruins the hearers.

2 Timothy 2.14

Have nothing to do with stupid, senseless controversies; you know that they breed quarrels.

2 Timothy 2.23

Aristocracy

By me kings reign,
    and rulers decree what is just;
by me princes rule,
    and nobles govern the earth.

Proverbs 8.15–16

For consider your call, brethren; not many of you were wise according to worldly standards, not many were powerful, not many were of noble birth.

1 Corinthians 1.26

First of all, then, I urge that supplications, prayers, intercessions, and thanksgivings be made for all men, for kings and all who are in high positions, that we may lead a quiet and peaceable life, godly and respectful in every way.

1 Timothy 2.1–2

Armaged'don

And they assembled them at the place which is called in Hebrew Armaged'don.

The seventh angel poured his bowl into the air, and a loud voice came out of the temple, from the throne, saying, 'It is done!' And there were flashes of lightning, voices, peals of thunder, and a great earthquake such as had never been since men were on the earth, so great was that earthquake. The great city was split into three parts, and the cities of the nations fell, and God remembered great Babylon, to make her drain the cup of the fury of his wrath. And every island fled away, and no mountains were to be found; and great hailstones, heavy as a hundredweight, dropped on men from heaven, till men cursed God for the plague of the hail, so fearful was that plague.

Revelation 16.16–21

Arrogance

See also **Egotism, Pride**

Talk no more so very proudly,
    let not arrogance come from your mouth;
for the Lord is a God of knowledge,
    and by him actions are weighed.

1 Samuel 2.3

Thou dost deliver a humble people,
    but thy eyes are upon the haughty to
        bring them down.

2 Samuel 22.28

Let not the foot of arrogance come upon
        me,
    nor the hand of the wicked drive me
        away.

Psalms 36.11

The man of haughty looks and arrogant
        heart
    I will not endure.

Psalms 101.5

For though the Lord is high, he regards the
        lowly;
    but the haughty he knows from afar.

Psalms 138.6

Trust in the Lord with all your heart,
    and do not rely on your own insight.

Proverbs 3.5

Pride and arrogance and the way of evil
    and perverted speech I hate.

Proverbs 8.13

Every one who is arrogant is an
abomination to the Lord.

Proverbs 16.5

Pride goes before destruction,
and a haughty spirit before a fall.

Proverbs 16.18

Before destruction a man's heart is
haughty,
but humility goes before honour.

Proverbs 18.12

Every way of a man is right in his own
eyes,
but the Lord weighs the heart.

Proverbs 21.2

Do you see a man who is wise in his own
eyes?
There is more hope for a fool than for
him.

Proverbs 26.12

The haughty looks of man shall be brought
low,
and the pride of men shall be humbled;
and the Lord alone will be exalted in that
day.

Isaiah 2.11

Woe to those who are wise in their own
eyes,
and shrewd in their own sight!

Isaiah 5.21

I will punish the world for its evil,
and the wicked for their iniquity;
I will put an end to the pride of the
arrogant,
and lay low the haughtiness of the
ruthless.

Isaiah 13.11

Thus says the Lord: 'Let not the wise man
glory in his wisdom, let not the mighty man
glory in his might, let not the rich man glory
in his riches.'

Jeremiah 9.23

Behold, I am against you, O proud one,
says the Lord God of hosts;
for your day has come.

Jeremiah 50.31

The pride of your heart has deceived you,
you who live in the clefts of the rock,
whose dwelling is high,
who say in your heart,
'Who will bring me down to the ground?'
Though you soar aloft like the eagle,
though your nest is set among the stars,
thence I will bring you down, says the
Lord.

Obadiah 3—4

He has scattered the proud in the imagination of their hearts, he has put down the
mighty from their thrones, and exalted
those of low degree.

Luke 1.51—52

For every one who exalts himself will be
humbled, and he who humbles himself will
be exalted.

Luke 14.11

God opposes the proud, but gives grace to
the humble.

James 4.6

Art

See also **Inspiration**

And I have filled him with the Spirit of
God, with ability and intelligence, with
knowledge and all craftsmanship, to devise
artistic designs, to work in gold, silver, and
bronze, in cutting stones for setting, and in
carving wood, for work in every craft.

Exodus 31.3—5

He has filled them with ability to do every
sort of work done by a craftsman or by a
designer or by an embroiderer in blue and
purple and scarlet stuff and fine twined
linen, or by a weaver — by any sort of
workman or skilled designer.

Exodus 35.35

A word fitly spoken
is like apples of gold in a setting of silver.
Like a gold ring or an ornament of gold
is a wise reprover to a listening ear.

Proverbs 25.11—12

For we are his workmanship, created in Christ Jesus for good works, which God prepared beforehand, that we should walk in them.

Ephesians 2.10

Asceticism

See also **Steadfastness**

'Yet even now,' says the Lord,
  'return to me with all your heart,
with fasting, with weeping, and with
      mourning.'

Joel 2.12

And he said to all, 'If any man would come after me, let him deny himself and take up his cross daily and follow me.'

Luke 9.23

For the mind that is set on the flesh is hostile to God; it does not submit to God's law, indeed it cannot; and those who are in the flesh cannot please God.

But you are not in the flesh, you are in the Spirit, if in fact the Spirit of God dwells in you. Any one who does not have the Spirit of Christ does not belong to him. But if Christ is in you, although your bodies are dead because of sin, your spirits are alive because of righteousness. If the Spirit of him who raised Jesus from the dead dwells in you, he who raised Christ Jesus from the dead will give life to your mortal bodies also through his Spirit which dwells in you.

Romans 8.7–11

But I pommel my body and subdue it, lest after preaching to others I myself should be disqualified.

1 Corinthians 9.27

Put to death therefore what is earthly in you: fornication, impurity, passion, evil desire, and covetousness, which is idolatry. On account of these the wrath of God is coming.

Colossians 3.5–6

Aspiration

Earnestly desire the higher gifts.

1 Corinthians 12.31

I press on toward the goal for the prize of the upward call of God in Christ Jesus.

Philippians 3.14

Aspire to live quietly, to mind your own affairs, and to work with your hands, as we charged you; so that you may command the respect of outsiders, and be dependent on nobody.

1 Thessalonians 4.11–12

Assassination

Cursed be he who takes a bribe to slay an innocent person.

Deuteronomy 27.25

Assault

Do not contend with a man for no reason, when he has done you no harm.

Proverbs 3.30

Assertiveness

In the fear of the Lord one has strong confidence,
    and his children will have a refuge.

Proverbs 14.26

You are the light of the world. A city set on a hill cannot be hid. Nor do men light a lamp and put it under a bushel, but on a stand, and it gives light to all in the house. Let your light so shine before men, that they may see your good works and give glory to your Father who is in heaven.

Matthew 5.14–16

And now, Lord, look upon their threats, and grant to thy servants to speak thy word with all boldness.

Acts 4.29

And if the bugle gives an indistinct sound, who will get ready for battle?

1 Corinthians 14.8

For it is not the man who commends himself that is accepted, but the man whom the Lord commends.

2 Corinthians 10.18

For he has said, 'I will never fail you nor forsake you.' Hence we can confidently say,
'The Lord is my helper,
I will not be afraid;
what can man do to me?'

Hebrews 13.5—6

Assurance

Therefore, brethren, since we have confidence to enter the sanctuary by the blood of Jesus, by the new and living way which he opened for us through the curtain, that is, through his flesh, and since we have a great priest over the house of God, let us draw near with a true heart in full assurance of faith, with our hearts sprinkled clean from an evil conscience and our bodies washed with pure water. Let us hold fast the confession of our hope without wavering, for he who promised is faithful.

Hebrews 10.19—23

Now faith is the assurance of things hoped for, the conviction of things not seen.

Hebrews 11.1—2

Astrology

See also **Occult**

Let them stand forth and save you,
those who divide the heavens,
who gaze at the stars,
who at the new moons predict
what shall befall you.
Behold, they are like stubble,
the fire consumes them;
they cannot deliver themselves
from the power of the flame.

Isaiah 47.13—14

Thus says the Lord:
'Learn not the way of the nations,
nor be dismayed at the signs of the
heavens
because the nations are dismayed at
them.'

Jeremiah 10.2

'Are you able to make known to me the dream that I have seen and its interpretation?' Daniel answered the king, 'No wise men, enchanters, magicians, or astrologers can show to the king the mystery which the king has asked, but there is a God in heaven who reveals mysteries.'

Daniel 2.26—28

Now when Jesus was born in Bethlehem of Judea in the days of Herod the king, behold, wise men from the East came to Jerusalem, saying, 'Where is he who has been born king of the Jews? For we have seen his star in the East, and have come to worship him.'

Matthew 2.1—2

Astronomy

When I look at thy heavens, the work of
thy fingers,
the moon and the stars which thou hast
established;
what is man that thou art mindful of him,
and the son of man that thou dost care
for him?

Psalms 8.3—4

The heavens are telling the glory of God;
and the firmament proclaims his handiwork.
Day to day pours forth speech,
and night to night declares knowledge.
There is no speech, nor are there words;
their voice is not heard;
yet their voice goes out through all the
earth,
and their words to the end of the world.
In them he has set a tent for the sun,
which comes forth like a bridegroom
leaving his chamber,
and like a strong man runs its course with
joy.

Psalms 19.1—5

To him who by understanding made the
    heavens,
  for his steadfast love endures for ever;
to him who spread out the earth upon the
    waters,
  for his steadfast love endures for ever;
to him who made the great lights,
  for his steadfast love endures for ever;
the sun to rule over the day,
  for his steadfast love endures for ever;
the moon and stars to rule over the night,
  for his steadfast love endures for ever.

Psalms 136.5−9

Lift up your eyes on high and see:
  who created these?
He who brings out their host by number,
  calling them all by name;
by the greatness of his might,
  and because he is strong in power
  not one is missing.

Isaiah 40.26

He who made the Plei'ades and Orion,
  and turns deep darkness into the
    morning,
  and darkens the day into night,
who calls for the waters of the sea,
  and pours them out upon the surface of
    the earth,
the Lord is his name.

Amos 5.8

Atheism

See also **Agnosticism, Cynicism, Heresy, Idolatry, Scepticism**

Curse God, and die.

Job 2.9

He . . . makes them wander in a pathless
    waste.
They grope in the dark without light;
  and he makes them stagger like a
    drunken man.

Job 12.24−25

In the pride of his countenance the wicked
    does not seek him;
  all his thoughts are, 'There is no God.'

Psalms 10.4

The fool says in his heart,
  'There is no God.'

Psalms 14.1

He who believes and is baptized will be saved; but he who does not believe will be condemned.

Mark 16.16

But he who denies me before men will be denied before the angels of God.

Luke 12.9

For God sent the Son into the world, not to condemn the world, but that the world might be saved through him. He who believes in him is not condemned; he who does not believe is condemned already, because he has not believed in the name of the only Son of God.

John 3.17−18

For every one who does evil hates the light, and does not come to the light, lest his deeds should be exposed.

John 3.20

He who is of God hears the words of God; the reason why you do not hear them is that you are not of God.

John 8.47

For the wrath of God is revealed from heaven against all ungodliness and wickedness of men who by their wickedness suppress the truth. For what can be known about God is plain to them, because God has shown it to them. Ever since the creation of the world his invisible nature, namely, his eternal power and deity, has been clearly perceived in the things that have been made. So they are without excuse.

Romans 1.18−20

For the word of the cross is folly to those who are perishing, but to us who are being saved it is the power of God.

1 Corinthians 1.18

Therefore God sends upon them a strong delusion, to make them believe what is false, so that all may be condemned who did not believe the truth but had pleasure in unrighteousness.

2 Thessalonians 2.11–12

Children . . . now many antichrists have come; therefore we know that it is the last hour.

1 John 2.18

Who is the liar but he who denies that Jesus is the Christ? This is the antichrist, he who denies the Father and the Son.

1 John 2.22

Athleticism

But they who wait for the Lord shall renew
    their strength,
  they shall mount up with wings like
    eagles,
they shall run and not be weary,
  they shall walk and not faint.

Isaiah 40.31

Well, I do not run aimlessly, I do not box as one beating the air; but I pommel my body and subdue it.

1 Corinthians 9.26–27

Train yourself in godliness; for while bodily training is of some value, godliness is of value in every way, as it holds promise for the present life and also for the life to come.

1 Timothy 4.8

Therefore, since we are surrounded by so great a cloud of witnesses, let us also lay aside every weight, and sin which clings so closely, and let us run with perseverance the race that is set before us.

Hebrews 12.1

Atonement

See **Reconciliation**

Attendance

Let us consider how to stir up one another to love and good works, not neglecting to meet together.

Hebrews 10.24–25

Attentiveness

Exhort one another every day, as long as it is called 'today,' that none of you may be hardened by the deceitfulness of sin.

Hebrews 3.13

Audacity

See also **Bravery, Courage**

The wicked flee when no one pursues,
  but the righteous are bold as a lion.

Proverbs 28.1

And now, Lord, look upon their threats, and grant to thy servants to speak thy word with all boldness.

Acts 4.29

Authority

See also **Government, Leadership, Power, Responsibility**

The Lord our God we will serve, and his voice we will obey.

Joshua 24.24

When one rules justly over men,
  ruling in the fear of God,
he dawns on them like the morning light.

2 Samuel 23.3

When the righteous are in authority, the
  people rejoice;
  but when the wicked rule, the people
  groan.

Proverbs 29.2

And call no man your father on earth, for you have one Father, who is in heaven. Neither be called masters, for you have one master, the Christ. He who is greatest among you shall be your servant; whoever exalts himself will be humbled, and whoever humbles himself will be exalted.

Matthew 23.9–12

And Jesus came and said to them, 'All authority in heaven and on earth has been given to me.'

Matthew 28.18

Take heed to yourselves and to all the flock, in which the Holy Spirit has made you overseers, to care for the church of God which he obtained with the blood of his own Son.

Acts 20.27—28

Let every person be subject to the governing authorities. For there is no authority except from God, and those that exist have been instituted by God. Therefore he who resists the authorities resists what God has appointed, and those who resist will incur judgment.

Romans 13.1—2

Then comes the end, when he delivers the kingdom to God the Father after destroying every rule and every authority and power . . . The last enemy to be destroyed is death.

1 Corinthians 15.24,26

Masters, do the same to them, and forbear threatening, knowing that he who is both their Master and yours is in heaven, and that there is no partiality with him.

Ephesians 6.9

For in him the whole fulness of deity dwells bodily, and you have come to fulness of life in him, who is the head of all rule and authority.

Colossians 2.9—10

Children, obey your parents in everything, for this pleases the Lord. Fathers, do not provoke your children, lest they become discouraged. Slaves, obey in everything those who are your earthly masters, not with eye-service, as men-pleasers, but in singleness of heart, fearing the Lord. Whatever your task, work heartily, as serving the Lord and not men, knowing that from the Lord you will receive the inheritance as your reward; you are serving the Lord Christ. For the wrongdoer will be paid back for the wrong he has done, and there is no partiality.

Colossians 3.20—25

Remember your leaders, those who spoke to you the word of God.

Hebrews 13.7

Obey your leaders and submit to them; for they are keeping watch over your souls, as men who will have to give account. Let them do this joyfully, and not sadly, for that would be of no advantage to you.

Hebrews 13.17

Be subject for the Lord's sake to every human institution, whether it be to the emperor as supreme, or to governors as sent by him to punish those who do wrong and to praise those who do right. For it is God's will that by doing right you should put to silence the ignorance of foolish men.

1 Peter 2.13—15

Awakening

See also **Regeneration**

Awake, my soul!
Awake, O harp and lyre!
  I will awake the dawn!

Psalms 108.1—2

My eyes fail with watching for thy
    salvation,
  and for the fulfilment of thy righteous
    promise.

Psalms 119.123

Morning by morning he wakens,
    he wakens my ear
  to hear as those who are taught.
The Lord God has opened my ear.

Isaiah 50.4—5

Awake, awake, put on strength,
  O arm of the Lord;
awake, as in days of old.

Isaiah 51.9

If you will not awake, I will come like a thief, and you will not know at what hour I will come upon you.

Revelation 3.3

Awareness

See **Care, Watchfulness**

Awe

You shall fear the Lord your God; you shall serve him, and swear by his name.

Deuteronomy 6.13

You shall walk after the Lord your God and fear him, and keep his commandments and obey his voice, and you shall serve him and cleave to him.

Deuteronomy 13.4

God is clothed with terrible majesty.

Job 37.22

Let all the earth fear the Lord,
   let all the inhabitants of the world stand
      in awe of him!

Psalms 33.8

O come, let us worship and bow down,
   let us kneel before the Lord, our Maker!

Psalms 95.6

He sent redemption to his people;
   he has commanded his covenant for ever.
   Holy and terrible is his name!

Psalms 111.9

Princes persecute me without cause, but my heart stands in awe of thy words. I rejoice at thy word.

Psalms 119.161–162

At the name of Jesus every knee should bow, in heaven and on earth and under the earth.

Philippians 2.10

Therefore let us be grateful for receiving a kingdom that cannot be shaken, and thus let us offer to God acceptable worship, with reverence and awe; for our God is a consuming fire.

Hebrews 12.28–29

B

Babies

See also **Children**

Thou whose glory above the heavens is
chanted
by the mouth of babes and infants.
Psalms 8.1

At that time Jesus declared, 'I thank thee,
Father, Lord of heaven and earth, that thou
hast hidden these things from the wise and
understanding and revealed them to babes.'
Matthew 11.25

Truly, I say to you, whoever does not
receive the kingdom of God like a child
shall not enter it.
Mark 10.15

Backsliding

You are the salt of the earth; but if salt has
lost its taste, how shall its saltness be restored? It is no longer good for anything
except to be thrown out and trodden under
foot by men.
Matthew 5.13

For it is impossible to restore again to
repentance those who have once been enlightened, who have tasted the heavenly
gift, and have become partakers of the Holy
Spirit, and have tasted the goodness of the
word of God and the powers of the age to
come, if they then commit apostasy, since
they crucify the Son of God on their own
account and hold him up to contempt.
Hebrews 6.4–6

Balance

Receive instruction in wise dealing,
righteousness, justice, and equity;
that prudence may be given to the simple,
knowledge and discretion to the youth.
Proverbs 1.3–4

I do not mean that others should be eased
and you burdened, but that as a matter of
equality your abundance at the present time
should supply their want, so that their
abundance may supply your want, that
there may be equality.
2 Corinthians 8.13–14

Baptism

I baptize you with water for repentance,
but he who is coming after me is mightier
than I, whose sandals I am not worthy to
carry; he will baptize you with the Holy
Spirit and with fire.
Matthew 3.11

Go therefore and make disciples of all
nations, baptizing them in the name of the
Father and of the Son and of the Holy
Spirit.
Matthew 28.19

He who believes and is baptized will be
saved.
Mark 16.16

Truly, truly, I say to you, unless one is
born of water and the Spirit, he cannot
enter the kingdom of God.
John 3.5

And Peter said to them, 'Repent, and be
baptized every one of you in the name of Jesus
Christ for the forgiveness of your sins; and you
shall receive the gift of the Holy Spirit.'
Acts 2.38

And now why do you wait? Rise and be
baptized, and wash away your sins, calling
on his name.
Acts 22.16

Do you not know that all of us who have been baptized into Christ Jesus were baptized into his death? We were buried therefore with him by baptism into death, so that as Christ was raised from the dead by the glory of the Father, we too might walk in newness of life.

Romans 6.3−4

For by one Spirit we were all baptized into one body — Jews or Greeks, slaves or free — and all were made to drink of one Spirit.

1 Corinthians 12.13

For in Christ Jesus you are all sons of God, through faith. For as many of you as were baptized into Christ have put on Christ.

Galatians 3.26−27

One Lord, one faith, one baptism.

Ephesians 4.5

You were buried with him in baptism, in which you were also raised with him through faith in the working of God, who raised him from the dead.

Colossians 2.12

Baptism, which corresponds to this, now saves you, not as a removal of dirt from the body but as an appeal to God for a clear conscience, through the resurrection of Jesus Christ.

1 Peter 3.21

The Spirit and the Bride say, 'Come.' And let him who hears say, 'Come.' And let him who is thirsty come, let him who desires take the water of life without price.

Revelation 22.17

Beauty

The sons of God saw that the daughters of men were fair.

Genesis 6.2

Worship the Lord in holy array.

1 Chronicles 16.29

One thing have I asked of the Lord,
  that will I seek after;
that I may dwell in the house of the Lord
  all the days of my life,
to behold the beauty of the Lord.

Psalms 27.4

Let the favour of the Lord our God be upon us.

Psalms 90.17

Honour and majesty are before him;
  strength and beauty are in his sanctuary.

Psalms 96.6

For the Lord takes pleasure in his people;
  he adorns the humble with victory.

Psalms 149.4

Do not desire her beauty in your heart,
  and do not let her capture you with her
    eyelashes;
for a harlot may be hired for a loaf of
    bread,
  but an adulteress stalks a man's very life.

Proverbs 6.25−26

Like a gold ring in a swine's snout
  is a beautiful woman without discretion.

Proverbs 11.22

Charm is deceitful, and beauty is vain,
  but a woman who fears the Lord is to be
    praised.

Proverbs 31.30

He has made everything beautiful in its time.

Ecclesiastes 3.11

In that day the branch of the Lord shall be beautiful and glorious, and the fruit of the land shall be the pride and glory of the survivors of Israel.

Isaiah 4.2

How beautiful upon the mountains
  are the feet of him who brings good
    tidings.

Isaiah 52.7

Your heart was proud because of your
    beauty;

you corrupted your wisdom for the sake
   of your splendour.
I cast you to the ground.

Ezekiel 28.17

For you are like whitewashed tombs,
which outwardly appear beautiful, but
within they are full of dead men's bones
and all uncleanness.

Matthew 23.27

How beautiful are the feet of those who
preach good news!

Romans 10.15

Whatever is lovely, whatever is gracious, if
there is any excellence, if there is anything
worthy of praise, think about these things.

Philippians 4.8

Begging

See also **Charity**

I delivered the poor who cried.

Job 29.12

I have been young, and now am old;
   yet I have not seen the righteous forsaken
   or his children begging bread.

Psalms 37.25

Belief

See also **Conviction, Faith, Trust**

Lord, I am not worthy to have you come
under my roof; but only say the word, and
my servant will be healed.

Matthew 8.8

Repent, and believe in the gospel.

Mark 1.15

I believe; help my unbelief!

Mark 9.24

Whoever causes one of these little ones
who believe in me to sin, it would be better
for him if a great millstone were hung

round his neck and he were thrown into the
sea.

Mark 9.42

He who believes and is baptized will be
saved.

Mark 16.16

And blessed is she who believed that there
would be a fulfilment of what was spoken to
her from the Lord.

Luke 1.45

For God so loved the world that he gave
his only Son, that whoever believes in him
should not perish but have eternal life.

John 3.16

I am the bread of life; he who comes to me
shall not hunger, and he who believes in me
shall never thirst.

John 6.35

I am the resurrection and the life; he who
believes in me, though he die, yet shall he
live, and whoever lives and believes in me
shall never die.

John 11.25–26

Did I not tell you that if you would believe
you would see the glory of God?

John 11.40

While you have the light, believe in the
light, that you may become sons of light.

John 12.36

Truly, truly I say to you, he who believes
in me will also do the works that I do; and
greater works than these will he do, because I go to the Father.

John 14.12

Blessed are those who have not seen and
yet believe.

John 20.29

To him all the prophets bear witness that
every one who believes in him receives
forgiveness of sins through his name.

Acts 10.43

Believe in the Lord Jesus, and you will be saved, you and your household.

Acts 16.31

And he who believes in him will not be put to shame.

Romans 9.33

The word is near you, on your lips and in your heart (that is, the word of faith which we preach); because, if you confess with your lips that Jesus is Lord and believe in your heart that God raised him from the dead, you will be saved.

Romans 10.8–9

Whoever would draw near to God must believe that he exists and that he rewards those who seek him.

Hebrews 11.6

You believe that God is one; you do well. Even the demons believe — and shudder.

James 2.19

Without having seen him you love him; though you do not now see him you believe in him and rejoice with unutterable and exalted joy. As the outcome of your faith you obtain the salvation of your souls.

1 Peter 1.8–9

Who is it that overcomes the world but he who believes that Jesus is the Son of God?

1 John 5.5

Belittling

He who belittles his neighbour lacks sense, but a man of understanding remains silent.

Proverbs 11.12

Benevolence

See also **Charity, Generosity, Goodness, Poverty**

If there is among you a poor man . . . you shall not harden your heart or shut your hand against your poor brother, but you shall open your hand to him, and lend him sufficient for his need.

Deuteronomy 15.7–8

What is man that thou art mindful of him, and the son of man that thou dost care for him?
Yet thou hast made him little less than God,
and dost crown him with glory and honour.

Psalms 8.4–5

Blessed is he who considers the poor!
The Lord delivers him in the day of trouble.

Psalms 41.1

If I give away all I have, and if I deliver my body to be burned, but have not love, I gain nothing.

1 Corinthians 13.3

For God is not so unjust as to overlook your work and the love which you showed for his sake in serving the saints, as you still do.

Hebrews 6.10

Bereavement

See also **Death, Grief**

But now he is dead; why should I fast? Can I bring him back again? I shall go to him, but he will not return to me.

2 Samuel 12.23

The Lord gave, and the Lord has taken away; blessed be the name of the Lord.

Job 1.21

Because I delivered the poor who cried, and the fatherless who had none to help him.
The blessing of him who was about to perish came upon me,
and I caused the widow's heart to sing for joy.

Job 29.12–13

Weeping may tarry for the night,
  but joy comes with the morning.

Psalms 30.5

Thou hast turned for me my mourning into
    dancing;
  thou hast loosed my sackcloth
  and girded me with gladness.

Psalms 30.11

Father of the fatherless and protector of
    widows
  is God in his holy habitation.

Psalms 68.5

The Lord watches over the sojourners,
  he upholds the widow and the fatherless.

Psalms 146.9

A time to weep, and a time to laugh;
  a time to mourn, and a time to dance.

Ecclesiastes 3.4

They shall obtain joy and gladness,
  and sorrow and sighing shall flee away.

Isaiah 35.10

For the Lord will be your everlasting light,
  and your days of mourning shall be
    ended.

Isaiah 60.20

He has sent me to bind up the broken-
    hearted . . .
  to comfort all who mourn;
to grant to those who mourn in Zion —
  to give them a garland instead of ashes,
the oil of gladness instead of mourning,
  the mantle of praise instead of a faint
    spirit.

Isaiah 61.1,2–3

Weep not for him who is dead,
  nor bemoan him.

Jeremiah 22.10

Blessed are those who mourn, for they
shall be comforted.

Matthew 5.4

Blessed are you that weep now, for you
shall laugh.

Luke 6.21

I will not leave you desolate; I will come to
you.

John 14.18

But we would not have you ignorant,
brethren, concerning those who are asleep,
that you may not grieve as others do who
have no hope. For since we believe that
Jesus died and rose again, even so, through
Jesus, God will bring with him those who
have fallen asleep . . . then we who are
alive, who are left, shall be caught up together with them in the clouds to meet the
Lord in the air; and so we shall always be
with the Lord. Therefore comfort one
another with these words.

1 Thessalonians 4.13–18

To visit orphans and widows in their affliction.

James 1.27

He will wipe away every tear from their
eyes, and death shall be no more, neither
shall there be mourning nor crying nor pain
any more.

Revelation 21.4

Bestiality

Whoever lies with a beast shall be put to
death.

Exodus 22.19

And you shall not lie with any beast and
defile yourself with it, neither shall any
woman give herself to a beast to lie with it:
it is perversion.

Leviticus 18.23

If a man lies with a beast, he shall be put to
death; and you shall kill the beast. If a
woman approaches any beast and lies with
it, you shall kill the woman and the beast;
they shall be put to death, their blood is
upon them.

Leviticus 20.15–16

Cursed be he who lies with any kind of
beast.

Deuteronomy 27.21

Betrayal

See also **Treachery**

If you have come to me to betray me to my adversaries, although there is no wrong in my hands, then may the God of our fathers see and rebuke you.

1 Chronicles 12.17

Thus says the Lord, 'You abandoned me, so I have abandoned you to the hand of Shishak.'

2 Chronicles 12.5

My God, my God, why hast thou forsaken me?

Psalms 22.1

For my father and my mother have forsaken me,
but the Lord will take me up.

Psalms 27.10

Give me not up to the will of my adversaries;
for false witnesses have risen against me,
and they breathe out violence . . .
Wait for the Lord;
be strong, and let your heart take courage;
yea, wait for the Lord!

Psalms 27.12,14

It is better to take refuge in the Lord
than to put confidence in man.
It is better to take refuge in the Lord
than to put confidence in princes.

Psalms 118.8−9

Do not plan evil against your neighbour
who dwells trustingly beside you.

Proverbs 3.29

A man who bears false witness against his neighbour
is like a war club, or a sword, or a sharp arrow.

Proverbs 25.18

Trust in a faithless man in time of trouble
is like a bad tooth or a foot that slips.

Proverbs 25.19

Your friend, and your father's friend, do not forsake.

Proverbs 27.10

But rebels and sinners shall be destroyed together,
and those who forsake the Lord shall be consumed.

Isaiah 1.28

'Woe to the rebellious children,' says the Lord,
'who carry out a plan, but not mine;
and who make a league, but not of my spirit.'

Isaiah 30.1

O Lord, the hope of Israel,
all who forsake thee shall be put to shame.

Jeremiah 17.13

To the Lord our God belong mercy and forgiveness; because we have rebelled against him.

Daniel 9.9

Put no trust in a neighbour,
have no confidence in a friend;
guard the doors of your mouth
from her who lies in your bosom;
for the son treats the father with contempt,
the daughter rises up against her mother,
the daughter-in-law against her mother-in-law;
a man's enemies are the men of his own house.
But as for me, I will look to the Lord.

Micah 7.5−7

Have we not all one father? Has not one God created us? Why then are we faithless to one another, profaning the covenant of our fathers?

Malachi 2.10

So take heed to yourselves and do not be faithless.

Malachi 2.16

And then many will fall away, and betray one another, and hate one another. And many false prophets will arise and lead many astray . . . But he who endures to the end will be saved.

Matthew 24.10−11,13

But woe to that man by whom the Son of man is betrayed! It would have been better for that man if he had not been born.

Matthew 26.24

And brother will deliver brother to death, and the father his child, and children will rise against parents and have them put to death . . .

Mark 13.12

Judas . . . went to the chief priests in order to betray him.

Mark 14.10

Judas, would you betray the Son of man with a kiss?

Luke 22.48

Betrothal

See also **Marriage**

Set me as a seal upon your heart,
  as a seal upon your arm;
for love is strong as death,
  jealousy is cruel as the grave.

Song of Solomon 8.6

And I will betroth you to me for ever; I will betroth you to me in righteousness and in justice, in steadfast love, and in mercy. I will betroth you to me in faithfulness; and you shall know the Lord.

Hosea 2.19−20

Bible

See also **Scripture**

And the tables were the work of God, and the writing was the writing of God.

Exodus 32.16

That he might make you know that man does not live by bread alone, but that man lives by everything that proceeds out of the mouth of the Lord.

Deuteronomy 8.3

This book of the law shall not depart out of your mouth, but you shall meditate on it day and night, that you may be careful to do according to all that is written in it; for then you shall make your way prosperous, and then you shall have good success.

Joshua 1.8

The promises of the Lord are promises
    that are pure,
  silver refined in a furnace on the ground,
  purified seven times.

Psalms 12.6

I have laid up thy word in my heart,
  that I might not sin against thee.

Psalms 119.11

Thy testimonies are my delight,
  they are my counsellors.

Psalms 119.24

I will also speak of thy testimonies before
    kings,
  and shall not be put to shame;
for I find my delight in thy commandments,
  which I love.
I revere thy commandments, which I love,
  and I will meditate on thy statutes.

Psalms 119.46−48

Thy word is a lamp to my feet
  and a light to my path.

Psalms 119.105

Thy testimonies are wonderful;
  therefore my soul keeps them.
The unfolding of thy words gives light;
  it imparts understanding to the simple.

Psalms 119.129−130

Every word of God proves true.

Proverbs 30.5

In that day the deaf shall hear
  the words of a book,
and out of their gloom and darkness
  the eyes of the blind shall see.

Isaiah 29.18

Seek and read from the book of the Lord.

Isaiah 34.16

For as the rain and the snow come down
    from the heaven,
  and return not thither but water the
    earth,

making it bring forth and sprout,
   giving seed to the sower and bread to the
     eater,
so shall my word be that goes forth from my
   mouth;
   it shall not return to me empty,
but it shall accomplish that which I purpose,
   and prosper in the thing for which I sent
     it.

Isaiah 55.10–11

Take a scroll and write on it all the words
that I have spoken to you . . .

Jeremiah 36.2

You are wrong, because you know neither
the scriptures nor the power of God.

Matthew 22.29

Heaven and earth will pass away, but my
words will not pass away.

Mark 13.31

You search the scriptures, because you
think that in them you have eternal life; and
it is they that bear witness to me; yet you
refuse to come to me that you may have
life.

John 5.39–40

Scripture cannot be broken.

John 10.35

Now Jesus did many other signs in the
presence of the disciples, which are not
written in this book; but these are written
that you may believe that Jesus is the
Christ, the Son of God, and that believing
you may have life in his name.

John 20.30–31

For whatever was written in former days
was written for our instruction, that by
steadfastness and by the encouragement of
the scriptures we might have hope.

Romans 15.4

You have been acquainted with the sacred
writings which are able to instruct you for
salvation through faith in Christ Jesus.

2 Timothy 3.15

All scripture is inspired by God and
profitable for teaching, for reproof, for
correction, and for training in righteousness, that the man of God may be complete, equipped for every good work.

2 Timothy 3.16–17

Receive with meekness the implanted
word, which is able to save your souls.

James 1.21

But the word of the Lord abides for ever.
That word is the good news which was
preached to you.

1 Peter 1.25

Blessed is he who reads aloud the words of
the prophecy, and blessed are those who
hear, and who keep what is written therein;
for the time is near.

Revelation 1.3

If any one takes away from the words of
the book of this prophecy, God will take
away his share in the tree of life and in the
holy city, which are described in this book.

Revelation 22.19

Bigotry

See also **Hypocrisy, Injustice**

Do I not hate them that hate thee, O
Lord? . . . I count them my enemies.

Psalms 139.21–22

Those who say, 'Keep to yourself,
   do not come near me, for I am set apart
     from you.'
. . . are a smoke in my nostrils,
   a fire that burns all the day.

Isaiah 65.1,5

And the scribes of the Pharisees, when
they saw that he was eating with sinners and
tax collectors, said to his disciples, 'Why
does he eat with tax collectors and sinners?'
And when Jesus heard it, he said to them
'Those who are well have no need of a
physician, but those who are sick; I came
not to call the righteous, but sinners.'

Mark 2.16–17

Let him who is without sin among you be the first to throw a stone at her.

John 8.7

You yourselves know how unlawful it is for a Jew to associate with or to visit any one of another nation; but God has shown me that I should not call any man common or unclean.

Acts 10.28

Birth

See also **Born Again**

Then the Lord God formed man of dust from the ground, and breathed into his nostrils the breath of life; and man became a living being.

Genesis 2.7

To the woman he said,
'I will greatly multiply your pain in childbearing . . .'

Genesis 3.16

But man is born to trouble
as the sparks fly upward.

Job 5.7

Man that is born of a woman is of few days, and full of trouble.
He comes forth like a flower, and withers; he flees like a shadow, and continues not.

Job 14.1–2

Yet thou art he who took me from the womb;
thou didst keep me safe upon my mother's breasts.
Upon thee was I cast from my birth,
and since my mother bore me thou hast been my God.

Psalms 22.9–10

The wicked go astray from the womb,
they err from their birth, speaking lies.

Psalms 58.3

A stupid son is a grief to a father;
and the father of a fool has no joy.

Proverbs 17.21

Let your father and mother be glad,
let her who bore you rejoice.

Proverbs 23.25

A good name is better than precious ointment;
and the day of death, than the day of birth.

Ecclesiastes 7.1

Shall I bring to the birth and not cause to bring forth?
says the Lord;
shall I, who cause to bring forth, shut the womb?
says your God.

Isaiah 66.9

Before I formed you in the womb I knew you,
and before you were born I consecrated you.

Jeremiah 1.5

They have dealt faithlessly with the Lord;
for they have borne alien children.
Now the new moon shall devour them with their fields.

Hosea 5.7

Truly, truly, I say to you, unless one is born anew, he cannot see the kingdom of God.

John 3.3

That which is born of the flesh is flesh, and that which is born of the Spirit is spirit.

John 3.6

When a woman is in travail she has sorrow, because her hour has come; but when she is delivered of the child, she no longer remembers the anguish, for joy that a child is born into the world.

John 16.21

For this I was born, and for this I have come into the world, to bear witness to the truth.

John 18.37

For though you have countless guides in Christ, you do not have many fathers. For I became your father in Christ Jesus through the gospel.

1 Corinthians 4.15

My little children, with whom I am again in travail until Christ be formed in you!

Galatians 4.19

Yet woman will be saved through bearing children, if she continues in faith and love and holiness, with modesty.

1 Timothy 2.15

You have been born anew, not of perishable seed but of imperishable, through the living and abiding word of God.

1 Peter 1.23

If you know that he is righteous, you may be sure that every one who does right is born of him.

1 John 2.29

No one born of God commits sin; for God's nature abides in him, and he cannot sin because he is born of God.

1 John 3.9

Blame

See also **Guilt, Judgment**

Though I am innocent, my own mouth
    would condemn me;
  though I am blameless, he would prove
    me perverse.

Job 9.20

Will you condemn him who is righteous and mighty.

Job 34.17

The Lord will not abandon him to his
    power,
  or let him be condemned when he is
    brought to trial.

Psalms 37.33

With my mouth I will give great thanks to
    the Lord;
  I will praise him in the midst of the
    throng.

For he stands at the right hand of the
    needy,
  to save him from those who condemn him
    to death.

Psalms 109.30−31

A good man obtains favour from the Lord,
  but a man of evil devices he condemns.

Proverbs 12.2

He who justifies the wicked and he who
    condemns the righteous
  are both alike an abomination to the
    Lord.

Proverbs 17.15

When a man's folly brings his way to ruin,
  his heart rages against the Lord.

Proverbs 19.3

Behold, the Lord God helps me;
  who will declare me guilty?

Isaiah 50.9

But he was wounded for our transgressions,
  he was bruised for our iniquities;
upon him was the chastisement that made
    us whole,
  and with his stripes we are healed.

Isaiah 53.5

And you shall confute every tongue that
    rises against you in judgment.
This is the heritage of the servants of the
    Lord.

Isaiah 54.17

Yet let no one contend,
  and let none accuse.

Hosea 4.4

Blessed are you when men revile you and persecute you and utter all kinds of evil against you falsely on my account.

Matthew 5.11

Judge not, and you will not be judged.

Luke 6.37

For God sent the Son into the world, not to condemn the world, but that the world might be saved through him.

John 3.17

Let him who is without sin among you be the first to throw a stone at her.

John 8.7

So then he has mercy upon whomever he wills, and he hardens the heart of whomever he wills.

You will say to me then, 'Why does he still find fault? For you can resist his will?' But who are you, a man, to answer back to God?

Romans 9.18−20

We put no obstacle in any one's way, so that no fault may be found with our ministry, but as servants of God we commend ourselves in every way.

2 Corinthians 6.3−4

For the sake of Christ, then, I am content with weaknesses, insults, hardships, persecutions, and calamities.

2 Corinthians 12.10

And may your spirit and soul and body be kept sound and blameless at the coming of our Lord Jesus Christ.

1 Thessalonians 5.23

By this we shall know that we are of the truth, and reassure our hearts before him whenever our hearts condemn us; for God is greater than our hearts, and he knows everything. Beloved, if our hearts do not condemn us, we have confidence before God.

1 John 3.19−21

Blamelessness

He who walks in the way that is blameless shall minister to me.

Psalms 101.6

But as servants of God we commend ourselves in every way . . . in honour and dishonour, in ill repute and good repute.

2 Corinthians 6.4,8

Blasphemy

You shall not take the name of the Lord your God in vain; for the Lord will not hold him guiltless who takes his name in vain.

Exodus 20.7

And you shall not swear by my name falsely, and so profane the name of your God.

Leviticus 19.12

Whoever curses his God shall bear his sin.

Leviticus 24.15

Curse God, and die.

Job 2.9

Why does the wicked renounce God,
    and say in his heart, 'Thou wilt not call to account'?

Psalms 10.13

They scoff and speak with malice;
    loftily they threaten oppression.
They set their mouths against the heavens,
    and their tongue struts through the earth.

Psalms 73.8−9

And an impious people reviles thy name.

Psalms 74.18

He loved to curse; let curses come on him!
    He did not like blessing; may it be far
        from him!

Psalms 109.17

Feed me with the food that is needful for
        me,
lest I be full, and deny thee,
    and say, 'Who is the Lord?'
or lest I be poor, and steal,
    and profane the name of my God.

Proverbs 30.8−9

Woe to him who strives with his Maker,
    an earthen vessel with the potter!
Does the clay say to him who fashions it,
    'What are you making'?
or 'Your work has no handles'?

Isaiah 45.9

Do not swear at all, either by heaven, for it is the throne of God, or by the earth, for it is his footstool . . . Let what you say be simply 'Yes' or 'No'; anything more than this comes from evil.

Matthew 5.34−35,37

Therefore I tell you, every sin and blasphemy will be forgiven men, but the blasphemy against the Spirit will not be forgiven.

Matthew 12.31

For out of the heart come evil thoughts, murder, adultery, fornication, theft, false witness, slander. These are what defile a man.

Matthew 15.19−20

Whoever, therefore, eats the bread or drinks the cup of the Lord in an unworthy manner will be guilty of profaning the body and blood of the Lord . . . For any one who eats and drinks without discerning the body eats and drinks judgment upon himself.

1 Corinthians 11.27,29

Therefore I want you to understand that no one speaking by the Spirit of God ever says 'Jesus be cursed!'

1 Corinthians 12.3

Let no evil talk come out of your mouths, but only such as is good for edifying, as fits the occasion, that it may impart grace to those who hear.

Ephesians 4.29

But now put them all away: anger, wrath, malice, slander, and foul talk from your mouth.

Colossians 3.8

And the man of lawlessness is revealed, the son of perdition, who opposes and exalts himself against every so-called god or object of worship, so that he takes his seat in the temple of God, proclaiming himself to be God.

2 Thessalonians 2.3−4

So that the name of God and the teaching may not be defamed.

1 Timothy 6.1

For men will be lovers of self, lovers of money, proud, arrogant, abusive, disobedient to their parents, ungrateful, unholy, inhuman, implacable, slanderers, profligates, fierce, haters of good, treacherous, reckless, swollen with conceit, lovers of pleasure rather than lovers of God.

2 Timothy 3.2−4

Bold and wilful, they are not afraid to revile the glorious ones.

2 Peter 2.10

Men gnawed their tongues in anguish and cursed the God of heaven for their pain and sores, and did not repent of their deeds.

Revelation 16.10−11

Blessings

See also **Happiness, Reward**

Because you have done this, and have not withheld your son, your only son, I will indeed bless you.

Genesis 22.16−17

By God Almighty who will bless you
　with blessings of heaven above,
blessings of the deep that couches beneath,
　blessing of the breasts and of the womb.
The blessings of your father
　are mighty beyond the blessings of the
　　eternal mountains,
　the bounties of the everlasting hills.

Genesis 49.25−26

If you walk in my statutes and observe my commandments and do them, then I will give you your rains in their season, and the land shall yield its increase, and the trees of the field shall yield their fruit. And your threshing shall last to the time of vintage, and the vintage shall last to the time for sowing; and you shall eat your bread to the full, and dwell in your land securely.

Leviticus 26.3−5

Know therefore that the Lord your God is God, the faithful God who keeps covenant and steadfast love with those who love him and keep his commandments, to a thousand generations . . . You shall be blessed above all peoples.

Deuteronomy 7.9,14

Behold, I set before you this day a blessing and a curse: the blessing, if you obey the commandments of the Lord your God, which I command you this day, and the curse, if you do not obey the commandments of the Lord your God.

Deuteronomy 11.26–28

And there you shall eat before the Lord your God, and you shall rejoice, you and your households, in all that you undertake, in which the Lord your God has blessed you.

Deuteronomy 12.7

Now therefore may it please thee to bless the house of thy servant, that it may continue for ever before thee; for what thou, O Lord, hast blessed is blessed for ever.

1 Chronicles 17.27

The hand of our God is for good upon all that seek him, and the power of his wrath is against all that forsake him.

Ezra 8.22

For thou dost meet him with goodly
    blessings;
  thou dost set a crown of fine gold upon
    his head.
He asked life of thee; thou gavest it to him,
  length of days for ever and ever.

Psalms 21.3–4

O save thy people, and bless thy heritage;
  be thou their shepherd, and carry them
    for ever.

Psalms 28.9

Thou visitest the earth and waterest it,
  thou greatly enrichest it;
the river of God is full of water;
  thou providest their grain.

Psalms 65.9

Blessed are the men whose strength is in
    thee,
  in whose heart are the highways to Zion.

Psalms 84.5

If you are willing and obedient,
  you shall eat the good of the land.

Isaiah 1.19

For I will pour water on the thirsty land,
  and streams on the dry ground;
I will pour my Spirit upon your
    descendants,
  and my blessing on your offspring.

Isaiah 44.3

And God is able to provide you with every blessing in abundance, so that you may always have enough of everything and may provide in abundance for every good work.

2 Corinthians 9.8

Every good endowment and every perfect gift is from above, coming down from the Father of lights.

James 1.17

Blindness (Moral/Physical/ Spiritual)

See also **Darkness, Light**

Who has made man's mouth? Who makes him dumb, or deaf, or seeing, or blind? Is it not I, the Lord?

Exodus 4.11

And you shall not take a bribe, for a bribe blinds the eyes of the wise and subverts the cause of the righteous.

Deuteronomy 16.19

Cursed be he who misleads a blind man on the road.

Deuteronomy 27.18

But to this day the Lord has not given you a mind to understand, or eyes to see, or ears to hear.

Deuteronomy 29.4

They have neither knowledge nor
    understanding,
  they walk about in darkness;
  all the foundations of the earth are
    shaken.

Psalms 82.5

The Lord opens the eyes of the blind.

Psalms 146.8

The way of the wicked is like deep
   darkness;
  they do not know over what they
   stumble.

Proverbs 4.19

Woe to those who call evil good
  and good evil,
who put darkness for light
  and light for darkness.

Isaiah 5.20

And he said, 'Go, and say to this people:
  "Hear and hear, but do not understand;
   see and see, but do not perceive."
Make the heart of this people fat,
  and their ears heavy,
  and shut their eyes;
lest they see with their eyes,
  and hear with their ears,
and understand with their hearts,
  and turn and be healed.'

Isaiah 6.9–10

In that day the deaf shall hear
  the words of a book,
and out of their gloom and darkness
  the eyes of the blind shall see.

Isaiah 29.18

Then the eyes of the blind shall be opened,
  and the ears of the deaf unstopped;
then shall the lame man leap like a hart,
  and the tongue of the dumb sing for joy.

Isaiah 35.5–6

I have given you as a covenant to the
   people,
  a light to the nations,
  to open the eyes that are blind.

Isaiah 42.6–7

And I will lead the blind
  in a way that they now not,
in paths that they have not known
  I will guide them.
I will turn the darkness before them into
   light,
  the rough places into level ground.

Isaiah 42.16

They know not, nor do they discern; for he
has shut their eyes, so that they cannot see,
and their minds, so that they cannot understand.

Isaiah 44.18

The eye is the lamp of the body. So, if
your eye is sound, your whole body will be
full of light; but if your eye is not sound,
your whole body will be full of darkness. If
then the light in you is darkness, how great
is the darkness!

Matthew 6.22–23

The blind receive their sight and the lame
walk, lepers are cleansed and the deaf hear,
and the dead are raised up, and the poor
have good news preached to them.

Matthew 11.5

And if a blind man leads a blind man, both
will fall into a pit.

Matthew 15.14

The Spirit of the Lord is upon me,
because he has anointed me to preach good
   news to the poor.
He has sent me to proclaim release to the
   captives
and recovering of sight to the blind.

Luke 4.18

For judgment I came into this world, that
those who do not see may see, and that
those who see may become blind.

John 9.39

To whom I send you to open their eyes,
that they may turn from darkness to light
and from the power of Satan to God.

Acts 26.17–18

And even if our gospel is veiled, it is
veiled only to those who are perishing. In
their case the god of this world has blinded
the minds of the unbelievers, to keep them
from seeing the light of the gospel of the
glory of Christ, who is the likeness of God.

2 Corinthians 4.3–4

That you must no longer live as the
Gentiles do, in the futility of their minds;

they are darkened in their understanding, alienated from the life of God because of the ignorance that is in them, due to their hardness of heart.

Ephesians 4.17—18

Therefore do not associate with them, for once you were darkness, but now you are light in the Lord; walk as children of light (for the fruit of light is found in all that is good and right and true).

Ephesians 5.7—9

He who loves his brother abides in the light, and in it there is no cause for stumbling. But he who hates his brother is in the darkness and walks in the darkness, and does not know where he is going, because the darkness has blinded his eyes.

1 John 2.9—11

For you say, I am rich, I have prospered, and I need nothing; not knowing that you are wretched, pitiable, poor, blind, and naked.

Revelation 3.17

Blood of Christ

See also **Eucharist**

And he took a cup, and when he had given thanks he gave it to them, and they all drank of it. And he said to them, 'This is my blood of the covenant, which is poured out for many.'

Mark 14.23—24

Truly, truly, I say to you, unless you eat the flesh of the Son of man and drink his blood, you have no life in you.

John 6.53

Take heed to yourselves and to all the flock, in which the Holy Spirit has made you overseers, to care for the church of God which he obtained with the blood of his own Son.

Acts 20.27—28

He entered once for all into the Holy Place, taking not the blood of goats and calves but his own blood, thus securing an eternal redemption.

Hebrews 9.12

But if we walk in the light, as he is in the light, we have fellowship with one another, and the blood of Jesus his Son cleanses us from all sin.

1 John 1.7

Boasting

See also **Arrogance, Pride, Vanity**

Talk no more so very proudly,
    let not arrogance come from your mouth;
for the Lord is a God of knowledge,
    and by him actions are weighed.

1 Samuel 2.3

The boastful may not stand before thy
        eyes;
    thou hatest all evildoers.

Psalms 5.5

For the wicked boasts of the desires of his heart.

Psalms 10.3

May the Lord cut off all flattering lips,
    the tongue that makes great boasts.

Psalms 12.3

My deadly enemies who surround me.
They close their hearts to pity;
    with their mouths they speak arrogantly.

Psalms 17.9—10

Some boast of chariots, and some of
        horses;
    but we boast of the name of the Lord our
        God.
They will collapse and fall;
    but we shall rise and stand upright.

Psalms 20.7—8

Why should I fear . . .
men who trust in their wealth
    and boast of the abundance of their
        riches?

Psalms 49.5—6

Why do you boast, O mighty man,
  of mischief done against the godly?
All the day you are plotting destruction.
  Your tongue is like a sharp razor,
  you worker of treachery.

Psalms 52.1–2

Let the righteous rejoice in the Lord,
  and take refuge in him!
Let all the upright in heart glory!

Psalms 64.10

I say to the boastful, 'Do not boast,'
  and to the wicked, 'Do not lift up your
    horn;
do not lift up your horn on high,
  or speak with insolent neck.'

Psalms 75.4–5

They pour out their arrogant words,
  they boast, all the evildoers.

Psalms 94.4

Many a man proclaims his own loyalty,
  but a faithful man who can find?

Proverbs 20.6

'It is bad, it is bad,' says the buyer;
  but when he goes away, then he boasts.

Proverbs 20.14

Do not boast about tomorrow,
  for you do not know what a day may
    bring forth.

Proverbs 27.1

Let another praise you, and not your own
    mouth;
  a stranger, and not your own lips.

Proverbs 27.2

Shall the axe vaunt itself over him who
    hews with it,
  or the saw magnify itself against him who
    wields it?
As if a rod should wield him who lifts it,
  or as if a staff should lift him who is not
    wood!

Isaiah 10.15

Thus says the Lord: Let not the wise man
glory in his wisdom, let not the mighty man
glory in his might, let not the rich man glory
in his riches; but let him who glories glory
in this, that he understands and knows me.

Jeremiah 9.23–24

And you magnified yourselves against me
with your mouth, and multiplied your
words against me; I heard it. Thus says the
Lord God: For the rejoicing of the whole
earth I will make you desolate.

Ezekiel 35.13–14

Then what becomes of our boasting? It is
excluded.

Romans 3.27

That no human being might boast in the
presence of God.

1 Corinthians 1.29

Let him who boasts, boast of the Lord.

1 Corinthians 1.31

So let no one boast of men.

1 Corinthians 3.21

If I must boast, I will boast of the things
that show my weakness.

2 Corinthians 11.30

But far be it from me to glory except in the
cross of our Lord Jesus Christ.

Galatians 6.14

For by grace you have been saved through
faith; and this is not your own doing, it is
the gift of God — not because of works,
lest any man should boast.

Ephesians 2.8–9

But understand this, that in the last days
there will come times of stress. For men will
be lovers of self, lovers of money, proud,
arrogant, abusive.

2 Timothy 3.1–2

The tongue is a little member and boasts
of great things.

James 3.5

You boast in your arrogance. All such
boasting is evil.

James 4.16

Body

His angels he charges with error;
how much more those who dwell in
　　houses of clay,
　whose foundation is in the dust,
　who are crushed before the moth.
Between morning and evening they are
　　destroyed.

Job 4.18−19

The eye is the lamp of the body. So, if
your eye is sound, your whole body will be
full of light.

Matthew 6.22

And do not fear those who kill the body
but cannot kill the soul; rather fear him
who can destroy both soul and body in hell.

Matthew 10.28

Let not sin therefore reign in your mortal
bodies, to make you obey their passions.
Do not yield your members to sin as instruments of wickedness.

Romans 6.12−13

But if Christ is in you, although your
bodies are dead because of sin, your spirits
are alive because of righteousness. If the
Spirit of him who raised Jesus from the
dead dwells in you, he who raised Christ
Jesus from the dead will give life to your
mortal bodies also through his Spirit which
dwells in you.

Romans 8.10−11

I appeal to you therefore, brethren, by the
mercies of God, to present your bodies as a
living sacrifice, holy and acceptable to God,
which is your spiritual worship.

Romans 12.1

For as in one body we have many members, and all the members do not have the
same function, so we, though many, are
one body in Christ, and individually members one of another.

Romans 12.4−5

Do you not know that your body is a
temple of the Holy Spirit within you, which

you have from God? You are not your own;
you were bought with a price. So glorify
God in your body.

1 Corinthians 6.19−20

Now you are the body of Christ and individually members of it. And God has
appointed in the church first apostles,
second prophets, third teachers, then
workers of miracles, then healers, helpers,
administrators, speakers in various kinds of
tongues.

1 Corinthians 12.27−28

Always carrying in the body the death of
Jesus, so that the life of Jesus may also be
manifested in our bodies.

2 Corinthians 4.10

For we know that if the earthly tent we live
in is destroyed, we have a building from
God, a house not made with hands, eternal
in the heavens.

2 Corinthians 5.1

We know that while we are at home in the
body we are away from the Lord.

2 Corinthians 5.6

For no man ever hates his own flesh, but
nourishes and cherishes it, as Christ does
the church, because we are members of his
body.

Ephesians 5.29−30

Lord Jesus Christ . . . will change our
lowly body to be like his glorious body.

Philippians 3.21

Boldness

And when they heard it, they lifted their
voices together to God and said, 'Sovereign
Lord, who didst make the heaven and the
earth and the sea and everything in them,
who by the mouth of our father David, thy
servant, didst say by the Holy Spirit,
　"Why did the Gentiles rage,
　　and the peoples imagine vain things?

The kings of the earth set themselves in
    array,
and the rulers were gathered together,
against the Lord and against his
    Anointed" —

for truly in this city there were gathered
together against thy holy servant Jesus,
whom thou didst anoint, both Herod and
Pontius Pilate, with the Gentiles and the
peoples of Israel, to do whatever thy hand
and thy plan had predestined to take place.
And now, Lord, look upon their threats,
and grant to thy servants to speak thy word
with all boldness, while thou stretchest out
thy hand to heal, and signs and wonders are
performed through the name of thy holy
servant Jesus.'

Acts 4.24–30

Boredom

Go to the ant, O sluggard;
    consider her ways, and be wise.

Proverbs 6.6

Let your foot be seldom in your
    neighbour's house,
lest he become weary of you and hate
    you.

Proverbs 25.17

The toil of a fool wearies him,
    so that he does not know the way to the
    city.

Ecclesiastes 10.15

Is it too little for you to weary men, that
you weary my God also?

Isaiah 7.13

And let us not grow weary in well-doing,
for in due season we shall reap, if we do not
lose heart.

Galatians 6.9

Would that you were cold or hot! So,
because you are lukewarm, and neither cold
nor hot, I will spew you out of my mouth.

Revelation 3.15–16

Born Again

Truly, truly, I say to you, unless one is
born anew, he cannot see the kingdom of
God . . . Truly, truly, I say to you, unless
one is born of water and the Spirit, he
cannot enter the kingdom of God. That
which is born of the flesh is flesh, and that
which is born of the Spirit is spirit. Do not
marvel that I said to you, 'You must be
born anew.' The wind blows where it wills,
and you hear the sound of it, but you do
not know whence it comes or whither it
goes; so it is with every one who is born of
the Spirit.

John 3.3,5–8

If any one is in Christ, he is a new creation;
the old has passed away, behold, the new
has come.

2 Corinthians 5.17

You have been born anew, not of perishable seed but of imperishable, through the
living and abiding word of God; for
    'All flesh is like grass . . .
    The grass withers . . .
    but the word of the Lord abides for ever.'

1 Peter 1.23–24

Borrowing

See also **Lending**

The wicked borrows, and cannot pay back,
    but the righteous is generous and gives.

Psalms 37.21

And the borrower is the slave of the
lender.

Proverbs 22.7

Give to him who begs from you, and do
not refuse him who would borrow from
you.

Matthew 5.42

Owe no one anything, except to love one
another.

Romans 13.8

Bravery

See also **Confidence**

Only be valiant for me and fight the Lord's battles.

1 Samuel 18.17

Now therefore let your hands be strong, and be valiant.

2 Samuel 2.7

Deal courageously, and may the Lord be with the upright!

2 Chronicles 19.11

The Lord is my light and my salvation;
   whom shall I fear?
The Lord is the stronghold of my life;
   of whom shall I be afraid?
. . . Though a host encamp against me,
   my heart shall not fear.

Psalms 27.1,3

Be strong, and let your heart take courage,
   all you who wait for the Lord!

Psalms 31.24

In God I trust without a fear.
   What can man do to me?

Psalms 56.11

With God we shall do valiantly;
   it is he who will tread down our foes.

Psalms 60.12

The wicked flee when no one pursues,
   but the righteous are bold as a lion.

Proverbs 28.1

In the world you have tribulation; but be of good cheer, I have overcome the world.

John 16.33

Bribery

And you shall take no bribe, for a bribe blinds the officials, and subverts the cause of those who are in the right.

Exodus 23.8

For the Lord your God is God of gods and Lord of lords, the great, the mighty, and the terrible God, who is not partial and takes no bribe.

Deuteronomy 10.17

You shall appoint judges . . . and they shall judge the people with righteous judgment.

Deuteronomy 16.18

Cursed be he who takes a bribe to slay an innocent person.

Deuteronomy 27.25

Now then, let the fear of the Lord be upon you; take heed what you do, for there is no perversion of justice with the Lord our God, or partiality, or taking bribes.

2 Chronicles 19.7

For the company of the godless is barren,
   and fire consumes the tents of bribery.

Job 15.34

Sweep me not away with sinners,
   nor my life with bloodthirsty men,
men in whose hands are evil devices,
   and whose right hands are full of bribes.

Psalms 26.9–10

He who is greedy for unjust gain makes
      trouble for his household,
   but he who hates bribes will live.

Proverbs 15.27

A bribe is like a magic stone in the eyes of
      him who gives it;
   wherever he turns he prospers.

Proverbs 17.8

A wicked man accepts a bribe from the
      bosom
   to pervert the ways of justice.

Proverbs 17.23

A man's gift makes room for him
   and brings him before great men.

Proverbs 18.16

A gift in secret averts anger;
   and a bribe in the bosom, strong wrath.

Proverbs 21.14

To show partiality is not good;
  but for a piece of bread a man will do
    wrong.

Proverbs 28.21

A bribe corrupts the mind.

Ecclesiastes 7.7

He . . . who despises the gain of
    oppressions,
who shakes his hands, lest they hold a
    bribe . . .
he will dwell on the heights.

Isaiah 33.15–16

Broadcasting

See also **Testifying**

What I tell you in the dark, utter in the
light; and what you hear whispered, proclaim upon the housetops.

Matthew 10.27

Brutality

See also **Cruelty, Violence**

Now the earth was corrupt in God's sight,
and the earth was filled with violence.

Genesis 6.11

The Lord tests the righteous and the
    wicked,
  and his soul hates him that loves
    violence.

Psalms 11.5

But thou, O God, wilt cast them down
  into the lowest pit;
men of blood and treachery
  shall not live out half their days.

Psalms 55.23

O God, insolent men have risen up against
    me;
  a band of ruthless men seek my life . . .
Show me a sign of thy favour,
that those who hate me may see and be
    put to shame
  because thou, Lord, hast helped me and
    comforted me.

Psalms 86.14,17

They crush thy people, O Lord,
  and afflict thy heritage.
They slay the widow and the sojourner,
  and murder the fatherless;
and they say, 'The Lord does not see;
the God of Jacob does not perceive.' . . .
He who planted the ear, does he not
    hear?
He who formed the eye, does he not see?

Psalms 94.5–7,9

Wipe them out for their wickedness;
  the Lord our God will wipe them out.

Psalms 94.23

Do not envy a man of violence
  and do not choose any of his ways.

Proverbs 3.31

From the fruit of his mouth a good man
    eats good,
  but the desire of the treacherous is for
    violence.

Proverbs 13.2

And do no wrong or violence to the alien,
the fatherless, and the widow, nor shed
innocent blood in this place.

Jeremiah 22.3

You . . . put far away the evil day,
  and bring near the seat of violence.

Amos 6.3

Destruction and violence are before me;
  strife and contention arise.

Habakkuk 1.3

Budget

For which of you, desiring to build a
tower, does not first sit down and count the
cost, whether he has enough to complete it?

Luke 14.28

Building

Wisdom builds her house,
  but folly with her own hands tears it
    down.

Proverbs 14.1

By wisdom a house is built,
  and by understanding it is established;
by knowledge the rooms are filled
  with all precious and pleasant riches.

Proverbs 24.3−4

Prepare your work outside,
  get everything ready for you in the field;
and after that build your house.

Proverbs 24.27

Woe to him who builds a town with blood,
  and founds a city on iniquity!

Habakkuk 2.12

For we are God's fellow workers; you are God's field, God's building.

1 Corinthians 3.9

So then you are no longer strangers and sojourners, but you are fellow citizens with the saints and members of the household of God . . . in whom you also are built into it for a dwelling place of God in the Spirit.

Ephesians 2.19,22

Burden

Cast your burden on the Lord,
  and he will sustain you.

Psalms 55.22

Come to me, all who labour and are heavy laden, and I will give you rest. Take my yoke upon you, and learn from me; for I am gentle and lowly in heart, and you will find rest for your souls. For my yoke is easy, and my burden is light.

Matthew 11.28−30

Bear one another's burdens, and so fulfil the law of Christ . . . For each man will have to bear his own load.

Galatians 6.2,5

Business

And all these blessings shall come upon you and overtake you, if you obey the voice of the Lord your God. Blessed shall you be in the city, and blessed shall you be in the field. Blessed shall be the fruit of your body, and the fruit of your ground, and the fruit of your beasts, the increase of your cattle, and the young of your flock.

Deuteronomy 28.2−4

The Lord will open to you his good treasury the heavens, to give the rain of your land in its season and to bless all the work of your hands.

Deuteronomy 28.12

Man goes forth to his work
  and to his labour until the evening.

Psalms 104.23

Some went down to the sea in ships,
  doing business on the great waters;
they saw the deeds of the Lord,
  his wondrous works in the deep.

Psalms 107.23−24

It is well with the man who deals
generously and lends,
  who conducts his affairs with justice.

Psalms 112.5

A slack hand causes poverty,
  but the hand of the diligent makes rich.

Proverbs 10.4

Wealth hastily gotten will dwindle,
  but he who gathers little by little will
    increase it.

Proverbs 13.11

In all toil there is profit.

Proverbs 14.23

Do you see a man skilful in his work?
  he will stand before kings.

Proverbs 22.29

It is God's gift to man that every one should eat and drink and take pleasure in all his toil.

Ecclesiastes 3.13

But we exhort you, brethren, to do so more and more, to aspire to live quietly, to mind your own affairs, and to work with your hands, as we charged you.

1 Thessalonians 4.10−11

Come now, you who say, 'Today or to-tomorrow we will go into such and such a town and spend a year there and trade and get gain' . . . you do not know about to-morrow. . . . Instead you ought to say, 'If the Lord wills, we shall live and we shall do this or that.'

James 4.13−14,15

C

Calendar/Seasons

See also **Time**

And God said, 'Let there be lights in the firmament of the heavens to separate the day from the night; and let them be for signs and for seasons and for days and years . . . And God made the two great lights, the greater light to rule the day, and the lesser light to rule the night.

Genesis 1.14,16

While the earth remains, seedtime and harvest, cold and heat, summer and winter, day and night, shall not cease.

Genesis 8.22

Remember the sabbath day, to keep it holy. Six days you shall labour, and do all your work; but the seventh day is a sabbath to the Lord your God.

Exodus 20.8–10

Thine is the day, thine also the night;
  thou hast established the luminaries and
    the sun.
Thou hast fixed all the bounds of the earth;
  thou hast made summer and winter.

Psalms 74.16–17

Thou hast made the moon to mark the
    seasons;
  the sun knows its time for setting.

Psalms 104.19

For everything there is a season, and a time for every matter under heaven.

Ecclesiastes 3.1

Yet he did not leave himself without witness, for he did good and gave you from heaven rains and fruitful seasons, satisfying your hearts with food and gladness.

Acts 14.17

Therefore let no one pass judgment on you in questions of food and drink or with regard to a festival or a new moon or a sabbath. These are only a shadow of what is to come; but the substance belongs to Christ.

Colossians 2.16–17

Calling

I cry to God Most High,
  to God who fulfils his purpose for me.

Psalms 57.2

Blessed is he whom thou dost choose and
    bring near,
  to dwell in thy courts!

Psalms 65.4

Because I have called and you refused to
    listen,
  have stretched out my hand and no one
    has heeded.

Proverbs 1.24

And I heard the voice of the Lord saying, 'Whom shall I send, and who will go for us?' Then I said, 'Here am I! Send me.'

Isaiah 6.8

I will give you the treasures of darkness
  and the hoards in secret places,
then you may know that it is I, the Lord,
  the God of Israel, who call you by your
    name.

Isaiah 45.3

Before I formed you in the womb I knew
you,
  and before you were born I consecrated
you;
I appointed you a prophet to the nations.

Jeremiah 1.5

For many are called, but few are chosen.

Matthew 22.14

Follow me.

Luke 5.27

No one can come to me unless the Father
who sent me draws him; and I will raise him
up at the last day.

John 6.44

You did not choose me, but I chose you
and appointed you that you should go and
bear fruit and that your fruit should abide.

John 15.16

And those whom he called he also justified; and those whom he justified he also
glorified.

Romans 8.30

For consider your call, brethren; not many
of you were wise according to worldly
standards, not many were powerful, not
many were of noble birth; but God chose
what is foolish in the world to shame the
wise, God chose what is weak in the world
to shame the strong.

1 Corinthians 1.26−27

You were bought with a price; do not
become slaves of men.

1 Corinthians 7.23

Having the eyes of your hearts enlightened, that you may know what is the hope
to which he has called you.

Ephesians 1.18

Lead a life worthy of the calling to which
you have been called.

Ephesians 4.1

There is one body and one Spirit, just as
you were called to the one hope.

Ephesians 4.4

I press on toward the goal for the prize of
the upward call of God in Christ Jesus.

Philippians 3.14

Lead a life worthy of God, who calls you
into his own kingdom and glory.

1 Thessalonians 2.12

To this end we always pray for you, that
our God may make you worthy of his call,
and may fulfil every good resolve and work
of faith by his power.

2 Thessalonians 1.11

To this he called you through our gospel,
so that you may obtain the glory of our
Lord Jesus Christ.

2 Thessalonians 2.14

Do not be ashamed then of testifying to
our Lord, nor of me his prisoner, but share
in suffering for the gospel in the power of
God, who saved us and called us with a
holy calling, not in virtue of our works but
in virtue of his own purpose . . .

2 Timothy 1.8−9

Therefore, holy brethren, who share in a
heavenly call, consider Jesus.

Hebrews 3.1

Therefore he is the mediator of a new
covenant, so that those who are called may
receive the promised eternal inheritance,
since a death has occurred which redeems
them from the transgressions under the first
covenant.

Hebrews 9.15

By faith Abraham obeyed when he was
called to go out to a place which he was to
receive as an inheritance; and he went out,
not knowing where he was to go.

Hebrews 11.8

But if when you do right and suffer for it
you take it patiently, you have God's
approval. For to this you have been called,
because Christ also suffered for you, leaving you an example, that you should follow
in his steps.

1 Peter 2.20−21

Therefore, brethren, be the more zealous to confirm your call and election, for if you do this you will never fall.

2 Peter 1.10

They will make war on the Lamb, and the Lamb will conquer them, for he is Lord of lords and King of kings, and those with him are called and chosen and faithful.

Revelation 17.14

Callousness

See also **Cruelty**

Love your neighbour as yourself.

Leviticus 19.18

For you have exacted pledges of your
    brothers for nothing,
  and stripped the naked of their clothing.
You have given no water to the weary to
    drink,
  and you have withheld bread from the
    hungry.
The man with power possessed the land,
  and the favoured man dwelt in it.
You have sent widows away empty,
  and the arms of the fatherless were
    crushed.
Therefore snares are round about you,
  and sudden terror overwhelms you;
your light is darkened, so that you cannot
    see,
  and a flood of water covers you.

Job 22.6−11

I looked for pity, but there was none;
  and for comforters, but I found none.
They gave me poison for food,
  and for my thirst they gave me vinegar to
    drink.
Let their own table before them become a
    snare;
  let their sacrificial feasts be a trap.

Psalms 69.20−22

May their camp be a desolation,
  let no one dwell in their tents.
For they persecute him whom thou hast
    smitten,
  and him whom thou hast wounded, they
    afflict still more.

Psalms 69.25−26

He who oppresses a poor man insults his
  Maker.

Proverbs 14.31

He who mocks the poor insults his Maker;
  he who is glad at calamity will not go
    unpunished.

Proverbs 17.5

He who closes his ear to the cry of the
    poor
  will himself cry out and not be heard.

Proverbs 21.13

But he who hardens his heart will fall into
  calamity.

Proverbs 28.14

Render true judgments, show kindness and mercy each to his brother, do not oppress the widow, the fatherless, the sojourner, or the poor . . . But they refused to hearken . . . and stopped their ears that they might not hear . . . Therefore great wrath came from the Lord of hosts. 'As I called, and they would not hear, so they called, and I would not hear,' says the Lord of hosts.

Zechariah 7.9−10,11−13

And many false prophets will arise and lead many astray. And because wickedness is multiplied, most men's love will grow cold.

Matthew 24.11−12

Then he will say to those at his left hand, 'Depart from me, you cursed, into the eternal fire prepared for the devil and his angels; for I was hungry and you gave me no food, I was thirsty and you gave me no drink, I was a stranger and you did not welcome me, naked and you did not clothe me, sick and in prison and you did not visit me . . . Truly, I say to you, as you did it not to one of the least of these, you did it not to me.'

Matthew 25.41−43,45

So then he has mercy upon whomever he wills, and he hardens the heart of whomever he wills.

Romans 9.18

But exhort one another every day, as long as it is called 'today,' that none of you may be hardened by the deceitfulness of sin.

Hebrews 3.13

But if any one has the world's goods and sees his brother in need, yet closes his heart against him, how does God's love abide in him?

1 John 3.17

Calmness

See also **Peace**

Be still, and know that I am God.

Psalms 46.10

Cast your burden on the Lord,
  and he will sustain you.

Psalms 55.22

Then they cried to the Lord in their
    trouble,
  and he delivered them from their distress;
he made the storm be still,
  and the waves of the sea were hushed.

Psalms 107.28–29

Return, O my soul, to your rest;
  for the Lord has dealt bountifully with
    you.

Psalms 116.7

But he who listens to me will dwell secure
  and will be at ease, without dread of evil.

Proverbs 1.33

For deference will make amends for great
    offences.

Ecclesiastes 10.4

Therefore I tell you, do not be anxious about your life, what you shall eat or what you shall drink, nor about your body, what you shall put on . . . do not be anxious about tomorrow, for tomorrow will be anxious for itself.

Matthew 6.25,34

And he awoke and rebuked the wind, and said to the sea, 'Peace! Be still!' And the wind ceased, and there was a great calm. He said to them, 'Why are you afraid? Have you no faith?'

Mark 4.39–40

You ought to be quiet and do nothing rash.

Acts 19.36

Have no anxiety about anything, but in everything by prayer and supplication with thanksgiving let your requests be made known to God.

Philippians 4.6

Therefore keep sane and sober for your prayers.

1 Peter 4.7

Cast all your anxieties on him, for he cares about you.

1 Peter 5.7

Be sober, be watchful. Your adversary the devil prowls around like a roaring lion, seeking some one to devour.

1 Peter 5.8

Candour

See also **Honesty, Integrity**

How many times shall I adjure you that you speak to me nothing but the truth in the name of the Lord?

1 Kings 22.16

No man who practises deceit
  shall dwell in my house;
no man who utters lies
  shall continue in my presence.

Psalms 101.7

But those who turn aside upon their
    crooked ways
  the Lord will lead away with evildoers!

Psalms 125.5

Let what you say be simply 'Yes' or 'No'; anything more than this comes from evil.

Matthew 5.37

I have said this to you in figures; the hour is coming when I shall no longer speak to you in figures but tell you plainly of the Father.

John 16.25

Let love be genuine.

Romans 12.9

If you in a tongue utter speech that is not intelligible, how will any one know what is said?

1 Corinthians 14.9

We have renounced disgraceful, underhanded ways; we refuse to practise cunning or to tamper with God's word, but by the open statement of the truth we would commend ourselves to every man's conscience in the sight of God.

2 Corinthians 4.2

Therefore, putting away falsehood, let every one speak the truth with his neighbour, for we are members one of another.

Ephesians 4.25

Capacity

See also **Ability**

If you have faith as a grain of mustard seed, you will say to this mountain, 'Move from here to there,' and it will move; and nothing will be impossible to you.

Matthew 17.20

For which of you, desiring to build a tower, does not first sit down and count the cost, whether he has enough to complete it? Otherwise, when he has laid a foundation, and is not able to finish, all who see it begin to mock him.

Luke 14.28−29

Capital

See also **Business, Money**

If riches increase, set not your heart on them.

Psalms 62.10

By your great wisdom in trade
you have increased your wealth,
and your heart has become proud in your
wealth.

Ezekiel 28.5

Again, the kingdom of heaven is like a merchant in search of fine pearls, who, on finding one pearl of great value, went and sold all that he had and bought it.

Matthew 13.45−46

A nobleman went into a far country to receive a Kingdom and then return. Calling ten of his servants, he gave them ten pounds, and said to them, 'Trade with these till I come.' . . . When he returned, . . . he commanded these servants . . . that he might know what they had gained by trading. The first came before him, saying, 'Lord, your pound has made ten pounds more.' And he said to him, 'Well done, good servant!'

Luke 19.12−13,15−17

I tell you, that to every one who has will more be given.

Luke 19.26

Captivity

Thou didst ascend the high mount,
leading captives in thy train,
and receiving gifts among men,
even among the rebellious, that the Lord
God may dwell there.

Psalms 68.18

The righteousness of the upright delivers
them,
but the treacherous are taken captive by
their lust.

Proverbs 11.6

Because the Lord has anointed me . . .
he has sent me . . .
to proclaim liberty to the captives,
and the opening of the prison to those
who are bound.

Isaiah 61.1

For I delight in the law of God, in my inmost self, but I see in my members another law at war with the law of my mind and making me captive to the law of sin which dwells in my members.

Romans 7.22–23

Take every thought captive to obey Christ.

2 Corinthians 10.5

And the Lord's servant must not be quarrelsome but kindly to every one, an apt teacher, forbearing, correcting his opponents with gentleness. God may perhaps grant that they will repent and come to know the truth, and they may escape from the snare of the devil, after being captured by him to do his will.

2 Timothy 2.24–26

Care

See also **Caution**

Only take heed, and keep your soul diligently.

Deuteronomy 4.9

Take good care to observe the commandment and the law which Moses the servant of the Lord commanded you.

Joshua 22.5

Consider what you do, for you judge not for man but for the Lord.

2 Chronicles 19.6

I said, 'I will guard my ways,
that I may not sin with my tongue.'

Psalms 39.1

Take heed that no one leads you astray. For many will come in my name, saying, 'I am the Christ,' and they will lead many astray.

Matthew 24.4–5

Watch and pray that you may not enter into temptation; the spirit indeed is willing, but the flesh is weak.

Matthew 26.41

Take heed what you hear; the measure you give will be the measure you get, and still more will be given you.

Mark 4.24

But take heed to yourselves lest you hearts be weighed down with dissipation and drunkenness and cares of this life, and that day come upon you suddenly like a snare . . . But watch at all times, praying that you may have strength to escape all these things that will take place.

Luke 21.34,36

Take heed to yourself and to your teaching; hold to that, for by so doing you will save both yourself and your hearers.

1 Timothy 4.16

Those who have believed in God may be careful to apply themselves to good deeds.

Titus 3.8

See to it that no one fail to obtain the grace of God.

Hebrews 12.15

Tend the flock of God that is your charge, not by constraint but willingly.

1 Peter 5.2

Career

But I do not account my life of any value nor as precious to myself, if only I may accomplish my course and the ministry which I received from the Lord Jesus.

Acts 20.24

Only, let every one lead the life which the Lord has assigned to him.

1 Corinthians 7.17

So, brethren, in whatever state each was called, there let him remain with God.

1 Corinthians 7.24

Do you not know that in a race all the runners compete, but only one receives the prize? So run that you may obtain it.

1 Corinthians 9.24

Let us also lay aside every weight, and sin which clings so closely, and let us run with perseverance the race that is set before us.

Hebrews 12.1

Carelessness

Therefore take good heed to yourselves. . . . beware lest you act corruptly.

Deuteronomy 4.15

Take heed lest you forget the Lord your God, by not keeping his commandments and his ordinances and his statutes.

Deuteronomy 8.11

My son, do not forget my teaching,
but let your heart keep my
commandments.

Proverbs 3.1

I will send fire . . . on those who dwell securely . . . and they shall know that I am the Lord.

Ezekiel 39.6

I tell you, on the day of judgment men will render account for every careless word they utter; for by your words you will be justified, and by your words you will be condemned.

Matthew 12.36−37

Therefore we must pay the closer attention to what we have heard, lest we drift away from it.

Hebrews 2.1

And we desire each one of you to show the same earnestness in realising the full assurance of hope until the end, so that you may not be sluggish.

Hebrews 6.11−12

Castration

He whose testicles are crushed or whose male member is cut off shall not enter the assembly of the Lord.

Deuteronomy 23.1

Caution

See also **Care**

I, wisdom, dwell in prudence,
and I find knowledge and discretion.

Proverbs 8.12

The simple believes everything,
but the prudent looks where he is going.

Proverbs 14.15

A prudent man sees danger and hides
himself;
but the simple go on, and suffer for it.

Proverbs 22.3

He who observes the wind will not sow;
and he who regards the clouds will not
reap.

Ecclesiastes 11.4

But if he had taken warning, he would have saved his life.

Ezekiel 33.5

Then if any one says to you, 'Lo, here is the Christ!' or 'There he is!' do not believe it.

Matthew 24.23

Take heed, watch; for you do not know when the time will come.

Mark 13.33

Look carefully then how you walk, not as unwise men but as wise.

Ephesians 5.15

Hold fast what is good, abstain from every form of evil.

1 Thessalonians 5.21

Let every man be quick to hear, slow to speak.

James 1.19

Be sober, be watchful. Your adversary the devil prowls around like a roaring lion, seeking some one to devour.

1 Peter 5.8

Awake, and strengthen what remains and is on the point of death.

Revelation 3.2

Celebration

See also **Joy, Rejoicing**

'This day is holy to the Lord your God; do not mourn or weep.' For all the people wept when they heard the words of the law. Then he said to them, 'Go your way, eat the fat and drink sweet wine and send portions to him for whom nothing is prepared; for this day is holy to our Lord; and do not be grieved, for the joy of the Lord is your strength.'

Nehemiah 8.9–10

Celibacy

See also **Chastity**

And I will betroth you to me for ever; I will betroth you to me in righteousness and in justice, in steadfast love, and in mercy. I will betroth you to me in faithfulness; and you shall know the Lord.

Hosea 2.19–20

For there are eunuchs who have been so from birth, and there are eunuchs who have been made eunuchs by men, and there are eunuchs who have made themselves eunuchs for the sake of the kingdom of heaven. He who is able to receive this, let him receive it.

Matthew 19.12

For in the resurrection they neither marry nor are given in marriage, but are like angels in heaven.

Matthew 22.30

It is well for a man not to touch a woman.

1 Corinthians 7.1

To the unmarried and the widows I say that it is well for them to remain single as I do. But if they cannot exercise self-control, they should marry. For it is better to marry than to be aflame with passion.

1 Corinthians 7.8–9

Now concerning the unmarried, I have no command of the Lord, but I give my opinion as one who by the Lord's mercy is trustworthy. I think that in view of the present distress it is well for a person to remain as he is. Are you bound to a wife? Do not seek to be free. Are you free from a wife? Do not seek marriage. But if you marry, you do not sin, and if a girl marries she does not sin. Yet those who marry will have wordly troubles, and I would spare you that.

1 Corinthians 7.25–28

The unmarried man is anxious about the affairs of the Lord, how to please the Lord; but the married man is anxious about worldly affairs, how to please his wife.

1 Corinthians 7.32–33

And the unmarried woman or girl is anxious about the affairs of the Lord, how to be holy in body and spirit; but the married woman is anxious about worldly affairs, how to please her husband.

1 Corinthians 7.34

Secure your undivided devotion to the Lord.

1 Corinthians 7.35

Whoever is firmly established in his heart, being under no necessity but having his desire under control, and has determined this in his heart, to keep her as his betrothed, he will do well. So that he who marries his betrothed does well; and he who refrains from marriage will do better.

A wife is bound to her husband as long as he lives. If the husband dies, she is free to be married to whom she wishes, only in the Lord. But in my judgment she is happier if she remains as she is.

1 Corinthians 7.37–40

Now the Spirit expressly says that in later times some will depart from the faith by giving heed to deceitful spirits and doctrines of demons . . . who forbid marriage.

1 Timothy 4.1,3

No one could learn that song except the hundred and forty-four thousand who had been redeemed from the earth. It is these who have not defiled themselves with women, for they are chaste.

Revelation 14.3–4

Ceremonial

And it was the duty of the trumpeters and singers to make themselves heard in unison in praise and thanksgiving to the Lord.

2 Chronicles 5.13

I wash my hands in innocence,
   and go about thy altar, O Lord,
singing aloud a song of thanksgiving,
   and telling all thy wondrous deeds.

Psalms 26.6–7

Ascribe to the Lord, O heavenly beings,
   ascribe to the Lord glory and strength.

Psalms 29.1

Then I will thank thee in the great
   congregation;
   in the mighty throng I will praise thee.

Psalms 35.18

Make a joyful noise to the Lord, all the
   lands!
   Serve the Lord with gladness!
   Come into his presence with singing!

Psalms 100.1–2

What shall I render to the Lord
   for all his bounty to me?
I will lift up the cup of salvation
   and call on the name of the Lord.

Psalms 116.12–13

Open to me the gates of righteousness,
   that I may enter through them
   and give thanks to the Lord.

Psalms 118.19

'What to me is the multitude of your
   sacrifices?'
   says the Lord . . .
'I cannot endure iniquity and solemn
   assembly. . . .
remove the evil of your doings
   from before my eyes;
cease to do evil,
   learn to do good.'

Isaiah 1.11,13,16–17

For I desire steadfast love and not
   sacrifice,
   the knowledge of God, rather than burnt
    offerings.

Hosea 6.6

I hate, I despise your feasts,
   and I take no delight in your solemn
    assemblies. . . .
But let justice roll down like waters,
   and righteousness like an everflowing
    stream.

Amos 5.21, 24

And when you pray, you must not be like the hypocrites; for they love to stand and pray in the synagogues and at the street corners, that they may be seen by men . . . But when you pray, go into your room and shut the door and pray to your Father who is in secret; and your Father who sees in secret will reward you.

Matthew 6.5–6

I desire mercy, and not sacrifice.

Matthew 9.13

Let us, therefore, celebrate the festival, not with the old leaven, the leaven of malice and evil, but with the unleavened bread of sincerity and truth.

1 Corinthians 5.8

All things should be done decently and in order.

1 Corinthians 14.40

Therefore let no one pass judgment on you . . . with regard to a festival or a new moon or a sabbath. These are only a shadow of what is to come; but the substance belongs to Christ.

Colossians 2.16–17

Certainty

A wicked man earns deceptive wages,
   but one who sows righteousness gets a
    sure reward.

Proverbs 11.18

In returning and rest you shall be saved;
  in quietness and in trust shall be your
    strength.

Isaiah 30.15

For I the Lord do not change.

Malachi 3.6

You . . . have come to know, that you are
the Holy One of God.

John 6.69

Their hearts may be encouraged as they
are knit together in love, to have all the
riches of assured understanding and the
knowledge of God's mystery.

Colossians 2.2

For our gospel came to you not only in
word, but also in power and in the Holy
Spirit and with full conviction.

1 Thessalonians 1.5

God's firm foundation stands.

2 Timothy 2.19

Jesus Christ is the same yesterday and
today and for ever.

Hebrews 13.8

Challenge

Then the Lord answered Job out of the
  whirlwind:
'Gird up your loins like a man;
  I will question you, and you declare
    to me.'

Job 40.7

Prove me, O Lord, and try me;
  test my heart and my mind.
For thy steadfast love is before my eyes,
  and I walk in faithfulness to thee.

Psalms 26.2–3

Search me, O God, and know my heart!
  Try me and know my thoughts!

Psalms 139.23

The fire will test what sort of work each
one has done. If the work which any man
has built on the foundation survives, he will
receive a reward. If any man's work is
burned up, he will suffer loss, though he

himself will be saved, but only as through
fire.

1 Corinthians 3.13–15

Count it all joy, my brethren, when you
meet various trials, for you know that the
testing of your faith produces steadfastness.
And let steadfastness have its full effect,
that you may be perfect and complete, lacking in nothing.

James 1.2–4

Though now for a little while you may
have to suffer various trials, so that the
genuineness of your faith, more precious
than gold which though perishable is tested
by fire, may redound to praise and glory
and honour at the revelation of Jesus
Christ.

1 Peter 1.6–7

Beloved, do not be surprised at the fiery
ordeal which comes upon you to prove you
. . . But rejoice in so far as you share
Christ's sufferings, that you may also rejoice and be glad when his glory is revealed.

1 Peter 4.12–14

The Lord knows how to rescue the godly
from trial.

2 Peter 2.9

Because you have kept my word of patient
endurance, I will keep you from the hour of
trial which is coming on the whole world.

Revelation 3.10

Champion

The Lord your God who goes before you
will himself fight for you.

Deuteronomy 1.30

Select the best and fittest of your master's
sons and set him on his father's throne, and
fight for your master's house.

2 Kings 10.3

Do not be afraid of them. Remember the
Lord, who is great and terrible, and fight
for your brethren, your sons, your daughters, your wives, and your homes.

Nehemiah 4.14

Rescue the weak and the needy;
  deliver them from the hand of the
    wicked.

Psalms 82.4

But the Lord is with me as a dread
    warrior;
  therefore my persecutors will stumble,
  they will not overcome me.

Jeremiah 20.11

In all things I have shown you that by so
toiling one must help the weak, remember-
ing the words of the Lord Jesus, how he
said, 'It is more blessed to give than to
receive.'

Acts 20.35

But if any one does sin, we have an
advocate with the Father, Jesus Christ the
righteous; and he is the expiation for our
sins, and not for ours only but also for the
sins of the whole world.

1 John 2.1−2

Chance

Again I saw that under the sun the race is
not to the swift, nor the battle to the strong,
nor bread to the wise, nor riches to the
intelligent, nor favour to the men of skill;
but time and chance happen to them all.

Ecclesiastes 9.11

'Lord . . . show which one of these two
thou hast chosen to take the place in this
ministry and apostleship from which Judas
turned aside . . .' And they cast lots for
them, and the lot fell on Matthi'as; and he
was enrolled with the eleven apostles.

Acts 1.24−26

Charity

See also **Alms, Altruism, Benevolence**

If there is among you a poor man . . . you
shall not harden your heart or shut your
hand against your poor brother, but you
shall open your hand to him, and lend him
sufficient for his need, whatever it may be.

Deuteronomy 15.7−8

Blessed is he who considers the poor!
  The Lord delivers him in the day of
    trouble.

Psalms 41.1

Do not withhold good from those to whom
    it is due,
  when it is in your power to do it.

Proverbs 3.27

He who gives to the poor will not want,
  but he who hides his eyes will get many a
    curse.

Proverbs 28.27

Is not this the fast that I choose . . .
to share your bread with the hungry,
  and bring the homeless poor into your
    house;
when you see the naked, to cover him,
  and not to hide yourself from your
    own flesh?

Isaiah 58.6,7

Give to him who begs from you, and do
not refuse him who would borrow from you.

Matthew 5.42

Thus, when you give alms, sound no
trumpet before you, as the hypocrites do
. . . that they may be praised by men . . .
But when you give alms, do not let your left
hand know what your right hand is doing, so
that your alms may be in secret; and your
Father who sees in secret will reward you.

Matthew 6.2−4

If you would be perfect, go, sell what you
possess and give to the poor, and you will
have treasure in heaven.

Matthew 19.21

He who has two coats, let him share with
him who has none; and he who has food, let
him do likewise.

Luke 3.11

He said also to the man who had invited
him, 'When you give a dinner or a banquet,
do not invite your friends or your brothers
or your kinsmen or rich neighbours, lest
they also invite you in return, and you be
repaid. But when you give a feast, invite

the poor, the maimed, the lame, the blind, and you will be blessed, because they cannot repay you. You will be repaid at the resurrection of the just.

Luke 14.12–14

If I give away all I have, and if I deliver my body to be burned, but have not love, I gain nothing.

1 Corinthians 13.3

I do not mean that others should be eased and you burdened, but that as a matter of equality your abundance at the present time should supply their want, so that their abundance may supply your want, that there may be equality.

2 Corinthians 8.13–14

He who sows sparingly will also reap sparingly, and he who sows bountifully will also reap bountifully. Each one must do as he has made up his mind, not reluctantly or under compulsion, for God loves a cheerful giver.

2 Corinthians 9.6–7

Do not neglect to do good and to share what you have, for such sacrifices are pleasing to God.

Hebrews 13.16

If a brother or sister is ill-clad and in lack of daily food, and one of you says to them, 'Go in peace, be warmed and filled,' without giving them the things needed for the body, what does it profit? So faith by itself, if it has no works, is dead.

James 2.15–17

But if any one has the world's goods and sees his brother in need, yet closes his heart against him, how does God's love abide in him?

1 John 3.17

Charm

Charm is deceitful.

Proverbs 31.30

Chastity

See also **Celibacy**

You shall not commit adultery.

Exodus 20.14

I have made a covenant with my eyes;
    how then could I look upon a virgin?

Job 31.1

Rejoice in the wife of your youth . . .
Why should you be infatuated, my son,
    with a loose woman?

Proverbs 5.18,20

But fornication and all impurity or covetousness must not even be named among you, as is fitting among saints.

Ephesians 5.3–4

For this is the will of God, your sanctification: that you abstain from unchastity; that each one of you know how to take a wife for himself in holiness and honour, not in the passion of lust like heathen who do not know God.

1 Thessalonians 4.3–5

And so train the young women to love their husbands and children, to be sensible, chaste.

Titus 2.4–5

Cheating

See also **Deceit**

If any one sins and commits a breach of faith against the Lord by deceiving his neighbour in a matter of deposit or security, or through robbery, or if he has oppressed his neighbour . . . he shall restore what he took by robbery, or what he got by oppression, or the deposit which was committed to him.

Leviticus 6.1–2,4

You shall not steal, nor deal falsely, nor lie to one another . . . The wages of a hired servant shall not remain with you all night until the morning.

Leviticus 19.11,13

The wicked borrows, and cannot pay back,
  but the righteous is generous and gives.

Psalms 37.21

Put no confidence in extortion,
  set no vain hopes on robbery.

Psalms 62.10

Do not say to your neighbour, 'Go, and
    come again,
  tomorrow I will give it' — when you have
    it with you.

Proverbs 3.28

A false balance is an abomination to the
    Lord,
  but a just weight is his delight.

Proverbs 11.1

They have taught their tongue to speak
    lies;
  they commit iniquity and are too weary
    to repent.

Jeremiah 9.5

A trader, in whose hands are false
    balances . . .
  loves to oppress.
E'phraim has said, 'Ah, but I am rich,
  I have gained wealth for myself';
but all his riches can never offset
  the guilt he has incurred.

Hosea 12.7–8

Hear this, you who trample upon the
    needy,
  and bring the poor of the land to an end,
saying, 'When will the new moon be over,
  that we may sell grain?
And the sabbath,
  that we may offer wheat for sale,
that we may make the ephah small and the
    shekel great,
  and deal deceitfully with false balances,
that we may buy the poor for silver
  and the needy for a pair of sandals,
  and sell the refuse of the wheat?'
The Lord has sworn by the pride of Jacob:
  'Surely I will never forget any of their
    deeds.'

Amos 8.4–7

Behold, the wages of the labourers who
mowed your fields, which you kept back by
fraud, cry out; and the cries of the harvesters have reached the ears of the Lord of
hosts.

James 5.4

Cheerfulness

See also **Happiness, Joy**

God has made laughter for me; every one
who hears will laugh over me.

Genesis 21.6

Behold, God will not reject a blameless
    man,
  nor take the hand of evildoers.
He will yet fill your mouth with laughter,
  and your lips with shouting.

Job 8.20–21

But let all who take refuge in thee rejoice,
  let them ever sing for joy;
and do thou defend them,
  that those who love thy name may exult
    in thee.

Psalms 5.11

Fill me with joy and gladness;
  let the bones which thou hast broken
    rejoice.

Psalms 51.8

Then our mouth was filled with laughter,
  and our tongue with shouts of joy . . .
The Lord has done great things for us;
  we are glad.

Psalms 126.2,3

A glad heart makes a cheerful
    countenance.

Proverbs 15.13

All the days of the afflicted are evil,
  but a cheerful heart has a continual feast.

Proverbs 15.15

A cheerful heart is a good medicine,
  but a downcast spirit dries up the bones.

Proverbs 17.22

He who blesses his neighbour with a loud
        voice,
    rising early in the morning,
    will be counted as cursing.

Proverbs 27.14

I know that there is nothing better for them
than to be happy and enjoy themselves as
long as they live.

Ecclesiastes 3.12

In the day of prosperity be joyful.

Ecclesiastes 7.14

And I commend enjoyment, for man has
no good thing under the sun but to eat, and
drink, and enjoy himself, for this will go
with him in his toil through the days of life
which God gives him under the sun.

Ecclesiastes 8.15

Go, eat your bread with enjoyment, and
drink your wine with a merry heart; for
God has already approved what you do.

Ecclesiastes 9.7

Rejoice, O young man, in your youth.

Ecclesiastes 11.9

In the world you have tribulation; but be of
good cheer, I have overcome the world.

John 16.33

Rejoice always.

1 Thessalonians 5.16

Childbearing

To the woman he said,
    'I will greatly multiply your pain in
        childbearing;
    in pain you shall bring forth children.'

Genesis 3.16

Give deliverance to the needy,
    and crush the oppressor!

Psalms 72.4

Yet woman will be saved through bearing
children, if she continues in faith and love
and holiness, with modesty.

1 Timothy 2.15

Children

See also **Babies, Family**

Honour your father and your mother.

Exodus 20.12

Thou whose glory above the heavens is
        chanted
    by the mouth of babes and infants.

Psalms 8.1–2

Lo, sons are a heritage from the Lord,
    the fruit of the womb a reward.
Like arrows in the hand of a warrior
    are the sons of one's youth.

Psalms 127.3–4

Blessed is every one who fears the Lord,
    who walks in his ways! . . .
Your wife will be like a fruitful vine
    within your house;
your children will be like olive shoots
    around your table.

Psalms 128.1,3

Hear, O sons, a father's instruction.

Proverbs 4.1

Grandchildren are the crown of the aged,
    and the glory of sons is their fathers.

Proverbs 17.6

A foolish son is ruin to his father.

Proverbs 19.13

A righteous man who walks in his
        integrity —
    blessed are his sons after him!

Proverbs 20.7

Even a child makes himself known by his
        acts,
    whether what he does is pure and right.

Proverbs 20.11

Train up a child in the way he should go,
    and when he is old he will not depart
        from it.

Proverbs 22.6

Folly is bound up in the heart of a child,
  but the rod of discipline drives it far from
    him.

Proverbs 22.15

Do not withhold discipline from a child;
  if you beat him with a rod, he will not
    die.
If you beat him with the rod
  you will save his life from Sheol.

Proverbs 23.13–14

He who begets a wise son will be glad.

Proverbs 23.24

The rod and reproof give wisdom,
  but a child left to himself brings shame to
    his mother.

Proverbs 29.15

Discipline your son, and he will give you
    rest;
  he will give delight to your heart.

Proverbs 29.17

All your sons shall be taught by the Lord,
  and great shall be the prosperity of your
    sons.

Isaiah 54.13

And what does he desire? Godly offspring.

Malachi 2.15

Truly, I say to you, unless you turn and
become like children, you will never enter
the kingdom of heaven. Whoever humbles
himself like this child, he is the greatest in
the kingdom of heaven.

Whoever receives one such child in my
name receives me; but whoever causes one
of these little ones who believe in me to sin,
it would be better for him to have a great
millstone fastened round his neck and to be
drowned in the depth of the sea.

Matthew 18.3–6

See that you do not despise one of these
little ones; for I tell you that in heaven their
angels always behold the face of my Father
who is in heaven. What do you think? If a
man has a hundred sheep, and one of them
has gone astray, does he not leave the
ninety-nine on the mountains and go in
search of the one that went astray? And if
he finds it, truly, I say to you, he rejoices
over it more than over the ninety-nine that
never went astray. So it is not the will of my
Father who is in heaven that one of these
little ones should perish.

Matthew 18.10–14

Let the children come to me, and do not
hinder them; for to such belongs the kingdom of heaven.

Matthew 19.14

Whoever receives this child in my name
receives me, and whoever receives me
receives him who sent me; for he who is
least among you all is the one who is great.

Luke 9.48

For children ought not to lay up for their
parents, but parents for their children.

2 Corinthians 12.14–15

Children, obey your parents in the Lord,
for this is right.

Ephesians 6.1

Fathers, do not provoke your children to
anger, but bring them up in the discipline
and instruction of the Lord.

Ephesians 6.4

Children or grandchildren, let them first
learn their religious duty to their own
family and make some return to their
parents; for this is acceptable in the sight of
God.

1 Timothy 5.4

Choice

I have set before you life and death, blessing and curse; therefore choose life, that
you and your descendants may live, loving
the Lord you God, obeying his voice, and
cleaving to him; for that means life to you.

Deuteronomy 30.19–20

The Lord our God we will serve, and his
voice we will obey.

Joshua 24.24

How long will you go limping with two different opinions? If the Lord is God, follow him.

1 Kings 18.21

Let us choose what is right;
   let us determine among ourselves what
     is good.

Job 34.4

Who is the man that fears the Lord?
   Him will he instruct in the way that he
     should choose.

Psalms 25.12

I have chosen the way of faithfulness,
   I set thy ordinances before me.
I cleave to thy testimonies, O Lord;
   let me not be put to shame!

Psalms 119.30–31

Let thy hand be ready to help me,
   for I have chosen thy precepts.

Psalms 119.173

He knows how to refuse the evil and choose the good.

Isaiah 7.15

I chose you out of the world.

John 15.19

But God chose what is foolish in the world to shame the wise, God chose what is weak in the world to shame the strong, God chose what is low and despised in the world, even things that are not, to bring to nothing things that are, so that no human being might boast in the presence of God.

1 Corinthians 1.27–29

Moses . . . choosing rather to share ill-treatment with the people of God than to enjoy the fleeting pleasures of sin.

Hebrews 11.24,25

Tend the flock of God that is your charge, not by constraint but willingly.

1 Peter 5.2

Chosen

The Lord has chosen you to be a people for his own possession, out of all the peoples that are on the face of the earth.

Deuteronomy 14.2

Here is the man of whom I spoke to you!

1 Samuel 9.17

Like grapes in the wilderness, I found
   Israel.
Like the first fruit on the fig tree, in its
   first season,
   I saw your fathers.
But they came to Ba'al-pe'or,
   and consecrated themselves to Ba'al,
   and became detestable like the thing
     they loved.

Hosea 9.10

For many are called, but few are chosen.

Matthew 22.14

So then he has mercy upon whomever he wills, and he hardens the heart of whomever he wills.

Romans 9.18

He chose us in him before the foundation of the world, that we should be holy and blameless before him.

Ephesians 1.4

God chose you from the beginning to be saved, through sanctification by the Spirit and belief in the truth.

2 Thessalonians 2.13

But you are a chosen race, a royal priesthood, a holy nation, God's own people, that you may declare the wonderful deeds of him who called you out of darkness into his marvellous light. Once you were no people but now you are God's people; once you had not received mercy but now you have received mercy.

1 Peter 2.9–10

Church

Yet have regard to the prayer of thy servant and to his supplication, O Lord my God, hearkening to the cry and to the prayer which thy servant prays before thee this day; that thy eyes may be open nigh and day toward this house, the place of which thou hast said, 'My name shall be there,' that thou mayest hearken to the prayer which thy servant offers toward this place.

1 Kings 8.28−29

I have built thee an exalted house,
a place for thee to dwell in for ever.

2 Chronicles 6.2

For now I have chosen and consecrated this house that my name may be there for ever; my eyes and my heart will be there for all time.

2 Chronicles 7.16

I was glad when they said to me,
'Let us go to the house of the Lord!'

Psalms 122.1

And I tell you, you are Peter, and on this rock I will build my church, and the powers of death shall not prevail against it.

Matthew 16.18

Take heed to yourselves and to all the flock, in which the Holy Spirit has made you overseers, to care for the church of God which he obtained with the blood of his own Son.

Acts 20.27−28

You are fellow citizens with the saints and members of the household of God, built upon the foundation of the apostles and prophets, Christ Jesus himself being the cornerstone, in whom the whole structure is joined together and grows into a holy temple in the Lord; in whom you also are built into it for a dwelling place of God in the Spirit.

Ephesians 2.19−22

Cleanliness (Moral/Physical)

And he who is to be cleansed shall wash his clothes . . . bathe himself in water, and he shall be clean.

Leviticus 14.8

Clear thou me from hidden faults.

Psalms 19.12

Who shall ascend the hill of the Lord?
And who shall stand in his holy place?
He who has clean hands and a pure heart,
who does not lift up his soul to what is
false.

Psalms 24.3−4

Have mercy on me, O God . . .
Wash me thoroughly from my iniquity,
and cleanse me from my sin!

Psalms 51.1−2

Purge me with hyssop, and I shall be clean;
wash me, and I shall be whiter than
snow.

Psalms 51.7

Create in me a clean heart, O God,
and put a new and right spirit within me.

Psalms 51.10

There are those who are pure in their own
eyes
but are not cleansed of their filth.

Proverbs 30.12

Wash yourselves; make yourselves clean.

Isaiah 1.16

O Jerusalem, wash your heart from
wickedness,
that you may be saved.

Jeremiah 4.14

Let us cleanse ourselves from every defilement of body and spirit, and make holiness perfect in the fear of God.

2 Corinthians 7.1

Cleanse your hands, you sinners, and purify your hearts, you men of double mind.

James 4.8

Clothes

See also **Adornment**

Then the eyes of both were opened, and they knew that they were naked; and they sewed fig leaves together and made themselves aprons.

Genesis 3.7

Thou didst clothe me with skin and flesh,
  and knit me together with bones and
    sinews.

Job 10.11

Bless the Lord, O my soul!
  O Lord my God, thou art very great!
Thou art clothed with honour and majesty,
  who coverest thyself with light as with a
    garment.

Psalms 104.1–2

A good wife who can find? . . .
Strength and dignity are her clothing.

Proverbs 31.10,25

I will greatly rejoice in the Lord,
  my soul shall exult in my God;
for he has clothed me with the garments of
    salvation,
  he has covered me with the robe of
    righteousness,

Isaiah 61.10

Consider the lilies of the field, how they
grow; they neither toil nor spin; yet I tell
you, even Solomon in all his glory was not
arrayed like one of these. But if God so
clothes the grass of the field, which today is
alive and tomorrow is thrown into the oven,
will he not much more clothe you, O men
of little faith?

Matthew 6.28–30

I desire . . . that women should adorn
themselves modestly and sensibly in seemly
apparel, not with braided hair or gold or
pearls or costly attire.

1 Timothy 2.8–9

But if we have food and clothing, with
these we shall be content.

1 Timothy 6.8

Clothe yourselves, all of you, with humility
toward one another.

1 Peter 5.5

Come-Uppance

These men lie in wait for their own blood,
  they set an ambush for their own lives.

Such are the ways of all who get gain by
    violence;
  it takes away the life of its possessors.

Proverbs 1.18–19

A worthless person, a wicked man,
  goes about with crooked speech,
winks with his eyes, scrapes with his feet,
  points with his finger,
with perverted heart devises evil,
  continually sowing discord;
therefore calamity will come upon him
    suddenly;
  in a moment he will be broken beyond
    healing.

Proverbs 6.12–15

He who digs a pit will fall into it,
  and a stone will come back upon him who
    starts it rolling.

Proverbs 26.27

Comfort

The eternal God is your dwelling place,
  and underneath are the everlasting arms.
And he thrust out the enemy before you.

Deuteronomy 33.27

Even though I walk through the valley of
    the shadow of death,
  I fear no evil;
for thou art with me;
  thy rod and thy staff,
  they comfort me.

Psalms 23.4

Because thou, Lord, hast helped me and
    comforted me.

Psalms 86.17

Say to the Lord, 'My refuge and my
    fortress;
  my God, in whom I trust.'

Psalms 91.3

When I thought, 'My foot slips,'
  thy steadfast love, O Lord, held me up.
When the cares of my heart are many,
thy consolations cheer my soul.

Psalms 94.18–19

Anxiety in a man's heart weighs him
    down,
    but a good word makes him glad.

Proverbs 12.25

A gentle tongue is a tree of life.

Proverbs 15.4

The Lord God has given me
    the tongue of those who are taught,
that I may know how to sustain with a word
    him that is weary.

Isaiah 50.4

I, I am he that comforts you.

Isaiah 51.12

For thus says the Lord: . . .
As one whom his mother comforts,
    so I will comfort you.

Isaiah 66.12,13

Blessed are those who mourn, for they
shall be comforted.

Matthew 5.4

I will not leave you desolate; I will come to
you.

John 14.18

In the world you have tribulation; but be of
good cheer, I have overcome the world.

John 16.33

Blessed be the God and Father of our
Lord Jesus Christ, the Father of mercies
and God of all comfort, who comforts us in
all our affliction, so that we may be able to
comfort those who are in any affliction,
with the comfort with which we ourselves
are comforted by God.

2 Corinthians 1.3–4

God . . . comforts the downcast.

2 Corinthians 7.6

Encourage the faint-hearted, help the
weak, be patient with them all.

1 Thessalonians 5.14

Now may our Lord Jesus Christ himself,
and God our Father . . . comfort your
hearts and establish them in every good
work and word.

2 Thessalonians 2.16–17

Commerce

See also **Business, Capital, Money**

Buy truth, and do not sell it.

Proverbs 23.23

A good wife who can find? . . .
She perceives that her merchandise is
    profitable.
    Her lamp does not go out at night.

Proverbs 31.10,18

For what will it profit a man, if he gains
the whole world and forfeits his life?

Matthew 16.26

Commitment

See also **Calling**

You shall fear the Lord your God; you
shall serve him and cleave to him, and by
his name you shall swear.

Deuteronomy 10.20

Take good care to observe the commandment . . . to love the Lord your God, and
to walk in all his ways . . . to cleave to him,
and to serve him with all your heart and
with all your soul.

Joshua 22.5

Cleave to the Lord your God as you have
done to this day.

Joshua 23.8

Follow me, and leave the dead to bury
their own dead.

Matthew 8.22

And every one who has left houses or
brothers or sisters or father or mother or
children or lands, for my name's sake, will
receive a hundredfold, and inherit eternal
life.

Matthew 19.29

Let us hold fast the confession of our hope
without wavering, for he who promised is
faithful.

Hebrews 10.23

I have not found your works perfect in the sight of my God. Remember then what you received and heard; keep that, and repent.

Revelation 3.2–3

Communications

A bad messenger plunges men into
    trouble,
  but a faithful envoy brings healing.

Proverbs 13.17

Communion

See **Eucharist**

Communism

But when they measured . . . he that gathered much had nothing over, and he that gathered little had no lack; each gathered according to what he could eat.

Exodus 16.18

Now the company of those who believed were of one heart and soul, and no one said that any of the things which he possessed was his own, but they had everything in common.

Acts 4.32

There was not a needy person among them, for as many as were possessors of lands or houses sold them, and brought the proceeds of what was sold and laid it at the apostles' feet; and distribution was made to each as any had need.

Acts 4.34–35

Let no one seek his own good, but the good of his neighbour.

1 Corinthians 10.24

But God has so composed the body . . . that there may be no discord in the body, but that the members may have the same care for one another. If one member suffers, all suffer together; if one member is honoured, all rejoice together.

1 Corinthians 12.24–26

But if any one has the world's goods and sees his brother in need, yet closes his heart against him, how does God's love abide in him?

1 John 3.17

Companionship

See also **Friendship**

Entreat me not to leave you or to return from following you; for where you go I will go, and where you lodge I will lodge; your people shall be my people, and your God my God; where you die I will die, and there will I be buried.

Ruth 1.16–17

I am a companion of all who fear thee,
  of those who keep thy precepts.

Psalms 119.63

Behold, how good and pleasant it is
  when brothers dwell in unity!

Psalms 133.1

He who walks with wise men becomes
    wise,
  but the companion of fools will suffer
    harm.

Proverbs 13.20

Iron sharpens iron,
  and one man sharpens another.

Proverbs 27.17

He who keeps the law is a wise son,
  but a companion of gluttons shames his
    father.

Proverbs 28.7

Two are better than one, because they have a good reward for their toil. For if they fall, one will lift up his fellow; but woe to him who is alone when he falls and has not another to lift him up. Again, if two lie together, they are warm; but how can one be warm alone? And though a man might prevail against one who is alone, two will withstand him. A threefold cord is not quickly broken.

Ecclesiastes 4.9–12

For where two or three are gathered in my name, there am I in the midst of them.

Matthew 18.20

I do not pray for these only, but also for those who believe in me through their word, that they may all be one.

John 17.20

Rejoice with those who rejoice, weep with those who weep.

Romans 12.15

So if there is any encouragement in Christ, any incentive of love, any participation in the Spirit, any affection and sympathy, complete my joy by being of the same mind, having the same love, being in full accord and of one mind.

Philippians 2.1−2

But if we walk in the light, as he is in the light, we have fellowship with one another.

1 John 1.7

Company

See also **Fellowship**

He who walks with wise men becomes wise,
 but the companion of fools will suffer harm.

Proverbs 13.20

Leave the presence of a fool,
 for there you do not meet words of knowledge.

Proverbs 14.7

Let a man meet a she-bear robbed of her cubs,
 rather than a fool in his folly.

Proverbs 17.12

Do not be mismated with unbelievers. For what partnership have righteousness and iniquity? Or what fellowship has light with darkness?

2 Corinthians 6.14

Compassion

See also **Mercy, Pity**

The Lord said in his heart, 'I will never again curse the ground because of man, for the imagination of man's heart is evil from his youth; neither will I ever again destroy every living creature as I have done.'

Genesis 8.21

And I will be gracious to whom I will be gracious, and will show mercy on whom I will show mercy.

Exodus 33.19

The Lord, the Lord, a God merciful and gracious, slow to anger, and abounding in steadfast love and faithfulness, keeping steadfast love for thousands, forgiving iniquity and transgression and sin.

Exodus 34.6−7

He who withholds kindness from a friend
 forsakes the fear of the Almighty.

Job 6.14

I sinned, and perverted what was right,
 and it was not requited to me.

Job 33.27

But thou, O lord, art a God merciful and gracious,
 slow to anger and abounding in steadfast love and faithfulness.
Turn to me and take pity on me.

Psalms 86.15−16

Let not loyalty and faithfulness forsake you;
 bind them about your neck,
 write them on the tablet of your heart.
So you will find favour and good repute
 in the sight of God and man.

Proverbs 3.3−4

He who despises his neighbour is a sinner,
 but happy is he who is kind to the poor.

Proverbs 14.21

He who is kind to the poor lends to the Lord,
 and he will repay him for his deed.

Proverbs 19.17

If your enemy is hungry, give him bread to
    eat;
  and if he is thirsty, give him water to
    drink.

Proverbs 25.21

The steadfast love of the Lord never
    ceases,
  his mercies never come to an end;
they are new every morning;
  great is thy faithfulness.

Lamentations 3.22−23

For the Lord will not
    cast off for ever,
but, though he cause grief, he will have
    compassion.

Lamentations 3.31−32

I took them up in my arms;
  but they did not know that I healed
    them.
I led them with cords of compassion,
  with the bands of love,
and I became to them as one
  who eases the yoke on their jaws,
  and I bent down to them and fed them.

Hosea 11.3−4

Render true judgments, show kindness
and mercy each to his brother.

Zechariah 7.9

Should not you have had mercy on your
fellow servant, as I had mercy on you?

Matthew 18.33

We who are strong ought to bear with the
failings of the weak, and not to please
ourselves; let each of us please his neighbour for his good, to edify him.

Romans 15.1−2

Love is patient and kind.

1 Corinthians 13.4

For you know the grace of our Lord Jesus
Christ, that though he was rich, yet for your
sake he became poor, so that by his poverty
you might become rich.

2 Corinthians 8.9

Put on then, as God's chosen ones, holy
and beloved, compassion, kindness, lowliness, meekness, and patience.

Colossians 3.12

Finally, all of you, have unity of spirit,
sympathy, love of the brethren, a tender
heart and a humble mind.

1 Peter 3.8

Competence

Not that we are competent of ourselves to
claim anything as coming from us; our
competence is from God, who has made us
competent to be ministers of a new
covenant.

2 Corinthians 3.5−6

Competition

See also **Conflict**

And the Lord had regard for Abel and his
offering, but for Cain and his offering he
had no regard. So Cain was very angry, and
his countenance fell.

Genesis 4.4−5

Let there be no strife between you and
me, and between your herdsmen and my
herdsmen; for we are kinsmen . . .
Separate yourself from me. If you take the
left hand, then I will go to the right; or if
you take the right hand, then I will go to
the left.

Genesis 13.8−9

Again I saw that under the sun the race is
not to the swift, nor the battle to the strong
. . . but time and chance happen to them
all.

Ecclesiastes 9.11

A dispute also arose among them, which
of them was to be regarded as the greatest.
And he said to them '. . . let the greatest
among you become as the youngest, and
the leader as one who serves.'

Luke 22.24−25,26

Outdo one another in showing honour.

Romans 12.10

Do you not know that in a race all the runners compete, but only one receives the prize? So run that you may obtain it.

1 Corinthians 9.24

An athlete is not crowned unless he competes according to the rules.

2 Timothy 2.5

Complacency

For the wicked boasts of the desires of
    his heart,
    and the man greedy for gain curses and
        renounces the Lord.
In the pride of his countenance the wicked
        does not seek him;
    all his thoughts are, 'There is no God.'
. . . He thinks in his heart, 'I shall not be
    moved.'

Psalms 10.3−4,6

This is the fate of those who have foolish
    confidence,
    the end of those who are pleased with
        their portion.
Like sheep they are appointed for Sheol;
    Death shall be their shepherd.

Psalms 49.13−14

Behold, these are the wicked;
    always at ease, they increase in riches.

Psalms 73.12

The complacence of fools destroys them.

Proverbs 1.32

The way of a fool is right in his own eyes,
    but a wise man listens to advice.

Proverbs 12.15

Every way of a man is right in his own
    eyes,
    but the Lord weighs the heart.

Proverbs 21.2

Do you see a man who is wise in his own
    eyes?
    There is more hope for a fool than for
        him.

Proverbs 26.12

The sluggard is wiser in his own eyes
    than seven men who can answer
        discreetly.

Proverbs 26.16

He who trusts in his own mind is a fool.

Proverbs 28.26

Tremble, you women who are at ease,
    shudder, you complacent ones;
strip, and make yourselves bare,
    and gird sackcloth upon your loins.

Isaiah 32.11

Now therefore hear this, you lover of
        pleasures,
    who sit securely,
who say in your heart,
    'I am, and there is no one besides me;
I shall not sit as a widow
    or know the loss of children':
These two things shall come to you in a
        moment, in one day;
the loss of children and widowhood
    shall come upon you in full measure.

Isaiah 47.8−9

'Rise up, advance against a nation at ease,
    that dwells securely,' says the Lord,
'that has no gates or bars,
    that dwells alone.'

Jeremiah 49.31

Woe to those who are at ease in Zion.

Amos 6.1

And I will punish the men
who are thickening upon their lees,
    those who say in their hearts,
'The Lord will not do good,
    nor will he do ill.'

Zephaniah 1.12

Every tree therefore that does not bear good fruit is cut down and thrown into the fire.

Matthew 3.10

Not every one who says to me, 'Lord, Lord,' shall enter the kingdom of heaven, but he who does the will of my Father who is in heaven.

Matthew 7.21

And every one who hears these words of mine and does not do them will be like a foolish man who built his house upon the sand; and the rain fell, and the floods came, and the winds blew and beat against that house, and it fell; and great was the fall of it.

Matthew 7.26−27

Why do you see the speck that is in your brother's eye, but do not notice the log that is in your own eye? Or how can you say to your brother, 'Brother, let me take out the speck that is in your eye,' when you yourself do not see the log that is in your own eye? You hypocrite, first take the log out of your own eye, and then you will see clearly to take out the speck that is in your brother's eye.

Luke 6.41−42

Therefore let any one who thinks that he stands take heed lest he fall.

1 Corinthians 10.12

Let such people understand . . . when they measure themselves by one another, and compare themselves with one another, they are without understanding . . . For it is not the man who commends himself that is accepted, but the man whom the Lord commends.

2 Corinthians 10.11−12,18

When people say, 'There is peace and security,' then sudden destruction will come upon them as travail comes upon a woman with child, and there will be no escape.

1 Thessalonians 5.3

I know your works: you are neither cold nor hot. Would that you were cold or hot! So, because you are lukewarm, and neither cold nor hot, I will spew you out of my mouth.

Revelation 3.15−17

Complaint

If I sin, what do I do to thee, thou watcher of men?
Why hast thou made me thy mark?

Job 7.20

Are the consolations of God too small . . .
Why does your heart carry you away,
and why . . . let such words go out of your mouth?

Job 15.11−13

God is greater than man.
Why do you contend against him,
saying, 'He will answer none of my words'?

Job 33.12−13

Rouse thyself! Why sleepest thou,
O Lord?
Awake! Do not cast us off for ever!
Why dost thou hide thy face?
Why dost thou forget our affliction and oppression?

Psalms 44.23−24

All in vain have I kept my heart clean
and washed my hands in innocence.
For all the day long I have been stricken,
and chastened every morning.

Psalms 73.13−14

When a man's folly brings his way to ruin,
his heart rages against the Lord.

Proverbs 19.3

Be not quick to anger,
for anger lodges in the bosom of fools.
Say not, 'Why were the former days better than these?'
For it is not from wisdom that you ask this.

Ecclesiastes 7.9−10

Why should a living man complain,
a man, about the punishment of his sins?

Lamentations 3.39

So if you are offering your gift at the altar, and there remember that your brother has something against you, leave your gift there before the altar and go; first be reconciled to your brother, and then come and offer your gift.

Matthew 5.23−24

Nor grumble, as some of them did and were destroyed by the Destroyer.

1 Corinthians 10.10

Do all things without grumbling or questioning, that you may be blameless and innocent.

Philippians 2.14–15

Put on then, as God's chosen ones, holy and beloved, compassion, kindness, lowliness, meekness and patience, forbearing one another and, if one has a complaint against another, forgiving each other; as the Lord has forgiven you, so you also must forgive.

Colossians 3.12–13

Practise hospitality ungrudgingly to one another.

1 Peter 4.9

These are grumblers, malcontents, following their own passions.

Jude 16

Conceit

Whoever loves discipline loves knowledge, but he who hates reproof is stupid.

Proverbs 12.1

Conciliation

A soft answer turns away wrath, but a harsh word stirs up anger.

Proverbs 15.1

Condition (of Man)

Cursed is the ground because of you;
in toil you shall eat of it all the days of your life;
thorns and thistles it shall bring forth to you;
and you shall eat the plants of the field.
In the sweat of your face
you shall eat bread
till you return to the ground.

Genesis 3.17–19

Man is born to trouble
as the sparks fly upward.

Job 5.7

Man that is born of a woman is of few days, and full of trouble.
He comes forth like a flower, and withers;
he flees like a shadow, and continues not.

Job 14.1–2

A perverse man will be filled with the fruit of his ways,
and a good man with the fruit of his deeds.

Proverbs 14.14

All things are full of weariness;
a man cannot utter it;
the eye is not satisfied with seeing,
nor the ear filled with hearing.
What has been is what will be,
and what has been done is what will be done;
and there is nothing new under the sun.
Is there a thing of which it is said,
'See, this is new'?
It has been already,
in the ages before us.
There is no remembrance of former things,
nor will there be any remembrance of
later things yet to happen
among those who come after.

Ecclesiastes 1.8–11

For the fate of the sons of men and the fate of beasts is the same; as one dies, so dies the other. They all have the same breath, and man has no advantage over the beasts; for all is vanity. All go to one place; all are from the dust, and all turn to dust again.

Ecclesiastes 3.19–20

I can will what is right, but I cannot do it. For I do not do the good I want, but the evil I do not want is what I do.

Romans 7.18–20

Confession

See also **Confidence**

O my God, I am ashamed and blush to lift my face to thee, my God, for our iniquities have risen higher than our heads, and our guilt has mounted up to the heavens.

Ezra 9.6

I acknowledged my sin to thee,
  and I did not hide my iniquity;
I said, 'I will confess my transgressions to
    the Lord';
  then thou didst forgive the guilt of my
    sin.

Psalms 32.5

My iniquities have overtaken me,
  till I cannot see . . .
Be pleased, O Lord, to deliver me!

Psalms 40.12–13

Have mercy on me, O God,
  according to thy steadfast love;
according to thy abundant mercy
  blot out my transgressions.
Wash me thoroughly from my iniquity,
  and cleanse me from my sin!

Psalms 51.1–2

The sacrifice acceptable to God is a broken
    spirit;
  a broken and contrite heart, O God, thou
    wilt not despise.

Psalms 51.17

O God, thou knowest my folly;
  the wrongs I have done are not hidden
    from thee.
Let not those who hope in thee be put to
    shame through me.

Psalms 69.5–6

He who conceals his transgressions will not
    prosper,
  but he who confesses and forsakes them
    will obtain mercy.

Proverbs 28.13

Let us test and examine our ways,
  and return to the Lord!
Let us lift up our hearts and hands
  to God in heaven.

Lamentations 3.40–41

And they were baptized by him in the river Jordan, confessing their sins.

Matthew 3.6

Since then we have a great high priest who has passed through the heavens, Jesus, the Son of God, let us hold fast our confession. For we have not a high priest who is unable to sympathize with our weaknesses, but one who in every respect has been tempted as we are, yet without sin. Let us then with confidence draw near to the throne of grace, that we may receive mercy and find grace to help in time of need.

Hebrews 4.14–16

If he has committed sins, he will be forgiven. Therefore confess your sins to one another, and pray for one another, that you may be healed.

James 5.15–16

If we say we have no sin, we deceive ourselves, and the truth is not in us. If we confess our sins, he is faithful and just, and will forgive our sins and cleanse us from all unrighteousness.

1 John 1.8–9

Confidence

See also **Trust**

It is better to take refuge in the Lord
  than to put confidence in man.
It is better to take refuge in the Lord
  than to put confidence in princes.

Psalms 118.8–9

If I take the wings of the morning
  and dwell in the uttermost parts of the
    sea,
even there thy hand shall lead me,
  and thy right hand shall hold me.

Psalms 139.9–10

Do not be afraid of sudden panic,
  or of the ruin of the wicked, when it
    comes;
for the Lord will be your confidence
  and will keep your foot from being
    caught.

Proverbs 3.25–26

He who walks in integrity walks securely.

Proverbs 10.9

In the fear of the Lord one has strong
confidence,
and his children will have a refuge.

Proverbs 14.26

He who gives heed to the word will
prosper,
and happy is he who trusts in the Lord.

Proverbs 16.20

And now, Lord, look upon their threats,
and grant to thy servants to speak thy word
with all boldness.

Acts 4.29

So we are always of good courage; we
know that while we are at home in the body
we are away from the Lord, for we walk by
faith, not by sight. We are of good courage,
and we would rather be away from the body
and at home with the Lord.

2 Corinthians 5.6–8

This was according to the eternal purpose
which he has realised in Christ Jesus our
Lord, in whom we have boldness and
confidence of access through our faith in
him.

Ephesians 3.11–12

I can do all things in him who strengthens
me.

Philippians 4.13

And we are his house if we hold fast our
confidence and pride in our hope.

Hebrews 3.6

For we share in Christ, if only we hold our
first confidence firm to the end.

Hebrews 3.14

For he has said, 'I will never fail you nor
forsake you.' Hence we can confidently say,
'The Lord is my helper,
I will not be afraid;
what can man do to me?'

Hebrews 13.5–6

And now, little children, abide in him, so
that when he appears we may have confidence and not shrink from him in shame at
his coming.

1 John 2.28

Beloved, if our hearts do not condemn us,
we have confidence before God.

1 John 3.21

And this is the confidence which we have
in him, that if we ask anything according to
his will he hears us.

1 John 5.14

Conflict

See also **Competition**

Do not contend with a man for no reason,
when he has done you no harm.

Proverbs 3.30

Hatred stirs up strife,
but love covers all offences.

Proverbs 10.12

By insolence the heedless make strife.

Proverbs 13.10

He who loves transgression loves strife.

Proverbs 17.19

A fool's lips bring strife,
and his mouth invites a flogging.

Proverbs 18.6

And a wife's quarrelling is a continual
dripping of rain.

Proverbs 19.13

It is an honour for a man to keep aloof
from strife.

Proverbs 20.3

For lack of wood the fire goes out;
and where there is no whisperer,
quarrelling ceases.

Proverbs 26.20

Nation shall not lift up sword against
nation,
neither shall they learn war any more.

Isaiah 2.4

Let us conduct ourselves becomingly . . .
not in quarrelling and jealousy.

Romans 13.13

Do nothing from selfishness or conceit, but in humility count others better than yourselves.

Philippians 2.3

For to this end we toil and strive, because we have our hope set on the living God.

1 Timothy 4.10

I any one teaches otherwise and does not agree with the sound words of our Lord Jesus Christ . . . he knows nothing; he has a morbid craving for controversy and for disputes about words, which produce envy, dissension, slander, base suspicions, and wrangling among men.

1 Timothy 6.3−5

Have nothing to do with stupid, senseless controversies; you know that they breed quarrels. And the Lord's servant must not be quarrelsome but kindly to every one, an apt teacher, forbearing, correcting his opponents with gentleness.

2 Timothy 2.23−25

Conformity

I appeal to you . . . Do not be conformed to this world but be transformed by the renewal of your mind.

Romans 12.1−2

I appeal to you . . . that all of you agree and that there be no dissensions among you, but that you be united in the same mind and the same judgment.

1 Corinthians 1.10

Any incentive of love, any participation in the Spirit, any affection and sympathy, complete my joy by being of the same mind, having the same love, being in full accord and of one mind.

Philippians 2.1−2

That I may know him and the power of his resurrection, and may share his sufferings, becoming like him in his death.

Philippians 3.10

Finally, all of you, have unity of spirit, sympathy . . . and a humble mind.

1 Peter 3.8

Confusion

See also **Anarchy**

Let them be put to shame and dishonour
  who seek after my life!
Let them be turned back and confounded
  who devise evil against me!

Psalms 35.4

Hear my cry, O God,
  listen to my prayer;
from the end of the earth I call to thee,
  when my heart is faint.
Lead thou me
  to the rock that is higher than I.

Psalms 61.1−2

Trust in the Lord with all your heart,
  and do not rely on your own insight.
In all your ways acknowledge him,
  and he will make straight your paths.

Proverbs 3.5−6

For the Lord God helps me;
  therefore I have not been confounded.

Isaiah 50.7

For God is not a God of confusion but of peace.

1 Corinthians 14.33

For where jealousy and selfish ambition exist, there will be disorder and every vile practice.

James 3.16

Conquest

And you shall destroy all the peoples that the Lord your God will give over to you, your eye shall not pity them.

Deuteronomy 7.16

Conscience

So I always take pains to have a clear conscience toward God and toward men.

Acts 24.16

When Gentiles who have not the law do by nature what the law requires, they are a law to themselves, even though they do not have the law. They show that what the law requires is written on their hearts, while their conscience also bears witness and their conflicting thoughts accuse or perhaps excuse them on that day when, according to my gospel, God judges the secrets of men by Christ Jesus.

Romans 2.14–16

Thus, sinning against your brethren and wounding their conscience when it is weak, you sin against Christ.

1 Corinthians 8.12

But by the open statement of the truth we would commend ourselves to every man's conscience in the sight of God.

2 Corinthians 4.2

The aim of our charge is love that issues from a pure heart and a good conscience and sincere faith.

1 Timothy 1.5

You may wage the good warfare, holding faith and a good conscience. By rejecting conscience, certain persons have made shipwreck of their faith.

1 Timothy 1.18–19

Some will depart from the faith by giving heed to deceitful spirits and doctrines of demons, through the pretensions of liars whose consciences are seared.

1 Timothy 4.1–2

To the pure all things are pure, but to the corrupt and unbelieving nothing is pure; their very minds and consciences are corrupted.

Titus 1.15

How much more shall the blood of Christ, who through the eternal Spirit offered himself without blemish to God, purify your conscience from dead works to serve the living God.

Hebrews 9.14

We are sure that we have a clear conscience, desiring to act honourably in all things.

Hebrews 13.18

But in your hearts reverence Christ as Lord. Always be prepared to make a defence to any one who calls you to account for the hope that is in you, yet do it with gentleness and reverence; and keep your conscience clear, so that, when you are abused, those who revile your good behaviour in Christ may be put to shame.

1 Peter 3.15–16

Little children, let us not love in word or speech but in deed and in truth.
By this we shall know that we are of the truth, and reassure our hearts before him whenever our hearts condemn us.

1 John 3.18–20

Conservatism

Will you keep to the old way
    which wicked men have trod?

Job 22.15

Do not remove an ancient landmark.

Proverbs 23.10

Stand by the roads, and look,
    and ask for the ancient paths,
where the good way is; and walk in it,
    and find rest for your souls.

Jeremiah 6.16

Can the Ethiopian change his skin
    or the leopard his spots?

Jeremiah 13.23

They have stumbled in their ways,
    in the ancient roads,
and have gone into bypaths,
    not the highway.

Jeremiah 18.15

So, for the sake of your tradition, you have made void the word of God.

Matthew 15.6

And no one puts new wine into old wineskins; if he does, the wine will burst the skins, and the wine is lost, and so are the skins; but new wine is for fresh skins.

Mark 2.22

Scoffers will come in the last days with scoffing, following their own passions and saying, 'Where is the promise of his coming? For ever since the fathers fell asleep, all things have continued as they were from the beginning of creation.'

2 Peter 3.3–4

Consolation

See also **Comfort, Pity**

When I thought, 'My foot slips,'
  thy steadfast love, O Lord, held me up.

Psalms 94.18

Comfort, comfort my people,
  says your God.

Isaiah 40.1

For as we share abundantly in Christ's sufferings, so through Christ we share abundantly in comfort too.

2 Corinthians 1.5

For we know that as you share in our sufferings, you will also share in our comfort.

2 Corinthians 1.7

Now may our Lord Jesus Christ himself, and God our Father, who loved us and gave us eternal comfort and good hope through grace, comfort your hearts and establish them in every good work and word.

2 Thessalonians 2.16–17

Conspicuousness

Let your light so shine before men, that they may see your good works and give glory to your Father who is in heaven.

Matthew 5.16

Beware of practising your piety before men in order to be seen by them; for then you will have no reward from your Father who is in heaven.

Matthew 6.1–3

Good deeds are conspicuous; and even when they are not, they cannot remain hidden.

1 Timothy 5.25

Constancy

I will establish his kingdom for ever if he continues resolute in keeping my commandments and my ordinances.

1 Chronicles 28.7

Yet the righteous holds to his way.

Job 17.9

The works of his hands are faithful and
      just;
  all his precepts are trustworthy.

Psalms 111.7

For he is the living God,
  enduring for ever;
his kingdom shall never be destroyed,
  and his dominion shall be to the end.

Daniel 6.26

And blessed is he who takes no offence at me.

Matthew 11.6

Therefore, my beloved brethren, be steadfast, immovable, always abounding in the work of the Lord, knowing that in the Lord your labour is not in vain.

1 Corinthians 15.58

For freedom Christ has set us free; stand fast therefore, and do not submit again to a yoke of slavery.

Galatians 5.1

Stand firm thus in the Lord.

Philippians 4.1

Stand firm and hold to the traditions.

2 Thessalonians 2.15

For we share in Christ, if only we hold our first confidence firm to the end.

Hebrews 3.14

We have this as a sure and steadfast anchor of the soul, a hope that enters into the inner shrine behind the curtain.

Hebrews 6.19

Beware lest you be carried away with the error of lawless men and lose your own stability.

2 Peter 3.17

Be faithful unto death, and I will give you the crown of life.

Revelation 2.10

Only hold fast what you have, until I come.

Revelation 2.25

Contempt

See also **Blame**

For those who honour me I will honour, and those who despise me shall be lightly esteemed.

1 Samuel 2.30

O Lord, who shall sojourn in thy tent?
  Who shall dwell on thy holy hill?
He . . . in whose eyes a reprobate is
    despised,
  but who honours those who fear the
    Lord.

Psalms 15.1–2,4

Let them go dumbfounded to Sheol.
Let the lying lips be dumb,
  which speak insolently against the
    righteous
  in pride and contempt.

Psalms 31.17–18

Take away from me their scorn and
    contempt,
  for I have kept thy testimonies.

Psalms 119.22

Have mercy upon us, O Lord, have mercy
    upon us,
  for we have had more than enough of
    contempt.
Too long our soul has been sated
  with the scorn of those who are at ease,
  the contempt of the proud.

Psalms 123.3–4

How long, O simple ones, will you love
    being simple?
How long will scoffers delight in their
    scoffing
  and fools hate knowledge?
Give heed to my reproof;
behold, I will pour out my thoughts to you;
  I will make my words known to you.
Because I have called and you refused to
    listen,
  have stretched out my hand and no one
    has heeded,
and you have ignored all my counsel
  and would have none of my reproof,
I also will laugh at your calamity.

Proverbs 1.22–26

He who belittles his neighbour lacks sense,
  but a man of understanding remains
    silent.

Proverbs 11.12

But one of perverse mind is despised.

Proverbs 12.8

He who despises the word brings
    destruction on himself.

Proverbs 13.13

He who despises his neighbour is a sinner.

Proverbs 14.21

When wickedness comes, contempt comes
    also;
  and with dishonour comes disgrace.

Proverbs 18.3

And many of those who sleep in the dust of the earth shall awake, some to everlasting life, and some to shame and everlasting contempt.

Daniel 12.2

Whoever insults his brother shall be liable to the council, and whoever says, 'You fool!' shall be liable to the hell of fire.

Matthew 5.22

He also told this parable to some who trusted in themselves that they were righteous and despised others: 'Two men went up into the temple to pray, one a Pharisee and the other a tax collector. The Pharisee stood and prayed thus with himself, "God, I thank thee that I am not like other men, extortioners, unjust, adulterers, or even like this tax collector. I fast twice a week, I give tithes of all that I get." But the tax collector, standing far off, would not even lift up his eyes to heaven, but beat his breast, saying, "God, be merciful to me a sinner!" I tell you, this man went down to his house justified rather than the other; for every one who exalts himself will be humbled, but he who humbles himself will be exalted.'

Luke 18.9–14

Contentment

Happy is the man who finds wisdom,
. . . Her ways are ways of pleasantness,
   and all her paths are peace.

Proverbs 3.13,17

There is great gain in godliness with contentment.

1 Timothy 6.6

Control

The Lord gave, and the Lord has taken away.

Job 1.21

A man's mind plans his way,
   but the Lord directs his steps.

Proverbs 16.9

I form light and create darkness,
   I make weal and create woe,
   I am the Lord, who do all these things.

Isaiah 45.7

Conversion

See also **Calling**

Restore to me the joy of thy salvation,
   and uphold me with a willing spirit.
Then I will teach transgressors thy ways,
   and sinners will return to thee . . .
thou God of my salvation.

Psalms 51.12–14

Let the wicked forsake his way,
   and the unrighteous man his thoughts;
let him return to the Lord, that he may
      have mercy on him,
   and to our God, for he will abundantly
      pardon.

Isaiah 55.7

Let us test and examine our ways,
   and return to the Lord!

Lamentations 3.40

Cast away from you all the transgressions which you have committed against me, and get yourselves a new heart and a new spirit!

Ezekiel 18.31

Unless you turn and become like children, you will never enter the kingdom of heaven.

Matthew 18.3

Unless one is born anew, he cannot see the kingdom of God.

John 3.3

Therefore, if any one is in Christ, he is a new creation; the old has passed away, behold, the new has come.

2 Corinthians 5.17

Be renewed in the spirit of your minds, and put on the new nature, created after the likeness of God in true righteousness and holiness.

Ephesians 4.23–24

If any one among you wanders from the truth and some one brings him back, let him know that whoever brings back a sinner from the error of his way will save his soul from death.

James 5.19–20

Conviction

See also **Certainty, Faith, Trust**

No distrust made him waver concerning the promise of God, but he grew strong in his faith as he gave glory to God, fully convinced that God was able to do what he had promised. That is why his faith was 'reckoned to him as righteousness.' . . . It will be reckoned to us who believe in him that raised from the dead Jesus our Lord.

Romans 4.20–25

For I am sure that neither death, nor life, nor angels, nor principalities, nor things present, nor things to come, nor powers, nor height, nor depth, nor anything else in all creation, will be able to separate us from the love of God in Christ Jesus our Lord.

Romans 8.38–39

But I am not ashamed, for I know whom I have believed, and I am sure that he is able to guard until that Day what has been entrusted to me.

2 Timothy 1.12

Coolness

He who restrains his words has
      knowledge,
   and he who has a cool spirit is a man of
      understanding.

Proverbs 17.27

Co-operation

See also **Companionship**

If you meet your enemy's ox or his ass going astray, you shall bring it back to him. If you see the ass of one who hates you lying under its burden, you shall refrain from leaving him with it, you shall help him to lift it up.

Exodus 23.4–5

Two are better than one, because they have a good reward for their toil. For if they fall, one will lift up his fellow; but woe to him who is alone when he falls and has not another to lift him up.

Ecclesiastes 4.9–10

Every one helps his neighbour,
   and says to his brother, 'Take courage!'
The craftsman encourages the goldsmith,
   and he who smooths with the hammer
   him who strikes the anvil.

Isaiah 41.6–7

If two of you agree on earth about anything they ask, it will be done for them by my Father in heaven.

Matthew 18.19

And all who believed were together and had all things in common.

Acts 2.44

We know that in everything God works for good with those who love him.

Romans 8.28

For we are God's fellow workers; you are God's field, God's building.

1 Corinthians 3.9

Correction

Because you have raged against me
   and your arrogance has come to my ears,
I will put my hook in your nose
   and my bit in your mouth,
and I will turn you back on the way by
      which you came.

Isaiah 37.29

My son, do not regard lightly the discipline of the Lord, nor lose courage when you are punished by him. For the Lord disciplines him whom he loves, and chastises every son whom he receives.

Hebrews 12.5–7

Corruption

See also **Bribery, Dishonesty**

All who act dishonestly, are an abomination to the Lord your God.

Deuteronomy 25.16

Help, Lord; for there is no longer any that
   is godly;
   for the faithful have vanished from
      among the sons of men.
Every one utters lies to his neighbour;
   with flattering lips and a double heart
      they speak.

Psalms 12.1–2

Put away from you crooked speech,
   and put devious talk far from you.

Proverbs 4.24

The way of the faithless is their ruin.

Proverbs 13.15

Ah, sinful nation,
   a people laden with iniquity,
offspring of evildoers,
   sons who deal corruptly!
They have forsaken the Lord.

Isaiah 1.4

Remove the evil of your doings
   from before my eyes;
cease to do evil.

Isaiah 1.16

Because you despise this word,
   and trust in oppression and perverseness,
   and rely on them;
therefore this iniquity shall be to you
   like a break in a high wall, bulging out,
   and about to collapse,

Isaiah 30.12–13

No one enters suit justly,
   no one goes to law honestly;
they rely on empty pleas, they speak lies,
   they conceive mischief and bring forth
      iniquity . . .
The way of peace they know not,
   and there is no justice in their paths;
they have made their roads crooked,
   no one who goes in them knows peace.

Isaiah 59.4,8

So, every sound tree bears good fruit, but
the bad tree bears evil fruit. A sound tree
cannot bear evil fruit, nor can a bad tree
bear good fruit. Every tree that does not
bear good fruit is cut down and thrown into
the fire. Thus you will know them by their
fruits.

Matthew 7.17–20

The good man out of his good treasure
brings forth good, and the evil man out of
his evil treasure brings forth evil.

Matthew 12.35

Bad company ruins good morals.

1 Corinthians 15.33

But I am afraid that as the serpent
deceived Eve by his cunning, your thoughts
will be led astray from a sincere and pure
devotion to Christ.

2 Corinthians 11.3

Put off your old nature which belongs to
your former manner of life and is corrupt
through deceitful lusts.

Ephesians 4.22

To the pure all things are pure, but to the
corrupt and unbelieving nothing is pure;
their very minds and consciences are corrupted.

Titus 1.15

See to it . . . that no 'root of bitterness'
spring up and cause trouble, and by it the
many become defiled.

Hebrews 12.15

He has granted to us his precious and very
great promises, that through these you may
escape from the corruption that is in the
world because of passion, and become partakers of the divine nature.

2 Peter 1.4

Courage

See also **Bravery**

Only be strong and very courageous, being
careful to do all according to the law . . .
that you may have good success wherever
you go.

Joshua 1.7

Be strong and of good courage; be not
frightened, neither be dismayed; for the
Lord your God is with you wherever you
go.

Joshua 1.9

Be of good courage, and let us play the man for our people, and for the cities of our God.

1 Chronicles 19.13

Be strong, and of good courage. Fear not; be not dismayed.

1 Chronicles 22.13–14

Deal courageously, and may the Lord be with the upright!

2 Chronicles 19.11

Do not be afraid of them. Remember the Lord, who is great and terrible, and fight for your brethren, your sons, your daughters, your wives, and your homes.

Nehemiah 4.14

Even though I walk through the valley of
    the shadow of death,
  I fear no evil;
for thou art with me;
  thy rod and thy staff,
  they comfort me.

Psalms 23.4

Wait for the Lord;
  be strong, and let your heart take
    courage;
  yea, wait for the Lord!

Psalms 27.14

Blessed are the men whose strength is in
    thee,
  in whose heart are the highways to Zion.

Psalms 84.5

You will not fear the terror of the night,
  nor the arrow that flies by day,
nor the pestilence that stalks in darkness,
  nor the destruction that wastes at
    noonday.

Psalms 91.5–6

Fear not, for I am with you,
  be not dismayed, for I am your God;
I will strengthen you, I will help you,
  I will uphold you with my victorious right
    hand.

Isaiah 41.10

I gave my back to the smiters,
  and my cheeks to those who pulled out
    the beard;
I hid not my face
  from shame and spitting.
For the Lord God helps me;
  therefore I have not been confounded;
therefore I have set my face like a flint,
  and I know that I shall not be put to
    shame;
  he who vindicates me is near.

Isaiah 50.6–8

Take heart, my son; your sins are forgiven.

Matthew 9.2

Courtesy

See also **Hospitality, Manners**

You shall rise up before the hoary head, and honour the face of an old man.

Leviticus 19.32

By insolence the heedless make strife.

Proverbs 13.10

If one of the unbelievers invites you to dinner and you are disposed to go, eat whatever is set before you without raising any question on the ground of conscience.

1 Corinthians 10.27

Lead a life worthy of the calling to which you have been called, with all lowliness and meekness, with patience.

Ephesians 4.1–2

Be ready . . . to show perfect courtesy toward all men.

Titus 3.1–2

The imperishable jewel of a gentle and quiet spirit . . . in God's sight is very precious.

1 Peter 3.4

Make a defence to any one who calls you to account . . . with gentleness and reverence.

1 Peter 3.15

Cowardice

See also **Fear**

What man is there that is fearful and fainthearted? Let him go back to his house, lest the heart of his fellows melt as his heart.

Deuteronomy 20.8

The wicked . . . knows that a day of darkness is ready at his hand;
 distress and anguish terrify him;
they prevail against him, like a king
 prepared for battle.

Job 15.20,23−24

The fear of man lays a snare,
 but he who trusts in the Lord is safe.

Proverbs 29.25

A living dog is better than a dead lion.

Ecclesiastes 9.4

I, I am he that comforts you;
 who are you that you are afraid of man
 who dies,
 of the son of man who is made like grass?

Isaiah 51.12

Peace I leave with you; my peace I give to you; not as the world gives do I give to you. Let not your hearts be troubled, neither let them be afraid.

John 14.27

Be at peace among yourselves . . . encourage the fainthearted.

1 Thessalonians 5.13−14

Rekindle the gift of God, that is within you through the laying on of my hands; for God did not give us a spirit of timidity but a spirit of power and love and self-control.

2 Timothy 1.6−7

But as for the cowardly . . . their lot shall be in the lake that burns with fire and sulphur, which is the second death.

Revelation 21.8

Creation

In the beginning God created the heavens and the earth.

Genesis 1.1

And God said, 'Let the waters under the heavens be gathered together into one place, and let the dry land appear.' And it was so. God called the dry land Earth, and the waters that were gathered together he called Seas. And God saw that it was good.

Genesis 1.9−10

And God said, 'Let the waters bring forth swarms of living creatures, and let birds fly above the earth across the firmament of the heavens.'

Genesis 1.20

And God said, 'Let the earth bring forth living creatures according to their kinds: cattle and creeping things and beasts of the earth according to their kinds.' And it was so.

Genesis 1.24

Then God said, 'Let us make man in our image, after our likeness; and let them have dominion over the fish of the sea, and over the birds of the air, and over the cattle, and over all the earth, and over every creeping thing that creeps upon the earth.' So God created man in his own image, in the image of God he created him; male and female he created them.

Genesis 1.26−27

And God saw everything that he had made, and behold, it was very good.

Genesis 1.31

Thou art the Lord, thou alone; thou hast made heaven, the heaven of heavens, with all their host, the earth and all that is on it, the seas and all that is in them . . . and the host of heaven worships thee.

Nehemiah 9.6

Where were you when I laid the
 foundation of the earth?
. . . On what were its bases sunk,
 or who laid its cornerstone,

when the morning stars sang together,
and all the sons of God shouted for joy?

Job 38.4,6−7

When I look at thy heavens, the work of
thy fingers,
the moon and the stars which thou hast
established;
what is man that thou art mindful of him,
and the son of man that thou dost care
for him?

Psalms 8.3−4

The heavens are telling the glory of God;
and the firmament proclaims his
handiwork.
Day to day pours forth speech,
and night to night declares knowledge.
There is no speech, nor are there words;
their voice is not heard;
yet their voice goes out through all the
earth,
and their words to the end of the world.

Psalms 19.1−4

Thou hast multiplied, O Lord my God,
thy wondrous deeds and thy thoughts
toward us;
none can compare with thee!
Were I to proclaim and tell of them,
they would be more than can be
numbered.

Psalms 40.5

In his hand are the depths of the earth;
the heights of the mountains are his also.
The sea is his, for he made it;
for his hands formed the dry land.
O come, let us worship and bow down,
let us kneel before the Lord, our Maker!

Psalms 95.4−6

Know that the Lord is God!
It is he that made us, and we are his;
we are his people, and the sheep of his
pasture.

Psalms 100.3

Bless the Lord, O my soul!
O Lord my God, thou art very great!
Thou art clothed with honour and majesty,
who coverest thyself with light as with a
garment,

who hast stretched out the heavens like a
tent,
who hast laid the beams of thy chambers
on the waters,
who makest the clouds thy chariot,
who ridest on the wings of the wind,
who makest the winds thy messengers,
fire and flame thy ministers.

Psalms 104.1−4

Thou dost cause the grass to grow for the
cattle,
and plants for man to cultivate,
that he may bring forth food from the
earth,
and wine to gladden the heart of man,
oil to make his face shine,
and bread to strengthen man's heart.

Psalms 104.14−15

O Lord, how manifold are thy works!
In wisdom hast thou made them all;
the earth is full of thy creatures.

Psalms 104.24

When thou hidest thy face, they are
dismayed;
when thou takest away their breath, they
die
and return to their dust.
When thou sendest forth thy Spirit, they are
created;
and thou renewest the face of the ground.

Psalms 104.29−30

May the Lord rejoice in his works.

Psalms 104.31

The Lord will fulfil his purpose for me;
thy steadfast love, O Lord, endures for
ever.
Do not forsake the work of thy hands.

Psalms 138.8

For thou didst form my inward parts,
thou didst knit me together in my
mother's womb.
I praise thee, for thou art fearful and
wonderful.
Wonderful are thy works!

Psalms 139.13−14

As you do not know how the spirit comes to the bones in the womb of a woman with child, so you do not know the work of God who makes everything.

Ecclesiastes 11.5

I am the Lord, and there is no other.
I form light and create darkness,
   I make weal and create woe.

Isaiah 45.6−7

For lo, he who forms the mountains, and creates the wind,
   and declares to man what is his thought;
who makes the morning darkness,
   and treads on the heights of the earth —
the Lord, the God of hosts, is his name!

Amos 4.13

In the beginning was the Word, and the Word was with God, and the Word was God. He was in the beginning with God; all things were made through him, and without him was not anything made that was made.

John 1.1−3

'You should turn from these vain things to a living God who made the heaven and the earth and the sea and all that is in them. In past generations he allowed all the nations to walk in their own ways; yet he did not leave himself without witness, for he did good and gave you from heaven rains and fruitful seasons, satisfying your hearts with food and gladness.' With these words they scarcely restrained the people from offering sacrifice to them.

Acts 14.15−18

The God who made the world and everything in it, being Lord of heaven and earth, does not live in shrines made by man, nor is he served by human hands.

Acts 17.24−25

Therefore, if any one is in Christ, he is a new creation; the old has passed away, behold, the new has come.

2 Corinthians 5.17

For we are his workmanship, created in Christ Jesus for good works, which God prepared beforehand, that we should walk in them.

Ephesians 2.10

He is the image of the invisible God, the first-born of all creation; for in him all things were created, in heaven and on earth, visible and invisible, whether thrones or dominions or principalities or authorities — all things were created through him and for him. He is before all things, and in him all things hold together.

Colossians 1.15−17

For everything created by God is good.

1 Timothy 4.4

By faith we understand that the world was created by the word of God, so that what is seen was made out of things which do not appear.

Hebrews 11.3

Worthy art thou, our Lord and God,
to receive glory and honour and power,
for thou didst create all things,
and by thy will they existed and were
      created.

Revelation 4.11

Criticism

See also **Blame, Judgment**

Then shall I have an answer for those who
      taunt me,
   for I trust in thy word.

Psalms 119.42

Whoever loves discipline loves knowledge,
   but he who hates reproof is stupid.

Proverbs 12.1

Be wise, my son, and make my heart glad,
   that I may answer him who reproaches
   me.

Proverbs 27.11

He who is often reproved,
   yet stiffens his neck
will suddenly be broken beyond healing.

Proverbs 29.1

Fear not the reproach of men,
 and be not dismayed at their revilings.
For the moth will eat them up like a
  garment,
 and the worm will eat them like wool.

Isaiah 51.7—8

Judge not, that you be not judged.

Matthew 7.1

Take heed to yourselves; if your brother
sins, rebuke him, and if he repents, forgive
him; and if he sins against you seven times
in the day, and turns to you seven times,
and says, 'I repent,' you must forgive him.

Luke 17.3—4

But who are you, a man, to answer back to
God? Will what is moulded say to its
moulder, 'Why have you made me thus?'

Romans 9.20

Who are you to pass judgment on the
servant of another? It is before his own
master that he stands or falls.

Romans 14.4

Why do you pass judgment on your
brother? . . . each of us shall give account
of himself to God.

Romans 14.10,12

Give the enemy no occasion to revile us.

1 Timothy 5.14

Do not grumble, brethren, against one
another, that you may not be judged.

James 5.9

Cruelty

See also **Brutality**

I cry to thee and thou dost not answer me;
 I stand, and thou dost not heed me.
Thou hast turned cruel to me;
 with the might of thy hand thou dost
   persecute me.

Job 30.20—21

A man who is kind benefits himself,
 but a cruel man hurts himself.

Proverbs 11.17

A righteous man has regard for the life of
  his beast,
 but the mercy of the wicked is cruel.

Proverbs 12.10

'What do you mean by crushing my people,
 by grinding the face of the poor?'
says the Lord God of hosts.

Isaiah 3.15

Because he practised extortion, robbed his
brother, and did what is not good among
his people, behold, he shall die for his
iniquity.

Ezekiel 18.18

Cults

If your brother, the son of your mother, or
your son, or your daughter, or the wife of
your bosom, or your friend who is as your
own soul, entices you secretly, saying, 'Let
us go and serve other gods,' which neither
you nor your fathers have known, some of
the gods of the peoples that are round
about you, whether near you or far off from
you, from the one end of the earth to the
other, you shall not yield to him or listen to
him, nor shall your eye pity him, nor shall
you spare him, nor shall you conceal him;
but you shall kill him; your hand shall be
first against him to put him to death, and
afterwards the hand of all the people.

Deuteronomy 13.6—9

But even if we, or an angel from heaven,
should preach to you a gospel contrary to
that which we preached to you, let him be
accursed. As we have said before, so now I
say again, If any one is preaching to you a
gospel contrary to that which you received,
let him be accursed.

Galatians 1.8—9

For the time is coming when people will
not endure sound teaching, but having itching ears they will accumulate for themselves
teachers to suit their own likings, and will
turn away from listening to the truth and
wander into myths.

2 Timothy 4.3—4

Cunning

See also **Worldly Wisdom**

Now the serpent was more subtle than any other wild creature that the Lord God had made. He said to the woman, 'Did God say, "You shall not eat of any tree of the garden" ?' . . .Then the Lord God said to the woman, 'What is this that you have done?' The woman said, 'The serpent beguiled me, and I ate.'

Genesis 3.1,13

He frustrates the devices of the crafty,
    so that their hands achieve no success.
He takes the wise in their own craftiness;
    and the schemes of the wily are brought
        to a quick end.
They meet with darkness in the daytime,
    and grope at noonday as in the night.

Job 5.12–14

Deceit is in the heart of those who devise evil.

Proverbs 12.20

The devising of folly is sin.

Proverbs 24.9

Woe to those who devise wickedness
    and work evil upon their beds!

Micah 2.1

Behold, I send you out as sheep in the midst of wolves; so be wise as serpents and innocent as doves.

Matthew 10.16

The sons of this world are more shrewd in dealing with their own generation than the sons of light.

Luke 16.8

But I am afraid that as the serpent deceived Eve by his cunning, your thoughts will be led astray from a sincere and pure devotion to Christ.

2 Corinthians 11.3

So that we may no longer be children, tossed to and fro and carried about with every wind of doctrine, by the cunning of men, by their craftiness in deceitful wiles.

Ephesians 4.14

Put on the whole armour of God, that you may be able to stand against the wiles of the devil.

Ephesians 6.11

And in their greed they will exploit you with false words; from of old their condemnation has not been idle, and their destruction has not been asleep.

2 Peter 2.3

Curiosity

Take heed . . . that you do not inquire about their gods, saying, 'How did these nations serve their gods? — that I also may do likewise.'

Deuteronomy 12.30

Say not, 'Why were the former days better
        than these?'
    For it is not from wisdom that you ask
        this.

Ecclesiastes 7.10

If any one teaches otherwise and does not agree with the sound words . . . he has a morbid craving for controversy and for disputes about words.

1 Timothy 6.3–4

Have nothing to do with stupid, senseless controversies; you know that they breed quarrels.

2 Timothy 2.23

Cynicism

See also **Agnosticism**

Blessed is the man
    who walks not in the counsel of the
        wicked,
nor stands in the way of sinners,
    nor sits in the seat of scoffers.

Psalms 1.

Toward the scorners he is scornful.

Proverbs 3.3

Do not reprove a scoffer, or he will hate
you.

Proverbs 9.8

If you are wise, you are wise for yourself;
if you scoff, you alone will bear it.

Proverbs 9.12

Condemnation is ready for scoffers,
and flogging for the backs of fools.

Proverbs 19.29

Drive out a scoffer, and strife will go out,
and quarrelling and abuse will cease.

Proverbs 22.10

The scoffer is an abomination to men.

Proverbs 24.9

For the ruthless shall come to naught and
the scoffer cease.

Isaiah 29.20

D

Damnation

See also **Hell, Judgment**

But the eyes of the wicked will fail;
   all way of escape will be lost to them,
   and their hope is to breathe their last.

Job 11.20

On the wicked he will rain coals of fire
      and brimstone;
   a scorching wind shall be the portion
      of their cup.

Psalms 11.6

If one curses his father or his mother,
   his lamp will be put out in utter darkness.

Proverbs 20.20

The day comes, burning like an oven, when all the arrogant and all evildoers will be stubble.

Malachi 4.1

Do not fear those who kill the body but cannot kill the soul; rather fear him who can destroy both soul and body in hell.

Matthew 10.28

The Son of man will send his angels, and they will gather out of his kingdom all causes of sin and all evildoers, and throw them into the furnace of fire; there men will weep and gnash their teeth.

Matthew 13.41–42

You are Peter, and on this rock I will build my church, and the powers of death shall not prevail against it.

Matthew 16.18

If your hand or your foot causes you to sin, cut it off and throw it away; it is better for you to enter life maimed or lame than with two hands or two feet to be thrown into the eternal fire.

Matthew 18.8

You serpents, you brood of vipers, how are you to escape being sentenced to hell?

Matthew 23.33

Whoever blasphemes against the Holy Spirit never has forgiveness, but is guilty of an eternal sin.

Mark 3.29

Scribes, who like to go about in long robes . . . who devour widows' houses and for a pretence make long prayers . . . will receive the greater condemnation.

Luke 20.46–47

The hour is coming when all who are in the tombs will hear his voice and come forth, those who have done good, to the resurrection of life, and those who have done evil, to the resurrection of judgment.

John 5.28–29

There is therefore now no condemnation for those who are in Christ Jesus.

Romans 8.1

He who has doubts is condemned, if he eats, because he does not act from faith; for whatever does not proceed from faith is sin.

Romans 14.23

The Lord Jesus is revealed from heaven with his mighty angels in flaming fire, inflicting vengeance upon those who do not know God and upon those who do not obey the gospel of our Lord Jesus.

2 Thessalonians 1.7–8

There will be false teachers among you, who will secretly bring in destructive heresies, even denying the Master who bought them, bringing upon themselves swift destruction.

2 Peter 2.1

God did not spare the angels when they sinned, but cast them into hell and committed them to pits of nether gloom to be kept until the judgment.

2 Peter 2.4

This is the second death, the lake of fire; and if any one's name was not found written in the book of life, he was thrown into the lake of fire.

Revelation 20.14–15

But as for the cowardly, the faithless, the polluted, as for murderers, fornicators, sorcerers, idolaters, and all liars, their lot shall be in the lake that burns with fire and sulphur, which is the second death.

Revelation 21.8

Dancing

Let them praise his name with dancing, making melody to him with timbrel and lyre!

Psalms 149.3

Praise him with timbrel and dance.

Psalms 150.4

There is . . . a time to mourn, and a time to dance.

Ecclesiastes 3.1,4

Again you shall adorn yourself with timbrels,
and shall go forth in the dance of the merrymakers.

Jeremiah 31.4

Then shall the maidens rejoice in the dance,
and the young men and the old shall be merry.
I will turn their mourning into joy.

Jeremiah 31.13

The old men have quit the city gate,
the young men their music.
The joy of our hearts has ceased;
our dancing has been turned to mourning.

Lamentations 5.14–15

Danger

See also **Fear**

Who shall separate us from the love of Christ? Shall tribulation, or distress, or persecution, or famine, or nakedness, or peril, or sword?

Romans 8.35

Why am I in peril every hour? I protest, brethren, by my pride in you which I have in Christ Jesus our Lord, I die every day!

1 Corinthians 15.30–31

I have been . . . in danger from rivers, danger from robbers, danger from my own people, danger from Gentiles, danger in the city, danger in the wilderness, danger at sea, danger from false brethren . . . If I must boast, I will boast of the things that show my weakness.

2 Corinthians 11.26,30

But understand this, that in the last days there will come times of stress.

2 Timothy 3.1

Darkness

See also **Blindness**

He uncovers the deeps out of darkness,
and brings deep darkness to light . . .
They grope in the dark without light;
and he makes them stagger like a drunken man.

Job 12.22,25

Yea, the light of the wicked is put out,
and the flame of his fire does not shine.

Job 18.5

He is thrust from light into darkness,
and driven out of the world.

Job 18.18

For his eyes are upon the ways of a man,
and he sees all his steps.
There is no gloom or deep darkness
where evildoers may hide themselves.

Job 34.21–22

Yea, thou dost light my lamp;
the Lord my God lightens my darkness.

Psalms 18.28

If I say, 'Let only darkness cover me,
and the light about me be night,'
even the darkness is not dark to thee,
the night is bright as the day.

Psalms 139.11–12

Delivering you from the way of evil,
from men of perverted speech,
who forsake the paths of uprightness
to walk in the ways of darkness.

Proverbs 2.12

The way of the wicked is like deep
darkness;
they do not know over what they
stumble.

Proverbs 4.19

The wise man has his eyes in his head, but
the fool walks in darkness.

Ecclesiastes 2.14

Woe to those who call evil good and good
evil,
who put darkness for light and light for
darkness.

Isaiah 5.20

The people who walked in darkness
have seen a great light;
those who dwelt in a land of deep darkness,
on them has light shined.

Isaiah 9.2

Woe to those who hide deep from the
Lord their counsel,
whose deeds are in the dark,
and who say, 'Who sees us? Who knows
us?'

Isaiah 29.15

Arise, shine; for your light has come,
and the glory of the Lord has risen upon
you.
For behold, darkness shall cover the earth,
and thick darkness the peoples.

Isaiah 60.1–2

Give glory to the Lord your God
before he brings darkness,
before your feet stumble
on the twilight mountains,
and while you look for light
he turns it into gloom.

Jeremiah 13.16

Walk while you have the light, lest the
darkness overtake you; he who walks in the
darkness does not know where he goes.

John 12.35

Let us then cast off the works of darkness
and put on the armour of light.

Romans 13.12

Take no part in the unfruitful works of
darkness, but instead expose them.

Ephesians 5.11

We are not of the night or of darkness. So
then let us not sleep, as others do, but let us
keep awake and be sober.

1 Thessalonians 5.5–6

Declare the wonderful deeds of him who
called you out of darkness into his marvellous light.

1 Peter 2.9

But he who hates his brother is in the
darkness and walks in the darkness, and
does not know where he is going, because
the darkness has blinded his eyes.

1 John 2.11

Day

See also **Light, Night**

God separated the light from the darkness. God called the light Day, and the darkness he called Night.

Genesis 1.4—5

And God said, 'Let there be lights in the firmament of the heavens to separate the day from the night; and let them be for signs and for seasons and for days and years.'

Genesis 1.14

O Lord, in the morning thou dost hear my voice;
in the morning I prepare a sacrifice for thee and watch.

Psalms 5.3

Thine is the day, thine also the night;
thou hast established the luminaries and the sun.

Psalms 74.16

For a day in thy courts is better
than a thousand elsewhere.

Psalms 84.10

O Give thanks to the Lord, for he is good,
. . . to him who made the great lights,
for his steadfast love endures for ever;
the sun to rule over the day,
for his steadfast love endures for ever.

Psalms 136.1,7—8

Give us each day our daily bread.

Luke 11.3

We must work the works of him who sent me, while it is day; night comes, when no one can work.

John 9.4

If any one walks in the day, he does not stumble, because he sees the light of this world.

John 11.9—10

The day of the Lord will come like a thief in the night . . . But you are not in darkness . . . you are all sons of light and sons of the day.

1 Thessalonians 5.2,4—5

And we have the prophetic word made more sure. You will do well to pay attention to this as to a lamp shining in a dark place, until the day dawns and the morning star rises in your hearts.

2 Peter 1.19

With the Lord one day is as a thousand years, and a thousand years as one day.

2 Peter 3.8

Daydream

See also **Visions**

A man of understanding sets his face
toward wisdom,
but the eyes of a fool are on the ends of the earth.

Proverbs 17.24

Death

See also **Decay**

You are dust,
and to dust you shall return.

Genesis 3.19

There the wicked cease from troubling,
and there the weary are at rest.

Job 3.17

Even though I walk through the valley of the shadow of death,
I fear no evil.

Psalms 23.4

Behold, the eye of the Lord is on those
who fear him,
on those who hope in his steadfast love,
that he may deliver their soul from death.

Psalms 33.18—19

Lord, let me know my end,
and what is the measure of my days;
let me know how fleeting my life is!

Psalms 39.4

But God will ransom my soul from the
  power of Sheol,
for he will receive me.

Psalms 49.15

And to God, the Lord, belongs escape
  from death.

Psalms 68.20

For my soul is full of troubles,
  and my life draws near to Sheol.
I am reckoned among those who go down
    to the Pit;
  I am a man who has no strength,
like one forsaken among the dead,
  like the slain that lie in the grave,
like those whom thou dost remember no
    more,
  for they are cut off from thy hand.
Thou hast put me in the depths of the Pit,
  in the regions dark and deep.
Thy wrath lies heavy upon me,
  and thou dost overwhelm me with all thy
    waves.
Thou hast caused my companions to shun
    me;
  thou hast made me a thing of horror to
    them.
I am shut in so that I cannot escape;
  my eye grows dim through sorrow.
Every day I call upon thee, O Lord;
  I spread out my hands to thee.
Dost thou work wonders for the dead?
  Do the shades rise up to praise thee?

Psalms 88.3–10

For all our days pass away under thy
    wrath,
  our years come to an end like a sigh.
The years of our life are threescore and ten,
  or even by reason of strength fourscore;
yet their span is but toil and trouble;
  they are soon gone, and we fly away.

Psalms 90.9–10

These all look to thee . . .
When thou hidest thy face, they are
    dismayed;
  when thou takest away their breath, they
    die
  and return to their dust.

When thou sendest forth thy Spirit, they are
    created;
  and thou renewest the face of the ground.

Psalms 104.27,29–30

All who hate me love death.

Proverbs 8.36

But the way of error leads to death.

Proverbs 12.28

The wicked is overthrown through his evil-
    doing,
  but the righteous finds refuge through his
    integrity.

Proverbs 14.32

There is a way which seems right to a man,
  but its end is the way to death.

Proverbs 16.25

Death and life are in the power of the
    tongue,
  and those who love it will eat its fruits.

Proverbs 18.21

A man who wanders from the way of
    understanding
  will rest in the assembly of the dead.

Proverbs 21.16

The wise man has his eyes in his head, but
the fool walks in darkness; and yet I perceived that one fate comes to all of them.

Ecclesiastes 2.14

There is . . . a time to be born, and a time
to die.

Ecclesiastes 3.1–2

No man has power to retain the spirit, or
authority over the day of death.

Ecclesiastes 8.8

For the living know that they will die, but
the dead know nothing, and they have no
more reward; but the memory of them is
lost. Their love and their hate and their
envy have already perished, and they have
no more for ever any share in all that is
done under the sun.

Ecclesiastes 9.5–6

The dust returns to the earth as it was, and the spirit returns to God who gave it.

Ecclesiastes 12.7

He will destroy . . . the covering that is cast over all peoples, the veil that is spread over all nations. He will swallow up death for ever.

Isaiah 25.7−8

I set before you the way of life and the way of death.

Jeremiah 21.8

Shall I ransom them from the power of
　　Sheol?
　Shall I redeem them from Death?
O Death, where are your plagues?
　O Sheol, where is your destruction?

Hosea 13.14

He is not God of the dead, but of the living.

Matthew 22.32

Lord, now lettest thou thy servant depart
　　in peace,
according to thy word;
for mine eyes have seen thy salvation
which thou hast prepared in the presence of
　　all peoples,
a light for revelation to the Gentiles,
and for glory to thy people Israel.

Luke 2.29−32

Truly, I say to you, today you will be with me in Paradise.

Luke 23.43

He who hears my word and believes him who sent me, has eternal life; he does not come into judgment, but has passed from death to life.

John 5.24

Truly, truly, I say to you, unless a grain of wheat falls into the earth and dies, it remains alone; but if it dies, it bears much fruit.

John 12.24

In my Father's house are many rooms; if it were not so, would I have told you that I go to prepare a place for you? And when I go and prepare a place for you, I will come again and will take you to myself, that where I am you may be also.

John 14.2−3

As sin came into the world through one man and death through sin . . . so death spread to all men because all men sinned.

Romans 5.12

So you also must consider yourselves dead to sin and alive to God in Christ Jesus.

Romans 6.11

For the wages of sin is death.

Romans 6.23

For the law of the Spirit of life in Christ Jesus has set me free from the law of sin and death.

Romans 8.2

To set the mind on the flesh is death, but to set the mind on the Spirit is life and peace.

Romans 8.6

The last enemy to be destroyed is death.

1 Corinthians 15.26

Flesh and blood cannot inherit the kingdom of God, nor does the perishable inherit the imperishable.

1 Corinthians 15.50

For this perishable nature must put on the imperishable, and this mortal nature must put on immortality.

1 Corinthians 15.53

When the perishable puts on the imperishable, and the mortal puts on immortality, then shall come to pass the saying that is written:
　'Death is swallowed up in victory.'
　'O death, where is thy victory?
　O death, where is thy sting?'

1 Corinthians 15.54−55

For godly grief produces a repentance that leads to salvation and brings no regret, but wordly grief produces death.

2 Corinthians 7.10

She who is self-indulgent is dead even while she lives.

1 Timothy 5.6

We brought nothing into the world, and we cannot take anything out of the world.

1 Timothy 6.7

It is appointed for men to die once, and after that comes judgment.

Hebrews 9.27

He who has an ear, let him hear what the Spirit says to the churches. He who conquers shall not be hurt by the second death.

Revelation 2.11

And in those days men will seek death and will not find it; they will long to die, and death will fly from them.

Revelation 9.6

Debauchery

See also **Promiscuity, Self-Indulgence**

You shall not lie carnally with your neighbour's wife, and defile yourself with her.

Leviticus 18.20

Every one who looks at a woman lustfully has already committed adultery with her in his heart.

Matthew 5.28

Let not sin therefore reign in your mortal bodies, to make you obey their passions.

Romans 6.12

For the mind that is set on the flesh is hostile to God; it does not submit to God's law.

Romans 8.7

But put on the Lord Jesus Christ, and make no provision for the flesh, to gratify its desires.

Romans 13.14

Love . . . does not rejoice at wrong.

1 Corinthians 13.5–6

Walk by the Spirit, and do not gratify the desires of the flesh.

Galatians 5.16

And those who belong to Christ Jesus have crucified the flesh with its passions and desires.

Galatians 5.24

No longer live as the Gentiles do, in the futility of their minds . . . they have become callous and have given themselves up to licentiousness, greedy to practise every kind of uncleanness.

Ephesians 4.17,19

Do not get drunk with wine, for that is debauchery.

Ephesians 5.18

Put to death therefore what is earthly in you: fornication, impurity, passion, evil desire . . . On account of these the wrath of God is coming.

Colossians 3.5–6

For this is the will of God . . . that you abstain from unchastity; that each one of you know how to take a wife for himself in holiness and honour, not in the passion of lust.

1 Thessalonians 4.3–5

What causes wars, and what causes fightings among you? Is it not your passions that are at war in your members?

James 4.1

Abstain from the passions of the flesh that wage war against your soul.

1 Peter 2.11

Keep the unrighteous under punishment until the day of judgment, and especially those who indulge in the lust of defiling passion and despise authority. Bold and wilful, they . . . will be destroyed . . . suffering wrong for their wrongdoing . . . They are blots and blemishes, revelling in their dissipation, carousing with you. They have eyes full of adultery, insatiable for sin.

2 Peter 2.9–10,12–14

Debt

See also **Borrowing, Interest, Lending, Usury**

The rich rules over the poor,
and the borrower is the slave of the
lender.

Proverbs 22.7

Be not one of those who give pledges,
who become surety for debts.
If you have nothing with which to pay,
why should your bed be taken from
under you?

Proverbs 22.26–27

If a man is righteous and does what is
lawful and right . . . restores to the debtor
his pledge . . . does not lend at interest or
take any increase . . . he is righteous.

Ezekiel 18.5,7–9

'Woe to him who heaps up what is not his
own —
for how long? —
and loads himself with pledges!'
Will not your debtors suddenly arise,
and those awake who will make you
tremble?
Then you will be booty for them.

Habakkuk 2.6–7

And forgive us our debts,
As we also have forgiven our debtors.

Matthew 6.12

Now to one who works, his wages are not
reckoned as a gift but as his due.

Romans 4.4

Pay all of them their dues, taxes to whom
taxes are due, revenue to whom revenue is
due, respect to whom respect is due,
honour to whom honour is due.

Romans 13.7

Decay

See also **Death**

You are dust,
and to dust you shall return.

Genesis 3.19

But man dies, and is laid low;
man breathes his last, and where is he?
. . . so man lies down and rises not again;
till the heavens are no more he will not
awake.

Job 14.10,12

Through sloth the roof sinks in,
and through indolence the house leaks.

Ecclesiastes 10.18

The grass withers, the flower fades;
but the word of our God will stand for
ever.

Isaiah 40.8

When the unclean spirit has gone out of a
man, he passes through waterless places
seeking rest, but he finds none. Then he
says, 'I will return to my house from which
I came.' And when he comes he finds it
empty, swept, and put in order. Then he
goes and brings with him seven other spirits
more evil than himself, and they enter and
dwell there; and the last state of that man
becomes worse than the first.

Matthew 12.43–45

For thou wilt not abandon my soul to
Hades,
nor let thy Holy One see corruption.

Acts 2.27

Creation itself will be set free from its
bondage to decay and obtain the glorious
liberty of the children of God.

Romans 8.21

Every athlete exercises self-control in all
things. They do it to receive a perishable
wreath, but we an imperishable.

1 Corinthians 9.25

So is it with the resurrection of the dead.
What is sown is perishable, what is raised is
imperishable.

1 Corinthians 15.42

Though our outer nature is wasting away,
our inner nature is being renewed every
day.

2 Corinthians 4.16

Whatever a man sows, that he will also reap. For he who sows to his own flesh will from the flesh reap corruption.

Galatians 6.7—8

Put off your old nature which belongs to your former manner of life and is corrupt through deceitful lusts.

Ephesians 4.22

Come now, you rich, weep and howl for the miseries that are coming upon you. Your riches have rotted and your garments are moth-eaten. Your gold and silver have rusted, and their rust will be evidence against you and will eat your flesh like fire.

James 5.1—3

Deceit

See also **Cheating, Dishonesty, Lie**

Thou hatest all evildoers.
Thou destroyest those who speak lies;
   the Lord abhors bloodthirsty and
     deceitful men.

Psalms 5.5—6

What man is there who desires life,
   and covets many days, that he may enjoy
     good?
Keep your tongue from evil,
   and your lips from speaking deceit.

Psalms 34.12—13

But to the wicked God says:
   'What right have you to recite my
     statutes,
   or take my covenant on your lips?
. . . You give your mouth free rein for evil,
   and your tongue frames deceit.'

Psalms 50.16,19

No man who practises deceit
   shall dwell in my house;
no man who utters lies
   shall continue in my presence.

Psalms 101.7

Deliver me, O Lord,
   from lying lips,
   from a deceitful tongue.

Psalms 120.2

Put away from you crooked speech,
   and put devious talk far from you.

Proverbs 4.24

The counsels of the wicked are
   treacherous.

Proverbs 12.5

A perverse tongue falls into calamity.

Proverbs 17.20

Bread gained by deceit is sweet to a man,
   but afterward his mouth will be full of
     gravel.

Proverbs 20.17

A harlot . . . lies in wait like a robber
   and increases the faithless among men.

Proverbs 23.28

Do not deceive with your lips.

Proverbs 24.27—28

He who hates, dissembles with his lips
   and harbours deceit in his heart.

Proverbs 26.24

The heart is deceitful above all things,
   and desperately corrupt;
who can understand it?

Jeremiah 17.9

Take heed that no one leads you astray.

Matthew 24.4

From within . . . come evil thoughts . . . deceit . . . slander . . . these evil things come from within, and they defile a man.

Mark 7.21—23

Let no one deceive you with empty words.

Ephesians 5.6

See to it that no one makes a prey of you by philosophy and empty deceit, according to human tradition, according to the elemental spirits of the universe, and no according to Christ.

Colossians 2.8

Evil men and impostors will go on from bad to worse, deceivers and deceived. Bu as for you, continue in what you have learned and have firmly believed.

2 Timothy 3.13−14

Decisiveness

Multitudes, multitudes,
in the valley of decision!
For the day of the Lord is near
in the valley of decision.
The sun and the moon are darkened,
and the stars withdraw their shining.

Joel 3.14−15

He who is not with me is against me, and he who does not gather with me scatters.

Matthew 12.30

Dedication

See also **Calling**

Today you have ordained yourselves for the service of the Lord . . . that he may bestow a blessing upon you this day.

Exodus 32.29

I have a treasure . . . and I give it to the house of my God . . . Who then will offer willingly, consecrating himself today to the Lord?

1 Chronicles 29.3,5

We will devote ourselves to prayer and to the ministry of the word.

Acts 6.4

Yield yourselves to God as men who have been brought from death to life.

Romans 6.13

Do you not know that if you yield yourselves to any one as obedient slaves, you are slaves of the one whom you obey, either of sin, which leads to death, or of obedience, which leads to righteousness? . . . For just as you once yielded your members to impurity and to greater and greater iniquity, so now yield your members to righteousness for sanctification.

Romans 6.16,19

I appeal to you therefore, brethren, by the mercies of God, to present your bodies as a living sacrifice, holy and acceptable to God.

Romans 12.1

So, whether you eat or drink, or whatever you do, do all to the glory of God. Give no offence to Jews or to Greeks or to the church of God.

1 Corinthians 10.31−32

And whatever you do, in word or deed, do everything in the name of the Lord Jesus, giving thanks to God the Father through him.

Colossians 3.17

As for you, man of God . . . aim at righteousness, godliness, faith, love, steadfastness, gentleness.

1 Timothy 6.11

By this we know love, that he laid down his life for us; and we ought to lay down our lives for the brethren.

1 John 3.16

Defeat

See also **Disgrace**

Look on every one that is proud, and bring
    him low;
  and tread down the wicked where they
    stand.

Job 40.12

Thou art my King and my God . . .
Through thee we push down our foes;
  through thy name we tread down our
    assailants.

Psalms 44.4−5

The wicked are overthrown and are no
    more,
  but the house of the righteous will stand.

Proverbs 12.7

Righteousness guards him whose way is
    upright,
  but sin overthrows the wicked.

Proverbs 13.6

When a strong man, fully armed, guards his own palace, his goods are in peace; but when one stronger than he assails him and overcomes him, he takes away his armour in which he trusted, and divides his spoil.

Luke 11.21—22

So in the present case I tell you, keep away from these men and let them alone; for if this plan or this undertaking is of men, it will fail; but if it is of God, you will not be able to overthrow them.

Acts 5.38—39

You are strong, and the word of God abides in you, and you have overcome the evil one.

1 John 2.14

For whatever is born of God overcomes the world; and this is the victory that overcomes the world, our faith.

1 John 5.4

Who is it that overcomes the world but he who believes that Jesus is the Son of God?

1 John 5.5

Defilement

See also **Degeneration**

What comes out of the mouth proceeds from the heart, and this defiles a man. For out of the heart come evil thoughts, murder, adultery, fornication, theft, false witness, slander. These are what defile a man; but to eat with unwashed hands does not defile a man.

Matthew 15.18—20

Degeneration

See also **Delinquency**

Take heed to yourselves lest your hearts be weighed down with dissipation and drunkenness and cares of this life, and that day come upon you suddenly like a snare.

Luke 21.34

Delay

See also **Hesitancy**

I hasten and do not delay
  to keep thy commandments.

Psalms 119.60

Do not say to your neighbour, 'Go, and
    come again,
  tomorrow I will give it' — when you have
    it with you.

Proverbs 3.28

Hope deferred makes the heart sick.

Proverbs 13.12

When you vow a vow to God, do not delay paying it; for he has no pleasure in fools. Pay what you vow. It is better that you should not vow than that you should vow and not pay.

Ecclesiastes 5.4—5

Whatever your hand finds to do, do it with your might.

Ecclesiastes 9.10

And now why do you wait? Rise and be baptized, and wash away your sins, calling on his name.

Acts 22.16

But my righteous one shall live by faith,
  and if he shrinks back,
  my soul has no pleasure in him.

Hebrews 10.38

The Lord is not slow about his promise as some count slowness, but is forbearing toward you, not wishing that any should perish.

2 Peter 3.9

Delight

See also **Joy, Pleasure**

Then you will delight yourself in the
    Almighty,
  and lift up your face to God.

Job 22.26

Blessed is the man
  who walks not in the counsel of the
    wicked . . .
but his delight is in the law of the Lord.

Psalms 1.1−2

I keep the Lord always before me;
. . . Therefore my heart is glad, and my
  soul rejoices.

Psalms 16.8−9

Take delight in the Lord,
  and he will give you the desires of your
    heart.

Psalms 37.4

The steps of a man are from the Lord,
  and he establishes him in whose way he
    delights.

Psalms 37.23

The Lord reigns; let the earth rejoice;
  let the many coastlands be glad!

Psalms 97.1

Great are the works of the Lord,
  studied by all who have pleasure in them.

Psalms 111.2

Blessed is the man who fears the Lord,
  who greatly delights in his
    commandments!

Psalms 112.1

As an apple tree among the trees of the
  wood,
so is my beloved among young men.
With great delight I sat in his shadow,
  and his fruit was sweet to my taste.

Song of Solomon 2.3

How fair and pleasant you are,
  O loved one, delectable maiden!

Song of Solomon 7.6

If you . . . call the sabbath a delight
  and the holy day of the Lord honourable;
. . . then you shall take delight in the Lord.

Isaiah 58.13−14

I am the Lord who practise steadfast love,
justice, and righteousness in the earth; for
in these things I delight, says the Lord.

Jeremiah 9.24

Who is a God like thee, pardoning iniquity
  and passing over transgression
  for the remnant of his inheritance?
He does not retain his anger for ever
  because he delights in steadfast love.

Micah 7.18

For I delight in the law of God, in my inmost self.

Romans 7.22

Delinquency

See also **Degeneration**

Discretion will watch over you;
  understanding will guard you;
delivering you . . .
  from men of perverted speech . . .
who rejoice in doing evil
  and delight in the perverseness of evil;
men whose paths are crooked,
  and who are devious in their ways.

Proverbs 2.11−12,14−15

There is severe discipline for him who
  forsakes the way;
he who hates reproof will die.

Proverbs 15.10

Now the parable is this: . . . The ones
along the path are those who have heard;
then the devil comes and takes away the
word from their hearts, that they may not
believe and be saved.

Luke 8.11−12

Deliverance

The Lord is my rock, and my fortress, and
  my deliverer.

Psalms 18.2

My times are in thy hand;
  deliver me from the hand of my enemies
    and persecutors!

Let thy face shine on thy servant;
    save me in thy steadfast love!

Psalms 31.15−16

When the righteous cry for help, the Lord
        hears,
    and delivers them out of all their
        troubles.

Psalms 34.17

The salvation of the righteous is from the
        Lord;
    he is their refuge in the time of trouble.
The Lord helps them and delivers them;
    he delivers them from the wicked, and
        saves them,
    because they take refuge in him.

Psalms 37.39−40

Deliver me from bloodguiltiness, O God,
    thou God of my salvation,
    and my tongue will sing aloud of thy
        deliverance.

Psalms 51.14

For he delivers the needy when he calls,
    the poor and him who has no helper.
He has pity on the weak and the needy,
    and saves the lives of the needy.

Psalms 72.12−13

The Lord preserves the simple;
    when I was brought low, he saved me.

Psalms 116.6

The righteousness of the upright delivers
        them.

Proverbs 11.6

The righteous is delivered from trouble.

Proverbs 11.8

The Lord has anointed me
to bring good tidings to the afflicted;
    he has sent me to bind up the broken-
        hearted,
to proclaim liberty to the captives,
    and the opening of the prison to those
        who are bound.

Isaiah 61.1

Our God whom we serve is able to deliver
us from the burning fiery furnace.

Daniel 3.17

And lead us not into temptation,
    But deliver us from evil.

Matthew 6.13

You will know the truth, and the truth will
make you free.

John 8.32

If the Son makes you free, you will be free
indeed.

John 8.36

You have been set free from sin and have
become slaves of God.

Romans 6.22

Who will deliver me from this body of
death?

Romans 7.24

For the law of the Spirit of life in Christ
Jesus has set me free from the law of sin
and death.

Romans 8.2

Creation itself will be set free from its
bondage to decay and obtain the glorious
liberty of the children of God.

Romans 8.21

God . . . raises the dead; he delivered us
from so deadly a peril, and he will deliver
us; on him we have set out hope that he will
deliver us again.

2 Corinthians 1.9−10

Where the Spirit of the Lord is, there is
freedom.

2 Corinthians 3.17

Grace to you and peace from God the
Father and our Lord Jesus Christ, who gave
himself for our sins to deliver us from the
present evil age, according to the will of our
God and Father.

Galatians 1.3−4

For freedom Christ has set us free; stand
fast therefore, and do not submit again to a
yoke of slavery.

Galatians 5.1

The Lord will rescue me from every evil and save me for his heavenly kingdom.

2 Timothy 4.18

Since therefore the children share in flesh and blood, he himself likewise partook of the same nature, that through death he might destroy him who has the power of death, that is, the devil, and deliver all those who through fear of death were subject to lifelong bondage.

Hebrews 2.14−15

Delusion

See also **Ignorance**

Transgression speaks to the wicked
   deep in his heart;
there is no fear of God
   before his eyes.
For he flatters himself in his own eyes
   that his iniquity cannot be found out and
     hated.

Psalms 36.1−2

Put false ways far from me;
   and graciously teach me thy law!

Psalms 119.29

Thou dost spurn all who go astray from thy
     statutes;
yea, their cunning is in vain.

Psalms 119.118

There is a way which seems right to a man,
   but its end is the way to death.

Proverbs 16.25

There are those who are pure in their own
    eyes
   but are not cleansed of their filth.

Proverbs 30.12

Do not deceive yourselves.

Jeremiah 37.9

I will say to my soul, 'Soul, you have ample goods laid up for many years; take your ease, eat, drink, be merry.' But God said to him, 'Fool! This night your soul is required of you; and the things you have prepared, whose will they be?'

Luke 12.19−20

The wrath of God is revealed from heaven against all ungodliness and wickedness of men who by their wickedness suppress the truth . . . So they are without excuse; for although they knew God they did not honour him . . . they exchanged the truth about God for a lie.

Romans 1.18,20−21,25

If any one among you thinks that he is wise in this age, let him become a fool that he may become wise.

1 Corinthians 3.18

I am not aware of anything against myself, but I am not thereby acquitted. It is the Lord who judges me.

1 Corinthians 4.4

For if any one thinks he is something, when he is nothing, he deceives himself.

Galatians 6.3

When people say, 'There is peace and security,' then sudden destruction will come upon them.

1 Thessalonians 5.3

Therefore God sends upon them a strong delusion, to make them believe what is false, so that all may be condemned who did not believe the truth but had pleasure in unrighteousness.

2 Thessalonians 2.11−12

Be doers of the word, and not hearers only, deceiving yourselves.

James 1.22

If any one thinks he is religious, and does not bridle his tongue but deceives his heart, this man's religion is vain.

James 1.26

If we say we have no sin, we deceive ourselves, and the truth is not in us.

1 John 1.8

Demeanour

Let your eyes look directly forward,
and your gaze be straight before you.

Proverbs 4.25

Haughty eyes and a proud heart,
the lamp of the wicked, are sin.

Proverbs 21.4

Democracy

See also **Freedom**

Hearken to the voice of the people in all
that they say to you.

1 Samuel 8.7

The rich and the poor meet together;
the Lord is the maker of them all.

Proverbs 22.2

Here there cannot be Greek and Jew,
circumcised and uncircumcised, barbarian,
Scyth'ian, slave, free man . . . above all
these put on love, which binds everything
together in perfect harmony.

Colossians 3.11,14

The perfect law, the law of liberty.

James 1.25

So speak and so act as those who are to be
judged under the law of liberty.

James 2.12

Live as free men, yet without using your
freedom as a pretext for evil; but live as
servants of God. Honour all men.

1 Peter 2.16

Demons

It is by the finger of God that I cast out
demons.

Luke 11.20

Denigration

Speak evil of no one.

Titus 3.2

Dependence

See also **Trust**

And he humbled you and let you hunger
and fed you with manna, which you did not
know, nor did your fathers know; that he
might make you know that man does not
live by bread alone, but that man lives by
everything that proceeds out of the mouth
of the Lord.

Deuteronomy 8.3

The Lord recompense you for what you
have done . . . under whose wings you have
come to take refuge!

Ruth 2.12

There is none like thee to help, between
the mighty and the weak. Help us, O Lord
our God, for we rely on thee.

2 Chronicles 14.11

God is our refuge and strength,
a very present help in trouble.

Psalms 46.1

If the Lord had not been my help,
my soul would soon have dwelt in the
land of silence.

Psalms 94.17

For the Lord will be your confidence
and will keep your foot from being
caught.

Proverbs 3.26

Man shall not live by bread alone,
but by every word that proceeds from the
mouth of God.

Matthew 4.4

Abide in me, and I in you. As the branch
cannot bear fruit by itself, unless it abides
in the vine, neither can you, unless you
abide in me. I am the vine, you are the
branches. He who abides in me, and I in
him, he it is that bears much fruit, for apart
from me you can do nothing.

John 15.4–5

For we cannot do anything against the
truth, but only for the truth.

2 Corinthians 13.8

If any of you lacks wisdom, let him ask God, who gives to all men generously and without reproaching, and it will be given him.

James 1.5

Depravity

See also **Corruption, Degeneration, Delinquency**

God saw the earth, and behold, it was corrupt; for all flesh had corrupted their way upon the earth.

Genesis 6.12

Behold, God puts no trust in his holy ones,
    and the heavens are not clean in his sight;
how much less one who is abominable and
        corrupt,
    a man who drinks iniquity like water!

Job 15.15–16

You are of your father the devil, and your will is to do your father's desires.

John 8.44

God gave them up to a base mind and to improper conduct. They were filled with all manner of wickedness, evil, covetousness, malice . . . they are . . . foolish, faithless, heartless, ruthless.

Romans 1.28–29,31

I see in my members another law at war with the law of my mind and making me captive to the law of sin.

Romans 7.22–23

If any one destroys God's temple, God will destroy him. for God's temple is holy, and that temple you are.

1 Corinthians 3.17

They promise them freedom, but they themselves are slaves of corruption; for whatever overcomes a man, to that he is enslaved. For if, after they have escaped the defilements of the world through the knowledge of our Lord and Saviour Jesus Christ, they are again entangled in them and overpowered, the last state has become worse for them than the first.

2 Peter 2.19–20

We know that we are of God, and the whole world is in the power of the evil one.

1 John 5.19

Depression

See also **Despair, Misery, Sadness**

Do not be grieved, for the joy of the Lord is your strength.

Nehemiah 8.10

Weeping may tarry for the night,
    but joy comes with the morning.

Psalms 30.5

The Lord is near to the brokenhearted,
    and saves the crushed in spirit.

Psalms 34.18

Why are you cast down, O my soul,
    and why are you disquieted within me?
Hope in God; for I shall again praise him,
    my help and my God.

Psalms 43.5

The sacrifice acceptable to God is a broken
        spirit;
    a broken and contrite heart, O God, thou
        wilt not despise.

Psalms 51.17

Cast your burden on the Lord,
    and he will sustain you.

Psalms 55.22

I called to the Lord, out of my distress,
    and he answered me;
out of the belly of Sheol I cried,
    and thou didst hear my voice.

Jonah 2.2

You will weep and lament, but the world will rejoice; you will be sorrowful, but your sorrow will turn into joy.

John 16.20

God, who comforts the downcast.

2 Corinthians 7.6

For godly grief produces a repentance that leads to salvation and brings no regret.

2 Corinthians 7.10

Be wretched and mourn and weep. Let your laughter be turned to mourning and your joy to dejection. Humble yourselves before the Lord and he will exalt you.

James 4.9–10

He will wipe away every tear from their eyes, and death shall be no more, neither shall there be mourning nor crying nor pain any more.

Revelation 21.4

Desertion

For my father and my mother have
  forsaken me,
  but the Lord will take me up.

Psalms 27.10

My friends and companions stand aloof
  from my plague,
  and my kinsmen stand afar off.

Psalms 38.11

But my eyes are toward thee, O Lord
  God;
  in thee I seek refuge; leave me not
  defenceless!

Psalms 141.8

I will scatter you like chaff
  driven by the wind from the desert . . .
  because you have forgotten me
  and trusted in lies.

Jeremiah 13.24–25

Woe to my worthless shepherd,
  who deserts the flock!

Zechariah 11.17

Now the Spirit expressly says that in later times some will depart from the faith by giving heed to deceitful spirits and doctrines of demons.

1 Timothy 4.1

Take care, brethren, lest there be in any of you an evil, unbelieving heart, leading you to fall away from the living God.

Hebrews 3.12

Forsaking the right way they have gone astray . . . These are waterless springs and mists driven by a storm; for them the nether gloom of darkness has been reserved.

2 Peter 2.15,17

And the angels that did not keep their own position but left their proper dwelling have been kept by him in eternal chains in the nether gloom until the judgment of the great day.

Jude 6

Desire

See also **Lust**

For the wicked boasts of the desires of his
  heart.

Psalms 10.3

O Lord, thou wilt hear the desire of the
  meek;
  thou wilt strengthen their heart,
  thou wilt incline thy ear.

Psalms 10.17

The ordinances of the Lord are true,
  and righteous altogether.
More to be desired are they than gold,
  even much fine gold.

Psalms 19.9–10

One thing have I asked of the Lord,
  that will I seek after;
that I may dwell in the house of the Lord
  all the days of my life.

Psalms 27.4

Take delight in the Lord,
  and he will give you the desires of your
  heart.

Psalms 37.4

Lord, all my longing is known to thee.

Psalms 38.9

O God, thou art my God, I seek thee,
  my soul thirsts for thee;
my flesh faints for thee.

Psalms 63.1

Grant not, O Lord, the desires of the
  wicked.

Psalms 140.8

But the desire of the righteous will be
  granted.

Proverbs 10.24

The desire of the righteous ends only in
  good;
  the expectation of the wicked in wrath.

Proverbs 11.23

Hope deferred makes the heart sick,
  but a desire fulfilled is a tree of life.

Proverbs 13.12

A desire fulfilled is sweet to the soul.

Proverbs 13.19

He who is estranged seeks pretexts
  to break out against all sound judgment.

Proverbs 18.1

The desire of the sluggard kills him
  for his hands refuse to labour.

Proverbs 21.25

O Lord, we wait for thee;
  thy memorial name
  is the desire of our soul.

Isaiah 26.8

Whatever you ask in prayer, believe that
you have received it, and it will be yours.

Mark 11.24

Make no provision for the flesh, to gratify
its desires.

Romans 13.14

Make love your aim, and earnestly desire
the spiritual gifts.

1 Corinthians 14.1

Walk by the Spirit, and do not gratify the
desires of the flesh.

Galatians 5.16

Set your minds on things that are above,
not on things that are on earth.

Colossians 3.2

For the love of money is the root of all
evils.

1 Timothy 6.10

They desire a better country, that is, a
heavenly one.

Hebrews 11.16

Desolation

See also **Depression, Loneliness**

My eyes are ever toward the Lord,
  for he will pluck my feet out of the net.
Turn thou to me, and be gracious to me;
  for I am lonely and afflicted.

Psalms 25.15−16

For the enemy has pursued me . . .
he has made me sit in darkness like
      those long dead.
Therefore my spirit faints within me;
  my heart within me is appalled . . .
Make haste to answer me, O Lord!
  My spirit fails!
Hide not thy face from me,
  lest I be like those who go down to
    the Pit.

Psalms 143.3−4,7

I will mock when panic strikes you . . .
  and your calamity comes like a
      whirlwind,
  when distress and anguish come upon
      you.
Then they will call upon me, but I will not
      answer;
  they will seek me diligently but will not
      find me.
Because they hated knowledge
  and did not choose the fear of the Lord.

Proverbs 1.26−29

What will you do on the day of
      punishment,
  in the storm which will come from afar?
To whom will you flee for help,
  and where will you leave your wealth?

Isaiah 10.3

This is the exultant city
    that dwelt secure,
  that said to herself,
    'I am and there is none else.'
What a desolation she has become,
    a lair for wild beasts!

Zephaniah 2.15

Every kingdom divided against itself is laid waste.

Matthew 12.25

Despair

See also **Depression, Misery, Sadness**

Kill me at once . . . that I may not see my wretchedness.

Numbers 11.15

And among these nations you shall find no ease, and there shall be no rest for the sole of your foot; but the Lord will give you there a trembling heart, and failing eyes, and a languishing soul; your life shall hang in doubt before you; night and day you shall be in dread, and have no assurance of your life.

Deuteronomy 28.65–66

O that my vexation were weighed,
    and all my calamity laid in the balances!
For then it would be heavier than the sand
        of the sea;
    therefore my words have been rash.

Job 6.1–3

I loathe my life;
    I will give free utterance to my
        complaint;
    I will speak in the bitterness of my soul.
I will say to God, Do not condemn me;
    let me know why thou dost contend
        against me.

Job 10.1–2

For what is the hope of the godless when God cuts him off.

Job 27.8

My God, my God, why hast thou forsaken me?

Psalms 22.1

Many are the pangs of the wicked;
    but steadfast love surrounds him who
        trusts in the Lord.

Psalms 32.10

My soul is cast down within me,
    therefore I remember thee . . .

I say to God, my rock:
    'Why hast thou forgotten me?
Why go I mourning
    because of the oppression of the enemy?'
. . . Why are you cast down, O my soul,
    and why are you disquieted within me?
Hope in God; for I shall again praise him,
    my help and my God.

Psalms 42.6,9,11

A man's spirit will endure sickness;
    but a broken spirit who can bear?

Proverbs 18.14

So I hated life, because what is done under the sun was grievous to me; for all is vanity and a striving after wind.

Ecclesiastes 2.17

So I turned about and gave my heart up to despair over all the toil of my labours under the sun, because sometimes a man who has toiled with wisdom and knowledge and skill must leave all to be enjoyed by a man who did not toil for it.

Ecclesiastes 2.20–21

Distress and darkness, the gloom of anguish.

Isaiah 8.22

O Lord, how long shall I cry for help,
    and thou wilt not hear?
Or cry to thee 'Violence!'
    and thou wilt not save?

Habakkuk 1.2

'My soul is very sorrowful even to death; remain here, and watch.' And going a little farther, he fell on the ground and prayed that, if it were possible, the hour might pass from him. And he said, 'Abba, Father, all things are possible to thee; remove this cup from me; yet not what I will, but what thou wilt.'

Mark 14.34–36

We are afflicted in every way, but not crushed; perplexed, but not driven to despair; persecuted, but not forsaken; struck down, but not destroyed; always carrying in the body the death of Jesus, so that the life of Jesus may also be manifested in our bodies.

2 Corinthians 4.8−10

Despondency

See also **Depression, Despair, Misery, Sadness**

But my eyes are toward thee, O Lord God;
  in thee I seek refuge; leave me not
    defenceless!

Psalms 141.8

Trust in a faithless man in time of trouble
  is like a bad tooth or a foot that slips.
He who sings songs to a heavy heart
  is like one who takes off a garment on a
    cold day,
  and like vinegar on a wound.

Proverbs 25.19−20

Despotism

See also **Oppression, Tyranny**

When the wicked are in authority,
  transgression increases;
  but the righteous will look upon their
    downfall.

Proverbs 29.16

Woe to those who decree iniquitous
  decrees,
  and the writers who keep writing
    oppression,
to turn aside the needy from justice.

Isaiah 10.1−2

I will put an end to the pride of the
  arrogant,
  and lay low the haughtiness of the
    ruthless.

Isaiah 13.11

Therefore because you trample upon the
  poor
  and take from him exactions of wheat,
you have built houses of hewn stone,
  but you shall not dwell in them;

you have planted pleasant vineyards,
  but you shall not drink their wine.

Amos 5.11

Destiny

See also **Chance**

The lot is cast into the lap,
  but the decision is wholly from the Lord.

Proverbs 16.33

A generation goes, and a generation
  comes,
  but the earth remains for ever.
The sun rises and the sun goes down,
. . . All streams run to the sea,
  but the sea is not full;
to the place where the streams flow,
  there they flow again.

Ecclesiastes 1.4,7

The race is not the the swift . . . but time
and chance happen to them all.

Ecclesiastes 9.11

Before I formed you in the womb I knew
  you,
and before you were born I consecrated
  you.

Jeremiah 1.5

Thus says the Lord:
Those who are for pestilence, to pestilence,
  and those who are for the sword, to the
    sword;
those who are for famine, to famine,
  and those who are for captivity, to
    captivity.

Jeremiah 15.2

For now we see in a mirror dimly, but then
face to face.

1 Corinthians 13.12

But you are a chosen race, a royal priesthood, a holy nation, God's own people, that you may declare the wonderful deeds of him who called you out of darkness into his marvellous light.

1 Peter 2.9

Destruction

I will blot out man whom I have created from the face of the ground, man and beast and creeping things and birds of the air, for I am sorry that I have made them.

Genesis 6.7

You did not obey the voice of the Lord your God. And as the Lord took delight in doing you good and multiplying you, so the Lord will take delight in bringing ruin upon you and destroying you.

Deuteronomy 28.62–63

The wicked man is spared in the day of
    calamity . . .
  he is rescued in the day of wrath.

Job 21.30

Thou hast given me the shield of thy
    salvation . . .
I pursued my enemies and overtook
    them;
  and did not turn back till they were
    consumed.
I thrust them through, so that they were not
    able to rise;
  they fell under my feet.

Psalms 18.35,37–38

Thou turnest man back to the dust,
  and sayest, 'Turn back, O children of
    men!'

Psalms 90.3

You will not fear the terror of the night,
  nor the arrow that flies by day,
nor the pestilence that stalks in darkness,
  nor the destruction that wastes at
    noonday.

Psalms 91.5–6

The complacence of fools destroys them.

Proverbs 1.32

The Lord tears down the house of the
  proud.

Proverbs 15.25

Pride goes before destruction,
  and a haughty spirit before a fall.

Proverbs 16.18

He will swallow up death for ever.

Isaiah 25.8

For the Lord is enraged against all the
    nations,
  and furious against all their host,
  he has doomed them, has given them
    over for slaughter.

Isaiah 34.2

These . . . things have befallen you —
  who will condole with you? —
devastation and destruction, famine and
    sword;
  who will comfort you?

Isaiah 51.19

The seed shrivels under the clods,
  the storehouses are desolate;
the granaries are ruined
  because the grain has failed.
. . . Unto thee, O Lord, I cry.

Joel 1.17,19

Do not lay up for yourselves treasures on earth, where moth and rust consume . . . but lay up for yourselves treasure in heaven.

Matthew 6.19–20

Do not fear those who kill the body but cannot kill the soul; rather fear him who can destroy both soul and body in hell.

Matthew 10.28

He has put down the mighty from their
    thrones,
  and exalted those of low degree.

Luke 1.52

The days will come when there shall not be left here one stone upon another that will not be thrown down.

Luke 21.6

The last enemy to be destroyed is death.

1 Corinthians 15.26

If you bite and devour one another take heed that you are not consumed by one another.

Galatians 5.15

The Lord Jesus will slay him [the lawless one] with the breath of his mouth and destroy him by his appearing and his coming.

2 Thessalonians 2.8

Another priest arises in the likeness of Melchiz'edek, who has become a priest, not according to a legal requirement concerning bodily descent but by the power of an indestructible life.

Hebrews 7.15–17

The day of the Lord will come like a thief, and then the heavens will pass away with a loud noise, and the elements will be dissolved with fire, and the earth and the works that are upon it will be burned up.

2 Peter 3.10

He who saved a people out of the land of Egypt, afterward destroyed those who did not believe.

Jude 5

The time . . . for destroying the destroyers of the earth.

Revelation 11.18

Determination

And your ears shall hear a word behind you, saying, 'This is the way, walk in it,' when you turn to the right or when you turn to the left.

Isaiah 30.21

For the Lord God helps me;
   therefore I have not been confounded;
therefore I have set my face like a flint,
   and I know that I shall not be put to
     shame;
   he who vindicates me is near.

Isaiah 50.7–8

And each went straight forward; wherever the spirit would go, they went, without turning as they went.

Ezekiel 1.12

No one who puts his hand to the plough and looks back is fit for the kingdom of God.

Luke 9.62

Therefore take the whole armour of God, that you may be able to withstand in the evil day, and having done all, to stand.

Ephesians 6.13

Forgetting what lies behind and straining forward to what lies ahead, I press on toward the goal for the prize of the upward call of God in Christ Jesus.

Philippians 3.13–14

We are not of those who shrink back and are destroyed, but of those who have faith and keep their souls.

Hebrews 10.39

Now who is there to harm you if you are zealous for what is right?

1 Peter 3.13

Deterrence

The man who acts presumptuously, by not obeying the priest who stands to minister there before the Lord your God, or the judge, that man shall die; so you shall purge the evil from Israel. And all the people shall hear, and fear, and not act presumptuously again.

Deuteronomy 17.12–13

Development

See also **Growth**

Blessed are the men whose strength is in
    thee,
in whose heart are the highways to Zion . . .
They go from strength to strength;
   the God of gods will be seen in Zion.

Psalms 84.5,7

The righteous flourish like the palm tree,
   and grow like a cedar in Lebanon.

Psalms 92.12

But the path of the righteous is like the
     light of dawn,
  which shines brighter and brighter until
     full day.

Proverbs 4.18

The least one shall become a clan,
  and the smallest one a mighty nation.

Isaiah 60.22

I will restore the fortunes of my people
     Israel,
  and they shall rebuild the ruined cities
     and inhabit them;
they shall plant vineyards and drink their
     wine,
  and they shall make gardens and eat their
     fruit.

Amos 9.14

The kingdom of heaven is like a grain of
mustard seed which a man took and sowed
in his field; it is the smallest of all seeds, but
when it has grown it is the greatest of
shrubs and becomes a tree, so that the birds
of the air come and make nests in its
branches.

Matthew 13.31–32

He who is faithful in a very little is faithful
also in much.

Luke 16.10

I have yet many things to say to you, but
you cannot bear them now. When the Spirit
of truth comes, he will guide you into all
the truth.

John 16.12–13

The whole structure is joined together and
grows into a holy temple in the Lord; in
whom you also are built into it for a dwelling place of God in the Spirit.

Ephesians 2.21–22

Speaking the truth in love, we are to grow
up in every way into him who is the head,
into Christ, from whom the whole body,
joined and knit together by every joint with
which it is supplied, when each part is
working properly, makes bodily growth and
upbuilds itself in love.

Ephesians 4.15–16

Love one another . . . more and more.

1 Thessalonians 4.10

Let us leave the elementary doctrine of
Christ and go on to maturity.

Hebrews 6.1

Grow in the grace and knowledge of our
Lord and Saviour Jesus Christ.

2 Peter 3.18

We are God's children now; it does not
yet appear what we shall be, but we know
that when he appears we shall be like him,
for we shall see him as he is.

1 John 3.2

Devil

See also **Damnation, Hell**

The Lord said to Satan, 'Whence have you
come?' Satan answered the Lord, 'From
going to and fro on the earth, and from
walking up and down on it.'

Job 1.7

How you are fallen from heaven,
  O Day Star, son of Dawn!
. . . You said in your heart,
  'I will ascend to heaven;
above the stars of God
  I will set my throne on high.'

Isaiah 14.12–13

Begone, Satan! for it is written,
  'You shall worship the Lord your God
  and him only shall you serve.'

Matthew 4.10

Get behind me, Satan! You are a hindrance to me; for you are not on the side of
God, but of men.

Matthew 16.23

These signs will accompany those who
believe: in my name they will cast out
demons; they will speak in new tongues;
they will pick up serpents, and if they drink
any deadly thing, it will not hurt them; they
will lay their hands on the sick, and they
will recover.

Mark 16.17–18

Lord, even the demons are subject to us in your name!

Luke 10.17

I saw Satan fall like lightning from heaven.

Luke 10.18

I have given you authority to tread upon serpents and scorpions, and over all the power of the enemy.

Luke 10.19

If Satan also is divided against himself, how will his kingdom stand . . . if I cast out demons by Be-el'zebul, by whom do your sons cast them out?

Luke 11.18–19

Why do you not understand what I say? It is because you cannot bear to hear my word. You are of your father the devil, and your will is to do your father's desires.

John 8.43–44

Now is the judgment of this world, now shall the ruler of this world be cast out.

John 12.31

The God of peace will soon crush Satan under your feet.

Romans 16.20

You cannot drink the cup of the Lord and the cup of demons. You cannot partake of the table of the Lord and the table of demons.

1 Corinthians 10.21

Keep Satan from gaining the advantage over us; for we are not ignorant of his designs.

2 Corinthians 2.11

Satan disguises himself as an angel of light.

2 Corinthians 11.14–15

Do not let the sun go down on your anger, and give no opportunity to the devil.

Ephesians 4.26–27

Put on the whole armour of God, that you may be able to stand against the wiles of the devil. For we are not contending against flesh and blood, but against the principalities, against the powers, against the world rulers of this present darkness, against the spiritual hosts of wickedness in the heavenly places.

Ephesians 6.11–12

The Lord is faithful; he will strengthen you and guard you from evil.

2 Thessalonians 3.3

In later times some will depart from the faith by giving heed to deceitful spirits and doctrines of demons.

1 Timothy 4.1

Since therefore the children share in flesh and blood, he himself likewise partook of the same nature, that through death he might destroy him who has the power of death, that is, the devil, and deliver all those who through fear of death were subject to lifelong bondage.

Hebrews 2.14–15

Submit yourselves therefore to God. Resist the devil and he will flee from you.

James 4.7

Be sober, be watchful. Your adversary the devil prowls around like a roaring lion, seeking some one to devour.

1 Peter 5.8

He who commits sin is of the devil; for the devil has sinned from the beginning.

1 John 3.8

We know that any one born of God does not sin, but He who was born of God keeps him, and the evil one does not touch him.

1 John 5.18

Behold, the devil is about to throw some of you into prison, that you may be tested . . . Be faithful unto death, and I will give you the crown of life.

Revelation 2.10

War arose in heaven, Michael and his angels fighting against the dragon; and the dragon and his angels fought, but they were defeated and there was no longer any place for them in heaven. And the great dragon was thrown down, that ancient serpent, who is called the Devil and Satan, the deceiver of the whole world — he was thrown down to the earth, and his angels were thrown down with him.

Revelation 12.7–9

Rejoice then, O heaven and you that dwell therein! But woe to you, O earth and sea, for the devil has come down to you in great wrath, because he knows that his time is short!

Relevation 12.12

Devoutness

You shall be holy; for I the Lord your God am holy.

Leviticus 19.2

The root of the righteous stands firm.

Proverbs 12.12

When you pray, go into your room and shut the door and pray to your Father who is in secret; and your Father who sees in secret will reward you.

Matthew 6.6

I urge that supplications, prayers, intercessions, and thanksgivings be made for all men, for kings and all who are in high positions, that we may lead a quiet and peaceable life, godly and respectful in every way.

1 Timothy 2.1–2

Train yourself in godliness; for while bodily training is of some value, godliness is of value in every way, as it holds promise for the present life and also for the life to come.

1 Timothy 4.7–8

Man of God, shun all this; aim at righteousness, godliness, faith, love, steadfastness, gentleness.

1 Timothy 6.11

The grace of God has appeared for the salvation of all men, training us to renounce irreligion and wordly passions, and to live sober, upright, and godly lives in this world.

Titus 2.11–12

Thus let us offer to God acceptable worship, with reverence and awe.

Hebrews 12.28

As he who called you is holy, be holy yourselves in all your conduct.

1 Peter 1.15

Devotion

Where you go I will go, and where you lodge I will lodge; your people shall be my people, and your God my God; where you die I will die, and there will I be buried.

Ruth 1.16–17

As the Lord lives, and as my lord the king lives, wherever my lord the king shall be, whether for death or for life, there also will your servant be.

2 Samuel 15.21

A friend loves at all times,
  and a brother is born for adversity.

Proverbs 17.17

Faithful are the wounds of a friend;
  profuse are the kisses of an enemy.

Proverbs 27.6

Set me as a seal upon your heart,
  as a seal upon your arm;
for love is strong as death,
  jealousy is cruel as the grave.
Its flashes are flashes of fire,
  a most vehement flame.
Many waters cannot quench love,
  neither can floods drown it.

Song of Solomon 8.6–7

Not every one who says to me, 'Lord, Lord,' shall enter the kingdom of heaven, but he who does the will of my Father who is in heaven.

Matthew 7.21

You shall love the Lord your God with all your heart, and with all your soul, and with all your mind. This is the great and first commandment. And a second is like it, You shall love your neighbour as yourself.

Matthew 22.37−39

I tell you, her sins, which are many, are forgiven, for she loved much; but he who is forgiven little, loves little.

Luke 7.47

Love one another as I have loved you. Greater love has no man than this, that a man lay down his life for his friends.

John 15.12−13

Difficulty

The way of the faithless is their ruin.

Proverbs 13.15

For the gate is narrow and the way is hard, that leads to life, and those who find it are few.

Matthew 7.14

How hard it will be for those who have riches to enter the kingdom of God! . . . It is easier for a camel to go through the eye of a needle than for a rich man to enter the kingdom of God!

Mark 10.23,25

Dignity

See also **Majesty**

Deck yourself with majesty and dignity; clothe yourself with glory and splendour.

Job 40.10

There is an evil which I have seen under the sun . . . folly is set in many high places.

Ecclesiastes 10.5−6

Bid the older women likewise to be reverent in behaviour . . . they are to teach what is good.

Titus 2.3

Diligence

Now set your mind and heart to seek the Lord your God. Arise and build the sanctuary of the Lord God.

1 Chronicles 22.19

A slack hand causes poverty,
but the hand of the diligent makes rich.

Proverbs 10.4

He who diligently seeks good seeks favour.

Proverbs 11.27

He who tills his land will have plenty of bread.

Proverbs 12.11

The hand of the diligent will rule, while the slothful will be put to forced labour.

Proverbs 12.24

The diligent man will get precious wealth.

Proverbs 12.27

The soul of the sluggard craves, and gets nothing,
while the soul of the diligent is richly supplied.

Proverbs 13.4

The path of the upright is a level highway.

Proverbs 15.19

The plans of the diligent lead surely to abundance.

Proverbs 21.5

He who tills his land will have plenty of bread,
but he who follows worthless pursuits will have plenty of poverty.

Proverbs 28.19

She looks well to the ways of her household,
and does not eat the bread of idleness.

Proverbs 31.27

We must work the works of him who sent me, while it is day.

John 9.4

Having gifts that differ according to the grace given to us, let us use them . . . he who exhorts, in his exhortation; he who contributes, in liberality; he who gives aid, with zeal; he who does acts of mercy, with cheerfulness.

Romans 12.6,8

Never flag in zeal, be aglow with the Spirit, serve the Lord.

Romans 12.11

Now as you excel in everything — in faith, in utterance, in knowledge, in all earnestness, and in your love for us — see that you excel in this gracious work also.

2 Corinthians 8.7

Let us not grow weary in well-doing, for in due season we shall reap, if we do not lose heart.

Galatians 6.9

I press on toward the goal for the prize of the upward call of God in Christ Jesus.

Philippians 3.14

We desire each one of you to show the same earnestness in realising the full assurance of hope until the end.

Hebrews 6.11

Be the more zealous to confirm your call and election.

2 Peter 1.10

Be zealous to be found by him without spot or blemish, and at peace.

2 Peter 3.14

Directness

Let your eyes look directly forward,
and your gaze be straight before you.

Proverbs 4.25

Disappointment

He frustrates the devices of the crafty,
so that their hands achieve no success.

Job 5.12

Without counsel plans go wrong.

Proverbs 15.22

You have looked for much, and, lo, it came to little; and when you brought it home, I blew it away.

Haggai 1.9

'You lack one thing; go, sell what you have, and give to the poor, and you will have treasure in heaven; and come, follow me.' At that saying his countenance fell, and he went away sorrowful; for he had great possessions.

Mark 10.21–22

Disarmament

See also **Pacifism, War**

The Lord saves not with sword and spear; for the battle is the Lord's and he will give you into our hand.

1 Samuel 17.47

He makes wars cease to the end of the earth;
he breaks the bow, and shatters the spear,
he burns the chariots with fire!

Psalms 46.9

Wisdom is better than weapons of war.

Ecclesiastes 9.18

He shall judge between the nations,
and shall decide for many peoples;
and they shall beat their swords into ploughshares,
and their spears into pruning hooks;
nation shall not lift up sword against nation,
neither shall they learn war any more.

Isaiah 2.4

Woe to those who go down to Egypt for help and rely on horses,
who trust in chariots because they are many
and in horsemen because they are very strong,
but do not look to the Holy One of Israel or consult the Lord!

Isaiah 31.1

No weapon that is fashioned against you shall prosper . . .

This is the heritage of the servants of
the Lord.

Isaiah 54.17

Thus says the Lord, the God of Israel:
Behold, I will turn back the weapons of war
which are in your hands.

Jeremiah 21.4

Blessed are the peacemakers, for they
shall be called sons of God.

Matthew 5.9

For all who take the sword will perish by
the sword.

Matthew 26.52

Be at peace with one another.

Mark 9.50

Would that even today you knew the
things that make for peace!

Luke 19.42

If possible, so far as it depends upon you,
live peaceably with all.

Romans 12.18

Never avenge yourselves, but leave it to
the wrath of God; for it is written, 'Vengeance is mine . . . says the Lord.'

Romans 12.19

Agree with one another, live in peace, and
the God of love and peace will be with you.

2 Corinthians 13.11

Discernment

See also **Wisdom**

He who has a cool spirit is a man of
understanding.

Proverbs 17.27

The wise man has his eyes in his head, but
the fool walks in darkness.

Ecclesiastes 2.14

The mind of a wise man will know the time
and way.

Ecclesiastes 8.5

They shall teach my people the difference
between the holy and the common, and

show them how to distinguish between the
unclean and the clean.

Ezekiel 44.23

Then once more you shall distinguish
between the righteous and the wicked, between one who serves God and one who
does not serve him.

Malachi 3.18

Do not give dogs what is holy; and do not
throw your pearls before swine, lest they
trample them under foot and turn to attack
you.

Matthew 7.6

When it is evening, you say, 'It will be fair
weather; for the sky is red.' And in the
morning, 'It will be stormy today, for the
sky is red and threatening.' You know how
to interpret the appearance of the sky, but
you cannot interpret the signs of the times.

Matthew 16.2–3

I appeal to you therefore, brethren, by the
mercies of God, to present your bodies as a
living sacrifice, holy and acceptable to God,
which is your spiritual worship.

Romans 12.1

The unspiritual man does not receive the
gifts of the Spirit of God, for they are folly
to him, and he is not able to understand
them because they are spiritually discerned.

1 Corinthians 2.14

The word of God is living and active . . .
discerning the thoughts and intentions of
the heart.

Hebrews 4.12

You need milk, not solid food; for every
one who lives on milk is unskilled in the
word of righteousness, for he is a child. But
solid food is for the mature, for those who
have their faculties trained by practice to
distinguish good from evil.

Hebrews 5.13–14

Discipleship

See also **Calling**

The Lord God has given me
the tongue of those who are taught,

that I may know how to sustain with a word
him that is weary.

Isaiah 50.4

A disciple is not above his teacher, nor a
servant above his master; it is enough for
the disciple to be like his teacher, and the
servant like his master.

Matthew 10.24–25

Therefore every scribe who has been
trained for the kingdom of heaven is like a
householder who brings out of his treasure
what is new and what is old.

Matthew 13.52

If any man would come after me, let him
deny himself and take up his cross and
follow me.

Matthew 16.24

Make disciples of all nations, baptizing
them in the name of the Father and of the
Son and of the Holy Spirit.

Matthew 28.19

Go, sell what you have, and give to the
poor, and you will have treasure in heaven;
and come, follow me.

Mark 10.21

He who hears you hears me, and he who
rejects you rejects me, and he who rejects
me rejects him who sent me.

Luke 10.16

I am the light of the world; he who follows
me will not walk in darkness, but will have
the light of life.

John 8.12

Discipline

See also **Self-Control**

Behold, happy is the man whom God
reproves;
therefore despise not the chastening of
the Almighty.

Job 5.17

Behold, God is mighty, and does not
despise any . . .

He opens their ears to instruction,
and commands that they return from
iniquity.
If they hearken, and serve him,
they complete their days in prosperity,
and their years in pleasantness.

Job 36.5,10–11

Blessed is the man whom thou dost
chasten, O Lord,
and whom thou dost teach out of thy law
to give him respite from days of trouble,
until a pit is dug for the wicked.

Psalms 94.12–13

It is good for me that I was afflicted,
that I might learn thy statutes.

Psalms 119.71

My son, do not despise the Lord's
discipline
or be weary of his reproof,
for the Lord reproves him whom he loves,
as a father the son in whom he delights.

Proverbs 3.11–12

Keep hold of instruction, do not let go;
guard her, for she is your life.

Proverbs 4.13

For the commandment is a lamp and the
teaching a light,
and the reproofs of discipline are the way
of life.

Proverbs 6.23

Whoever loves discipline loves knowledge,
but he who hates reproof is stupid.

Proverbs 12.1

He who spares the rod hates his son,
but he who loves him is diligent to
discipline him.

Proverbs 13.24

The wisdom of a prudent man is to discern
his way.

Proverbs 14.8

Folly is bound up in the heart of a child,
but the rod of discipline drives it far from
him.

Proverbs 22.15

A whip for the horse, a bridle for the ass,
and a rod for the back of fools.

Proverbs 26.3

The rod and reproof give wisdom,
but a child left to himself brings shame to
his mother.

Proverbs 29.15

Discipline your son, and he will give you
rest;
he will give delight to your heart.

Proverbs 29.17

Correct me, O Lord, but in just measure;
not in thy anger, lest thou bring me to
nothing.

Jeremiah 10.24

When we are judged by the Lord, we are
chastened so that we may not be condemned along with the world.

1 Corinthians 11.32

Fathers, do not provoke your children to
anger, but bring them up in the discipline
and instruction of the Lord.

Ephesians 6.4

The Lord's servant must not be quarrelsome but kindly to every one, an apt
teacher, forbearing, correcting his opponents with gentleness.

2 Timothy 2.24−25

For there are many insubordinate men,
empty talkers and deceivers, especially the
circumcision party; they must be silenced,
since they are upsetting whole families by
teaching for base gain what they have no
right to teach.

Titus 1.10−11

My son, do not regard lightly the
discipline of the Lord,
nor lose courage when you are punished
by him.
For the Lord disciplines him whom
he loves,
and chastises every son whom he
receives.
It is for discipline that you have to endure.

Hebrews 12.5−7

We have had earthly fathers to discipline
us and we respected them. Shall we not
much more be subject to the Father of
spirits and live?

Hebrews 12.9

For the moment all discipline seems pain-
ful rather than pleasant; later it yields the
peaceful fruit of righteousness to those who
have been trained by it.

Hebrews 12.11

Discontent

See also **Complaint, Disappointment**

When the Lord gives you in the evening
flesh to eat and in the morning bread to the
full, because the Lord has heard your
murmurings which you murmur against him
— what are we? Your murmurings are not
against us but against the Lord.

Exodus 16.8

I pour out my complaint before him,
I tell my trouble before him.
When my spirit is faint,
thou knowest my way!

Psalms 142.2−3

When a man's folly brings his way to ruin,
his heart rages against the Lord.

Proverbs 19.3

Sheol and Abaddon are never satisfied,
and never satisfied are the eyes of man.

Proverbs 27.20

Say not, 'Why were the former days better
than these?'
For it is not from wisdom that you ask
this.

Ecclesiastes 7.10

Nor grumble, as some of them did and
were destroyed by the Destroyer.

1 Corinthians 10.10

Do all things without grumbling or questioning, that you may be blameless and
innocent, children of God without blemish.

Philippians 2.14−15

Discord

See also **Argument, Quarrelling**

Do not contend with a man for no reason,
when he has done you no harm.

Proverbs 3.30

A worthless person, a wicked man,
. . . with perverted heart devises evil,
continually sowing discord;
therefore calamity will come upon him
suddenly;
in a moment he will be broken beyond
healing.

Proverbs 6.12,14−15

The Lord hates . . .
a man who sows discord among
brothers.

Proverbs 6.16,19

A hot-tempered man stirs up strife,
but he who is slow to anger quiets
contention.

Proverbs 15.18

Better is a dry morsel with quiet
than a house full of feasting with strife.

Proverbs 17.1

It is better to live in a desert land
than with a contentious and fretful
woman.

Proverbs 21.19

Drive out a scoffer, and strife will go out,
and quarrelling and abuse will cease.

Proverbs 22.10

Brother will deliver up brother to death,
and the father his child, and children will
rise against parents and have them put to
death; and you will be hated by all for my
name's sake.

Matthew 10.21−22

Do not think that I have come to bring
peace on earth; I have not come to bring
peace, but a sword. For I have come to set
a man against his father, and a daughter
against her mother, and a daughter-in-law
against her mother-in-law; and a man's foes
will be those of his own household.

Matthew 10.34−36

Every kingdom divided against itself is laid
waste.

Matthew 12.25

As for the man who is weak in faith,
welcome him, but not for disputes over
opinions.

Romans 14.1

Let us then pursue what makes for peace
and for mutual upbuilding.

Romans 14.19

Take note of those who create dissensions
and difficulties, in opposition to the doctrine which you have been taught.

Romans 16.17

Avoid disputing about words, which does
no good, but only ruins the hearers.

2 Timothy 2.14

Discouragement

The Lord your God has set the land before
you; go up, take possession, as the Lord,
the God of your fathers, has told you; do
not fear or be dismayed.

Deuteronomy 1.21

It is the Lord who goes before you; he will
be with you, he will not fail you or forsake
you; do not fear or be dismayed.

Deuteronomy 31.8

He will faithfully bring forth justice.
He will not fail or be discouraged
till he has established justice in the earth.

Isaiah 42.3−4

Discovery

I rejoice at thy word
like one who finds great spoil . . .
I love thy law.

Psalms 119.162−163

You will seek me and find me; when you seek me with all your heart.

Jeremiah 29.13

He who finds his life will lose it, and he who loses his life for my sake will find it.

Matthew 10.39

Discretion

See also **Discernment, Tact**

Teach me good judgment and knowledge, for I believe in thy commandments.

Psalms 119.66

For wisdom will come into your heart, and knowledge will be pleasant to your soul; discretion will watch over you.

Proverbs 2.10–11

Keep sound wisdom and discretion.

Proverbs 3.21

O simple ones, learn prudence; O foolish men, pay attention.

Proverbs 8.5

Like a gold ring in a swine's snout is a beautiful woman without discretion.

Proverbs 11.22

The wisdom of a prudent man is to discern his way.

Proverbs 14.8

A soft answer turns away wrath, but a harsh word stirs up anger.

Proverbs 15.1

Good sense makes a man slow to anger.

Proverbs 19.11

A soft tongue will break a bone.

Proverbs 25.15

Do you see a man who is hasty in his words?
There is more hope for a fool than for him.

Proverbs 29.20

If you have been foolish, exalting yourself, or if you have been devising evil, put your hand on your mouth.

Proverbs 30.32

Even in your thought, do not curse the king, nor in your bedchamber curse the rich; for a bird of the air will carry your voice, or some winged creature tell the matter.

Ecclesiastes 10.20

To the weak I became weak, that I might win the weak. I have become all things to all men, that I might by all means save some.

1 Corinthians 9.22

Discrimination

See also **Apartheid, Racism, Xenophobia**

You shall not be partial in judgment; you shall hear the small and the great alike.

Deuteronomy 1.17

You yourselves know how unlawful it is for a Jew to associate with or to visit any one of another nation; but God has shown me that I should not call any man common or unclean.

Acts 10.28

For if a man with gold rings and in fine clothing comes into your assembly, and a poor man in shabby clothing also comes in, and you pay attention to the one who wears the fine clothing and say, 'Have a seat here, please,' while you say to the poor man, 'Stand there,' or, 'Sit at my feet,' have you not made distinctions among yourselves, and become judges with evil thoughts.?

James 2.2–4

If you show partiality, you commit sin.

James 2.9

Disease

For he wounds, but he binds up; he smites, but his hands heal.

Job 5.18

The Lord sustains him on his sickbed.

Psalms 41.3

If the Lord had not been my help,
my soul would soon have dwelt in the
land of silence.

Psalms 94.17

A leper came to him and knelt before him,
saying, 'Lord, if you will, you can make me
clean.' And he stretched out his hand and
touched him, saying, 'I will; be clean.'

Matthew 8.2–3

To keep me from being too elated by the
abundance of revelations, a thorn was given
me in the flesh.

2 Corinthians 12.7

Disgrace

See also **Blame**

Let them be put to shame and confusion
altogether
who rejoice at my calamity!
Let them be clothed with shame and
dishonour
who magnify themselves against me!

Psalms 35.26

All day long my disgrace is before me,
and shame has covered my face.

Psalms 44.15

Thou knowest my reproach,
and my shame and my dishonour;
my foes are all known to thee.
Insults have broken my heart,
so that I am in despair.

Psalms 69.19–20

In thee, O Lord, do I take refuge;
let me never be put to shame!

Psalms 71.1

May my accusers be clothed with
dishonour;
may they be wrapped in their own shame
as in a mantle!

Psalms 109.29

Lord . . . we have sinned against thee.
Do not spurn us, for thy name's sake;
do not dishonour thy glorious throne;
remember . . . thy covenant.

Jeremiah 14.20–21

Then they left the presence of the council,
rejoicing that they were counted worthy to
suffer dishonour for the name.

Acts 5.41

You who boast in the law, do you dishonour God by breaking the law?

Romans 2.23

God chose what is foolish in the world to
shame the wise.

1 Corinthians 1.27

So is it with the resurrection of the dead.
What is sown is perishable, what is raised is
imperishable. It is sown in dishonour, it is
raised in glory.

1 Corinthians 15.42–43

Little children, abide in him, so that when
he appears we may have confidence and not
shrink from him in shame at his coming.

1 John 2.28

Dishonesty

See also **Cheating, Deceit**

You shall not steal, nor deal falsely, nor lie
to one another.

Leviticus 19.11

You shall not oppress your neighbour or
rob him.

Leviticus 19.13

For all who . . . act dishonestly, are an
abomination to the Lord your God.

Deuteronomy 25.16

Behold, the wicked man conceives evil,
and is pregnant with mischief,
and brings forth lies.
He makes a pit, digging it out,
and falls into the hole which he has
made.

His mischief returns upon his own head,
and on his own pate his violence
descends.

Psalms 7.14–16

The wicked borrows, and cannot pay back,
but the righteous is generous and gives.

Psalms 37.21

He who walks in integrity walks securely,
but he who perverts his ways will be
found out.

Proverbs 10.9

A false balance is an abomination to the
Lord.

Proverbs 11.1

A righteous man hates falsehood,
but a wicked man acts shamefully and
disgracefully.

Proverbs 13.5

An evildoer listens to wicked lips;
and a liar gives heed to a mischievous
tongue.

Proverbs 17.4

A false witness will not go unpunished,
and he who utters lies will perish.

Proverbs 19.9

The getting of treasures by a lying tongue
is a fleeting vapour and a snare of death.

Proverbs 21.6

The violence of the wicked will sweep
them away,
because they refuse to do what is just.

Proverbs 21.7

The knaveries of the knave are evil;
he devises wicked devices
to ruin the poor with lying words.

Isaiah 32.7

Will you steal . . . swear falsely . . . and
then come and stand before me in this
house, which is called by my name?

Jeremiah 7.9–10

Like the partridge that gathers a brood
which she did not hatch,

so is he who gets riches but not by right;
in the midst of his days they will leave him,
and at his end he will be a fool.

Jeremiah 17.11

Woe to him who builds his house by
unrighteousness,
and his upper rooms by injustice.

Jeremiah 22.13

In you men take bribes to shed blood; you
take interest and increase and make gain of
your neighbours by extortion; and you have
forgotten me. . . . Can your courage endure, or can your hands be strong, in the
days that I shall deal with you?

Ezekiel 22.12,14

You who trample upin the needy . . .
bring the poor of the land to an end . . .
and deal deceitfully with false balances . . .
The Lord has sworn by the pride of Jacob:
'Surely I will never forget any of their
deeds.'

Amos 8.4,5,7

Dismay

See also **Depression, Doubt, Fear**

It is the Lord who goes before you; he will
be with you, he will not fail you or forsake
you; do not fear or be dismayed.

Deuteronomy 31.8

I had said in my alarm,
'I am driven far from thy sight.'
But thou didst hear my supplications,
when I cried to thee for help.

Psalms 31.22

Strengthen the weak hands,
and make firm the feeble knees.
Say to those who are of a fearful heart,
'Be strong, fear not!'

Isaiah 35.3–4

Be not dismayed, for I am your God;
I will strengthen you, I will help you.

Isaiah 41.10

Nor be dismayed at the signs of the
   heavens
  because the nations are dismayed at
   them.

Jeremiah 10.2

Let not your hearts be troubled; believe in
God, believe also in me.

John 14.1

Disobedience

See also **Betrayal**

So shall you perish, because you would not
obey the voice of the Lord your God.

Deuteronomy 8.20

I set before you a . . . curse, if you do not
obey the commandments of the Lord your
God, but turn aside from the way which I
command you this day, to go after other
gods which you have not known.

Deuteronomy 11.26,28

The man who acts presumptuously, by not
obeying the priest who stands to minister
there before the Lord your God, or the
judge, that man shall die; so you shall purge
the evil from Israel. And all the people
shall hear, and fear, and not act presumptuously again.

Deuteronomy 17.12−13

If you will not hearken to the voice of the
Lord, but rebel against the commandment
of the Lord, then the hand of the Lord will
be against you.

1 Samuel 12.15

For rebellion is as the sin of divination.

1 Samuel 15.23

If they hearken and serve him,
  they complete their days in
   prosperity . . .
But if they do not hearken, they perish by
   the sword,
  and die without knowledge.

Job 36.11−12

Poverty and disgrace come to him who
  ignores instruction.

Proverbs 13.18

The eye that mocks a father
  and scorns to obey a mother
will be picked out by the ravens of the
   valley
  and eaten by the vultures.

Proverbs 30.17

If you are willing and obedient,
  you shall eat the good of the land;
but if you refuse and rebel,
  you shall be devoured by the sword.

Isaiah 1.19−20

As by one man's disobedience many were
made sinners, so by one man's obedience
many will be made righteous.

Romans 5.19

All day long I have held out my hands to
a disobedient and contrary people.

Romans 10.21

For God has consigned all men to disobedience, that he may have mercy upon
all.

Romans 11.32

The wrath of God comes upon the sons of
disobedience.

Ephesians 5.6

The Lord Jesus is revealed from heaven
with his mighty angels in flaming fire, inflicting vengeance upon those who do not
know God and upon those who do not obey
the gospel of our Lord Jesus.

2 Thessalonians 1.7−8

The corrupt and unbelieving . . . profess to
know God, but . . . they are detestable,
disobedient, unfit for any good deed.

Titus 1.15−16

If the message declared by angels was valid
and every transgression or disobedience
received a just retribution, how shall we
escape if we neglect such a great salvation?

Hebrews 2.2−3

Take care, brethren, lest there be in any of
you an evil, unbelieving heart, leading you
to fall away from the living God.

Hebrews 3.12

To whom did he swear that they should never enter his rest, but to those who were disobedient?

Hebrews 3.18

Disorder

In the beginning God created the heavens and the earth. The earth was without form and void.

Genesis 1.1

There is an evil which I have seen under the sun, as it were an error proceeding from the ruler: folly is set in many high places, and the rich sit in a low place. I have seen slaves on horses, and princes walking on foot like slaves.

Ecclesiastes 10.5–7

Disrespect

Cursed be he who dishonours his father or his mother.

Deuteronomy 27.16

The eye that mocks a father
    and scorns to obey a mother
will be picked out by the ravens of the
        valley
    and eaten by the vultures.

Proverbs 30.17

I honour my Father, and you dishonour me.

John 8.49

Do not rebuke an older man.

1 Timothy 5.1

Dissatisfaction

The young lions suffer want and hunger;
    but those who seek the Lord lack no
        good thing.

Psalms 34.10

Surely man goes about as a shadow!
    Surely for naught are they in turmoil.

Psalms 39.6

Sheol and Abaddon are never satisfied,
    and never satisfied are the eyes of man.

Proverbs 27.20

Three things are never satisfied;
    four never say, 'Enough':
Sheol, the barren womb,
    the earth ever thirsty for water,
    and the fire which never says, 'Enough.'

Proverbs 30.15–16

The eye is not satisfied with seeing,
    nor the ear filled with hearing.

Ecclesiastes 1.8

Then I considered all that my hands had done and the toil I had spent in doing it, and behold, all was vanity and a striving after wind, and there was nothing to be gained under the sun.

Ecclesiastes 2.11

He who loves money will not be satisfied with money; nor he who loves wealth, with gain.

Ecclesiastes 5.10

All the toil of man is for his mouth, yet his appetite is not satisfied.

Ecclesiastes 6.7

Dissipation

The gate is wide and the way is easy, that leads to destruction, and those who enter by it are many.

Matthew 7.13

Distortion

Put away from you crooked speech,
    and put devious talk far from you.

Proverbs 4.24

He who justifies the wicked and he who
        condemns the righteous
are both alike an abomination to the
        Lord.

Proverbs 17.15

Woe to those who call evil good and good
  evil,
who put darkness for light
  and light for darkness,
who put bitter for sweet
  and sweet for bitter!

Isaiah 5.20

To the pure all things are pure, but to the
corrupt and unbelieving nothing is pure;
their very minds and consciences are
corrupted.

Titus 1.15

Distress
See also **Dismay**

In my distress I called upon the Lord;
  to my God I called.
From his temple he heard my voice,
  and my cry came to his ears.

2 Samuel 22.7

For thou hast been to me a fortress
  and a refuge in the day of my distress.

Psalms 59.16

Distribution (of Wealth)
See also **Communism**

There was not a needy person among
them, for as many as were possessors of
lands or houses sold them, and brought the
proceeds of what was sold and laid it at the
apostles' feet; and distribution was made to
each as any had need.

Acts 4.34–35

Divinity

The Lord said '. . . man shall not see me
and live.'

Exodus 33.17,20

Can you find out the deep things of God?

Job 11.7

Ever since the creation of the world his
invisible nature, namely, his eternal power
and deity, has been clearly perceived in the
things that have been made.

Romans 1.20

There are many 'gods' and many 'lords' —
yet for us there is one God, the Father,
from whom are all things and for whom we
exist, and one Lord, Jesus Christ, through
whom are all things and through whom we
exist.

1 Corinthians 8.6

God is one.

Galatians 3.20

In him the whole fulness of deity dwells
bodily, and you have come to fulness of life
in him, who is the head of all rule and
authority.

Colossians 2.9–10

His divine power has granted to us all
things that pertain to life and godliness,
through the knowledge of him.

2 Peter 1.3

No man has ever seen God; if we love one
another, God abides in us and his love is
perfected in us.

1 John 4.12

The Son of God has come and has given us
understanding, to know him who is true.

1 John 5.20

He who does good is of God.

3 John 11

Division
See also **Anarchy**

He who forgives an offence seeks love,
  but he who repeats a matter alienates a
    friend.

Proverbs 17.9

Every kingdom divided against itself is laid
waste, and no city or house divided against
itself will stand.

Matthew 12.25

The angels will come out and separate the evil from the righteous.

Matthew 13.49

Before him will be gathered all the nations, and he will separate them one from another as a shepherd separates the sheep from the goats, and he will place the sheep at his right hand, but the goats at the left.

Matthew 25.32–33

Do you think that I have come to give peace on earth? No, I tell you, but rather division.

Luke 12.51–52

I appeal to you, brethren, by the name of our Lord Jesus Christ, that all of you agree and that there be no dissensions among you, but that you be united in the same mind and the same judgment.

1 Corinthians 1.10

God has so composed the body . . . that there may be no discord in the body, but that the members may have the same care for one another.

1 Corinthians 12.24–25

He is our peace, who has made us both one, and has broken down the dividing wall of hostility.

Ephesians 2.14

Divorce

When a man takes a wife and marries her, if then she finds no favour in his eyes because he has found some indecency in her . . . he writes her a bill of divorce and puts it in her hand and sends her out of his house.

Deuteronomy 24.1

If a man divorces his wife
  and she goes from him
and becomes another man's wife,
  will he return to her?
Would not that land be greatly polluted?

Jeremiah 3.1

Has not the one God made and sustained for us the spirit of life? And what does he

desire? Godly offspring. So take heed to yourselves, and let none be faithless to the wife of his youth. For I hate divorce, says the Lord the God of Israel.

Malachi 2.15–16

It was also said, 'Whoever divorces his wife, let him give her a certificate of divorce.' But I say to you that every one who divorces his wife, except on the ground of unchastity, makes her an adulteress; and whoever marries a divorced woman commits adultery.

Matthew 5.31–32

'Have you not read that he who made them from the beginning made them male and female, and said, "For this reason a man shall leave his father and mother and be joined to his wife, and the two shall become one"? So they are no longer two but one flesh. What therefore God has joined together, let not man put asunder.' They said to him, 'Why then did Moses command one to give a certificate of divorce, and to put her away?' He said to them, 'For your hardness of heart Moses allowed you to divorce your wives, but from the beginning it was not so. And I say to you: whoever divorces his wife, except for unchastity, and marries another, commits adultery.'

Matthew 19.4–9

Jesus said to her, 'Go, call your husband, and come here.' The woman answered him, 'I have no husband.' Jesus said to her, 'You are right in saying, "I have no husband"; for you have had five husbands, and he whom you now have is not your husband; this you said truly.'

John 4.16–18

The wife should not separate from her husband (but if she does, let her remain single or else be reconciled to her husband) — and . . . the husband should not divorce his wife.

1 Corinthians 7.10–11

Are you bound to a wife? Do not seek to be free.

1 Corinthians 7.27

Domesticity

The Lord grant that you may find a home, each of you in the house of her husband!

Ruth 9

He who troubles his household will inherit wind.

Proverbs 11.29

Like a bird that strays from its nest,
  is a man who strays from his home.

Proverbs 27.8

Doom

Thus says the Lord God: Disaster after disaster! Behold, it comes. An end has come, the end has come; it has awakened against you. Behold, it comes. Your doom has come to you, O inhabitant of the land; the time has come, the day is near, a day of tumult, and not of joyful shouting upon the mountains. Now I will soon pour out my wrath upon you, and spend my anger against you, and judge you according to your ways; and I will punish you for all your abominations. And my eye will not spare, nor will I have pity; I will punish you according to your ways, while your abominations are in your midst. Then you will know that I am the Lord, who smite.

Ezekiel 7.5–9

Doubt

Your words have upheld him who was
    stumbling . . .
But now it has come to you, and you
    are impatient;
  it touches you, and you are dismayed.

Job 4.4–5

But Zion said, 'The Lord has forsaken me,
  my Lord has forgotten me.'
Can a woman forget her sucking child,
    that she should have no compassion on
      the son of her womb?
Even these may forget,
  yet I will not forget you.

Isaiah 49.14–15

Jesus said to him, 'Again it is written, "You shall not tempt the Lord your God." '

Matthew 4.7

An evil and adulterous generation seeks for a sign.

Matthew 12.39

He cried out, 'Lord, save me.' Jesus immediately reached out his hand and caught him, saying to him, 'O man of little faith, why did you doubt?'

Matthew 14.30–31

If you have faith and never doubt . . . even if you say to this mountain, 'Be taken up and cast into the sea,' it will be done.

Matthew 21.21

I believe; help my unbelief!

Mark 9.24

Thomas . . . said . . . 'Unless I see in his hands the print of the nails, and place my finger in the mark of the nails, and place my hand in his side, I will not believe.' . . . Jesus came and stood among them, and said . . . to Thomas, 'Put your finger here, and see my hands; and put out your hand, and place it in my side; do not be faithless, but believing.' Thomas answered him, 'My Lord and my God!'

John 20.25–28

As for the man who is weak in faith, welcome him, but not for disputes over opinions.

Romans 14.1

He who has doubts is condemned, if he eats, because he does not act from faith.

Romans 14.23

Let us hold fast the confession of our hope without wavering.

Hebrews 10.23

He who doubts is like a wave of the sea that is driven and tossed by the wind. For that person must not suppose that a double-minded man, unstable in all his ways, will receive anything from the Lord.

James 1.6–8

Cleanse your hands, you sinners, and purify your hearts, you men of double mind.

James 4.8

Convince some, who doubt.

Jude 22

Dread

See also **Dismay, Fear**

Jacob . . . was afraid, and said, 'How awesome is this place! This is none other than the house of God, and this is the gate of heaven.'

Genesis 28.16−17

What the wicked dreads will come upon him.

Proverbs 10.24

Do not fear what they fear, nor be in dread. But the Lord of hosts, him you shall regard as holy; let him be your fear, and let him be your dread.

Isaiah 8.12−13

Dreams

See also **Nightmare**

If there is a prophet among you, I the Lord make myself known to him in a vision, I speak with him in a dream.

Numbers 12.6

The exulting of the wicked is short . . .
he will fly away like a dream, and not
be found;
he will be chased away like a vision of
the night.

Job 20.5,8

For God speaks in one way,
and in two, though man does not
perceive it.
In a dream, in a vision of the night,
when deep sleep falls upon men, while
they slumber on their beds,
then he opens the ears of men,
and terrifies them with warnings,
that he may turn man aside from his deed,

and cut off pride from man;
he keeps back his soul from the Pit,
his life from perishing by the sword.

Job 33.14−18

He who follows worthless pursuits has no sense.

Proverbs 12.11

For a dream comes with much business, and a fool's voice with many words.

Ecclesiastes 5.3

For when dreams increase, empty words grow many.

Ecclesiastes 5.7

I slept, but my heart was awake.

Song of Solomon 5.2

Do not let your prophets and your diviners who are among you deceive you, and do not listen to the dreams which they dream, for it is a lie which they are prophesying to you in my name.

Jeremiah 29.8−9

Drunkenness

See also **Alcohol, Wine**

How long will you be drunken? Put away your wine from you.

1 Samuel 1.14

Wine is a mocker, strong drink a brawler;
and whoever is led astray by it is not
wise.

Proverbs 20.1

Be not among winebibbers . . .
for the drunkard and the glutton will
come to poverty,
and drowsiness will clothe a man with
rags.

Proverbs 23.20−21

Who has woe? Who has sorrow?
Who has strife? Who has complaining?
Who has wounds without cause?
Who has redness of eyes?

Those who tarry long over wine,
those who go to try mixed wine.

Proverbs 23.29–30

Let us conduct ourselves becomingly as in the day, not in revelling and drunkenness.

Romans 13.13

I wrote to you not to associate with any one who bears the name of brother if he is . . . an idolator, drunkard or robber—not even to eat with such a one.

1 Corinthians 5.11

Nor drunkards . . . will inherit the kingdom of God.

1 Corinthians 6.10

Do not get drunk with wine, for that is debauchery; but be filled with the Spirit.

Ephesians 5.18

For those who sleep sleep at night, and those who get drunk are drunk at night. But, since we belong to the day, let us be sober.

1 Thessalonians 5.7–8

For a bishop, as God's steward, must be blameless; he must not be . . . a drunkard or violent.

Titus 1.7

Duty

You shall do what is right and good in the sight of the Lord, that it may go well with you.

Deuteronomy 6.18

You shall therefore love the Lord your God, and keep his charge, his statutes, his ordinances, and his commandments always.

Deuteronomy 11.1

Fear God, and keep his commandments; for this is the whole duty of man.

Ecclesiastes 12.13

He has showed you, O man, what is good; and what does the Lord require of you but to do justice, and to love kindness, and to walk humbly with your God?

Micah 6.8

Render therefore to Caesar the things that are Caesar's, and to God the things that are God's.

Matthew 22.21

When you have done all that is commanded you, say, 'We are unworthy servants; we have only done what was our duty.'

Luke 17.10

If you love me, you will keep my commandments.

John 14.15

We must obey God rather than men.

Acts 5.29

We who are strong ought to bear with the failings of the weak, and not to please ourselves.

Romans 15.

Husbands should love their wives as their own bodies.

Ephesians 5.2

He laid down his life for us; and we ought to lay down our lives for the brethren.

1 John 3.1

Beloved, if God so loved us, we also ought to love one another.

1 John 4.1

E

Eagerness

See also **Earnestness, Zeal**

Know the God of your father, and serve him with a whole heart and with a willing mind; for the Lord searches all hearts, and understands every plan and thought.

1 Chronicles 28.9

It is for thy sake that I have borne
    reproach . . .
I have become a stranger to my
    brethren . . .
For zeal for thy house has consumed me.

Psalms 69.7–9

Never flag in zeal, be aglow with the Spirit, serve the Lord.

Romans 12.11

Let the word of Christ dwell in you richly, teach and admonish one another in, all wisdom, and sing psalms and hymns and spiritual songs with thankfulness in your hearts to God.

Colossians 3.16

Whatever your task, work heartily, as serving the Lord and not men, knowing that from the Lord you will receive the inheritance as your reward.

Colossians 3.23–24

I preferred to do nothing without your consent in order that your goodness might not be by compulsion but of your own free will.

Philemon 14

Having purified your souls by your obedience to the truth for a sincere love of the brethren, love one another earnestly from the heart.

1 Peter 1.22

Earnestness

See also **Eagerness, Zeal**

You will seek me and find me; when you seek me with all your heart.

Jeremiah 29.13

'Yet even now,' says the Lord,
  'return to me with all your heart.'

Joel 2.12

A sower went out to sow his seed; and as he sowed, some fell along the path . . . some fell on the rock . . . some fell among thorns. . . . And some fell into good soil and grew, and yielded a hundredfold.

Luke 8.5–8

And as for that in the good soil, they are those who, hearing the word, hold it fast in an honest and good heart, and bring forth fruit with patience.

Luke 8.15

Earnestly desire the higher gifts.

1 Corinthians 12.31

We know that if the earthly tent we live in is destroyed, we have a building from God, a house not made with hands, eternal in the heavens. Here indeed we groan, and long to put on our heavenly dwelling.

2 Corinthians 5.1–2

Slaves, be obedient to those who are your earthly masters, with fear and trembling, in singleness of heart, as to Christ; not in the way of eyeservice, as men-pleasers, but as servants of Christ, doing the will of God.

Ephesians 6.5–6

We must pay the closer attention to what we have heard, lest we drift away from it.

Hebrews 2.1

Earth

See also **Creation, Nature**

In the beginning God created the heavens and the earth. The earth was without form and void, and darkness was upon the face of the deep; and the Spirit of God was moving over the face of the waters.

Genesis 1.1—2

Cursed is the ground because of you;
in toil you shall eat of it all the days of
your life;
thorns and thistles it shall bring forth to
you;
and you shall eat the plants of the field.
In the sweat of your face
you shall eat bread
till you return to the ground,
for out of it you were taken;
you are dust,
and to dust you shall return.

Genesis 3.17—19

When I bring clouds over the earth and the bow is seen in the clouds, I will remember my covenant which is between me and you and every living creature of all flesh.

Genesis 9.14—15

Thou hast made heaven, the heaven of heavens, with all their host, the earth and all that is on it, the seas and all that is in them; and thou preservest all of them; and the host of heaven worships thee.

Nehemiah 9.6

Those who wait for the Lord shall possess the land.

Psalms 37.9

God is our refuge and strength,
a very present help in trouble.
Therefore we will not fear though the earth
should change,
though the mountains shake in the heart
of the sea.

Psalms 46.1—2

Of old thou didst lay the foundation of the
earth,
and the heavens are the work of thy
hands.

They will perish, but thou dost endure;
they will all wear out like a garment.

Psalms 102.25—26

The Lord created me at the beginning of
his work,
the first of his acts of old.
Ages ago I was set up,
at the first, before the beginning of the
earth.

Proverbs 8.22—23

For behold, I create new heavens and a
new earth;
and the former things shall not be
remembered
or come into mind.

Isaiah 65.17

Thus says the Lord:
'Heaven is my throne
and the earth is my footstool;
what is the house which you would build for
me,
and what is the place of my rest?'

Isaiah 66.1

Thy kingdom come,
Thy will be done,
On earth as it is in heaven.

Matthew 6.10

Then I saw a new heaven and a new earth;
for the first heaven and the first earth had
passed away, and the sea was no more.

Revelation 21.1

Easter

See also **Resurrection**

Why do you seek the living among the dead? Remember how he told you, while he was still in Galilee, that the Son of man must be delivered into the hands of sinful men, and be crucified, and on the third day rise.

Luke 24.5—7

I am the resurrection and the life; he who believes in me, though he die, yet shall he live, and whoever lives and believes in me shall never die.

John 11.25—26

Do you not know that all of us who have been baptized into Christ Jesus were baptized into his death? We were buried therefore with him by baptism into death, so that as Christ was raised from the dead by the glory of the Father, we too might walk in newness of life.

For if we have been united with him in a death like his, we shall certainly be united with him in a resurrection like his.

Romans 6.3—5

If the Spirit of him who raised Jesus from the dead dwells in you, he who raised Christ Jesus from the dead will give life to your mortal bodies also through his Spirit which dwells in you.

Romans 8.11

Christ, our paschal lamb, has been sacrificed. Let us, therefore, celebrate the festival, not with the old leaven, the leaven of malice and evil, but with the unleavened bread of sincerity and truth.

1 Corinthians 5.7—8

For I delivered to you as of first importance what I also received, that Christ died for our sins in accordance with the scriptures, that he was buried, that he was raised on the third day in accordance with the scriptures, and that he appeared to Cephas, then to the twelve.

1 Corinthians 15.3—5

If Christ has not been raised, then our preaching is in vain and your faith is in vain.

1 Corinthians 15.14

But in fact Christ has been raised from the dead, the first fruits of those who have fallen asleep.

1 Corinthians 15.20

Blessed be the God and Father of our Lord Jesus Christ! By his great mercy we have been born anew to a living hope through the resurrection of Jesus Christ

from the dead, and to an inheritance which is imperishable, undefiled, and unfading, kept in heaven for you.

1 Peter 1.3—4

Ecstasy

See also **Delight, Joy**

Thou dost show me the path of life;
in thy presence there is fullness of joy,
in thy right hand are pleasures for
evermore.

Psalms 16.11

Then I will go to the altar of God,
to God my exceeding joy;
and I will praise thee with the lyre.

Psalms 43.4

Then shall the maidens rejoice in the
dance,
and the young men and the old shall be
merry.
I will turn their mourning into joy,
I will comfort them, and give them
gladness for sorrow.

Jeremiah 31.13

Bring the full tithes into the storehouse, that there may be food in my house; and thereby put me to the test, says the Lord of hosts, if I will not open the windows of heaven for you and pour down for you an overflowing blessing.

Malachi 3.10

Rejoice in that day, and leap for joy, for behold, your reward is great in heaven.

Luke 6.23

So you have sorrow now, but I will see you again and your hearts will rejoice, and no one will take your joy from you.

John 16.22

May the God of hope fill you with all joy and peace in believing, so that by the power of the Holy Spirit you may abound in hope.

Romans 15.13

I know a man in Christ who . . . was caught up to the third heaven . . . I know that this man was caught up into Paradise . . . and he heard things that cannot be told, which man may not utter.

2 Corinthians 1.2–4

We all, with unveiled face, beholding the glory of the Lord, are being changed into his likeness from one degree of glory to another.

2 Corinthians 3.18

Without having seen him you love him; though you do not now see him you believe in him and rejoice with unutterable and exalted joy.

1 Peter 1.8

and will make her wilderness like Eden, her desert like the garden of the Lord.

Isaiah 51.3

The land that was desolate shall be tilled, instead of being the desolation that it was in the sight of all who passed by. And they will say, 'This land that was desolate has become like the garden of Eden; and the waste and desolate and ruined cities are now inhabited and fortified.'

Ezekiel 36.34–35

He who has an ear, let him hear what the Spirit says to the churches. To him who conquers I will grant to eat of the tree of life, which is in the paradise of God.

Revelation 2.7

Eden

The Lord God planted a garden in Eden, in the east; and there he put the man whom he had formed. And out of the ground the Lord God made to grow every tree that is pleasant to the sight and good for food, the tree of life also in the midst of the garden, and the tree of the knowledge of good and evil.

Genesis 2.8–9

The Lord God took the man and put him in the garden of Eden to till it and keep it.

Genesis 2.15

Then the Lord God said, 'Behold, the man has become like one of us, knowing good and evil; and now, lest he put forth his hand and take also of the tree of life, and eat, and live for ever' — therefore the Lord God sent him forth from the garden of Eden, to till the ground from which he was taken. He drove out the man; and at the east of the garden of Eden he placed the cherubim, and a flaming sword which turned every way, to guard the way to the tree of life.

Genesis 3.22–24

For the Lord will comfort Zion; he will comfort all her waste places,

Edification

See also **Education, Learning, Wisdom**

The way of a fool is right in his own eyes, but a wise man listens to advice.

Proverbs 12.15

Let us then pursue what makes for peace and for mutual unbuilding.

Romans 14.19

Let each of us please his neighbour for his good, to edify him.

Romans 15.2

Knowledge puffs up, but love builds up.

1 Corinthians 8.1

'All things are lawful,' but not all things are helpful. 'All things are lawful,' but not all things build up.

1 Corinthians 10.23

He who prophesies speaks to men for their unbuilding and encouragement and consolation.

1 Corinthians 14.3

He who prophesies edifies the church.

1 Corinthians 14.4

Since you are eager for manifestations of the Spirit, strive to excel in building up the church.

1 Corinthians 14.12

When you come together, each one has a hymn, a lesson, a revelation. . . . Let all things be done for edification.

1 Corinthians 14.26

Let no evil talk come out of your mouths, but only such as is good for edifying, as fits the occasion, that it may impart grace to those who hear.

Ephesians 4.29

I urged you . . . that you may charge certain persons not to teach any different doctrine, nor to occupy themselves with myths and endless genealogies which promote speculations rather than the divine training that is in faith.

1 Timothy 1.3—4

Education

See also **Edification, Learning**

All the congregation of the people of Israel moved on from the wilderness of Sin by stages, according to the commandment of the Lord.

Exodus 17.1

These words which I command you this day shall be upon your heart; and you shall teach them diligently to your children, and shall talk of them when you sit in your house, and when you walk by the way, and when you lie down, and when you rise.

Deuteronomy 6.6—7

I will instruct you and teach you
the way you should go;
I will counsel you with my eye upon you.

Psalms 32.8

Then I will teach transgressors thy ways,
and sinners will return to thee.

Psalms 51.13

The wise man also may hear and increase
in learning,
and the man of understanding acquire
skill.

Proverbs 1.5

The fear of the Lord is the beginning of
knowledge;
fools despise wisdom and instruction.

Proverbs 1.7

Train up a child in the way he should go,
and when he is old he will not depart
from it.

Proverbs 22.6

Folly is bound up in the heart of a child,
but the rod of discipline drives it far from
him.

Proverbs 22.15

Apply your mind to instruction
and your ear to words of knowledge.

Proverbs 23.12

Buy truth, and do not sell it;
buy wisdom, instruction, and
understanding.

Proverbs 23.23

I applied my mind to seek and to search out by wisdom all that is done under heaven; it is an unhappy business that God has given to the sons of men to be busy with.

Ecclesiastes 1.13

The sayings of the wise are like goads.

Ecclesiastes 12.11

Go therefore and make disciples of all nations . . . teaching them to observe all that I have commanded you.

Matthew 28.19—20

A disciple is not above his teacher, but every one when he is fully taught will be like his teacher.

Luke 6.40

Formerly, when you did not know God, you were in bondage to beings that by nature are no gods; but now that you have come to know God, or rather to be known by God, how can you turn back again to the weak . . . spirits whose slaves you want to be once more.

Galatians 4.8–9

Let him who is taught the word share all good things with him who teaches.

Galatians 6.6

Fathers, do not provoke your children to anger, but bring them up in the discipline and instruction of the Lord.

Ephesians 6.4

How great . . . are the riches . . . of this mystery, which is Christ in you, the hope of glory. Him we proclaim, warning every man and teaching every man in all wisdom, that we may present every man mature in Christ.

Colossians 1.27–28

Effort

Unless the Lord builds the house,
    those who build it labour in vain.
Unless the Lord watches over the city,
    the watchman stays awake in vain.

Psalms 127.1

The wage of the righteous leads to life,
    the gain of the wicked to sin.

Proverbs 10.16

Wealth hastily gotten will dwindle,
    but he who gathers little by little will
        increase it.

Proverbs 13.11

A worker's appetite works for him;
    his mouth urges him on.

Proverbs 16.26

It is God's gift to man that every one should eat and drink and take pleasure in all his toil.

Ecclesiastes 3.13

Sweet is the sleep of a labourer, whether he eats little or much; but the surfeit of the rich will not let him sleep.

Ecclesiastes 5.12

The spirit indeed is willing, but the flesh is weak.

Matthew 26.41

Strive to enter by the narrow door; for many, I tell you, will seek to enter and will not be able.

Luke 13.24

Never flag in zeal, be aglow with the Spirit, serve the Lord.

Romans 12.11

He who plants and he who waters are equal, and each shall receive his wages according to his labour.

1 Corinthians 3.8

We make it our aim to please him. For we must all appear before the judgment seat of Christ, so that each one may receive good or evil, according to what he has done in the body.

2 Corinthians 5.9–10

Respect those who labour among you and are over you in the Lord and admonish you, and to esteem them very highly in love because of their work.

1 Thessalonians 5.12–13

For God is not so unjust as to overlook your work and the love which you showed for his sake in serving the saints.

Hebrews 6.10

'Blessed are the dead who die in the Lord henceforth.' 'Blessed indeed,' says the Spirit, 'that they may rest from their labours, for their deeds follow them!'

Revelation 14.13

Egalitarianism

For consider your call, brethren; not many of you were wise according to worldly standards, not many were powerful, not many were of noble birth; but God chose what is foolish in the world to shame the wise, God chose what is weak in the world to shame the strong, God chose what is low and despised in the world, even things that are not, to bring to nothing things that are, so that no human being might boast in the presence of God.

1 Corinthians 1.26–29

Honour all men.

1 Peter 2.17

Egotism

See also **Arrogance, Pride**

Talk no more so very proudly,
 let not arrogance come from your mouth;
for the Lord is a God of knowledge,
 and by him actions are weighed.

1 Samuel 2.3

The man of haughty looks and arrogant
  heart
 I will not endure.

Psalms 101.5

Every one who is arrogant is an
  abomination to the Lord;
 be assured, he will not go unpunished.

Proverbs 16.5

A man's pride will bring him low,
 but he who is lowly in spirit will obtain
  honour.

Proverbs 29.23

I will punish the world for its evil,
 and the wicked for their iniquity;
I will put an end to the pride of the
  arrogant,
 and lay low the haughtiness of the
  ruthless.

Isaiah 13.11

You said in your heart,
 'I will ascend to heaven;
above the stars of God
 I will set my throne on high . . .'
But you are brought down to Sheol,
 to the depths of the Pit.

Isaiah 14.13,15

Now therefore hear this, you lover of
  pleasures,
 who sit securely,

who say in your heart,
 'I am, and there is no one besides me;
I shall not sit as a widow
 or know the loss of children':
These two things shall come to you
 in a moment, in one day.

Isaiah 47.8–9

He has shown strength with his arm,
 he has scattered the proud in the
  imagination of their hearts.

Luke 1.51

He who speaks on his own authority seeks
his own glory.

John 7.18

Love is not jealous or boastful; it is not
arrogant or rude.

1 Corinthians 13.4

Do nothing from selfishness or conceit, but
in humility count others better than yourselves. Let each of you look not only to his
own interests, but also to the interests of
others.

Philippians 2.3–4

Eloquence

May my teaching drop as the rain,
 my speech distil as the dew,
as the gentle rain upon the tender grass,
 and as the showers upon the herb.
For I will proclaim the name of the Lord.

Deuteronomy 32.2–3

Should a multitude of words go
  unanswered,
 and a man full of talk be vindicated?

Job 11.2

His speech was smoother than butter,
 yet war was in his heart;
his words were softer than oil,
 yet they were drawn swords.

Psalms 55.21

Men shall proclaim the might of thy
  terrible acts,
 and I will declare thy greatness.

Psalms 145.6

The tongue of the righteous is choice
  silver.

Proverbs 10.20

From the fruit of his mouth a good man
  eats good.

Proverbs 13.2

To make an apt answer is a joy to a man,
  and a word in season, how good it is!

Proverbs 15.23

Pleasant words are like a honeycomb,
  sweetness to the soul and health to the
  body.

Proverbs 16.24

Fine speech is not becoming to a fool.

Proverbs 17.7

The words of a man's mouth are deep
  waters;
  the fountain of wisdom is a gushing
  stream.

Proverbs 18.4

Death and life are in the power of the
  tongue,
  and those who love it will eat its fruits.

Proverbs 18.21

He who gives a right answer
  kisses the lips.

Proverbs 24.26

A word fitly spoken
  is like apples of gold in a setting of silver.

Proverbs 25.11

Like the glaze covering an earthen vessel
  are smooth lips with an evil heart.

Proverbs 26.23

There is . . . a time to keep silence, and a
time to speak.

Ecclesiastes 3.3,7

When they bring you before the synagogues and the rulers and the authorities,
do not be anxious how or what you are to
answer or what you are to say; for the Holy
Spirit will teach you in that very hour what
you ought to say.

Luke 12.11–12

Take note of those who create dissensions
and difficulties in opposition to the doctrine
which you have been taught . . . such
persons do not serve our Lord Christ, but
their own appetites, and by fair and flattering words they deceive the hearts of the
simple-minded.

Romans 16.17–18

And my speech and my message were not
implausible words of wisdom, but in
demonstration of the Spirit and power.

1 Corinthians 2.4

If I speak in the tongues of men and of
angels, but have not love, I am a noisy gong
or a clanging cymbal.

1 Corinthians 13.1

Conduct yourselves wisely toward outsiders. . . . Let your speech always be
gracious, seasoned with salt, so that you
may know how you ought to answer every
one.

Colossians 4.5–6

Let every man be quick to hear, slow to
speak.

James 1.19

Empathy

To the weak I became weak, that I might
win the weak.

1 Corinthians 9.22

Employment

See also **Work**

The wages of a hired servant shall not
remain with you all night until the morning.

Leviticus 19.13

You shall not oppress a hired servant who
is poor and needy . . . you shall give him
his hire on the day he earns it, before the
sun goes down (for he is poor, and sets his
heart upon it).

Deuteronomy 24.14–15

Has not man a hard service upon earth,
and are not his days like the days of a
hireling?
Like a slave who longs for the shadow,
and like a hireling who looks for his
wages.

Job 7.1−2

If I have rejected the cause of my
manservant or my maidservant,
when they brought a complaint against
me;
what then shall I do when God rises up?

Job 31.13−14

The labourer deserves his food.

Matthew 10.10

Let the thief no longer steal, but rather let
him labour, doing honest work with his
hands.

Ephesians 4.28

Whatever your task, work heartily, as
serving the Lord and not men, knowing that
from the Lord you will receive the inheritance as your reward.

Colossians 3.23−24

Aspire to live quietly, to mind your own
affairs, and to work with your hands . . . so
that you may command the respect of outsiders.

1 Thessalonians 4.11,12

Do your best to present yourself to God as
one approved, a workman who has no need
to be ashamed.

2 Timothy 2.15

Emptiness

The earth was without form and void.

Genesis 1.2

Emulation

As obedient children, do not be conformed to the passions of your former
ignorance, but as he who called you is holy,
be holy yourselves in all your conduct.

1 Peter 1.14−15

Encouragement

I am the God of Abraham your father; fear
not, for I am with you.

Genesis 26.24

Fear not, for those who are with us are
more than those who are with them.

2 Kings 6.16

Be strong, and let your heart take courage,
all you who wait for the Lord!

Psalms 31.24

The light of the eyes rejoices the heart.

Proverbs 15.30

Fear not, for I have redeemed you;
I have called you by name, you are mine.
When you pass through the waters I will be
with you;
and through the rivers, they shall not
overwhelm you;
when you walk through fire you shall not be
burned,
and the flame shall not consume you.
For I am the Lord your God,
the Holy One of Israel, your Saviour.

Isaiah 43.1−3

I am with you always, to the close of the
age.

Matthew 28.20

Strengthen your brethren.

Luke 22.32

Be mutually encouraged by each other's
faith.

Romans 1.12

Let us then pursue what makes for peace
and for mutual upbuilding.

Romans 14.19

Prophesy one by one, so that all may learn
and all be encouraged.

1 Corinthians 14.31

As we have opportunity, let us do good to
all men, and especially to those who are of
the household of faith.

Galatians 6.10

Whatever is true, whatever is honourable, whatever is just, whatever is pure, whatever is lovely, whatever is gracious, if there is any excellence, if there is anything worthy of praise, think about these things.

Philippians 4.8

Encourage one another and build one another up.

1 Thessalonians 5.11

Admonish the idlers, encourage the fainthearted, help the weak, be patient with them all.

1 Thessalonians 5.14

Exhort one another every day, as long as it is called 'today,' that none of you may be hardened by the deceitfulness of sin.

Hebrews 3.13

When God desired to show more convincingly to the heirs of the promise the unchangeable character of his purpose, he interposed with an oath, so that ... we who have fled for refuge might have strong encouragement to seize the hope set before us.

Hebrews 6.17–18

Let us consider how to stir up one another to love and good works, not neglecting to meet together, as is the habit of some, but encouraging one another, and all the more as you see the Day drawing near.

Hebrews 10.24–25

End

See also **Death, Judgment**

He cannot find out what God has done from the beginning to the end.

Ecclesiastes 3.11

It is better to go to the house of mourning
than to go to the house of feasting;
for this is the end of all men.

Ecclesiastes 7.2

Better is the end of a thing than its beginning.

Ecclesiastes 7.8

The harvest is the close of the age, and the reapers are angels. Just as the weeds are gathered and burned with fire, so will it be at the close of the age.

Matthew 13.39–40

So it will be at the close of the age. The angels will come out and separate the evil from the righteous, and throw them into the furnace of fire; there men will weep and gnash their teeth.

Matthew 13.49–50

Lo, I am with you always, to the close of the age.

Matthew 28.20

For this is the will of my Father, that everyone who sees the Son and believes in him should have eternal life; and I will raise him up.

John 6.40

For as in Adam all die, so also in Christ shall all be made alive. But each in his own order: Christ the first fruits, then at his coming those who belong to Christ. Then comes the end, when he delivers the kingdom to God the Father after destroying every rule and every authority and power.

1 Corinthians 15.22–24

As the outcome of your faith you obtain the salvation of your souls.

1 Peter 1.9

Set your hope fully upon the grace that is coming to you at the revelation of Jesus Christ.

1 Peter 1.13

For the time has come for judgment to begin with the household of God; and if it begins with us, what will be the end of those who do not obey the gospel of God?

1 Peter 4.17

He who conquers and who keeps my works until the end, I will give him power over the nations.

Revelation 2.26

I am the Alpha and the Omega, the beginning and the end.

Revelation 21.6

Endeavour

See also **Effort**

Strive to enter by the narrow door; for many, I tell you, will seek to enter and will not be able.

Luke 13.24

Do you not know that in a race all the runners compete, but only one receives the prize? So run that you may obtain it.

1 Corinthians 9.24

I . . . beg you to lead a life worthy of the calling . . . eager to maintain the unity of the Spirit in the bond of peace.

Ephesians 4.1,3

Stand firm in one spirit, with one mind striving side by side for the faith of the gospel, and not frightened in anything by your opponents.

Philippians 1.27–28

Train yourself in godliness; for while bodily training is of some value, godliness is of value in every way.

1 Timothy 4.7–8

An athlete is not crowned unless he competes according to the rules.

2 Timothy 2.5

There remains a sabbath rest for the people of God . . . Let us therefore strive to enter that rest.

Hebrews 4.9,11

We desire each one of you to show the same earnestness . . . until the end, so that you may not be sluggish, but imitators of those who through faith and patience inherit the promises.

Hebrews 6.11–12

Endurance

See also **Strength**

Seek the Lord and his strength,
    seek his presence continually!

1 Chronicles 16.11

He who endures to the end will be saved.

Matthew 10.22

Love bears all things, believes all things, hopes all things, endures all things.

1 Corinthians 13.7

Stand firm in your faith, be courageous, be strong.

1 Corinthians 16.13

May you be strengthened with all power, according to his glorious might, for all endurance and patience with joy.

Colossians 1.11

Share in suffering as a good soldier of Christ Jesus.

2 Timothy 2.3

Jesus offered up prayers and supplications . . . to him that was able to save him from death, and he was heard for his godly fear. Although he was a Son, he learned obedience through what he suffered; and being made perfect he became the source of eternal salvation to all who obey him.

Hebrews 5.7–9

You have need of endurance, so that you may do the will of God and receive what is promised.

Hebrews 10.36

Let us also lay aside every weight, and sin which clings so closely, and let us run with perseverance the race that is set before us.

Hebrews 12.1

As an example of suffering and patience, brethren, take the prophets who spoke in the name of the Lord. Behold, we call those happy who were steadfast. You have heard of the steadfastness of Job, and you have seen the purpose of the Lord, how the Lord is compassionate and merciful.

James 5.10–11

If when you do right and suffer for it you take it patiently, you have God's approval. For to this you have been called.

1 Peter 2.20–21

Enemy

If you meet your enemy's ox or his ass going astray, you shall bring it back to him. If you see the ass of one who hates you lying under its burden, you shall refrain from leaving him with it, you shall help him to lift it up.

Exodus 23.4—5

If you hearken attentively . . . and do all that I say, then I will be an enemy to your enemies and an adversary to your adversaries . . . my angel goes before you.

Exodus 23.22—23

The Lord your God is he that goes with you, to fight for you against your enemies, to give you the victory.

Deuteronomy 20.4

The eternal God is your dwelling place,
  and underneath are the everlasting arms.
And he thrust out the enemy before you.

Deuteronomy 33.27

Lead me, O Lord, in thy righteousness
  because of my enemies;
  make thy way straight before me.

Psalms 5.8

But the wicked perish;
  the enemies of the Lord are like the glory
    of the pastures,
  they vanish — like smoke they vanish
    away.

Psalms 37.20

For thou art my refuge,
  a strong tower against the enemy.

Psalms 61.3

When a man's ways please the Lord,
  he makes even his enemies to be at peace
    with him.

Proverbs 16.7

Do not rejoice when your enemy falls,
  and let not your heart be glad when he
    stumbles;
lest the Lord see it, and be displeased,
  and turn away his anger from him.

Proverbs 24.17—18

If your enemy is hungry, give him bread
    to eat;
  and if he is thirsty, give him water
    to drink;
for you will heap coals of fire on his head,
  and the Lord will reward you.

Proverbs 25.21—22

Faithful are the wounds of a friend; profuse are the kisses of an enemy.

Proverbs 27.6

A man's enemies are the men of his own house.

Micah 7.6

Love your enemies and pray for those who persecute you, so that you may be sons of your Father who is in heaven.

Matthew 5.44—45

The last enemy to be destroyed is death.

1 Corinthians 15.26

For many . . . live as enemies of the cross of Christ. Their end is destruction.

Philippians 3.18—19

If any one refuses to obey . . . note that man, and have nothing to do with him, that he may be ashamed. Do not look on him as an enemy, but warn him as a brother.

2 Thessalonians 3.14—15

Do you not know that friendship with the world is enmity with God?

James 4.4

Energy

See also **Eagerness**

The God of Israel,
  he gives power and strength to his
    people.
Blessed be God!

Psalms 68.35

He does not faint or grow weary,
his understanding is unsearchable.
He gives power to the faint,
and to him who has no might he increases
strength.
Even youths shall faint and be weary,
and young men shall fall exhausted;
but they who wait for the Lord shall renew
their strength,
they shall mount up with wings like
eagles,
they shall run and not be weary,
they shall walk and not faint.

Isaiah 40.28−31

You will seek me and find me; when you
seek me with all your heart.

Jeremiah 29.13

The people who know their God shall
stand firm and take action.

Daniel 11.32

I am filled with power,
with the Spirit of the Lord,
and with justice and might.

Micah 3.8

Be steadfast, immovable, always abounding in the work of the Lord, knowing that in
the Lord your labour is not in vain.

1 Corinthians 15.58

Neither circumcision nor uncircumcision is
of any avail, but faith working through
love.

Galatians 5.6

To him who by the power at work within
us is able to do far more abundantly than all
that we ask or think . . . be glory.

Ephesians 3.20−21

Be strong in the Lord and in the strength
of his might.

Ephesians 6.10

The word of God is living and active.

Hebrews 4.12

The prayer of a righteous man has great
power in its effects.

James 5.16

Enforcement

See also **Law**

Whoever will not obey the law of your
God and the law of the king, let judgment
be strictly executed upon him.

Ezra 7.26

Execute justice in the morning,
and deliver from the hand of the
oppressor
him who has been robbed.

Jeremiah 21.12

Render in your gates judgments that are
true and make for peace.

Zechariah 8.16

It is not the hearers of the law who are
righteous before God, but the doers of the
law who will be justified.

Romans 2.13

He who loves his neighbour has fulfilled
the law. . . . Love does no wrong to a
neighbour; therefore love is the fulfilling of
the law.

Romans 13.8,10

Bear one another's burdens, and so fulfil
the law of Christ.

Galatians 6.2

Enigma

See also **Mystery, Paradox**

Three things are too wonderful for me;
four I do not understand:
the way of an eagle in the sky,
the way of a serpent on a rock,
the way of a ship on the high seas,
and the way of a man with a maiden.

Proverbs 30.18−19

According to my gospel and the preaching
of Jesus Christ, according to the revelation
of the mystery which was kept secret for
long ages but is now disclosed and through
the prophetic writings is made known to all
nations, according to the command of the
eternal God, to . . . God be glory for evermore.

Romans 16.25−27

We impart a secret and hidden wisdom of God, which God decreed before the ages.

1 Corinthians 2.7

As it is written,
'What no eye has seen, nor ear heard,
  nor the heart of man conceived . . .
God has prepared for those who love
  him.'

1 Corinthians 2.9

The Spirit searches everything, even the depths of God.

1 Corinthians 2.10

If I have prophetic powers, and understand all mysteries and all knowledge . . . but have not love, I am nothing.

1 Corinthians 13.2

I tell you a mystery. We shall not all sleep, but we shall all be changed, in a moment, in the twinkling of an eye, at the last trumpet. For the trumpet will sound, and the dead will be raised imperishable, and we shall be changed.

1 Corinthians 15.51–52

He has made known to us in all wisdom and insight the mystery of his will, according to his purpose which he set forth in Christ as a plan for the fulness of time.

Ephesians 1.9–10

I was made a minister according to the gift of God's grace . . . to make all men see what is the plan of the mystery hidden for ages in God who created all things; that through the church the manifold wisdom of God might now be made known to the principalities and powers in the heavenly places.

Ephesians 3.7,9–10

To have all the riches of assured understanding and the knowledge of God's mystery, of Christ, in whom are hid all the treasures of wisdom and knowledge.

Colossians 2.2–3

Great indeed, we confess, is the mystery of our religion:
  He was manifested in the flesh,
  vindicated in the Spirit,

seen by angels,
preached among the nations,
believed on in the world,
taken up in glory.

1 Timothy 3.16

Enjoyment

See also **Delight, Pleasure**

How precious is thy steadfast love,
  O God!
  The children of men take refuge
  in the shadow of thy wings.
They feast on the abundance of thy house,
  and thou givest them drink from the river
  of thy delights.

Psalms 36.7–8

I said to myself, 'Come now, I will make a test of pleasure; enjoy yourself.' But behold, this also was vanity.

Ecclesiastes 2.1

There is nothing better for a man than that he should eat and drink, and find enjoyment in his toil.

Ecclesiastes 2.24

Who can have enjoyment? . . . to the man who pleases him God gives wisdom and knowledge and joy.

Ecclesiastes 2.26

It is God's gift to man that every one should eat and drink and take pleasure in all his toil.

Ecclesiastes 3.13

But be glad and rejoice for ever
  in that which I create.

Isaiah 65.18

As for the rich in this world, charge them not to be haughty, nor to set their hopes on uncertain riches but on God who richly furnishes us with everything to enjoy.

1 Timothy 6.17

He that would love life
  and see good days,
let him keep his tongue from evil
  and his lips from speaking guile.

1 Peter 3.10

Enlightenment

See also **Wisdom**

Yea, thou art my lamp, O Lord,
  and my God lightens my darkness.

2 Samuel 22.29

He has redeemed my soul from going
    down into the Pit,
  and my life shall see the light.

Job 33.28

The commandment of the Lord is pure,
  enlightening the eyes.

Psalms 19.8

The Lord is my light and my salvation;
  whom shall I fear?

Psalms 27.1

For with thee is the fountain of life;
  in thy light do we see light.

Psalms 36.9

Oh send out thy light and thy truth;
  let them lead me.

Psalms 43.3

Light dawns for the righteous,
  and joy for the upright in heart.

Psalms 97.11

The unfolding of thy words gives light;
  it imparts understanding to the simple.

Psalms 119.130

The poor man and the oppressor meet
    together;
  the Lord gives light to the eyes of both.

Proverbs 29.13

Come, let us walk
in the light of the Lord.

Isaiah 2.5

The people who walked in darkness
  have seen a great light;
those who dwelt in a land of deep darkness,
  on them has light shined.

Isaiah 9.2

The sun shall be no more
  your light by day,
nor for brightness shall the moon
  give light to you by night;
but the Lord will be your everlasting light,
  and your God will be your glory.

Isaiah 60.19

Blessed be the name of God for ever and
    ever . . .
he gives wisdom to the wise
  and knowledge to those who have
    understanding.

Daniel 2.20−21

You are the light of the world. A city set
on a hill cannot be hid. . . . Let your light
so shine before men, that they may see your
good works and give glory to your Father
who is in heaven.

Matthew 5.14,16

And you, child, will be called the prophet
    of the Most High;
for you will go before the Lord to prepare
    his ways,
to give knowledge of salvation to his people
in the forgiveness of their sins . . .
to give light to those who sit in
    darkness
and in the shadow of death.

Luke 1.76−77,79

Be careful lest the light in you be
darkness.

Luke 11.35

In him was life, and the life was the light of
men. The light shines in the darkness, and
the darkness has not overcome it.

John 1.4−5

The true light that enlightens every man
. . . He was in the world, and the world was
made through him, yet the world knew him
not.

John 1.9−10

For every one who does evil hates the light, and does not come to the light, lest his deeds should be exposed. But he who does what is true comes to the light, that it may be clearly seen that his deeds have been wrought in God.

John 3.20–21

I am the light of the world; he who follows me will not walk in darkness, but will have the light of life.

John 8.12

For it is the God who said, 'Let light shine out of darkness,' who has shone in our hearts to give the light of the knowledge of the glory of God in the face of Christ.

2 Corinthians 4.6

Having the eyes of your hearts enlightened . . . you may know what is the hope to which he has called you . . . and what is the immeasurable greatness of his power.

Ephesians 1.18–19

Once you were darkness, but now you are light in the Lord; walk as children of light (for the fruit of light is found in all that is good and right and true).

Ephesians 5.8–9

For it is impossible to restore again to repentance those who have once been enlightened, who have tasted the heavenly gift, and have become partakers of the Holy Spirit . . . if they then commit apostasy.

Hebrews 6.4,6

Ennui

All things are full of weariness;
a man cannot utter it.

Ecclesiastes 1.8

Enrichment

The earth has yielded its increase;
God, our God, has blessed us.
God has blessed us;
let all the ends of the earth fear him!

Psalms 67.6–7

To get wisdom is better than gold;
to get understanding is to be chosen
rather than silver.

Proverbs 16.16

Do not lay up for yourselves treasures on earth, where moth and rust consume and where thieves break in and steal, but lay up for yourselves treasure in heaven, where neither moth nor rust consumes and where thieves do not break in and steal. For where your treasure is, there will your heart be also.

Matthew 6.19–21

If then you have not been faithful in the unrighteous mammon, who will entrust to you the true riches?

Luke 16.11

He who supplies seed to the sower and bread for food will supply and multiply your resources and increase the harvest of your righteousness. You will be enriched in every way for great generosity, which through us will produce thanksgiving to God.

2 Corinthians 9.10–11

Enticement

See also **Seduction**

If a man seduces a virgin who is not betrothed, and lies with her, he shall give the marriage present for her, and make her his wife.

Exodus 22.16

If your brother . . . or your son, or your daughter, or the wife of your bosom, or your friend who is as your own soul, entices you secretly, saying, 'Let us go and serve other gods,' . . . you shall not yield to him or listen to him, nor shall your eye pity him, nor shall you spare him, nor shall you conceal him.

Deuteronomy 13.6,8

My son, if sinners entice you,
do not consent.

Proverbs 1.10

Discretion will watch over you . . .
You will be saved from the loose
    woman,
  from the adventuress with her smooth
    words . . .
none who go to her come back
  nor do they regain the paths of life.

Proverbs 2.11,16,19

A man of violence entices his neighbour
  and leads him in a way that is not good.

Proverbs 16.29

I say this in order that no one may delude
you with beguiling speech.

Colossians 2.4

Each person is tempted when he is lured
and enticed by his own desire.

James 1.14

Uttering loud boasts of folly, they entice
with licentious passions of the flesh men
who have barely escaped from those who
live in error.

2 Peter 2.18

Entreaty

See also **Begging, Petition**

You shall not afflict any widow or orphan.
If you do afflict them, and they cry out to
me, I will surely hear their cry.

Exodus 22.22−23

Answer me when I call, O God of my
    right!
  Thou hast given me room when I was in
    distress.
Be gracious to me, and hear my prayer.

Psalms 4.1

For he who avenges blood is mindful of
    them;
  he does not forget the cry of the afflicted.

Psalms 9.12

May the Lord fulfil all your petitions!

Psalms 20.5

Blessed be the Lord!
  for he has heard the voice of my
    supplications.

Psalms 28.6

Hear my prayer, O Lord;
  let my cry come to thee!

Psalms 102.1

Let my cry come before thee, O Lord.

Psalms 119.169

The Lord is just in all his ways,
  and kind in all his doings.
The Lord is near to all who call upon him,
  to all who call upon him in truth.
He fulfils the desire of all who fear him,
  he also hears their cry, and saves them.

Psalms 145.17−19

The poor use entreaties,
  but the rich answer roughly.

Proverbs 18.23

Seek the Lord while he may be found,
  call upon him while he is near.

Isaiah 55.6

Ask, and it will be given you; seek, and
you will find; knock, and it will be opened
to you.

Matthew 7.7

Pray at all times in the Spirit, with all
prayer and supplication. To that end keep
alert with all perseverance, making supplication for all the saints.

Ephesians 6.18

Have no anxiety about anything, but in
everything by prayer and supplication with
thanksgiving let your requests be made
known to God.

Philippians 4.6

Envy

See also **Discontent, Jealousy**

The Lord had regard for Abel and his
offering, but for Cain and his offering he
had no regard. So Cain was very angry, and

his countenance fell. The Lord said to Cain, 'Why are you angry, and why has your countenance fallen? If you do well, will you not be accepted? And if you do not do well, sin is couching at the door; its desire is for you, but you must master it.'

Cain said to Abel his brother, 'Let us to out to the field.' And when they were in the field, Cain rose up against his brother Abel, and killed him.

Genesis 4.4–8

Surely vexation kills the fool,
 and jealousy slays the simple.

Job 5.2

Fret not yourself because of the wicked,
 be not envious of wrongdoers!
For they will soon fade like the grass,
 and wither like the green herb.

Psalms 37.1–2

But as for me, my feet had almost
  stumbled,
 my steps had well nigh slipped.
For I was envious of the arrogant,
 when I saw the prosperity of the wicked.

Psalms 73.2–3

Do not envy a man of violence
 and do not choose any of his ways.

Proverbs 3.31

A tranquil mind gives life to the flesh,
 but passion makes the bones rot.

Proverbs 14.30

Let not your heart envy sinners,
 but continue in the fear of the Lord all
  the day.

Proverbs 23.17

Be not envious of evil men,
 nor desire to be with them;
for their minds devise violence,
 and their lips talk of mischief.

Proverbs 24.1–2

Then I saw that all toil and all skill in work come from a man's envy of his neighbour. This also is vanity and a striving after wind.

Ecclesiastes 4.4

If we live by the Spirit, let us also walk by the Spirit. Let us have no self-conceit, no provoking of one another, no envy of one another.

Galatians 5.25–26

Do not grumble, brethren, against one another, that you may not be judged.

James 5.9

So put away all malice and all guile and insincerity and envy and all slander.

1 Peter 2.1

Equality

The man called his wife's name Eve, because she was the mother of all living.

Genesis 3.20

If I have rejected the cause of my
  manservant or my maidservant,
 when they brought a complaint against
  me;
what then shall I do when God rises up?
 When he makes inquiry, what shall I
  answer him?
Did not he who made me in the womb
  make him?
 And did not one fashion us in the womb?

Job 31.13–15

The rich and the poor meet together;
 the Lord is the maker of them all.

Proverbs 22.2

Partiality in judging is not good.

Proverbs 24.23

The poor man and the oppressor meet
  together;
 the Lord gives light to the eyes of both.

Proverbs 29.13

Have we not all one father? Has not one God created us?

Malachi 2.10

Take what belongs to you, and go; choose to give to this last as I give to you.

Matthew 20.1

You have one teacher, and you are all
brethren. And call no man your father on
earth, for you have one Father, who is in
heaven.

Matthew 23.8–9

You yourselves know how unlawful it is
for a Jew to associate with or to visit any
one of another nation; but God has shown
me that I should not call any man common
or unclean.

Acts 10.28

He made from one every nation of men.

Acts 17.26

God shows no partiality.

Romans 2.11

The same Lord is Lord of all and bestows
his riches upon all who call upon him. For,
'every one who calls upon the name of the
Lord will be saved.'

Romans 10.12–13

The fire will test what sort of work each
one has done.

1 Corinthians 3.13

There is neither Jew nor Greek, there is
neither slave nor free, there is neither male
nor female; for you are all one in Christ
Jesus.

Galatians 3.28

We are members one of another.

Ephesians 4.25

Whatever good any one does, he will
receive the same again from the Lord,
whether he is a slave or free.

Ephesians 6.8

If you show partiality, you commit sin, and
are convicted by the law as transgressors.

James 2.9

Error

Are you not ashamed to wrong me? . . .
even if it be true that I have erred, my error
remains with myself.

Job 19.3–4

But who can discern his errors?
Clear thou me from hidden faults.

Psalms 19.12

Thou dost spurn all who go astray from thy
        statutes;
yea, their cunning is in vain.

Psalms 119.118

Cease, my son, to hear instruction
only to stray from the words of
    knowledge.

Proverbs 19.27

Let not your mouth lead you into sin, and
do not say before the messenger that it was
a mistake; why should God be angry at
your voice, and destroy the work of your
hands?

Ecclesiastes 5.6

And those who err in spirit will come to
        understanding,
and those who murmur will accept
    instruction.

Isaiah 29.24

For the fool speaks folly,
    and his mind plots iniquity:
to practise ungodliness,
    to utter error concerning the Lord.

Isaiah 32.6

Every goldsmith is put to shame by his
        idols;
for his images are false,
and there is no breath in them.
They are worthless, a work of delusion;
    at the time of their punishment they shall
    perish.

Jeremiah 10.14–15

You are wrong, because you know neither
the scriptures nor the power of God.

Matthew 22.29

Do not be deceived; God is not mocked,
for whatever a man sows, that he will also
reap.

Galatians 6.7

For the love of money is the root of all evils; it is through this craving that some have wandered away from the faith and pierced their hearts with many pangs.

1 Timothy 6.10

Avoid the godless chatter and contradictions of what is falsely called knowledge, for by professing it some have missed the mark as regards the faith.

1 Timothy 6.20–21

Rebuke, and exhort, be unfailing in patience.

2 Timothy 4.2

If any one among you wanders from the truth and some one brings him back, let him know that whoever brings back a sinner from the error of his way will save his soul from death and will cover a multitude of sins.

James 5.19–20

You were straying like sheep, but have now returned to the Shepherd and Guardian of your souls.

1 Peter 2.25

It is better to suffer for doing right, if that should be God's will, than for doing wrong.

1 Peter 3.17

If we say we have no sin, we deceive ourselves, and the truth is not in us.

1 John 1.8

We are of God. Whoever knows God listens to us, and he who is not of God does not listen to us. By this we know the spirit of truth and the spirit of error.

1 John 4.6

Esteem

A disciple is not above his teacher, nor a servant above his master; it is enough for the disciple to be like his teacher and the servant like his master.

Matthew 10.24–25

What is exalted among men is an abomination in the sight of God.

Luke 16.15

Glory and honour and peace for every one who does good.

Romans 2.10

In humility count others better than yourselves.

Philippians 2.3

Respect those who labour among you and are over you in the Lord and admonish you, and . . . esteem them very highly in love because of their work.

1 Thessalonians 5.12–13

Honour all men. Love the brotherhood. Fear God.

1 Peter 2.17

Eternity

Lest he put forth his hand and take also of the tree of life, and eat, and live for ever . . . God sent him forth from the garden.

Genesis 3.22–23

The Lord will reign for ever and ever.

Exodus 15.18

The Lord knows the days of the blameless, and their heritage will abide for ever.

Psalms 37.18

May his name endure for ever,
his fame continue as long as the sun!

Psalms 72.17

For a day in thy courts is better
than a thousand elsewhere.

Psalms 84.10

Before the mountains were brought forth,
or . . . thou hadst formed the earth and
the world,
from everlasting to everlasting thou art
God.

Psalms 90.2

But the steadfast love of the Lord is from
everlasting to everlasting
upon those who fear him.

Psalms 103.17

Lead me in the way everlasting!

Psalms 139.24

Thy kingdom is an everlasting kingdom,
and thy dominion endures throughout all
generations.

Psalms 145.13

He has made everything beautiful in its
time; also he has put eternity into man's
mind, yet so that he cannot find out what
God has done from the beginning to the
end.

Ecclesiastes 3.11

I am the first and I am the last;
beside me there is no god.

Isaiah 44.6

The high and lofty One
who inhabits eternity, whose name is
Holy.

Isaiah 57.15

For he is the living God,
enduring for ever;
his kingdom shall never be destroyed,
and his dominion shall be to the end.

Daniel 6.26

The saints of the Most High shall receive
the kingdom, and possess the kingdom for
ever, for ever and ever.

Daniel 7.18

But you, O Bethlehem Eph'rathah,
who are little to be among the clans
of Judah,
from you shall come forth for me
one who is to be ruler in Israel,
whose origin is from of old,
from ancient days.

Micah 5.2

They will go away into eternal punishment,
but the righteous into eternal life.

Matthew 25.46

Lo, I am with you always, to the close of
the age.

Matthew 28.20

He will reign over the house of Jacob for
ever;
and of his kingdom there will be no end.

Luke 1.33

For God so loved the world that he gave
his only Son, that whoever believes in him
should not perish but have eternal life.

John 3.16

Whoever drinks of the water that I shall
give him will never thirst; the water that I
shall give him will become in him a spring
of water welling up to eternal life.

John 4.14

This is eternal life, that they know thee the
only true God, and Jesus Christ whom thou
hast sent.

John 17.3

As many as were ordained to eternal life
believed.

Acts 13.48

Now to him who is able to strengthen you
according to my gospel and the preaching of
Jesus Christ, according to the revelation of
the mystery which was kept secret for long
ages . . . to . . . God be glory.

Romans 16.25,27

This perishable nature must put on the
imperishable, and this mortal nature must
put on immortality.

1 Corinthians 15.53

To preach . . . the unsearchable riches of
Christ, and to make all men see . . . the
plan of the mystery hidden for ages in God.

Ephesians 3.8−9

With the Lord one day is as a thousand
years, and a thousand years as one day.

2 Peter 3.8

The world passes away, and the lust of it;
but he who does the will of God abides for
ever.

1 John 2.17

'I am the Alpha and the Omega,' says the Lord God, who is and who was and who is to come, the Almighty.

Revelation 1.8

Then I saw another angel flying in mid-heaven, with an eternal gospel to proclaim to those who dwell on earth.

Revelation 14.6

The devil . . . was thrown into the lake of fire and sulphur where the beast and the false prophet were, and they will be tormented day and night for ever and ever.

Revelation 20.10

Eucharist
See also **Blood of Christ**

Now as they were eating, Jesus took bread, and blessed, and broke it, and gave it to the disciples and said, 'Take, eat; this is my body.' And he took a cup, and when he had given thanks he gave it to them, saying, 'Drink of it, all of you; for this is my blood of the covenant, which is poured out for many for the forgiveness of sins.'

Matthew 26.26−28

He took bread, and when he had given thanks he broke it and gave it to them, saying, 'This is my body which is given for you. Do this in remembrance of me.'

Luke 22.19

I am the bread of life; he who comes to me shall not hunger.

John 6.35

I am the living bread which came down from heaven; if any one eats of this bread, he will live for ever; and the bread which I shall give for the life of the world is my flesh.

John 6.51

Unless you eat the flesh of the Son of man and drink his blood, you have no life in you; he who eats my flesh and drinks my blood has eternal life, and I will raise him up at the last day.

John 6.53−54

He who eats my flesh and drinks my blood abides in me, and I in him.

John 6.56

As the living Father sent me, and I live because of the Father, so he who eats me will live because of me.

John 6.57

The cup of blessing which we bless, is it not a participation in the blood of Christ? The bread which we break, is it not a participation in the body of Christ? Because there is one bread, we who are many are one body, for we all partake of the one bread.

1 Corinthians 10.16−17

Jesus on the night when he was betrayed took bread, and when he had given thanks, he broke it, and said, 'This is my body which is for you. Do this in remembrance of me.' . . . For as often as you eat this bread and drink the cup, you proclaim the Lord's death until he comes.

1 Corinthians 11.23−24,26

Whoever, therefore, eats the bread or drinks the cup of the Lord in an unworthy manner will be guilty of profaning the body and blood of the Lord. . . . For any one who eats and drinks without discerning the body eats and drinks judgment upon himself.

1 Corinthians 11.27,29

Euthanasia
See **Murder, Suicide**

Evangelism
See also **Gospel, Mission, Preaching**

Then I will teach transgressors thy ways,
    and sinners will return to thee.

Psalms 51.13

The Lord gives the command.

Psalms 68.11

Tell of his salvation from day to day.
Declare his glory among the nations,
    his marvellous works among all the
        peoples!

Psalms 96.2−3

How beautiful upon the mountains
   are the feet of him who brings good
      tidings,
who publishes peace, who brings good
      tidings of good,
   who publishes salvation.

Isaiah 52.7

Blow the trumpet through the land;
   cry aloud.

Jeremiah 4.5

Stand in the gate of the Lord's house, and proclaim there this word, and say, Hear the word of the Lord, all you men of Judah who enter these gates to worship the Lord.

Jeremiah 7.2

Hear the word of the Lord, O nations,
   and declare it in the coastlands afar off.

Jeremiah 31.10

Declare among the nations and proclaim,
   set up a banner and proclaim,
      conceal it not.

Jeremiah 50.2

Those who are wise shall shine like the brightness of the firmament; and those who turn many to righteousness, like the stars for ever and ever.

Daniel 12.3

Follow me, and I will make you fishers of men.

Matthew 4.19

Preach as you go, saying, 'The kingdom of heaven is at hand.'

Matthew 10.7

This gospel of the kingdom will be preached throughout the whole world, as a testimony to all nations.

Matthew 24.14

Go therefore and make disciples of all nations, baptizing them in the name of the Father and of the Son and of the Holy Spirit.

Matthew 28.19

The time is fulfilled, and the kingdom of God is at hand; repent, and believe in the gospel.

Mark 1.15

The gospel must first be preached to all nations.

Mark 13.10

Go into all the world and preach the gospel to the whole creation.

Mark 16.15

Go and proclaim the kingdom of God.

Luke 9.60

I am not ashamed of the gospel: it is the power of God for salvation to every one who has faith.

Romans 1.16

How are men to call upon him in whom they have not believed? And how are they to believe in him of whom they have never heard? And how are they to hear without a preacher? And how can men preach unless they are sent?

Romans 10.14–15

But I will come to you soon, if the Lord wills, and I will find out not the talk of these arrogant people but their power. For the kingdom of God does not consist in talk but in power.

1 Corinthians 4.19–20

Those who proclaim the gospel should get their living by the gospel.

1 Corinthians 9.14

Even if our gospel is veiled, it is veiled only to those who are perishing. In their case the god of this world has blinded the minds of the unbelievers, to keep them from seeing the light of the gospel of the glory of Christ, who is the likeness of God. For what we preach is not ourselves, but Jesus Christ as Lord.

2 Corinthians 4.3–5

His gifts were that some should be apostles, some prophets, some evangelists.

Ephesians 4.11

You are all partakers . . . in the defence and confirmation of the gospel.

Philippians 1.7

Preach the word, be urgent in season and out of season, convince, rebuke, and exhort, be unfailing in patience and in teaching.

2 Timothy 4.2

Do the work of an evangelist, fulfil your ministry.

2 Timothy 4.5

Whoever brings back a sinner from the error of his way will save his soul from death and will cover a multitude of sins.

James 5.20

That which we have seen and heard we proclaim also to you, so that you may have fellowship with us; and our fellowship is with the Father and with his Son Jesus Christ.

1 John 1.3

Evil

See also **Sin, Ungodliness**

Even though I walk through the valley of
     the shadow of death,
I fear no evil.

Psalms 23.4

Refrain from anger, and forsake wrath!
Fret not yourself; it tends only to evil.

Psalms 37.8

The Lord loves those who hate evil.

Psalms 97.10

Depart from me, you evildoers,
     that I may keep the commandments of
     my God.

Psalms 119.115

Let evil hunt down the violent man
     speedily!

Psalms 140.11

The fear of the Lord is hatred of evil.

Proverbs 8.13

No ill befalls the righteous,
     but the wicked are filled with trouble.

Proverbs 12.21

Fret not yourself because of evildoers,
     and be not envious of the wicked;
for the evil man has no future;
     the lamp of the wicked will be put out.

Proverbs 24.19−20

Remove the evil of your doings
     from before my eyes;
cease to do evil,
     learn to do good.

Isaiah 1.16−17

Woe to those who call evil good
     and good evil.

Isaiah 5.20

May the descendants of evildoers
     nevermore be named!

Isaiah 14.20

Seek good, and not evil,
     that you may live;
and so the Lord, the God of hosts, will be
     with you.

Amos 5.14

Hate evil, and love good,
     and establish justice in the gate.

Amos 5.15

Let every one turn from his evil way and from the violence which is in his hands.

Jonah 3.8

Return from your evil ways and from your evil deeds.

Zechariah 1.4

Let none of you devise evil against his brother in your heart.

Zechariah 7.10

If your eye is not sound, your whole body will be full of darkness.

Matthew 6.23

Every sound tree bears good fruit, but the bad tree bears evil fruit.

Matthew 7.17

Example 165

For out of the heart come evil thoughts, murder, adultery, fornication, theft, false witness, slander. These are what defile a man.

Matthew 15.19–20

The evil man out of his evil treasure produces evil; for out of the abundance of the heart his mouth speaks.

Luke 6.45

The light has come into the world, and men loved darkness rather than light, because their deeds were evil.

John 3.19

There will be tribulation and distress for every human being who does evil.

Romans 2.9

Let love be genuine; hate what is evil.

Romans 12.9

Repay no one evil for evil.

Romans 12.17

Do not be overcome by evil, but overcome evil with good.

Romans 12.21

Bad company ruins good morals.

1 Corinthians 15.33

We pray God that you may not do wrong.

2 Corinthians 13.7

Our Lord Jesus Christ, who gave himself for our sins to deliver us from the present evil age.

Galatians 1.4

We are not contending against flesh and blood, but against the principalities, against the powers, against the world rulers of this present darkness, against the spiritual hosts of wickedness in the heavenly places.

Ephesians 6.12

Look out for the evil-workers.

Philippians 3.2

Hold fast what is good, abstain from every form of evil.

1 Thessalonians 5.21–22

The love of money is the root of all evils.

1 Timothy 6.10

For God cannot be tempted with evil.

James 1.13

No human being can tame the tongue — a restless evil, full of deadly poison.

James 3.8

The face of the Lord is against those that do evil.

1 Peter 3.12

He who does evil has not seen God.

3 John 11

Examination

The Lord is in his holy temple,
   the Lord's throne is in heaven;
his eyes behold, his eyelids test,
   the children of men.

Psalms 11.4

The Lord tests the righteous and the
   wicked.

Psalms 11.5

I the Lord search the mind
   and try the heart,
to give to every man according to his ways,
   according to the fruit of his doings.

Jeremiah 17.10

Example

See also **Imitation**

You are the light of the world. A city set on a hill cannot be hid. Nor do men light a lamp and put it under a bushel, but on a stand, and it gives light to all in the house. Let your light so shine before men, that they may see your good works and give glory to your Father who is in heaven.

Matthew 5.14–16

Do you not know that a little leaven leavens the whole lump?

1 Corinthians 5.6

Bad company ruins good morals.

1 Corinthians 15.33

Do all things without grumbling or questioning, that you may be blameless and innocent, children of God without blemish in the midst of a crooked and perverse generation, among whom you shine as lights in the world, holding fast the word of life.

Philippians 2.14–15

Set the believers an example in speech and conduct, in love, in faith, in purity.

1 Timothy 4.12

Bid the older women . . . to be reverent in behaviour, not to be slanderers or slaves to drink; they are to teach what is good, and so train the young women to love their husbands and children, to be sensible, chaste, domestic.

Titus 2.3–5

Show yourself in all respects a model of good deeds, and in your teaching show integrity, gravity, and sound speech that cannot be censured.

Titus 2.7–8

Therefore, since we are surrounded by so great a cloud of witnesses, let us also lay aside every weight, and sin which clings so closely.

Hebrews 12.1

As an example of suffering and patience, brethren, take the prophets who spoke in the name of the Lord.

James 5.10

For it is God's will that by doing right you should put to silence the ignorance of foolish men.

1 Peter 2.15

Because Christ also suffered for you, leaving you an example, that you should follow in his steps.

1 Peter 2.21

Tend the flock of God that is your charge . . . not as domineering over those in your charge but being examples to the flock.

1 Peter 5.2–3

We may be sure that we are in him: he who says he abides in him ought to walk in the same way in which he walked.

1 John 2.5–6

Sodom and Gomor'rah . . . serve as an example by undergoing a punishment of eternal fire.

Jude 7

Excuses

He who is estranged seeks pretexts
    to break out against all sound judgment.

Proverbs 18.1

When one of those who sat at table with him heard this, he said to him, 'Blessed is he who shall eat bread in the kingdom of God!' But he said to him, 'A man once gave a great banquet, and invited many; and at the time for the banquet he sent his servant to say to those who had been invited, "Come; for all is now ready." But they all alike began to make excuses. The first said to him, "I have bought a field, and I must go out and see it; I pray you, have me excused." And another said, "I have bought five yoke of oxen, and I go to examine them; I pray you, have me excused." And another said, "I have married a wife, and therefore I cannot come." So the servant came and reported this to his master. Then the householder in anger said to his servant, "Go out quickly to the streets and lanes of the city, and bring in the poor and maimed and blind and lame." And the servant said, "Sir, what you commanded has been done, and still there is room." And the master said to the servant, "Go out to the highways and hedges, and compel people to come in, that my house may be filled. For I tell you, none of those men who were invited shall taste my banquet." '

Luke 14.15–24

If I had not come and spoken to them, they would not have sin; but now they have no excuse for their sin.

John 15.22

Exhortation

If you have any word of exhortation for the people, say it.

Acts 13.15

He who prophesies speaks to men for their upbuilding and encouragement and consolation.

1 Corinthians 14.3

Preach the word, be urgent in season and out of season, convince, rebuke, and exhort, be unfailing in patience and in teaching.

2 Timothy 4.2

For a bishop . . . must hold firm to the sure word as taught, so that he may be able to give instruction in sound doctrine and also to confute those who contradict it.

Titus 1.7,9

Urge the younger men to control themselves.

Titus 2.6

For the grace of God has appeared . . . training us to renounce irreligion and worldly passions, and to live sober, upright, and godly lives in this world . . . Declare these things; exhort and reprove with all authority.

Titus 2.11–12,15

Exhort one another every day, as long as it is called 'today'.

Hebrews 3.13

Let us consider how to stir up one another to love and good works.

Hebrews 10.24

I appeal to you, brethren, bear with my word of exhortation.

Hebrews 13.22

Exile

By the waters of Babylon, there we sat down and wept,
when we remembered Zion.

Psalms 137.1

How shall we sing the Lord's song in a foreign land?

Psalms 137.4

Therefore, son of man, prepare for yourself an exile's baggage, and go into exile by day in their sight; you shall go like an exile from your place to another place in their sight.

Ezekiel 12.3

Through him we both have access in one Spirit to the Father. So then you are no longer strangers and sojourners.

Ephesians 2.18–19

People who speak thus make it clear that they are seeking a homeland. If they had been thinking of that land from which they had gone out, they would have had opportunity to return. But as it is, they desire a better country, that is, a heavenly one.

Hebrews 11.14–16

Beloved, I beseech you as aliens and exiles to abstain from the passions of the flesh that wage war against your soul.

1 Peter 2.11

Exploitation

Let them be put to shame and confusion altogether
who rejoice at my calamity!

Psalms 35.26

Exposure

Take no part in the unfruitful works of darkness, but instead expose them. For it is a shame even to speak of the things that they do in secret; but when anything is exposed by the light it becomes visible, for anything that becomes visible is light.

Ephesians 5.11–13

Extravagance

See also **Luxury, Self-Indulgence**

One man gives freely, yet grows all the
richer;
another withholds what he should give,
and only suffers want.

Proverbs 11.24

He who loves pleasure will be a poor man;
he who loves wine and oil will not be
rich.

Proverbs 21.17

Why do you spend your money for that
which is not bread,
and your labour for that which does not
satisfy?

Isaiah 55.2

Woe to those who lie upon beds of ivory,
and stretch themselves upon their
couches,
and eat lambs from the flock,
and calves from the midst of the stall;
who sing idle songs to the sound of the
harp,
and like David invent for themselves
instruments of music;
who drink wine in bowls,
and anoint themselves with the finest oils,
. . . Therefore they shall now be the first of
those to go into exile,
and the revelry of those who stretch
themselves shall pass away.

Amos 6.4–6,7

As for what fell among the thorns, they
are those who hear, but as they go on their
way they are choked by the cares and riches
and pleasures of life, and their fruit does
not mature.

Luke 8.14

She who is self-indulgent is dead even
while she lives.

1 Timothy 5.6

In the last days . . . men will be . . . reckless, swollen with conceit, lovers of pleasure
rather than lovers of God.

2 Timothy 3.1–2,4

Come now, you rich, weep and howl for
the miseries that are coming upon you. . . .
You have lived on the earth in luxury and
in pleasure; you have fattened your hearts
in a day of slaughter.

James 5.1,5

F

Failure

See also **Degeneration, Fall**

Not one of all the good promises which the Lord had made to the house of Israel had failed; all came to pass.

Joshua 21.45

I will not remove from him my steadfast
  love,
  or be false to my faithfulness.

Psalms 89.33

If you faint in the day of adversity,
  your strength is small.

Proverbs 24.10

All who forsake thee shall be put to
  shame;
  those who turn away from thee shall be
  written in the earth.

Jeremiah 17.13

You have been weighed in the balances and found wanting.

Daniel 5.27

Thus says the Lord of hosts: Consider how you have fared. You have looked for much, and, lo, it came to little; and when you brought it home, I blew it away. Why? . . . Because . . . my house . . . lies in ruins, while you busy yourselves each with his own house.

Haggai 1.7,9

Then many will fall away . . . but he who endures to the end will be saved.

Matthew 24.10,13

No one who puts his hand to the plough and looks back is fit for the kingdom of God.

Luke 9.62

Provide yourselves with purses that do not grow old, with a treasure in the heavens that does not fail, where no thief approaches and no moth destroys.

Luke 12.33

If I speak in the tongues of men and of angels, but have not love, I am a noisy gong or a clanging cymbal.

1 Corinthians 13.1

Love never ends; as for prophecies, they will pass away; as for tongues, they will cease; as for knowledge, it will pass away.

1 Corinthians 13.8

Examine yourselves, to see whether you are holding to your faith. Test yourselves. Do you not realise that Jesus Christ is in you? — unless indeed you fail to meet the test!

2 Corinthians 13.5

For land which . . . bears thorns and thistles, is worthless and near to being cursed; its end is to be burned.

Hebrews 6.7–8

For if we sin deliberately after receiving the knowledge of the truth, there no longer remains a sacrifice for sins.

Hebrews 10.26

For we all make many mistakes, and if any one makes no mistakes in what he says he is a perfect man, able to bridle the whole body also.

James 3.2

Faintness

Let not your heart faint; do not fear, or tremble, or be in dread of them; for the Lord your God is he that goes with you, to fight for you against your enemies, to give you the victory.

Deuteronomy 20.3–4

What man is there that is fearful and fainthearted? Let him go back to his house, lest the heart of his fellows melt as his heart.

Deuteronomy 20.8

Your words have upheld him who was stumbling,
  and you have made firm the feeble knees.

Job 4.4

The Lord is the everlasting God
. . . He does not faint or grow weary,
. . . He gives power to the faint,
  and to him who has no might he increases strength.

Isaiah 40.28–29

Always to pray and not lose heart.

Luke 18.1

Having this ministry by the mercy of God, we do not lose heart.

2 Corinthians 4.1

We too believe . . . that he who raised the Lord Jesus will raise us also with Jesus and bring us with you into his presence. . . . So we do not lose heart. Though our outer nature is wasting away, our inner nature is being renewed every day.

2 Corinthians 4.13–14,16

Let us not grow weary in well-doing, for in due season we shall reap, if we do not lose heart.

Galatians 6.9

Consider him who endured from sinners such hostility against himself, so that you may not grow weary or faint-hearted.

Hebrews 12.3

My son, do not regard lightly the
  discipline of the Lord,
  nor lose courage when you are punished
  by him.
For the Lord disciplines him whom he
  loves.

Hebrews 12.5–6

Lift your drooping hands and strengthen your weak knees . . . so that what is lame may not be put out of joint but rather be healed.

Hebrews 12.12–13

Fairness

See also **Justice**

You shall not be partial in judgment; you shall hear the small and the great alike.

Deuteronomy 1.17

Justice, and only justice, you shall follow, that you may live and inherit the land which the Lord your God gives you.

Deuteronomy 16.20

When one rules justly over men,
  ruling in the fear of God,
he dawns on them like the morning light.

2 Samuel 23.3–4

Blessings are on the head of the righteous.

Proverbs 10.6

The mouth of the righteous brings forth
  wisdom.

Proverbs 10.31

A false balance is an abomination to the
  Lord,
  but a just weight is his delight.

Proverbs 11.1

When justice is done, it is a joy to the
  righteous.

Proverbs 21.15

If a man is righteous and does what is lawful and right . . . does not oppress any one, but restores to the debtor his pledge, commits no robbery . . . executes true justice between man and man, walks in my statutes, and is careful to observe my ordinances — he is righteous.

Ezekiel 18.5,7—9

Collect no more than is appointed you . . . Rob no one by violence or by false accusation, and be content with your wages.

Luke 3.13—14

Masters, treat your slaves justly and fairly, knowing that you also have a Master in heaven.

Colossians 4.1

Faith

See also **Belief, Trust**

And Abram . . . believed the Lord; and he reckoned it to him as righteousness.

Genesis 15.3,6

Believe in the Lord your God, and you will be established; believe his prophets, and you will succeed.

2 Chronicles 20.20

Blessed are the men whose strength is in thee,
   in whose heart are the highways to Zion.

Psalms 84.5

In returning and rest you shall be saved;
   in quietness and in trust shall be your
      strength.

Isaiah 30.15

Behold, he whose soul is not upright in
      him shall fail,
   but the righteous shall live by his faith.

Habakkuk 2.4

A woman who had suffered from a hemorhage for twelve years came up behind him and touched the fringe of his garment; for she said to herself, 'If I only touch his garment, I shall be made well.' Jesus turned, and seeing her he said, 'Take heart, daughter; your faith has made you well.'

Matthew 9.20—22

If you have faith as a grain of mustard seed, you will say to this mountain, 'Move from here to there,' and it will move; and nothing will be impossible to you.

Matthew 17.20

Truly, I say to you, if you have faith and never doubt, you will not only do what has been done to the fig tree, but even if you say to this mountain, 'Be taken up and cast into the sea,' it will be done. And whatever you ask in prayer, you will receive, if you have faith.

Matthew 21.21—22

I believe; help my unbelief.

Mark 9.24

Your faith has saved you; go in peace.

Luke 7.50

I am not ashamed of the gospel: it is the power of God for salvation to every one who has faith . . . the righteousness of God is revealed through faith for faith . . . He who through faith is righteous shall live.

Romans 1.16—17

For we hold that a man is justified by faith apart from works of law.

Romans 3.28

Now to one who works, his wages are not reckoned as a gift but as his due. And to one who does not work but trusts him who justifies the ungodly, his faith is reckoned as righteousness.

Romans 4.4—5

Since we are justified by faith, we have peace with God through our Lord Jesus Christ. Through him we have obtained access to this grace in which we stand.

Romans 5.1—2

For Christ is the end of the law, that every one who has faith may be justified.

Romans 10.4

Faith comes from what is heard, and what is heard comes by the preaching of Christ.

Romans 10.17

You stand fast only through faith.

Romans 11.20

As for the man who is weak in faith, welcome him, but not for disputes over opinions.

Romans 14.1

The faith that you have, keep between yourself and God.

Romans 14.22

May the God of hope fill you with all joy and peace in believing, so that by the power of the Holy Spirit you may abound in hope.

Romans 15.13

We are always of good courage . . . for we walk by faith, not by sight.

2 Corinthians 5.6–7

For in Christ Jesus you are all sons of God, through faith.

Galatians 3.26

For in Christ Jesus neither circumcision nor uncircumcision is of any avail, but faith working through love.

Galatians 5.6

For by grace you have been saved through faith; and this is not your own doing, it is the gift of God.

Ephesians 2.8

Fight the good fight of the faith; take hold of the eternal life.

1 Timothy 6.12

Now faith is the assurance of things hoped for, the conviction of things not seen.

Hebrews 11.1

By faith we understand that the world was created by the word of God, so that what is seen was made out of things which do not appear.

Hebrews 11.3

Without faith it is impossible to please him. For whoever would draw near to God must believe that he exists and that he rewards those who seek him.

Hebrews 11.6

Looking to Jesus the pioneer and perfecter of our faith.

Hebrews 12.2

Faith by itself, if it has no works, is dead.

James 2.17

The prayer of faith will save the sick man, and the Lord will raise him up.

James 5.15

Without having seen him you love him; though you do not now see him you believe in him and rejoice with unutterable and exalted joy. As the outcome of your faith you obtain the salvation of your souls.

1 Peter 1.8–9

This is the victory that overcomes the world, our faith.

1 John 5.4

We know that the Son of God has come and has given us understanding, to know him who is true.

1 John 5.20

Faithfulness

Fear the Lord, and serve him faithfully with all your heart.

1 Samuel 12.24

With the loyal thou dost show thyself loyal.

Psalms 18.25

Love the Lord, all you his saints!
 The Lord preserves the faithful,
 but abundantly requites him who acts
  haughtily.

Psalms 31.23

I will look with favour on the faithful in the
  land,
 that they may dwell with me.

Psalms 101.6

But the steadfast love of the Lord is from
everlasting to everlasting
upon those who fear him,
and his righteousness to children's
children,
to those who keep his covenant
and remember to do his commandments.

Psalms 103.17—18

The Lord is . . . kind in all his doings.
The Lord is near to all who call upon
him,
to all who call upon him in truth.

Psalms 145.17—18

By loyalty and faithfulness iniquity is
atoned for.

Proverbs 16.6

Set me as a seal upon your heart,
as a seal upon your arm.

Song of Solomon 8.6

Behold, he whose soul is not upright in
him shall fail,
but the righteous shall live by his faith.

Habakkuk 2.4

Let none be faithless to the wife of his
youth.

Malachi 2.15

Well done, good and faithful servant; you
have been faithful over a little, I will set
you over much.

Matthew 25.21

God is faithful.

1 Corinthians 1.9

Let us draw near with a true heart in full
assurance of faith, with our hearts sprinkled
clean from an evil conscience and our
bodies washed with pure water.

Hebrews 10.22

If we confess our sins, he is faithful and
just, and will forgive our sins.

1 John 1.9

Be faithful unto death, and I will give you
the crown of life.

Revelation 2.10

Fall

See also **Failure**

Let us fall into the hand of the Lord, for
his mercy is great; but let me not fall into
the hand of man.

2 Samuel 24.14

For thou hast delivered my soul from
death,
my eyes from tears,
my feet from stumbling;
I walk before the Lord
in the land of the living.

Psalms 116.8—9

The Lord upholds all who are falling,
and raises up all who are bowed down.

Psalms 145.14

The wicked falls by his own wickedness.

Proverbs 11.5

Where there is no guidance, a people falls;
but in an abundance of counsellors there
is safety.

Proverbs 11.14

He who trusts in his riches will wither.

Proverbs 11.28

One with a perverse tongue falls into
calamity.

Proverbs 17.20

The mouth of a loose woman is a deep pit;
he with whom the Lord is angry will fall
into it.

Proverbs 22.14

For a righteous man falls seven times, and
rises again;
but the wicked are overthrown by
calamity.

Proverbs 24.16

He who digs a pit will fall into it.

Proverbs 26.27

He who is perverse in his ways will fall
into a pit.

Proverbs 28.18

When the wicked are in authority,
  transgression increases;
 but the righteous will look upon their
  downfall.

Proverbs 29.16

A divided household falls.

Luke 11.17

Sin came into the world through one man
and death through sin, and so death spread
to all men because all men sinned.

Romans 5.12

Never . . . put a stumbling block or hindrance in the way of a brother.

Romans 14.13

Let any one who thinks that he stands take
heed lest he fall.

1 Corinthians 10.12

The serpent deceived Eve by his cunning.

2 Corinthians 11.3

It is a fearful thing to fall into the hands of
the living God.

Hebrews 10.31

Be the more zealous to confirm your call
and election, for if you do this you will
never fall.

2 Peter 1.10

Beware lest you be carried away with the
error of lawless men and lose your own
stability.

2 Peter 3.17

To him who is able to keep you from
falling and to present you without blemish
before the presence of his glory with rejoicing, to the only God, our Saviour through
Jesus Christ our Lord, be glory.

Jude 24−25

Falsehood

See also **Deceit, Lie**

You shall not bear false witness against
your neighbour.

Exodus 20.16

You shall not utter a false report.

Exodus 23.1

Keep far from a false charge.

Exodus 23.7

Give me not up to the will of my
  adversaries;
 for false witnesses have risen against me,
 and they breathe out violence.

Psalms 27.12

He who speaks the truth gives honest
  evidence,
 but a false witness utters deceit.

Proverbs 12.17

A righteous man hates falsehood,
 but a wicked man acts shamefully and
  disgracefully.

Proverbs 13.5

An evildoer listens to wicked lips;
 and a liar gives heed to a mischievous
  tongue.

Proverbs 17.4

A false witness will not go unpunished,
 and he who utters lies will not escape.

Proverbs 19.5

A false witness will perish.

Proverbs 21.28

This is the curse that goes out over the face
of the whole land . . . according to it . . .
every one who swears falsely shall be cut off
henceforth.

Zechariah 5.3

Love no false oath, for . . . these things I
hate, says the Lord.

Zechariah 8.17

Blessed are you when men revile you and
persecute you and utter all kinds of evil
against you falsely on my account.

Matthew 5.11

For out of the heart come evil thoughts
. . . false witness, slander. These are what
defile a man.

Matthew 15.19−20

Therefore, putting away falsehood, let every one speak the truth with his neighbour, for we are members one of another.

Ephesians 4.25

Now the Spirit expressly says that in later times some will depart from the faith by giving heed to deceitful spirits and doctrines of demons, through the pretensions of liars whose consciences are seared.

1 Timothy 4.1−2

Family

See also **Children, Parenthood**

God blessed them, and God said to them, 'Be fruitful and multiply, and fill the earth.'

Genesis 1.28

Take heed . . . lest you forget the things which your eyes have seen, and lest they depart from your heart all the days of your life; make them known to your children and your children's children.

Deuteronomy 4.9

He raises up the needy out of affliction,
    and makes their families like flocks.

Psalms 107.41

For I have come to set a man against his father, and a daughter against her mother, and a daughter-in-law against her mother-in-law; and a man's foes will be those of his own household. He who loves father or mother more than me is not worthy of me.

Matthew 10.35−37

While he was still speaking to the people, behold, his mother and his brothers stood outside, asking to speak to him. But he replied to the man who told him, 'Who is my mother, and who are my brothers?' And stretching out his hand toward his disciples, he said, 'Here are my mother and my brothers! For whoever does the will of my father in heaven is my brother, and sister, and mother.'

Matthew 12.46−50

A prophet is not without honour, except in his own country and among his own kin, and in his own house.

Mark 6.4

You will be delivered up even by parents and brothers and kinsmen and friends.

Luke 21.16

We are indeed his offspring.

Acts 17.28

The Father, from whom every family in heaven and on earth is named.

Ephesians 3.15

If any one does not provide for his relatives, and especially for his own family, he has disowned the faith and is worse than an unbeliever.

1 Timothy 5.8

Farming

The Lord God took the man and put him in the garden of Eden to till it and keep it.

Genesis 2.15

He who tills his land will have plenty of
    bread,
    but he who follows worthless pursuits will
    have plenty of poverty.

Proverbs 28.19

Fasting

'Yet even now,' says the Lord,
    'return to me with all your heart,
with fasting, with weeping, and with
        mourning;
    and rend your hearts and not your
        garments.'

Joel 2.12−13

And when you fast, do not look dismal, like the hypocrites, for they disfigure their faces that their fasting may be seen by men. Truly, I say to you, they have received their reward. But when you fast, anoint your head and wash your face, that your fasting may not be seen by men but by your Father who is in secret; and your Father who sees in secret will reward you.

Matthew 6.16–18

Fatalism

What has been is what will be,
   and what has been done is what will be
      done;
   and there is nothing new under the sun.
Is there a thing of which it is said, 'See, this
      is new'?

Ecclesiastes 1.9–10

But all this I laid to heart, examining it all, how the righteous and the wise and their deeds are in the hand of God; whether it is love or hate man does not know. Everything before them is vanity, since one fate comes to all, to the righteous and the wicked, to the good and the evil, to the clean and the unclean, to him who sacrifices and him who does not sacrifice. As is the good man, so is the sinner; and he who swears is as he who shuns an oath.

Ecclesiastes 9.1–2

Fault

See also **Sin**

I remember my faults today.

Genesis 1.9

But who can discern his errors?
   Clear thou me from hidden faults.

Psalms 19.12

For I know my transgressions,
   and my sin is ever before me.

Psalms 51.3

If your brother sins against you, go and tell him his fault, between you and him alone.

Matthew 18.15

If a man is overtaken in any trespass, you who are spiritual should restore him in a spirit of gentleness.

Galatians 6.1

Now to him who is able to keep you from falling and to present you without blemish before the presence of his glory with rejoicing, to the only God, our Saviour through Jesus Christ our Lord, be glory.

Jude 24–25

These have been redeemed from mankind as first fruits for God and the Lamb, and in their mouth no lie was found, for they are spotless.

Revelation 14.4–5

Favour

For his anger is but for a moment,
   and his favour is for a lifetime.

Psalms 30.5

By thy favour, O Lord,
   thou hadst established me as a strong
      mountain.

Psalms 30.7

Let not loyalty and faithfulness forsake
      you . . .
So you will find favour and good repute
   in the sight of God and man.

Proverbs 3.3–4

For he who finds me finds life
   and obtains favour from the Lord.

Proverbs 8.35

He who diligently seeks good seeks
   favour.

Proverbs 11.27

A good man obtains favour from the Lord.

Proverbs 12.2

Good sense wins favour.

Proverbs 13.15

In the light of a king's face there is life,
   and his favour is like the clouds that bring
      the spring rain.

Proverbs 16.15

He who rebukes a man will afterward find
      more favour
   than he who flatters with his tongue.

Proverbs 28.23

If favour is shown to the wicked,
he does not learn righteousness.

Isaiah 26.10

For to him who has will more be given,
and he will have abundance; but from him
who has not, even what he has will be taken
away.

Matthew 13.12

My soul magnifies the Lord,
and my spirit rejoices in God my Saviour,
for he has regarded the low estate of his
handmaiden.
For behold, henceforth all generations
will call me blessed;
for he who is mighty has done great things
for me.

Luke 1.46—49

Favouritism

See also **Jealousy**

When his brothers saw that their father
loved him more than all his brothers, they
hated him, and could not speak peaceably
to him.

Genesis 37.4

I perceive that God shows no partiality, but
in every nation any one who fears him and
does what is right is acceptable to him.

Acts 10.34—35

In the presence of God and of Christ Jesus
and of the elect angels I charge you to keep
these rules without favour, doing nothing
from partiality.

1 Timothy 5.21

Fear

See also **Cowardice, Dismay, Distress**

If you walk in my statutes and observe my
commandments and do them . . . I will give
peace in the land, and you shall lie down,
and none shall make you afraid.

Leviticus 26.3,6

Do not be in dread or afraid of them. The
Lord your God who goes before you will
himself fight for you.

Deuteronomy 1.29—30

You shall fear the Lord your God; you
shall serve him and cleave to him, and by
his name you shall swear.

Deuteronomy 10.20

Be strong and of good courage, do not fear
. . . for it is the Lord your God who goes
with you; he will not fail you or forsake
you.

Deuteronomy 31.6

O Lord, let thy ear be attentive to the
prayer of thy servant, and to the prayer of
thy servants who delight to fear thy name;
and give success to thy servant today, and
grant him mercy in the sight of this man.

Nehemiah 1.11

If iniquity is in your hand, put it far away,
and let not wickedness dwell in your
tents.
Surely then you will lift up your face
without blemish;
you will be secure, and will not fear.

Job 11.14—15

Withdraw thy hand far from me,
and let not dread of thee terrify me.

Job 13.21

The wicked man writhes in pain all his
days . . .
He knows that a day of darkness is
ready at his hand;
distress and anguish terrify him.

Job 15.20,23—24

The Lord is my light and my salvation;
whom shall I fear?
The Lord is the stronghold of my life;
of whom shall I be afraid?

Psalms 27.1

I had said in my alarm,
'I am driven far from thy sight.'
But thou didst hear my supplications,
when I cried to thee for help.

Psalms 31.22

I sought the Lord, and he answered me,
   and delivered me from all my fears.

Psalms 34.4

God is our refuge and strength,
   a very present help in trouble.
Therefore we will not fear though the earth
      should change,
   though the mountains shake in the heart
      of the sea;
though its waters roar and foam,
   though the mountains tremble with its
      tumult.

Psalms 46.1−3

When I am afraid,
   I put my trust in thee.
In God, whose word I praise,
   in God I trust without a fear.
   What can flesh do to me?

Psalms 56.3−4

You will not fear the terror of the night,
   nor the arrow that flies by day,
nor the pestilence that stalks in darkness,
   nor the destruction that wastes at
      noonday . . .
For he will give his angels charge of you
   to guard you in all your ways.

Psalms 91.5−6,11

The fear of the Lord is the beginning of
   wisdom.

Psalms 111.10

With the Lord on my side I do not fear.
   What can man do to me?

Psalms 118.6

He who listens to me will dwell secure
   and will be at ease, without dread of evil.

Proverbs 1.33

Do not be afraid of sudden panic,
   or of the ruin of the wicked, when it
      comes;
for the Lord will be your confidence
   and will keep your foot from being
      caught.

Proverbs 3.25−26

The fear of the Lord is hatred of evil.

Proverbs 8.13

What the wicked dreads will come upon
      him,
   but the desire of the righteous will be
      granted.

Proverbs 10.24

Like a muddied spring or a polluted
      fountain
   is a righteous man who gives way before
      the wicked.

Proverbs 25.26

The fear of man lays a snare,
   but he who trusts in the Lord is safe.

Proverbs 29.25

The Lord of hosts, him you shall regard as
holy; let him be your fear, and let him be
your dread.

Isaiah 8.13

I, I am he that comforts you;
   who are you that you are afraid of man
      who dies,
of the son of man who is made like grass.

Isaiah 51.12

Son of man, eat your bread with quaking,
and drink water with trembling and with
fearfulness; and say of the people of the
land, Thus says the Lord God concerning
the inhabitants of Jerusalem in the land of
Israel: They shall eat their bread with fearfulness, and drink water in dismay.

Ezekiel 12.18−19

Do not fear those who kill the body but
cannot kill the soul; rather fear him who
can destroy both soul and body in hell.

Matthew 10.28

Remember the oath which he swore to our
      father Abraham, to grant us
that we, being delivered from the hand of
      our enemies,
might serve him without fear,
in holiness and righteousness before him all
      the days of our life.

Luke 1.72−73

My peace I give to you; not as the world gives do I give to you. Let not your hearts be troubled, neither let them be afraid.

John 14.27

God did not give us a spirit of timidity but a spirit of power and love and self-control.

2 Timothy 1.7

Consider him who endured from sinners such hostility against himself, so that you may not grow weary or faint-hearted.

Hebrews 12.3

He has said, 'I will never fail you nor forsake you.' Hence we can confidently say,
'The Lord is my helper,
I will not be afraid;
what can man do to me?'

Hebrews 13.5−6

Fear God.

1 Peter 2.17

Let nothing terrify you.

1 Peter 3.6

There is no fear in love, but perfect love casts out fear. For fear has to do with punishment, and he who fears is not perfected in love. We love, because he first loved us.

1 John 4.18−19

Fellowship

See also **Co-operation, Friendship**

I will make my abode among you, and my soul shall not abhor you. And I will walk among you, and will be your God, and you shall be my people.

Leviticus 26.11−12

I am a companion of all who fear thee,
of those who keep thy precepts.

Psalms 119.63

Two are better than one, because they have a good reward for their toil. For if they fall, one will lift up his fellow; but woe to him who is alone when he falls and has not another to lift him up.

Ecclesiastes 4.9−10

Whoever does the will of my Father in heaven is my brother, and sister, and mother.

Matthew 12.50

Where two or three are gathered in my name, there am I in the midst of them.

Matthew 18.20

Abide in me, and I in you. As the branch cannot bear fruit by itself, unless it abides in the vine, neither can you, unless you abide in me. I am the vine, you are the branches.

John 15.4−5

Holy Father, keep them in thy name, which thou hast given me, that they may be one, even as we are one.

John 17.11

The glory which thou hast given me I have given to them, that they may be one even as we are one, I in them and thou in me, that they may become perfectly one, so that the world may know that thou hast sent me and hast loved them even as thou hast loved me.

John 17.22−23

They devoted themselves to the apostles' teaching and fellowship.

Acts 2.42

It is the Spirit himself bearing witness with our spirit that we are children of God, and if children, then heirs, heirs of God and fellow heirs with Christ, provided we suffer with him in order that we may also be glorified with him.

Romans 8.16−17

So we, though many, are one body in Christ, and individually members one of another.

Romans 12.5

May the God of steadfastness and encouragement grant you to live in such harmony with one another, in accord with Christ Jesus, that together you may with one voice glorify the God and Father of our Lord Jesus Christ.

Romans 15.5−6

God is faithful, by whom you were called into the fellowship of his Son, Jesus Christ our Lord.

1 Corinthians 1.9

Do you not know that your bodies are members of Christ?

1 Corinthians 6.15

Just as the body is one and has many members, and all the members of the body, though many, are one body, so it is with Christ. For by one Spirit we were all baptized into one body — Jews or Greeks, slaves or free — and all were made to drink of one Spirit.

1 Corinthians 12.12—13

Now you are the body of Christ and individually members of it.

1 Corinthians 12.27

As we have opportunity, let us do good to all men, and especially to those who are of the household of faith.

Galatians 6.10

Let every one speak the truth with his neighbour, for we are members one of another.

Ephesians 4.25

If there is any encouragement in Christ . . . any participation in the Spirit . . . complete my joy by being of the same mind, having the same love, being in full accord and of one mind.

Philippians 2.1—2

That which we have seen and heard we proclaim also to you, so that you may have fellowship with us; and our fellowship is with the Father and with his son Jesus Christ.

1 John 1.3

God is light and in him is no darkness at all. If we say we have fellowship with him while we walk in darkness, we lie and do not live according to the truth; but if we walk in the light, as he is in the light, we have fellowship with one another, and the blood of Jesus his Son cleanses us from all sin.

1 John 1.5—7

Fertility

Be fruitful and multiply, and fill the earth and subdue it.

Genesis 1.28

God Almighty . . . will bless you
  with blessings of heaven above . . .
blessings of the breasts and of the womb.

Genesis 49.25

He raises up the needy out of affliction,
  and makes their families like flocks.

Psalms 107.41

The wilderness and the dry land shall be
    glad,
  the desert shall rejoice and blossom;
like the crocus it shall blossom abundantly,
  and rejoice with joy and singing.

Isaiah 35.1—2

Has not the one God made and sustained for us the spirit of life? And what does he desire? Godly offspring.

Malachi 2.15

Fervour

See also **Eagerness**

As a hart longs
  for flowing streams,
so longs my soul
  for thee, O God.

Psalms 42.1

Never flag in zeal, be aglow with the Spirit, serve the Lord.

Romans 12.11

Love one another earnestly from the heart.

1 Peter 1.22

Above all hold unfailing your love for one another, since love covers a multitude of sins.

1 Peter 4.8

Fickleness

Your love is like a morning cloud,
like the dew that goes early away.

Hosea 6.4

Fidelity

See also **Faithfulness**

A man leaves his father and his mother
and cleaves to his wife, and they become
one flesh.

Genesis 2.24

Where you go I will go, and where you
lodge I will lodge; your people shall be my
people, and your God my God; where you
die I will die, and there will I be buried.

Ruth 1.16–17

Rejoice in the wife of your youth,
a lovely hind, a graceful doe.
Let her affection fill you at all times with
delight,
be infatuated always with her love.
Why should you be infatuated, my son,
with a loose woman
and embrace the bosom of an
adventuress?

Proverbs 5.18–20

Enjoy life with the wife whom you love, all
the days of your vain life which he has given
you.

Ecclesiastes 9.9

Set me as a seal upon your heart,
as a seal upon your arm;
for love is strong as death,
jealousy is cruel as the grave.

Song of Solomon 8.6

Take heed to yourselves, and let none be
faithless to the wife of his youth.

Malachi 2.15

It is well for a man not to touch a woman.
But because of the temptation to immorality, each man should have his own wife and
each woman her own husband.

1 Corinthians 7.1–2

The wife should not separate from her
husband (but if she does, let her remain
single or else be reconciled to her husband)
— and . . . the husband should not divorce
his wife.

1 Corinthians 7.10–11

Husbands, love your wives, as Christ loved
the church and gave himself up for her.

Ephesians 5.25

Let marriage be held in honour among all,
and let the marriage bed be undefiled; for
God will judge the immoral and adulterous.

Hebrews 13.4

Fight

See also **War**

When men quarrel and one strikes the
other with a stone or with his fist and the
man does not die but keeps his bed, then if
the man rises again and walks abroad with
his staff, he that struck him shall be clear;
only he shall pay for the loss of his time,
and shall have him thoroughly healed.

Exodus 21.18–19

When a man causes a disfigurement in his
neighbour, as he has done it shall be done
to him, fracture for fracture, eye for eye,
tooth for tooth; as he has disfigured a man,
he shall be disfigured.

Leviticus 24.19–20

When men fight with one another, and the
wife of the one draws near to rescue her
husband from the hand of him who is beating him, and puts out her hand and seizes
him by the private parts, then you shall cut
off her hand; your eye shall have no pity.

Deuteronomy 25.11–12

One man of you puts to flight a thousand,
since it is the Lord your God who fights for
you, as he promised you.

Joshua 23.10

The Lord saves not with sword and spear;
for the battle is the Lord's and he will give
you into our hand.

1 Samuel 17.47

Remember the Lord, who is great and terrible, and fight for your brethren, your sons, your daughters, your wives, and your homes.

Nehemiah 4.14

I have fought the good fight, I have finished the race, I have kept the faith.

2 Timothy 4.7

Firmness

If you set your heart aright,
    you will stretch out your hands toward
      him . . .
Surely then you will lift up your face
      without blemish;
    you will be secure, and will not fear.

Job 11.13,15

His breath kindles coals . . .
The folds of his flesh cleave together,
    firmly cast upon him and immovable.

Job 41.21,23

Live in him . . . established in the faith, just as you were taught, abounding in thanksgiving.

Colossians 2.7

If we endure, we shall also reign with him.

2 Timothy 2.12

Fitness

It is fitting for us to fulfil all righteousness.

Matthew 3.15

Flattery

I will not show partiality to any person
    or use flattery toward any man.
For I do not know how to flatter,
    else would my Maker soon put an end
      to me.

Job 32.21−22

May the Lord cut off all flattering lips,
    the tongue that makes great boasts.

Psalms 12.3

The reproofs of discipline are the way of
      life,
    to preserve you from the evil woman,
from the smooth tongue of the adventuress.

Proverbs 6.23−24

It is not good to eat much honey,
    so be sparing of complimentary words.

Proverbs 25.27

A flattering mouth works ruin.

Proverbs 26.28

The crucible is for silver, and the furnace is
      for gold,
    and a man is judged by his praise.

Proverbs 27.21

A man who flatters his neighbour
    spreads a net for his feet.

Proverbs 29.5

Woe to you, when all men speak well of you.

Luke 6.26

These are grumblers, malcontents, following their own passions, loudmouthed boasters, flattering people to gain advantage.

Jude 16

Flesh

See also **Mortality**

If he should take back his spirit to himself,
    and gather to himself his breath,
all flesh would perish together,
    and man would return to dust.

Job 34.14−15

To thee shall all flesh come
    on account of sins.

Psalms 65.2

Remove vexation from your mind, and put away pain from your body.

Ecclesiastes 11.10

All flesh is grass,
    and all its beauty is like the flower of the
      field.

The grass withers, the flower fades . . .
but the word of our God will stand for
ever.

Isaiah 40.6–8

The spirit indeed is willing, but the flesh is
weak.

Matthew 26.41

The Word became flesh and dwelt among
us, full of grace and truth; we have beheld
his glory, glory as of the only Son from the
Father.

John 1.14

That which is born of the flesh is flesh, and
that which is born of the Spirit is spirit.

John 3.6

It is the spirit that gives life, the flesh is of
no avail; the words that I have spoken to
you are spirit and life.

John 6.63

Flesh and blood cannot inherit the kingdom of God, nor does the perishable also
inherit the imperishable.

1 Corinthians 15.50

For though we live in the world we are not
carrying on a wordly war, for the weapons
of our warfare are not worldly but have
divine power to destroy strongholds.

2 Corinthians 10.3–4

Flight

See also **Exile**

The wicked flee when no one pursues,
but the righteous are bold as a lion.

Proverbs 28.1

For you shall not go out in haste,
and you shall not go in flight,
for the Lord will go before you.

Isaiah 52.12

Submit yourselves . . . to God. Resist the
devil and he will flee from you. Draw near
to God.

James 4.7–8

Followers

See also **Discipleship**

How long will you go limping with two
different opinions? If the Lord is God,
follow him.

1 Kings 18.21

Follow me, and I will make you fishers of
men.

Matthew 4.19

If any man would come after me, let him
deny himself and take up his cross daily and
follow me.

Luke 9.23

I am the light of the world; he who follows
me will not walk in darkness, but will have
the light of life.

John 8.12

If you continue in my word, you are truly
my disciples, and you will know the truth,
and the truth will make you free.

John 8.31–32

Folly

The fool says in his heart,
'There is no God.'

Psalms 14.1

Fools despise wisdom and instruction.

Proverbs 1.7

The iniquities of the wicked ensnare him,
and he is caught in the toils of his sin.
He dies for lack of discipline,
and because of his great folly he is lost.

Proverbs 5.22–23

The babbling of a fool brings ruin near.

Proverbs 10.14

He who conceals hatred has lying lips,
and he who utters slander is a fool.

Proverbs 10.18

Fools die for lack of sense.

Proverbs 10.21

A prudent man conceals his knowledge,
but fools proclaim their folly.

Proverbs 12.23

To turn away from evil is an abomination
to fools.

Proverbs 13.19

He who walks with wise men becomes
wise,
but the companion of fools will suffer
harm.

Proverbs 13.20

The folly of fools is deceiving.

Proverbs 14.8

He who is slow to anger has great
understanding,
but he who has a hasty temper exalts
folly.

Proverbs 14.29

Folly is a joy to him who has no sense.

Proverbs 15.21

Let a man meet a she-bear robbed of her
cubs,
rather than a fool in his folly.

Proverbs 17.12

Even a fool who keeps silent is considered
wise;
when he closes his lips, he is deemed
intelligent.

Proverbs 17.28

A fool takes no pleasure in understanding,
but only in expressing his opinion.

Proverbs 18.2

If one gives answer before he hears,
it is his folly and shame.

Proverbs 18.13

When a man's folly brings his way to ruin,
his heart rages against the Lord.

Proverbs 19.3

The devising of folly is sin.

Proverbs 24.9

Answer not a fool according to his folly,
lest you be like him yourself.

Proverbs 26.4

A stone is heavy, and sand is weighty,
but a fool's provocation is heavier than
both.

Proverbs 27.3

Crush a fool in a mortar with a pestle
along with crushed grain,
yet his folly will not depart from him.

Proverbs 27.22

He who trusts in his own mind is a fool.

Proverbs 28.26

The fool walks in darkness.

Ecclesiastes 2.14

The heart of the wise is in the house of
mourning;
but the heart of fools is in the house of
mirth.
It is better for a man to hear the rebuke of
the wise
than to hear the song of fools.
For as the crackling of thorns under a pot,
so is the laughter of the fools;
this also is vanity.

Ecclesiastes 7.4−6

Dead flies make the perfumer's ointment
give off an evil odour;
so a little folly outweighs wisdom and
honour.

Ecclesiastes 10.1

There is an evil which I have seen under
the sun, as it were an error proceeding from
the ruler: folly is set in many high places.

Ecclesiastes 10.5

The words of a wise man's mouth win him
favour,
but the lips of a fool consume him.
The beginning of the words of his mouth is
foolishness,
and the end of his talk is wicked
madness.
A fool multiplies words.

Ecclesiastes 10.12−14

Every one who hears these words of mine and does not do them will be like a foolish man who built his house upon the sand; and the rain fell, and the floods came, and the winds blew and beat against that house, and it fell; and great was the fall of it.

Matthew 7.26–27

Has not God made foolish the wisdom of the world? For since, in the wisdom of God, the world did not know God through wisdom, it pleased God through the folly of what we preach to save those who believe.

1 Corinthians 1.20–21

The foolishness of God is wiser than men.

1 Corinthians 1.25

God chose what is foolish in the world to shame the wise.

1 Corinthians 1.27

If any one among you thinks that he is wise in this age, let him become a fool that he may become wise. For the wisdom of this world is folly with God.

1 Corinthians 3.18–19

Food

God said, 'Behold, I have given you every plant yielding seed which is upon the face of all the earth, and every tree with seed in its fruit; you shall have them for food. And to every beast of the earth, and to every bird of the air, and to everything that creeps on the earth, everything that has the breath of life, I have given every green plant for food.'

Genesis 1.29–30

Every moving thing that lives shall be food for you; and as I gave you the green plants, I give you everything.

Genesis 9.3

Thou preparest a table before me
  in the presence of my enemies;
thou anointest my head with oil,
  my cup overflows.

Psalms 23.5

Yet he commanded the skies above,
  and opened the doors of heaven;
and he rained down upon them manna to
    eat,
  and gave them the grain of heaven.
Man ate of the bread of the angels;
  he sent them food in abundance.

Psalms 78.23–25

Thou dost cause the grass to grow for the
    cattle,
  and plants for man to cultivate,
that he may bring forth food from the
    earth,
  and wine to gladden the heart of man,
oil to make his face shine,
  and bread to strengthen man's heart.

Psalms 104.14–15

He provides food for those who fear him;
  he is ever mindful of his covenant.

Psalms 111.5

The eyes of all look to thee,
  and thou givest them their food in due
    season.
Thou openest thy hand,
  thou satisfiest the desire of every living
    thing.

Psalms 145.15–16

Better is a dinner of herbs where love is
  than a fatted ox and hatred with it.

Proverbs 15.17

Better is a dry morsel with quiet
  than a house full of feasting with strife.

Proverbs 17.1

Do not desire his delicacies,
  for they are deceptive food.

Proverbs 23.3

He who is sated loathes honey,
  but to one who is hungry everything
    bitter is sweet.

Proverbs 27.7

Feed me with the food that is needful
    for me,
  lest I be full, and deny thee,
and say, 'Who is the Lord?'

Proverbs 30.8–9

Bread is made for laughter.

Ecclesiastes 10.19

Hearken diligently to me, and eat what is good,
and delight yourselves in fatness.

Isaiah 55.2

You shall eat in plenty and be satisfied,
and praise the name of the Lord your God,
who has dealt wondrously with you.

Joel 2.26

Give us this day our daily bread.

Matthew 6.11

He has filled the hungry with good things,
and the rich he has sent empty away.

Luke 1.53

He who has two coats, let him share with him who has none; and he who has food, let him do likewise.

Luke 3.11

For my flesh is food indeed, and my blood is drink indeed. He who eats my flesh and drinks my blood abides in me, and I in him.

John 6.55–56

He did not leave himself without witness, for he did good and gave you from heaven rains and fruitful seasons, satisfying your hearts with food and gladness.

Acts 14.17

He who supplies seed to the sower and bread for food will supply and multiply your resources and increase the harvest of your righteousness.

2 Corinthians 9.10

For everything created by God is good, and nothing is to be rejected if it is received with thanksgiving; for then it is consecrated by the word of God and prayer.

1 Timothy 4.4

If we have food and clothing, with these we shall be content.

1 Timothy 6.8

Forbearance

See also **Patience**

A fool gives full vent to his anger,
but a wise man quietly holds it back.

Proverbs 29.11

Do not resist one who is evil. But if any one strikes you on the right cheek, turn to him the other also; and if any one would sue you and take your coat, let him have your cloak as well.

Matthew 5.39–40

If I wish to boast, I shall not be a fool, for I shall be speaking the truth. But I refrain from it, so that no one may think more of me than he sees in me or hears from me.

2 Corinthians 12.6

Lead a life worthy of the calling to which you have been called, with all lowliness and meekness, with patience, forbearing one another in love.

Ephesians 4.1–2

Put on . . . patience, forbearing one another and, if one has a complaint against another, forgiving each other.

Colossians 3.12–13

Do not return evil for evil or reviling for reviling; but on the contrary bless.

1 Peter 3.9

Forgetfulness

There is no remembrance of former things,
nor will there be any remembrance
of later things yet to happen
among those who come after.

Ecclesiastes 1.11

Forgiveness

Thou art a God ready to forgive, gracious and merciful, slow to anger and abounding in steadfast love.

Nehemiah 9.17

I sinned, and perverted what was right,
　and it was not requited to me.
He has redeemed my soul from going down
　　into the Pit,
　and my life shall see the light.

Job 33.27—28

Blessed is he whose transgression is
　　forgiven,
　whose sin is covered.

Psalms 32.1

To thee shall all flesh come
　on account of sins.
When our transgressions prevail over us,
　thou dost forgive them.

Psalms 65.2—3

So great is his steadfast love toward those
　　who fear him;
as far as the east is from the west,
so far does he remove our transgressions
　　from us.

Psalms 103.11

He who forgives an offence seeks love,
　but he who repeats a matter alienates a
　　friend.

Proverbs 17.9

Good sense makes a man slow to anger,
　and it is his glory to overlook an offence.

Proverbs 19.11

Though your sins are like scarlet,
　they shall be as white as snow;
though they are red like crimson,
　they shall become like wool.

Isaiah 1.18

Thou hast held back my life
　from the pit of destruction,
for thou hast cast all my sins
　behind thy back.

Isaiah 38.17

I, I am He
　who blots out your transgressions for my
　　own sake,
　and I will not remember your sins.

Isaiah 43.25

To the Lord our God belong mercy and
forgiveness; because we have rebelled
against him, and have not obeyed the voice
of the Lord our God.

Daniel 9.9—10

On that day there shall be a fountain
opened for the house of David and the
inhabitants of Jerusalem to cleanse them
from sin and uncleanness.

Zechariah 13.1

If you forgive men their trespasses, your
heavenly Father also will forgive you; but if
you do not forgive men their trespasses,
neither will your Father forgive your trespasses.

Matthew 6.14—15

Take heart, my son; your sins are forgiven.

Matthew 9.2

The Son of man has authority on earth to
forgive sins.

Matthew 9.6

'Lord, how often shall my brother sin
against me, and I forgive him? As many as
seven times?' Jesus said to him, 'I do not
say to you seven times, but seventy times
seven.'

Matthew 18.21—22

And he took a cup, and when he had given
thanks he gave it to them, saying, 'Drink of
it, all of you; for this is my blood of the
covenant, which is poured out for many for
the forgiveness of sins.'

Matthew 26.27—28

Whenever you stand praying, forgive, if
you have anything against any one; so that
your Father also who is in heaven may
forgive you your trespasses.

Mark 11.25

Forgive, and you will be forgiven.

Luke 6.37

Her sins, which are many, are forgiven,
for she loved much; but he who is forgiven
little, loves little.

Luke 7.47

If your brother sins, rebuke him, and if he repents, forgive him; and if he sins against you seven times in the day, and turns to you seven times, and says, 'I repent,' you must forgive him.

Luke 17.3−4

Father, forgive them; for they know not what they do.

Luke 23.34

Let it be known to you therefore, brethren, that through this man forgiveness of sins is proclaimed to you.

Acts 13.38

And God who knows the heart bore witness to them, giving them the Holy Spirit just as he did to us; and he made no distinction between us and them, but cleansed their hearts by faith.

Acts 15.8−9

Bless those who persecute you; bless and do not curse them.

Romans 12.14

In him we have redemption through his blood, the forgiveness of our trespasses.

Ephesians 1.7

Be kind to one another, tenderhearted, forgiving one another, as God in Christ forgave you.

Ephesians 4.32

Put on . . . patience, forbearing one another and, if one has a complaint against another, forgiving each other; as the Lord has forgiven you, so you also must forgive.

Colossians 3.12−13

Do not return evil for evil or reviling for reviling; but on the contrary bless.

1 Peter 3.9

If we confess our sins, he is faithful and just, and will forgive our sins and cleanse us from all unrighteousness.

1 John 1.9

Your sins are forgiven for his sake.

1 John 2.12

Fornication

See also **Adultery, Lust**

From within, out of the heart of man, come evil thoughts, fornication . . . adultery . . . licentiousness. . . . All these evil things come from within, and they defile a man.

Mark 7.21−23

Abstain from . . . unchastity.

Acts 15.20

Let us conduct ourselves becomingly as in the day, not in . . . debauchery and licentiousness.

Romans 13.13

I wrote . . . not to associate with any one who bears the name of brother if he is guilty of immorality . . . not even to eat with such a one.

1 Corinthians 5.11

Neither the immoral . . . nor adulterers . . . will inherit the kingdom of God.

1 Corinthians 6.9−10

The body is not meant for immorality, but for the Lord.

1 Corinthians 6.13

Shun immorality. Every other sin which a man commits is outside the body; but the immoral man sins against his own body. Do you not know that your body is a temple of the Holy Spirit . . . You are not your own; you were bought with a price. So glorify God in your body.

1 Corinthians 6.18−20

Because of the temptation to immorality, each man should have his own wife and each woman her own husband.

1 Corinthians 7.2

We must not indulge in immorality as some of them did, and twenty-three thousand fell in a single day.

1 Corinthians 10.8

Fornication and all impurity or covetousness must not even be named among you, as is fitting among saints.

Ephesians 5.3

Put to death therefore what is earthly in you: fornication, impurity, passion . . . On account of these the wrath of God is coming.

Colossians 3.5–6

This is the will of God . . . that you abstain from unchastity; that each one of you know how to take a wife for himself in holiness and honour.

1 Thessalonians 4.3–4

Just as Sodom and Gomor'rah . . . acted immorally and indulged in unnatural lust, serve as an example by undergoing a punishment of eternal fire.

Jude 7

Forthrightness

He who winks the eye causes trouble,
    but he who boldly reproves makes peace.

Proverbs 10.10

Therefore, having this ministry by the mercy of God, we do not lose heart. We have renounced disgraceful, underhanded ways; we refuse to practise cunning or to tamper with God's word, but by the open statement of the truth we would commend ourselves to every man's conscience in the sight of God.

2 Corinthians 4.1–2

Forwardness

Do not put yourself forward in the king's
        presence,
    or stand in the place of the great;
for it is better to be told, 'Come up here,'
    than to be put lower in the presence of
        the prince.

Proverbs 25.6–7

Fraternity

See also Fellowship

If your brother sins against you, go and tell him his fault, between you and him alone. If he listens to you, you have gained your brother.

Matthew 18.15

Then Peter came up and said to him, 'Lord, how often shall my brother sin against me, and I forgive him? As many as seven times?' Jesus said to him, 'I do not say to you seven times, but seventy times seven.'

Matthew 18.21–22

Love one another.

Romans 12.10

Fraud

You shall not have in your bag two kinds of weights, a large and a small. You shall not have in your house two kinds of measures, a large and a small. A full and just weight you shall have, a full and just measure you shall have; that your days may be prolonged in the land which the Lord your God gives you.

Deuteronomy 25.13–15

A false balance is an abomination to the
        Lord,
    but a just weight is his delight.

Proverbs 11.1

Bread gained by deceit is sweet to a man,
    but afterward his mouth will be full of
        gravel.

Proverbs 20.17

The getting of treasures by a lying tongue
    is a fleeting vapour and a snare of death.

Proverbs 21.6

Shall I acquit the man with wicked scales
    and with a bag of deceitful weights?

Micah 6.11

Free Will

For this reason the Father loves me, because I lay down my life, that I may take it again. No one takes it from me, but I lay it down of my own accord. I have power to lay it down, and I have power to take it again; this charge I have received from my Father.

John 10.17–18

Freedom

Rise up early in the morning and stand before Pharaoh, and say to him, 'Thus says the Lord, the God of the Hebrews, "Let my people go, that they may serve me." '

Exodus 9.13

Proclaim liberty throughout the land to all its inhabitants.

Leviticus 25.10

Is not this the fast that I choose:
to loose the bonds of wickedness,
to undo the thongs of the yoke,
to let the oppressed go free,
and to break every yoke?

Isaiah 58.6

The Lord has anointed me . . .
to proclaim liberty to the captives,
and the opening of the prison to those
who are bound.

Isaiah 61.1

You will know the truth, and the truth will make you free.

John 8.32

If the Son makes you free, you will be free indeed.

John 8.36

Let it be known to you therefore, brethren, that through this man forgiveness of sins is proclaimed to you, and by him every one that believes is freed from everything from which you could not be freed by the law of Moses.

Acts 13.38−39

You . . . having been set free from sin, have become slaves of righteousness.

Romans 6.17−18

Now that you have been set free from sin and have become slaves of God, the return you get is sanctification and its end, eternal life.

Romans 6.22

The law of the Spirit of life in Christ Jesus has set me free from the law of sin and death.

Romans 8.2

The creation itself will be set free from its bondage to decay and obtain the glorious liberty of the children of God.

Romans 8.21

He who was called in the Lord as a slave is a freedman of the Lord. Likewise he who was free when called is a slave of Christ.

1 Corinthians 7.22

Take care lest this liberty of yours somehow become a stumbling block to the weak.

1 Corinthians 8.9

Though I am free from all men I have made myself a slave to all, that I might win the more.

1 Corinthians 9.19

Where the Spirit of the Lord is, there is freedom.

2 Corinthians 3.17

For freedom Christ has set us free; stand fast therefore, and do not submit again to a yoke of slavery.

Galatians 5.1

You were called to freedom, brethren; only do not use your freedom as an opportunity for the flesh.

Galatians 5.13

In him we have redemption through his blood, the forgiveness of our trespasses.

Ephesians 1.7

He who looks into the perfect law, the law of liberty, and perseveres, being no hearer that forgets but a doer that acts, he shall be blessed in his doing.

James 1.25

So speak and so act as those who are to be judged under the law of liberty.

James 2.12

Live as free men, yet without using your freedom as a pretext for evil; but live as servants of God.

1 Peter 2.16

Friendship

See also **Companionship**

Very pleasant have you been to me;
  your love to me was wonderful, passing
    the love of women.

2 Samuel 1.26

A whisperer separates close friends.

Proverbs 16.28

He who forgives an offence seeks love,
  but he who repeats a matter alienates a
    friend.

Proverbs 17.9

A friend loves at all times,
  and a brother is born for adversity.

Proverbs 17.17

There are friends who pretend to be
    friends,
  but there is a friend who sticks closer
    than a brother.

Proverbs 18.24

Wealth brings many new friends.

Proverbs 19.4

Make no friendship with a man given to
    anger,
  nor go with a wrathful man,
lest you learn his ways
  and entangle yourself in a snare.

Proverbs 22.24−25

Faithful are the wounds of a friend;
  profuse are the kisses of an enemy.

Proverbs 27.6

Your friend, and your father's friend, do
    not forsake;
  and do not go to your brother's house in
    the day of your calamity.
Better is a neighbour who is near than a
    brother who is far away.

Proverbs 27.10

Greater love has no man than this, that a
man lay down his life for his friends.

John 15.13

You are my friends if you do what I
command you. No longer do I call you
servants, for the servant does not know
what his master is doing; but I have called
you friends, for all that I have heard from
my Father I have made known to you.

John 15.14−15

Welcome one another, therefore, as Christ
has welcomed you, for the glory of God.

Romans 15.7

Do you not know that friendship with the
world is enmity with God?

James 4.4

Futility

My days are swifter than a weaver's
    shuttle,
  and come to their end without hope.

Job 7.6

Surely every man stands as a mere breath!
  Surely man goes about as a shadow!

Psalms 39.5−6

Men of low estate are but a breath,
  men of high estate are a delusion;
in the balances they go up;
  they are together lighter than a breath.

Psalms 62.9

The years of our life are threescore and
    ten,
  or even by reason of strength fourscore;
yet their span is but toil and trouble;
  they are soon gone, and we fly away.

Psalms 90.10

All is vanity.
  What does man gain by all the toil
  at which he toils under the sun?

Ecclesiastes 1.2−3

I have seen everything that is done under
the sun; and behold, all is vanity and a
striving after wind.

Ecclesiastes 1.14

I said of laughter, 'It is mad,' and of
pleasure, 'What use is it?'

Ecclesiastes 2.2

Who knows what is good for man while he lives the few days of his vain life, which he passes like a shadow?

Ecclesiastes 6.12

You should turn from these vain things to a living God.

Acts 14.15

This I affirm and testify in the Lord, that you must no longer live as the Gentiles do, in the futility of their minds.

Ephesians 4.17

Let no one deceive you with empty words.

Ephesians 5.6

G

Gain

Such are the ways of all who get gain by
   violence;
   it takes away the life of its possessors.

Proverbs 1.19

For the gain from it [wisdom] is better than
   gain from silver
   and its profit better than gold.

Proverbs 3.14

He who is greedy for unjust gain makes
trouble for his household.

Proverbs 15.27

For what will it profit a man, if he gains
the whole world and forfeits his life?

Matthew 16.26

If any one teaches otherwise . . . he has a
morbid craving for controversy and for disputes about words, which produce envy,
dissension, slander, base suspicions, and
wrangling among men who are depraved in
mind and bereft of the truth, imagining that
godliness is a means of gain.

1 Timothy 6.3−5

Generosity

See also **Altruism, Charity**

If there is among you a poor man, one of
your brethren, in any of your towns within your land which the Lord your God gives
you, you shall not harden your heart or
shut your hand against your poor brother,
but you shall open your hand to him, and
lend him sufficient for his need, whatever it
may be.

Deuteronomy 15.7−8

For the poor will never cease out of the
land; therefore I command you, You shall
open wide your hand to your brother, to
the needy and to the poor, in the land.

Deuteronomy 15.11

Every man shall give as he is able,
according to the blessing of the Lord your
God which he has given you.

Deuteronomy 16.17

The wicked borrows, and cannot pay back,
   but the righteous is generous and gives.

Psalms 37.21

He has distributed freely, he has given to
   the poor;
   his righteousness endures for ever;
   his horn is exalted in honour.

Psalms 112.9

The eyes of all look to thee,
   and thou givest them their food in due
      season.
Thou openest thy hand,
   thou satisfiest the desire of every living
      thing.

Psalms 145.15−16

A man who is kind benefits himself,
   but a cruel man hurts himself.

Proverbs 11.17

A liberal man will be enriched,
   and one who waters will himself be
      watered.

Proverbs 11.25

Many seek the favour of a generous man,
   and every one is a friend to a man who
      gives gifts.

Proverbs 19.6

He who is kind to the poor lends to the
  Lord,
  and he will repay him for his deed.

Proverbs 19.17

He who has a bountiful eye will be
  blessed,
  for he shares his bread with the poor.

Proverbs 22.9

Cast your bread upon the waters,
  for you will find it after many days.
Give a portion to seven, or even to eight,
  for you know not what evil may happen
    on earth.

Ecclesiastes 11.1–2

If any one forces you to go one mile, go
with him two miles. Give to him who begs
from you, and do not refuse him who would
borrow from you.

Matthew 5.41–42

Give to him who begs from you, and do
not refuse him who would borrow from
you.

Matthew 6.42

You received without paying, give without
pay.

Matthew 10.8

If you would be perfect, go, sell what you
possess and give to the poor, and you will
have treasure in heaven.

Matthew 19.21

Then the King will say to those at his right
hand, 'Come, O blessed of my Father, inherit the kingdom prepared for you from
the foundation of the world; for I was
hungry and you gave me food, I was thirsty
and you gave me drink, I was a stranger
and you welcomed me, I was naked and
you clothed me, I was sick and you visited
me, I was in prison and you came to me
. . . Truly, I say to you, as you did it to one
of the least of these my brethren, you did it
to me.'

Matthew 25.34–36,40

Give to every one who begs from you; and
of him who takes away your goods do not
ask them again.

Luke 6.30

Give, and it will be given to you; good
measure, pressed down, shaken together,
running over, will be put into your lap. For
the measure you give will be the measure
you get back.

Luke 6.38

He looked up and saw the rich putting
their gifts into the treasury; and he saw a
poor widow put in two copper coins. And
he said, 'Truly I tell you, this poor widow
has put in more than all of them; for they
all contributed out of their abundance, but
she out of her poverty put in all the living
that she had.'

Luke 21.1–4

In all things I have shown you that by so
toiling one must help the weak, remember-
ing the words of the Lord Jesus, how he
said, 'It is more blessed to give than to
receive.'

Acts 20.35

Their abundance of joy and their extreme
poverty have overflowed in a wealth of
liberality on their part.

2 Corinthians 8.2

For you know the grace of our Lord Jesus
Christ, that though he was rich, yet for your
sake he became poor, so that by his poverty
you might become rich.

2 Corinthians 8.9

The point is this: he who sows sparingly
will also reap sparingly, and he who sows
bountifully will also reap bountifully. Each
one must do as he has made up his mind,
not reluctantly or under compulsion, for
God loves a cheerful giver. And God is able
to provide you with every blessing in abundance, so that you may always have enough
of everything and may provide in abundance for every good work. As it is written,
'He scatters abroad, he gives to the poor;
  his righteousness endures for ever.'

He who supplies seed to the sower and bread for food will supply and multiply your resources and increase the harvest of your righteousness. You will be enriched in every way for great generosity, which through us will produce thanksgiving to God.

2 Corinthians 9.6−11

God . . . gives grace to the humble.

James 4.6

Geniality

See also **Courtesy**

Good sense makes a man slow to anger,
  and it is his glory to overlook an offence.

Proverbs 19.11

It is an honour for a man to keep aloof
    from strife;
  but every fool will be quarrelling.

Proverbs 20.3

Gentleness

See also **Comfort**

Thou hast given me the shield of thy
    salvation,
  and thy right hand supported me,
  and thy help made me great.

Psalms 18.35

He will feed his flock like a shepherd,
  he will gather the lambs in his arms,
he will carry them in his bosom,
  and gently lead those that are with
    young.

Isaiah 40.11

Take my yoke upon you, and learn from me; for I am gentle and lowly in heart, and you will find rest for your souls. For my yoke is easy, and my burden is light.

Matthew 11.29−30

By the meekness and gentleness of Christ.

2 Corinthians 10.1

But the fruit of the Spirit is love, joy, peace, patience, kindness, goodness, faithfulness, gentleness, self-control; against such there is no law.

Galatians 5.22−23

Brethren, if a man is overtaken in any trespass, you who are spiritual should restore him in a spirit of gentleness.

Galations 6.1

Let all bitterness and wrath and anger and clamour and slander be put away from you, with all malice, and be kind to one another, tenderhearted, forgiving one another, as God in Christ forgave you.

Ephesians 4.31−32

And the Lord's servant must not be quarrelsome but kindly to every one, an apt teacher, forbearing, correcting his opponents with gentleness.

2 Timothy 2.24−25

But the wisdom from above is first pure, then peaceable, gentle, open to reason, full of mercy and good fruits, without uncertainty or insincerity.

James 3.17

Let not yours be the outward adorning with braiding of hair, decoration of gold, and wearing of fine clothing, but let it be the hidden person of the heart with the imperishable jewel of a gentle and quiet spirit, which in God's sight is very precious.

1 Peter 3.3−4

Gifts

For jealousy makes a man furious,
  and he will not spare when he takes
    revenge.
He will accept no compensation,
  nor be appeased though you multiply
    gifts.

Proverbs 6.34−35

A man's gift makes room for him
  and brings him before great men.

Proverbs 18.16

Many seek the favour of a generous man, and every one is a friend to a man who gives gifts.

Proverbs 19.6

A gift in secret averts anger.

Proverbs 21.14

If you then, who are evil, know how to give good gifts to your children, how much more will your Father who is in heaven give good things to those who ask him!

Matthew 7.11

These signs will accompany those who believe: in my name they will cast out demons; they will speak in new tongues; they will pick up serpents, and if they drink any deadly thing, it will not hurt them; they will lay their hands on the sick, and they will recover.

Mark 16.17—18

For the gifts and the call of God are irrevocable.

Romans 11.29

Having gifts that differ according to the grace given to us, let us use them: if prophecy, in proportion to our faith; if service, in our serving; he who teaches, in his teaching.

Romans 12.6—7

Now there are varieties of gifts, but the same Spirit; and there are varieties of service, but the same Lord; and there are varieties of working, but it is the same God who inspires them all in every one.

1 Corinthians 12.4—6

But grace was given to each of us according to the measure of Christ's gift. Therefore it is said,
'When he ascended on high he led a host of captives,
and he gave gifts to men.' . . .
to equip the saints for the work of ministry, for building up the body of Christ.

Ephesians 4.7—8,12

Every good endowment and every perfect gift is from above, coming down from the Father of lights with whom there is no variation or shadow due to change.

James 1.17

As each has received a gift, employ it for one another, as good stewards of God's varied grace: whoever speaks, as one who utters oracles of God; whoever renders service, as one who renders it by the strength which God supplies; in order that in everything God may be glorified through Jesus Christ.

1 Peter 4.10—11

Giving

The measure you give will be the measure you get, and still more will be given you.

Mark 4.24

Gladness

See also **Joy**

Be glad in the Lord, and rejoice,
O righteous,
and shout for joy, all you upright in heart!

Psalms 32.11

But may all who seek thee
rejoice and be glad in thee.

Psalms 40.16

Let the righteous rejoice in the Lord,
and take refuge in him!
Let all the upright in heart glory!

Psalms 64.10

But let the righteous be joyful;
let them exult before God;
let them be jubilant with joy!

Psalms 68.3

The Lord reigns; let the earth rejoice;
let the many coastlands be glad!

Psalms 97.1

Make a joyful noise to the Lord,
all the lands!
Serve the Lord with gladness!
Come into his presence with singing!

Psalms 100.1—2

Anxiety in a man's heart weighs
    him down,
  but a good word makes him glad.

Proverbs 12.25

When the righteous triumph, there is great
glory.

Proverbs 28.12

But be glad and rejoice for ever
  in that which I create.

Isaiah 65.18

Fear not, O land;
  be glad and rejoice,
  for the Lord has done great things!

Joel 2.21

If a man has a hundred sheep, and one of
them has gone astray, does he not leave the
ninety-nine on the mountains and go in
search of the one that went astray? And if
he finds it, truly, I say to you, he rejoices
over it more than over the ninety-nine that
never went astray.

Matthew 18.12–13

Yet he did not leave himself without
witness, for he did good and gave you from
heaven rains and fruitful seasons, satisfying
your hearts with food and gladness.

Acts 14.17

Rejoice in your hope, be patient in tribulation, be constant in prayer.

Romans 12.12

Thou hast loved righteousness and hated
  lawlessness;
therefore God, thy God, has anointed thee
  with the oil of gladness beyond thy
  comrades.

Hebrews 1.9

But rejoice in so far as you share Christ's
sufferings, that you may also rejoice and be
glad when his glory is revealed.

1 Peter 4.13

For the Lord our God the Almighty reigns.
Let us rejoice and exult and give him the
  glory.

Revelation 19.6–7

Gloating

He who mocks the poor insults his Maker;
  he who is glad at calamity will not go
  unpunished.

Proverbs 17.5

Glory

Ascribe to the Lord, O families of the
  peoples,
  ascribe to the Lord glory and strength!
Ascribe to the Lord the glory due his name.

1 Chronicles 16.28–29

The glory of the Lord filled the temple.
And the priests could not enter the house of
the Lord, because the glory of the Lord
filled the Lord's house.

2 Chronicles 7.1–2

God is clothed with terrible majesty.

Job 37.22

But thou, O Lord, art a shield about me,
  my glory, and the lifter of my head.

Psalms 3.3

On God rests my deliverance and my
    honour;
  my mighty rock, my refuge is God.

Psalms 62.7

Surely his salvation is at hand for those
    who fear him,
  that glory may dwell in our land.

Psalms 85.9

Glorious things are spoken of you.

Psalms 87.3

Declare his glory among the nations,
  his marvellous works among all the
    peoples!

Psalms 96.3

Glory in his holy name.

Psalms 105.3

The glory of young men is their strength.

Proverbs 20.29

Give glory to the Lord your God
  before he brings darkness,
before your feet stumble
  on the twilight mountains.

Jeremiah 13.16

Behold, the glory of the God of Israel
came from the east; and the sound of his
coming was like the sound of many waters;
and the earth shone with his glory.

Ezekiel 43.2

The more they increased,
  the more they sinned against me;
  I will change their glory into shame.

Hosea 4.7

And the Word became flesh and dwelt
among us, full of grace and truth; we have
beheld his glory, glory as of the only Son
from the Father.

John 1.14

He who speaks on his own authority seeks
his own glory; but he who seeks the glory of
him who sent him is true, and in him there
is no falsehood.

John 7.18

Did I not tell you that if you would
believe you would see the glory of God?

John 11.40

Father, the hour has come; glorify thy Son
that the Son may glorify thee.

John 17.1

The glory which thou hast given me I have
given to them, that they may be one even as
we are one.

John 17.22

Glory and honour and peace for every one
who does good.

Romans 2.10

But we impart a secret and hidden wisdom
of God, which God decreed before the ages
for our glorification.

1 Corinthians 2.7

And we all, with unveiled face, beholding
the glory of the Lord, are being changed
into his likeness from one degree of glory to
another; for this comes from the Lord who
is the Spirit.

2 Corinthians 3.18

For this slight momentary affliction is
preparing for us an eternal weight of glory
beyond all comparison.

2 Corinthians 4.17

When Christ who is our life appears, then
you also will appear with him in glory.

Colossians 3.4

Lead a life worthy of God, who calls you
into his own kingdom and glory.

1 Thessalonians 2.12

For it was fitting that he, for whom and by
whom all things exist, in bringing many sons
to glory, should make the pioneer of their
salvation perfect through suffering.

Hebrews 2.10

Through him you have confidence in God,
who raised him from the dead and gave him
glory, so that your faith and hope are in
God.

1 Peter 1.21

All flesh is like grass
  and all its glory like the flower of grass.
  The grass withers, and the flower falls.

1 Peter 1.24

Worthy art thou, our Lord and God,
  to receive glory and honour and power,
  for thou didst create all things,
  and by thy will they existed and were
    created.

Revelation 4.11

To him who sits upon the throne and to
the Lamb be blessing and honour and glory
and might for ever and ever!

Revelation 5.13

Gluttony

See also **Greed**

And put a knife to your throat
  if you are a man given to appetite.

> *Proverbs 23.2*

Do not desire his delicacies,
  for they are deceptive food.

> *Proverbs 23.3*

Be not among winebibbers,
  or among gluttonous eaters of meat;
for the drunkard and the glutton will come
    to poverty,
  and drowsiness will clothe a man with
    rags.

> *Proverbs 23.20–21*

If you have found honey, eat only enough
    for you,
  lest you be sated with it and vomit it.

> *Proverbs 25.16*

He who is sated loathes honey,
  but to one who is hungry everything
    bitter is sweet.

> *Proverbs 27.7*

Woe to you, O land, when your king is a
    child,
  and your princes feast in the morning!

> *Ecclesiastes 10.16*

Let us eat and drink,
  for tomorrow we die.

> *Isaiah 22.13*

For such persons do not serve our Lord
Christ, but their own appetites.

> *Romans 16.18*

Their end is destruction, their god is the
belly, and they glory in their shame, with
minds set on earthly things.

> *Philippians 3.19*

These are blemishes on your love feasts, as
they boldly carouse together, looking after
themselves.

> *Jude 12*

Goal

I keep the Lord always before me;
  because he is at my right hand, I shall not
    be moved.

> *Psalms 16.8*

Let your eyes look directly forward,
  and your gaze be straight before you
. . . Do not swerve to the right or to
    the left;
  turn your foot away from evil.

> *Proverbs 4.25,27*

But I do not account my life of any value
nor as precious to myself, if only I may
accomplish my course and the ministry
which I received from the Lord Jesus, to
testify to the gospel of the grace of God.

> *Acts 20.24*

Do you not know that in a race all the
runners compete, but only one receives the
prize? So run that you may obtain it.

> *1 Corinthians 9.24–25*

And he died for all, that those who live
might live no longer for themselves but for
him who for their sake died and was raised.

> *2 Corinthians 5.15*

Not that I have already obtained this or
am already perfect; but I press on to make
it my own, because Christ Jesus has made
me his own.

> *Philippians 3.12*

If then you have been raised with Christ,
seek the things that are above, where Christ
is, seated at the right hand of God.

> *Colossians 3.1*

Godlessness

See also **Blasphemy**

Know therefore that the Lord your God is
God, the faithful God who keeps covenant
and steadfast love with those who love him
and keep his commandments, to a thousand
generations, and requites to their face those
who hate him.

> *Deuteronomy 7.9–10*

The Lord declares '. . . those who honour me I will honour, and those who despise me shall be lightly esteemed.'

1 Samuel 2.30

Can papyrus grow where there is
    no marsh?
  Can reeds flourish where there is no
    water?
While yet in flower and not cut down,
  they wither before any other plant.
Such are the paths of all who forget God;
  the hope of the godless man shall perish.
His confidence breaks in sunder,
  and his trust is a spider's web.
He leans against his house, but it does not
    stand;
  he lays hold of it, but it does not endure.
He thrives before the sun,
  and his shoots spread over his garden.
His roots twine about the stoneheap;
  he lives among the rocks.

Job 8.11–17

For the wicked boasts of the desires of his
    heart,
  and the man greedy for gain curses and
    renounces the Lord.
In the pride of his countenance the wicked
    does not seek him;
  all his thoughts are, 'There is no God.'

Psalms 10.3–4

Because they do not regard the works of
    the Lord,
  or the work of his hands,
he will break them down and build them up
    no more.

Psalms 28.5

'Woe to the rebellious children,' says the
    Lord,
  'who carry out a plan, but not mine;
and who make a league, but not of my
    spirit,
  that they may add sin to sin.'

Isaiah 30.1

But I know that you have not the love of God within you. I have come in my Father's name, and you do not receive me; if another comes in his own name, him you will receive.

John 5.42–43

He who hates me hates my Father also.

John 15.23

For the wrath of God is revealed from heaven against all ungodliness and wickedness of men who by their wickedness suppress the truth.

Romans 1.18

So they are without excuse; for although they knew God they did not honour him as God or give thanks to him, but they became futile in their thinking and their senseless minds were darkened.

Romans 1.20–21

Now this I affirm and testify in the Lord, that you must no longer live as the Gentiles do, in the futility of their minds; they are darkened in their understanding, alienated from the life of God because of the ignorance that is in them, due to their hardness of heart.

Ephesians 4.17–18

For if we sin deliberately after receiving the knowledge of the truth, there no longer remains a sacrifice for sins.

Hebrews 10.26

He did not spare the ancient world, but preserved Noah, a herald of righteousness, with seven other persons, when he brought a flood upon the world of the ungodly.

2 Peter 2.5

In the last time there will be scoffers, following their own ungodly passions.

Jude 18

Godliness

Man does not live by bread alone, but . . . man lives by everything that proceeds out of the mouth of the Lord.

Deuteronomy 8.3

But know that the Lord has set apart the
    godly for himself;
  the Lord hears when I call to him.

Psalms 4.3

First of all, then, I urge that supplications, prayers, intercessions, and thanksgivings be made for all men, for kings and all who are in high positions, that we may lead a quiet and peaceable life, godly and respectful in every way. This is good, and it is acceptable in the sight of God our Saviour.

1 Timothy 2.1−3

Have nothing to do with godless and silly myths. Train yourself in godliness; for while bodily training is of some value, godliness is of value in every way, as it holds promise for the present life and also for the life to come.

1 Timothy 4.7−8

There is great gain in godliness with contentment.

1 Timothy 6.6

But as for you, man of God, shun all this; aim at righteousness, godliness, faith, love, steadfastness, gentleness.

1 Timothy 6.11

For the grace of God has appeared for the salvation of all men, training us to renounce irreligion and worldly passions, and to live sober, upright, and godly lives in this world.

Titus 2.11−12

May grace and peace be multiplied to you in the knowledge of God and of Jesus our Lord.

2 Peter 1.2

Make every effort to supplement your faith with virtue, and virtue with knowledge, and knowledge with self-control, and self-control with steadfastness, and steadfastness with godliness.

2 Peter 1.5−6

Goodness

See also **Righteousness, Virtue**

Surely goodness and mercy shall follow me all the days of my life.

Psalms 23.6

Depart from evil, and do good; seek peace, and pursue it.

Psalms 34.14

Trust in the Lord, and do good.

Psalms 37.3

So you will walk in the way of good men and keep to the paths of the righteous.

Proverbs 2.20

Misfortune pursues sinners, but prosperity rewards the righteous.

Proverbs 13.21

To do righteousness and justice is more acceptable to the Lord than sacrifice.

Proverbs 21.3

'I will feast the soul of the priests with abundance, and my people shall be satisfied with my goodness,' says the Lord.

Jeremiah 31.14

Seek good, and not evil, that you may live.

Amos 5.14

So, every sound tree bears good fruit, but the bad tree bears evil fruit.

Matthew 7.17

Why do you ask me about what is good? One there is who is good.

Matthew 19.17

No one is good but God alone.

Mark 10.18

And if you do good to those who do good to you, what credit is that to you? For even sinners do the same . . . But love your enemies, and do good, and lend, expecting nothing in return; and your reward will be great, and you will be sons of the Most High.

Luke 6.33,35

The good man out of the good treasure of his heart produces good.

Luke 6.45

Do you not know that God's kindness is meant to lead you to repentance?

Romans 2.4

Let love be genuine; hate what is evil, hold fast to what is good.

Romans 12.9

Do not be overcome by evil, but overcome evil with good.

Romans 12.21

I would have you wise as to what is good and guileless as to what is evil.

Romans 16.19

So then, as we have opportunity, let us do good to all men, and especially to those who are of the household of faith.

Galatians 6.10

For we are his workmanship, created in Christ Jesus for good works, which God prepared beforehand, that we should walk in them.

Ephesians 2.10

For the fruit of light is found in all that is good and right and true.

Ephesians 5.9

Whatever good any one does, he will receive the same again from the Lord.

Ephesians 6.8

See that none of you repays evil for evil, but always seek to do good to one another and to all.

1 Thessalonians 5.15

To this end we always pray for you, that our God may make you worthy of his call, and may fulfil every good resolve and work of faith by his power.

2 Thessalonians 1.11

I desire . . . that those who have believed in God may be careful to apply themselves to good deeds; these are excellent and profitable to men.

Titus 3.8

Now may the God of peace . . . equip you with everything good that you may do his will, working in you that which is pleasing in his sight.

Hebrews 13.20−21

Now who is there to harm you if you are zealous for what is right? But even if you do suffer for righteousness' sake, you will be blessed.

1 Peter 3.13−14

Beloved, do not imitate evil but imitate good.

3 John 11

Gospel

See also **Bible, Evangelism, Scripture**

And this gospel of the kingdom will be preached throughout the whole world, as a testimony to all nations; and then the end will come.

Matthew 24.14

The time is fulfilled, and the kingdom of God is at hand; repent, and believe in the gospel.

Mark 1.15

For I am not ashamed of the gospel: it is the power of God for salvation to every one who has faith, to the Jew first and also to the Greek.

Romans 1.16

How beautiful are the feet of those who preach good news!

Romans 10.15

In the same way, the Lord commanded that those who proclaim the gospel should get their living by the gospel.

1 Corinthians 9.14

And even if our gospel is veiled, it is veiled only to those who are perishing. In their case the god of this world has blinded the minds of the unbelievers, to keep them from seeing the light of the gospel of the glory of Christ, who is the likeness of God.

2 Corinthians 4.3−4

All this is from God, who gave us the ministry of reconciliation.

2 Corinthians 5.18

If any one is preaching to you a gospel contrary to that which you received, let him be accursed.

Galatians 1.9

Only let your manner of life be worthy of the gospel of Christ.

Philippians 1.27

The word of the truth, the gospel . . . has come to you, as indeed in the whole world it is bearing fruit and growing.

Colossians 1.6

Continue in the faith, stable and steadfast, not shifting from the hope of the gospel which you heard.

Colossians 1.23

Christ Jesus . . . abolished death and brought life and immortality to light through the gospel.

2 Timothy 1.10

The grass withers, and the flower falls, but the word of the Lord abides for ever.
   That word is the good news which was preached to you.

1 Peter 1.24−25

For this is why the gospel was preached even to the dead, that though judged in the flesh like men, they might live in the spirit like God.

1 Peter 4.6

Then I saw another angel flying in midheaven, with an eternal gospel to proclaim to those who dwell on earth, to every nation and tribe and tongue and people; and he said with a loud voice, 'Fear God and give him glory . . .'

Revelation 14.6−7

Gossip

See also **Slander**

When words are many, transgression is
   not lacking,
   but he who restrains his lips is prudent.

Proverbs 10.19

He who goes about as a talebearer reveals
   secrets,
   but he who is trustworthy in spirit keeps a
   thing hidden.

Proverbs 11.13

And a whisperer separates close friends.

Proverbs 16.28

The words of a whisperer are like delicious morsels.

Proverbs 18.8

He who goes about gossiping reveals
   secrets;
   therefore do not associate with one who
   speaks foolishly.

Proverbs 20.19

The north wind brings forth rain;
   and a backbiting tongue, angry looks.

Proverbs 25.23

Let every one beware of his neighbour,
   and put no trust in any brother;
for every brother is a supplanter,
   and every neighbour goes about as a
   slanderer.

Jeremiah 9.4

I tell you, on the day of judgment men will render account for every careless word they utter.

Matthew 12.36

Bid the older women likewise to be reverent in behaviour, not to be slanderers or slaves to drink.

Titus 2.3

No human being can tame the tongue — a restless evil, full of deadly poison.

James 3.8

Government

When one rules justly over men,
  ruling in the fear of God,
he dawns on them like the morning light.

2 Samuel 23.3–4

For dominion belongs to the Lord,
  and he rules over the nations.

Psalms 22.28

By me kings reign,
  and rulers decree what is just;
by me princes rule,
  and nobles govern the earth.

Proverbs 8.15–16

Where there is no guidance, a people falls;
  but in an abundance of counsellors there
    is safety.

Proverbs 11.14

When the righteous are in authority, the
    people rejoice;
  but when the wicked rule, the people
    groan.

Proverbs 29.2

And the government will be upon his
    shoulder,
  and his name will be called
'Wonderful Counsellor, Mighty God,
  Everlasting Father, Prince of Peace.'
Of the increase of his government and of
    peace
  there will be no end.

Isaiah 9.6–7

Render therefore to Caesar the things that
are Caesar's, and to God the things
that are God's.

Matthew 22.21

Let every person be subject to the governing authorities. For there is no authority
except from God, and those that exist have
been instituted by God. Therefore he who
resists the authorities resists what God has
appointed, and those who resist will incur
judgment. For rulers are not a terror to
good conduct, but to bad. Would you have
no fear of him who is in authority? Then do
what is good, and you will receive his
approval, for he is God's servant for your
good.

Romans 13.1–4

Pay all of them their dues, taxes to whom
taxes are due, revenue to whom revenue is
due, respect to whom respect is due,
honour to whom honour is due.

Romans 13.7

Remind them to be submissive to rulers
and authorities, to be obedient.

Titus 3.1

Remember your leaders, those who spoke
to you the word of God.

Hebrews 13.7

Obey your leaders and submit to them; for
they are keeping watch over your souls, as
men who will have to give account.

Hebrews 13.17

Be subject for the Lord's sake to every
human institution, whether it be to the
emperor as supreme, or to governors as
sent by him to punish those who do wrong
and to praise those who do right. For it is
God's will that by doing right you should
put to silence the ignorance of foolish men.

1 Peter 2.13–15

Grace

See also **Chosen**

Moses said, 'I pray thee, show me thy
glory.' And he said, 'I will make all my
goodness pass before you, and will proclaim
before you my name "The Lord"; and I will
be gracious to whom I will be gracious, and
will show mercy on whom I will show
mercy.'

Exodus 33.18–19

The Lord make his face to shine upon
you, and be gracious to you.

Numbers 6.2.

It was not because you were more in
number than any other people that the
Lord set his love upon you and chose you

for you were the fewest of all peoples; but it is because the Lord loves you.

> *Deuteronomy 7.7–9*

For the Lord God is a sun and shield;
  he bestows favour and honour.
No good thing does the Lord withhold
  from those who walk uprightly.

> *Psalms 84.11*

The Lord is merciful and gracious,
  slow to anger and abounding in steadfast
  love . . .
He does not deal with us according
  to our sins,
  nor requite us according to our iniquities.

> *Psalms 103.8,10*

Therefore the Lord waits to be gracious to
  you;
  therefore he exalts himself to show mercy
  to you.
For the Lord is a God of justice;
  blessed are all those who wait for him.

> *Isaiah 30.18*

We do not present our supplications before thee on the ground of our righteousness, but on the ground of thy great mercy.

> *Daniel 9.18*

Like grapes in the wilderness,
  I found Israel.
Like the first fruit on the fig tree,
  in its first season.

> *Hosea 9.10*

And from his fulness have we all received, grace upon grace. For the law was given through Moses; grace and truth came through Jesus Christ.

> *John 1.16–17*

We believe that we shall be saved through the grace of the Lord Jesus.

> *Acts 15.11*

And now I commend you to God and to the word of his grace, which is able to build you up and to give you the inheritance among all those who are sanctified.

> *Acts 20.32*

Since all have sinned and fall short of the glory of God, they are justified by his grace as a gift, through the redemption which is in Christ Jesus.

> *Romans 3.23–24*

Through him we have obtained access to this grace in which we stand, and we rejoice in our hope of sharing the glory of God.

> *Romans 5.2*

But the free gift is not like the trespass. For if many died through one man's trespass, much more have the grace of God and the free gift in the grace of that one man Jesus Christ abounded for many. And the free gift is not like the effect of that one man's sin. For the judgment following one trespass brought condemnation, but the free gift following many trespasses brings justification.

> *Romans 5.15–16*

As sin reigned in death, grace also might reign through righteousness to eternal life through Jesus Christ our Lord.

> *Romans 5.21*

For sin will have no dominion over you, since you are not under law but under grace.

> *Romans 6.14*

So it depends not upon man's will or exertion, but upon God's mercy. For the scripture says to Pharaoh, 'I have raised you up for the very purpose of showing my power in you, so that my name may be proclaimed in all the earth.'

> *Romans 9.16–17*

So too at the present time there is a remnant, chosen by grace. But if it is by grace, it is no longer on the basis of works; otherwise grace would no longer be grace.

> *Romans 11.5–6*

Working together with him, then, we entreat you not to accept the grace of God in vain.

> *2 Corinthians 6.1*

And God is able to provide you with every blessing in abundance, so that you may always have enough of everything and may provide in abundance for every good work.

2 Corinthians 9.8

Thanks be to God for his inexpressible gift!

2 Corinthians 9.15

My grace is sufficient for you, for my power is made perfect in weakness.

2 Corinthians 12.9

The grace of the Lord Jesus Christ and the love of God and the fellowship of the Holy Spirit be with you all.

2 Corinthians 13.14

Blessed be God the Father of our Lord Jesus Christ, who has blessed us in Christ with every spiritual blessing in the heavenly places . . . his glorious grace which he freely bestowed on us in the Beloved. In him we have redemption through his blood, the forgiveness of our trespasses, according to the riches of his grace which he lavished upon us.

Ephesians 1.3,6−8

By grace you have been saved.

Ephesians 2.6

For by grace you have been saved through faith; and this is not your own doing, it is the gift of God.

Ephesians 2.8

But grace was given to each of us according to the measure of Christ's gift.

Ephesians 4.7

Grace be with all who love our Lord Jesus Christ with love undying.

Ephesians 6.24

Now may our Lord Jesus Christ himself, and God our Father, who loved us and gave us eternal comfort and good hope through grace, comfort your hearts and establish them in every good work and word.

2 Thessalonians 2.16−17

God . . . who saved us and called us with a holy calling, not in virtue of our works but in virtue of his own purpose and the grace which he gave us in Christ Jesus ages ago.

2 Timothy 1.9

Be strong in the grace that is in Christ Jesus.

2 Timothy 2.1

For the grace of God has appeared for the salvation of all men.

Titus 2.11

But when the goodness and loving kindness of God our Saviour appeared, he saved us, not because of deeds done by us in righteousness, but in virtue of his own mercy, by the washing of regeneration and renewal in the Holy Spirit, which he poured out upon us richly through Jesus Christ our Saviour, so that we might be justified by his grace and become heirs in hope of eternal life.

Titus 3.4−7

Since . . . we have a great high priest who has passed through the heavens, Jesus, the Son of God, let us hold fast our confession . . . Let us . . . with confidence draw near to the throne of grace, that we may receive mercy and find grace to help in time of need.

Hebrews 4.14,16

Do not be led away by diverse and strange teachings; for it is well that the heart be strengthened by grace.

Hebrews 13.9

Therefore gird up your minds, be sober, set your hope fully upon the grace that is coming to you at the revelation of Jesus Christ.

1 Peter 1.13

Graciousness

A gracious woman gets honour.

Proverbs 11.16

Grandchildren

Grandchildren are the crown of the aged,
and the glory of sons is their fathers.

Proverbs 17.6

Gratitude

See also **Thankfulness**

And you shall eat and be full, and you
shall bless the Lord your God for the good
land he has given you.

Deuteronomy 8.10

O give thanks to the Lord, for he is good;
for his steadfast love endures for ever!

1 Chronicles 16.34

Offer to God a sacrifice of thanksgiving.

Psalms 50.14

It is good to give thanks to the Lord,
to sing praises to thy name, O Most
High;
to declare thy steadfast love in the morning,
and thy faithfulness by night.

Psalms 92.1–2

O sing to the Lord a new song,
for he has done marvellous things!

Psalms 98.1

Make a joyful noise to the Lord, all the
lands!
Serve the Lord with gladness!
Come into his presence with singing!

Psalms 100.1–2

Surely the righteous shall give thanks to
thy name.

Psalms 140.13

But thanks be to God, who gives us the
victory through our Lord Jesus Christ.

1 Corinthians 15.57

But thanks be to God, who in Christ
always leads us in triumph.

2 Corinthians 2.14

He who raised the Lord Jesus will raise us
also with Jesus and bring us with you into
his presence. For it is all for your sake, so
that as grace extends to more and more
people it may increase thanksgiving, to the
glory of God.

2 Corinthians 4.14–15

Be filled with the Spirit . . . singing . . .
with all your heart, always and for everything giving thanks in the name of our Lord
Jesus Christ to God the Father.

Ephesians 5.19–20

Have no anxiety about anything, but in
everything by prayer and supplication with
thanksgiving let your requests be made
known to God.

Philippians 4.6

May you be strengthened with all power,
according to his glorious might, for all
endurance and patience with joy, giving
thanks to the Father, who has qualified us
to share in the inheritance of the saints in
light.

Colossians 1.11–12

And let the peace of Christ rule in your
hearts, to which indeed you were called in
the one body. And be thankful.

Colossians 3.15

Give thanks in all circumstances; for this is
the will of God in Christ Jesus for you.

1 Thessalonians 5.17–18

First of all, then, I urge that supplications,
prayers, intercessions, and thanksgivings be
made for all men.

1 Timothy 2.1

Gravity

See also **Sobriety**

So then let us not sleep, as others do, but
let us keep awake and be sober.

1 Thessalonians 5.6

Bid the older men be temperate, serious,
sensible, sound in faith, in love, and in
steadfastness.

Titus 2.2

The end of all things is at hand; therefore keep sane and sober for your prayers.

1 Peter 4.7

Greatness

Whoever would be great among you must be your servant, and whoever would be first among you must be your slave; even as the Son of man came not to be served but to serve, and to give his life as a ransom for many.

Matthew 20.26–28

Greed

You shall not covet your neighbour's house; you shall not covet your neighbour's wife, or his manservant, or his maidservant, or his ox, or his ass, or anything that is your neighbour's.

Exodus 20.17

For the wicked boasts of the desires of his heart,
and the man greedy for gain curses and renounces the Lord.

Psalms 10.3

Incline my heart to thy testimonies, and not to gain!

Psalms 119.36

The people curse him who holds back grain,
but a blessing is on the head of him who sells it.

Proverbs 11.26

He who is greedy for unjust gain makes trouble for his household.

Proverbs 15.27

All day long the wicked covets.

Proverbs 21.26

Sheol and Abaddon are never satisfied,
and never satisfied are the eyes of man.

Proverbs 27.20

A ruler who lacks understanding is a cruel oppressor; but he who hates unjust gain will prolong his days.

Proverbs 28.16

A greedy man stirs up strife.

Proverbs 28.25

When goods increase, they increase who eat them.

Ecclesiastes 5.11

Woe to those who join house to house,
who add field to field,
until there is no more room,
and you are made to dwell alone in the
midst of the land.

Isaiah 5.8

Woe to those who devise wickedness
and work evil upon their beds!
When the morning dawns, they perform it,
because it is in the power of their hand.
They covet fields, and seize them;
and houses, and take them away;
they oppress a man and his house,
a man and his inheritance.
Therefore thus says the Lord:
Behold, against this family I am devising
evil.

Micah 2.1–3

Woe to him who gets evil gain for his
house,
to set his nest on high,
to be safe from the reach of harm!

Habakkuk 2.9

Do not lay up for yourselves treasures or earth, where moth and rust consume and where thieves break in and steal, but lay up for yourselves treasure in heaven, where neither moth nor rust consumes and where thieves do not break in and steal. For where your treasure is, there will your heart be also.

Matthew 6.19–2

'Take heed, and beware of all covetousness; for a man's life does not consist in the abundance of his possessions.' And he told them a parable, saying, 'The land of rich man brought forth plentifully; and he thought to himself, "What shall I do, fo

I have nowhere to store my crops?" And he said, "I will do this: I will pull down my barns, and build larger ones; and there I will store all my grain and my goods. And I will say to my soul, Soul, you have ample goods laid up for many years; take your ease, eat, drink, be merry." But God said to him, "Fool! This night your soul is required of you; and the things you have prepared, whose will they be?" So is he who lays up treasure for himself, and is not rich toward God.'

Luke 12.15−21

But those who desire to be rich fall into temptation, into a snare, into many senseless and hurtful desires that plunge men into ruin and destruction. For the love of money is the root of all evils; it is through this craving that some have wandered away from the faith and pierced their hearts with many pangs.

1 Timothy 6.9−10

Keep your life free from love of money, and be content with what you have.

Hebrews 13.5

Greeting

See also **Welcome**

Greet one another with a holy kiss.

Romans 16.16

Grief

See also **Bereavement, Mourning, Sadness**

O that my vexation were weighed,
  and all my calamity laid in the balances!
For then it would be heavier than the sand
    of the sea;
  therefore my words have been rash.

Job 6.2−3

Be gracious to me, O Lord, for I am in
    distress;
  my eye is wasted from grief,
  my soul and my body also.

Psalms 31.9

The Lord is near to the brokenhearted,
  and saves the crushed in spirit.

Psalms 34.18

May those who sow in tears
  reap with shouts of joy!

Psalms 126.5

For in much wisdom is much vexation,
  and he who increases knowledge
    increases sorrow.

Ecclesiastes 1.18

You shall weep no more. He will surely be gracious to you at the sound of your cry; when he hears it, he will answer you.

Isaiah 30.19

Surely he has borne our griefs
  and carried our sorrows.

Isaiah 53.4

Blessed are those who mourn, for they shall be comforted.

Matthew 5.4

Blessed are you that weep now, for you shall laugh.

Luke 6.21

You will weep and lament, but the world will rejoice; you will be sorrowful, but your sorrow will turn into joy.

John 16.20

So you should . . . turn to forgive and comfort him, or he may be overwhelmed by excessive sorrow.

2 Corinthians 2.7

Let no evil talk come out of your mouths, but only such as is good for edifying . . . And do not grieve the Holy Spirit of God.

Ephesians 4.29−30

Obey your leaders and submit to them; for they are keeping watch over your souls, as men who will have to give account. Let them do this joyfully, and not sadly, for that would be of no advantage to you.

Hebrews 13.17

Be wretched and mourn and weep. Let your laughter be turned to mourning and your joy to dejection.

James 4.9

He will wipe away every tear from their eyes, and death shall be no more, neither shall there be mourning nor crying nor pain any more.

Revelation 21.4

Growth

See also **Development**

But I am like a green olive tree
  in the house of God.
I trust in the steadfast love of God
  for ever and ever.

Psalms 52.8

The righteous flourish like the palm tree,
  and grow like a cedar in Lebanon.

Psalms 92.12

The least one shall become a clan,
  and the smallest one a mighty nation.

Isaiah 60.22

The kingdom of God . . . is like a grain of mustard seed, which, when sown upon the ground, is the smallest of all the seeds on earth; yet when it is sown it grows up and becomes the greatest of all shrubs, and puts forth large branches, so that the birds of the air can make nests in its shade.

Mark 4.30–32

Jesus increased in wisdom and in stature, and in favour with God and man.

Luke 2.52

And now I commend you to God and to the word of his grace, which is able to build you up and to give you the inheritance among all those who are sanctified.

Acts 20.32

What you sow does not come to life unless it dies. And what you sow is not the body which is to be, but a bare kernel, perhaps of wheat or of some other grain. But God gives it a body as he has chosen . . . So is it with the resurrection of the dead. What is sown is perishable, what is raised is imperishable.

1 Corinthians 15.36–38,42

You are fellow citizens . . . of the household of God . . . Christ Jesus himself being the cornerstone, in whom the whole structure is joined together and grows into a holy temple in the Lord; in whom you also are built into it for a dwelling place of God in the Spirit.

Ephesians 2.19–22

Rather, speaking the truth in love, we are to grow up in every way into him who is the head, into Christ, from whom the whole body, joined and knit together by every joint with which it is supplied, when each part is working properly, makes bodily growth and upbuilds itself in love.

Ephesians 4.15–16

Although he was a Son, he learned obedience through what he suffered; and being made perfect he became the source of eternal salvation to all who obey him.

Hebrews 5.8–9

Like newborn babes, long for the pure spiritual milk, that by it you may grow up to salvation.

1 Peter 2.2

But grow in the grace and knowledge of our Lord and Saviour Jesus Christ.

2 Peter 3.18

Grudge

You shall not hate your brother in your heart, but you shall reason with your neighbour, lest you bear sin because of him. You shall not take vengeance or bear any grudge against the sons of your own people.

Leviticus 19.17–1̸

He who is estranged seeks pretexts
  to break out against all sound judgment.

Proverbs 18..

Grumbling

We must not put the Lord to the test, as some of them did and were destroyed by serpents; nor grumble, as some of them did and were destroyed by the Destroyer.

1 Corinthians 10.9−10

Guests

See also **Hospitality**

Do not eat the bread of a man who is
    stingy . . .
'Eat and drink!' he says to you;
but his heart is not with you.

Proverbs 23.6−7

Let your foot be seldom in your
    neighbour's house,
lest he become weary of you and hate
    you.

Proverbs 25.17

Bring the homeless poor into your house.

Isaiah 58.7

Whatever town or village you enter, find out who is worthy in it, and stay with him until you depart. As you enter the house, salute it. And if the house is worthy, let your peace come upon it; but if it is not worthy, let your peace return to you.

Matthew 10.11−13

But when you are invited, go and sit in the lowest place, so that when your host comes he may say to you, 'Friend, go up higher'; then you will be honoured in the presence of all who sit at table with you.

Luke 14.10

When you give a dinner or a banquet, do not invite your friends or your brothers or your kinsmen or rich neighbours, lest they also invite you in return, and you be repaid. But when you give a feast, invite the poor, the maimed, the lame, the blind and you will be blessed, because they cannot repay you. You will be repaid at the resurrection of the just.

Luke 14.12−14

Contribute to the needs of the saints, practise hospitality.

Romans 12.13

So then you are no longer strangers and sojourners, but you are fellow citizens with the saints and members of the household of God.

Ephesians 2.19

A widow . . . must be well attested for her good deeds, as one who has brought up children, shown hospitality, washed the feet of the saints, relieved the afflicted, and devoted herself to doing good in every way.

1 Timothy 5.9−10

Do not neglect to show hospitality to strangers, for thereby some have entertained angels unawares.

Hebrews 13.1−2

Practise hospitality ungrudgingly to one another.

1 Peter 4.9

Guidance

For we are powerless against this great multitude that is coming against us. We do not know what to do, but our eyes are upon thee.

2 Chronicles 20.12

The Lord is my shepherd . . .
He leads me in paths of righteousness
    for his name's sake.

Psalms 23.1,3

Make me to know thy ways, O Lord;
    teach me thy paths.
Lead me in thy truth, and teach me,
    for thou art the God of my salvation.

Psalms 25.4−5

He leads the humble in what is right,
    and teaches the humble his way.

Psalms 25.9

Yea, thou art my rock and my fortress;
   for thy name's sake lead me and
      guide me.

Psalms 31.3

The steps of a man are from the Lord,
  and he establishes him in whose way he
    delights;
though he fall, he shall not be cast
    headlong,
  for the Lord is the stay of his hand.

Psalms 37.23 — 24

Oh send out thy light and thy truth;
  let them lead me,
let them bring me to thy holy hill
  and to thy dwelling!

Psalms 43.3

This is God,
our God for ever and ever.
  He will be our guide for ever.

Psalms 48.14

Thou dost guide me with thy counsel,
  and afterward thou wilt receive me to
    glory.

Psalms 73.24

Lead me in the way everlasting!

Psalms 139.24

Teach me to do thy will,
  for thou art my God!
Let thy good spirit lead me
  on a level path!

Psalms 143.10

My son, keep your father's
    commandment,
  and forsake not your mother's teaching.
Bind them upon your heart always;
  tie them about your neck.
When you walk, they will lead you;
  when you lie down, they will watch over
    you;
  and when you awake, they will talk with
    you.

Proverbs 6.20 — 22

The integrity of the upright guides them.

Proverbs 11.3

Where there is no guidance, a people falls.

Proverbs 11.14

A man's steps are ordered by the Lord;
  how then can man understand his way?

Proverbs 20.24

Hear, my son, and be wise,
  and direct your mind in the way.

Proverbs 23.19

He will surely be gracious to you at the
sound of your cry; when he hears it, he will
answer you. And though the Lord give you
the bread of adversity and the water of
affliction, yet your Teacher will not hide
himself any more, but your eyes shall see
your Teacher. And your ears shall hear a
word behind you, saying, 'This is the way,
walk in it,' when you turn to the right or
when you turn to the left.

Isaiah 30.19 — 21

Thus says the Lord,
  your Redeemer, the Holy One of Israel:
'I am the Lord your God,
  who teaches you to profit,
  who leads you in the way you should go.'

Isaiah 48.17

And the Lord will guide you continually,
  and satisfy your desire with good things.

Isaiah 58.11

And if a blind man leads a blind man, both
will fall into a pit.

Matthew 15.14

You will go before the Lord . . .
when the day shall dawn upon us from on
    high
to give light to those who sit in darkness
    and in the shadow of death,
to guide our feet into the way of peace.

Luke 1.76,78 — 79

When the Spirit of truth comes, he will
guide you into all the truth.

John 16.13

Philip . . . asked, 'Do you understand
what you are reading?' And he said, 'How
can I, unless some one guides me?'

Acts 8.30 — 31

We walk by faith, not by sight.

2 Corinthians 5.7

May the Lord direct your hearts to the love of God and to the steadfastness of Christ.

2 Thessalonians 3.5

Guilt

See also **Blame, Judgment, Remorse**

If any one sins, doing any of the things which the Lord has commanded not to be done, though he does not know it, yet he is guilty and shall bear his iniquity.

Leviticus 5.17

O my God, I am ashamed and blush to lift my face to thee, my God, for our iniquities have risen higher than our heads, and our guilt has mounted up to the heavens.

Ezra 9.6

Behold, we are before thee in our guilt, for none can stand before thee because of this.

Ezra 9.15

You have given no water to the weary to drink,
and you have withheld bread from the hungry . . .
You have sent widows away empty,
and the arms of the fatherless were crushed.

Therefore snares are round about you,
and sudden terror overwhelms you;
your light is darkened, so that you cannot see,
and a flood of water covers you.

Job 22.7,9–11

Have mercy on me, O God,
according to thy steadfast love;
according to thy abundant mercy
blot out my transgressions.

Psalms 51.1

He does not deal with us according to our sins,
nor requite us according to our iniquities.

Psalms 103.10

Their heart is false;
now they must bear their guilt.
The Lord will break down their altars,
and destroy their pillars.

Hosea 10.2

The Lord is slow to anger and of great might,
and the Lord will by no means clear the guilty.

Nahum 1.3

For whoever keeps the whole law but fails in one point has become guilty of all of it.

James 2.10

H

Hair

Does not nature itself teach you that for a man to wear long hair is degrading to him, but if a woman has long hair, it is her pride? For her hair is given to her for a covering.

1 Corinthians 11.14–15

Half-Heartedness

So, because you are lukewarm, and neither cold nor hot, I will spew you out of my mouth.

Revelation 3.16

Happiness

See also **Contentment, Joy, Pleasure**

Only be strong and very courageous, being careful to do according to all the law which Moses my servant commanded you; turn not from it to the right hand or to the left, that you may have good success wherever you go.

Joshua 1.7

Behold, happy is the man whom God reproves.

Job 5.17

Why do the wicked live,
  reach old age, and grow mighty in
    power? . . .
They sing to the tambourine and the
  lyre,
  and rejoice to the sound of the pipe.
They spend their days in prosperity,
  and in peace they go down to Sheol.

Job 21.7,12–13

Thou dost show me the path of life;
  in thy presence there is fullness of joy,
  in thy right hand are pleasures for
    evermore.

Psalms 16.11

Satisfy us in the morning with thy steadfast
  love,
  that we may rejoice and be glad all our
    days.

Psalms 90.14

Blessed is every one who fears the Lord,
  who walks in his ways!
You shall eat the fruit of the labour of your
  hands;
  you shall be happy, and it shall be well
    with you.

Psalms 128.1–2

Happy the people to whom such blessings
  fall!
  Happy the people whose God is the
    Lord!

Psalms 144.15

Happy is he whose help is the God of
  Jacob,
  whose hope is in the Lord his God.

Psalms 146.5

Happy is the man who finds wisdom,
  and the man who gets understanding . . .
Her ways are ways of pleasantness,
  and all her paths are peace.
She is a tree of life to those who lay hold of
  her;
  those who hold her fast are called happy.

Proverbs 3.13,17–18

Happy is he who is kind to the poor.

Proverbs 14.21

He who gives heed to the word will
    prosper,
  and happy is he who trusts in the Lord.

Proverbs 16.20

I know that there is nothing better for them than to be happy and enjoy themselves as long as they live; also that it is God's gift to man that every one should eat and drink and take pleasure in all his toil.

Ecclesiastes 3.12−13

Remove vexation from your mind, and put away pain from your body; for youth and the dawn of life are vanity.

Ecclesiastes 11.10

And the ransomed of the Lord shall
    return,
  and come to Zion with singing;
everlasting joy shall be upon their heads;
  they shall obtain joy and gladness,
  and sorrow and sighing shall flee away.

Isaiah 35.10

So you have sorrow now, but I will see you again and your hearts will rejoice, and no one will take your joy from you.

John 16.22

Rejoice in the Lord always; again I will say, Rejoice.

Philippians 4.4

Rejoice always, pray constantly, give thanks in all circumstances.

1 Thessalonians 5.16−17

As for the rich in this world, charge them not to be haughty, not to set their hopes on uncertain riches but on God who richly furnishes us with everything to enjoy.

1 Timothy 6.17

Hardness

See also **Toughness**

He who hardens his heart will fall into calamity.

Proverbs 28.14

So then he has mercy upon whomever he wills, and he hardens the heart of whomever he wills.

Romans 9.18

Gentiles . . . are darkened in their understanding, alienated from the life of God because of the ignorance that is in them, due to their hardness of heart.

Ephesians 4.17−18

Do not harden your hearts as in the rebellion,
on the day of testing in the wilderness.

Hebrews 3.8

But exhort one another every day . . . that none of you may be hardened by the deceitfulness of sin.

Hebrews 3.13

Today, when you hear his voice,
do not harden your hearts.

Hebrews 4.7

Hardship

See also **Poverty**

When you are in tribulation, and all these things come upon you in the latter days, you will return to the Lord your God and obey his voice, for the Lord your God is a merciful God; he will not fail you or destroy you.

Deuteronomy 4.30−31

The Lord is a stronghold for the
    oppressed,
  a stronghold in times of trouble.

Psalms 9.9

This poor man cried, and the Lord heard
    him,
  and saved him out of all his troubles.

Psalms 34.6

Many are the afflictions of the righteous;
  but the Lord delivers him out of them all.
He keeps all his bones;
  not one of them is broken.

Psalms 34.19−20

The salvation of the righteous is from the
　　Lord;
　he is their refuge in the time of trouble.
The Lord helps them and delivers them;
　he delivers them from the wicked, and
　　saves them,
　because they take refuge in him.

Psalms 37.39—40

Though I walk in the midst of trouble,
　thou dost preserve my life;
thou dost stretch out thy hand against the
　　wrath of my enemies,
　and thy right hand delivers me.

Psalms 138.7

When you pass through the waters I will
　　be with you;
　and through the rivers, they shall not
　　overwhelm you;
when you walk through fire you shall not be
　　burned,
　and the flame shall not consume you.
For I am the Lord your God,
　the Holy One of Israel, your Saviour.

Isaiah 43.2—3

In the world you have tribulation; but be of
good cheer, I have overcome the world.

John 16.33

Through many tribulations we must enter
the kingdom of God.

Acts 14.22

We rejoice in our sufferings.

Romans 5.3

For this slight momentary affliction is
preparing for us an eternal weight of glory
beyond all comparison.

2 Corinthians 4.17

Share in suffering as a good soldier of
Christ Jesus.

2 Timothy 2.3

Remember those who are in prison, as
though in prison with them; and those who
are ill-treated, since you also are in the
body.

Hebrews 13.3

Harm

May my accusers be put to shame and
　　consumed;
　with scorn and disgrace may they be
　　covered
　who seek my hurt.

Psalms 71.13

Because you have made the Lord your
　　refuge,
　the Most High your habitation,
no evil shall befall you,
　no scourge come near your tent.
For he will give his angels charge of you
　to guard you in all your ways.
On their hands they will bear you up,
　lest you dash your foot against a stone.
You will tread on the lion and the adder,
　the young lion and the serpent you will
　　trample under foot.

Psalms 91.9—13

Do not contend with a man for no reason,
　when he has done you no harm.

Proverbs 3.30

Behold, I have given you authority to
tread upon serpents and scorpions, and
over all the power of the enemy; and nothing shall hurt you.

Luke 10.19

Now who is there to harm you if you are
zealous for what is right?

1 Peter 3.13

Harmony

See also **Co-operation**

Steadfast love and faithfulness will meet;
　righteousness and peace will kiss each
　　other.

Psalms 85.10

Behold, how good and pleasant it is
　when brothers dwell in unity!

Psalms 133.1

The wolf shall dwell with the lamb,
　and the leopard shall lie down with the
　　kid,

and the calf and the lion and the fatling
    together,
    and a little child shall lead them.
The cow and the bear shall feed . . .
They shall not hurt or destroy in all
        my holy mountain;
    for the earth shall be full of the
        knowledge of the Lord
        as the waters cover the sea.

Isaiah 11.6–7,9

If two of you agree on earth about anything
they ask, it will be done for them by my
Father in heaven.

Matthew 18.19

For as in one body we have many members, and all the members do not have the
same function, so we, though many, are
one body in Christ, and individually members one of another.

Romans 12.4–5

If possible, so far as it depends upon you,
live peaceably with all.

Romans 12.18

May the God of steadfastness and
encouragement grant you to live in such
harmony with one another, in accord with
Christ Jesus, that together you may with
one voice glorify the God and Father of our
Lord Jesus Christ.

Romans 15.5–6

Mend your ways, heed my appeal, agree
with one another, live in peace, and the
God of love and peace will be with you.

2 Corinthians 13.11

Lead a life worthy of the calling to which
you have been called, with all lowliness and
meekness, with patience, forbearing one
another in love, eager to maintain the unity
of the Spirit in the bond of peace.

Ephesians 4.1–3

Complete my joy by being of the same
mind, having the same love, being in full
accord and of one mind.

Philippians 2.2

Be at peace among yourselves.

1 Thessalonians 5.13

Harvest

While the earth remains, seedtime and
harvest, cold and heat, summer and winter,
day and night, shall not cease.

Genesis 8.22

As I have seen, those who plough iniquity
and sow trouble reap the same.

Job 4.8

He that goes forth weeping,
    bearing the seed for sowing,
shall come home with shouts of joy,
    bringing his sheaves with him.

Psalms 126.6

Honour the Lord with your substance
    and with the first fruits of all your
        produce;
then your barns will be filled with plenty,
    and your vats will be bursting with wine.

Proverbs 3.9–10

A son who gathers in summer is prudent,
    but a son who sleeps in harvest brings
        shame.

Proverbs 10.5

Sow for yourselves righteousness,
    reap the fruit of steadfast love;
    break up your fallow ground,
for it is the time to seek the Lord,
    that he may come and rain salvation
        upon you.

Hosea 10.12

The kingdom of heaven may be compared
to a man who sowed good seed in his field;
but while men were sleeping, his enemy
came and sowed weeds among the wheat,
and went away. So when the plants came up
and bore grain, then the weeds appeared
also . . . The servants said to him, '. . . do
you want us to go and gather them?' But he
said, 'No; lest in gathering the weeds you
root up the wheat along with them. Let
both grow together until the harvest; and at
harvest time I will tell the reapers, Gather
the weeds first and bind them in bundles to
be burned, but gather the wheat into my
barn.'

Matthew 13.24–26,28–30

He who sows the good seed is the Son of man; the field is the world, and the good seed means the sons of the kingdom; the weeds are the sons of the evil one, and the enemy who sowed them is the devil; the harvest is the close of the age, and the reapers are angels.

Matthew 13.37–39

The harvest is plentiful, but the labourers are few; pray therefore the Lord of the harvest to send out labourers into his harvest.

Luke 10.2

Lift up your eyes, and see how the fields are already ripe for harvest. He who reaps receives wages, and gathers fruit for eternal life, so that sower and reaper may rejoice together.

John 4.35–36

He who sows sparingly will also reap sparingly, and he who sows bountifully will also reap bountifully.

2 Corinthians 9.6

Do not be deceived; God is not mocked, for whatever a man sows, that he will also reap. For he who sows to his own flesh will from the flesh reap corruption; but he who sows to the Spirit will from the Spirit reap eternal life.

Galatians 6.7–8

Then I looked, and lo, a white cloud, and seated on the cloud one like a son of man, with a golden crown on his head, and a sharp sickle in his hand. And another angel came out of the temple, calling with a loud voice to him who sat upon the cloud, 'Put in your sickle, and reap, for the hour to reap has come, for the harvest of the earth is fully ripe.' So he who sat upon the cloud swung his sickle on the earth, and the earth was reaped.

Revelation 14.14–16

Hatred

You shall not hate your brother in your heart.

Leviticus 19.17

Those who hate the righteous will be condemned.

Psalms 34.21

Your divine throne endures for ever and ever.
Your royal sceptre is a sceptre of equity;
you love righteousness and hate wickedness.

Psalms 45.6–7

Hatred stirs up strife,
but love covers all offences.

Proverbs 10.12

He who conceals hatred has lying lips,
and he who utters slander is a fool.

Proverbs 10.18

Better is a dinner of herbs where love is
than a fatted ox and hatred with it.

Proverbs 15.17

He who hates, dissembles with his lips
and harbours deceit in his heart;
when he speaks graciously, believe him not,
for there are seven abominations in his heart;
though his hatred be covered with guile,
his wickedness will be exposed in the assembly.

Proverbs 26.24–26

Love your enemies and pray for those who persecute you . . . For if you love those who love you, what reward have you?

Matthew 5.44,46

You will be hated by all for my name's sake. But he who endures to the end will be saved.

Matthew 10.22

Blessed are you when men hate you, and when they exclude you and revile you, and cast out your name as evil, on account of the Son of man! Rejoice in that day, and leap for joy, for behold, your reward is great in heaven; for so their fathers did to the prophets.

Luke 6.22–23

If the world hates you, know that it has hated me before it hated you. If you were of the world, the world would love its own; but because you are not of the world, but I chose you out of the world, therefore the world hates you.

John 15.18–19

He who says he is in the light and hates his brother is in the darkness still. He who loves his brother abides in the light, and in it there is no cause for stumbling. But he who hates his brother is in the darkness and walks in the darkness, and does not know where he is going, because the darkness has blinded his eyes.

1 John 2.9–11

He who does not love abides in death.

1 John 3.14

Any one who hates his brother is a murderer, and you know that no murderer has eternal life abiding in him.

1 John 3.15

If any one says, 'I love God,' and hates his brother, he is a liar; for he who does not love his brother whom he has seen, cannot love God whom he has not seen.

1 John 4.19–20

Healing

See also **Illness**

I am the Lord, your healer.

Exodus 15.26

I kill and I make alive;
   I wound and I heal;
   and there is none that can deliver out of
     my hand.

Deuteronomy 32.39

O Lord my God, I cried to thee for help,
   and thou hast healed me.

Psalms 30.2

O Lord, be gracious to me;
   heal me, for I have sinned against thee!

Psalms 41.4

Bless the Lord, O my soul,
   and forget not all his benefits,
who forgives all your iniquity,
   who heals all your diseases.

Psalms 103.2–3

He gathers the outcasts of Israel.
He heals the brokenhearted,
   and binds up their wounds.

Psalms 147.2–3

For everything there is a season,
and a time for every matter under
     heaven . . .
a time to kill, and a time to heal.

Ecclesiastes 3.1,3

Then shall your light break forth like
     the dawn,
   and your healing shall spring up speedily.

Isaiah 58.8

Heal me, O Lord, and I shall be healed;
   save me, and I shall be saved;
   for thou art my praise.

Jeremiah 17.14

For I will restore health to you,
   and your wounds I will heal, says the
     Lord.

Jeremiah 30.17

Come, let us return to the Lord;
   for he has torn, that he may heal us;
   he has stricken, and he will bind us up.

Hosea 6.1

Heal the sick, raise the dead, cleanse lepers.

Matthew 10.8

Your faith has made you well.

Mark 5.34

Now, Lord, look upon their threats, and grant to thy servants to speak thy word with all boldness, while thou stretchest out thy hand to heal, and signs and wonders are performed through the name of thy holy servant Jesus.

Acts 4.29–30

Jesus Christ heals you.

Acts 9.34

To one is given through the Spirit the utterance of wisdom . . . to another gifts of healing by the one Spirit.

1 Corinthians 12.8—9

Therefore lift your drooping hands and strengthen your weak knees, and make straight paths for your feet, so that what is lame may not be put out of joint but rather be healed.

Hebrews 12.12—13

Is any among you sick? Let him call for the elders of the church, and let them pray over him, anointing him with oil in the name of the Lord; and the prayer of faith will save the sick man, and the Lord will raise him up.

James 5.14—15

Pray for one another, that you may be healed. The prayer of a righteous man has great power in its effects.

James 5.16

He himself bore our sins in his body on the tree, that we might die to sin and live to righteousness. By his wounds you have been healed.

1 Peter 2.24

Then he showed me the river of the water of life, bright as crystal, flowing from the throne of God and of the Lamb through the middle of the street of the city; also, on either side of the river, the tree of life . . . the leaves of the tree were for the healing of the nations.

Revelation 22.1—2

Health

You shall walk in all the way which the Lord your God has commanded you, that you may live, and that it may go well with you, and that you may live long in the land which you shall possess.

Deuteronomy 5.33

The righteous flourish like the palm tree,
and grow like a cedar in Lebanon.
They are planted in the house of the Lord,
they flourish in the courts of our God.
They still bring forth fruit in old age,
they are ever full of sap and green.

Psalms 92.12—14

Fear the Lord, and turn away from evil.
It will be healing to your flesh
and refreshment to your bones.

Proverbs 3.7—8

My son, be attentive to my words;
incline your ear to my sayings.
Let them not escape from your sight;
keep them within your heart.
For they are life to him who finds them,
and healing to all his flesh.

Proverbs 4.20—22

The tongue of the wise brings healing.

Proverbs 12.18

A cheerful heart is a good medicine,
but a downcast spirit dries up the bones.

Proverbs 17.22

Beloved, I pray that all may go well with you and that you may be in health; I know that it is well with your soul.

3 John 2

Heart

You shall love the Lord your God with all your heart, and with all your soul, and with all your might.

Deuteronomy 6.5

The Lord sees not as man sees; man looks on the outward appearance, but the Lord looks on the heart.

1 Samuel 16.7

For thou, thou only, knowest the hearts of all the children of men.

1 Kings 8.39

Know the God of your father, and serve him with a whole heart and with a willing mind; for the Lord searches all hearts, and understands every plan and thought.

1 Chronicles 28.9

I know, my God, that thou triest the heart, and hast pleasure in uprightness; in the uprightness of my heart I have freely offered all these things, and now I have seen thy people, who are present here, offering freely and joyously to thee. O Lord, the God of Abraham, Isaac, and Israel, our fathers, keep for ever such purposes and thoughts in the hearts of thy people, and direct their hearts toward thee.

1 Chronicles 29.17–18

Let the words of my mouth and the
        meditation of my heart
be acceptable in thy sight.

Psalms 19.14

If we had forgotten the name of our God,
    or spread forth our hands to a strange
        god,
would not God discover this?
    For he knows the secrets of the heart.

Psalms 44.20–21

Create in me a clean heart, O God,
    and put a new and right spirit within me.

Psalms 51.10

His speech was smoother than butter,
    yet war was in his heart;
his words were softer than oil,
    yet they were drawn swords.

Psalms 55.21

You who seek God, let your hearts revive.

Psalms 69.32

Truly God is good to the upright,
    to those who are pure in heart.

Psalms 73.1

I commune with my heart in the night;
    I meditate and search my spirit.

Psalms 77.6

Do good, O Lord, to those who are good,
    and to those who are upright in their
        hearts!

Psalms 125.4

Keep your heart with all vigilance;
    for from it flow the springs of life.

Proverbs 4.23

The heart knows its own bitterness,
    and no stranger shares its joy.

Proverbs 14.10

A glad heart makes a cheerful
        countenance.

Proverbs 15.13

All the days of the afflicted are evil,
    but a cheerful heart has a continual feast.

Proverbs 15.15

Who can say, 'I have made my heart
        clean;
    I am pure from my sin'?

Proverbs 20.9

The king's heart is a steam of water in the
        hand of the Lord;
    he turns it wherever he will.

Proverbs 21.1

The Lord weighs the heart.

Proverbs 21.2

O Jerusalem, wash your heart from
        wickedness,
    that you may be saved.

Jeremiah 4.14

Blessed are the pure in heart, for they shall see God.

Matthew 5.8

For out of the heart come evil thoughts, murder, adultery, fornication, theft, false witness, slander. These are what defile a man.

Matthew 15.19

You have neither part nor lot in this matter, for your heart is not right before God. Repent therefore of this wickedness of yours, and pray to the Lord that, if possible, the intent of your heart may be forgiven you.

Acts 8.21–22

If you confess with your lips that Jesus is Lord and believe in your heart that God raised him from the dead, you will be saved. For man believes with his heart and so is justified, and he confesses with his lips and so is saved.

Romans 10.9–10

In your hearts reverence Christ as Lord.

1 Peter 3.15

Heaven

See also **Resurrection**

To you it was shown, that you might know that the Lord is God; there is no other besides him. Out of heaven he let you hear his voice, that he might discipline you.

Deuteronomy 4.35–36

And hearken thou to the supplication of thy servant . . . yea, hear thou in heaven thy dwelling place.

1 Kings 8.30

The Lord is in his holy temple,
   the Lord's throne is in heaven.

Psalms 11.4

Now I know that the Lord will help his
      anointed;
   he will answer him from his holy heaven
   with mighty victories by his right hand.

Psalms 20.6

God is in heaven, and you upon earth.

Ecclesiastes 5.2

Heaven is my throne
   and the earth is my footstool;
what is the house which you would build for
      me,
   and what is the place of my rest?

Isaiah 66.1

Blessed are the poor in spirit, for theirs is the kingdom of heaven.

Matthew 5.3

Blessed are those who are persecuted for righteousness' sake, for theirs is the kingdom of heaven.

Matthew 5.10

Whoever then relaxes one of the least of these commandments and teaches men so, shall be called least in the kingdom of heaven; but he who does them and teaches them shall be called great in the kingdom of heaven.

Matthew 5.19

Our Father who art in heaven.

Matthew 6.9

Lay up for yourselves treasure in heaven, where neither moth nor rust consumes and where thieves do not break in and steal.

Matthew 6.20

Not every one who says to me, 'Lord, Lord,' shall enter the kingdom of heaven, but he who does the will of my Father who is in heaven.

Matthew 7.21

I tell you, many will come from east and west and sit at table with Abraham, Isaac, and Jacob in the kingdom of heaven.

Matthew 8.11

The kingdom of heaven is like a grain of mustard seed which a man took and sowed in his field; it is the smallest of all seeds, but when it has grown it is the greatest of shrubs and becomes a tree, so that the birds of the air come and make nests in its branches.

Matthew 13.31–32

Again, the kingdom of heaven is like a net which was thrown into the sea and gathered fish of every kind; when it was full, men drew it ashore and sat down and sorted the good into vessels but threw away the bad. So it will be at the close of the age. The angels will come out and separate the evil from the righteous, and throw them into the furnace of fire; there men will weep and gnash their teeth.

Matthew 13.47–50

To you has been given the secret of the kingdom of God.

Mark 4.11

No one can receive anything except what is given him from heaven.

John 3.27

For the kingdom of God is . . . righteousness and peace and joy in the Holy Spirit.

Romans 14.17

For we know that if the earthly tent we live in is destroyed, we have a building from God, a house not made with hands, eternal in the heavens.

2 Corinthians 5.1

Blessed be the God and Father of our Lord Jesus Christ, who has blessed us in Christ with every spiritual blessing in the heavenly places.

Ephesians 1.3

But God, who is rich in mercy, out of the great love with which he loved us . . . raised us up with him, and made us sit with him in the heavenly places in Christ Jesus.

Ephesians 2.4,6

Now war arose in heaven, Michael and his angels fighting against the dragon; and the dragon and his angels fought, but they were defeated and there was no longer any place for them in heaven.

Revelation 12.7–8

In the Spirit he carried me away to a great, high mountain, and showed me the holy city Jerusalem coming down out of heaven from God, having the glory of God, its radiance like a most rare jewel, like a jasper, clear as crystal. It had a great, high wall, with twelve gates, and at the gates twelve angels, and on the gates the names of the twelve tribes of the sons of Israel were inscribed; on the east three gates, on the north three gates, on the south three gates, and on the west three gates. And the wall of the city had twelve foundations, and on them the twelve names of the twelve apostles of the Lamb.

Revelation 21.10–14

And I saw no temple in the city, for its temple is the Lord God the Almighty and the Lamb. And the city has no need of sun or moon to shine upon it, for the glory of God is its light, and its lamp is the Lamb. By its light shall the nations walk; and the kings of the earth shall bring their glory into it, and its gates shall never be shut by day – and there shall be no night there; they shall bring into it the glory and the honour of the nations. But nothing unclean shall enter it, nor any one who practises abomination or falsehood, but only those who are written in the Lamb's book of life.

Revelation 21.22–27

The throne of God and of the Lamb shall be in it, and his servants shall worship him; they shall see his face, and his name shall be on their foreheads. And night shall be no more; they need no light of lamp or sun, for the Lord God will be their light, and they shall reign for ever and ever.

Revelation 22.3–5

Blessed are those who wash their robes, that they may have the right to the tree of life and that they may enter the city by the gates.

Revelation 22.14

Hedonism

He who loves pleasure will be a poor man; he who loves wine and oil will not be rich.

Proverbs 21.17

Go, eat your bread with enjoyment, and drink your wine with a merry heart; for God has already approved what you do.

Ecclesiastes 9.7

Hell

See also **Damnation, Devil**

Sheol is naked before God, and Abaddon has no covering.

Job 26.6

The wicked shall depart to Sheol, all the nations that forget God.

Psalms 9.17

For thou dost not give me up to Sheol,
  or let thy godly one see the Pit.

Psalms 16.10

I give thanks to thee, O Lord my God,
  with my whole heart,
and I will glorify thy name for ever.
For great is thy steadfast love toward me;
  thou hast delivered my soul from the
    depths of Sheol.

Psalms 86.12–13

Say to wisdom, 'You are my sister,'
  and call insight your intimate friend;
to preserve you from the loose woman,
  from the adventuress with her smooth
    words.

Proverbs 7.4–5

For many a victim has she laid low;
  yea, all her slain are a mighty host.
Her house is the way to Sheol,
  going down.to the chambers of death.

Proverbs 7.26–27

There is severe discipline for him who
    forsakes the way;
  he who hates reproof will die.
Sheol and Abaddon lie open before the
    Lord,
  how much more the hearts of men!

Proverbs 15.10–11

Sheol and Abaddon are never satisfied,
  and never satisfied are the eyes of man.

Proverbs 27.20

Those who go down to the pit cannot hope
for thy faithfulness.

Isaiah 38.18

Every one who is angry with his brother
shall be liable to judgment . . . and whoever says, 'You fool!' shall be liable to the
hell of fire.

Matthew 5.22

It is better that you lose one of your
members than that your whole body go into
hell.

Matthew 5.30

The rich man also died and was buried;
and in Hades, being in torment, he lifted up
his eyes, and saw Abraham far off and
Laz'arus in his bosom. And he called out,
'Father Abraham, have mercy upon me,
and send Laz'arus to dip the end of his
finger in water and cool my tongue; for I
am in anguish in this flame.' But Abraham
said, 'Son, remember that you in your lifetime received your good things, and
Laz'arus in like manner evil things; but now
he is comforted here, and you are in
anguish. And besides all this, between us
and you a great chasm has been fixed, in
order that those who would pass from here
to you may not be able, and none may cross
from there to us.' And he said, 'Then I beg
you, father, to send him to my father's
house, for I have five brothers, so that he
may warn them, lest they also come into
this place of torment.' But Abraham said,
'They have Moses and the prophets; let
them hear them.' And he said, 'No, father
Abraham; but if some one goes to them
from the dead, they will repent.' He said to
him, 'If they do not hear Moses and the
prophets, neither will they be convinced if
some one should rise from the dead.'

Luke 16.22–31

The tongue is an unrighteous world among
our members, staining the whole body,
setting on fire the cycle of nature, and set
on fire by hell.

James 3.6

For if God did not spare the angels when
they sinned, but cast them into hell and
committed them to pits of nether gloom to
be kept until the judgment . . . then the
Lord knows how to rescue the godly from
trial, and to keep the unrighteous under
punishment until the day of judgment.

2 Peter 2.4,9

Sodom and Gomor'rah and the surround-
ing cities, which likewise acted immorally
and indulged in unnatural lust, serve as an
example by undergoing a punishment of
eternal fire.

Jude 7

Help

See also **Charity, Guidance, Protection**

If you meet your enemy's ox or his ass going astray, you shall bring it back to him. If you see the ass of one who hates you lying under its burden, you shall refrain from leaving him with it, you shall help him to lift it up.

Exodus 23.4–5

O Lord, there is none like thee to help, between the mighty and the weak. Help us, O Lord our God, for we rely on thee, and in thy name we have come against this multitude.

2 Chronicles 14.11

Behold, God will not reject a blameless man,
nor take the hand of evildoers.

Job 8.20

Our soul waits for the Lord;
he is our help and shield.

Psalms 33.20

God is our refuge and strength,
a very present help in trouble.

Psalms 46.1

O grant us help against the foe,
for vain is the help of man!

Psalms 108.12

Let me live that I may praise thee,
and let thy ordinances help me.

Psalms 119.175

I lift up my eyes to the hills.
From whence does my help come?
My help comes from the Lord,
who made heaven and earth.

Psalms 121.1–2

He fulfils the desire of all who fear him,
he also hears their cry, and saves them.

Psalms 145.19

Two are better than one . . . For if they fall, one will lift up his fellow.

Ecclesiastes 4.9–10

The way of the righteous is level;
thou dost make smooth the path of the righteous.

Isaiah 26.7

Likewise the Spirit helps us in our weakness; for we do not know how to pray as we ought, but the Spirit himself intercedes for us with sighs too deep for words.

Romans 8.26

Bear one another's burdens, and so fulfil the law of Christ.

Galatians 6.2

Let us then with confidence draw near to the throne of grace, that we may receive mercy and find grace to help in time of need.

Hebrews 4.16

The Lord is my helper,
I will not be afraid;
what can man do to me?

Hebrews 13.6

Helplessness

See also **Weakness**

Be gracious to me, O Lord, for I am languishing.

Psalms 6.2

While we were still weak, at the right time Christ died for the ungodly.

Romans 5.6

I was with you in weakness and in much fear and trembling; and my speech and my message were not in plausible words of wisdom, but in demonstration of the Spirit.

1 Corinthians 2.3–4

Heredity

See also **Ancestors, Parenthood**

For I the Lord your God am a jealous God, visiting the iniquity of the fathers upon the children to the third and the fourth generation of those who hate me.

Exodus 20.5

Who can bring a clean thing out of an unclean?

Job 14.4

You say, 'God stores up their iniquity for
  their sons.'
  Let him recompense it to themselves,
    that they may know it.

Job 21.19

Behold, I was brought forth in iniquity,
  and in sin did my mother conceive me.

Psalms 51.5

The soul that sins shall die. The son shall
not suffer for the iniquity of the father, nor
the father suffer for the iniquity of the son.

Ezekiel 18.20

That which is born of the flesh is flesh, and
that which is born of the Spirit is spirit.

John 3.6

Sin came into the world through one man
and death through sin, and so death spread
to all men because all men sinned.

Romans 5.12

Heresy

See also **Blasphemy, Godlessness**

As for a man who is factious, after admon-
ishing him once or twice, have nothing
more to do with him, knowing that such a
person is perverted and sinful; he is self-
condemned.

Titus 3.10–11

But false prophets also arose among the
people, just as there will be false teachers
among you, who will secretly bring in destructive heresies, even denying the Master
who brought them, bringing upon themselves swift destruction.

2 Peter 2.1

They went out from us, but they were not
of us; for if they had been of us, they would
have continued with us; but they went out
that it might be plain that they all are not of
us.

1 John 2.19

Hesitancy

See also **Doubt**

How long will you go limping with two
different opinions? If the Lord is God,
follow him.

1 Kings 18.21

No one who puts his hand to the plough
and looks back is fit for the kingdom of
God.

Luke 9.62

Let us hold fast the confession of our hope
without wavering.

Hebrews 10.23

'But my righteous one shall live by faith,
  and if he shrinks back,
  my soul has no pleasure in him.'
But we are not of those who shrink back
    and are destroyed, but of those who
    have faith and keep their souls.

Hebrews 10.38–39

If any of you lacks wisdom, let him ask
God, who gives to all men generously and
without reproaching, and it will be given
him. But let him ask in faith, with no
doubting, for he who doubts is like a wave
of the sea that is driven and tossed by the
wind.

James 1.5–6

I know your works: you are neither cold
nor hot. Would that you were cold or hot
So, because you are lukewarm, and neither
cold nor hot, I will spew you out of my
mouth.

Revelation 3.15–16

High-Mindedness

See also **Transcendence**

If then you have been raised with Christ
seek the things that are above, where Chris
is, seated at the right hand of God. Set you
minds on things that are above, not o
things that are on earth.

Colossians 3.1–

History

See also **Ancestors**

Remember the days of old,
  consider the years of many generations;
ask your father, and he will show you;
  your elders, and they will tell you.

Deuteronomy 32.7

For inquire, I pray you, of bygone ages,
and consider what the fathers have found.

Job 8.8

Remove not the ancient landmark
  which your fathers have set.

Proverbs 22.28

What has been is what will be,
  and what has been done is what will be
    done;
  and there is nothing new under the sun.

Ecclesiastes 1.9

Stand by the roads, and look,
  and ask for the ancient paths,
where the good way is.

Jeremiah 6.16

Holiness

See also **Godliness**

Remember the sabbath day, to keep it
holy.

Exodus 20.8

Consecrate yourselves therefore, and be
holy; for I am the Lord your God.

Leviticus 20.7

The Lord will establish you as a people
holy to himself, as he has sworn to you, if
you keep the commandments of the Lord
your God, and walk in his ways.

Deuteronomy 28.9

Worship the Lord in holy array.

Psalms 29.2

Rejoice in the Lord, O you righteous,
  and give thanks to his holy name!

Psalms 97.12

And a highway shall be there,
  and it shall be called the Holy Way;
the unclean shall not pass over it,
  and fools shall not err therein.

Isaiah 35.8

Do not give dogs what is holy; and do not
throw your pearls before swine, lest they
trample them under foot and turn to attack
you.

Matthew 7.6

Remember . . . the oath which he swore to
    our father Abraham, to grant us
that we, being delivered from the hand of
    our enemies,
might serve him without fear,
in holiness and righteousness before him all
    the days of our life.

Luke 1.72–75

I appeal to you therefore, brethren, by the
mercies of God, to present your bodies as a
living sacrifice, holy and acceptable to God,
which is your spiritual worship.

Romans 12.1

Do you not know that you are God's
temple and that God's Spirit dwells in you?
If any one destroys God's temple, God will
destroy him. For God's temple is holy, and
that temple you are.

1 Corinthians 3.16–17

Since we have these promises, beloved, let
us cleanse ourselves from every defilement
of body and spirit, and make holiness
perfect in the fear of God.

2 Corinthians 7.1

Be renewed in the spirit of your minds,
and put on the new nature, created after
the likeness of God in true righteousness
and holiness.

Ephesians 4.23–24

For God has not called us for uncleanness,
but in holiness.

1 Thessalonians 4.7

Strive for peace with all men, and for the
holiness without which no one will see the
Lord.

Hebrews 12.14

Be holy yourselves in all your conduct; since it is written, 'You shall be holy, for I am holy.'

1 Peter 1.15–16

He himself bore our sins in his body on the tree, that we might die to sin and live to righteousness.

1 Peter 2.24

He who does right is righteous, as he is righteous. He who commits sin is of the devil.

1 John 3.7

Let . . . the righteous still do right, and the holy still be holy.

Revelation 22.11

Holy Spirit

Unless one is born of water and the Spirit, he cannot enter the kingdom of God.

John 3.5

The wind blows where it wills, and you hear the sound of it, but you do not know whence it comes or whither it goes; so it is with every one who is born of the Spirit.

John 3.8

And I will pray the Father, and he will give you another Counsellor, to be with you for ever, even the Spirit of truth, whom the world cannot receive, because it neither sees him nor knows him; you know him, for he dwells with you, and will be in you.

John 14.16–17

When the Counsellor comes, whom I shall send to you from the Father, even the Spirit of truth, who proceeds from the Father, he will bear witness to me.

John 15.26

When the Spirit of truth comes, he will guide you into all the truth; for he will not speak on his own authority, but whatever he hears he will speak, and he will declare to you the things that are to come. He will glorify me, for he will take what is mine and declare it to you.

John 16.13–14

When the day of Pentecost had come, they were all together in one place. And suddenly a sound came from heaven like the rush of a mighty wind, and it filled all the house where they were sitting. And there appeared to them tongues as of fire, distributed and resting on each one of them. And they were all filled with the Holy Spirit and began to speak in other tongues, as the Spirit gave them utterance.

Acts 2.1–4

Being therefore exalted at the right hand of God, and having received from the Father the promise of the Holy Spirit, he has poured out this which you see and hear.

Acts 2.33

If the Spirit of him who raised Jesus from the dead dwells in you, he who raised Christ Jesus from the dead will give life to your mortal bodies also through his Spirit which dwells in you.

Romans 8.11

For the kingdom of God is . . . righteousness and peace and joy in the Holy Spirit.

Romans 14.17

God has revealed to us through the Spirit. For the Spirit searches everything, even the depths of God.

1 Corinthians 2.10

For by one Spirit we were all baptized into one body — Jews or Greeks, slaves or free — and all were made to drink of one Spirit.

1 Corinthians 12.13

The Spirit gives life.

2 Corinthians 3.6

But I say, walk by the Spirit, and do not gratify the desires of the flesh. For the desires of the flesh are against the Spirit, and the desires of the Spirit are against the flesh; for these are opposed to each other, to prevent you from doing what you would.

Galatians 5.16–17

But the fruit of the Spirit is love, joy, peace, patience, kindness, goodness, faithfulness, gentleness, self-control.

Galatians 5.22–23

If we live by the Spirit, let us also walk by the Spirit.

Galatians 5.25

Home

See also **Domesticity**

The Lord grant that you may find a home, each of you in the house of her husband!

Ruth 1.9

Homelessness

Like a bird that strays from its nest,
is a man who strays from his home.

Proverbs 27.8

Foxes have holes, and birds of the air have nests; but the Son of man has nowhere to lay his head.

Matthew 8.20

Homosexuality

You shall not lie with a male as with a woman; it is an abomination.

Leviticus 18.22

I am distressed for you, my brother Jonathan;
very pleasant have you been to me;
your love to me was wonderful,
passing the love of women.

2 Samuel 1.26

For this reason God gave them up to dishonourable passions. Their women exchanged natural relations for unnatural, and the men likewise gave up natural relations with women and were consumed with passion for one another, men committing shameless acts with men and receiving in their own persons the due penalty for their error.

Romans 1.26–27

Do you not know that the unrighteous will not inherit the kingdom of God? . . . neither the immoral, nor idolaters, nor adulterers, nor sexual perverts.

1 Corinthians 6.9

Honesty

See also **Integrity, Justice**

You shall do no wrong in judgment, in measures of length or weight or quantity. You shall have just balances, just weights.

Leviticus 19.25–36

I know, my God, that thou triest the heart, and hast pleasure in uprightness.

1 Chronicles 29.17

He . . . who swears to his own hurt and
    does not change;
who does not put out his money at interest,
    and does not take a bribe against the
    innocent.
He who does these things shall never be
    moved.

Psalms 15.1,4–5

Let your eyes look directly forward,
    and your gaze be straight before you.
Take heed to the path of your feet,
    then all your ways will be sure.
Do not swerve to the right or to the left;
    turn your foot away from evil.

Proverbs 4.25–27

A false balance is an abomination to the
    Lord,
    but a just weight is his delight.

Proverbs 11.1

The integrity of the upright guides them,
    but the crookedness of the treacherous
    destroys them.

Proverbs 11.3

Lying lips are an abomination to the Lord,
    but those who act faithfully are his
    delight.

Proverbs 12.22

Righteous lips are the delight of a king,
    and he loves him who speaks what is
    right.

Proverbs 16.13

Diverse weights and diverse measures
    are both alike an abomination to the
    Lord.

Proverbs 20.10

I am the Lord, and there is no other.
I did not speak in secret,
  in a land of darkness . . .
I the Lord speak the truth,
  I declare what is right.

Isaiah 45.18–19

Tax collectors also came to be baptized, and said to him, 'Teacher, what shall we do?' And he said to them, 'Collect no more than is appointed you.'

Luke 3.12–13

He who is faithful in a very little is faithful also in much; and he who is dishonest in a very little is dishonest also in much.

Luke 16.10

So I always take pains to have a clear conscience toward God and toward men.

Acts 24.16

We have renounced disgraceful, underhanded ways; we refuse to practise cunning or to tamper with God's word, but by the open statement of the truth we would commend ourselves to every man's conscience in the sight of God.

2 Corinthians 4.2

But we pray God that you may not do wrong.

2 Corinthians 13.7

Honour

See also **Respect, Reverence**

Honour your father and your mother.

Exodus 20.12

Thine, O Lord, is the greatness, and the power, and the glory, and the victory, and the majesty; for all that is in the heavens and in the earth is thine; thine is the kingdom, O Lord, and thou art exalted as head above all.

1 Chronicles 29.11

But the Lord made the heavens.
Honour and majesty are before him;
  strength and beauty are in his sanctuary.

Psalms 96.5–6

Happy is the man who finds wisdom . . .
Long life is in her right hand;
  in her left hand are riches and honour.

Proverbs 3.13,16

The wise will inherit honour,
  but fools get disgrace.

Proverbs 3.35

Prize her [wisdom] highly, and she will
  exalt you;
  she will honour you if you embrace her.

Proverbs 4.8

Riches and honour are with me [wisdom],
  enduring wealth and prosperity.

Proverbs 8.18

A gracious woman gets honour.

Proverbs 11.16

Humility goes before honour.

Proverbs 15.33

He who pursues righteousness and kindness will find life and honour.

Proverbs 21.21

He who is lowly in spirit will obtain honour.

Proverbs 29.23

Glory and honour and peace for every one who does good.

Romans 2.10

Pray for us, for we are sure that we have a clear conscience, desiring to act honourably in all things.

Hebrews 13.18

Honour all men.

1 Peter 2.17

Hope

And you will have confidence, because
    there is hope;
  you will be protected and take your rest
    in safety.
You will lie down, and none will make you
    afraid;

many will entreat your favour.
But the eyes of the wicked will fail;
    all way of escape will be lost to them,
    and their hope is to breathe their last.

Job 11.18—20

I believe that I shall see the goodness of
    the Lord
    in the land of the living!
Wait for the Lord;
    be strong, and let your heart take
        courage;
    yea, wait for the Lord!

Psalms 27.13

Weeping may tarry for the night,
    but joy comes with the morning.

Psalms 30.5

Let thy steadfast love, O Lord, be upon
    us,
    even as we hope in thee.

Psalms 33.22

Those who wait for the Lord shall possess
the land.

Psalms 37.9

Why are you cast down, O my soul,
    and why are you disquieted within me?
Hope in God; for I shall again praise him,
    my help and my God.

Psalms 42.5—6

Why are you case down, O my soul,
    and why are you disquieted within me?
Hope in God; for I shall again praise him,
    my help and my God.

Psalms 43.5

O God of our salvation,
who art the hope of all the ends of the
    earth.

Psalms 65.5

I hope in thy word.
My eyes fail with watching for thy promise.

Psalms 119.81—82

Happy is he . . . whose hope is in the Lord
his God.

Psalms 146.5

When the wicked dies, his hope perishes.

Proverbs 11.7

Hope deferred makes the heart sick,
    but a desire fulfilled is a tree of life.

Proverbs 13.12

Wait for the Lord, and he will help you.

Proverbs 20.22

Blessed is the man who trusts in the Lord,
whose trust is the Lord.

Jeremiah 17.7

Let us know, let us press on to know the
    Lord;
    his going forth is sure as the dawn;
he will come to us as the showers,
    as the spring rains that water the earth.

Hosea 6.3

We rejoice in our sufferings, knowing that
suffering produces endurance, and endurance produces character, and character
produces hope, and hope does not dis-
appoint us, because God's love has been
poured into our hearts through the Holy
Spirit which has been given to us.

Romans 5.3—5

For in this hope we were saved. Now hope
that is seen is not hope. For who hopes for
what he sees? But if we hope for what we
do not see, we wait for it with patience.

Romans 8.24—25

For whatever was written in former days
was written for our instruction, that by
steadfastness and by the encouragement of
the scriptures we might have hope.

Romans 15.4

May the God of hope fill you with all joy
and peace in believing, so that by the power
of the Holy Spirit you may abound in hope.

Romans 15.13

We are afflicted in every way, but not
crushed; perplexed, but not driven to
despair.

2 Corinthians 4.8

For through the Spirit, by faith, we wait for the hope of righteousness.

Galatians 5.5

Christ was faithful over God's house as a son. And we are his house if we hold fast our confidence and pride in our hope.

Hebrews 3.6

And we desire each one of you to show the same earnestness in realising the full assurance of hope until the end.

Hebrews 6.11

We have this as a sure and steadfast anchor of the soul, a hope that enters into the inner shrine behind the curtain.

Hebrews 6.19

On the one hand, a former commandment is set aside . . . on the other hand, a better hope is introduced, through which we draw near to God.

Hebrews 7.19

Blessed be the God and Father of our Lord Jesus Christ! By his great mercy we have been born anew to a living hope through the resurrection of Jesus Christ from the dead, and to an inheritance which is imperishable, undefiled, and unfading.

1 Peter 1.3−4

Therefore gird up your minds, be sober, set your hope fully upon the grace that is coming to you at the revelation of Jesus Christ.

1 Peter 1.13

Beloved, we are God's children now; it does not yet appear what we shall be, but we know that when he appears we shall be like him, for we shall see him as he is. And every one who thus hopes in him purifies himself as he is pure.

1 John 3.2−3

Hospitality

See also **Guests**

He . . . loves the sojourner, giving him food and clothing. Love the sojourner therefore; for you were sojourners in the land of Egypt.

Deuteronomy 10.18−19

He you receives you receives me, and he who receives me receives him who sent me. He who receives a prophet because he is a prophet shall receive a prophet's reward, and he who receives a righteous man because he is a righteous man shall receive a righteous man's reward. And whoever gives to one of these little ones even a cup of cold water because he is a disciple, truly, I say to you, he shall not lose his reward.

Matthew 10.40−42

Love one another with brotherly affection . . . practise hospitality.

Romans 12.10,13

Do not neglect to show hospitality to strangers, for thereby some have enterained angels unawares.

Hebrews 13.1−2

Practise hospitality ungrudgingly to one another.

1 Peter 4.9

Beloved, it is a loyal thing you do when you render any service to the brethren, especially to strangers, who have testified to your love before the church . . . we ought to support such men, that we may be fellow workers in the truth.

3 John 5−6,8

Hostility

See also **Hatred**

And blessed is he who takes no offence at me.

Matthew 11.6

Human Nature

Can the Ethiopian change his skin
  or the leopard his spots?

Jeremiah 13.23

Humility

O Lord, thou wilt hear the desire of the
    meek;
  thou wilt strengthen their heart,
    thou wilt incline thy ear.

Psalms 10.17

O Lord, my heart is not lifted up,
  my eyes are not raised too high;
I do not occupy myself with things
  too great and too marvellous for me.
But I have calmed and quieted my soul,
  like a child quieted at its mother's breast;
  like a child that is quieted is my soul.

Psalms 131.1−2

For though the Lord is high, he regards the
    lowly;
  but the haughty he knows from afar.

Psalms 138.6

Humility goes before honour.

Proverbs 15.33

It is better to be of a lowly spirit with the
    poor
  than to divide the spoil with the proud.

Proverbs 16.19

The reward for humility and fear of the
    Lord
  is riches and honour and life.

Proverbs 22.4

He who is lowly in spirit will obtain
honour.

Proverbs 29.23

The meek shall obtain fresh joy in the
Lord.

Isaiah 29.19

For thus says the high and lofty One
  who inhabits eternity, whose name is
    Holy;
I dwell in the high and holy place,
  and also with him who is of a contrite and
    humble spirit,
to revive the spirit of the humble,
  and to revive the heart of the contrite.'

Isaiah 57.15

And what does the Lord require of you
but to do justice, and to love kindness,
  and to walk humbly with your God?

Micah 6.8

Blessed are the poor in spirit, for theirs is
the kingdom of heaven.

Matthew 5.3

Unless you turn and become like children,
you will never enter the kingdom of
heaven. Whoever humbles himself like this
child, he is the greatest in the kingdom of
heaven.

Matthew 18.3−4

Whoever exalts himself will be humbled,
and whoever humbles himself will be
exalted.

Matthew 23.12

He has put down the mighty from their
    thrones,
  and exalted those of low degree.

Luke 1.52

Now he told a parable to those who were
invited, when he marked how they chose
the places of honour, saying to them,
'When you are invited by any one to a
marriage feast, do not sit down in a place of
honour, lest a more eminent man than you
be invited by him; and he who invited you
both will come and say to you, "Give place
to this man," and then you will begin with
shame to take the lowest place. But when
you are invited, go and sit in the lowest
place, so that when your host comes he may
say to you, "Friend, go up higher"; then
you will be honoured in the presence of all
who sit at table with you. For every one
who exalts himself will be humbled, and
he who humbles himself will be exalted.'

Luke 14.7−11

I bid every one among you not to think of
himself more highly than he ought to think,
but to think with sober judgment, each
according to the measure of faith which
God has assigned him.

Romans 12.3

Do nothing from selfishness or conceit, but in humility count others better than yourselves. Let each of you look not only to his own interests, but also to the interests of others. Have this mind among yourselves, which is yours in Christ Jesus, who, though he was in the form of God, did not count equality with God a thing to be grasped, but emptied himself, taking the form of a servant, being born in the likeness of men. And being found in human form he humbled himself and became obedient unto death, even death on a cross.

Philippians 2.3—8

Put on then, as God's chosen ones, holy and beloved, compassion, kindness, lowliness, meekness, and patience.

Colossians 3.12

Humble yourselves before the Lord and he will exalt you.

James 4.10

Clothe yourselves, all of you, with humility toward one another, for 'God opposes the proud, but gives grace to the humble.'

Humble yourselves therefore under the mighty hand of God, that in due time he may exalt you.

1 Peter 5.5—6

Hunger

See also **Need, Poverty**

Let them thank the Lord for his steadfast love,
　for his wonderful works to the sons of men!
For he satisfies him who is thirsty,
　and the hungry he fills with good things.

Psalms 107.8—9

He turns a desert into pools of water,
　a parched land into springs of water.
And there he lets the hungry dwell,
　and they establish a city to live in.

Psalms 107.35—36

The Lord . . . keeps faith for ever . . .
　gives food to the hungry.

Psalms 146.5—7

An idle person will suffer hunger.

Proverbs 19.15

He who is sated loathes honey,
　but to one who is hungry everything
　　bitter is sweet.

Proverbs 27.7

If you pour yourself out for the hungry
　and satisfy the desire of the afflicted,
then shall your light rise in the darkness
　and your gloom be as the noonday.

Isaiah 58.10

Blessed are those who hunger and thirst for righteousness, for they shall be satisfied.

Matthew 5.6

He has filled the hungry with good things, and the rich he has sent empty away.

Luke 1.53

Blessed are you that hunger now, for you shall be satisfied.

Luke 6.21

Woe to you that are full now, for you shall hunger.

Luke 6.25

I am the bread of life; he who comes to me shall not hunger.

John 6.35

They shall hunger no more, neither thirst any more; the sun shall not strike them, nor any scorching heat.

Revelation 7.16

Hurry

He who makes haste with his feet misses his way.

Proverbs 19.2

The plans of the diligent lead surely to abundance,
　but every one who is hasty comes only to want.

Proverbs 21.5

O Lord, hear; O Lord, forgive; O Lord, give heed and act; delay not, for thy own sake, O my God, because thy city and thy people are called by thy name.

Daniel 9.19

Hymn

See also **Music, Praise**

Praise the Lord with the lyre,
  make melody to him with the harp of ten
    strings!
Sing to him a new song,
  play skilfully on the strings, with loud
    shouts.

Psalms 33.2−3

I will bless thee as long as I live . . .
  and my mouth praises thee with
    joyful lips.

Psalms 63.4−5

O come, let us sing to the Lord;
  let us make a joyful noise to the rock of
    our salvation!
Let us come into his presence with
    thanksgiving;
  let us make a joyful noise to him with
    songs of praise!

Psalms 95.1−2

Sing to the Lord with thanksgiving;
  make melody to our God upon the lyre!

Psalms 147.7

Be filled with the Spirit, addressing one another in psalms and hymns and spiritual songs, singing and making melody to the Lord with all your heart.

Ephesians 5.19

Sing psalms and hymns and spiritual songs with thankfulness in your hearts to God.

Colossians 3.16

I will proclaim thy name to my brethren,
in the midst of the congregation I will praise
thee.

Hebrews 2.12

Hypocrisy

For there is no truth in their mouth;
  their heart is destruction,
their throat is an open sepulchre,
  they flatter with their tongue.
Make them bear their guilt, O God.

Psalms 5.9−10

But they flattered him with their mouths;
  they lied to him with their tongues.
Their heart was not steadfast toward him;
  they were not true to his covenant.

Psalms 78.36−37

I hate double-minded men.

Psalms 119.113

'It is bad, it is bad,' says the buyer;
  but when he goes away, then he boasts.

Proverbs 20.14

Trust in a faithless man in time of trouble
  is like a bad tooth or a foot that slips.

Proverbs 25.19

Like the glaze covering an earthen vessel
  are smooth lips with an evil heart.

Proverbs 26.23

Woe to those who call evil good and good
    evil,
who put darkness for light and light for
    darkness.

Isaiah 5.20

Woe to those who hide deep from the
    Lord their counsel,
  whose deeds are in the dark, and who
    say,
'Who sees us? Who knows us?'
  You turn things upside down!

Isaiah 29.15−16

Its heads give judgment for a bribe,
  its priests teach for hire,
  its prophets divine for money;
yet they lean upon the Lord and say,
  'Is not the Lord in the midst of us?
  No evil shall come upon us.'

Micah 3.11

When you pray, you must not be like the hypocrites; for they love to stand and pray in the synagogues and at the street corners, that they may be seen by men. Truly, I say to you, they have received their reward.

Matthew 6.5

Why do you see the speck that is in your brother's eye, but do not notice the log that is in your own eye? Or how can you say to your brother, 'Let me take the speck out of your eye,' when there is the log in your own eye? You hypocrite, first take the log out of your own eye, and then you will see clearly to take the speck out of your brother's eye.

Matthew 7.3–5

You brood of vipers! how can you speak good, when you are evil? For out of the abundance of the heart the mouth speaks. The good man out of his good treasure brings forth good, and the evil man out of his evil treasure brings forth evil. I tell you, on the day of judgment men will render account for every careless word they utter; for by your words you will be justified, and by your words you will be condemned.

Matthew 12.34–37

Woe to you, scribes and Pharisees, hypocrites! for you are like whitewashed tombs, which outwardly appear beautiful, but within they are full of dead men's bones and all uncleanness. So you also outwardly appear righteous to men, but within you are full of hypocrisy and iniquity . . . You serpents, you brood of vipers, how are you to escape being sentenced to hell?

Matthew 23.27–28,33

But if that wicked servant says to himself, 'My master is delayed,' and begins to beat his fellow servants, and eats and drinks with the drunken, the master of that servant will come on a day when he does not expect him and at an hour he does not know, and will punish him, and put him with the hypocrites; there men will weep and gnash their teeth.

Matthew 24.48–51

Stop making crooked the straight paths of the Lord.

Acts 13.10

Therefore you have no excuse, O man, whoever you are, when you judge another; for in passing judgment upon him you condemn yourself, because you, the judge, are doing the very same things.

Romans 2.1

But be doers of the word, and not hearers only, deceiving yourselves.

James 1.22

What does it profit, my brethren, if a man says he has faith but has not works? Can his faith save him?

James 2.14

So put away all malice and all guile and insincerity and envy and all slander.

1 Peter 2.1

If any one says, 'I love God,' and hates his brother, he is a liar.

1 John 4.20

You have the name of being alive, and you are dead.

Revelation 3.1

I

Ideal

See also **Perfection**

I am God Almighty; walk before me, and be blameless. And I will . . . multiply you exceedingly.

Genesis 17.1−2

Mark the blameless man, and behold the upright.

Psalms 37.37

Where there is no prophecy the people cast off restraint.

Proverbs 29.18

Mend your ways, heed my appeal, agree with one another, live in peace, and the God of love and peace will be with you.

2 Corinthians 13.11

And his gifts were . . . for building up the body of Christ, until we all attain to the unity of the faith and of the knowledge of the Son of God, to mature manhood, to the measure of the stature of the fulness of Christ.

Ephesians 4.11−13

Christ also suffered for you, leaving you an example, that you should follow in his steps. He committed no sin; no guile was found on his lips. When he was reviled, he did not revile in return; when he suffered, he did not threaten; but he trusted to him who judges justly. He himself bore our sins in his body on the tree, that we might die to sin and live to righteousness.

1 Peter 2.21−24

Idleness

See also **Laziness**

Go to the ant, O sluggard;
   consider her ways, and be wise.

Proverbs 6.6

How long will you lie there, O sluggard?
   When will you arise from your sleep?
A little sleep, a little slumber,
   a little folding of the hands to rest,
and poverty will come upon you like a
      vagabond,
   and want like an armed man.

Proverbs 6.9−11

A slack hand causes poverty,
   but the hand of the diligent makes rich.

Proverbs 10.4

A son who gathers in summer is prudent,
   but a son who sleeps in harvest brings
      shame.

Proverbs 10.5

Like vinegar to the teeth, and smoke to
      the eyes,
   so is the sluggard to those who send him.

Proverbs 10.26

Better is a man of humble standing who
      works for himself
   than one who plays the great man but
      lacks bread.

Proverbs 12.9

Slothfulness casts into a deep sleep,
   and an idle person will suffer hunger.

Proverbs 19.15

The sluggard does not plough in the
      autumn;
   he will seek at harvest and have nothing.

Proverbs 20.4

Through sloth the roof sinks in,
and through indolence the house leaks.

Ecclesiastes 10.18

Rise up, you women who are at ease, hear
my voice . . .
In a little more than a year
you will shudder, you complacent
women;
for the vintage will fail,
the fruit harvest will not come.

Isaiah 32.9–10

Never flag in zeal, be aglow with the
Spirit, serve the Lord.

Romans 12.11

Admonish the idlers, encourage the faint-
hearted, help the weak, be patient with
them all.

1 Thessalonians 5.14

Keep away from any brother who is living
in idleness and not in accord with the tradition.

2 Thessalonians 3.6

For even when we were with you, we gave
you this command: If any one will not
work, let him not eat. For we hear that
some of you are living in idleness, mere
busybodies, not doing any work. Now such
persons we command and exhort in the
Lord Jesus Christ to do their work in quietness and to earn their own living.

2 Thessalonians 3.10–12

Do you want to be shown . . . that faith
apart from works is barren?

James 2.20

Idolatry

You shall not make for yourself a graven
image, or any likeness of anything that is in
heaven above, or that is in the earth
beneath or that is in the water under the
earth; you shall not bow down to them or
serve them; for I the Lord your God am a
jealous God.

Exodus 20.4–5

Do not turn to idols or make for yourselves molten gods: I am the Lord your
God.

Leviticus 19.4

You shall make for yourselves no idols and
erect no graven image or pillar, and you
shall not set up a figured stone in your land,
to bow down to them; for I am the Lord
your God.

Leviticus 26.1

And if in spite of this you will not hearken
to me, but walk contrary to me . . . I will
destroy your high places, and cut down
your incense altars . . . and my soul will
abhor you.

Leviticus 26.27,30

They have stirred me to jealousy with what
is no god;
they have provoked me with their idols.

Deuteronomy 32.21

For rebellion is as the sin of divination,
and stubbornness is as iniquity and
idolatry.

1 Samuel 15.23

Who shall ascend the hill of the Lord?
And who shall stand in his holy place?
He . . . who does not lift up his soul to
what is false.

Psalms 24.3–4

Thou hatest those who pay regard to vain
idols.

Psalms 31.6

All worshippers of images are put to
shame,
who make their boast in worthless idols.

Psalms 97.7

The makers of idols go in confusion together.

Isaiah 45.16

What profit is an idol
when its maker has shaped it,
a metal image, a teacher of lies?
For the workman trusts in his own creation
when he makes dumb idols!

Habakkuk 2.18

They exchanged the truth about God for a lie and worshipped and served the creature rather than the Creator.

Romans 1.25

I wrote to you not to associate with any one who bears the name of brother if he is guilty of immorality or greed, or is an idolater.

1 Corinthians 5.11

We know that 'an idol has no real existence,' and that 'there is no God but one.'

1 Corinthians 8.4

Shun the worship of idols.

1 Corinthians 10.14

Be sure of this, that no fornicator or impure man, or one who is covetous (that is, an idolater), has any inheritance in the kingdom of Christ and of God.

Ephesians 5.5

Keep yourselves from idols.

1 John 5.21

But as for the cowardly, the faithless, the polluted, as for murderers, fornicators, sorcerers, idolaters, and all liars, their lot shall be in the lake that burns with fire and sulphur, which is the second death.

Revelation 21.8

Ignominy

Draw near to me, redeem me,
    set me free because of my enemies!

Psalms 69.18

He who commits adultery has no sense;
    he who does it destroys himself.
Wounds and dishonour will he get,
    and his disgrace will not be wiped away.

Proverbs 6.32–33

A servant who deals wisely has the king's
    favour,
    but his wrath falls on one who acts
        shamefully.

Proverbs 14.35

When wickedness comes, contempt
    comes also;
    and with dishonour comes disgrace.

Proverbs 18.3

Woe to him who makes his neighbours
    drink . . .
You will be sated with contempt
    instead of glory . . .
The cup in the Lord's right hand
    will come around to you,
    and shame will come upon your glory!

Habakkuk 2.15–16

Ignorance

And the priest shall make atonement before the Lord for the person who commits an error, when he sins unwittingly, to make atonement for him; and he shall be forgiven.

Numbers 15.28

We are but of yesterday, and know
    nothing,
    for our days on earth are a shadow.

Job 8.9

Can you find out the deep things of God?
    Can you find out the limit of the
        Almighty?
It is higher than heaven — what can you
    do?
    Deeper than Sheol — what can you
        know?

Job 11.7–8

But where shall wisdom be found?
    And where is the place of understanding?
Man does not know the way to it,
    and it is not found in the land of the
        living.

Job 28.12–13

Be not like a horse or a mule, without
    understanding,
    which must be curbed with bit and bridle,
    else it will not keep with you.

Psalms 32.9

The unfolding of thy words gives light;
  it imparts understanding to the simple.

Psalms 119.130

He cannot find out what God has done from the beginning to the end.

Ecclesiastes 3.11

And I thought the dead who are already dead more fortunate than the living who are still alive; but better than both is he who has not yet been, and has not seen the evil deeds that are done under the sun.

Ecclesiastes 4.2–3

As you do not know how the spirit comes to the bones in the womb of a woman with child, so you do not know the work of God who makes everything.

Ecclesiastes 11.5

These are only the poor, they have no
  sense;
for they do not know the way of the Lord,
  the law of their God.

Jeremiah 5.4

And Jesus said, 'Father, forgive them; for they know not what they do.'

Luke 23.34

Come to your right mind, and sin no more. For some have no knowledge of God.

1 Corinthians 15.34

You must no longer live as the Gentiles do, in the futility of their minds; they are darkened in their understanding, alienated from the life of God because of the ignorance that is in them, due to their hardness of heart.

Ephesians 4.17–18

Every high priest . . . can deal gently with the ignorant and wayward, since he himself is beset with weakness.

Hebrews 5.1–2

For it is God's will that by doing right you should put to silence the ignorance of foolish men.

1 Peter 2.15

But these, like irrational animals, creatures of instinct, born to be caught and killed, reviling in matters of which they are ignorant, will be destroyed in the same destruction with them, suffering wrong for their wrongdoing.

2 Peter 2.12–13

Illness

See also **Disease**

And the Lord will take away from you all sickness.

Deuteronomy 7.15

Man is . . . chastened with pain upon
  his bed,
  and with continual strife in his bones.

Job 33.19

Blessed is he who considers the poor!
  The Lord delivers him in the day of
    trouble . . .
The Lord sustains him on his sickbed;
  in his illness thou healest all his
    infirmities.

Psalms 41.1,3

A man's spirit will endure sickness;
  but a broken spirit who can bear?

Proverbs 18.14

And these signs will accompany those who believe: in my name they will cast out demons; they will speak in new tongues; they will pick up serpents, and if they drink any deadly thing, it will not hurt them; they will lay their hands on the sick, and they will recover.

Mark 16.17–18

Is any among you sick? Let him call for the elders of the church, and let them pray over him, anointing him with oil in the name of the Lord; and the prayer of faith will save the sick man, and the Lord will raise him up.

James 5.14–15

Imagination

The Lord searches all hearts, and understands every plan and thought.

1 Chronicles 28.9

When your eyes light upon it, it is gone;
for suddenly it takes to itself wings,
flying like an eagle toward heaven.

Proverbs 23.5

Do not listen to the words of the prophets who prophesy to you, filling you with vain hopes; they speak visions of their own minds, not from the mouth of the Lord. They say continually to those who despise the word of the Lord, 'It shall be well with you'.

Jeremiah 23.16—17

Every one who looks at a woman lustfully has already committed adultery with her in his heart.

Matthew 5.28

So they are without excuse; for although they knew God they did not honour him as God or give thanks to him, but they became futile in their thinking and their senseless minds were darkened.

Romans 1.20—21

If any one imagines that he knows something, he does not yet know as he ought to know.

1 Corinthians 8.2

Therefore let any one who thinks that he stands take heed lest he fall.

1 Corinthians 10.12

For if any one thinks he is something, when he is nothing, he deceives himself.

Galatians 6.3

Imitation (of Christ)

See also **Example**

Be imitators of me, as I am of Christ.

1 Corinthians 11.1

Have this mind among yourselves, which is yours in Christ Jesus, who, though he was in the form of God, did not count equality with God a thing to be grasped, but emptied himself, taking the form of a servant, being born in the likeness of men.

Philippians 2.5—8

As obedient children, do not be conformed to the passions of your former ignorance, but as he who called you is holy, be holy yourselves in all your conduct; since it is written, 'You shall be holy, for I am holy.'

1 Peter 1.14—16

But if when you do right and suffer for it you take it patiently, you have God's approval. For to this you have been called, because Christ also suffered for you, leaving you an example, that you should follow in his steps.

1 Peter 2.20—21

He who says he abides in him ought to walk in the same way in which he walked.

1 John 2.6

Imminence

The days are at hand, and the fulfilment of every vision. For there shall be no more any false vision or flattering divination within the house of Israel. But I the Lord will speak the word which I will speak, and it will be performed. It will no longer be delayed, but in your days, O rebellious house, I will speak the word and perform it, says the Lord God.

Ezekiel 12.23—25

For still the vision awaits its time;
it hastens to the end — it will not lie.
If it seem slow, wait for it;
it will surely come, it will not delay.

Habakkuk 2.3

Behold, now is the acceptable time; behold, now is the day of salvation.

2 Corinthians 6.2

Behold, the Judge is standing at the doors.

James 5.9

The end of all things is at hand; therefore keep sane and sober for your prayers.

1 Peter 4.7

Immodesty

See also **Promiscuity**

The Lord said:
Because the daughters of Zion are
haughty
and walk with outstretched necks,
glancing wantonly with their eyes,
mincing along as they go,
tinkling with their feet;
the Lord will smite with a scab
the heads of the daughters of Zion,
and the Lord will lay bare their secret
parts.
In that day the Lord will take away the
finery of the anklets, the headbands, and
the crescents; the pendants, the bracelets,
and the scarfs; the headdresses, the armlets,
the sashes, the perfume boxes, and the
amulets; the signet rings and nose rings; the
festal robes, the mantles, the cloaks, and
the handbags; the garments of gauze, the
linen garments, the turbans, and the veils.
Instead of perfume there will be
rottenness;
and instead of a girdle, a rope;
and instead of well-set hair, baldness;
and instead of a rich robe, a girding of
sackcloth;
instead of beauty, shame.

Isaiah 3.16−24

Immorality

See also **Sin, Wrong**

Transgression speaks to the wicked
deep in his heart;
there is no fear of God
before his eyes . . .
The words of his mouth are mischief
and deceit;
he has ceased to act wisely and do good.
He plots mischief while on his bed;
he sets himself in a way that is not good;
he spurns not evil.

Psalms 36.1,3−4

Why do you boast, O mighty man,
of mischief done against the godly?
. . . You love evil more than good,
and lying more than speaking the truth.
You love all words that devour,
O deceitful tongue.
But God will break you down for ever . . .
he will uproot you from the land of the
living.

Psalms 52.1,3−5

Discretion will watch over you;
understanding will guard you;
delivering you from the way of evil,
from men of perverted speech . . .
who rejoice in doing evil
and delight in the perverseness of evil;
men whose paths are crooked,
and who are devious in their ways.

Proverbs 2.11−12,14−15

He who is steadfast in righteousness will
live,
but he who pursues evil will die.

Proverbs 11.19

He who justifies the wicked and he who
condemns the righteous
are both alike an abomination to the
Lord.

Proverbs 17.15

Woe to those who call evil good and good
evil,
who put darkness for light and light for
darkness,
who put bitter for sweet and sweet for
bitter!

Isaiah 5.20

And since they did not see fit to acknow
ledge God, God gave them up to a base
mind and to improper conduct. They were
filled with all manner of wickedness, evil
covetousness, malice. Full of envy, murder
strife, deceit, malignity, they are gossip
. . . boastful, inventors of evil, disobedient
to parents, foolish, faithless, heartless, ruth
less. Though they know God's decree that
those who do such things deserve to die
they not only do them but approve those
who practise them.

Romans 1.28−32

Immortality

See also **Life, Resurrection**

Depart from evil, and do good;
so shall you abide for ever.

Psalms 37.27

And many of those who sleep in the dust of the earth shall awake, some to everlasting life, and some to shame and everlasting contempt.

Daniel 12.2

And every one who has left houses or brothers or sisters or father or mother or children or lands, for my name's sake, will receive a hundredfold, and inherit eternal life.

Matthew 19.29

For God so loved the world that he gave his only Son, that whoever believes in him should not perish but have eternal life.

John 3.16

Every one who drinks of this water will thirst again, but whoever drinks of the water that I shall give him will never thirst; the water that I shall give him will become in him a spring of water welling up to eternal life.

John 4.13–14

Unless you eat the flesh of the Son of man and drink his blood, you have no life in you; he who eats my flesh and drinks my blood has eternal life, and I will raise him up at the last day.

John 6.53–54

Truly, truly, I say to you, if any one keeps my word, he will never see death.

John 8.51

My sheep hear my voice, and I know them, and they follow me; and I give them eternal life, and they shall never perish, and no one shall snatch them out of my hand.

John 10.27–28

For he will render to every man according to his works: to those who by patience in well-doing seek for glory and honour and immortality, he will give eternal life.

Romans 2.6–7

As sin reigned in death, grace also might reign through righteousness to eternal life through Jesus Christ our Lord.

Romans 5.21

For the wages of sin is death, but the free gift of God is eternal life in Christ Jesus our Lord.

Romans 6.23

When the perishable puts on the imperishable, and the mortal puts on immortality, then shall come to pass the saying that is written: 'Death is swallowed up in victory.'

1 Corinthians 15.54

Whatever a man sows, that he will also reap . . . he who sows to the Spirit will from the Spirit reap eternal life.

Galatians 6.7–8

Our Saviour Christ Jesus . . . abolished death and brought life and immortality to light through the gospel.

2 Timothy 1.10

And this is what he has promised us, eternal life.

1 John 2.25

God gave us eternal life, and this life is in his Son.

1 John 5.11

Immutability

Thou art the same, and thy years have no end.
The children of thy servants shall dwell secure;
their posterity shall be established before thee.

Psalms 102.27–28

What is crooked cannot be made straight, and what is lacking cannot be numbered.

Ecclesiastes 1.15

For I the Lord do not change.

Malachi 3.6

Jesus Christ is the same yesterday and today and for ever.

Hebrews 13.8

Every good endowment and every perfect gift is from above, coming down from the Father of lights with whom there is no variation or shadow due to change.

James 1.17

Impartiality

Truly I perceive that God shows no partiality, but in every nation any one who fears him and does what is right is acceptable to him.

Acts 10.34–35

For God shows no partiality.

Romans 2.11

Impatience

Be still before the Lord, and wait patiently for him;
  fret not yourself over him who prospers in his way,
  over the man who carries out evil devices!
Refrain from anger, and forsake wrath!
  Fret not yourself; it tends only to evil.
For the wicked shall be cut off;
  but those who wait for the Lord shall possess the land.

Psalms 37.7–9

Hope deferred makes the heart sick,
  but a desire fulfilled is a tree of life.

Proverbs 13.12

He who has a hasty temper exalts folly.

Proverbs 14.29

Do you see a man who is hasty in his words?
  There is more hope for a fool than for him.

Proverbs 29.20

The patient in spirit is better than the proud in spirit.
Be not quick to anger,
  for anger lodges in the bosom of fools.

Ecclesiastes 7.8–9

Count it all joy, my brethren, when you meet various trials, for you know that the testing of your faith produces steadfastness. And let steadfastness have its full effect, that you may be perfect and complete, lacking in nothing.

James 1.2–4

Impenitence

See also **Hardness**

There are those that rebel against the light,
  who are not acquainted with its ways,
  and do not stay in its paths.

Job 24.13

The man greedy for gain curses and renounces the Lord.

Psalms 10.3

Why do you boast, O mighty man,
  of mischief done against the godly?

Psalms 52.1

Because I have called and you refused to listen,
  have stretched out my hand and no one has heeded,
and you have ignored all my counsel
  and would have none of my reproof,
I also will laugh at your calamity;
  I will mock when panic strikes you.

Proverbs 1.24–26

He who conceals his transgressions will not prosper,
  but he who confesses and forsakes them will obtain mercy.
Blessed is the man who fears the Lord always;
  but he who hardens his heart will fall into calamity.

Proverbs 28.13–14

He who is often reproved, yet stiffens his
 neck
 will suddenly be broken beyond healing.

Proverbs 29.1

You dwell in the midst of a rebellious
house, who have eyes to see, but see not,
who have ears to hear, but hear not; for
they are a rebellious house.

Ezekiel 12.2–3

If any one who hears the sound of the
trumpet does not take warning, and the
sword comes and takes him away, his blood
shall be upon his own head.

Ezekiel 33.4

Do you not know that God's kindness is
meant to lead you to repentance? But by
your hard and impenitent heart you are
storing up wrath for yourself on the day of
wrath when God's righteous judgment will
be revealed.

Romans 2.4–5

Impetuosity

See also **Impatience**

Do you see a man who is hasty in his
 words?
There is more hope for a fool than for him.

Proverbs 29.20

You ought to be quiet and do nothing
rash.

Acts 19.26

Impossibility

No one can serve two masters; for either
he will hate the one and love the other, or
he will be devoted to the one and despise
the other. You cannot serve God and
mammon.

Matthew 6.24

If you have faith as a grain of mustard
seed, you will say to this mountain, 'Move
from here to there,' and it will move; and
nothing will be impossible to you.

Matthew 17.20

For with God nothing will be impossible.

Luke 1.37

What is impossible with men is possible
with God.

Luke 18.27

And without faith it is impossible to please
him. For whoever would draw near to God
must believe that he exists and and that he
rewards those who seek him.

Hebrews 11.6

Incarnation

See also **Immortality**

He was in the world, and the world was
made through him, yet the world knew him
not. He came to his own home, and his own
people received him not. But to all who
received him, who believed in his name, he
gave power to become children of God;
who were born, not of blood nor of the will
of the flesh nor of the will of man, but of
God.

   And the Word became flesh and dwelt
among us, full of grace and truth; we have
beheld his glory, glory as of the only Son
from the Father.

John 1.10–14

For God has done what the law, weakened
by the flesh, could not do: sending his own
Son in the likeness of sinful flesh and for
sin, he condemned sin in the flesh.

Romans 8.3

But when the time had fully come, God
sent forth his Son, born of woman, born
under the law, to redeem those who were
under the law, so that we might receive
adoption as sons.

Galatians 4.4–5

Christ Jesus came into the world to save
sinners.

1 Timothy 1.15

He was manifested in the flesh,
vindicated in the Spirit,
 seen by angels,

preached among the nations,
believed on in the world, taken up in glory.

1 Timothy 3.16

The reason the Son of God appeared was to destroy the works of the devil.

1 John 3.8

God sent his only Son into the world, so that we might live through him. In this is love, not that we loved God but that he loved us and sent his Son to be the expiation for our sins . . . if God so loved us, we also ought to love one another.

1 John 4.9–11

Incest

None of you shall approach any one near of kin to him to uncover nakedness . . . You shall not uncover the nakedness of your father, which is the nakedness of your mother; she is your mother, you shall not uncover her nakedness. You shall not uncover the nakedness of your father's wife; it is your father's nakedness. You shall not uncover the nakedness of your sister, the daughter of your father or the daughter of your mother, whether born at home or born abroad. You shall not uncover the nakedness of your son's daughter or of your daughter's daughter, for their nakedness is your own nakedness. You shall not uncover the nakedness of your father's wife's daughter, begotten by your father, since she is your sister. You shall not uncover the nakedness of your father's sister; she is your father's near kinswoman. You shall not uncover the nakedness of your mother's sister, for she is your mother's near kinswoman. You shall not uncover the nakedness of your father's brother, that is, you shall not approach his wife; she is your aunt. You shall not uncover the nakedness of your daughter-in-law; she is your son's wife, you shall not uncover her nakedness. You shall not uncover the nakedness of your brother's wife; she is your brother's nakedness. You shall not uncover the nakedness of a woman and of her daughter, and you shall not take her son's daughter or her daughter's daughter to uncover her nakedness; they are your near kinswomen; it is wickedness. And you shall not take a woman as a rival wife to her sister, uncovering her nakedness while her sister is yet alive.

Leviticus 18.6–18

The man who lies with his father's wife has uncovered his father's nakedness; both of them shall be put to death, their blood is upon them. If a man lies with his daughter-in-law, both of them shall be put to death; they have committed incest, their blood is upon them. If a man lies with a male as with a woman, both of them have committed an abomination; they shall be put to death, their blood is upon them. If a man takes a wife and her mother also, it is wickedness; they shall be burned with fire, both he and they, that there may be no wickedness among you.

Leviticus 20.11–14

A man shall not take his father's wife, nor shall he uncover her who is his father's.

Deuteronomy 22.30

Cursed be he who lies with his sister, whether the daughter of his father or the daughter of his mother.

Deuteronomy 27.22

Cursed be he who lies with his mother-in-law.

Deuteronomy 27.23

It is actually reported that there is immorality among you, and of a kind that is not found among pagans; for a man is living with his father's wife.

1 Corinthians 5.1

Indecision

See also **Doubt, Hesitancy**

How long will you go limping with two different opinions? If the Lord is God, follow him; but if Ba'al, then follow him.

1 Kings 18.21

Do not swerve to the right or to the left; turn your foot away from evil.

Proverbs 4.27

He who observes the wind will not sow;
  and he who regards the clouds will not
    reap.

Ecclesiastes 11.4

No one who puts his hand to the plough
and looks back is fit for the kingdom of
God.

Luke 9.62

Remember Lot's wife.

Luke 17.32

Therefore we must pay the closer attention
to what we have heard, lest we drift away
from it.

Hebrews 2.1

For that person must not suppose that a
double-minded man, unstable in all his
ways, will receive anything from the Lord.

James 1.7–8

Independence

But we exhort you, brethren, to do so
more and more, to aspire to live quietly, to
mind your own affairs, and to work with
your hands, as we charged you; so that you
may command the respect of outsiders, and
be dependent on nobody.

1 Thessalonians 4.10–12

Indifference

If any one will not receive you or listen to
your words, shake off the dust from your
feet as you leave that house or town. Truly,
I say to you, it shall be more tolerable on
the day of judgment for the land of Sodom
and Gomor'rah than for that town.

Matthew 10.14–15

Indignation

See also **Anger**

Pour forth the overflowings of your anger,
  and look on every one that is proud, and
    abase him.

Job 40.11

But the Lord is the true God;
  he is the living God and the everlasting
    King.
At his wrath the earth quakes,
  and the nations cannot endure his
    indignation.

Jeremiah 10.10

By what that righteous man saw and heard
as he lived among them, he was vexed in his
righteous soul day after day with their lawless deeds.

2 Peter 2.8

Indiscipline

The iniquities of the wicked ensnare him,
  and he is caught in the toils of his sin.
He dies for lack of discipline,
  and because of his great folly he is lost.

Proverbs 5.22–23

He who spares the rod hates his son,
  but he who loves him is diligent to
    discipline him.

Proverbs 13.24

Individuality

For as in one body we have many members, and all the members do not have the
same function, so we, though many, are
one body in Christ, and individually members one of another.

Romans 12.4–5

By the grace of God I am what I am.

1 Corinthians 15.10

Inexorability

He who flees from the terror
  shall fall into the pit,
and he who climbs out of the pit
  shall be caught in the snare.

Jeremiah 48.44

Though they dig into Sheol,
  from there shall my hand take them;
though they climb up to heaven,
  from there I will bring them down.

Though they hide themselves on the top of
  Carmel,
    from there I will search out and take
      them;
and though they hide from my sight at the
    bottom of the sea,
  there I will command the serpent, and it
    shall bite them.
And though they go into captivity before
    their enemies,
  there I will command the sword, and it
    shall slay them;
and I will set my eyes upon them
  for evil and not for good.

Amos 9.2−4

Infatuation

Why should you be infatuated, my son,
  with a loose woman
and embrace the bosom of an
    adventuress?

Proverbs 5.20

Infirmity

See also Weakness

Remember also your Creator in the days
of your youth, before the evil days come,
and the years draw nigh, when you will say,
'I have no pleasure in them'; before the sun
and the light and the moon and the stars are
darkened and the . . . strong men are bent.

Ecclesiastes 12.1−3

The Spirit helps us in our weakness; for we
do not know how to pray as we ought, but
the Spirit himself intercedes for us with
sighs too deep for words.

Romans 8.26

We who are strong ought to bear with the
failings of the weak, and not to please
ourselves.

Romans 15.1

The Lord . . . said to me, '. . . my power
is made perfect in weakness.' I will all the
more gladly boast of my weaknesses, that
the power of Christ may rest upon me. For
the sake of Christ, then, I am content with

weaknesses, insults, hardships, persecutions, and calamities; for when I am weak,
then I am strong.

2 Corinthians 12.8−10

Influence

The Lord our God be with us, as he was
with our fathers; may he not leave us or
forsake us; that he may incline our hearts to
him, to walk in all his ways, and to keep his
commandments, his statutes, and his ordinances, which he commanded our fathers.

1 Kings 8.57−58

O Lord, the God of Abraham, Isaac, and
Israel, our fathers, keep for ever such purposes and thoughts in the hearts of thy
people, and direct their hearts toward thee.

1 Chronicles 29.18

The Lord opened her heart to give heed to
what was said.

Acts 16.14

Ingratitude

Take heed lest you forget the Lord your
God . . . lest, when you have eaten and
are full, and have built goodly houses and
live in them, and when your herds and
flocks multiply, and your silver and gold is
multiplied, and all that you have is multiplied, then your heart be lifted up, and you
forget the Lord your God.

Deuteronomy 8.11−1

Because you did not serve the Lord your
God with joyfulness and gladness of heart
by reason of the abundance of all things
therefore you shall serve your enemie
whom the Lord will send against you, i
hunger and thirst, in nakedness, and i
want of all things; and he will put a yoke o
iron upon your neck, until he has destroye
you.

Deuteronomy 28.47−4

Our fathers, when they were in Egypt,
  did not consider thy wonderful works;

they did not remember the abundance of
    thy steadfast love.

Psalms 106.7

If a man returns evil for good,
    evil will not depart from his house.

Proverbs 17.13

Love your enemies, do good to those who
hate you, bless those who curse you, pray
for those who abuse you.

Luke 6.27–28

He came to his own home, and his own
people received him not.

John 1.11

In the last days there will come times of
stress. For men will be lovers of self, lovers
of money, proud, arrogant, abusive, disobedient to their parents, ungrateful,
unholy . . . Avoid such people.

2 Timothy 3.1–2,5

Iniquity

See also **Sin, Wickedness, Wrong**

Those who plough iniquity
    and sow trouble reap the same.

Job 4.8

If iniquity is in your hand, put it far away,
    and let not wickedness dwell in your
        tents.

Job 11.14

For his eyes are upon the ways of a man,
    and he sees all his steps.
There is no gloom or deep darkness
    where evildoers may hide themselves.

Job 34.21–22

Take heed, do not turn to iniquity.

Job 36.21

For thou art not a God who delights in
    wickedness;
    evil may not sojourn with thee . . .
thou hatest all evildoers.

Psalms 5.4–5

Take me not off with the wicked,
    with those who are workers of evil,
who speak peace with their neighbours,
    while mischief is in their hearts.
Requite them according to their work,
    and according to the evil of their deeds;
requite them according to the work of their
        hands;
    render them their due reward.
Because they do not regard the works of
        the Lord,
    or the work of his hands,
he will break them down and build them up
        no more.

Psalms 28.3–5

Fret not yourself because of the wicked,
    be not envious of wrongdoers!
For they will soon fade like the grass,
    and wither like the green herb.

Psalms 37.1–2

Though the wicked sprout like grass
    and all evildoers flourish,
they are doomed to destruction for ever,
    but thou, O Lord, art on high for ever.
For, lo, thy enemies, O Lord,
    for, lo, thy enemies shall perish;
    all evildoers shall be scattered.

Psalms 92.7–9

Keep steady my steps according to thy
        promise,
    and let no iniquity get dominion over me.

Psalms 119.133

The iniquities of the wicked ensnare him,
    and he is caught in the toils of his sin.

Proverbs 5.22

The Lord is a stronghold to him whose way
    is upright,
    but destruction to evildoers.

Proverbs 10.29

All who watch to do evil shall be cut off.

Isaiah 29.20

But if you warn the wicked, and he does
not turn from his wickedness, or from his
wicked way, he shall die in his iniquity.

Ezekiel 3.19

But when a righteous man turns away from his righteousness and commits iniquity and does the same abominable things that the wicked man does, shall he live? None of the righteous deeds which he has done shall be remembered; for the treachery of which he is guilty and the sin he has committed, he shall die.

Ezekiel 18.24

Woe to those who devise wickedness.

Micah 2.1

Let every one who names the name of the Lord depart from iniquity.

2 Timothy 2.19

Injustice

See also **Corruption**

You shall not utter a false report. You shall not join hands with a wicked man, to be a malicious witness. You shall not follow a multitude to do evil; nor shall you bear witness in a suit, turning aside after a multitude, so as to pervert justice; nor shall you be partial to a poor man in his suit.

Exodus 23.1–3

You shall do no injustice in judgment; you shall not be partial to the poor or defer to the great, but in righteousness shall you judge your neighbour.

Leviticus 19.15

You shall not pervert the justice due to the sojourner or to the fatherless, or take a widow's garment in pledge.

Deuteronomy 24.17

Cursed be he who perverts the justice due to the sojourner, the fatherless, and the widow.

Deuteronomy 27.19

How long will you judge unjustly?

Psalms 82.2

He who justifies the wicked and he who condemns the righteous

are both alike an abomination to the Lord.

Proverbs 17.15

He who sows injustice will reap calamity.

Proverbs 22.8

He who oppresses the poor to increase his own wealth, or gives to the rich, will only come to want.

Proverbs 22.16

He who says to the wicked, 'You are innocent,'
will be cursed by peoples, abhorred by nations.

Proverbs 24.24

If one turns away his ear from hearing the law,
even his prayer is an abomination.

Proverbs 28.9

If you see in a province the poor oppressed and justice and right violently taken away, do not be amazed at the matter; for the high official is watched by a higher, and there are yet higher ones over them. But in all, a king is an advantage to a land with cultivated fields.

Ecclesiastes 5.8–9

Woe to those who decree iniquitous decrees,
and the writers who keep writing oppression,
to turn aside the needy from justice
and to rob the poor of my people of their right.

Isaiah 10.1–2

O you who turn justice to wormwood,
and cast down righteousness to the earth!
. . . They hate him who reproves in the gate,
and they abhor him who speaks the truth.

Amos 5.7,10

Soldiers also asked him, 'And we, what shall we do?' And he said to them, 'Rob no one by violence or by false accusation, and be content with your wages.'

Luke 3.14

For one is approved if, mindful of God, he endures pain while suffering unjustly.

1 Peter 2.19

Innocence

Let not wickedness dwell in your tents.
Surely then you will lift up your face
without blemish;
you will be secure, and will not fear . . .
Your life will be brighter than the
noonday;
its darkness will be like the morning.
And you will have confidence, because
there is hope;
you will be protected and take your rest
in safety.
You will lie down, and none will make you
afraid;
many will entreat your favour.

Job 11.14−15,17−19

He delivers the innocent man;
you will be delivered through the
cleanness of your hands.

Job 22.30

Let me be weighed in a just balance,
and let God know my integrity!

Job 31.6

I shall be blameless,
and innocent of great transgressions.

Psalms 19.13

Who shall ascend the hill of the Lord?
And who shall stand in his holy place?
He who has clean hands and a pure heart,
who does not lift up his soul to what is
false,
and does not swear deceitfully.
He will receive blessing from the Lord,
and vindication from the God of his
salvation.

Psalms 24.3−5

Blessed is the man to whom the Lord
imputes no iniquity,
and in whose spirit there is no deceit.

Psalms 32.2

Mark the blameless man, and behold the
upright,
for there is posterity for the man of
peace.
But transgressors shall be altogether
destroyed.

Psalms 37.37−38

The . . . blameless shall minister to me.

Psalms 101.6

Blessed are those whose way is blameless,
who walk in the law of the Lord!
Blessed are those who keep his testimonies,
who seek him with their whole heart.

Psalms 119.1−2

For the upright will inhabit the land,
and men of integrity will remain in it;
but the wicked will be cut off from the land,
and the treacherous will be rooted out
of it.

Proverbs 2.21−22

Blessed are the pure in heart, for they
shall see God.

Matthew 5.8

As you once yielded your members to
impurity and to greater and greater iniquity, so now yield your members to righteousness for sanctification.

Romans 6.19

Brethren, do not be children in your thinking; be babes in evil, but in thinking be
mature.

1 Corinthians 14.20

He chose us in him before the foundation
of the world, that we should be holy and
blameless before him.

Ephesians 1.4

Do all things without grumbling or questioning, that you may be blameless and
innocent, children of God without blemish
in the midst of a crooked and perverse
generation.

Philippians 2.14−15

May the God of peace himself sanctify you
wholly; and may your spirit and soul and

body be kept sound and blameless at the coming of our Lord Jesus Christ.

1 Thessalonians 5.23

A bishop . . . must be blameless.

Titus 1.7

Religion that is pure and undefiled before God and the Father is this: to visit orphans and widows in their affliction, and to keep oneself unstained from the world.

James 1.27

Innuendo

A worthless person, a wicked man, goes about with crooked speech, winks with his eyes, scrapes with his feet, points with his finger, with perverted heart devises evil, continually sowing discord; therefore calamity will come upon him suddenly; in a moment he will be broken beyond healing.

Proverbs 6.12–15

Insensitivity

He who sings songs to a heavy heart is like one who takes off a garment on a cold day, and like vinegar on a wound.

Proverbs 25.20

Insight

See also **Discretion, Wisdom**

For he knows worthless men; when he sees iniquity, will he not consider it?

Job 11.11

Trust in the Lord with all your heart, and do not rely on your own insight.

Proverbs 3.5

For he has made known to us in all wisdom and insight the mystery of his will.

Ephesians 1.9

Insignificance

How then can man be righteous before God?
How can he who is born of woman be clean?
Behold, even the moon is not bright and the stars are not clean in his sight;
how much less man, who is a maggot, and the son of man, who is a worm!

Job 25.4–6

When I look at thy heavens, the work of thy fingers,
the moon and the stars which thou hast established;
what is man that thou art mindful of him, and the son of man that thou dost care for him?

Psalms 8.3–4

Insolence

See also **Arrogance, Injustice, Pride**

I send you to the people of Israel, to a nation of rebels, who have rebelled against me; they and their fathers . . . are impudent and stubborn.

Ezekiel 2.3–4

Inspiration

Who has made man's mouth? Who makes him dumb, or deaf, or seeing, or blind? Is it not I, the Lord? Now therefore go, and I will be with your mouth and teach you what you shall speak.

Exodus 4.11–12

The Spirit of the Lord speaks by me, his word is upon my tongue.

2 Samuel 23.2

And when the minstrel played, the power of the Lord came upon him.

2 Kings 3.15

But it is the spirit in a man,
   the breath of the Almighty,
     that makes him understand.

Job 32.8

The Lord God has given me
   the tongue of those who are taught,
that I may know how to sustain with a word
   him that is weary.
Morning by morning he wakens,
   he wakens my ear
   to hear as those who are taught.

Isaiah 50.4

Behold, I have put my words in your
     mouth.
See, I have set you this day over nations
     and over kingdoms,
   to pluck up and to break down,
   to destroy and to overthrow,
   to build and to plant.

Jeremiah 1.9—10

When they deliver you up, do not be anxious how you are to speak or what you are to say; for what you are to say will be given to you in that hour; for it is not you who speak, but the Spirit of your Father speaking through you.

Matthew 10.19—20

And when they bring you before the synagogues and the rulers and the authorities, do not be anxious how or what you are to answer or what you are to say; for the Holy Spirit will teach you in that very hour what you ought to say.

Luke 12.11—12

The wind blows where it wills, and you hear the sound of it, but you do not know whence it comes or whither it goes; so it is with every one who is born of the Spirit.

John 3.8

Now we have received not the spirit of the world, but the Spirit which is from God, that we might understand the gifts bestowed on us by God. And we impart this in words not taught by human wisdom but taught by the Spirit.

1 Corinthians 2.12—13

There are varieties of working, but it is the same God who inspires them all in every one.

1 Corinthians 12.6

Be filled with the Spirit.

Ephesians 5.19

Let the word of Christ dwell in you richly, teach and admonish one another in all wisdom.

Colossians 3.16

All scripture is inspired by God.

2 Timothy 3.16

Instability

When a land transgresses
   it has many rulers.

Proverbs 28.2

Instinct

Out of my understanding a spirit answers me.

Job 20.3

He who trusts in his own mind is a fool.

Proverbs 28.26

Can the Ethiopian change his skin
   or the leopard his spots?

Jeremiah 13.23

Instruction

See also **Education, Learning, Teaching**

To you it was shown, that you might know that the Lord is God; there is no other besides him. Out of heaven he let you hear his voice, that he might discipline you.

Deuteronomy 4.35—36

I will instruct you and teach you
   the way you should go;
I will counsel you with my eye upon you.

Psalms 32.8

Hear, my son, your father's instruction,
  and reject not your mother's teaching;
for they are a fair garland for your head,
  and pendants for your neck.

Proverbs 1.8—9

Hear instruction and be wise,
  and do not neglect it.

Proverbs 8.33

If you are sure that you are a guide to the blind, a light to those who are in darkness, a corrector of the foolish, a teacher of children, having in the law the embodiment of knowledge and truth — you then who teach others, will you not teach yourself?

Romans 2.19—21

The Lord's servant must not be quarrelsome but kindly to every one, an apt teacher, forbearing, correcting his opponents with gentleness.

2 Timothy 2.24—25

All scripture is inspired by God and profitable for teaching, for reproof, for correction, and for training in righteousness, that the man of God may be complete, equipped for every good work.

2 Timothy 3.16—17

Insult

See also **Abuse, Arrogance, Gossip, Slander**

Let thy steadfast love come to me,
    O Lord,
  thy salvation according to thy promise;
then shall I have an answer for those who
    taunt me,
  for I trust in thy word.

Psalms 119.41—42

The vexation of a fool is known at once,
  but the prudent man ignores an insult.

Proverbs 12.16

For the Lord God helps me;
  therefore I have not been confounded.

Isaiah 50.7

Hearken to me, you who know
    righteousness,
  the people in whose heart is my law;
fear not the reproach of men,
  and be not dismayed at their revilings.

Isaiah 51.7

Whoever insults his brother shall be liable to the council, and whoever says, 'You fool!' shall be liable to the hell of fire.

Matthew 5.22

But now put them all away; anger, wrath, malice, slander, and foul talk from your mouth.

Colossians 3.8

He [who does not agree with Jesus Christ] has a morbid craving for controversy and for disputes about words, which produce envy, dissension, slander, base suspicions, and wrangling among men who are depraved in mind and bereft of the truth.

1 Timothy 6.4—5

Is it not the rich who oppress you, is it not they who drag you into court? Is it not they who blaspheme the honourable name which was invoked over you?
  If you really fulfil the royal law, according to the scripture, 'You shall love your neighbour as yourself,' you do well.

James 2.6—8

Maintain good conduct among the Gentiles, so that in case they speak against you as wrongdoers, they may see your good deeds and glorify God on the day of visitation.

1 Peter 2.12

If you are reproached for the name of Christ, you are blessed, because the spirit of glory and of God rests upon you.

1 Peter 4.14

But these, like irrational animals, creatures of instinct, born to be caught and killed, reviling in matters of which they are ignorant, will be destroyed in the same destruction with them, suffering wrong for their wrongdoing.

2 Peter 2.12—1

Integrity

See also **Honesty**

Moreover choose able men from all the people, such as fear God, men who are trustworthy and who hate a bribe; and place such men over the people as rulers.

Exodus 18.21

I hold fast my righteousness, and will not
    let it go;
    my heart does not reproach me for any of
      my days.

Job 27.6

He who walks blamelessly, and does what
    is right,
    and speaks truth from his heart;
who does not slander with his tongue,
    and does no evil to his friend,
    nor takes up a reproach against his
      neighbour;
in whose eyes a reprobate is despised,
    but who honours those who fear
    the Lord;
who swears to his own hurt and does not
    change;
who does not put out his money at interest,
    and does not take a bribe against the
      innocent.
He who does these things shall never be
    moved.

Psalms 15.2–5

If thou triest my heart, if thou visitest me
    by night,
    if thou testest me, thou wilt find no
      wickedness in me;
    my mouth does not transgress.

Psalms 17.3

For the word of the Lord is upright;
    and all his work is done in faithfulness.

Psalms 33.4

Behold, thou desirest truth in the inward
    being.

Psalms 51.6

No good thing does the Lord withhold
    from those who walk uprightly.

Psalms 84.11

He who walks in integrity walks securely,
    but he who perverts his ways will be
      found out.

Proverbs 10.9

The integrity of the upright guides them.

Proverbs 11.3

Men of perverse mind are an abomination
    to the Lord,
    but those of blameless ways are his
      delight.

Proverbs 11.20

The righteous finds refuge through his integrity.

Proverbs 14.32

Better is a poor man who walks in his
    integrity
    than a man who is perverse in speech,
    and is a fool.

Proverbs 19.1

A righteous man who walks in his
    integrity —
blessed are his sons after him!

Proverbs 20.7

Better is a poor man who walks in his
    integrity
    than a rich man who is perverse in his
    ways.

Proverbs 28.6

He who walks in integrity will be delivered.

Proverbs 28.18

For when thy judgments are in the earth,
    the inhabitants of the world learn
      righteousness.

Isaiah 26.9

Hearken to me, you who know
    righteousness,
    the people in whose heart is my law;
fear not the reproach of men,
    and be not dismayed at their revilings.
For the moth will eat them up like
    a garment,
    and the worm will eat them like wool;

but my deliverance will be for ever,
and my salvation to all generations.

Isaiah 51.7—8

Keep justice, and do righteousness . . .
Blessed is the man who does this.

Isaiah 56.1—2

Do justice and righteousness.

Jeremiah 22.3

Let justice roll down like waters,
and righteousness like an everflowing
stream.

Amos 5.24

You fools! Did not he who made the outside make the inside also? But give for alms
those things which are within; and behold,
everything is clean for you.

Luke 11.40—41

He who speaks on his own authority seeks
his own glory; but he who seeks the glory of
him who sent him is true, and in him there
is no falsehood.

John 7.18

Intemperance

See also **Self-Indulgence**

Wine is a mocker, strong drink a brawler;
and whoever is led astray by it is not
wise.

Proverbs 20.1

Be not among winebibbers,
or among gluttonous eaters of meat;
for the drunkard and the glutton will come
to poverty,
and drowsiness will clothe a man with
rags.

Proverbs 23.20—21

But take heed to yourselves lest your
hearts be weighed down with dissipation
and drunkenness and cares of this life, and
that day come upon you suddenly like a
snare.

Luke 21.34

Let us conduct ourselves becomingly as in
the day, not in revelling and drunkenness,
not in debauchery and licentiousness, not in
quarrelling and jealousy.

Romans 13.13

Now the works of the flesh are . . . drunkenness, carousing, and the like. I warn you
. . . that those who do such things shall not
inherit the kingdom of God.

Galatians 5.19,21

And do not get drunk with wine, for that
is debauchery; but be filled with the Spirit.

Ephesians 5.18

For those who sleep sleep at night, and
those who get drunk are drunk at night.
But, since we belong to the day, let us be
sober.

1 Thessalonians 5.7—8

Therefore put away all filthiness and rank
growth of wickedness and receive with
meekness the implanted word, which is able
to save your souls.

James 1.21

Intercession

See also **Petition**

The Lord bless you and keep you:
The Lord make his face to shine upon you,
and be gracious to you:
The Lord lift up his countenance upon you,
and give you peace.

Numbers 6.24

Moreover as for me, far be it from me
that I should sin against the Lord by ceasing
to pray for you.

1 Samuel 12.23

For he is not a man, as I am, that I might
answer him,
that we should come to trial together.
There is no umpire between us,
who might lay his hand upon us both.

Job 9.32—3

My eye pours out tears to God,
that he would maintain the right of a man
    with God,
  like that of a man with his neighbour.

Job 16.20–21

Likewise the Spirit helps us in our weakness; for we do not know how to pray as we ought, but the Spirit himself intercedes for us with sighs too deep for words. And he who searches the hearts of men knows what is the mind of the Spirit, because the Spirit intercedes for the saints according to the will of God.

Romans 8.26–27

Is it Christ Jesus, who died, yes, who was raised from the dead, who is at the right hand of God, who indeed intercedes for us?

Romans 8.34

Keep alert with all perseverance, making supplication for all the saints.

Ephesians 6.18

I urge that supplications, prayers, intercessions, and thanksgivings be made for all men, for kings and all who are in high positions.

1 Timothy 2.1–2

Consequently he is able for all time to save those who draw near to God through him, since he always lives to make intercession for them.

Hebrews 7.25

The prayer of faith will save the sick man, and the Lord will raise him up.

James 5.15

If any one sees his brother committing what is not a mortal sin, he will ask, and God will give him life for those whose sin is not mortal.

1 John 5.16

He who conquers shall be clad thus in white garments, and I will not blot his name out of the book of life; I will confess his name before my Father and before his angels.

Revelation 3.5

Interdependence

None of us lives to himself, and none of us dies to himself.

Romans 14.7

If one member suffers, all suffer together; if one member is honoured, all rejoice together.

1 Corinthians 12.26

Interest

See also **Usury**

If you lend money to any of my people with you who is poor, you shall not be to him as a creditor, and you shall not exact interest from him.

Exodus 22.25

And if your brother becomes poor, and cannot maintain himself with you, you shall maintain him; as a stranger and a sojourner he shall live with you. Take no interest from him.

Leviticus 25.35–36

He . . . who does not put out his money at
    interest,
and does not take a bribe against the
    innocent . . .
shall never be moved.

Psalms 15.2,5

He who augments his wealth by interest
    and increase
gathers it for him who is kind to the poor.

Proverbs 28.8

If a man . . . does not lend at interest or take any increase . . . he is righteous.

Ezekiel 18.5,8–9

You take interest and increase and make gain of your neighbours by extortion; and you have forgotten me, says the Lord God.

Ezekiel 22.12

Interference

He who meddles in a quarrel not his own
   is like one who takes a passing dog by the
   ears.

Proverbs 26.17

Mind your own affairs.

1 Thessalonians 4.11

Internationalism

Clap your hands, all peoples!
   Shout to God with loud songs of joy!
For the Lord, the Most High, is terrible,
   a great king over all the earth.

Psalms 47.1−2

Go therefore and make disciples of all
nations, baptizing them in the name of the
Father and of the Son and of the Holy
Spirit, teaching them to observe all that I
have commanded you; and lo, I am with
you always, to the close of the age.

Matthew 28.19−20

For mine eyes have seen thy salvation
which thou hast prepared in the presence of
all peoples, a light for revelation to the
Gentiles, and for glory to thy people Israel.

Luke 2.30−32

Intimacy

If two lie together, they are warm; but how
can one be warm alone?

Ecclesiastes 4.11

Guard the doors of your mouth
   from her who lies in your bosom.

Micah 7.5

Invisibility

You cannot see my face; for man shall not
see me and live.

Exodus 33.20

No one has ever seen God; the only Son,
who is in the bosom of the Father, he has
made him known.

John 1.18

No man has ever seen God.

1 John 4.12

Invulnerability

For he will give his angels charge of you
   to guard you in all your ways.
On their hands they will bear you up,
   lest you dash your foot against a stone.
You will tread on the lion and the adder,
   the young lion and the serpent you will
      trample under foot.

Psalms 91.11−13

When you pass through the waters I will
      be with you;
   and through the rivers, they shall not
      overwhelm you;
when you walk through fire you shall not
      be burned,
   and the flame shall not consume you.

Isaiah 43.2

They will pick up serpents, and if they
drink any deadly thing, it will not hurt
them; they will lay their hands on the sick,
and they will recover.

Mark 16.18

Behold, I have given you authority to
tread upon serpents and scorpions, and
over all the power of the enemy; and nothing shall hurt you.

Luke 10.19

J

Jealousy

See also **Envy**

I the Lord your God am a jealous God.

Exodus 20.5

You shall not . . . bear any grudge against
the sons of your own people, but you shall
love your neighbour as yourself.

Leviticus 19.18

For jealousy makes a man furious,
and he will not spare when he takes
revenge.
He will accept no compensation,
nor be appeased though you multiply
gifts.

Proverbs 6.34–35

Wrath is cruel, anger is overwhelming;
but who can stand before jealousy?

Proverbs 27.4

I saw that all toil and all skill in work come
from a man's envy of his neighbour.

Ecclesiastes 4.4

Love is strong as death,
jealousy is cruel as the grave.
Its flashes are flashes of fire,
a most vehement flame.

Song of Solomon 8.6

Let us conduct ourselves becomingly as in
the day . . . not in quarrelling and jealousy.

Romans 13.13

For while there is jealousy and strife
among you, are you not of the flesh?

1 Corinthians 3.3

Love is patient and kind; love is not
jealous.

1 Corinthians 13.4

If you have bitter jealousy . . . in your
hearts, do not . . . be false to the truth.
This wisdom is not such as comes down
from above, but is earthly, unspiritual,
devilish.

James 3.14–15

For where jealousy and selfish ambition
exist, there will be disorder and every vile
practice.

James 3.16

Jewellery

The price of wisdom is above pearls.

Job 28.18

There is gold, and abundance of costly
stones;
but the lips of knowledge are a precious
jewel.

Proverbs 20.15

A good wife who can find?
She is far more precious than jewels.

Proverbs 31.10

I will make your pinnacles of agate,
your gates of carbuncles,
and all your wall of precious stones.
All your sons shall be taught by the
Lord . . .
In righteousness you shall be established.

Isaiah 54.12–14

Again, the kingdom of heaven is like a
merchant in search of fine pearls, who, on

finding one pearl of great value, went and sold all that he had and bought it.

Matthew 13.45–46

No other foundation can any one lay than that which is laid, which is Jesus Christ. Now if any one builds on the foundation with gold, silver, precious stones, wood, hay, straw — each man's work will become manifest; for the Day will disclose it.

1 Corinthians 3.11–13

Women should adorn themselves modestly and sensibly in seemly apparel, not with braided hair or gold or pearls or costly attire but by good deeds, as befits women who profess religion.

1 Timothy 2.9–10

Jokes

You shall not curse the deaf or put a stumbling block before the blind, but you shall fear your God: I am the Lord.

Leviticus 19.14

Cursed be he who misleads a blind man on the road.

Deuteronomy 27.18

Like a madman who throws firebrands, arrows, and death,
is the man who deceives his neighbour
and says, 'I am only joking!'

Proverbs 26.18–19

Joy

See also **Delight, Pleasure**

The Lord took delight in doing you good and multiplying you.

Deuteronomy 28.63

The joy of the Lord is your strength.

Nehemiah 8.10

Behold, God will not reject a blameless man,
nor take the hand of evildoers.

He will yet fill your mouth with laughter,
and your lips with shouting.

Job 8.20–21

In thy presence there is fullness of joy,
in thy right hand are pleasures for
evermore.

Psalms 16.11

Weeping may tarry for the night,
but joy comes with the morning.

Psalms 30.5

Then my soul shall rejoice in the Lord,
exulting in his deliverance.

Psalms 35.9

Clap your hands, all peoples!
Shout to God with loud songs of joy!
For the Lord, the Most High, is terrible,
a great king over all the earth.

Psalms 47.1–2

Let the nations be glad and sing for joy,
for thou dost judge the peoples with
equity.

Psalms 67.4

Let the heavens be glad, and let the earth
rejoice;
let the sea roar, and all that fills it;
let the field exult, and everything in it!
Then shall all the trees of the wood sing for
joy
before the Lord, for he comes,
for he comes to judge the earth.
He will judge the world with righteousness,
and the peoples with his truth.

Psalms 96.11–13

Light dawns for the righteous,
and joy for the upright in heart.

Psalms 97.11

Make a joyful noise to the Lord, all the
earth;
break forth into joyous song and sing
praises!
Sing praises to the Lord with the lyre,
with the lyre and the sound of melody!
With trumpets and the sound of the horn
make a joyful noise before the King, the
Lord!

Let the sea roar, and all that fills it;
  the world and those who dwell in it!
Let the floods clap their hands;
  let the hills sing for joy together.

Psalms 98.4—8

Make a joyful noise to the Lord, all the
    lands!
  Serve the Lord with gladness!
  Come into his presence with singing!

Psalms 100.1—2

Enter his gates with thanksgiving,
  and his courts with praise!
  Give thanks to him, bless his name!

Psalms 100.4

The hope of the righteous ends in gladness.

Proverbs 10.28

To the man who pleases him God gives
wisdom and knowledge and joy.

Ecclesiastes 2.26

He will not much remember the days of
his life because God keeps him occupied
with joy in his heart.

Ecclesiastes 5.20

With joy you will draw water from the
wells of salvation.

Isaiah 12.3

The ransomed of the Lord shall return,
  and come to Zion with singing;
everlasting joy shall be upon their heads;
  they shall obtain joy and gladness,
  and sorrow and sighing shall flee away.

Isaiah 35.10

For you shall go out in joy,
  and be led forth in peace;
he mountains and the hills before you
  shall break forth into singing,
  and all the trees of the field shall clap
    their hands.

Isaiah 55.12

Blessed are you when men hate you, and
when they exclude you and revile you, and
cast out your name as evil, on account of
he Son of man! Rejoice in that day, and
leap for joy, for behold, your reward is
great in heaven.

Luke 6.22—23

There will be more joy in heaven over one
sinner who repents than over ninety-nine
righteous persons who need no repentance.

Luke 15.7

If you keep my commandments, you will
abide in my love, just as I have kept my
Father's commandments and abide in his
love. These things I have spoken to you,
that my joy may be in you, and that your
joy may be full.

John 15.10—11

I will see you again and your hearts will
rejoice, and no one will take your joy from
you.

John 16.22

We . . . rejoice in God through our Lord
Jesus Christ, through whom we have now
received our reconciliation.

Romans 5.11

Rejoice with those who rejoice.

Romans 12.15

The kingdom of God is . . . righteousness
and peace and joy in the Holy Spirit.

Romans 14.17

May the God of hope fill you with all joy
and peace in believing, so that by the power
of the Holy Spirit you may abound in hope.

Romans 15.13

Rejoice in the Lord always; again I will
say, Rejoice.

Philippians 4.4

May you be strengthened, with all power,
according to his glorious might, for all
endurance and patience with joy, giving
thanks to the Father.

Colossians 1.11

Without having seen him you love him;
though you do not now see him you believe
in him and rejoice with unutterable and
exalted joy.

1 Peter 1.8

Judgment

There is a dispute between men, and they come into court, and the judges decide between them, acquitting the innocent and condemning the guilty.

Deuteronomy 25.1

Consider what you do, for you judge not for man but for the Lord; he is with you in giving judgment. Now then, let the fear of the Lord be upon you; take heed what you do, for there is no perversion of justice with the Lord our God, or partiality, or taking bribes.

2 Chronicles 19.6–7

Teach me good judgment and knowledge, for I believe in thy commandments.

Psalms 119.66

Search me, O God, and know my heart!
Try me and know my thoughts!
And see if there be any wicked way in me,
and lead me in the way everlasting!

Psalms 139.23–24

The lot is cast into the lap,
but the decision is wholly from the Lord.

Proverbs 16.33

God will bring every deed into judgment, with every secret thing, whether good or evil.

Ecclesiastes 12.14

For thus says the Lord God: '. . . I send upon Jerusalem my four sore acts of judgment, sword, famine, evil beasts, and pestilence, to cut off from it man and beast! Yet, if there should be left in it any survivors to lead out sons and daughters, when they come forth to you, and you see their ways and their doings, you will be consoled for the evil that I have brought upon Jerusalem, for all that I have brought upon it. They will console you, when you see their ways and their doings; and you shall know that I have not done without cause all that I have done in it, says the Lord God.'

Ezekiel 14.21–23

Behold, I judge between sheep and sheep, rams and he-goats.

Ezekiel 34.17

You are not my people and I am not your God.

Hosea 1.9

Behold, I am setting a plumb line in the midst of my people Israel.

Amos 7.8

The nations shall see and be ashamed of all
their might;
they shall lay their hands on their
mouths;
their ears shall be deaf;
they shall lick the dust like a serpent,
like the crawling things of the earth;
they shall come trembling out of their
strongholds.

Micah 7.16–17

On that day every prophet will be ashamed of his vision when he prophesies; he will not put on a hairy mantle in order to deceive, but he will say, 'I am no prophet, I am a tiller of the soil; for the land has been my possession since my youth.' And if one asks him, 'What are these wounds on your back?' he will say, 'The wounds I received in the house of my friends.'

Zechariah 13.4–6

On that day there shall be neither cold nor frost. And there shall be continuous day (it is known to the Lord), not day and not night, for at evening time there shall be light.
    On that day living waters shall flow out from Jerusalem, half of them to the eastern sea and half of them to the western sea; it shall continue in summer as in winter.
    And the Lord will become king over all the earth; on that day the Lord will be one and his name one.

Zechariah 14.6–9

Their flesh shall rot while they are still on their feet, their eyes shall rot in their sockets, and their tongues shall rot in their mouths. And on that day a great panic from the Lord shall fall on them, so that each will lay hold on the hand of his fellow, and the hand of the one will be raised against the hand of the other.

Zechariah 14.12–13

Then I will draw near to you for judgment; I will be a swift witness against the sorcerers, against the adulterers, against those who swear falsely, against those who oppress the hireling in his wages, the widow and the orphan, against those who thrust aside the sojourner, and do not fear me, says the Lord of hosts.

Malachi 3.5

A book of remembrance was written before him of those who feared the Lord and thought on his name.

Malachi 3.16

For behold, the day comes, burning like an oven, when all the arrogant and all evildoers will be stubble; the day that comes shall burn them up, says the Lord of hosts.

Malachi 4.1

With the judgment you pronounce you will be judged, and the measure you give will be the measure you get.

Matthew 7.2

Let him who is without sin among you be the first to throw a stone at her.

John 8.7

I judge no one.

John 8.15

Jesus said, 'For judgment I came into this world, that those who do not see may see, and that those who see may become blind.'

John 9.39

Now is the judgment of this world, now shall the ruler of this world be cast out; and I, when I am lifted up from the earth, will draw all men to myself.

John 12.31–32

He who rejects me and does not receive my sayings has a judge; the word that I have spoken will be his judge on the last day.

John 12.48

Therefore you have no excuse, O man, whoever you are, when you judge another; for in passing judgment upon him you condemn yourself, because you, the judge, are doing the very same things. We know that the judgment of God rightly falls upon those who do such things. Do you suppose, O man, that when you judge those who do such things and yet do them yourself, you will escape the judgment of God?

Romans 2.1–3

Let us no more pass judgment on one another, but rather decide never to put a stumbling block or hindrance in the way of a brother.

Romans 14.13

The spiritual man judges all things, but is himself to be judged by no one.

1 Corinthians 2.15

It is the Lord who judges me. Therefore do not pronounce judgment before the time, before the Lord comes.

1 Corinthians 4.4–5

Is it not those inside the church whom you are to judge? God judges those outside.

1 Corinthians 5.12–13

Do not be deceived; God is not mocked, for whatever a man sows, that he will also reap.

Galatians 6.7

For the word of God is living and active, sharper than any two-edged sword, piercing to the division of soul and spirit, of joints and marrow, and discerning the thoughts and intentions of the heart. And before him no creature is hidden, but all are open and laid bare to the eyes of him with whom we have to do.

Hebrews 4.12–13

There is one lawgiver and judge, he who is able to save and to destroy. But who are you that you judge your neighbour?

James 4.12

Judgment (Last)

The Lord will judge the ends of the earth.

1 Samuel 2.10

But the Lord sits enthroned for ever,
  he has established his throne for
    judgment;
and he judges the world with righteousness,
  he judges the peoples with equity.

Psalms 9.7−8

Our God comes, he does not keep silence,
  before him is a devouring fire,
    round about him a mighty tempest.
He calls to the heavens above
  and to the earth, that he may judge his
    people . . .
The heavens declare his righteousness,
  for God himself is judge!

Psalms 50.3−4,6

The Lord . . . comes
    to judge the earth.
He will judge the world with righteousness,
  and the peoples with his truth.

Psalms 96.13

If one curses his father or his mother,
  his lamp will be put out in utter darkness.

Proverbs 20.20

I said in my heart, God will judge the
righteous and the wicked, for he has
appointed a time for every matter, and for
every work.

Ecclesiastes 3.17

God will bring every deed into judgment,
with every secret thing, whether good or
evil.

Ecclesiastes 12.14

As I looked,
thrones were placed
  and one that was ancient of days took his
    seat;
his raiment was white as snow,
  and the hair of his head like pure wool;
his throne was fiery flames,
  its wheels were burning fire.
A stream of fire issued
  and came forth from before him;

a thousand thousands served him,
  and ten thousand times ten thousand
    stood before him;
the court sat in judgment,
  and the books were opened.

Daniel 7.9−10

At that time shall arise Michael, the great
prince who has charge of your people. And
there shall be a time of trouble, such as
never has been since there was a nation till
that time; but at that time your people shall
be delivered, every one whose name shall
be found written in the book. And many of
those who sleep in the dust of the earth
shall awake, some to everlasting life, and
some to shame and everlasting contempt.
And those who are wise shall shine like the
brightness of the firmament; and those who
turn many to righteousness, like the stars
for ever and ever.

Daniel 12.1−3

You are not my people and I am not your
God.

Hosea 1.9

Alas for the day!
For the day of the Lord is near,
  and as destruction from the Almighty it
    comes.

Joel 1.15

Woe to you who desire the day of the
    Lord!
  Why would you have the day of the
    Lord?
It is darkness, and not light;
  as if a man fled from a lion,
    and a bear met him;
or went into the house and leaned
  with his hand against the wall,
and a serpent bit him.
Is not the day of the Lord darkness, and no
    light,
  and gloom with no brightness in it?

Amos 5.18−2

'And on that day,' says
    the Lord God,
  'I will make the sun go down at noon,
    and darken the earth in broad daylight.
I will turn your feasts into mourning,

and all your songs into lamentation;
I will bring sackcloth upon all loins,
  and baldness on every head;
I will make it like the mourning for an only
    son,
  and the end of it like a bitter day.'

Amos 8.9–10

Though they dig into Sheol,
  from there shall my hand take them;
though they climb up to heaven,
  from there I will bring them down.
Though they hide themselves on the top of
    Carmel,
  from there I will search out and take
    them;
and though they hide from my sight at the
    bottom of the sea,
  there I will command the serpent, and it
    shall bite them.
And though they go into captivity before
    their enemies,
  there I will command the sword, and it
    shall slay them;
and I will set my eyes upon them
  for evil and not for good.

Amos 9.2–4

The great day of the Lord is near,
  near and hastening fast;
the sound of the day of the Lord is bitter,
  the mighty man cries aloud there.
A day of wrath is that day,
  a day of distress and anguish,
a day of ruin and devastation,
  a day of darkness and gloom,
a day of clouds and thick darkness.

Zephaniah 1.14–15

He will baptize you with the Holy Spirit
and with fire. His winnowing fork is in his
hand, and he will clear his threshing floor
and gather his wheat into the granary, but
the chaff he will burn with unquenchable
fire.

Matthew 3.12

I tell you, on the day of judgment men will
render account for every careless word they
utter; for by your words you will be justified, and by your words you will be condemned.

Matthew 12.36–37

Of that day and hour no one knows, not
even the angels of heaven, nor the Son, but
the Father only.

Matthew 24.36

When the Son of man comes in his glory,
and all the angels with him, then he will sit
on his glorious throne. Before him will be
gathered all the nations, and he will separate them one from another as a shepherd
separates the sheep from the goats, and he
will place the sheep at his right hand, but
the goats at the left. Then the King will say
to those at his right hand, 'Come, O blessed
of my Father, inherit the kingdom prepared
for you from the foundation of the world.'
. . . Then he will say to those at his left
hand, 'Depart from me, you cursed, into
the eternal fire prepared for the devil and
his angels . . .' And they will go away into
eternal punishment, but the righteous into
eternal life.

Matthew 25.31–34,41,46

He who rejects me and does not receive
my sayings has a judge; the word that I
have spoken will be his judge on the last
day.

John 12.48

He has fixed a day on which he will judge
the world in righteousness by a man whom
he has appointed, and of this he has given
assurance to all men by raising him from
the dead.

Acts 17.31

By your hard and impenitent heart you are
storing up wrath for yourself on the day of
wrath when God's righteous judgment will
be revealed.

Romans 2.5

We shall all stand before the judgment
    seat of God; for it is written,
  'As I live, says the Lord, every knee shall
    bow to me,
  and every tongue shall give praise
    to God.'
So each of us shall give account of himself
    to God.

Romans 14.10–12

Each man's work will become manifest; for the Day will disclose it, because it will be revealed with fire, and the fire will test what sort of work each one has done. If the work which any man has built on the foundation survives, he will receive a reward. If any man's work is burned up, he will suffer loss, though he himself will be saved, but only as through fire.

1 Corinthians 3.13—15

We must all appear before the judgment seat of Christ, so that each one may receive good or evil, according to what he has done in the body.

2 Corinthians 5.10

Then the lawless one will be revealed, and the Lord Jesus will slay him with the breath of his mouth and destroy him by his appearing and his coming.

2 Thessalonians 2.8

Christ Jesus . . . is to judge the living and the dead.

2 Timothy 4.1

It is appointed for men to die once, and after that comes judgment.

Hebrews 9.27

I saw the dead, great and small, standing before the throne, and books were opened. Also another book was opened, which is the book of life. And the dead were judged by what was written in the books, by what they had done . . . if any one's name was not found written in the book of life, he was thrown into the lake of fire.

Revelation 20.12,15

Justice

Shall not the Judge of all the earth do right?

Genesis 18.25

Choose able men from all the people, such as fear God, men who are trustworthy and who hate a bribe; and place such men over the people as rulers . . . let them judge the people at all times.

Exodus 18.21—22

You shall do no injustice in judgment.

Leviticus 19.15

You shall do no wrong in judgment, in measures of length or weight or quantity.

Leviticus 19.35

Hear the cases between your brethren, and judge righteously between a man and his brother or the alien that is with him. You shall not be partial in judgment; you shall hear the small and the great alike.

Deuteronomy 1.16—17

You shall appoint judges and officers in all your towns which the Lord your God gives you, according to your tribes; and they shall judge the people with righteous judgment. You shall not pervert justice; you shall not show partiality; and you shall not take a bribe, for a bribe blinds the eyes of the wise and subverts the cause of the righteous. Justice, and only justice, you shall follow, that you may live and inherit the land which the Lord your God gives you.

Deuteronomy 16.18—20

If there is a dispute between men, and they come into court . . . the judges decide between them, acquitting the innocent and condemning the guilty.

Deuteronomy 25.1

Cursed be he who perverts the justice due to the sojourner, the fatherless, and the widow.

Deuteronomy 27.19

Give thy servant therefore an understanding mind to govern thy people.

1 Kings 3.9

Judge thy servants, condemning the guilty by bringing his conduct upon his own head, and vindicating the righteous by rewarding him according to his righteousness.

1 Kings 8.32

Take heed what you do, for there is no perversion of justice with the Lord our God, or partiality, or taking bribes.

2 Chronicles 19.7

God is clothed with terrible majesty . . .
  he is great in power and justice,
  and abundant righteousness he
    will not violate.

Job 37.22—23

He loves righteousness and justice;
  the earth is full of the steadfast love of
    the Lord.

Psalms 33.5

Men will say, 'Surely there is a reward for
    the righteous;
  surely there is a God who judges on
    earth.'

Psalms 58.11

Give the king thy justice, O God,
  and thy righteousness to the royal son!
May he judge thy people with
    righteousness,
  and thy poor with justice!

Psalms 72.1—2

Give justice to the weak and the
    fatherless;
  maintain the right of the afflicted and the
    destitute.

Psalms 82.3

Righteousness and justice are the
    foundation of thy throne;
  steadfast love and faithfulness go before
    thee.

Psalms 89.14

Blessed are they who observe justice,
  who do righteousness at all times!

Psalms 106.3

To do righteousness and justice
  is more acceptable to the Lord than
    sacrifice.

Proverbs 21.3

Partiality in judging is not good.
He who says to the wicked, 'You are
    innocent,'
  will be cursed by peoples, abhorred by
    nations.

Proverbs 24.23—24

Open your mouth, judge righteously,
  maintain the rights of the poor and
    needy.

Proverbs 31.9

Learn to do good;
  seek justice,
correct oppression;
  defend the fatherless,
plead for the widow.

Isaiah 1.16—17

The Lord of hosts will be . . . a spirit of
justice to him who sits in judgment.

Isaiah 28.5—6

The effect of righteousness will be peace,
  and the result of righteousness, quietness
    and trust for ever.

Isaiah 32.17

Thus says the Lord:
Keep justice, and do righteousness,
  for soon my salvation will come,
  and my deliverance be revealed.

Isaiah 56.1

Let justice roll down like waters,
  and righteousness like an everflowing
    stream.

Amos 5.24

What does the Lord require of you
  but to do justice?

Micah 6.8

Do not be deceived; God is not mocked,
for whatever a man sows, that he will also
reap.

Galatians 6.7

Justification

See also **Salvation**

He believed the Lord; and he reckoned it
to him as righteousness.

Genesis 15.6

He who vindicates me is near.

Isaiah 50.8

Let it be known to you therefore, brethren, that through this man forgiveness of sins is proclaimed to you, and by him every one that believes is freed from everything from which you could not be freed by the law of Moses.

Acts 13.38—39

It is not the hearers of the law who are righteous before God, but the doers of the law who will be justified.

Romans 2.13

Since all have sinned and fall short of the glory of God, they are justified by his grace as a gift, through the redemption which is in Christ Jesus, whom God put forward as an expiation by his blood, to be received by faith. This was to show God's righteousness, because in his divine forbearance he had passed over former sins; it was to prove at the present time that he himself is righteous and that he justifies him who has faith in Jesus.

Romans 3.23—26

Jesus our Lord . . . was put to death for our trespasses and raised for our justification.

Romans 4.24—25

Christ died for us. Since, therefore, we are now justified by his blood, much more shall we be saved by him from the wrath of God.

Romans 5.8—9

As one man's trespass led to condemnation for all men, so one man's act of righteousness leads to acquittal and life for all men.

Romans 5.18

It is God who justifies; who is to condemn?

Romans 8.34

You were washed, you were sanctified, you were justified in the name of the Lord Jesus Christ and in the Spirit of our God.

1 Corinthians 6.11

We . . . who know that a man is not justified by works of the law but through faith in Jesus Christ, even we have believed in Christ Jesus, in order to be justified by faith in Christ, and not by works of the law, because by works of the law shall no one be justified.

Galatians 2.15—16

When the goodness and loving kindness of God our Saviour appeared, he saved us, not because of deeds done by us in righteousness, but in virtue of his own mercy, by the washing of regeneration and renewal in the Holy Spirit, which he poured out upon us richly through Jesus Christ our Saviour, so that we might be justified by his grace and become heirs in hope of eternal life.

Titus 3.4—7

You see that a man is justified by works and not by faith alone . . . For as the body apart from the spirit is dead, so faith apart from works is dead.

James 2.24,26

K

Kidnap

Whoever steals a man, whether he sells him or is found in possession of him, shall be put to death.

Exodus 21.16

Kindness

See also **Altruism, Charity, Generosity**

As a father pities his children,
   so the Lord pities those who fear him.

Psalms 103.13

Let not loyalty and faithfulness forsake you.

Proverbs 3.3

A man who is kind benefits himself,
   but a cruel man hurts himself.

Proverbs 11.17

Happy is he who is kind to the poor.

Proverbs 14.21

He who is kind to the poor lends to the Lord,
   and he will repay him for his deed.

Proverbs 19.17

What is desired in a man is loyalty.

Proverbs 19.22

He who pursues righteousness and kindness
   will find life and honour.

Proverbs 21.21

A good wife who can find?
. . . She opens her mouth with wisdom,
and the teaching of kindness is on her tongue.

Proverbs 31.10,26

Render true judgments, show kindness and mercy each to his brother.

Zechariah 7.9

Love your enemies, and do good, and lend, expecting nothing in return; and your reward will be great, and you will be sons of the Most High; for he is kind to the ungrateful and the selfish.

Luke 6.35

Do you presume upon the riches of his kindness and forbearance and patience? Do you not know that God's kindness is meant to lead you to repentance?

Romans 2.4

Note then the kindness and the severity of God: severity toward those who have fallen, but God's kindness to you, provided you continue in his kindness; otherwise you too will be cut off.

Romans 11.22

Love is patient and kind.

1 Corinthians 13.4

Be kind to one another, tenderhearted, forgiving one another, as God in Christ forgave you.

Ephesians 4.32

Put on then, as God's chosen ones, holy and beloved, compassion, kindness, lowliness, meekness, and patience.

Colossians 3.12

When the goodness and loving kindness of God our Saviour appeared, he saved us, not because of deeds done by us in righteousness, but in virtue of his own mercy.

Titus 3.4–5

Kingdom

The Lord reigns; let the earth rejoice;
  let the many coastlands be glad!
Clouds and thick darkness are round about
    him;
  righteousness and justice are the
    foundations of his throne.

Psalms 97.1

Blessed are the poor in spirit, for theirs is the kingdom of heaven.

Blessed are those who mourn, for they shall be comforted.

Blessed are the meek, for they shall inerit the earth.

Blessed are those who hunger and thirst for righteousness, for they shall be satisfied.

Blessed are the merciful, for they shall obtain mercy.

Blessed are the pure in heart, for they shall see God.

Blessed are the peacemakers, for they shall be called the sons of God.

Blessed are those who are persecuted for righteousness' sake, for theirs is the kingdom of heaven.

Blessed are you when men revile you . . . on my account. Rejoice and be glad, for your reward is great in heaven.

Matthew 5.3–12

Another parable he put before them, saying, 'The kingdom of heaven may be compared to a man who sowed good seed in his field; but while men were sleeping, his enemy came and sowed weeds among the wheat, and went away. So when the plants came up and bore grain, then the weeds appeared also. And the servants of the householder came and said to him, "Sir, did you not sow good seed in your field? How then has it weeds?" He said to them, "An enemy has done this." The servants said to him, "Then do you want us to go and gather them?" But he said, "No; lest in gathering the weeds you root up the wheat along with them. Let both grow together until the harvest; and at harvest time I will tell the reapers, Gather the weeds first and bind them in bundles to be burned, but gather the wheat into my barn." '

Another parable he put before them, saying, 'The kingdom of heaven is like a grain of mustard seed which a man took and sowed in his field; it is the smallest of all seeds, but when it has grown it is the greatest of shrubs and becomes a tree, so that the birds of the air come and make nests in its branches.'

He told them another parable. 'The kingdom of heaven is like leaven which a woman took and hid in three measures of flour, till it was all leavened.'

All this Jesus said to the crowds in parables; indeed he said nothing to them without a parable. This was to fulfil what was spoken by the prophet:
'I will open my mouth in parables,
I will utter what has been hidden since the
    foundation of the world.'

Then he left the crowds and went into the house. And his disciples came to him, saying, 'Explain to us the parable of the weeds of the field.' He answered, 'He who sows the good seed is the Son of man; the field is the world, and the good seed means the sons of the kingdom; the weeds are the sons of the evil one, and the enemy who sowed them is the devil; the harvest is the close of the age, and the reapers are angels. Just as the weeds are gathered and burned with fire, so will it be at the close of the age. The Son of man will send his angels, and they will gather out of his kingdom all causes of sin and all evildoers, and throw them into the furnace of fire; there men will weep and gnash their teeth. Then the righteous will shine like the sun in the kingdom of their Father. He who has ears, let him hear.

'The kingdom of heaven is like treasure hidden in a field, which a man found and covered up; then in his joy he goes and sells all that he has and buys that field.

'Again, the kingdom of heaven is like a merchant in search of fine pearls, who, on finding one pearl of great value, went and sold all that he had and bought it.

'Again, the kingdom of heaven is like a
et which was thrown into the sea and
athered fish of every kind; when it was
ull, men drew it ashore and sat down and
orted the good into vessels but threw away
ae bad. So it will be at the close of the age.
he angels will come out and separate the
vil from the righteous, and throw them
to the furnace of fire; there men will weep
ad gnash their teeth.
'Have you understood all this?' They said
o him, 'Yes.' And he said to them, 'There-
ore every scribe who has been trained for
ae kingdom of heaven is like a householder
ho brings out of his treasure what is new
ad what is old.'

Matthew 13.18–52

And he said, 'The kingdom of God is as if
man should scatter seed upon the ground,
ad should sleep and rise night and day,
ad the seed should sprout and grow, he
aows not how.'

Mark 4.26–27

Blessed is the kingdom of our father David
aat is coming! Hosanna in the highest!

Mark 11.10

tell you, among those born of women
one is greater than John; yet he who
least in the kingdom of God is greater
an he.

Luke 7.28

And when a great crowd came together
ad people from town after town came to
m, he said in a parable: 'A sower went
at to sow his seed; and as he sowed, some
ll along the path, and was trodden under
ot, and the birds of the air devoured it.
nd some fell on the rock; and as it grew
o, it withered away, because it had no
oisture. And some fell among thorns; and
e thorns grew with it and choked it. And
me fell into good soil and grew, and
elded a hundredfold.' As he said this, he
lled out, 'He who has ears to hear, let
m hear.'
And when his disciples asked him what
is parable meant, he said, 'To you it has
een given to know the secrets of the king-
om of God; but for others they are in

parables, so that seeing they may not see,
and hearing they may not understand. Now
the parable is this: The seed is the word of
God. The ones along the path are those
who have heard; then the devil comes and
takes away the word from their hearts, that
they may not believe and be saved. And the
ones on the rock are those who, when they
hear the word, receive it with joy; but these
have no root, they believe for a while and
in time of temptation fall away. And as for
what fell among the thorns, they are those
who hear, but as they go on their way they
are choked by the cares and riches and
pleasures of life, and their fruit does not
mature. And as for that in the good soil,
they are those who, hearing the word, hold
it fast in an honest and good heart, and
bring forth fruit with patience.'

Luke 8.4–15

The law and the prophets were until John;
since then the good news of the kingdom of
God is preached, and every one enters it
violently.

Luke 16.16

Being asked by the Pharisees when the
kingdom of God was coming, he answered
them, 'The kingdom of God is not coming
with signs to be observed; nor will they say,
"Lo, here it is!" or "There!" for behold, the
kingdom of God is in the midst of you.'

Luke 17.20–21

The Lord will rescue me from every evil
and save me for his heavenly kingdom.

2 Timothy 4.18

Kinship

See also **Family**

Let there be no strife between you
and me . . . for we are kinsmen.

Genesis 13.8

Behold, how good and pleasant it is
when brothers dwell in unity!

Psalms 133.1

The Lord hates . . . a man who sows discord among brothers.

Proverbs 6.16,19

Have we not all one father? Has not one God created us?

Malachi 2.10

You have one teacher, and you are all brethren. And call no man your father on earth, for you have one Father, who is in heaven. Neither be called masters, for you have one master, the Christ.

Matthew 23.8–10

Whoever does the will of God is my brother, and sister, and mother.

Mark 3.35

A prophet is not without honour, except in his own country, and among his own kin, and in his own house.

Mark 6.4

God . . . gives to all men life and breath and everything. And he made from one every nation of men to live on all the face of the earth.

Acts 17.24–26

We are members one of another.

Ephesians 4.26

Kissing

See also **Greeting**

Greet one another with a holy kiss.

Romans 16.16

Knowledge

See also **Wisdom**

You may freely eat of every tree of the garden; but of the tree of the knowledge of good and evil you shall not eat, for in the day that you eat of it you shall die.

Genesis 2.16–17

The serpent said to the woman, 'You will not die. For God knows that when you eat

of it your eyes will be opened, and you will be like God, knowing good and evil.'

Genesis 3.4–5

The Lord is a God of knowledge.

1 Samuel 2.3

Teach me good judgment and knowledge, for I believe in thy commandments.

Psalms 119.66

The fear of the Lord is the beginning of knowledge.

Proverbs 1.7

If you cry out for insight
and raise your voice for understanding,
if you seek it like silver
and search for it as for hidden treasures;
then you will understand the fear of the
Lord
and find the knowledge of God.
For the Lord gives wisdom;
from his mouth come knowledge and
understanding.

Proverbs 2.3–6

The Lord by wisdom founded the earth;
by understanding he established the
heavens;
by his knowledge the deeps broke forth,
and the clouds drop down the dew.

Proverbs 3.19–20

Wise men lay up knowledge.

Proverbs 10.14

The mind of him who has understanding seeks knowledge.

Proverbs 15.14

My son, eat honey, for it is good,
and the drippings of the honeycomb are
sweet to your taste.
Know that wisdom is such to your soul;
if you find it, there will be a future,
and your hope will not be cut off.

Proverbs 24.13–1

To the man who pleases him God give wisdom and knowledge and joy.

Ecclesiastes 2.2

The earth shall be full of the knowledge of
the Lord
as the waters cover the sea.

Isaiah 11.9

I will give you shepherds after my own
heart, who will feed you with knowledge
and understanding.

Jeremiah 3.15

My people are destroyed for lack of
knowledge;
because you have rejected knowledge,
I reject you from being a priest to me.

Hosea 4.6

Now I know in part; then I shall understand fully, even as I have been fully
understood.

1 Corinthians 13.12

Come to your right mind, and sin no more.
For some have no knowledge of God. I say
this to your shame.

1 Corinthians 15.34

It is the God who said, 'Let light shine out
of darkness,' who has shone in our hearts to
give the light of the knowledge of the glory
of God in the face of Christ.

2 Corinthians 4.6

It is my prayer that your love may abound
more and more, with knowledge and all
discernment.

Philippians 1.9

We have not ceased to pray for you,
asking that you may be filled with the
knowledge of his will in all spiritual wisdom
and understanding, to lead a life worthy of
the Lord, fully pleasing to him, bearing
fruit in every good work and increasing in
the knowledge of God.

Colossians 1.9–10

Their hearts . . . have . . . the knowledge
. . . of Christ, in whom are hid all the
treasures of wisdom and knowledge.

Colossians 2.2–3

Grow in the grace and knowledge of our
Lord and Saviour Jesus Christ.

2 Peter 3.18

L

Labour

See also **Employment, Work**

In the sweat of your face
  you shall eat bread
till you return to the ground.

Genesis 3.19

Six days you shall labour, and do all your work; but the seventh day is a sabbath to the Lord your God.

Exodus 20.9—10

Man goes forth to his work
  and to his labour until the evening.

Psalms 104.23

Blessed is every one who fears the Lord,
  who walks in his ways!
You shall eat the fruit of the labour of your
  hands;
  you shall be happy, and it shall be well
  with you.

Psalms 128.1—2

From the fruit of his words a man is
  satisfied with good,
  and the work of a man's hand comes back
  to him.

Proverbs 12.14

In all toil there is profit.

Proverbs 14.23

There is nothing better for a man than that he should eat and drink, and find enjoyment in his toil.

Ecclesiastes 2.24

Sweet is the sleep of a labourer, whether he eats little or much.

Ecclesiastes 5.12

They shall not labour in vain . . .
for they shall be the offspring of the
  blessed of the Lord.

Isaiah 65.23

Come to me, all who labour and are heavy laden, and I will give you rest.

Matthew 11.28

The labourer deserves his wages.

Luke 10.7

Do not labour for the food which perishes, but for the food which endures to eternal life, which the Son of man will give to you.

John 6.27

Each shall receive his wages according to his labour. For we are God's fellow workers; you are God's field, God's building.

1 Corinthians 3.8—9

Be steadfast, immovable, always abounding in the work of the Lord, knowing that in the Lord your labour is not in vain.

1 Corinthians 15.58

Let the thief no longer steal, but rather let him labour, doing honest work with his hands.

Ephesians 4.28

Aspire to live quietly, to mind your own affairs, and to work with your hands.

1 Thessalonians 4.11

But we beseech you, brethren, to respect those who labour among you.

1 Thessalonians 5.12

You yourselves know how you ought to imitate us; we were not idle when we were with you . . . with toil and labour we worked night and day, that we might not burden any of you.

2 Thessalonians 3.7–8

It is the hard-working farmer who ought to have the first share of the crops.

2 Timothy 2.6

Language

Now the whole earth had one language and . . . men . . . said . . . 'Let us build ourselves a city, and a tower with its top in the heavens . . .' And the Lord came down to see the city and . . . said, 'Behold, they are one people, and they have all one language; and this is only the beginning of what they will do; and nothing that they propose to do will now be impossible for them. Come, let us go down, and there confuse their language, that they may not understand one another's speech.' So the Lord scattered them abroad from there over the face of all the earth, and they left off building the city. Therefore its name was called Babel, because there the Lord confused the language of all the earth.

Genesis 11.1–9

The heavens are telling the glory of God;
   and the firmament proclaims his
     handiwork.
Day to day pours speech,
   and night to night declares knowledge.
There is no speech, nor are there words;
   their voice is not heard;
yet their voice goes out through all the
     earth,
   and their words to the end of the world.

Psalms 19.1–4

Yea, at that time I will change the speech
   of the peoples
to a pure speech,
that all of them may call on the name of the
   Lord.

Zephaniah 3.9

Those who believe . . . will speak in new tongues.

Mark 16.17

There appeared to them tongues as of fire, distributed and resting on each one of them. And they were all filled with the Holy Spirit and began to speak in other tongues, as the Spirit gave them utterance.

Acts 2.3–4

If I speak in the tongues of men and of angels, but have not love, I am a noisy gong or a clanging cymbal.

1 Corinthians 13.1

One who speaks in a tongue speaks not to men but to God; for no one understands him, but he utters mysteries in the Spirit.

1 Corinthians 14.2

When you come together, each one has a hymn, a lesson, a revelation, a tongue, or an interpretation. Let all things be done for edification.

1 Corinthians 14.26

For thou wast slain and by thy blood didst
   ransom men for God
from every tribe and tongue and people
   and nation.

Revelation 5.9

Then I saw another angel flying in mid-heaven, with an eternal gospel to proclaim to those who dwell on earth, to every nation and tribe and tongue and people.

Revelation 14.6

Lapsing

See also **Backsliding, Degeneration**

The Lord is with you, while you are with him. If you seek him, he will be found by you, but if you forsake him, he will forsake you.

2 Chronicles 15.2

For lo, those who are far from thee shall
   perish;
thou dost put an end to those who are
   false to thee.

Psalms 73.27

All who forsake thee shall be put
   to shame;

those who turn away from thee shall be
    written in the earth,
for they have forsaken the Lord, the
    fountain of living water.

Jeremiah 17.13

When a righteous man turns away from his righteousness and commits iniquity and does the same abominable things that the wicked man does, shall he live? None of the righteous deeds which he has done shall be remembered; for the treachery of which he is guilty and the sin he has committed, he shall die.

Ezekiel 18.24

From the days of your fathers you have turned aside from my statutes and have not kept them. Return to me, and I will return to you, says the Lord of hosts.

Malachi 3.7

You are the salt of the earth; but if salt has lost its taste, how shall its saltness be restored? It is no longer good for anything except to be thrown out and trodden under foot by men.

Matthew 5.13

These . . . are the ones sown upon rocky ground, who, when they hear the word, immediately receive it with joy; and they have no root in themselves, but endure for a while; then, when tribulation or persecution arises on account of the word, immediately they fall away.

Mark 4.16–17

When the unclean spirit has gone out of a man, he passes through waterless places seeking rest; and finding none he says, 'I will return to my house from which I came.' And when he comes he finds it swept and put in order. Then he goes and brings seven other spirits more evil than himself, and they enter and dwell there; and the last state of that man becomes worse than the first.

Luke 11.24–26

On that day, let him who is on the house-top, with his goods in the house, not come down to take them away; and likewise let him who is in the field not turn back. Remember Lot's wife.

Luke 17.31–32

It is impossible to restore again to repentance those who have once been enlightened, who have tasted the heavenly gift, and have become partakers of the Holy Spirit, and have tasted the goodness of the word of God and the powers of the age to come, if they then commit apostasy.

Hebrews 6.4–5

My righteous one shall live by faith,
    and if he shrinks back,
my soul has no pleasure in him.

Hebrews 10.38

If, after they have escaped the defilements of the world through the knowledge of our Lord and Saviour Jesus Christ, they are again entangled in them and overpowered, the last state has become worse for them than the first.

2 Peter 2.20

Laughter

God has made laughter for me; every one who hears will laugh over me.

Genesis 21.6

Behold, God will not reject a blameless
    man,
    nor take the hand of evildoers.
He will yet fill your mouth with laughter,
    and your lips with shouting.

Job 8.20–21

He who sits in the heavens laughs.

Psalms 2.4

When the Lord restored the fortunes of
    Zion,
    we were like those who dream.
Then our mouth was filled with laughter,
    and our tongue with shouts of joy.

Psalms 126.1–2

Even in laughter the heart is sad,
    and the end of joy is grief.

Proverbs 14.1.

I said of laughter, 'It is mad,' and of pleasure, 'What use is it?'

Ecclesiastes 2.2

There is . . . a time to weep, and a time to laugh.

Ecclesiastes 3.1,4

Sorrow is better than laughter,
for by sadness of countenance, the heart is made glad.

Ecclesiastes 7.3

The heart of the wise is in the house of mourning;
but the heart of fools is in the house of mirth.

Ecclesiastes 7.4

Surely oppression makes the wise man foolish,
and a bribe corrupts the mind.

Ecclesiastes 7.7

Bread is made for laughter.

Ecclesiastes 10.19

Blessed are you that weep now, for you shall laugh.

Luke 6.21

Woe to you that are full now, for you shall hunger.
Woe to you that laugh now, for you shall mourn and weep.

Luke 6.25

Law

Be strong and very courageous, being careful to do according to all the law which Moses my servant commanded you; turn not from it to the right hand or to the left, that you may have good success wherever you go. This book of the law shall not depart out of your mouth, but you shall meditate on it day and night, that you may be careful to do according to all that is written in it; for then you shall make your way prosperous, and then you shall have good success.

Joshua 1.7–8

Blessed is the man
who walks not in the counsel of the wicked . . .
but his delight is in the law of the Lord,
and on his law he meditates day and night.
He is like a tree
planted by streams of water,
that yields its fruit in its season,
and its leaf does not wither.
In all that he does, he prospers.

Psalms 1.1–3

The law of the Lord is perfect,
reviving the soul.

Psalms 19.7

Great peace have those who love thy law;
nothing can make them stumble.

Psalms 119.165

He who justifies the wicked and he who condemns the righteous
are both alike an abomination to the Lord.

Proverbs 17.15

What your eyes have seen
do not hastily bring into court;
for what will you do in the end,
when your neighbour puts you to shame?

Proverbs 25.7–8

He who keeps the law is a wise son.

Proverbs 28.7

Think not that I have come to abolish the law and the prophets; I have come not to abolish them but to fulfil them. For truly, I say to you, till heaven and earth pass away, not an iota, not a dot, will pass from the law until all is accomplished. Whoever then relaxes one of the least of these commandments and teaches men so, shall be called least in the kingdom of heaven; but he who does them and teaches them shall be called great in the kingdom of heaven.

Matthew 5.17–19

All who have sinned without the law will also perish without the law, and all who have sinned under the law will be judged by the law. For it is not the hearers of the law who are righteous before God, but the doers of the law who will be justified.

Romans 2.12–13

We hold that a man is justified by faith apart from works of law . . . Do we then overthrow the law by this faith? By no means! On the contrary, we uphold the law.

Romans 3.28,31

The law is holy, and the commandment is holy and just and good.

Romans 7.12

The law of the Spirit of life in Christ Jesus has set me free from the law of sin and death.

Romans 8.2

Christ is the end of the law, that every one who has faith may be justified.

Romans 10.4

The law was our custodian until Christ came, that we might be justified by faith.

Galatians 3.24

If you really fulfil the royal law, according to the Scripture, 'You shall love your neighbour as yourself,' you do well. But if you show partiality, you commit sin, and are convicted by the law as transgressors. For whoever keeps the whole law but fails in one point has become guilty of all of it.

James 2.8–10

Every one who commits sin is guilty of lawlessness; sin is lawlessness.

1 John 3.4

Laziness

See also **Idleness**

Go to the ant, O sluggard;
   consider her ways, and be wise.
Without having any chief,
   officer or ruler,
she prepares her food in summer,
   and gathers her sustenance in harvest.

Proverbs 6.6–8

How long will you lie there, O sluggard?
   When will you arise from your sleep?

Proverbs 6.9

A little sleep, a little slumber,
   a little folding of the hands to rest,
and poverty will come upon you like a
      vagabond,
   and want like an armed man.

Proverbs 6.10–11

A slack hand causes poverty.

Proverbs 10.4

The hand of the diligent will rule,
   while the slothful will be put to forced
      labour.

Proverbs 12.24

The soul of the sluggard craves, and gets
   nothing.

Proverbs 13.4

The way of a sluggard is overgrown with
   thorns.

Proverbs 15.19

He who is slack in his work
   is a brother to him who destroys.

Proverbs 18.9

Slothfulness casts into a deep sleep,
   and an idle person will suffer hunger.

Proverbs 19.15

The sluggard does not plough in the
      autumn;
   he will seek at harvest and have nothing.

Proverbs 20.4

The desire of the sluggard kills him
   for his hands refuse to labour.

Proverbs 21.25

Let not your hands grow weak.

Zephaniah 3.16

Keep away from any brother who is living
in idleness.

2 Thessalonians 3.6

If any one will not work, let him not eat.

2 Thessalonians 3.10

Leadership

See also **Government**

Choose able men from all the people, such as fear God, men who are trustworthy and who hate a bribe; and place such men over the people as rulers.

Exodus 18.21

You shall not revile God, nor curse a ruler of your people.

Exodus 22.28

You are Peter, and on this rock I will build my church, and the powers of death shall not prevail against it. I will give you the keys of the kingdom of heaven, and whatever you bind on earth shall be bound in heaven.

Matthew 16.18–19

You know that the rulers of the Gentiles lord it over them, and their great men exercise authority over them. It shall not be so among you; but whoever would be great among you must be your servant, and whoever would be first among you must be your slave.

Matthew 20.25–27

Let the greatest among you become as the youngest, and the leader as one who serves. For which is the greater, one who sits at table, or one who serves? Is it not the one who sits at table? But I am among you as one who serves.

Luke 22.26–27

Never flag in zeal, be aglow with the Spirit.

Romans 12.11

It is required of stewards that they be found trustworthy.

1 Corinthians 4.2

The saying is sure: If any one aspires to the office of bishop, he desires a noble task. Now a bishop must be above reproach, the husband of one wife, temperate, sensible, dignified, hospitable, an apt teacher, no drunkard, not violent but gentle, nor quarrelsome, and no lover of money.

1 Timothy 3.1–3

Let the elders who rule well be considered worthy of double honour, especially those who labour in preaching and teaching.

1 Timothy 5.17

A bishop, as God's steward, must be blameless; he must not be arrogant or quick-tempered or a drunkard or violent or greedy for gain, but hospitable, a lover of goodness, master of himself, upright, holy, and self-controlled; he must hold firm to the sure word as taught, so that he may be able to give instruction in sound doctrine and also to confute those who contradict it.

Titus 1.7–9

Jesus Christ . . . made us . . . priests to his God and Father.

Revelation 1.5–6

Learning

See also **Education, Teaching**

The Lord said to me, 'Gather the people to me, that I may let them hear my words, so that they may learn to fear me all the days that they live upon the earth, and that they may teach their children so.'

Deuteronomy 4.10

You shall therefore lay up these words of mine in your heart and in your soul; and you shall bind them as a sign upon your hand, and they shall be as frontlets between your eyes.

Deuteronomy 11.18

The wise man . . . may hear and increase in learning.

Proverbs 1.5

Give instruction to a wise man, and he will be still wiser.

Proverbs 9.9

Learn to do good;
    seek justice,
Correct oppression;
    defend the fatherless,
plead for the widow.

Isaiah 1.17

For when thy judgments are in the earth,
  the inhabitants of the world learn
    righteousness.

Isaiah 26.9

And the Lord said:
'Because this people draw near with their
    mouth
  and honour me with their lips,
    while their hearts are far from me,
and their fear of me is a commandment
    of men learned by rote;
therefore, behold, I will again do
    marvellous things with this people,
  wonderful and marvellous;
and the wisdom of their wise men shall
    perish,
  and the discernment of their discerning
    men shall be hid.'

Isaiah 29.13–14

Take my yoke upon you, and learn from
me; for I am gentle and lowly in heart.

Matthew 11.29

It is written in the prophets, 'And they
shall all be taught by God.' Every one who
has heard and learned from the Father
comes to me.

John 6.45

Whatever was written in former days was
written for our instruction, that by steadfastness and by the encouragement of the
scriptures we might have hope.

Romans 15.4

You can all prophesy one by one, so that
all may learn and all be encouraged.

1 Corinthians 14.31

Continue in what you have learned and
have firmly believed, knowing from whom
you learned it and how from childhood you
have been acquainted with the sacred writings which are able to instruct you for
salvation through faith in Christ Jesus.

2 Timothy 3.14–15

Who is wise and understanding among
you? By his good life let him show his
works in the meekness of wisdom.

James 3.13

Legislation

Woe to those who decree iniquitous
    decrees,
  and the writers who keep writing
    oppression.

Isaiah 10.1

Leisure

Six days you shall do your work, but on the
seventh day you shall rest; that your ox and
your ass may have rest, and the son of your
bondmaid, and the alien, may be refreshed.

Exodus 23.12

O that I had wings like a dove!
  I would fly away and be at rest.

Psalms 55.6

Come to me, all who labour and are heavy
laden, and I will give you rest.

Matthew 11.28

Lending

See also **Borrowing, Interest, Usury**

If you lend money to any of my people
with you who is poor, you shall not be to
him as a creditor, and you shall not exact
interest from him.

Exodus 22.25

If your brother becomes poor, and cannot
maintain himself with you, you shall maintain him . . . Take no interest from him or
increase.

Leviticus 25.35–36

I have been young, and now am old;
  yet I have not seen the righteous forsaken
    or his children begging bread.
He is ever giving liberally and lending,
  and his children become a blessing.

Psalms 37.25–26

He who is kind to the poor lends to the
    Lord,
  and he will repay him for his deed.

Proverbs 19.17

Give to him who begs from you, and do not refuse him who would borrow from you.

Matthew 5.42

If you lend to those from whom you hope to receive, what credit is that to you? Even sinners lend to sinners, to receive as much again. But . . . lend, expecting nothing in return.

Luke 6.34−35

Lie

See also **Deceit**

You shall not steal, nor deal falsely, nor lie to one another.

Leviticus 19.11

Let the wicked be put to shame,
  let them go dumbfounded to Sheol.
Let the lying lips be dumb,
  which speak insolently against the
    righteous.

Psalms 31.17−18

The wicked go astray from the womb,
  they err from their birth, speaking lies.

Psalms 58.3

All who swear by him shall glory;
  for the mouths of liars will be stopped.

Psalms 63.11

No man who utters lies
  shall continue in my presence.

Psalms 101.7

Lying lips are an abomination to the Lord.

Proverbs 12.22

A righteous man hates falsehood,
  but a wicked man acts shamefully and
    disgracefully.

Proverbs 13.5

A false witness will not go unpunished,
  and he who utters lies will perish.

Proverbs 19.9

The getting of treasures by a lying tongue
  is a fleeting vapour and a snare of death.

Proverbs 21.6

A lying tongue hates its victims.

Proverbs 26.28

Do not trust in . . . deceptive words.

Jeremiah 7.4

Thus says the Lord God: Because you have uttered delusions and seen lies, therefore behold, I am against you . . . My hand will be against the prophets who see delusive visions and who give lying divinations; they shall not be in the council of my people.

Ezekiel 13.8−9

Putting away falsehood, let every one speak the truth with his neighbour, for we are members one of another.

Ephesians 4.25

Do not lie to one another, seeing that you have put off the old nature.

Colossians 3.9

God . . . never lies.

Titus 1.2

Do not boast and be false to the truth.

James 3.14

Who is the liar but he who denies that Jesus is the Christ? This is the antichrist.

1 John 2.22

As for the . . . sorcerers, idolaters, and all liars, their lot shall be in the lake that burns with fire and sulphur, which is the second death.

Revelation 21.8

Blessed are those who wash their robes, that they may have the right to the tree of life and that they may enter the city by the gates. Outside are . . . every one who loves and practises falsehood.

Revelation 22.14−15

Life

The Lord God formed man of dust from the ground, and breathed into his nostrils the breath of life; and man became a living being.

Genesis 2.7

I call heaven and earth to witness against you this day, that I have set before you life and death, blessing and curse; therefore choose life, that you and your descendants may live, loving the Lord your God, obeying his voice, and cleaving to him; for that means life to you.

Deuteronomy 30.19−20

Thou dost show me the path of life;
  in thy presence there is fullness of joy,
  in thy right hand are pleasures for
    evermore.

Psalms 16.11

The Lord is the stronghold of my life.

Psalms 27.1

Lord, let me know my end,
  and what is the measure of my days.

Psalms 39.4

Bless our God, O peoples,
  let the sound of his praise be heard,
who has kept us among the living,
  and has not let our feet slip.

Psalms 66.8−9

For he who finds me finds life
  and obtains favour from the Lord.

Proverbs 8.35

The fruit of the righteous is a tree of life.

Proverbs 11.30

In the path of righteousness is life.

Proverbs 12.28

The fear of the Lord is a fountain of life,
  that one may avoid the snares of death.

Proverbs 14.27

I hated life, because what is done under the sun was grievous to me; for all is vanity and a striving after wind.

Ecclesiastes 2.17

Who knows what is good for man while he lives the few days of his vain life, which he passes like a shadow?

Ecclesiastes 6.12

Has not the one God made and sustained for us the spirit of life?

Malachi 2.15

Enter by the narrow gate; for the gate is wide and the way is easy, that leads to destruction, and those who enter by it are many. For the gate is narrow and the way is hard, that leads to life, and those who find it are few.

Matthew 7.13−14

He who finds his life will lose it, and he who loses his life for my sake will find it.

Matthew 10.39

If you would enter life, keep the commandments.

Matthew 19.17

In him was life, and the life was the light of men.

John 1.4

The Son gives life to whom he will.

John 5.21

He who hears my word and believes him who sent me, has eternal life; he does not come into judgment, but has passed from death to life.

John 5.24

I am the bread of life; he who comes to me shall not hunger, and he who believes in me shall never thirst.

John 6.35

Again Jesus spoke to them, saying, 'I am the light of the world; he who follows me will not walk in darkness, but will have the light of life.'

John 8.12

I am the resurrection and the life; he who believes in me, though he die, yet shall he live, and whoever lives and believes in me shall never die.

John 11.25−26

I am the way, and the truth, and the life; no one comes to the Father, but by me.

John 14.6

Believe that Jesus is the Christ, the Son of God, and . . . you may have life in his name.

John 20.31

But I do not account my life of any value nor as precious to myself, if only I may accomplish my course and the ministry which I received from the Lord Jesus, to testify to the gospel of the grace of God.

Acts 20.24

You also must consider yourselves dead to sin and alive to God in Christ Jesus.

Romans 6.11

To set the mind on the flesh is death, but to set the mind on the Spirit is life and peace.

Romans 8.6

If you live according to the flesh you will die, but if by the Spirit you put to death the deeds of the body you will live.

Romans 8.13

He is the source of your life in Christ Jesus, whom God made our wisdom, our righteousness and sanctification and redemption.

1 Corinthians 1.30

The Spirit gives life.

2 Corinthians 3.6

For in him the whole fulness of deity dwells bodily, and you have come to fulness of life in him, who is the head of all rule and authority.

Colossians 2.9−10

His divine power has granted to us all things that pertain to life.

2 Peter 1.3

That which was from the beginning, which we have heard, which we have seen with our eyes, which we have looked upon and touched with our hands, concerning the word of life — the life was made manifest, and we saw it, and testify to it, and proclaim to you the eternal life which was with the Father and was made manifest to us.

1 John 1.1−2

He who has the Son has life; he who has not the Son of God has not life.

1 John 5.12

He who has an ear, let him hear what the Spirit says to the churches. To him who conquers I will grant to eat of the tree of life, which is in the paradise of God.

Revelation 2.7

Life (Eternal)

For he will render to every man according to his works: to those who by patience in well-doing seek for glory and honour and immortality, he will give eternal life.

Romans 2.6−7

But now that you have been set free from sin and have become slaves of God, the return you get is sanctification and its end, eternal life. For the wages of sin is death, but the free gift of God is eternal life in Christ Jesus our Lord.

Romans 6.22−23

He who sows to his own flesh will from the flesh reap corruption; but he who sows to the Spirit will from the Spirit reap eternal life.

Galatians 6.8

Blessed is the man who endures trial, for when he has stood the test he will receive the crown of life which God has promised to those who love him.

James 1.12

And this is the testimony, that God gave us eternal life, and this life is in his Son. He who has the Son has life; he who has not the Son of God has not life.

1 John 5.11−12

To him who conquers I will grant to eat of the tree of life, which is in the paradise of God.

Revelation 2.7

Be faithful unto death, and I will give you the crown of life.

Revelation 2.10

He who conquers shall be clad thus in white garments, and I will not blot his name out of the book of life; I will confess his name before my Father and before his angels.

Revelation 3.5

Then I saw a great white throne and him who sat upon it; from his presence earth and sky fled away, and no place was found for them. And I saw the dead, great and small, standing before the throne, and books were opened. Also another book was opened, which is the book of life. And the dead were judged by what was written in the books, by what they had done.

Revelation 20.11–12

Light

God said, 'Let there be light'; and there was light. And God saw that the light was good; and God separated the light from the darkness. God called the light Day, and the darkness he called Night.

Genesis 1.3–5

Yea, thou art my lamp, O Lord,
and my God lightens my darkness.

2 Samuel 22.29

The Lord is my light and my salvation;
whom shall I fear?

Psalms 27.1

Light dawns for the righteous,
and joy for the upright in heart.

Psalms 97.11

Thy word is a lamp to my feet
and a light to my path.

Psalms 119.105

But the path of the righteous is like the
light of dawn,
which shines brighter and brighter until
full day.

Proverbs 4.18

My son, keep your father's
commandment . . .
For the commandment is a lamp and
the teaching a light.

Proverbs 6.20,23

The light of the righteous rejoices,
but the lamp of the wicked will be put
out.

Proverbs 13.9

I saw that wisdom excels folly as light
excels darkness.

Ecclesiastes 2.13

I will give you as a light to the nations,
that my salvation may reach to the end of
the earth.

Isaiah 49.6

The sun shall be no more
your light by day,
nor for brightness shall the moon
give light to you by night;
but the Lord will be your everlasting light,
and your God will be your glory.

Isaiah 60.19

The people who sat in darkness
have seen a great light,
and for those who sat in the region and
shadow of death
light has dawned.

Matthew 4.16

Your eye is the lamp of your body; when
your eye is sound, your whole body is full
of light; but when it is not sound, your body
is full of darkness.

Luke 11.34

In him was life, and the life was the light of
men. The light shines in the darkness, and
the darkness has not overcome it.

John 1.4–5

I am the light of the world; he who follows me will not walk in darkness, but will have the light of life.'

John 8.12

The Lord . . . will bring to light the things now hidden in darkness and will disclose the purposes of the heart.

1 Corinthians 4.5

It is the God who said, 'Let light shine out of darkness,' who has shone in our hearts to give the light of the knowledge of the glory of God in the face of Christ.

2 Corinthians 4.6

Once you were darkness, but now you are light in the Lord; walk as children of light (for the fruit of light is found in all that is good and right and true).

Ephesians 5.8−9

Thanks to the Father, who has qualified us to share in the inheritance of the saints in light.

Colossians 1.12

Every good endowment and every perfect gift is from above, coming down from the Father of lights with whom there is no variation or shadow due to change.

James 1.17

God is light and in him is no darkness at all. If we say we have fellowship with him while we walk in darkness, we lie and do not live according to the truth; but if we walk in the light, as he is in the light, we have fellowship with one another, and the blood of Jesus his Son cleanses us from all sin.

1 John 1.5−7

The city has no need of sun or moon to shine upon it, for the glory of God is its light, and its lamp is the Lamb.

Revelation 21.23

Lip Service

Not every one who says to me, 'Lord, Lord,' shall enter the kingdom of heaven.

Matthew 7.21

Listening

Speak, for thy servant hears.

1 Samuel 3.10

Guard your steps when you go to the house of God; to draw near to listen is better than to offer the sacrifice of fools; for they do not know that they are doing evil.

Ecclesiastes 5.1

The Lord God has opened my ear, and I was not rebellious,
I turned not backward.

Isaiah 50.5

He who has ears to hear, let him hear.

Matthew 11.15

And a cloud overshadowed them, and a voice came out of the cloud, 'This is my beloved Son; listen to him.'

Mark 9.7

Whoever knows God listens to us.

1 John 4.6

Behold, I stand at the door and knock; if any one hears my voice and opens the door, I will come in to him and eat with him, and he with me.

Revelation 3.20

Litigation

See also **Law**

The beginning of strife is like letting out water;
  so quit before the quarrel breaks out.
He who justifies the wicked and he who condemns the righteous
  are both alike an abomination to the Lord.

Proverbs 17.14−15

To have lawsuits at all with one another is defeat for you. Why not rather suffer wrong? Why not rather be defrauded?

1 Corinthians 6.7−8

Loneliness

The Lord God said, 'It is not good that the man should be alone; I will make him a helper fit for him.'

Genesis 2.18

Be strong and of good courage . . . the Lord your God . . . goes with you; he will not fail you or forsake you.

Deuteronomy 31.6

I fear no evil;
   for thou are with me;
thy rod and thy staff,
   they comfort me.

Psalms 23.4

God gives the desolate a home to dwell in.

Psalms 68.6

The heart knows its own bitterness,
   and no stranger shares its joy.

Proverbs 14.10

Again, I saw vanity under the sun: a person who has no one, either son or brother, yet there is no end to all his toil, and his eyes are never satisfied with riches, so that he never asks, 'For whom am I toiling and depriving myself of pleasure?' This also is vanity and an unhappy business.

Ecclesiastes 4.7−8

Fear not, for I am with you,
   be not dismayed, for I am your God;
I will strengthen you, I will help you,
   I will uphold you with my victorious right hand.

Isaiah 41.10

I am with you always, to the close of the age.

Matthew 28.20

I will not leave you desolate; I will come to you.

John 14.18

I am not alone, for the Father is with me.

John 16.32

Longevity

See also **Age**

Honour your father and your mother, that your days may be long in the land which the Lord your God gives you.

Exodus 20.12

You shall know also that your descendants
      shall be many,
   and your offspring as the grass of the
      earth.
You shall come to your grave in ripe old
      age,
   as a shock of grain comes up to the
      threshing floor in its season.

Job 5.25−26

What man is there who desires life,
   and covets many days, that he may enjoy
      good?
Keep your tongue from evil,
   and your lips from speaking deceit.
Depart from evil, and do good;
   seek peace, and pursue it.

Psalms 34.12−14

I will rescue him and honour him.
   With long life I will satisfy him.

Psalms 91.15−16

Long life is in her [wisdom's] right hand;
   in her left hand are riches and honour.

Proverbs 3.16

Hear, my son, and accept my words,
   that the years of your life may be many.

Proverbs 4.1

For by me your days will be multiplied,
   and years will be added to your life.

Proverbs 9.1

Righteousness delivers from death.

Proverbs 10.

The fear of the Lord prolongs life,
   but the years of the wicked will be short.

Proverbs 10.2

Loss

If any man's work is burned up, he w suffer loss.

1 Corinthians 3.

Indeed I count everything as loss becau of the surpassing worth of knowing Chri Jesus my Lord.

Philippians 3

Love

You shall love your neighbour as yourself.

Leviticus 19.18

You shall love the Lord your God with all your heart, and with all your soul, and with all your might.

Deuteronomy 6.5

I love those who love me,
  and those who seek me diligently
    find me.

Proverbs 8.17

Love covers all offences.

Proverbs 10.12

Better is a dinner of herbs where love is
  than a fatted ox and hatred with it.

Proverbs 15.17

If your enemy is hungry, give him bread
    to eat;
  and if he is thirsty, give him water
    to drink.

Proverbs 25.21

Better is open rebuke
  than hidden love.

Proverbs 27.5

Faithful are the wounds of a friend;
  profuse are the kisses of an enemy.

Proverbs 27.6

Three things are too wonderful for me;
  four I do not understand:
the way of an eagle in the sky,
  the way of a serpent on a rock,
the way of a ship on the high seas,
  and the way of a man with a maiden.

Proverbs 30.18–19

Love is strong as death . . .
Its flashes are flashes of fire,
  a most vehement flame.
Many waters cannot quench love,
  neither can floods drown it.

Song of Solomon 8.6–7

You shall love the Lord your God with all your heart, and with all your soul, and with all your mind. This is the great and first commandment. And a second is like it, You shall love your neighbour as yourself. On these two commandments depend all the law and the prophets.

Matthew 22.37–40

Her sins, which are many, are forgiven, for she loved much; but he who is forgiven little, loves little.

Luke 7.47

And behold, a lawyer stood up to put him to the test, saying, 'Teacher, what shall I do to inherit eternal life?' He said to him, 'What is written in the law? How do you read?' And he answered, 'You shall love the Lord your God with all your heart, and with all your soul, and with all your strength, and with all your mind; and your neighbour as yourself.' And he said to him, 'You have answered right; do this, and you will live.'

But he, desiring to justify himself, said to Jesus, 'And who is my neighbour?' Jesus replied, 'A man was going down from Jerusalem to Jericho, and he fell among robbers, who stripped him and beat him, and departed, leaving him half dead. Now by chance a priest was going down that road; and when he saw him he passed by on the other side. So likewise a Levite, when he came to the place and saw him, passed by on the other side. But a Samaritan, as he journeyed, came to where he was; and when he saw him, he had compassion, and went to him and bound up his wounds, pouring on oil and wine; then he set him on his own beast and brought him to an inn, and took care of him. And the next day he took out two denarii and gave them to the innkeeper, saying, "Take care of him; and whatever more you spend, I will repay you when I come back." Which of these three, do you think, proved neighbour to the man who fell among the robbers?' He said, 'The one who showed mercy on him.' And Jesus said to him, 'Go and do likewise.'

Luke 10.25–37

God so loved the world that he gave his only Son, that whoever believes in him should not perish but have eternal life.

John 3.16

A new commandment I give to you, that you love one another; even as I have loved you, that you also love one another. By this all men will know that you are my disciples, if you have love for one another.

John 13.34—35

As the Father has loved me, so have I loved you; abide in my love. If you keep my commandments, you will abide in my love, just as I have kept my Father's commandments and abide in his love.

John 15.9—10

Greater love has no man than this, that a man lay down his life for his friends.

John 15.13

God's love has been poured into our hearts through the Holy Spirit which has been given to us.

Romans 5.5

God shows his love for us in that while we were yet sinners Christ died for us.

Romans 5.8

Neither death, nor life, nor angels, nor principalities, nor things present, nor things to come, nor powers, nor height, nor depth, nor anything else in all creation, will be able to separate us from the love of God in Christ Jesus our Lord.

Romans 8.38—39

Let love be genuine; hate what is evil, hold fast to what is good; love one another with brotherly affection.

Romans 12.9—10

Owe no one anything, except to love one another.

Romans 13.8

Love does no wrong to a neighbour; therefore love is the fulfilling of the law.

Romans 13.10

As it is written,
'What no eye has seen, nor ear heard,
   nor the heart of man conceived . . .
God has prepared for those who love him.'

1 Corinthians 2.9

If I speak in the tongues of men and of angels, but have not love, I am a noisy gong or a clanging cymbal. And if I have prophetic powers, and understand all mysteries and all knowledge, and if I have all faith, so as to remove mountains, but have not love, I am nothing. If I give away all I have, and if I deliver my body to be burned, but have not love, I gain nothing.

1 Corinthians 13.1—3

Love is patient and kind; love is not jealous or boastful; it is not arrogant or rude. Love does not insist on its own way; it is not irritable or resentful; it does not rejoice at wrong, but rejoices in the right. Love bears all things, believes all things, hopes all things, endures all things. Love never ends.

1 Corinthians 13.4—8

Faith, hope, love abide, these three; but the greatest of these is love.

1 Corinthians 13.13

Make love your aim.

1 Corinthians 14.1

Let all that you do be done in love.

1 Corinthians 16.14

Through love be servants of one another. For the whole law is fulfilled in one word. 'You shall love your neighbour as yourself.'

Galatians 5.13—1

You, being rooted . . . in love, may have power to comprehend with all the saint what is the breadth and length and heigh and depth, and to know the love of Chris which surpasses knowledge, that you ma be filled with all the fulness of God.

Ephesians 3.17—1

Be imitators of God, as beloved children And walk in love, as Christ loved us an gave himself up for us, a fragrant offerin and sacrifice to God.

Ephesians 5.1—

And above all these put on love, whic binds everything together in perfect ha mony.

Colossians 3.1

May the Lord make you increase and abound in love to one another and to all men.

1 Thessalonians 3.12

You yourselves have been taught by God to love one another.

1 Thessalonians 4.9

Bid the older women likewise to . . . train the young women to love their husbands and children.

Titus 2.3—4

Let brotherly love continue.

Hebrews 13.1

Without having seen him you love him; though you do not now see him you believe in him and rejoice with unutterable and exalted joy.

1 Peter 1.8

Above all hold unfailing your love for one another, since love covers a multitude of sins.

1 Peter 4.8

He who loves his brother abides in the light, and in it there is no cause for stumbling.

1 John 2.10

Let us love one another; for love is of God, and he who loves is born of God and knows God. He who does not love does not know God; for God is love.

1 John 4.7—8

If we love one another, God abides in us and his love is perfected in us.

1 John 4.12

God is love, and he who abides in love abides in God, and God abides in him.

1 John 4.16

There is no fear in love, but perfect love casts out fear.

1 John 4.18

This commandment we have from him, that he who loves God should love his brother also.

1 John 4.21

Loyalty

I am with you.

Genesis 28.15

Take heed to all that I have said to you; and make no mention of the names of other gods, nor let such be heard out of your mouth.

Exodus 23.13

The Lord your God is a merciful God; he will not fail you or destroy you or forget the covenant with your fathers which he swore to them.

Deuteronomy 4.31

You shall have no other gods before me.

Deuteronomy 5.7

If you forget the Lord your God and go after other gods and serve them and worship them . . . you shall surely perish.

Deuteronomy 8.19

You shall fear the Lord your God; you shall serve him and cleave to him, and by his name you shall swear.

Deuteronomy 10.20

As I was with Moses, so I will be with you.

Joshua 1.5

Where you go I will go, and where you lodge I will lodge; your people shall be my people, and your God my God.

Ruth 1.16

Serve him with a whole heart and with a willing mind; for the Lord searches all hearts.

1 Chronicles 28.9

Those who know thy name put their trust in thee,
for thou, O Lord, hast not forsaken those who seek thee.

Psalms 9.10

For the Lord is good;
his steadfast love endures for ever,
and his faithfulness to all generations.

Psalms 100.5

Let not loyalty and faithfulness forsake
　　you;
　bind them about your neck,
　write them on the tablet of your heart.
So you will find favour and good repute
　in the sight of God and man.

Proverbs 3.3—4

By loyalty and faithfulness iniquity is
　　atoned for.

Proverbs 16.6

A friend loves at all times,
　and a brother is born for adversity.

Proverbs 17.17

What is desired in a man is loyalty.

Proverbs 19.22

A faithful man will abound with blessings.

Proverbs 28.20

No one can serve two masters; for either
he will hate the one and love the other, or
he will be devoted to the one and despise
the other. You cannot serve God and
mammon.

Matthew 6.24

Not every one who says to me, 'Lord,
Lord,' shall enter the kingdom of heaven,
but he who does the will of my Father who
is in heaven.

Matthew 7.21

I will not leave you desolate; I will come to
you.

John 14.18

He who calls you is faithful.

1 Thessalonians 5.24

The Lord is faithful; he will strengthen and
guard you from evil.

2 Thessalonians 3.3

He has said, 'I will never fail you nor
forsake you.'

Hebrews 13.5

Luck

But you who forsake the Lord,
　who forget my holy mountain,
who set a table for Fortune
　and fill cups of mixed wine for Destiny;
I will destine you to the sword.

Isaiah 65.11—12

Lust

See also **Adultery, Promiscuity**

If my heart has been enticed to a woman,
　and I have lain in wait at my neighbour's
　　door;
then let my wife grind for another,
　and let others bow down upon her.

Job 31.9—10

For the commandment is a lamp and the
　　teaching a light,
　and the reproofs of discipline are the way
　　of life,
to preserve you from the evil woman,
　from the smooth tongue of the
　　adventuress.
Do not desire her beauty in your heart,
　and do not let her capture you with her
　　eyelashes;
for a harlot may be hired for a loaf of
　　bread,
　but an adulteress stalks a man's very life.
Can a man carry fire in his bosom
　and his clothes not be burned?

Proverbs 6.23—2

Every one who looks at a woman lustfull
has already committed adultery with her i
his heart.

Matthew 5.2

From within, out of the heart of man
come evil thoughts, fornication . . . adul
tery . . . All these evil things come fron
within, and they defile a man.

Mark 7.21,2

Let not sin . . . reign in your morta
bodies, to make you obey their passions.

Romans 6.

Put on the Lord Jesus Christ, and make no provision for the flesh, to gratify its desires.

Romans 13.14

If they cannot exercise self-control, they should marry. For it is better to marry than to be aflame with passion.

1 Corinthians 7.9

Shun youthful passions and aim at right-eousness, faith, love, and peace.

2 Timothy 2.22

Each person is tempted when he is lured and enticed by his own desire. The desire when it has conceived gives birth to sin; and sin when it is full-grown brings forth death.

James 1.14—15

What causes wars, and what causes fight-ings among you? Is it not your passions that are at war in your members? You desire and do not have; so you kill.

James 4.1—2

All that is in the world, the lust of the flesh and the lust of the eyes and the pride of life, is not of the Father but is of the world.

1 John 2.16

Luxury

It is not fitting for a fool to live in luxury.

Proverbs 19.10

Woe to those who lie upon beds of ivory,
  and stretch themselves upon their
    couches,
and eat lambs from the flock,
  and calves from the midst of the stall;
who sing idle songs to the sound of the
    harp,
  and like David invent for themselves
    instruments of music;
who drink wine in bowls,
  and anoint themselves with the finest oils.

Amos 6.4—6

Come now, you rich, weep and howl for the miseries that are coming upon you . . . You have lived on the earth in luxury and in pleasure; you have fattened your hearts in a day of slaughter.

James 5.1,5

M

Magic

See also **Witchcraft**

You shall not practice augury or witchcraft.

Leviticus 19.26

Rebellion is as the sin of divination.

1 Samuel 15.23

Saul died for his unfaithfulness; he was
unfaithful to the Lord . . . and also con-
sulted a medium, seeking guidance.

1 Chronicles 10.13

When they say to you, 'Consult the
mediums and the wizards who chirp and
mutter,' should not a people consult their
God? Should they consult the dead on
behalf of the living? . . . They . . . curse
their king and their God, and . . . will be
thrust into thick darkness.

Isaiah 8.19−22

I am the Lord . . .
who frustrates the omens of liars,
  and makes fools of diviners;
who turns wise men back,
  and makes their knowledge foolish.

Isaiah 44.24−25

I will cut off sorceries from your hand,
  and you shall have no more soothsayers.

Micah 5.12

The works of the flesh are plain: . . .
idolatry, sorcery . . . those who do such
things shall not inherit the kingdom of God.

Galatians 5.19−21

Sorcerers, idolaters . . . shall be in the lake
that burns with fire and sulphur, which is
the second death.

Revelation 21.8

Majesty

Thine, O Lord, is the greatness, and the
power, and the glory, and the victory, and
the majesty; for all that is in the heavens
and in the earth is thine; thine is the kingdom, O Lord, and thou art exalted as head
above all.

1 Chronicles 29.11

O Lord, our Lord,
  how majestic is thy name in all the earth!

Psalms 8.1

Clap your hands, all peoples!
  Shout to God with loud songs of joy!
For the Lord, the Most High, is terrible,
  a great king over all the earth.

Psalms 47.1−2

The clouds poured out water;
  the skies gave forth thunder;
  thy arrows flashed on every side.
The crash of thy thunder was in the
    whirlwind;
  thy lightnings lighted up the world;
  the earth trembled and shook.

Psalms 77.17−18

Bless the Lord, O my soul!
  O Lord my God, thou art very great!
Thou art clothed with honour and majesty,
  who coverest thyself with light as with a
    garment,
who hast stretched out the heavens like a
    tent,

who hast laid the beams of thy chambers
    on the waters,
who makest the clouds thy chariot,
    who ridest on the wings of the wind,
who makest the winds thy messengers,
    fire and flame thy ministers.

Psalms 104.1−4

As I looked,
thrones were placed
    and one that was ancient of days took his
        seat;
his raiment was white as snow,
    and the hair of his head like pure wool;
his throne was fiery flames,
    its wheels were burning fire.
A stream of fire issued
    and came forth from before him;
a thousand thousands served him,
    and ten thousand times ten thousand
        stood before him;
the court sat in judgment,
    and the books were opened.

Daniel 7.9−10

I saw in the night visions,
and behold, with the clouds of heaven
    there came one like a son of man,
and he came to the Ancient of Days
    and was presented before him.
And to him was given dominion
    and glory and kingdom,
that all peoples, nations, and languages
    should serve him;
his dominion is an everlasting dominion,
    which shall not pass away,
and his kingdom one
    that shall not be destroyed.

Daniel 7.13−14

They shall go after the Lord,
    he will roar like a lion;
yea, he will roar,
    and his sons shall come trembling from
        the west.

Hosea 11.10

His brightness was like the light,
    rays flashed from his hand.

Habakkuk 3.4

After this I looked, and lo, in heaven an
open door! And the first voice, which I had
heard speaking to me like a trumpet, said,

'Come up hither, and I will show you what
must take place after this.' At once I was in
the Spirit, and lo, a throne stood in heaven,
with one seated on the throne! And he who
sat there appeared like jasper and carne-
lian, and round the throne was a rainbow
that looked like an emerald. Round the
throne were twenty-four thrones, and
seated on the thrones were twenty-four
elders, clad in white garments, with golden
crowns upon their heads. From the throne
issue flashes of lightning, and voices and
peals of thunder, and before the throne
burn seven torches of fire, which are the
seven spirits of God; and before the throne
there is as it were a sea of glass, like crystal.

Revelation 4.1−6

Malice

You shall not curse the deaf or put a
stumbling block before the blind.

Leviticus 19.14

I have rejoiced at the ruin of him that
        hated me . . .
exulted when evil overtook him
(I have not let my mouth sin
    by asking for his life with a curse).

Job 31.29−30

Behold, the wicked man conceives evil,
    and is pregnant with mischief,
    and brings forth lies.
He makes a pit, digging it out,
    and falls into the hole which he
        has made.
His mischief returns upon his own head,
    and on his own pate his violence
        descends.

Psalms 7.14−16

Keep your tongue from evil,
    and your lips from speaking deceit.

Psalms 34.13

Be not silent, O God of my praise!
    For wicked and deceitful mouths are
        opened against me,
    speaking against me with lying tongues.
They beset me with words of hate,
    and attack me without cause.

Psalms 109.1−3

Deliver me, O Lord, from evil men . . .
They make their tongue sharp as a
    serpent's,
  and under their lips is the poison of
    vipers.

Psalms 140.1,3

Do not plan evil against your neighbour
  who dwells trustingly beside you.

Proverbs 3.29

Do not enter the path of the wicked,
and do not walk in the way of evil men . . .
For they cannot sleep unless they have
    done wrong;
  they are robbed of sleep unless they have
    made some one stumble.

Proverbs 4.14,16

The mouth of the wicked pours out evil
    things.

Proverbs 15.28

The soul of the wicked desires evil;
  his neighbour finds no mercy in his eyes.

Proverbs 21.10

Do not rejoice when your enemy falls,
  and let not your heart be glad when he
    stumbles.

Proverbs 24.17

Do not devise evil in your hearts against
one another . . . for . . . these things I hate,
says the Lord.

Zechariah 8.17

Let all bitterness and wrath and anger and
clamour and slander be put away from you.

Ephesians 4.31

Put away all malice and all guile and
insincerity and envy and all slander. Like
newborn babes, long for the pure spiritual
milk, that by it you may grow up to salvation.

1 Peter 2.1–2

Do not return evil for evil or reviling for
reviling; but on the contrary bless.

1 Peter 3.9

Mankind

God said, 'Let us make man in our image,
after our likeness; and let them have
dominion over the fish of the sea, and over
the birds of the air, and over the cattle, and
over all the earth, and over every creeping
thing that creeps upon the earth.'

Genesis 1.26

God created man in his own image, in the
image of God he created him; male and
female he created them.

Genesis 1.27

The Lord God formed man of dust from
the ground, and breathed into his nostrils
the breath of life; and man became a living
being.

Genesis 2.7

As the man is, so is his strength.

Judges 8.21

In his hand is the life of every living thing
  and the breath of all mankind.

Job 12.10

How then can man be righteous before
    God?
  How can he who is born of woman be
    clean?
Behold, even the moon is not bright
  and the stars are not clean in his sight;
how much less man, who is a maggot,
  and the son of man, who is a worm!

Job 25.4–6

What is man that thou art mindful of him,
  and the son of man that thou dost care
    for him?
Yet thou hast made him little less than
    God,
  and dost crown him with glory and
    honour.
Thou has given him dominion over the
    works of thy hands;
  thou hast put all things under his feet,
all sheep and oxen,
  and also the beasts of the field,

the birds of the air, and the fish of the sea,
whatever passes along the paths of the
sea.

Psalms 8.4—8

The Lord looks down from heaven,
he sees all the sons of men;
from where he sits enthroned he looks forth
on all the inhabitants of the earth,
he who fashions the hearts of them all,
and observes all their deeds.

Psalms 33.13—15

Know that the Lord is God!
It is he that made us, and we are his;
we are his people, and the sheep of his
pasture.

Psalms 100.3

A man's steps are ordered by the Lord;
how then can man understand his way?

Proverbs 20.24

The spirit of man is the lamp of the Lord,
searching all his innermost parts.

Proverbs 20.27

I said in my heart with regard to the sons of
men that God is testing them to show them
that they are but beasts.

Ecclesiastes 3.18

God made man upright, but they have
sought out many devices.

Ecclesiastes 7.29

The hearts of men are full of evil, and
madness is in their hearts while they live.

Ecclesiastes 9.3

Yet, O Lord, thou art our Father;
we are the clay, and thou art our potter;
we are all the work of thy hand.

Isaiah 64.8

What person knows a man's thoughts
except the spirit of the man which is in him?

1 Corinthians 2.11

There is neither Jew nor Greek, there is
neither slave nor free, there is neither male
nor female; for you are all one in Christ
Jesus.

Galatians 3.28

Manners

See also **Courtesy**

Love is . . . not arrogant or rude.

1 Corinthians 13.4

You . . . know how one ought to behave
in the household of God, which is the
church of the living God, the pillar and
bulwark of the truth.

1 Timothy 3.15

Practise hospitality ungrudgingly to one
another.

1 Peter 4.9

Marital Rights

Do not refuse one another except perhaps
by agreement for a season, that you may
devote yourselves to prayer; but then come
together again, lest Satan tempt you
through lack of self-control.

1 Corinthians 7.5

Marriage

The Lord God said, 'It is not good that the
man should be alone; I will make him a
helper fit for him.'

Genesis 2.18

The man said,
'This at last is bone of my bones
and flesh of my flesh;
she shall be called Woman,
because she was taken out of Man.'
Therefore a man leaves his father and his
mother and cleaves to his wife, and they
become one flesh.

Genesis 2.23—24

To the woman he said,
'I will greatly multiply your pain in
childbearing;
in pain you shall bring forth children,
yet your desire shall be for your husband,
and he shall rule over you.'

Genesis 3.16

'They have taken some of their daughters to be wives for themselves and for their sons; so that the holy race has mixed itself with the peoples of the lands. And in this faithlessness the hand of the officials and chief men has been foremost.' When I heard this, I rent my garments and my mantle, and pulled hair from my head and beard, and sat appalled.

Ezra 9.2—3

We have broken faith with our God and have married foreign women from the peoples of the land, but even now there is hope for Israel in spite of this. Therefore let us make a covenant with our God to put away all these wives and their children, according to the counsel of my lord and of those who tremble at the commandment of our God.

Ezra 10.2—3

You have trespassed and married foreign women, and so increased the guilt of Israel.

Ezra 10.10

A good wife is the crown of her husband,
    but she who brings shame is like
        rottenness in his bones.

Proverbs 12.4

He who finds a wife finds a good thing,
    and obtains favour from the Lord.

Proverbs 18.22

A wife's quarrelling is a continual dripping
    of rain.

Proverbs 19.13

House and wealth are inherited from
    fathers,
    but a prudent wife is from the Lord.

Proverbs 19.14

A good wife who can find?
    She is far more precious than jewels.
The heart of her husband trusts in her,
    and he will have no lack of gain.
She does him good, and not harm,
    all the days of her life.
She seeks wool and flax,
    and works with willing hands.

She is like the ships of the merchant,
    she brings her food from afar.
She rises while it is yet night
    and provides food for her household
    and tasks for her maidens.
She considers a field and buys it;
    with the fruit of her hands she plants a
        vineyard.
She girds her loins with strength and makes
    her arms strong.
She perceives that her merchandise is
    profitable.
Her lamp does not go out at night.
She puts her hands to the distaff,
    and her hands hold the spindle.
She opens her hand to the poor,
    and reaches out her hands to the needy.
She is not afraid of snow for her household,
    for all her household are clothed in
        scarlet.
She makes herself coverings;
    her clothing is fine linen and purple.
Her husband is known in the gates,
    when he sits among the elders of the
        land.
She makes linen garments and sells them;
    she delivers girdles to the merchant.
Strength and dignity are her clothing,
    and she laughs at the time to come.
She opens her mouth with wisdom,
    and the teaching of kindness is on her
        tongue.
She looks well to the ways of her
    household,
    and does not eat the bread of idleness.
Her children rise up and call her blessed;
    her husband also, and he praises her:
'Many women have done excellently,
    but you surpass them all.'

Proverbs 31.10—29

Enjoy life with the wife whom you love, all the days of your vain life which he has given you under the sun.

Ecclesiastes 9.9

Take wives and have sons and daughters; take wives for your sons, and give your daughters in marriage, that they may bear sons and daughters; multiply there, and do not decrease.

Jeremiah 29.6

Have you not read that he who made them from the beginning made them male and female, and said, 'For this reason a man shall leave his father and mother and be joined to his wife, and the two shall become one flesh'? So they are no longer two but one flesh. What therefore God has joined together, let not man put asunder.

Matthew 19.4–6

In the resurrection they neither marry nor are given in marriage, but are like angels in heaven.

Matthew 22.30

Because of the temptation to immorality, each man should have his own wife and each woman her own husband. The husband should give to his wife her conjugal rights, and likewise the wife to her husband.

1 Corinthians 7.2–3

The wife does not rule over her own body, but the husband does; likewise the husband does not rule over his own body, but the wife does.

1 Corinthians 7.4

If any brother has a wife who is an unbeliever, and she consents to live with him, he should not divorce her. If any woman has a husband who is an unbeliever, and he consents to live with her, she should not divorce him. For the unbelieving husband is consecrated through his wife, and the unbelieving wife is consecrated through her husband . . . Wife, how do you know whether you will save your husband? Husband, how do you know whether you will save your wife?

1 Corinthians 7.12–14,16

Are you bound to a wife? Do not seek to be free. Are you free from a wife? Do not seek marriage. But if you marry, you do not sin, and if a girl marries she does not sin. Yet those who marry will have worldly troubles.

1 Corinthians 7.27–28

Husbands, love your wives, as Christ loved the church and gave himself up for her, that he might sanctify her, having cleansed her by the washing of water with the word, that he might present the church to himself in splendour, without spot or wrinkle or any such thing, that she might be holy and without blemish. Even so husbands should love their wives as their own bodies. He who loves his wife loves himself.

Ephesians 5.25–28

Let each one of you love his wife as himself, and let the wife see that she respects her husband.

Ephesians 5.33

I would have younger widows marry, bear children, rule their households, and give the enemy no occasion to revile us.

1 Timothy 5.14

Train the young women to love their husbands and children, to be sensible, chaste, domestic, kind, and submissive to their husbands, that the word of God may not be discredited.

Titus 2.4–5

Let marriage be held in honour among all, and let the marriage bed be undefiled.

Hebrews 13.4

Husbands, live considerately with your wives, bestowing honour on the woman as the weaker sex, since you are joint heirs of the grace of life, in order that your prayers may not be hindered.

1 Peter 3.7

Blessed are those who are invited to the marriage supper of the Lamb.

Revelation 19.9

Martyrdom

See also **Persecution**

Nay, for thy sake we are slain all the day long,
and accounted as sheep for the slaughter.
Rouse thyself! Why sleepest thou, O Lord?
Awake! Do not cast us off for ever!

Psalms 44.22–23

Brother will deliver up brother to death, and the father his child, and children will rise against parents and have them put to death; and you will be hated by all for my name's sake. But he who endures to the end will be saved.

Matthew 10.21–22

He who finds his life will lose it, and he who loses his life for my sake will find it.

Matthew 10.39

As they were stoning Stephen, he prayed, 'Lord Jesus, receive my spirit.' And he knelt down and cried with a loud voice, 'Lord, do not hold this sin against them.' And when he had said this, he fell asleep.

Acts 7.59–60

If I give away all I have, and if I deliver my body to be burned, but have not love, I gain nothing.

1 Corinthians 13.3

They have conquered him by the blood of the Lamb and by the word of their testimony, for they loved not their lives even unto death.

Revelation 12.11

Materialism

See also **Worldliness**

Man does not live by bread alone, but . . . man lives by everything that proceeds out of the mouth of the Lord.

Deuteronomy 8.3

For thou hast no delight in sacrifice;
   were I to give a burnt offering, thou
      wouldst not be pleased.
The sacrifice acceptable to God is a broken
   spirit;
   a broken and contrite heart, O God, thou
      wilt not despise.

Psalms 51.16–17

Man shall not live by bread alone,
but by every word that proceeds from the
   mouth of God.

Matthew 4.4

As for what was sown among thorns, this is he who hears the word, but the cares of the world and the delight in riches choke the word, and it proves unfruitful.

Matthew 13.22

What will it profit a man, if he gains the whole world and forfeits his life? Or what shall a man give in return for his life?

Matthew 16.26

The cares of the world, and the delight in riches, and the desire for other things, enter in and choke the word, and it proves unfruitful.

Mark 4.19

Beware of all covetousness; for a man's life does not consist in the abundance of his possessions . . . The land of a rich man brought forth plentifully; and he thought to himself, 'What shall I do, for I have nowhere to store my crops?' And he said, 'I will do this: I will pull down my barns, and build larger ones; and there I will store all my grain and my goods. And I will say to my soul, Soul, you have ample goods laid up for many years; take your ease, eat, drink, be merry.' But God said to him, 'Fool! This night your soul is required of you; and the things you have prepared, whose will they be?' So is he who lays up treasure for himself, and is not rich toward God.

Luke 12.15–21

You cannot serve God and mammon.

Luke 16.13

Do not love the world or the things in the world. If any one loves the world, love for the Father is not in him.

1 John 2.15

Maturity

See also **Development, Growth**

When the perfect comes, the imperfect will pass away. When I was a child, I spoke like a child, I thought like a child, I reasoned like a child; when I became a man, I gave up childish ways. For now we see in a mirror dimly, but then face to face. Now I know in part; then I shall understand fully, even as I have been fully understood.

1 Corinthians 13.10–12

Do not be children in your thinking; be babes in evil, but in thinking be mature.

1 Corinthians 14.20

We all attain to the unity of the faith and of the knowledge of the Son of God, to mature manhood, to the measure of the stature of the fulness of Christ.

Ephesians 4.13

Him we proclaim, warning every man and teaching every man in all wisdom, that we may present every man mature in Christ.

Colossians 1.28

Every one who lives on milk is unskilled in the word of righteousness, for he is a child. But solid food is for the mature, for those who have their faculties trained by practice to distinguish good from evil.

Hebrews 5.13–14

Therefore let us leave the elementary doctrine of Christ and go on to maturity.

Hebrews 6.1

Like newborn babes, long for the pure spiritual milk, that by it you may grow up to salvation.

1 Peter 2.2

Meanness

The people curse him who holds back grain,
but a blessing is on the head of him who sells it.

Proverbs 11.26

Meddling

Why should you provoke trouble so that you fall?

2 Kings 14.10

He who meddles in a quarrel not his own is like one who takes a passing dog by the ears.

Proverbs 26.17

Why do you see the speck that is in your brother's eye, but do not notice the log that is in your own eye?

Matthew 7.3

Some of you are living in idleness, mere busybodies, not doing any work. Now such persons we command and exhort in the Lord Jesus Christ to do their work in quietness and to earn their own living.

2 Thessalonians 3.11–12

Younger widows . . . learn to be . . . gossips and busybodies.

1 Timothy 5.11,13

Mediation

For he is not a man, as I am, that I might answer him,
that we should come to trial together.
There is no umpire between us.

Job 9.32–33

I will send you Eli'jah the prophet before the great and terrible day of the Lord comes. And he will turn the hearts of fathers to their children and the hearts of children to their fathers, lest I come and smite the land with a curse.

Malachi 4.5–6

Christ reconciled us to himself and gave us the ministry of reconciliation; that is, in Christ God was reconciling the world to himself, not counting their trespasses against them, and entrusting to us the message of reconciliation.

2 Corinthians 5.18–19

There is one God, and there is one mediator between God and men, the man Christ Jesus.

1 Timothy 2.5

He is able for all time to save those who draw near to God through him, since he always lives to make intercession for them.

Hebrews 7.25

The covenant he mediates is better, since it is enacted on better promises.

Hebrews 8.6

He is the mediator of a new covenant, so that those who are called may receive the promised eternal inheritance.

Hebrews 9.15

Meditation

See also **Prayer**

This book of the law shall not depart out of your mouth, but you shall meditate on it day and night, that you may be careful to do according to all that is written in it.

Joshua 1.8

Commune with your own hearts on your beds, and be silent.

Psalms 4.4

Let the words of my mouth and the
      meditation of my heart
  be acceptable in thy sight,
O Lord, my rock and my redeemer.

Psalms 19.14

My soul is feasted . . .
when I think of thee upon my bed,
  and meditate on thee in the watches
      of the night;
for thou hast been my help,
  and in the shadow of thy wings I
      sing for joy.

Psalms 63.6−7

I commune with my heart in the night;
  I meditate and search my spirit.

Psalms 77.6

I will meditate on all thy work,
  and muse on thy mighty deeds.
Thy way, O God, is holy.
  What god is great like our God?

Psalms 77.12−13

May my meditation be pleasing to him,
  for I rejoice in the Lord.

Psalms 104.34

With my whole heart I seek thee;
  let me not wander from thy
      commandments!
I have laid up thy word in my heart.

Psalms 119.10−11

I will meditate on thy precepts,
  and fix my eyes on thy ways.

Psalms 119.15

Whatever is true, whatever is honourable, whatever is just, whatever is pure, whatever is lovely, whatever is gracious, if there is any excellence, if there is anything worthy of praise, think about these things.

Philippians 4.8

Meekness

See also **Humility**

He leads the humble in what is right,
  and teaches the humble his way.

Psalms 25.9

The Lord lifts up the downtrodden,
  he casts the wicked to the ground.

Psalms 147.6

For the Lord takes pleasure in his people;
  he adorns the humble with victory.

Psalms 149.4

Seek the Lord, all you humble of the land,
  who do his commands;
seek righteousness, seek humility;
  perhaps you may be hidden
  on the day of the wrath of the Lord.

Zephaniah 2.3

Blessed are the meek, for they shall inherit the earth.

Matthew 5.5

Come to me, all who are heavy laden, and I will give you rest. Take my yoke upon you, and learn from me; for I am gentle and lowly in heart, and you will find rest for your souls. For my yoke is easy, and my burden is light.

Matthew 11.28–30

Put away all filthiness and rank growth of wickedness and receive with meekness the implanted word, which is able to save your souls.

James 1.21

Mercy

See also **Compassion, Pity**

The Lord is slow to anger, and abounding in steadfast love, forgiving iniquity and transgression.

Numbers 14.18

The Lord your God is a merciful God.

Deuteronomy 4.31

Thou art a God ready to forgive, gracious and merciful, slow to anger and abounding in steadfast love.

Nehemiah 9.17

Know then that God exacts of you less than your guilt deserves.

Job 11.6

Steadfast love surrounds him who trusts in the Lord.

Psalms 32.10

His compassion is over all that he has made.

Psalms 145.9

Happy is he who is kind to the poor.

Proverbs 14.21

Now therefore, O our God, hearken to the prayer of thy servant and to his supplications, and for thy own sake, O Lord, cause thy face to shine upon thy sanctuary, which is desolate. O my God, incline thy ear and hear; open thy eyes and behold our desolations, and the city which is called by thy name; for we do not present our suppli-cations before thee on the ground of our righteousness, but on the ground of thy great mercy.

Daniel 9.17–18

Who is a God like thee, pardoning iniquity and passing over transgression
for the remnant of his inheritance?
He does not retain his anger for ever
because he delights in steadfast love.

Micah 7.18

Blessed are the merciful, for they shall obtain mercy.

Matthew 5.7

I desire mercy.

Matthew 9.13

And his mercy is on those who fear him from generation to generation.

Luke 1.50

He is kind to the ungrateful and the selfish. Be merciful, even as your Father is merciful.

Luke 6.35–36

There was a rich man, who was clothed in purple and fine linen and who feasted sumptuously every day. And at his gate lay a poor man named Laz'arus, full of sores, who desired to be fed with what fell from the rich man's table; moreover the dogs came and licked his sores. The poor man died and was carried by the angels to Abraham's bosom. The rich man also died and was buried; and in Hades, being in torment, he lifted up his eyes, and saw Abraham far off and Laz'arus in his bosom. And he called out, 'Father Abraham, have mercy upon me, and send Laz'arus to dip the end of his finger in water and cool my tongue; for I am in anguish in this flame.' But Abraham said, 'Son, remember that you in your lifetime received your good things, and Laz'arus in like manner evil things; but now he is comforted here, and you are in anguish.'

Luke 16.19–25

God has consigned all men to disobedience, that he may have mercy upon all.

Romans 11.32

Judgment is without mercy to one who has shown no mercy; yet mercy triumphs over judgment.

James 2.13

Merit

The labourer deserves his food.

Matthew 10.10

Who then is the faithful and wise steward, whom his master will set over his household, to give them their portion of food at the proper time? Blessed is that servant whom his master when he comes will find so doing. Truly, I say to you, he will set him over all his possessions.

Luke 12.42–44

Would you have no fear of him who is in authority? Then do what is good, and you will receive his approval.

Romans 13.3

We always pray for you, that our God may make you worthy of his call, and may fulfil every good resolve and work of faith by his power.

2 Thessalonians 1.11

Let the elders who rule well be considered worthy of double honour, especially those who labour in preaching and teaching; for the scripture says, 'You shall not muzzle an ox when it is treading out the grain,' and 'The labourer deserves his wages.'

1 Timothy 5.17–18

Ministry

But I do not account my life of any value nor as precious to myself, if only I may accomplish my course and the ministry which I received from the Lord Jesus, to testify to the gospel of the grace of God.

Acts 20.24

All this is from God, who through Christ reconciled us to himself and gave us the ministry of reconciliation; that is, in Christ God was reconciling the world to himself, not counting their trespasses against them, and entrusting to us the message of reconciliation.

2 Corinthians 5.18–19

Fulfil your ministry.

2 Timothy 4.5

Minutiae

He who is faithful in a very little is faithful also in much.

Luke 16.10

Miracles

Believe the works, that you may know and understand that the Father is in me and I am in the Father.

John 10.38

Mischief

See also **Meddling**

They conceive mischief and bring forth evil
  and their heart prepares deceit.

Job 15.35

Take me not off with the wicked,
  with those who are workers of evil,
who speak peace with their neighbours,
  while mischief is in their hearts.

Psalms 28.3

The Lord hates . . . a heart that devises
    wicked plans,
  feet that make haste to run to evil.

Proverbs 6.16,18

It is like sport to a fool to do wrong.

Proverbs 10.23

Evil comes to him who searches for it.

Proverbs 11.27

No ill befalls the righteous,
  but the wicked are filled with trouble.

Proverbs 12.21

A worthless man plots evil,
   and his speech is like a scorching fire.

Proverbs 16.27

Be not envious of evil men,
   nor desire to be with them;
for their minds devise violence,
   and their lips talk of mischief.

Proverbs 24.1−2

Misery

See also **Depression, Despair**

If you set your heart aright . . .
You will forget your misery;
   you will remember it as waters that have
      passed away.

Job 11.13,16

The wicked man writhes in pain all his
      days.

Job 15.20

Be gracious to me, O Lord, for I am in
      distress;
   my eye is wasted from grief,
   my soul and my body also.
For my life is spent with sorrow,
   and my years with sighing;
my strength fails because of my misery,
   and my bones waste away.

Psalms 31.9−10

For my days pass away like smoke,
   and my bones burn like a furnace.
My heart is smitten like grass, and
      withered;
   I forget to eat my bread.
Because of my loud groaning
   my bones cleave to my flesh.
I am like a vulture of the wilderness,
   like an owl of the waste places;
I lie awake,
   I am like a lonely bird on the housetop.
All the day my enemies taunt me,
   those who deride me use my name for a
      curse.
For I eat ashes like bread,
   and mingle tears with my drink,
because of thy indignation and anger;

for thou hast taken me up and thrown me
      away.
My days are like an evening shadow;
   I wither away like grass.

Psalms 102.3−11

Misfortune

My days are past, my plans are
      broken off . . .
   where then is my hope?

Job 17.11,15

For evils have encompassed me without
      number . . .
Be pleased, O Lord, to deliver me!

Psalms 40.12−13

Mission

See also **Calling, Evangelism**

This day is a day of good news . . . let us
go and tell the king's household.

2 Kings 7.9

Sing to the Lord, all the earth!
   Tell of his salvation from day to day.
Declare his glory among the nations,
   his marvellous works among all the
      peoples!

1 Chronicles 16.23−24

I will tell of the decree of the Lord:
   He said to me, 'You are my son,
   today I have begotten you.
Ask of me, and I will make the nations your
      heritage,
   and the ends of the earth your
      possession.'

Psalms 2.7−8

Say among the nations, 'The Lord reigns!'

Psalms 96.10

I heard the voice of the Lord saying,
'Whom shall I send, and who will go for
us?' Then I said, 'Here am I! Send me.'

Isaiah 6.8

A voice cries:
'In the wilderness prepare the way of the
    Lord,
    make straight in the desert a highway for
        our God.
Every valley shall be lifted up,
    and every mountain and hill be made
        low;
the uneven ground shall become level,
    and the rough places a plain.
And the glory of the Lord shall be revealed,
    and all flesh shall see it together.'

Isaiah 40.3—5

Behold, I have put my words in your
        mouth.
See, I have set you this day over nations
        and over kingdoms,
to pluck up and to break down,
to destroy and to overthrow,
to build and to plant.

Jeremiah 1.9—10

The harvest iş plentiful, but the labourers
are few; pray therefore the Lord of the
harvest to send out labourers into his
harvest.

Matthew 9.37—38

These twelve Jesus sent out, charging
them, 'Go nowhere among the Gentiles,
and enter no town of the Samaritans, but go
rather to the lost sheep of the house of
Israel. And preach as you go, saying, "The
kingdom of heaven is at hand." Heal the
sick, raise the dead, cleanse lepers, cast out
demons. You received without paying, give
without pay. Take no gold, nor silver, nor
copper in your belts, no bag for your journey, nor two tunics, nor sandals, nor a staff;
for the labourer deserves his food. And
whatever town or village you enter, find out
who is worthy in it, and stay with him until
you depart. As you enter the house, salute
it. And if the house is worthy, let your
peace come upon it; but if it is not worthy,
let your peace return to you. And if any
one will not receive you or listen to your
words, shake off the dust from your feet as
you leave that house or town. Truly, I say
to you, it shall be more tolerable on the day
of judgment for the land of Sodom and
Gomor'rah than for that town.

'Behold, I send you out as sheep in the
midst of wolves; so be wise as serpents and
innocent as doves. Beware of men; for they
will deliver you up to councils, and flog you
in their synagogues, and you will be
dragged before governors and kings for my
sake, to bear testimony before them and
the Gentiles. When they deliver you up, do
not be anxious how you are to speak or
what you are to say; for what you are to say
will be given to you in that hour; for it is
not you who speak, but the Spirit of your
Father speaking through you. Brother will
deliver up brother to death, and the father
his child, and children will rise against
parents and have them put to death; and
you will be hated by all for my name's sake.
But he who endures to the end will be
saved. When they persecute you in one
town, flee to the next; for truly, I say to
you, you will not have gone through all the
towns of Israel, before the Son of man
comes.'

Matthew 10.5—23

Make disciples of all nations, baptizing
them in the name of the Father and of the
Son and of the Holy Spirit, teaching them
to observe all that I have commanded you.

Matthew 28.19—20

The gospel must first be preached to all
nations.

Mark 13.10

Go into all the world and preach the
gospel to the whole creation. He who believes and is baptized will be saved; but he
who does not believe will be condemned.

Mark 16.15—16

You, child, will be called the prophet of
        the Most High;
for you will go before the Lord to prepare
        his ways.

Luke 1.76

It is written, that the Christ should suffer
and on the third day rise from the dead,
and that repentance and forgiveness of sins
should be preached in his name to all
nations.

Luke 24.46—47

I have other sheep, that are not of this fold; I must bring them also, and they will heed my voice. So there shall be one flock, one shepherd.

John 10.16

As thou didst send me into the world, so I have sent them into the world . . . I do not pray for these only, but also for those who believe in me through their word, that they may all be one.

John 17.18,20

As the Father has sent me, even so I send you.

John 20.21

And now, Lord, look upon their threats, and grant to thy servants to speak thy word with all boldness, while thou stretchest out thy hand to heal, and signs and wonders are performed through the name of thy holy servant Jesus.

Acts 4.29—30

I have set you to be a light for
     the Gentiles,
that you may bring salvation to the
     uttermost parts of the earth.

Acts 13.47

God had called us to preach the gospel.

Acts 16.10

But I do not account my life of any value nor as precious to myself, if only I may accomplish my course and the ministry which I received from the Lord Jesus, to testify to the gospel of the grace of God.

Acts 20.24

We are ambassadors for Christ, God making his appeal through us. We beseech you on behalf of Christ, be reconciled to God.

2 Corinthians 5.20

Stand therefore, having girded your loins with truth, and having put on the breastplate of righteousness, and having shod your feet with the equipment of the gospel of peace.

Ephesians 6.14—15

Do not be ashamed then of testifying to our Lord.

2 Timothy 1.8

Mob

You shall not follow a multitude to do evil.

Exodus 23.2

Mockery

See also **Scorn**

God scorns the wicked,
     but the upright enjoy his favour.

Proverbs 14.9

He who mocks the poor insults his Maker;
     he who is glad at calamity will not go
          unpunished.

Proverbs 17.5

The eye that mocks a father
     and scorns to obey a mother
will be picked out by the ravens of the
          valley
     and eaten by the vultures.

Proverbs 30.17

Do not scoff,
     lest your bonds be made strong.

Isaiah 28.22

Then my enemy will see,
     and shame will cover her who said to me,
     'Where is the Lord your God?'
My eyes will gloat over her;
     now she will be trodden down
     like the mire of the streets.

Micah 7.10

For the word of the cross is folly to those who are perishing, but to us who are being saved it is the power of God.

1 Corinthians 1.18

Scoffers will come in the last days with scoffing, following their own passions and saying, 'Where is the promise of his coming?'

2 Peter 3.3—4

Moderation

See also **Temperance**

If you have found honey, eat only enough
for you,
  lest you be sated with it and vomit it.

Proverbs 25.16

Be not righteous overmuch, and do not
make yourself overwise; why should you
destroy yourself?

Ecclesiastes 7.16

He argued about justice and self-control
and future judgment.

Acts 24.25

Do not get drunk with wine, for that is
debauchery; but be filled with the Spirit.

Ephesians 5.18

Bid the older men be temperate, serious,
sensible, sound in faith, in love, and in
steadfastness.

Titus 2.2

Urge the younger men to control themselves.

Titus 2.6

Live sober, upright, and godly lives in this
world.

Titus 2.12

Modesty

See also **Humility**

Do not put yourself forward in the king's
    presence
  or stand in the place of the great;
for it is better to be told, 'Come up here,'
  than to be put lower in the presence of
    the prince.

Proverbs 25.6−7

Let another praise you, and not your own
    mouth;
  a stranger, and not your own lips.

Proverbs 27.2

Women should adorn themselves modestly
and sensibly in seemly apparel.

1 Timothy 2.9

Monarchy

See also **Majesty**

When you come to the land which the
Lord your God gives you, and you possess
it and dwell in it, and then say, 'I will set a
king over me, like all the nations that are
round about me'; you may indeed set as
king over you him whom the Lord your
God will choose. One from among your
brethren you shall set as king over you; you
may not put a foreigner over you, who is
not your brother.

Deuteronomy 17.14−15

And you shall reign over the people of the
Lord and you will save them from the hand
of their enemies round about.

1 Samuel 10.1

In the light of a king's face there is life,
  and his favour is like the clouds that bring
    the spring rain.

Proverbs 16.15

The king's heart is a stream of water in the
    hand of the Lord;
  he turns it wherever he will.

Proverbs 21.1

But in all, a king is an advantage to a land
with cultivated fields.

Ecclesiastes 5.9

Money

See also **Wealth**

He . . . swears to his own hurt and does
    not change . . .
does not put out his money at interest,
  and does not take a bribe against the
    innocent.
He who does these things shall never be
    moved.

Psalms 15.2,4−5

He who loves money will not be satisfied
with money; nor he who loves wealth, with
gain: this also is vanity.

Ecclesiastes 5.10

Money answers everything.

Ecclesiastes 10.19

Give alms . . . in secret; and your Father who sees in secret will reward you.

Matthew 6.3−4

You cannot serve God and mammon.

Matthew 6.24

Make friends for yourselves by means of unrighteous mammon, so that when it fails they may receive you into the eternal habitations.

Luke 16.9

If then you have not been faithful in the unrighteous mammon, who will entrust to you the true riches?

Luke 16.11

Your silver perish with you, because you thought you could obtain the gift of God with money!

Acts 8.20

A bishop must be . . . no lover of money.

1 Timothy 3.2−3

Those who desire to be rich fall into temptation, into a snare, into many senseless and hurtful desires that plunge men into ruin and destruction. For the love of money is the root of all evils; it is through this craving that some have wandered away from the faith and pierced their hearts with many pangs.

1 Timothy 6.9−10

Keep your life free from love of money, and be content with what you have.

Hebrews 13.5

Monogamy

See also **Marriage**

A married woman . . . will be called an adulteress if she lives with another man while her husband is alive.

Romans 7.2−3

Each man should have his own wife and each woman her own husband.

1 Corinthians 7.2

Let deacons be the husband of one wife.

1 Timothy 3.12

Monopoly

Woe to those who join house to house,
    who add field to field,
until there is no more room.

Isaiah 5.8

Monotheism

You shall have no other gods before me.

Exodus 20.3

The Lord is God; there is no other besides him.

Deuteronomy 4.35

Hear, O Israel: The Lord our God is one Lord; and you shall love the Lord your God with all your heart, and with all your soul, and with all your might.

Deuteronomy 6.4−5

Let these words of mine, wherewith I have made supplication before the Lord, be near to the Lord our God day and night, and may he maintain the cause of his servant, and the cause of his people Israel, as each day requires; that all the peoples of the earth may know that the Lord is God; there is no other.

1 Kings 8.59−60

Thou art the Lord, thou alone; thou hast made heaven, the heaven of heavens, with all their host, the earth and all that is on it, the seas and all that is in them; and thou preservest all of them; and the host of heaven worships thee.

Nehemiah 9.6

O Lord of hosts, God of Israel, who art enthroned above the cherubim, thou art the God, thou alone, of all the kingdoms of the earth; thou hast made heaven and earth.

Isaiah 37.16

'You are my witnesses,' says the Lord,
    'and my servant whom I have chosen,
that you may know and believe me

and understand that I am He.
Before me no god was formed,
   nor shall there be any after me.
I, I am the Lord,
   and besides me there is no saviour.'

Isaiah 43.10—11

I am the first and I am the last;
   besides me there is no god.

Isaiah 44.6

I am the Lord, and there is no other.

Isaiah 45.7

Turn to me and be saved,
   all the ends of the earth!
For I am God, and there is no other.

Isaiah 45.22

I saw in the night visions,
   and behold, with the clouds of heaven
   there came one like a son of man,
and he came to the Ancient of Days
   and was presented before him.
And to him was given dominion
   and glory and kingdom,
that all peoples, nations, and languages
   should serve him;
his dominion is an everlasting dominion,
   which shall not pass away,
and his kingdom one
   that shall not be destroyed.

Daniel 7.13—14

I am the Lord your God
   from the land of Egypt;
you know no God but me,
   and besides me there is no saviour.

Hosea 13.4

Have we not all one father? Has not one
God created us?

Malachi 2.10

Is God the God of Jews only? Is he not the
God of Gentiles also? Yes, of Gentiles also,
since God is one.

Romans 3.29—30

There is no God but one.

1 Corinthians 8.4

There is one God, the Father, from whom
are all things and for whom we exist.

1 Corinthians 8.6

There is . . . one Lord, one faith, one
baptism, one God and Father of us all, who
is above all and through all and in all.

Ephesians 4.4—6

Morality

See also **Righteousness**

You shall do what is right and good in the
sight of the Lord, that it may go well with
you.

Deuteronomy 6.18

O Lord, who shall sojourn in thy tent?
   Who shall dwell on thy holy hill?
He who walks blamelessly, and does what is
   right,
   and speaks truth from his heart.

Psalms 15.1—2

The righteous flourish like the palm tree,
   and grow like a cedar in Lebanon.
They are planted in the house of the Lord,
   they flourish in the courts of our God.
They still bring forth fruit in old age,
   they are ever full of sap and green.

Psalms 92.12—14

Blessed are they who observe justice,
   who do righteousness at all times!

Psalms 106.3

Righteousness delivers from death.

Proverbs 10.2

He who diligently seeks good seeks
   favour.

Proverbs 11.27

The way of the wicked is an abomination
   to the Lord,
   but he loves him who pursues
   righteousness.

Proverbs 15.9

He who pursues righteousness and
  kindness
will find life and honour.

Proverbs 21.21

Come to your right mind, and sin no more.

1 Corinthians 15.34

Aim at righteousness, godliness, faith,
love, steadfastness, gentleness.

1 Timothy 6.11

Mortality

See also **Death**

In the sweat of your face
  you shall eat bread
till you return to the ground,
  for out of it you were taken;
you are dust,
  and to dust you shall return.

Genesis 3.19

He drove out the man; and at the east of
the garden of Eden he placed the cherubim,
and a flaming sword which turned every
way, to guard the way to the tree of life.

Genesis 3.24

Has not man a hard service upon earth,
  and are not his days like the days of a
    hireling?

Job 7.1

As the cloud fades and vanishes,
  so he who goes down to Sheol does not
    come up.

Job 7.9

We are but of yesterday, and know
    nothing,
  for our days on earth are a shadow.

Job 8.9

Remember that thou hast made me of
    clay;
  and wilt thou turn me to dust again?

Job 10.9

Man that is born of a woman is of few
days, and full of trouble.

He comes forth like a flower, and withers;
  he flees like a shadow, and continues not.

Job 14.1-2

Lord, let me know my end,
  and what is the measure of my days;
  let me know how fleeting my life is!
Behold, thou hast made my days a few
    handbreadths,
  and my lifetime is as nothing in thy sight.
Surely every man stands as a mere breath!
  Surely man goes about as a shadow!

Psalms 39.4-6

Remember, O Lord, what the measure of
    life is,
  for what vanity thou hast created all the
    sons of men!
What man can live and never see death?
  Who can deliver his soul from the power
    of Sheol?

Psalms 89.47-48

Our years come to an end like a sigh.
The years of our life are threescore and ten,
  or even by reason of strength fourscore;
yet their span is but toil and trouble;
  they are soon gone, and we fly away.

Psalms 90.9-10

As for man, his days are like grass;
  he flourishes like a flower of the field;
for the wind passes over it, and it is gone,
  and its place knows it no more.

Psalms 103.15-16

O Lord, what is man that thou dost regard
    him,
  or the son of man that thou dost think of
    him?
Man is like a breath,
  his days are like a passing shadow.

Psalms 144.3-4

All go to one place; all are from the dust,
and all turn to dust again.

Ecclesiastes 3.20

The living know that they will die, but the
dead know nothing.

Ecclesiastes 9.5

A voice says, 'Cry!'
  And I said, 'What shall I cry?'
All flesh is grass,
  and all its beauty is like the flower of the
    field.
The grass withers, the flower fades,
  when the breath of the Lord blows
    upon it;
  surely the people is grass.
The grass withers, the flower fades;
  but the word of our God will stand for
    ever.

Isaiah 40.6−8

Who will deliver me from this body of
death?

Romans 7.24

While we are still in this tent, we sigh with
anxiety; not that we would be unclothed,
but that we would be further clothed, so
that what is mortal may be swallowed up by
life.

2 Corinthians 5.4

It is appointed for men to die once.

Hebrews 9.27

You do not know about tomorrow. What
is your life? For you are a mist that appears
for a little time and then vanishes.

James 4.14

Motherhood

See also **Parenthood**

He gives the barren woman a home,
  making her the joyous mother of
    children.

Psalms 113.9

The rod and reproof give wisdom,
  but a child left to himself brings shame to
    his mother.

Proverbs 29.15

A good wife who can find?
. . . Her children rise up and call her
    blessed.

Proverbs 31.10,28

Can a woman forget her sucking child,
  that she should have no compassion on
    the son of her womb?

Isaiah 49.15

Train the young women to love their . . .
children.

Titus 2.4

Motive

The purpose in a man's mind is like deep
    water,
  but a man of understanding will draw it
    out.

Proverbs 20.5

Mourning

See also **Bereavement, Grief, Sadness**

O Lord, be thou my helper!
Thou hast turned for me my mourning into
    dancing;
  thou hast loosed my sackcloth
  and girded me with gladness.

Psalms 30.10−11

There is . . . a time to mourn, and a time
to dance.

Ecclesiastes 3.1,4

It is better to go to the house of mourning
    than to go to the house of feasting;
for this is the end of all men,
  and the living will lay it to heart.

Ecclesiastes 7.2

The heart of the wise is in the house of
mourning.

Ecclesiastes 7.4

Your sun shall no more go down,
  nor your moon withdraw itself;
for the Lord will be your everlasting light,
  and your days of mourning shall be
    ended.

Isaiah 60.20

Comfort all who mourn . . .
give them a garland instead of ashes,

the oil of gladness instead of mourning,
the mantle of praise instead of a faint
spirit.

Isaiah 61.2–3

I will turn their mourning into joy,
I will comfort them, and give them
gladness for sorrow.

Jeremiah 31.13

Blessed are those who mourn, for they
shall be comforted.

Matthew 5.4

Purify your hearts . . . Be wretched and
mourn and weep.

James 4.8–9

Murder

See also **Violence**

The voice of your brother's blood is crying
to me from the ground. And now you are
cursed from the ground, which has opened
its mouth to receive your brother's blood
from your hand. When you till the ground,
it shall no longer yield to you its strength;
you shall be a fugitive and a wanderer on
the earth.

Genesis 4.10–12

Whoever sheds the blood of man, by man
shall his blood be shed; for God made man
in his own image.

Genesis 9.6

You shall not kill.

Exodus 20.13

Whoever strikes a man so that he dies
shall be put to death.

Exodus 21.12

Whoever strikes his father or his mother
shall be put to death.

Exodus 21.15

Do not slay the innocent and righteous.

Exodus 23.7

Blood pollutes the land, and no expiation
can be made for the land, for the blood that
is shed in it, except by the blood of him
who shed it.

Numbers 35.33

Cursed be he who takes a bribe to slay an
innocent person.

Deuteronomy 27.25

If sinners entice you,
do not consent.
If they say, 'Come with us, let us lie in wait
for blood,
let us wantonly ambush the innocent . . .'
do not walk in the way with them,
hold back your foot from their paths;
for their feet run to evil,
and they make haste to shed blood . . .
these men lie in wait for their own blood,
they set an ambush for their own lives.

Proverbs 1.10–11,15–16,18

If a man is burdened with the blood of
another,
let him be a fugitive until death;
let no one help him.

Proverbs 28.17

For every boot of the tramping warrior in
battle tumult
and every garment rolled in blood
will be burned as fuel for the fire.

Isaiah 9.5

For behold, the Lord is coming forth out
of his place
to punish the inhabitants of the earth for
their iniquity,
and the earth will disclose the blood shed
upon her,
and will no more cover her slain.

Isaiah 26.21

I will prepare you for blood, and blood
shall pursue you; because you are guilty of
blood, therefore blood shall pursue you.

Ezekiel 35.6

If you . . . kill, you have become a transgressor of the law.

James 2.11

Let none of you suffer as a murderer.

1 Peter 4.15

Any one who hates his brother is a murderer, and you know that no murderer has eternal life abiding in him.

1 John 3.15

As for murderers . . . their lot shall be in the lake that burns with fire and sulphur, which is the second death.

Revelation 21.8

Music

See also **Hymn**

And when the minstrel played, the power of the Lord came upon him.

2 Kings 3.15

David . . . commanded the chiefs of the Levites to appoint their brethren as the singers who should play loudly on musical instruments, on harps and lyres and cymbals, to raise sounds of joy.

1 Chronicles 15.16

Praise the Lord with the lyre,
  make melody to him with the harp of ten
    strings!
Sing to him a new song,
  play skilfully on the strings, with loud
    shouts.

Psalms 33.2-3

Sing to God, sing praises to his name.

Psalms 68.4

Sing aloud to God our strength;
  shout for joy to the God of Jacob!
Raise a song, sound the timbrel,
  the sweet lyre with the harp.
Blow the trumpet at the new moon,
  at the full moon, on our feast day.

Psalms 81.1-3

It is good to give thanks to the Lord,
  to sing praises to thy name,
    O Most High;
to declare thy steadfast love in the morning,
  and thy faithfulness by night,

to the music of the lute and the harp,
  to the melody of the lyre.

Psalms 92.1-3

Sing praises to the Lord with the lyre,
  with the lyre and the sound of melody!
With trumpets and the sound of the horn
  make a joyful noise before the King, the
    Lord!

Psalms 98.5-6

Praise him with trumpet sound;
  praise him with lute and harp!
Praise him with timbrel and dance;
  praise him with strings and pipe!
Praise him with sounding cymbals.

Psalms 150.3-5

The old men have quit the city gate,
  the young men their music.
The joy of our hearts has ceased;
  our dancing has been turned to
    mourning.

Lamentations 5.14-15

I will sing with the spirit and I will sing with the mind also.

1 Corinthians 14.15

Be filled with the Spirit, addressing one another in psalms and hymns and spiritual songs, singing and making melody to the Lord with all your heart.

Ephesians 5.19

I heard a voice from heaven like the sound of many waters and like the sound of loud thunder; the voice I heard was like the sound of harpers playing on their harps, and they sing a new song before the throne . . . No one could learn that song except the hundred and forty-four thousand who had been redeemed from the earth.

Revelation 14.2-

Mystery

See also **Paradox**

The Lord has said that he would dwell in thick darkness.

2 Chronicles 6

Can you find out the deep things of God?
  Can you find out the limit of the
    Almighty?
It is higher than heaven — what can
    you do?
  Deeper than Sheol — what can
    you know?

Job 11.7—8

Behold, I go forward, but he is not there;
  and backward, but I cannot perceive him;
on the left hand I seek him, but I cannot
    behold him;
  I turn to the right hand, but I cannot see
    him.

Job 23.8—9

By his wind the heavens were made fair;
  his hand pierced the fleeing serpent.
Lo, these are but the outskirts of his ways;
  and how small a whisper do we hear of
    him!
But the thunder of his power who can
    understand?

Job 26.13—14

Behold, God is great, and we know him
    not;
  the number of his years is unsearchable.

Job 36.26

He has made everything beautiful in its
time; also he has put eternity into man's
mind ... so that he cannot find out what
God has done from the beginning to the
end.

Ecclesiastes 3.11

As you do not know how the spirit comes
to the bones in the womb of a woman with
child, so you do not know the work of God
who makes everything.

Ecclesiastes 11.5

And the vision of all this has become to
you like the words of a book that is sealed.
When men give it to one who can read,
saying, 'Read this,' he says, 'I cannot, for it
is sealed.'
  And when they give the book to one who
cannot read, saying, 'Read this,' he says, 'I
cannot read.'

Isaiah 29.11—12

The words are shut up and sealed until the
time of the end.

Daniel 12.9

Jesus declared, 'I thank thee, Father, Lord
of heaven and earth, that thou hast hidden
these things from the wise and understanding and revealed them to babes.'

Matthew 11.25

To you it has been given to know the
secrets of the kingdom of heaven, but to
them it has not been given.

Matthew 13.11

The wind blows where it wills, and you
hear the sound of it, but you do not know
whence it comes or whither it goes; so it is
with every one who is born of the Spirit.

John 3.8

How unsearchable are his judgments and
how inscrutable his ways!

Romans 11.33

Among the mature we do impart wisdom
... a secret and hidden wisdom of God,
which God decreed before the ages for our
glorification.

1 Corinthians 2.6—7

This is how one should regard us, as
servants of Christ and stewards of the
mysteries of God.

1 Corinthians 4.1

If I have prophetic powers, and understand
all mysteries and all knowledge, and if I
have all faith, so as to remove mountains,
but have not love, I am nothing.

1 Corinthians 13.2

Now we see in a mirror dimly, but then
face to face.

1 Corinthians 13.12

Lo! I tell you a mystery. We shall not all
sleep, but we shall all be changed.

1 Corinthians 15.51

He has made known to us in all wisdom and insight the mystery of his will, according to his purpose which he set forth in Christ as a plan for the fulness of time.

Ephesians 1.9

And the peace of God, which passes all understanding, will keep your hearts and your minds in Christ Jesus.

Philippians 4.7

I strive for you . . . to have . . . the knowledge of God's mystery, of Christ, in whom are hid all the treasures of wisdom.

Colossians 2.1–3

Deacons . . . must hold the mystery of the faith with a clear conscience.

1 Timothy 3.8–9

Great indeed, we confess, is the mystery of our religion:
He was manifested in the flesh,
vindicated in the Spirit,
    seen by angels,
preached among the nations,
believed on in the world,
    taken up in glory.

1 Timothy 3.16

Mysticism

The secret things belong to the Lord our God; but the things that are revealed belong to us and to our children for ever, that we may do all the words of this law.

Deuteronomy 29.29

And behold, the Lord passed by, and a great and strong wind rent the mountains, and broke in pieces the rocks before the Lord, but the Lord was not in the wind; and after the wind an earthquake, but the Lord was not in the earthquake; and after the earthquake a fire, but the Lord was not in the fire; and after the fire a still small voice.

1 Kings 19.11–12

The friendship of the Lord is for those who fear him,
    and he makes known to them his covenant.

Psalms 25.14

The upright are in his confidence.

Proverbs 3.32

I will give you the treasures of darkness
    and the hoards in secret places,
that you may know that it is I, the Lord.

Isaiah 45.3

Does evil befall a city,
    unless the Lord has done it?
Surely the Lord God does nothing,
    without revealing his secret
    to his servants the prophets.

Amos 3.6–7

The Spirit searches everything, even the depths of God.

1 Corinthians 2.10

The mystery was made known to me by revelation . . . the mystery of Christ . . . was not made known to the sons of men in other generations as it has now been revealed to his holy apostles and prophets by the Spirit . . . I was made a minister . . . to preach to the Gentiles the unsearchable riches of Christ, and to make all men see what is the plan of the mystery hidden for ages in God who created all things; that through the church the manifold wisdom of God might now be made known to the principalities and powers . . . So I ask you not to lose heart.

Ephesians 3.3–5,7–10,1.

N

Nagging

A continual dripping on a rainy day
  and a contentious woman are alike;
to restrain her is to restrain the wind
  or to grasp oil in his right hand.

Proverbs 7.15

It is better to live in a corner of the
      housetop
  than in a house shared with a contentious
    woman.

Proverbs 21.9

It is better to live in a desert land
  than with a contentious and fretful
    woman.

Proverbs 21.19

Nakedness

The eyes of both were opened, and they
knew that they were naked; and they sewed
fig leaves together and made themselves
aprons.

Genesis 3.7

Naked I came from my mother's womb,
and naked shall I return.

Job 1.21

For you have exacted pledges of your
      brothers for nothing,
and stripped the naked of their clothing . . .
Therefore snares are round about you,
  and sudden terror overwhelms you.

Job 22.6,10

When you see the naked . . . cover
  him . . .
Then shall your light break forth like
    the dawn, and . . .
your righteousness shall go before
  you.

Isaiah 57.7–8

Come, O blessed of my Father, inherit the
kingdom prepared for you from the foundation of the world; for I was . . . a stranger
and you welcomed me, I was naked and
you clothed me . . . I say to you, as you did
it to one of the least of these my brethren,
you did it to me.

Matthew 25.34–36,40

Before him no creature is hidden, but all
are open and laid bare to the eyes of him
with whom we have to do.

Hebrews 4.13

If a brother or sister is ill-clad . . . and one
of you says to them, 'Go in peace, be
warmed and filled,' without giving them the
things needed for the body, what does it
profit? So faith by itself, if it has no works,
is dead.

James 2.15–17

You say, I am rich, I have prospered, and
I need nothing; not knowing that you are
wretched, pitiable, poor, blind, and naked.

Revelation 3.17

Nation

Righteousness exalts a nation,
  but sin is a reproach to any people.

Proverbs 14.34

I will give you as a light to the nations.

Isaiah 49.6

I am coming to gather all nations and
tongues; and they shall come and shall see
my glory.

Isaiah 66.18

Mine eyes have seen thy salvation
which thou hast prepared in the presence of
    all peoples,
a light for revelation to the Gentiles,
and for glory to thy people Israel.

Luke 2.30–32

You are a chosen race, a royal priesthood,
a holy nation, God's own people, that you
may declare the wonderful deeds of him
who called you out of darkness into his
marvellous light.

1 Peter 2.9

Nature

See also **Creation, Earth**

God said, 'Let the earth put forth vegeta-
tion, plants yielding seed, and fruit trees
bearing fruit in which is their seed, each
according to its kind, upon the earth.' And
it was so.

Genesis 1.11

God blessed them, and God said to them,
'Be fruitful and multiply, and fill the earth
and subdue it; and have dominion over the
fish of the sea and over the birds of the air
and over every living thing that moves upon
the earth.' And God said, 'Behold, I have
given you every plant yielding seed which is
upon the face of all the earth, and every
tree with seed in its fruit; you shall have
them for food. And to every beast of the
earth, and to every bird of the air, and to
everything that creeps on the earth, everything that has the breath of life, I have
given every green plant for food.' And it
was so. And God saw everything that he
had made, and behold, it was very good.

Genesis 1.28–31

But ask the beasts, and they will teach
    you;
  the birds of the air, and they will tell you;
or the plants of the earth, and they will
    teach you;
  and the fish of the sea will declare to you.
Who among all these does not know
  that the hand of the Lord has done this?

In his hand is the life of every living thing
  and the breath of all mankind.

Job 12.7–10

The heavens are telling the glory of God;
  and the firmament proclaims his
    handiwork.

Psalms 19.1

By dread deeds thou dost answer us with
    deliverance,
  O God of our salvation,
who art the hope of all the ends of the
    earth . . .
who by thy strength hast established
    the mountains,
  being girded with might;
who dost still the roaring of the seas,
  the roaring of their waves.

Psalms 65.5–7

Thou visitest the earth and waterest it,
  thou greatly enrichest it;
the river of God is full of water;
  thou providest their grain,
  for so thou hast prepared it.
Thou waterest its furrows abundantly,
  settling its ridges,
softening it with showers.

Psalms 65.9–1

Thou crownest the year with thy bounty;
  the tracks of thy chariot drip with fatness
The pastures of the wilderness drip,
  the hills gird themselves with joy,
the meadows clothe themselves with flock
  the valleys deck themselves with grain.

Psalms 65.11–1

Thou makest springs gush forth in the
    valleys;
  they flow between the hills,
they give drink to every beast of the field;
  the wild asses quench their thirst.
By them the birds of the air have their
    habitation;
  they sing among the branches.

Psalms 104.10–

From thy lofty abode thou waterest the
    mountains;
  the earth is satisfied with the fruit of thy
    work.

Thou dost cause the grass to grow for the
cattle,
and plants for man to cultivate,
hat he may bring forth food from the
earth.

Psalms 104.13—14

The trees of the Lord are watered
abundantly,
the cedars of Lebanon which he planted.
n them the birds build their nests;
the stork has her home in the fir trees.
he high mountains are for the wild goats;
the rocks are a refuge for the badgers.

Psalms 104.16—18

) Lord, how manifold are thy works!
In wisdom hast thou made them all;
the earth is full of thy creatures.
'onder is the sea, great and wide,
which teems with things innumerable,
living things both small and great.

Psalms 104.24—25

He did not leave himself without witness,
r he did good and gave you from heaven
ins and fruitful seasons, satisfying your
arts with food and gladness.

Acts 14.17

ver since the creation of the world his
visible nature, namely, his eternal power
d deity, has been clearly perceived in the
ings that have been made.

Romans 1.20

ecessities (of Life)

ive us this day our daily bread.

Matthew 6.11

herefore I tell you, do not be anxious
out your life, what you shall eat or what
u shall drink, nor about your body, what
u shall put on. Is not life more than food,
d the body more than clothing? Look at
birds of the air: they neither sow nor
p nor gather into barns, and yet your
avenly Father feeds them. Are you not of
re value than they? And which of you by
ng anxious can add one cubit to his span
life? And why are you anxious about

clothing? Consider the lilies of the field,
how they grow; they neither toil nor spin;
yet I tell you, even Solomon in all his glory
was not arrayed like one of these. But if
God so clothes the grass of the field, which
today is alive and tomorrow is thrown into
the oven, will he not much more clothe
you, O men of little faith? Therefore do not
be anxious, saying, 'What shall we eat?' or
'What shall we drink?' or 'What shall we
wear?' For the Gentiles seek all these
things; and your heavenly Father knows
that you need them all. But seek first his
kingdom and his righteousness, and all
these things shall be yours as well.

Matthew 6.25—33

Necessity

It was necessary for the Christ to suffer and
to rise from the dead.

Acts 17.3

The parts of the body which seem to be
weaker are indispensable.

1 Corinthians 12.22

He must be well thought of by outsiders,
or he may fall into reproach.

1 Timothy 3.7

Need

The Lord will provide.

Genesis 22.14

The poor will never cease out of the land;
therefore I command you, You shall open
wide your hand to your brother, to the
needy and to the poor.

Deuteronomy 15.11

For the needy shall not always be
forgotten,
and the hope of the poor shall not perish
for ever.

Psalms 9.18

Give deliverance to the needy.

Psalms 72.4

For he delivers the needy when he calls,
  the poor and him who has no helper.
He has pity on the weak and the needy,
  and saves the lives of the needy.

Psalms 72.12–13

Maintain the right of the afflicted and the
  destitute.
Rescue the weak and the needy;
  deliver them from the hand of the
    wicked.

Psalms 82.3–4

Maintain the rights of the poor and needy.

Proverbs 31.9

For thou hast been a stronghold to the
  poor,
a stronghold to the needy in his distress,
  a shelter from the storm and a shade
    from the heat.

Isaiah 25.4

When the poor and needy seek water,
  and there is none,
  and their tongue is parched with thirst,
I the Lord will answer them,
  I the God of Israel will not forsake them.

Isaiah 41.17

Hear this, you who trample upon
  the needy,
and bring the poor of the land to
  an end . . .
The Lord has sworn by the pride of Jacob:
  Surely I will never forget any of their
    deeds.

Amos 8.4,7

Your Father knows what you need before
you ask him.

Matthew 6.8

All who believed were together and had
all things in common; and they sold their
possessions and goods and distributed them
to all, as any had need.

Acts 2.44–45

Contribute to the needs of the saints,
practise hospitality.

Romans 12.13

Let the thief no longer steal, but rather let
him labour, doing honest work with his
hands, so that he may be able to give to
those in need.

Ephesians 4.28

God will supply every need of yours
according to his riches in glory in Christ
Jesus.

Philippians 4.19

If any one has the world's goods and sees
his brother in need, yet closes his heart
against him, how does God's love abide in
him?

1 John 3.17

Neglect

Take heed lest you forget the Lord your
God, by not keeping his commandments
and his ordinances and his statutes.

Deuteronomy 8.11

A child left to himself brings shame to his
mother.

Proverbs 29.15

Woe to you, scribes and Pharisees, hypocrites! For you tithe mint and dill and
cummin, and have neglected the weightier
matters of the law, justice and mercy and
faith.

Matthew 23.23

That servant who knew his master's will
but did not make ready or act according to
his will, shall receive a severe beating.

Luke 12.47

Do not neglect the gift you have.

1 Timothy 4.14

We must pay the closer attention to what
we have heard, lest we drift away from it.
For if the message declared by angels was
valid and every transgression or disobedience received a just retribution, how shall
we escape if we neglect such a great salvation?

Hebrews 2.1

Whoever knows what is right to do and fails to do it, for him it is sin.

James 4.17

Negligence

Do not now be negligent, for the Lord has chosen you to stand in his presence, to minister to him.

2 Chronicles 29.11

Cursed is he who does the work of the Lord with slackness.

Jeremiah 48.10

Then the kingdom of heaven shall be compared to ten maidens who took their lamps and went to meet the bridegroom. Five of them were foolish, and five were wise. For when the foolish took their lamps, they took no oil with them; but the wise took flasks of oil with their lamps . . . at midnight there was a cry, 'Behold, the bridegroom! Come out to meet him.' Then all those maidens rose and trimmed their lamps. And the foolish said to the wise, 'Give us some of your oil, for our lamps are going out.' But the wise replied, 'Perhaps there will not be enough for us and for you; go rather to the dealers and buy for yourselves.' And while they went to buy, the bridegroom came, and those who were ready went in with him to the marriage feast; and the door was shut. Afterward the other maidens came also, saying, 'Lord, Lord, open to us.' But he replied, 'Truly, I say to you, I do not know you.'

Matthew 25.1–12

He . . . who had received the one talent came forward, saying, 'Master, I knew you to be a hard man . . . so I was afraid, and I went and hid your talent in the ground. Here you have what is yours.' But his master answered him, 'You wicked and slothful servant! . . . you ought to have invested my money with the bankers, and at my coming I should have received what was my own with interest. So take the talent from him, and give it to him who has the ten talents.'

Matthew 25.24–28

Neighbours

You shall not covet your neighbour's house; you shall not covet your neighbour's wife, or his manservant, or his maidservant, or his ox, or his ass, or anything that is your neighbour's.

Exodus 20.17

You shall love your neighbour as yourself.

Leviticus 19.18

Do not plan evil against your neighbour who dwells trustingly beside you.

Proverbs 3.29

He who belittles his neighbour lacks sense.

Proverbs 11.12

He who despises his neighbour is a sinner.

Proverbs 14.21

Be not a witness against your neighbour without cause.

Proverbs 24.28

Love does no wrong to a neighbour; therefore love is the fulfilling of the law.

Romans 13.10

Let each of us please his neighbour for his good, to edify him.

Romans 15.2

If you really fulfil the royal law, according to the scripture, 'You shall love your neighbour as yourself,' you do well. But if you show partiality, you commit sin, and are convicted by the law as transgressors.

James 2.8–9

There is one lawgiver and judge, he who is able to save and to destroy. But who are you that you judge your neighbour?

James 4.12

Newness

Remember not the former things.

Isaiah 43.18

From this time forth I make you hear new things,

hidden things which you have not known.
They are created now, not long ago;
  before today you have never heard of
    them,
  lest you should say, 'Behold, I knew
    them.'
You have never heard, you have never
    known,
  from of old your ear has not been
    opened.

Isaiah 48.6—8

For behold, I create new heavens and a
    new earth;
and the former things shall not be
    remembered
  or come into mind.

Isaiah 65.17

Behold, the days are coming, says the
Lord, when I will make a new covenant
with the house of Israel and the house of
Judah, not like the covenant which I made
with their fathers when I took them by the
hand to bring them out of the land of
Egypt, my covenant which they broke,
though I was their husband, says the Lord.

Jeremiah 31.31—32

And no one puts a piece of unshrunk cloth
on an old garment, for the patch tears away
from the garment, and a worse tear is
made. Neither is new wine put into old
wineskins; if it is, the skins burst, and the
wine is spilled, and the skins are destroyed;
but new wine is put into fresh wineskins,
and so both are preserved.

Matthew 9.16—17

Now we are discharged from the law, dead
to that which held us captive, so that we
serve not under the old written code but in
the new life of the Spirit.

Romans 7.6

If any one is in Christ, he is a new creation;
the old has passed away, behold, the new
has come.

2 Corinthians 5.17

Put on the new nature.

Ephesians 4.24

News

Like cold water to a thirsty soul,
  so is good news from a far country.

Proverbs 25.25

How beautiful upon the mountains
  are the feet of him who brings good
    tidings.

Isaiah 52.7

Night

See also **Darkness**

God separated the light from the darkness
God called the light Day, and the darkness
he called Night.

Genesis 1.4—5

God made the two great lights, the greater
light to rule the day, and the lesser light to
rule the night.

Genesis 1.1

The heavens are telling the glory of
    God . . .
Day to day pours forth speech,
  and night to night declares knowledge.

Psalms 19.1—

By day the Lord commands his steadfast
    love;
  and at night his song is with me,
  a prayer to the God of my life.

Psalms 42

Thou makest darkness, and it is night,
  when all the beasts of the forest creep
    forth.

Psalms 104.

The moon and stars . . . rule over the
    night.

Psalms 136

If I say, 'Let only darkness cover me,
  and the light about me be night,'
even the darkness is not dark to thee,
  the night is bright as the day.

Psalms 139.11—

We must work the works of him who sent me, while it is day; night comes, when no one can work.

John 9.4

If any one walks in the night, he stumbles, because the light is not in him.

John 11.10

The night is far gone, the day is at hand. Let us then cast off the works of darkness and put on the armour of light.

Romans 13.12

You are all sons of light and sons of the day; we are not of the night or of darkness. So then let us not sleep, as others do, but let us keep awake and be sober.

1 Thessalonians 5.5−6

Its gates shall never be shut by day — and there shall be no night there.

Revelation 21.25

Nightmare

See also **Dreams**

Amid thoughts from visions of the night,
    when deep sleep falls on men,
dread came upon me, and trembling,
    which made all my bones shake.
A spirit glided past my face;
    the hair of my flesh stood up.

Job 4.13−15

When I say, 'My bed will comfort me,
    my couch will ease my complaint,'
then thou dost scare me with dreams
    and terrify me with visions.

Job 7.13−14

He will cover you with his pinions,
and under his wings you will find refuge . . .

You will not fear the terror of the night . . .
For he will give his angels charge of you
    to guard you in all your ways.

Psalms 91.4−5,11

Noise

A foolish woman is noisy.

Proverbs 9.13

Nonsense

See also **Folly**

A soft answer turns away wrath . . .
    but the mouths of fools pour out folly.

Proverbs 15.1−2

Answer a fool according to his folly,
    lest he be wise in his own eyes.

Proverbs 26.5

For every one is godless and an evildoer,
    and every mouth speaks folly.

Isaiah 9.17

Although they knew God they did not honour him as God or give thanks to him, but they became futile in their thinking and their senseless minds were darkened.

Romans 1.21

There are many insubordinate men, empty talkers and deceivers, especially the circumcision party; they must be silenced, since they are upsetting whole families by teaching for base gain what they have no right to teach.

Titus 1.10−11

Nostalgia

Say not, 'Why were the former days better
    than these?'
For it is not from wisdom that you ask
    this.

Ecclesiastes 7.10

O

Oaths

You shall not take the name of the Lord your God in vain.

Exodus 20.7

You shall not swear by my name falsely, and so profane the name of your God.

Leviticus 19.12

You shall fear the Lord your God; you shall serve him, and swear by his name.

Deuteronomy 6.13

You know in your hearts and souls, all of you, that not one thing has failed of all the good things which the Lord your God promised concerning you.

Joshua 23.14

If a man sins against his neighbour and is made to take an oath, and comes and swears his oath before thine altar in this house, then hear thou in heaven, and act, and judge thy servants, condemning the guilty by bringing his conduct upon his own head, and vindicating the righteous by rewarding him according to his righteousness.

1 Kings 8.31–32

If you swear, 'As the Lord lives,'
in truth, in justice, and in uprightness,
then nations shall bless themselves in him,
and in him shall they glory.
For thus says the Lord.

Jeremiah 4.2–3

You have heard that it was said to the men of old, 'You shall not swear falsely, but shall perform to the Lord what you have sworn.' But I say to you, Do not swear at all, either by heaven, for it is the throne of God, or by the earth, for it is his footstool, or by Jerusalem, for it is the city of the great King. And do not swear by your head, for you cannot make one hair white or black. Let what you say be simply 'Yes' or 'No'; anything more than this comes from evil.

Matthew 5.33–37

Blessed be the Lord God of Israel,
for he has visited and redeemed his
        people . . .
to perform the mercy promised to our
        fathers,
and to remember his holy covenant,
the oath which he swore to our father
        Abraham, to grant us
that we, being delivered from the
        hand of our enemies,
might serve him without fear,
in holiness and righteousness before
        him all the days of our life.

Luke 1.68,72–7?

When God made a promise to Abraham, since he had no one greater by whom to swear, he swore by himself, saying, 'Surely I will bless you and multiply you.'

Hebrews 6.13–1?

Men indeed swear by a greater than themselves, and in all their disputes an oath is final for confirmation. So when God desired to show more convincingly to the heirs of the promise the unchangeable character of his purpose, he interposed with an oath, so that . . . we . . . might have strong encouragement.

Hebrews 6.16–1?

Do not swear . . . that you may not fall under condemnation.

James 5.1?

Obedience

If you will obey my voice and keep my covenant, you shall be my own possession among all peoples; for all the earth is mine.

Exodus 19.5

When you are in tribulation . . . you will return to the Lord your God and obey his voice.

Deuteronomy 4.30

I set before you this day a blessing and a curse: the blessing, if you obey the commandments of the Lord your God . . . and the curse, if you do not obey the commandments of the Lord your God.

Deuteronomy 11.26–28

I have not departed from the
    commandment of his lips;
I have treasured in my bosom the words
    of his mouth.

Job 23.12

All the paths of the Lord are steadfast love
    and faithfulness,
for those who keep his covenant and his
    testimonies.

Psalms 25.10

In the roll of the book it is written of me;
delight to do thy will, O my God;
thy law is within my heart.

Psalms 40.7–8

Blessed are those who keep his
    testimonies,
who seek him with their whole heart.

Psalms 119.2

He who respects the commandment will be
    rewarded.

Proverbs 13.13

He who keeps the law is a wise son.

Proverbs 28.7

If you are willing and obedient,
    you shall eat the good of the land;
but if you refuse and rebel,
    you shall be devoured by the sword;
for the mouth of the Lord has spoken.

Isaiah 1.19–20

Obey my voice, and I will be your God, and you shall be my people; and walk in all the way that I command you, that it may be well with you.

Jeremiah 7.23

Every one then who hears these words of mine and does them will be like a wise man who built his house upon the rock; and the rain fell, and the floods came, and the winds blew and beat upon that house, but it did not fall, because it had been founded on the rock. And every one who hears these words of mine and does not do them will be like a foolish man who built his house upon the sand; and the rain fell, and the floods came, and the winds blew and beat against that house, and it fell; and great was the fall of it.

Matthew 7.24–27

Not as I will, but as thou wilt.

Matthew 26.39

If you love me, you will keep my commandments.

John 14.15

The Holy Spirit . . . God has given to those who obey him.

Acts 5.32

The will of the Lord be done.

Acts 21.14

As by one man's disobedience many were made sinners, so by one man's obedience many will be made righteous.

Romans 5.19

Do you not know that if you yield yourselves to any one as obedient slaves, you are slaves of the one whom you obey, either of sin, which leads to death, or of obedience, which leads to righteousness?

Romans 6.16

Let every person be subject to the governing authorities. For there is no authority except from God, and those that exist have been instituted by God. Therefore he who resists the authorities resists what God has appointed.

Romans 13.1–2

Destroy . . . every . . . obstacle to the knowledge of God, and take every thought captive to obey Christ, being ready to punish every disobedience, when your obedience is complete.

2 Corinthians 10.5–6

Children, obey your parents in the Lord, for this is right.

Ephesians 6.1

Slaves, be obedient to those who are your earthly masters, with fear and trembling, in singleness of heart, as to Christ; not in the way of eye-service, as men-pleasers, but as servants of Christ, doing the will of God.

Ephesians 6.5–6

Although he was a Son, he learned obedience through what he suffered; and being made perfect he became the source of eternal salvation to all who obey him.

Hebrews 5.8–9

Obey your leaders and submit to them; for they are keeping watch over your souls, as men who will have to give account. Let them do this joyfully, and not sadly, for that would be of no advantage to you.

Hebrews 13.17

We may be sure that we know him, if we keep his commandments. He who says, 'I know him' but disobeys his commandments is a liar, and the truth is not in him; but whoever keeps his word, in him truly love for God is perfected.

1 John 2.3–5

Obligation

If God so loved us, we also ought to love one another.

1 John 4.11

Obscenity

Now put them all away: anger, wrath, malice, slander, and foul talk from your mouth.

Colossians 3.8

Obstinacy

If you walk contrary to me, and will not hearken to me, I will bring more plagues upon you, sevenfold as many as your sins.

Leviticus 26.21

The Lord, the God of their fathers, sent persistently to them by his messengers, because he had compassion on his people and on his dwelling place; but they kept mocking the messengers of God, despising his words and scoffing at his prophets, till the wrath of the Lord rose against his people, till there was no remedy.

2 Chronicles 36.15–16

God is a righteous judge,
    and a God who has indignation every
        day.
If a man does not repent, God will whet
        his sword.

Psalms 7.11–12

Be not like a horse or a mule, without
        understanding,
    which must be curbed with bit and bridle,
    else it will not keep with you.

Psalms 32.9

Because I have called and you refused to
        listen,
    have stretched out my hand and no one
        has heeded . . .
I also will laugh at your calamity;
    I will mock when panic strikes you.

Proverbs 1.24,26

He who is often reproved, yet stiffens his
        neck
    will suddenly be broken beyond healing.

Proverbs 29.1

Because they have forsaken my law which I set before them, and have not obeyed my voice, or walked in accord with it, but have stubbornly followed their own hearts . . . will feed this people with wormwood, and give them poisonous water to drink. I will scatter them among the nations whom neither they nor their fathers have known; and I will send the sword after them, until I have consumed them.

Jeremiah 9.13–16

If you warn the wicked, and he does not turn from his wickedness, or from his wicked way, he shall die in his iniquity; but you will have saved your life.

Ezekiel 3.19

In anger and wrath I will execute
vengeance
upon the nations that did not obey.

Micah 5.15

They refused to hearken, and turned a stubborn shoulder, and stopped their ears that they might not hear. They made their hearts like adamant lest they should hear the law and the words which the Lord of hosts had sent by his Spirit through the former prophets. Therefore great wrath came from the Lord of hosts. 'As I called, and they would not hear, so they called, and I would not hear,' says the Lord of hosts, 'and I scattered them with a whirlwind among all the nations which they had not known. Thus the land they left was desolate, so that no one went to and fro, and the pleasant land was made desolate.'

Zechariah 7.11–14

If they do not hear Moses and the prophets, neither will they be convinced if some one should rise from the dead.

Luke 16.31

By your hard and impenitent heart you are storing up wrath for yourself on the day of wrath when God's righteous judgment will be revealed.

Romans 2.5

Occult

See also **Magic, Witchcraft**

You shall not permit a sorceress to live.

Exodus 22.18

Do not turn to mediums or wizards; do not seek them out, to be defiled by them.

Leviticus 19.31

If a person turns to mediums and wizards, playing the harlot after them, I will set my face against that person, and will cut him off from among his people.

Leviticus 20.6

Then you shall do according to what they declare to you from that place which the Lord will choose; and you shall be careful to do according to all that they direct you; according to the instructions which they give you, and according to the decision which they pronounce to you, you shall do; you shall not turn aside from the verdict which they declare to you, either to the right hand or to the left. The man who acts presumptuously, by not obeying the priest who stands to minister there before the Lord your God . . . shall die.

Deuteronomy 17.10–12

There shall not be found among you any one who burns his son or his daughter as an offering, any one who practises divination, a soothsayer, or an augur . . . or a medium, or a wizard, or a necromancer. For whoever does these things is an abomination to the Lord.

Deuteronomy 18.10–12

Let them stand forth and save you,
those who divide the heavens,
	who gaze at the stars,
who at the new moons predict
	what shall befall you.
Behold, they are like stubble,
	the fire consumes them;
they cannot deliver themselves
	from the power of the flame.

Isaiah 47.13–14

Do not listen to your prophets, your diviners, your dreamers, your soothsayers, or your sorcerers . . . it is a lie which they are prophesying to you.

Jeremiah 27.9–10

I will cut off sorceries from your hand,
	and you shall have no more soothsayers.

Micah 5.12

I will be a swift witness against the sorcerers.

Malachi 3.5

I do not want you to be partners with demons. You cannot drink the cup of the Lord and the cup of demons. You cannot partake of the table of the Lord and the table of demons.

1 Corinthians 10.20–21

Idolatry, sorcery . . . those who do such things shall not inherit the kingdom of God.

Galatians 5.20–21

Now the Spirit expressly says that in later times some will depart from the faith by giving heed to deceitful spirits and doctrines of demons, through the pretensions of liars whose consciences are seared.

1 Timothy 4.1–2

Offence

You shall not bring an abominable thing into your house, and become accursed like it; you shall utterly detest and abhor it; for it is an accursed thing.

Deuteronomy 7.26

An unjust man is an abomination to the
　　righteous,
　but he whose way is straight is an
　　abomination to the wicked.

Proverbs 29.27

He will become a sanctuary, and a stone of offence, and a rock of stumbling to both houses of Israel.

Isaiah 8.14

Oh, do not do this abominable thing that I hate!

Jeremiah 44.4

If your right eye causes you to sin, pluck it out and throw it away; it is better that you lose one of your members than that your whole body be thrown into hell.

Matthew 5.29

Whoever causes one of these little ones who believe in me to sin, it would be better for him to have a great millstone fastened round his neck and to be drowned in the depth of the sea.

Matthew 18.6

Take note of those who create dissensions and difficulties in opposition to the doctrine which you have been taught; avoid them.

Romans 16.17

We preach Christ crucified, a stumbling block to Jews and folly to Gentiles.

1 Corinthians 1.23

Give no offence to Jews or to Greeks or to the church of God, just as I try to please all men.

1 Corinthians 10.32

We put no obstacle in any one's way, so that no fault may be found with our ministry, but as servants of God we commend ourselves in every way.

2 Corinthians 6.3–4

We all make many mistakes, and if any one makes no mistakes in what he says he is a perfect man.

James 3.2

Old Testament

For truly, I say to you, till heaven and earth pass away, not an iota, not a dot, will pass from the law until all is accomplished. Whoever then relaxes one of the least of these commandments and teaches men so, shall be called least in the kingdom of heaven; but he who does them and teaches them shall be called great in the kingdom of heaven.

Matthew 5.18–19

Omnipotence

See also **Power**

Is anything too hard for the Lord?

Genesis 18.14

Thou hast only begun to show thy servant thy . . . mighty hand; for what god is there . . . who can do such works and mighty acts as thine?

Deuteronomy 3.24

To you it was shown, that you might know that the Lord is God; there is no other besides him.

Deuteronomy 4.35

For the Lord your God is God of gods and Lord of lords, the great, the mighty, and the terrible God, who is not partial and takes no bribe.

Deuteronomy 10.17

No man shall be able to stand against you; the Lord your God will lay the fear of you and the dread of you upon all the land that you shall tread, as he promised you.

Deuteronomy 11.25

Thine, O Lord, is the greatness, and the power, and the glory, and the victory, and the majesty; for all that is in the heavens and in the earth is thine; thine is the kingdom, O Lord, and thou art exalted as head above all. Both riches and honour come from thee, and thou rulest over all. In thy hand are power and might; and in thy hand it is to make great and to give strength to all.

1 Chronicles 29.11−12

Thou art the Lord, thou alone; thou hast made heaven, the heaven of heavens, with all their host, the earth and all that is on it, the seas and all that is in them; and thou preservest all of them; and the host of heaven worships thee.

Nehemiah 9.6

The Lord gave, and the Lord has taken away.

Job 1.21

In his hand is the life of every living thing
and the breath of all mankind.

Job 12.10

I know that thou canst do all things,
and that no purpose of thine can be
thwarted.

Job 42.2

Ah Lord God! It is thou who hast made the heavens and the earth by thy great power and by thy outstretched arm! Nothing is too hard for thee.

Jeremiah 32.17−18

He rose and rebuked the winds and the sea; and there was a great calm. And the men marvelled, saying 'What sort of man is this, that even winds and sea obey him?'

Matthew 8.26−27

With God all things are possible.

Matthew 19.26

Jesus came and said to them, 'All authority in heaven and on earth has been given to me.'

Matthew 28.18

Abba, Father, all things are possible to thee.

Mark 14.36

Father, the hour has come; glorify thy Son that the Son may glorify thee, since thou hast given him power over all flesh, to give eternal life to all whom thou hast given him. And this is eternal life, that they know thee the only true God.

John 17.1−3

The King of kings and Lord of lords, who alone has immortality and dwells in unapproachable light.

1 Timothy 6.15−16

I heard what seemed to be the voice of a great multitude, like the sound of many waters and like the sound of mighty thunderpeals, crying,
'Hallelujah! For the Lord our God the Almighty reigns.'

Revelation 19.6

Omnipresence

Will God indeed dwell on the earth? Behold, heaven and the highest heaven cannot contain thee.

1 Kings 8.27

Whither shall I go from thy Spirit?
Or whither shall I flee from thy presence?
If I ascend to heaven, thou art there!
If I make my bed in Sheol, thou art
there!
If I take the wings of the morning
and dwell in the uttermost parts of the
sea,

even there thy hand shall lead me,
  and thy right hand shall hold me.

Psalms 139.7–10

Am I a God at hand, says the Lord, and
not a God afar off? Can a man hide himself
in secret places so that I cannot see him?
says the Lord. Do I not fill heaven and
earth? says the Lord.

Jeremiah 23.23–24

The God who made the world and everything in it, being Lord of heaven and earth,
does not live in shrines made by man.

Acts 17.24

Omniscience

The Lord is a God of knowledge,
  and by him actions are weighed.

1 Samuel 2.3

The Lord sees not as man sees; man looks
on the outward appearance, but the Lord
looks on the heart.

1 Samuel 16.7

Thou, thou only, knowest the hearts of all
the children of men.

1 Kings 8.39

The Lord searches all hearts, and understands every plan and thought.

1 Chronicles 28.9

Thine, O Lord, is the greatness.

1 Chronicles 29.11

For he knows worthless men;
  when he sees iniquity, will he not
    consider it?

Job 11.11

For he looks to the ends of the earth,
  and sees everything under the heavens.

Job 28.24

He knows the secrets of the heart.

Psalms 44.21

O God, thou knowest my folly;
  the wrongs I have done are not hidden
    from thee.

Psalms 69.5

Understand, O dullest of the people!
  Fools, when will you be wise?
He who planted the ear, does he not hear?
He who formed the eye, does he not see?
He who chastens the nations, does he not
    chastise?
He who teaches men knowledge,
  the Lord, knows the thoughts of man,
  that they are but a breath.

Psalms 94.8–11

The eyes of the Lord are in every place,
  keeping watch on the evil and the good.

Proverbs 15.3

Sheol and Abaddon lie open before the
    Lord,
  how much more the hearts of men!

Proverbs 15.11

Does not he who weighs the heart
    perceive it?
Does not he who keeps watch over your
    soul know it.

Proverbs 24.12

Woe to those who hide deep from the
    Lord their counsel,
  whose deeds are in the dark,
  and who say, 'Who sees us?
    Who knows us?'
You turn things upside down!

Isaiah 29.15–16

I know your sitting down
  and your going out and coming in,
  and your raging against me.
Because you have raged against me
  and your arrogance has come to my ears,
I will put my hook in your nose
  and my bit in your mouth,
and I will turn you back on the way
  by which you came.

Isaiah 37.28–29

You are those who justify yourselves
before men, but God knows your hearts;
for what is exalted among men is an abomination in the sight of God.

Luke 16.15

God is greater than our hearts, and he knows everything.

1 John 3.20

Openness

See also **Forthrightness**

Better is open rebuke
than hidden love.

Proverbs 27.5

Opinions

A fool takes no pleasure in understanding,
but only in expressing his opinion.

Proverbs 18.2

Opportunity

See also **Freedom**

As we have opportunity, let us do good to all men, and especially to those who are of the household of faith.

Galatians 6.10

Oppression

See also **Tyranny**

You shall not wrong a stranger or oppress him, for you were strangers in the land of Egypt. You shall not afflict any widow or orphan. If you do afflict them, and they cry out to me, I will surely hear their cry; and my wrath will burn, and I will kill you with the sword, and your wives shall become widows and your children fatherless.

Exodus 22.21–24

The Lord is a stronghold for the
oppressed,
a stronghold in times of trouble.

Psalms 9.9

O Lord, thou wilt hear the desire of the
meek;
thou wilt strengthen their heart, thou wilt
incline thy ear
to do justice to the fatherless and the
oppressed,

so that man who is of the earth may
strike terror no more.

Psalms 10.17–18

'Because the poor are despoiled, because
the needy groan,
I will now arise,' says the Lord;
'I will place him in the safety for which he
longs.'

Psalms 12.5

Put no confidence in extortion,
set no vain hopes on robbery.

Psalms 62.10

Give deliverance to the needy,
and crush the oppressor!

Psalms 72.4

He has pity on the weak and the needy,
and saves the lives of the needy.
From oppression and violence he redeems
their life;
and precious is their blood in his sight.

Psalms 72.13–14

He who oppresses a poor man insults his
Maker.

Proverbs 14.31

He who oppresses the poor to increase his
own wealth,
or gives to the rich, will only come to
want.

Proverbs 22.16

Surely oppression makes the wise
man foolish.

Ecclesiastes 7.7

Correct oppression.

Isaiah 1.17

'What do you mean by crushing
my people,
by grinding the face of the poor?' says the
Lord God of hosts.

Isaiah 3.15

Woe to those who decree iniquitous
decrees,
and the writers who keep writing
oppression,
to turn aside the needy from justice
and to rob the poor of my people of their
right,

that widows may be their spoil,
  and that they may make the fatherless
    their prey!

Isaiah 10.1–2

He who walks righteously and speaks
    uprightly,
  who despises the gain of oppressions . . .
he will dwell on the heights;
  his place of defence will be the fortresses
    of rocks.

Isaiah 33.15,16

O afflicted one, storm-tossed, and
    not comforted,
  behold, I will set your stones in
    antimony,
and lay your foundations with
    sapphires . . .
In righteousness you shall be
    established;
  you shall be far from oppression, for you
    shall not fear;
  and from terror, for it shall not come
    near you.

Isaiah 54.11,14

If you do not oppress the alien, the fatherless or the widow, or shed innocent blood in
this place . . . then I will let you dwell in
this place, in the land that I gave of old to
your fathers for ever.

Jeremiah 7.6–7

I will punish all who oppress them.

Jeremiah 30.20

Hear this word, you . . .
  who oppress the poor, who crush the
    needy,
  who say to their husbands,
    'Bring, that we may drink!'
The Lord God has sworn by his holiness
  that, behold, the days are coming
    upon you,
  when they shall take you away with hooks,
    even the last of you with fishhooks.

Amos 4.1–2

Do not oppress the widow, the fatherless,
the sojourner, or the poor.

Zechariah 7.10

The Spirit of the Lord is upon me,
  because he has anointed me to preach
    good news to the poor . . .
to set at liberty those who are oppressed.

Luke 4.18

Remember . . . those who are ill-treated,
since you also are in the body.

Hebrews 13.3

Optimism

See also **Hope**

May all who seek thee
  rejoice and be glad in thee!
May those who love thy salvation
  say evermore, 'God is great!'

Psalms 70.4

I will hope continually,
  and will praise thee yet more and more.

Psalms 71.14

Rejoice in your hope.

Romans 12.12

Love bears all things, believes all things,
hopes all things, endures all things.

1 Corinthians 13.7

Order

All things should be done decently and in
order.

1 Corinthians 14.40

In Christ shall all be made alive. But each
in his own order: Christ the first fruits, then
at his coming those who belong to Christ.

1 Corinthians 15.22–23

Amend what was defective, and appoint
elders in every town.

Titus 1.5

Orphans

You shall not afflict any widow or orphan. If you do afflict them, and they cry out to me, I will surely hear their cry; and my wrath will burn, and I will kill you with the sword, and your wives shall become widows and your children fatherless.

Exodus 22.22–24

He executes justice for the fatherless and the widow.

Deuteronomy 10.18

Cursed be he who perverts the justice due to the sojourner, the fatherless, and the widow.

Deuteronomy 27.19

There are those who snatch the fatherless child from the breast . . .
yet God pays no attention to their prayer.

Job 24.9,12

For my father and my mother have forsaken me,
    but the Lord will take me up.

Psalms 27.10

Father of the fatherless and protector of widows
    is God in his holy habitation.

Psalms 68.5

I will not leave you desolate; I will come to you.

John 14.18

Religion that is pure and undefiled before God and the Father is this: to visit orphans and widows in their affliction.

James 1.27

Outcasts

The Lord God sent him forth from the garden of Eden, to till the ground from which he was taken. He drove out the man.

Genesis 3.23–24

Make your shade like night
    at the height of noon;
hide the outcasts,
    betray not the fugitive.

Isaiah 16.3

Bring the homeless poor into your
        house . . .
Then shall your light break forth like
    the dawn.

Isaiah 58.7–8

For I will restore health to you,
    and your wounds I will heal, says the
        Lord,
because they have called you an outcast:
    'It is Zion, for whom no one cares!'

Jeremiah 30.17

When the king came in to look at the guests, he saw there a man who had no wedding garment; and he said to him, 'Friend, how did you get in here without a wedding garment?' And he was speechless. Then the king said to the attendants, 'Bind him hand and foot, and cast him into the outer darkness; there men will weep and gnash their teeth.' For many are called, but few are chosen.

Matthew 22.11–14

P

Pacifism

See also **Disarmament**

He makes wars cease to the end of the
　　earth;
　he breaks the bow, and shatters the
　　　spear,
　he burns the chariots with fire!
'Be still, and know that I am God.'

Psalms 46.9—10

Those who plan good have joy.

Proverbs 12.20

Cursed is he who does the work of the
Lord with slackness; and cursed is he who
keeps back his sword from bloodshed.

Jeremiah 48.10

Blessed are the peacemakers, for they
shall be called sons of God.

Matthew 5.9

You have heard that it was said, 'An eye
for an eye and a tooth for a tooth.' But I
say to you, Do not resist one who is evil.
But if any one strikes you on the right
cheek, turn to him the other also.

Matthew 5.38—39

All who take the sword will perish by the
sword.

Matthew 26.52

Pain

The wicked man writhes in pain all his
days.

Job 15.20

Man is also chastened with pain upon his
　　bed,
　and with continual strife in his bones . . .

If there be for him an angel,
　a mediator, one of the thousand,
　to declare to man what is right for him;
and he is gracious to him, and says,
　'Deliver him from going down into
　　　the Pit . . .'
then man prays to God . . .
Behold, God does all these things,
　twice, three times, with a man,
to bring back his soul from the Pit,
　that he may see the light of life.

Job 33.19,23—24,26,29—30

Turn thou to me, and be gracious to me;
　for I am lonely and afflicted.
Relieve the troubles of my heart,
　and bring me out of my distresses.
Consider my affliction and my trouble,
　and forgive all my sins.

Psalms 25.16—18

Pour out thy indignation upon them,
　and let thy burning anger overtake
　　　them . . .
For they persecute him whom thou hast
　　　smitten,
　and him whom thou hast wounded, they
　　　afflict still more.

Psalms 69.24,26

I love the Lord, because he has heard
　my voice and my supplications.
Because he inclined his ear to me,
　therefore I will call on him as long as I
　　　live.
The snares of death encompassed me;
　the pangs of Sheol laid hold on me;
　I suffered distress and anguish.
Then I called on the name of the Lord:
　'O Lord, I beseech thee, save my life!'

Psalms 116.1—4

They brought him all the sick, those afflicted with various diseases and pains, demoniacs, epileptics, and paralytics, and he healed them.

Matthew 4.24

We know that the whole creation has been groaning in travail together until now; and not only the creation, but we ourselves, who have the first fruits of the Spirit, groan inwardly as we wait for adoption as sons, the redemption of our bodies.

Romans 8.22–23

Although he was a Son, he learned obedience through what he suffered.

Hebrews 5.8

Paradox

See also **Mystery**

The beginning of wisdom is this:
  Get wisdom.

Proverbs 4.7

One man pretends to be rich, yet has
    nothing;
another pretends to be poor, yet has
    great wealth.

Proverbs 13.7

He who finds his life will lose it, and he who loses his life for my sake will find it.

Matthew 10.39

If any one would be first, he must be last of all and servant of all.

Mark 9.35

He who loves his life loses it, and he who hates his life in this world will keep it for eternal life.

John 12.25

Has not God made foolish the wisdom of the world? For since, in the wisdom of God, the world did not know God through wisdom, it pleased God through the folly of what we preach to save those who believe.

1 Corinthians 1.20–21

If any one among you thinks that he is wise in this age, let him become a fool that he may become wise.

1 Corinthians 3.18

I will all the more gladly boast of my weaknesses, that the power of Christ may rest upon me. For the sake of Christ, then, I am content with weaknesses . . . for when I am weak, then I am strong.

2 Corinthians 12.9–10

But whatever gain I had, I counted as loss for the sake of Christ.

Philippians 3.7

Paranoia

The wicked flee when no one pursues,
  but the righteous are bold as a lion.

Proverbs 28.1

Parenthood

See also **Motherhood**

Honour your father and your mother.

Exodus 20.12

Whoever curses his father or his mother shall be put to death.

Exodus 21.17

If a man has a stubborn and rebellious son, who will not obey the voice of his father or the voice of his mother, and, though they chastise him, will not give heed to them, then his father and his mother shall take hold of him and bring him out to the elders of his city at the gate of the place where he lives, and they shall say to the elders of his city, 'This our son is stubborn and rebellious, he will not obey our voice; he is a glutton and a drunkard.' Then all the men of the city shall stone him to death with stones.

Deuteronomy 21.18–21

Cursed be he who dishonours his father or his mother.

Deuteronomy 27.16

Lay to heart all the words which I enjoin upon you this day, that you may command them to your children, that they may be careful to do all the words of this law.

Deuteronomy 32.46

As a father pities his children,
  so the Lord pities those who fear him.

Psalms 103.13

For the Lord reproves him whom he loves,
  as a father the son in whom he delights.

Proverbs 3.12

A good man leaves an inheritance to his
  children's children.

Proverbs 13.22

If one curses his father or his mother,
  his lamp will be put out in utter darkness.

Proverbs 20.20

Train up a child in the way he should go,
  and when he is old he will not depart
    from it.

Proverbs 22.6

Hearken to your father who begat you,
  and do not despise your mother when she
    is old.

Proverbs 23.22

Let your father and mother be glad,
  let her who bore you rejoice.

Proverbs 23.25

The eye that mocks a father
  and scorns to obey a mother
will be picked out by the ravens of the
    valley
  and eaten by the vultures.

Proverbs 30.17

The living, the living, he thanks thee,
  as I do this day;
the father makes known to the children
  thy faithfulness.

Isaiah 38.19

Can a woman forget her sucking child,
  that she should have no compassion on
    the son of her womb?

Isaiah 49.15

As one whom his mother comforts,
  so I will comfort you.

Isaiah 66.13

He who loves father or mother more than me is not worthy of me; and he who loves son or daughter more than me is not worthy of me.

Matthew 10.37

What father among you, if his son asks for a fish, will instead of a fish give him a serpent; or if he asks for an egg, will give him a scorpion? If you then, who are evil, know how to give good gifts to your children, how much more will the heavenly Father give the Holy Spirit to those who ask him!

Luke 11.11−13

Children ought not to lay up for their parents, but parents for their children.

2 Corinthians 12.14

Fathers, do not provoke your children to anger, but bring them up in the discipline and instruction of the Lord.

Ephesians 6.4

Fathers, do not provoke your children, lest they become discouraged.

Colossians 3.21

A bishop must . . . manage his own household well, keeping his children submissive and respectful in every way.

1 Timothy 3.2,4

Participation

Because there is one bread, we who are many are one body, for we all partake of the one bread.

1 Corinthians 10.17

We know that as you share in our sufferings, you will also share in our comfort.

2 Corinthians 1.7

You were called in the one body.

Colossians 3.15

Do not . . . participate in another man's sins.

1 Timothy 5.22

Since therefore the children share in flesh and blood, he himself likewise partook of the same nature, that through death he might destroy him who has the power of death, that is, the devil, and deliver all those who through fear of death were subject to lifelong bondage.

Hebrews 2.14−15

That which we have seen and heard we proclaim also to you, so that you may have fellowship with us; and our fellowship is with the Father and with his Son Jesus Christ.

1 John 1.3

If we say we have fellowship with him while we walk in darkness, we lie and do not live according to the truth; but if we walk in the light, as he is in the light, we have fellowship with one another, and the blood of Jesus his Son cleanses us from all sin.

1 John 1.6−7

Passion

A tranquil mind gives life to the flesh,
  but passion makes the bones rot.

Proverbs 14.30

So shun youthful passions and aim at righteousness, faith, love, and peace, along with those who call upon the Lord.

2 Timothy 2.22

Patience

Be still before the Lord, and wait patiently
  for him.

Psalms 37.7

Wait for the Lord, and keep to his
  way . . .
ou will look on the destruction of the
  wicked.

Psalms 37.34

With patience a ruler may be persuaded,
  and a soft tongue will break a bone.

Proverbs 25.15

The patient in spirit is better than the proud in spirit.

Ecclesiastes 7.8

The Lord is good to those who wait for
  him,
  to the soul that seeks him.
It is good that one should wait quietly
  for the salvation of the Lord.

Lamentations 3.25−26

Suffering produces endurance, and endurance produces character, and character produces hope.

Romans 5.4

If we hope for what we do not see, we wait for it with patience.

Romans 8.25

Be patient in tribulation.

Romans 12.12

Love is patient and kind.

1 Corinthians 13.4

The Spirit is . . . patience.

Galatians 5.22

Lead a life worthy of the calling to which you have been called, with all lowliness and meekness, with patience.

Ephesians 4.1−2

Be patient with them all.

1 Thessalonians 5.14

May the Lord direct your hearts to the love of God and to the steadfastness of Christ.

2 Thessalonians 3.5

The Lord's servant . . . must . . . be . . . forbearing.

2 Timothy 2.24

The testing of your faith produces steadfastness.

James 1.3

Be patient, therefore, brethren, until the coming of the Lord. Behold, the farmer waits for the precious fruit of the earth, being patient over it until it receives the early and the late rain. You also be patient. Establish your hearts.

James 5.7–8

As an example of suffering and patience, brethren, take the prophets who spoke in the name of the Lord.

James 5.10

We call those happy who were steadfast. You have heard of the steadfastness of Job, and you have seen the purpose of the Lord, how the Lord is compassionate and merciful.

James 5.11

What credit is it, if when you do wrong and are beaten for it you take it patiently? But if when you do right and suffer for it you take it patiently, you have God's approval.

1 Peter 2.20

Peace

Rest assured, do not be afraid.

Genesis 43.23

If you walk in my statutes and observe my commandments and do them, then I will give you . . . peace in the land, and you shall lie down, and none shall make you afraid; and I will remove evil beasts from the land, and the sword shall not go through your land.

Leviticus 26.3,6

Agree with God, and be at peace; thereby good will come to you.

Job 22.21

Dominion and fear are with God; he makes peace in his high heaven.

Job 25.2

In peace I will both lie down and sleep; for thou alone, O Lord, makest me dwell in safety.

Psalms 4.8

The Lord is my shepherd, I shall not want; he makes me lie down in green pastures. He leads me beside still waters; he restores my soul.

Psalms 23.1–3

May the Lord bless his people with peace!

Psalms 29.11

Seek peace, and pursue it.

Psalms 34.14

Shout for joy and be glad, and say evermore, 'Great is the Lord, who delights in the welfare of his servant!'

Psalms 35.27

In his days may righteousness flourish, and peace abound, till the moon be no more!

Psalms 72.7

Great peace have those who love thy law.

Psalms 119.165

When a man's ways please the Lord, he makes even his enemies to be at peace with him.

Proverbs 16.7

Better is a dry morsel with quiet than a house full of feasting with strife.

Proverbs 17.1

Open the gates, that the righteous nation which keeps faith may enter in. Thou dost keep him in perfect peace, whose mind is stayed on thee, because he trusts in thee.

Isaiah 26.2–3

The effect of righteousness will be peace, and the result of righteousness, quietness and trust for ever.

Isaiah 32.17

How beautiful upon the mountains are the feet of him who brings good tidings,

who publishes peace, who brings good
    tidings of good,
  who publishes salvation,
  who says to Zion, 'Your God reigns.'

                  Isaiah 52.7

For the mountains may depart
  and the hills be removed,
but my steadfast love shall not depart from
    you,
  and my covenant of peace shall not be
    removed,
  says the Lord, who has compassion on
    you.

                Isaiah 54.10

For the righteous man is taken away from
    calamity,
  he enters into peace.

                Isaiah 57.1–2

He shall judge between many peoples,
  and shall decide for strong nations afar
    off;
and they shall beat their swords into
    ploughshares,
  and their spears into pruning hooks;
nation shall not lift up sword against nation,
  neither shall they learn war any more;
but they shall sit every man under his vine
    and under his fig tree,
  and none shall make them afraid;
  for the mouth of the Lord of hosts has
    spoken.

                Micah 4.3–4

Render in your gates judgments that are
true and make for peace.

                Zechariah 8.16

Love truth and peace.

                Zechariah 8.19

Blessed are the peacemakers, for they
shall be called sons of God.

                Matthew 5.9

Do not think that I have come to bring
peace on earth; I have not come to bring
peace, but a sword. For I have come to set
a man against his father, and a daughter
against her mother, and a daughter-in-law
against her mother-in-law; and a man's foes
will be those of his own household.

                Matthew 10.34–36

Be at peace with one another.

                Mark 9.50

Glory to God in the highest,
  and on earth peace among men with
    whom he is pleased!

                Luke 2.14

Lord, now lettest thou thy servant depart
    in peace,
according to thy word;
for mine eyes have seen thy salvation
which thou hast prepared in the presence of
    all peoples,
a light for revelation to the Gentiles,
and for glory to thy people Israel.

                Luke 2.29–32

Whatever house you enter, first say,
'Peace be to this house!' And if a son of
peace is there, your peace shall rest upon
him; but if not, it shall return to you.

                Luke 10.5–6

Peace I leave with you; my peace I give to
you; not as the world gives do I give to you.

                John 14.27

Since we are justified by faith, we have
peace with God through our Lord Jesus
Christ.

                Romans 5.1

If possible, so far as it depends upon you,
live peaceably with all.

                Romans 12.18

Let us then pursue what makes for peace
and for mutual upbuilding.

                Romans 14.19

The God of peace be with you all.

                Romans 15.33

God has called us to peace.

                1 Corinthians 7.15

God is not a God of confusion but of
peace.

                1 Corinthians 14.33

Agree with one another, live in peace, and the God of love and peace will be with you.

2 Corinthians 13.11

Maintain the unity of the Spirit in the bond of peace.

Ephesians 4.3

The peace of God, which passes all understanding, will keep your hearts and your minds in Christ Jesus.

Philippians 4.7

Let the peace of Christ rule in your hearts, to which indeed you were called in the one body.

Colossians 3.15

Be at peace among yourselves.

1 Thessalonians 5.13

God deems it just to repay with affliction those who afflict you, and to grant rest with us to you who are afflicted.

2 Thessalonians 1.6−7

Strive for peace with all men, and for the holiness without which no one will see the Lord.

Hebrews 12.14

The harvest of righteousness is sown in peace by those who make peace.

James 3.18

Let him seek peace and pursue it.

1 Peter 3.11

Penitence

See also **Confession, Remorse, Repentance**

If you return to the Almighty and humble yourself,
if you remove unrighteousness far from your tents . . .
then you will delight yourself in the Almighty,
and lift up your face to God.

Job 22.23,26

The Lord has heard the sound of my weeping.

The Lord has heard my supplication;
the Lord accepts my prayer.

Psalms 6.8−9

I acknowledged my sin to thee,
and I did not hide my iniquity;
I said, 'I will confess my transgressions to the Lord';
then thou didst forgive the guilt of my sin.

Psalms 32.5

The sacrifice acceptable to God is a broken spirit;
a broken and contrite heart, O God, thou wilt not despise.

Psalms 51.17

If a wicked man turns away from all his sins which he has committed and keeps all my statutes and does what is lawful and right, he shall surely live; he shall not die.

Ezekiel 18.21

If we confess our sins, he is faithful and just, and will forgive our sins and cleanse us from all unrighteousness.

1 John 1.9

Percipience

The eye is the lamp of the body. So, if your eye is sound, your whole body will be full of light; but if your eye is not sound, your whole body will be full of darkness. If then the light in you is darkness, how great is the darkness!

Matthew 6.22−23

Perfection

See also **Ideal**

I am God Almighty; walk before me, and be blameless.

Genesis 17.1

For I will proclaim the name of the Lord.
Ascribe greatness to our God!
The Rock, his work is perfect;
for all his ways are justice.

A God of faithfulness and without iniquity,
  just and right is he.

  Deuteronomy 32.3–4

This God — his way is perfect.

  2 Samuel 22.31

A blameless and upright man . . . fears
God and turns away from evil.

  Job 1.8

Behold, God will not reject a blameless
  man,
  nor take the hand of evildoers.

  Job 8.20

God . . . girded me with strength,
  and made my way safe.

  Psalms 18.32

The law of the Lord is perfect.

  Psalms 19.7

Out of Zion, the perfection of beauty,
  God shines forth.

  Psalms 50.2

He who walks in the way that is blameless
  shall minister to me.

  Psalms 101.6

The righteousness of the blameless keeps
  his way straight.

  Proverbs 11.5

You, therefore, must be perfect, as your
heavenly Father is perfect.

  Matthew 5.48

Jesus said to him, 'If you would be perfect,
go, sell what you possess and give to the
poor, and you will have treasure in heaven;
and come, follow me.'

  Matthew 19.21

Do not be conformed to this world but be
transformed by the renewal of your mind,
that you may prove what is the will of God,
what is good and acceptable and perfect.

  Romans 12.2

Let us cleanse ourselves from every
defilement of body and spirit, and make
holiness perfect in the fear of God.

  2 Corinthians 7.1

Mend your ways, heed my appeal, agree
with one another, live in peace.

  2 Corinthians 13.11

When he ascended on high he led a host
  of captives,
  and he gave gifts to men . . . and his gifts
  were . . .
to equip the saints for the work of ministry,
for building up the body of Christ, until we
all attain to the unity of the faith and of the
knowledge of the Son of God, to mature
manhood, to the measure of the stature of
the fulness of Christ.

  Ephesians 4.8,12–13

Him we proclaim, warning every man and
teaching every man in all wisdom, that we
may present every man mature in Christ.

  Colossians 1.28

Let steadfastness have its full effect, that
you may be perfect and complete, lacking
in nothing.

  James 1.4

Every good endowment and every perfect
gift is from above.

  James 1.17

If any one makes no mistakes in what he
says he is a perfect man, able to bridle the
whole body also.

  James 3.2

Whoever keeps his word, in him truly love
for God is perfected.

  1 John 2.5

If we love one another, God abides in us
and his love is perfected in us.

  1 John 4.12

Perfume

Oil and perfume make the heart glad.

  Proverbs 27.9

Perjury

See also **Deceit, Injustice, Lie**

You shall not bear false witness against your neighbour.

Exodus 20.16

You shall not utter a false report. You shall not join hands with a wicked man, to be a malicious witness.

Exodus 23.1

You shall not swear by my name falsely, and so profane the name of your God.

Leviticus 19.12

A false witness will not go unpunished.

Proverbs 19.5

A worthless witness mocks at justice.

Proverbs 19.28

Because he despised the oath and broke the covenants, because . . . he did all these things, he shall not escape.

Ezekiel 17.18

They utter mere words;
    with empty oaths they make covenants;
so judgment springs up like poisonous
        weeds
    in the furrows of the field.

Hosea 10.4

This is the curse . . . I will send it forth, says the Lord of hosts, and it shall enter the house of the thief, and the house of him who swears falsely by my name; and it shall abide in his house and consume it, both timber and stones.

Zechariah 5.3−4

Love no false oath.

Zechariah 8.17

The law is not laid down for the just but for the lawless . . . liars, perjurers, and whatever else is contrary to sound doctrine, in accordance with the glorious gospel of the blessed God.

1 Timothy 1.9−11

Persecution

See also **Martyrdom**

My times are in thy hand;
    deliver me from the hand of my enemies
        and persecutors!

Psalms 31.15

The wicked watches the righteous,
    and seeks to slay him.
The Lord will not abandon him to his
        power,
    or let him be condemned when he is
        brought to trial.

Psalms 37.32−33

Nay, for thy sake we are slain all the day
        long,
    and accounted as sheep for the slaughter.
Rouse thyself! Why sleepest thou, O Lord?
    Awake! Do not cast us off for ever!

Psalms 44.22−23

For he did not remember to show
        kindness,
    but pursued the poor and needy
    and the brokenhearted to their death.
He loved to curse; let curses come on him!
    He did not like blessing; may it be far
        from him!

Psalms 109.16−1?

Bloodthirsty men hate one who is
        blameless.

Proverbs 29.1?

I gave my back to the smiters,
    and my cheeks to those who pulled out
        the beard;
I hid not my face
    from shame and spitting.
For the Lord God helps me;
    therefore I have not been confounded;
therefore I have set my face like a flint,
    and I know that I shall not be put to
        shame;
    he who vindicates me is near.
Who will contend with me?
    Let us stand up together.
Who is my adversary?

Let him come near to me.
Behold, the Lord God helps me;
   who will declare me guilty?

                Isaiah 50.6−9

Why dost thou look on faithless men,
   and art silent when the wicked
      swallows up
the man more righteous than he?

              Habakkuk 1.13

Blessed are those who are persecuted for
righteousness' sake, for theirs is the kingdom of heaven.

              Matthew 5.10

Blessed are you when men revile you and
persecute you and utter all kinds of evil
against you falsely on my account. Rejoice
and be glad, for your reward is great in
heaven, for so men persecuted the prophets
who were before you.

            Matthew 5.11−12

Pray for those who persecute you.

              Matthew 5.44

Behold, I send you out as sheep in the
midst of wolves; so be wise as serpents and
innocent as doves. Beware of men; for they
will deliver you up to councils, and flog you
in their synagogues, and you will be
dragged before governors and kings for my
sake, to bear testimony before them and
the Gentiles. When they deliver you up, do
not be anxious how you are to speak or
what you are to say; for what you are to say
will be given to you in that hour; for it is
not you who speak, but the Spirit of your
Father speaking through you. Brother will
deliver up brother to death, and the father
his child, and children will rise against
parents and have them put to death; and
you will be hated by all for my name's sake.
But he who endures to the end will be
saved. When they persecute you in one
town, flee to the next; for truly, I say to
you, you will not have gone through all the
towns of Israel, before the Son of man
comes.

           Matthew 10.16−23

Who shall separate us from the love of
Christ? Shall tribulation, or distress, or
persecution . . . or peril, or sword?

              Romans 8.35

Bless those who persecute you; bless and
do not curse them.

             Romans 12.14

When persecuted, we endure.

        1 Corinthians 4.12−13

We are afflicted in every way, but not
crushed . . . persecuted, but not forsaken;
struck down, but not destroyed.

        2 Corinthians 4.8−9

All who desire to live a godly life in Christ
Jesus will be persecuted.

            2 Timothy 3.12

They were stoned, they were sawn in two,
they were killed with the sword . . . destitute, afflicted, ill-treated . . . though well
attested by their faith.

          Hebrews 11.37,39

These are they who have come out of the
great tribulation; they have washed their
robes and made them white in the blood of
the Lamb.
   Therefore are they before the throne of
      God,
  and serve him day and night within his
      temple.

           Revelation 7.14−15

Perseverance

See also **Earnestness**

Seek the Lord and his strength,
   seek his presence continually!

           1 Chronicles 16.11

He that has clean hands grows stronger
and stronger.

               Job 17.9

Nevertheless I am continually with thee;
   thou dost hold my right hand.
Thou dost guide me with thy counsel,

and afterward thou wilt receive me to glory.

Psalms 73.23−24

Then I shall not be put to shame, having my eyes fixed on all thy commandments.

Psalms 119.6

They shall be my people, and I will be their God . . . I will not turn away from doing good to them.

Jeremiah 32.38,40

He who endures to the end will be saved.

Matthew 24.13

As for that in the good soil, they are those who, hearing the word, hold it fast in an honest and good heart, and bring forth fruit with patience.

Luke 8.15

By your endurance you will gain your lives.

Luke 21.19

I am the vine, you are the branches. He who abides in me, and I in him, he it is that bears much fruit, for apart from me you can do nothing. If a man does not abide in me, he is cast forth as a branch and withers; and the branches are gathered, thrown into the fire and burned. If you abide in me, and my words abide in you, ask whatever you will, and it shall be done for you.

John 15.5−7

Be steadfast, immovable, always abounding in the work of the Lord, knowing that in the Lord your labour is not in vain.

1 Corinthians 15.58

Let us not grow weary in well-doing, for in due season we shall reap, if we do not lose heart.

Galatians 6.9

Pray at all times in the Spirit, with all prayer and supplication. To that end keep alert with all perseverance, making supplication for all the saints.

Ephesians 6.18

Hold fast what is good.

1 Thessalonians 5.21

Do your best to present yourself to God as one approved.

2 Timothy 2.15

We desire each one of you to show the same earnestness in realising the full assurance of hope until the end, so that you may not be sluggish, but imitators of those who through faith and patience inherit the promises.

Hebrews 6.11−12

Let us also lay aside every weight, and sin which clings so closely, and let us run with perseverance the race that is set before us, looking to Jesus the pioneer and perfecter of our faith.

Hebrews 12.1−2

I am coming soon; hold fast what you have, so that no one may seize your crown. He who conquers, I will make him a pillar in the temple of my God; never shall he go out of it, and I will write on him the name of my God, and the name of the city of my God, the new Jerusalem which comes down from my God out of heaven, and my own new name.

Revelation 3.11−1:

Persistence

And he told them a parable, to the effec that they ought always to pray and no lose heart. He said, 'In a certain city ther was a judge who neither feared God no regarded man; and there was a widow i that city who kept coming to him an saying, "Vindicate me against my adve: sary." For a while he refused; but afterwar he said to himself, "Though I neither fea God nor regard man, yet because th' widow bothers me, I will vindicate her, c she will wear me out by her continu; coming." ' And the Lord said, 'Hear wh; the unrighteous judge says. And will n' God vindicate his elect, who cry to him da and night? Will he delay long over them? tell you, he will vindicate them speedily.'

Luke 18.1−

For he will render to every man according to his works: to those who by patience in well-doing seek for glory and honour and immortality, he will give eternal life.

Romans 2.6−7

And let us not grow weary in well-doing, for in due season we shall reap, if we do not lose heart. So then, as we have opportunity, let us do good to all men, and especially to those who are of the household of faith.

Galatians 6.9−10

And this is the confidence which we have in him, that if we ask anything according to his will he hears us. And if we know that he hears us in whatever we ask, we know that we have obtained the requests made of him.

1 John 5.14−15

Perversion

See also **Bestiality, Homosexuality**

Do you not know that the unrighteous will not inherit the kingdom of God? Do not be deceived; neither the immoral, nor idolators, nor adulterers, nor sexual perverts.

1 Corinthians 6.9

Perversity

Perverseness of heart shall be far from me; I will know nothing of evil.

Psalms 101.4

For the perverse man is an abomination to the Lord,
but the upright are in his confidence.

Proverbs 3.32

Men of perverse mind are an abomination to the Lord,
but those of blameless ways are his delight.

Proverbs 11.20

Thorns and snares are in the way of the perverse;
he who guards himself will keep far from them.

Proverbs 22.5

It hurts you to kick against the goads.

Acts 26.14

Petition

Keep me as the apple of the eye;
hide me in the shadow of thy wings.

Psalms 17.8

Ask, and it will be given you; seek, and you will find; knock, and it will be opened to you. For every one who asks receives, and he who seeks finds, and to him who knocks it will be opened. Or what man of you, if his son asks him for bread, will give him a stone? Or if he asks for a fish, will give him a serpent? If you then, who are evil, know how to give good gifts to your children, how much more will your Father who is in heaven give good things to those who ask him! So whatever you wish that men would do to you, do so to them; for this is the law and the prophets.

Matthew 7.7−12

Again I say to you, if two of you agree on earth about anything they ask, it will be done for them by my Father in heaven. For where two or three are gathered in my name, there am I in the midst of them.

Matthew 18.19−20

Whatever you ask in prayer, you will receive, if you have faith.

Matthew 21.22

Whatever you ask in my name, I will do it.

John 14.13

Philosophy

It is the glory of God to conceal things,
but the glory of kings is to search things out.

Proverbs 25.2

Claiming to be wise, they became fools, and exchanged the glory of the immortal God for images resembling mortal man.

Romans 1.22−23

Christ did not send me to baptize but to preach the gospel, and not with eloquent wisdom, lest the cross of Christ be emptied of its power.

For the word of the cross is folly to those who are perishing, but to us who are being saved it is the power of God. For it is written,
'I will destroy the wisdom of the wise,
and the cleverness of the clever I will
thwart.'
Where is the wise man? Where is the scribe? Where is the debater of this age? Has not God made foolish the wisdom of the world?

1 Corinthians 1.17−20

My speech and my message were not in plausible words of wisdom.

1 Corinthians 2.4

The Lord knows that the thoughts of the wise are futile.

1 Corinthians 3.20

See to it that no one makes a prey of you by philosophy and empty deceit, according to human tradition, according to the elemental spirits of the universe.

Colossians 2.8

Avoid such godless chatter, for it will lead people into more and more ungodliness.

2 Timothy 2.16

Pity

See also **Compassion, Sympathy**

He who withholds kindness from a friend
forsakes the fear of the Almighty.

Job 6.14

His soul draws near the Pit,
and his life to those who bring death.
If there be for him an angel . . .
and he is gracious to him, and says,
'Deliver him from going down into
the Pit,
I have found a ransom . . .'
then man prays to God.

Job 33.22,24,26

With everlasting love I will have
compassion on you,
says the Lord, your Redeemer.

Isaiah 54.8

In his love and in his pity he redeemed
them.

Isaiah 63.9

Should not you have had mercy on your fellow servant, as I had mercy on you?

Matthew 18.33

The Lord is compassionate and merciful.

James 5.11

Have unity of spirit, sympathy, love of the brethren, a tender heart and a humble mind.

1 Peter 3.8

Plan

All the congregation of the people of Israel moved on from the wilderness of Sin by stages, according to the commandment of the Lord.

Exodus 17.1

I cry to God Most High,
to God who fulfils his purpose for me.

Psalms 57.2

O Lord, thou art my God;
I will exalt thee, I will praise thy name;
for thou hast done wonderful things,
plans formed of old, faithful and sure.

Isaiah 25.1

My counsel shall stand,
and I will accomplish all my purpose.

Isaiah 46.10

For he has made known to us in all wisdom and insight the mystery of his will, according to his purpose which he set forth in Christ as a plan for the fulness of time, to unite all things in him, things in heaven and things on earth.

Ephesians 1.9−10

To me, though I am the very least of all the saints, this grace was given, to preach to the Gentiles the unsearchable riches of Christ, and to make all men see what is the plan of the mystery hidden for ages in God who created all things; that through the church the manifold wisdom of God might now be made known to the principalities and powers in the heavenly places. This was according to the eternal purpose which he has realised in Christ Jesus our Lord, in whom we have boldness and confidence of access through our faith in him.

Ephesians 3.8–12

He was destined before the foundation of the world but was made manifest at the end of the times for your sake.

1 Peter 1.20

Plants

And God said, 'Behold, I have given you every plant yielding seed which is upon the face of all the earth, and every tree with seed in its fruit; you shall have them for food.'

Genesis 1.29

Pleasure

See also **Delight, Enjoyment**

Why do the wicked live,
    reach old age, and grow mighty in
        power? . . .
They sing to the tambourine and the
        lyre,
    and rejoice to the sound of the pipe.
They spend their days in prosperity,
    and in peace they go down to Sheol.

Job 21.7,12–13

In thy presence there is fullness of joy,
    in thy right hand are pleasures for
        evermore.

Psalms 16.11

He who loves pleasure will be a poor man.

Proverbs 21.17

I said to myself, 'Come now, I will make a test of pleasure; enjoy yourself.' But behold, this also was vanity. I said of laughter, 'It is mad,' and of pleasure, 'What use is it?'

Ecclesiastes 2.1–2

There is nothing better for a man than that he should eat and drink, and find enjoyment in his toil. This also, I saw, is from the hand of God; for apart from him who can eat or who can have enjoyment?

Ecclesiastes 2.24–25

In that day the Lord God of hosts
    called to weeping and mourning,
    to baldness and girding with sackcloth;
and behold, joy and gladness.

Isaiah 22.12–13

Now therefore hear this, you lover of
        pleasures,
    who sit securely,
who say in your heart,
    'I am, and there is no one besides me;
I shall not sit as a widow
    or know the loss of children':
These two things shall come to you
    in a moment, in one day.

Isaiah 47.8–9

She who is self-indulgent is dead even while she lives.

1 Timothy 5.6

In the last days there will come times of stress. For men will be lovers of self, lovers of money . . . lovers of pleasure rather than lovers of God.

2 Timothy 3.1–2,4

Plenty

See also **Prosperity**

The Lord your God is bringing you into a good land, a land of brooks of water, of fountains and springs, flowing forth in valleys and hills, a land of wheat and barley, of vines and fig trees and pomegranates, a land of olive trees and honey, a land in which you will eat bread without scarcity, in which you will lack nothing, a land whose stones are iron, and out of whose hills you can dig copper. And you shall eat and be full, and you shall bless the Lord your God for the good land he has given you.

Deuteronomy 8.7–10

God has given it into your hands, a place where there is no lack of anything that is in the earth.

Judges 18.10

The Lord is my shepherd, I shall not want.

Psalms 23.1

O fear the Lord, you his saints,
   for those who fear him have no want!
The young lions suffer want and hunger;
   but those who seek the Lord lack no
      good thing.

Psalms 34.9–10

Pollution

You shall not defile the land in which you
   live.

Numbers 35.34

The earth mourns and withers,
   the world languishes and withers;
   the heavens languish together with the
      earth.
The earth lies polluted
   under its inhabitants;
for they have transgressed the laws,
   violated the statutes,
   broken the everlasting covenant.
Therefore a curse devours the earth,
   and its inhabitants suffer for their guilt.

Isaiah 24.4–6

You have polluted the land
   with your vile harlotry.
Therefore the showers have been withheld,
   and the spring rain has not come;
yet you have a harlot's brow,
   you refuse to be ashamed.

Jeremiah 3.2–3

How long will the land mourn,
   and the grass of every field wither?

For the wickedness of those who dwell in it
   the beasts and the birds are swept away.

Jeremiah 12.4

Thy wrath came, and the time . . . for destroying the destroyers of the earth.

Revelation 11.18

Let the . . . filthy still be filthy.

Revelation 22.11

Polygamy

See also **Marriage, Monogamy**

If he takes another wife to himself, he shall not diminish her food, her clothing, or her marital rights.

Exodus 21.10

He shall not multiply wives for himself, lest his heart turn away.

Deuteronomy 17.1?

Popularity

When it goes well with the righteous, the
      city rejoices;
   and when the wicked perish there are
      shouts of gladness.

Proverbs 11.10

Positiveness

As surely as God is faithful, our word to you has not been Yes and No. For the Son of God, Jesus Christ, whom we preached among you, Silv'anus and Timothy and I was not Yes and No; but in him it is always Yes. For all the promises of God find their Yes in him.

2 Corinthians 1.18–2

One thing I do, forgetting what lies behind and straining forward to what lies ahead, I press on toward the goal for the prize of the **upward call of God in Christ Jesus.**

Philippians 3.13–1

Possessions

See also **Riches, Wealth**

Jesus said to him, 'If you would be perfect, go, sell what you possess and give to the poor, and you will have treasure in heaven; and come, follow me.' When the young man heard this he went away sorrowful; for he had great possessions.

And Jesus said to his disciples, 'Truly, I say to you, it will be hard for a rich man to enter the kingdom of heaven. Again I tell you, it is easier for a camel to go through the eye of a needle than for a rich man to enter the kingdom of God.' When the disciples heard this they were greatly astonished, saying, 'Who then can be saved?' But Jesus looked at them and said to them, 'With men this is impossible, but with God all things are possible.' Then Peter said in reply, 'Lo, we have left everything and followed you. What then shall we have?' Jesus said to them, 'Truly, I say to you, in the new world, when the Son of man shall sit on his glorious throne, you who have followed me will also sit on twelve thrones, judging the twelve tribes of Israel. And every one who has left houses or brothers or sisters or father or mother or children or lands, for my name's sake, will receive a hundredfold, and inherit eternal life. But many that are first will be last, and the last first.

Matthew 19.21—30

A man's life does not consist in the abundance of his possessions.

Luke 12.15

And all who believed were together and had all things in common; and they sold their possessions and goods and distributed them to all, as any had need.

Acts 2.44—45

There was not a needy person among them, for as many as were possessors of lands or houses sold them, and brought the proceeds of what was sold and laid it at the apostles' feet; and distribution was made to each as any had need.

Acts 4.34—35

Possibility

All things are possible to him who believes.

Mark 9.23

All things are possible with God.

Mark 10.27

Poverty

See also **Need**

If your brother becomes poor, and cannot maintain himself with you, you shall maintain him; as a stranger and a sojourner he shall live with you.

Leviticus 25.35

But there will be no poor among you (for the Lord will bless you in the land which the Lord your God gives you for an inheritance to possess), if only you will obey the voice of the Lord your God, being careful to do all this commandment which I command you this day.

Deuteronomy 15.4—5

The poor will never cease out of the land; therefore I command you, You shall open wide your hand to your brother, to the needy and to the poor, in the land.

Deuteronomy 15.11

He raises up the poor from the dust;
    he lifts the needy from the ash heap,
to make them sit with princes and inherit
    a seat of honour.
For the pillars of the earth are the Lord's,
    and on them he has set the world.

1 Samuel 2.8

He saves . . . the needy from the hand of
    the mighty.
So the poor have hope.

Job 5.15—16

For the needy shall not always be
    forgotten,

and the hope of the poor shall not perish
   for ever.

Psalms 9.18

This poor man cried, and the Lord heard
   him,
   and saved him out of all his troubles.

Psalms 34.6

All my bones shall say,
   'O Lord, who is like thee,
thou who deliverest the weak
   from him who is too strong for him,
   the weak and needy from him who
      despoils him?'

Psalms 35.10

Blessed is he who considers the poor!
   The Lord delivers him in the day of
      trouble;
the Lord protects him and keeps him alive;
   he is called blessed in the land;
   thou dost not give him up to the will of
      his enemies.
The Lord sustains him on his sickbed;
   in his illness thou healest all his
      infirmities.

Psalms 41.1–3

In thy goodness, O God, thou didst
   provide for the needy.

Psalms 68.10

For the Lord hears the needy.

Psalms 69.33

With my mouth I will give great thanks to
   the Lord . . .
For he stands at the right hand of the
   needy,
to save him from those who condemn him
   to death.

Psalms 109.30–31

I know that the Lord maintains the cause
   of the afflicted,
   and executes justice for the needy.

Psalms 140.12

A little sleep, a little slumber,
   a little folding of the hands to rest,

and poverty will come upon you like a
   vagabond,
   and want like an armed man.

Proverbs 6.10–11

The ransom of a man's life is his wealth,
   but a poor man has no means of
      redemption.

Proverbs 13.8

Poverty and disgrace come to him who
   ignores instruction,
   but he who heeds reproof is honoured.

Proverbs 13.18

The poor is disliked even by his neighbour,
   but the rich has many friends.

Proverbs 14.20

He who despises his neighbour is a sinner,
   but happy is he who is kind to the poor.

Proverbs 14.21

He who oppresses a poor man insults his
   Maker.

Proverbs 14.31

Better is a little with righteousness
   than great revenues with injustice.

Proverbs 16.8

Better is a poor man who walks in his
   integrity
   than a rich man who is perverse in his
      ways.

Proverbs 28.6

A righteous man knows the rights of the
   poor;
   a wicked man does not understand such
      knowledge.

Proverbs 29.7

Remove far from me falsehood and lying;
   give me neither poverty nor riches;
feed me with the food that is
   needful for me,
lest I be full, and deny thee.

Proverbs 30.8

The poor among men shall exult in the
   Holy One of Israel.

Isaiah 29.19

When the poor and needy seek water,
  and there is none,
  and their tongue is parched with thirst,
 the Lord will answer them.

Isaiah 41.17

Sing to the Lord;
  praise the Lord!
For he has delivered the life of the needy
  from the hand of evildoers.

Jeremiah 20.13

And he sat down opposite the treasury,
nd watched the multitude putting money
nto the treasury. Many rich people put in
arge sums. And a poor widow came, and
ut in two copper coins, which make a
enny. And he called his disciples to him,
nd said to them, 'Truly, I say to you, this
oor widow has put in more than all those
ho are contributing to the treasury. For
ey all contributed out of their abundance;
ut she out of her poverty has put in every-
ing she had, her whole living.'

Mark 12.41–44

ou always have the poor with you, and
henever you will, you can do good to
em.

Mark 14.7

lessed are you poor, for yours is the
gdom of God.

Luke 6.20

ou know the grace of our Lord Jesus
rist, that though he was rich, yet for your
e he became poor, so that by his poverty
u might become rich.

2 Corinthians 8.9

emember the poor.

Galatians 2.10

as not God chosen those who are poor in
world to be rich in faith.

James 2.5

Power

See also **Ability, Strength**

Beware lest you say in your heart, 'My power and the might of my hand have gotten me this wealth.' You shall remember the Lord your God, for it is he who gives you power to get wealth.

Deuteronomy 8.17–18

This God is my strong refuge,
  and has made my way safe . . .
I pursued my enemies and destroyed
    them,
  and did not turn back until they were
    consumed.

2 Samuel 22.33,38

Honour and majesty are before him;
  strength and joy are in his place.

1 Chronicles 16.27

Thine, O Lord, is the greatness, and the power, and the glory, and the victory, and the majesty; for all that is in the heavens and in the earth is thine; thine is the kingdom, O Lord, and thou art exalted as head above all. Both riches and honour come from thee, and thou rulest over all. In thy hand are power and might; and in thy hand it is to make great and to give strength to all. And now we thank thee, our God, and praise thy glorious name.

1 Chronicles 29.11–13

With God are wisdom and might.

Job 12.13

Behold, God is mighty, and does not despise any . . .
He . . . gives the afflicted their right.

Job 36.5–6

Behold, God is exalted in his power;
  who is a teacher like him?

Job 36.22

The voice of the Lord is powerful.

Psalms 29.4

There did we rejoice in him,
  who rules by his might for ever.

Psalms 66.6–7

Summon thy might, O God;
> show thy strength, O God, thou who hast
>> wrought for us.

Psalms 68.28

Ascribe power to God,
> whose majesty is over Israel,
> and his power is in the skies.
Terrible is God in his sanctuary,
> the God of Israel,
> he gives power and strength to his
>> people.

Psalms 68.34–35

Great is our Lord, and abundant in power.

Psalms 147.5

Do not withhold good from those to whom
> it is due,
when it is in your power to do it.

Proverbs 3.27

No man has power to retain the spirit, or
authority over the day of death.

Ecclesiastes 8.8

He gives power to the faint,
> and to him who has no might he increases
>> strength.

Isaiah 40.29

Behold, I have given you authority to
tread upon serpents and scorpions, and
over all the power of the enemy; and nothing shall hurt you.

Luke 10.19

But to all who received him, who believed
in his name, he gave power to become
children of God.

John 1.12

But you shall receive power when the Holy
Spirit has come upon you; and you shall be
my witnesses.

Acts 1.8

For the kingdom of God does not consist
in talk but in power.

1 Corinthians 4.20

For it is the God who said, 'Let light shine
out of darkness,' who has shone in our
hearts to give the light of the knowledge of
the glory of God in the face of Christ.
But we have this treasure in earthen
vessels, to show that the transcenden
power belongs to God and not to us.

2 Corinthians 4.6–

My power is made perfect in weakness.

2 Corinthians 12.

God . . . may give you . . . wisdom . .
that you may know . . . what is the im
measurable greatness of his power in u
who believe, according to the working o
his great might which he accomplished i
Christ when he raised him from the dead.

Ephesians 1.17–2

According to the riches of his glory he ma
grant you to be strengthened with mig
through his Spirit in the inner man.

Ephesians 3.

Finally, be strong in the Lord and in th
strength of his might.

Ephesians 6.

To this end we always pray for you, th
our God may make you worthy of his ca
and may fulfil every good resolve and wo
of faith by his power.

2 Thessalonians 1.

God did not give us a spirit of timidity b
a spirit of power and love and self-contro

2 Timothy

He who conquers and who keeps
works until the end, I will give him pow
over the nations, and he shall rule th
with a rod of iron, as when earthen pots a
broken in pieces, even as I myself ha
received power from my Father; and I v
give him the morning star.

Revelation 2.26–

Practicality

See also **Ability**

Arise and be doing! The Lord be with y

1 Chronicles 22

The people who know their God shall stand firm and take action.

Daniel 11.32

For he will render to every man according to his works.

Romans 2.6

Complete what a year ago you began not only to do but to desire, so that your readiness in desiring it may be matched by your completing it out of what you have.

2 Corinthians 8.10−11

And let our people learn to apply themselves to good deeds, so as to help cases of urgent need, and not to be unfruitful.

Titus 3.14

So faith by itself, if it has no works, is dead.

James 2.17

Little children, let us not love in word or speech but in deed and in truth.

1 John 3.18

Praise

See also **Hymn, Worship**

Let the heavens be glad, and let the earth rejoice,
and let them say among the nations, 'The Lord reigns!'
Let the sea roar, and all that fills it,
let the field exult, and everything in it!
Then shall the trees of the wood sing for joy before the Lord.

1 Chronicles 16.31−33

Thine, O Lord, is the greatness, and the power, and the glory, and the victory, and the majesty; for all that is in the heavens and in the earth is thine; thine is the kingdom, O Lord, and thou art exalted as head above all.

1 Chronicles 29.11

I call upon the Lord, who is worthy to be praised,
and I am saved from my enemies.

Psalms 18.3

You who fear the Lord, praise him!

Psalms 22.23

Those who seek him shall praise the Lord!

Psalms 22.26

Rejoice in the Lord, O you righteous!
Praise befits the upright.

Psalms 33.1

Clap your hands, all peoples!
Shout to God with loud songs of joy!
For the Lord, the Most High, is terrible,
a great king over all the earth.

Psalms 47.1−2

He who brings thanksgiving as his sacrifice honours me;
to him who orders his way aright
I will show the salvation of God!

Psalms 50.23

O Lord, open thou my lips,
and my mouth shall show forth thy praise.

Psalms 51.15

Because thy steadfast love is better than life,
my lips will praise thee.
So I will bless thee as long as I live.

Psalms 63.3−4

Sing to God, sing praises to his name;
lift up a song to him who rides upon the clouds;
his name is the Lord, exult before him!

Psalms 68.4

Make a joyful noise to the Lord, all the earth;
break forth into joyous song and sing praises!
Sing praises to the Lord with the lyre,
with the lyre and the sound of melody!
With trumpets and the sound of the horn
make a joyful noise before the King, the Lord!
Let the sea roar, and all that fills it;
the world and those who dwell in it!
Let the floods clap their hands;
let the hills sing for joy together.

Psalms 98.4−8

Make a joyful noise to the Lord, all the
    lands!
  Serve the Lord with gladness!
  Come into his presence with singing!

Psalms 100.1–2

Enter his gates with thanksgiving,
  and his courts with praise!
  Give thanks to him, bless his name!

Psalms 100.4

Bless the Lord, O you his angels.

Psalms 103.20

His praise endures for ever!

Psalms 111.10

I will extol thee, my God and King,
  and bless thy name for ever and ever.

Psalms 145.1

My mouth will speak the praise of the
    Lord,
  and let all flesh bless his holy name for
    ever and ever.

Psalms 145.21

Praise the Lord!
  For it is good to sing praises to our God;
  for he is gracious, and a song of praise is
    seemly.

Psalms 147.1

Praise the Lord!
  Praise the Lord from the heavens,
  praise him in the heights!
Praise him, all his angels,
  praise him, all his host!

Psalms 148.1–2

Kings of the earth and all peoples,
  princes and all rulers of the earth!
Young men and maidens together,
  old men and children!
Let them praise the name of the Lord,
  for his name alone is exalted;
  his glory is above earth and heaven.

Psalms 148.11–13

Praise him with trumpet sound;
  praise him with lute and harp!
Praise him with timbrel and dance;
  praise him with strings and pipe!

Praise him with sounding cymbals;
  praise him with loud clashing cymbals!
Let everything that breathes praise
    the Lord!
  Praise the Lord!

Psalms 150.3–6

Let another praise you, and not your own
    mouth;
  a stranger, and not your own lips.

Proverbs 27.2

Charm is deceitful, and beauty is vain,
  but a woman who fears the Lord is to be
    praised.
Give her of the fruit of her hands,
  and let her works praise her in the gates.

Proverbs 31.30–31

O Lord, thou art my God;
  I will exalt thee, I will praise thy name;
for thou hast done wonderful things,
  plans formed of old, faithful and sure.

Isaiah 25.

For as the earth brings forth its shoots,
  and as a garden causes what is sown in it
    to spring up,
so the Lord God will cause righteousness
    and praise
  to spring forth before all the nations.

Isaiah 61.1

Therefore do not pronounce judgmen
before the time, before the Lord come
who will bring to light the things no
hidden in darkness and will disclose th
purposes of the heart. Then every man wi
receive his commendation from God.

1 Corinthians 4.

Through him then let us continually offe
up a sacrifice of praise to God, that is, th
fruit of lips that acknowledge his name.

Hebrews 13.

But you are a chosen race, a royal pries
hood, a holy nation, God's own peop!
that you may declare the wonderful dee
of him who called you out of darkness in
his marvellous light.

1 Peter 2

Day and night they never cease to sing,
'Holy, holy, holy, is the Lord God
Almighty,
who was and is and is to come!'

Revelation 4.8

Prayer

See also **Intercession, Mediation**

Whatever prayer, whatever supplication is
made by any man or by all thy people
Israel, each knowing the affliction of his
own heart and stretching out his hands
toward this house; then hear thou in heaven
thy dwelling place, and forgive, and act,
and render to each whose heart thou
knowest, according to all his ways (for
thou, thou only, knowest the hearts of all
the children of men).

1 Kings 8.38–39

Let these words of mine, wherewith I have
made supplication before the Lord, be near
to the Lord our God day and night, and
may he maintain the cause of his servant,
and the cause of his people Israel, as each
day requires; that all the peoples of the
earth may know that the Lord is God; there
is no other. Let your heart therefore be
wholly true to the Lord our God, walking in
his statutes and keeping his commandments, as at this day.

1 Kings 8.59–61

If my people who are called by my name
humble themselves, and pray and seek my
face, and turn from their wicked ways, then
I will hear from heaven, and will forgive
their sin.

2 Chronicles 7.14

O Lord, let thy ear be attentive to the
prayer of thy servant, and to the prayer of
thy servants who delight to fear thy name;
and give success to thy servant today, and
grant him mercy in the sight of this man.

Nehemiah 1.11

Then you will delight yourself in the
Almighty,
and lift up your face to God.

You will make your prayer to him, and he
will hear you.

Job 22.26–27

Surely God does not hear an empty cry,
nor does the Almighty regard it.

Job 35.13

In my distress I called upon the Lord;
to my God I cried for help.
From his temple he heard my voice,
and my cry to him reached his ears.

Psalms 18.6

And to thee shall vows be performed,
O thou who hearest prayer!

Psalms 65.1–2

Give ear, O Lord, to my prayer;
hearken to my cry of supplication.
In the day of my trouble I call on thee,
for thou dost answer me.

Psalms 86.6–7

Hear my prayer, O Lord;
let my cry come to thee!
Do not hide thy face from me
in the day of my distress!
Incline thy ear to me;
answer me speedily in the day when I
call!

Psalms 102.1–2

He will regard the prayer of the destitute,
and will not despise their supplication.

Psalms 102.17

He fulfils the desire of all who fear him.

Psalms 145.19

The prayer of the upright is his delight.

Proverbs 15.8

The Lord is far from the wicked,
but he hears the prayer of the righteous.

Proverbs 15.29

Now therefore, O our God, hearken to the
prayer of thy servant and to his supplications, and for thy own sake, O Lord, cause
thy face to shine upon thy sanctuary, which
is desolate. O my God, incline thy ear
and hear; open thy eyes and behold our

desolations, and the city which is called by thy name; for we do not present our supplications before thee on the ground of our righteousness, but on the ground of thy great mercy. O Lord, hear; O Lord, forgive; O Lord, give heed and act; delay not, for thy own sake, O my God, because thy city and thy people are called by thy name.

Daniel 9.17–19

And when you pray, you must not be like the hypocrites; for they love to stand and pray in the synagogues and at the street corners, that they may be seen by men. Truly, I say to you, they have received their reward. But when you pray, go into your room and shut the door and pray to your Father who is in secret; and your Father who sees in secret will reward you.

And in praying do not heap up empty phrases as the Gentiles do; for they think that they will be heard for their many words. Do not be like them, for your Father knows what you need before you ask him. Pray then like this:
Our Father who art in heaven,
Hallowed be thy name.
Thy kingdom come,
Thy will be done,
　On earth as it is in heaven.
Give us this day our daily bread;
And forgive us our debts,
　As we also have forgiven our debtors;
And lead us not into temptation,
　But deliver us from evil.
For if you forgive men their trespasses, your heavenly Father also will forgive you; but if you do not forgive men their trespasses, neither will your Father forgive your trespasses.

Matthew 6.5–15

Whatever you ask in prayer, you will receive, if you have faith.

Matthew 21.22

Watch and pray that you may not enter into temptation; the spirit indeed is willing, but the flesh is weak.

Matthew 26.41

Ask, and it will be given you; seek, and you will find; knock, and it will be opened to you. For every one who asks receives, and he who seeks finds, and to him who knocks it will be opened.

Luke 11.9–10

Pray and [do] not lose heart.

Luke 18.1

But watch at all times, praying that you may have strength to escape all these things that will take place, and to stand before the Son of man.

Luke 21.36

Whatever you ask the Father in my name, he may give it to you.

John 15.16

Likewise the Spirit helps us in our weakness; for we do not know how to pray as we ought, but the Spirit himself intercedes for us with sighs too deep for words.

Romans 8.26

Be constant in prayer.

Romans 12.12

Pray at all times in the Spirit, with all prayer and supplication.

Ephesians 6.18

Have no anxiety about anything, but in everything by prayer and supplication with thanksgiving let your requests be made known to God.

Philippians 4.6

Continue steadfastly in prayer, being watchful in it with thanksgiving.

Colossians 4.2

Pray constantly.

1 Thessalonians 5.17

First of all, then, I urge that supplications, prayers, intercessions, and thanksgivings be made for all men, for kings and all who are in high positions, that we may lead a quiet and peaceable life, godly and respectful in every way. This is good, and it is acceptable in the sight of God our Saviour.

1 Timothy 2.1–

I desire then that in every place the men should pray, lifting holy hands without anger or quarrelling.

1 Timothy 2.8

If any of you lacks wisdom, let him ask God, who gives to all men generously and without reproaching, and it will be given him. But let him ask in faith, with no doubting.

James 1.5—6

Is anyone among you suffering? Let him pray. Is any cheerful? Let him sing praise. Is any among you sick? Let him call for the elders of the church, and let them pray over him, anointing him with oil in the name of the Lord; and the prayer of faith will save the sick man, and the Lord will raise him up; and if he has committed sins, he will be forgiven. Therefore confess your sins to one another, and pray for one another, that you may be healed. The prayer of a righteous man has great power in its effects.

James 5.13—16

Preaching

See also **Evangelism**

I have told the glad news of deliverance
   in the great congregation;
lo, I have not restrained my lips,
   as thou knowest, O Lord.
I have not hid thy saving help within my
   heart,
I have spoken of thy faithfulness and thy
   salvation;
I have not concealed thy steadfast love and
   thy faithfulness
   from the great congregation.

Psalms 40.9—10

The Spirit of the Lord God is upon me,
   because the Lord has anointed me
to bring good tidings to the afflicted;
   he has sent me to bind up the brokenhearted,
to proclaim liberty to the captives,
   and the opening of the prison to those
   who are bound;
to proclaim the year of the Lord's favour,
   and the day of vengeance of our God.

Isaiah 61.1—2

And preach as you go, saying, 'The kingdom of heaven is at hand.'

Matthew 10.7

What I tell you in the dark, utter in the light; and what you hear whispered, proclaim upon the housetops.

Matthew 10.27

This gospel of the kingdom will be preached throughout the whole world.

Matthew 24.14

Leave the dead to bury their own dead; but as for you, go and proclaim the kingdom of God.

Luke 9.60

And he commanded us to preach to the people, and to testify that he is the one ordained by God to be judge of the living and the dead.

Acts 10.42

God had called us to preach the gospel.

Acts 16.10

The word is near you, on your lips and in your heart (that is, the word of faith which we preach).

Romans 10.8

The Lord commanded that those who proclaim the gospel should get their living by the gospel.

1 Corinthians 9.14

Woe to me if I do not preach the gospel!

1 Corinthians 9.16

Therefore, having this ministry by the mercy of God, we do not lose heart. We have renounced disgraceful, underhanded ways; we refuse to practise cunning or to tamper with God's word, but by the open statement of the truth we would commend ourselves to every man's conscience in the sight of God.

2 Corinthians 4.1—2

But even if we, or an angel from heaven, should preach to you a gospel contrary to that which we preached to you, let him be accursed.

Galatians 1.8

Preach the word, be urgent in season and out of season.

2 Timothy 4.2

That word is the good news which was preached to you.

1 Peter 1.25

Predestination

See also **Destiny**

I will be gracious to whom I will be gracious, and will show mercy on whom I will show mercy.

Exodus 33.19

His days are determined,
  and the number of his months is
    with thee,
  and thou hast appointed his bounds that
    he cannot pass.

Job 14.5

But he is unchangeable and who can turn
    him?
  What he desires, that he does.

Job 23.13

Blessed is the nation whose God is the
    Lord,
  the people whom he has chosen as his
    heritage!

Psalms 33.12

Blessed is he whom thou dost choose and
    bring near,
  to dwell in thy courts!

Psalms 65.4

The Lord has made everything for its
    purpose,
  even the wicked for the day of trouble.

Proverbs 16.4

A man's steps are ordered by the Lord;
  how then can man understand his way?

Proverbs 20.24

Before I formed you in the womb I knew
    you,
and before you were born I consecrated
    you.

Jeremiah 1.5

You will drink my cup, but to sit at my right hand and at my left is not mine to grant, but it is for those for whom it has been prepared by my Father.

Matthew 20.23

Come, O blessed of my Father, inherit the kingdom prepared for you from the foundation of the world.

Matthew 25.34

You did not choose me, but I chose you and appointed you that you should go and bear fruit and that your fruit should abide.

John 15.16

And he made from one every nation of men to live on all the face of the earth, having determined allotted periods and the boundaries of their habitation.

Acts 17.26

We know that in everything God works for good with those who love him, who are called according to his purpose. For those whom he foreknew he also predestined to be conformed to the image of his Son, in order that he might be the first-born among many brethren. And those whom he predestined he also called; and those whom he called he also justified; and those whom he justified he also glorified.

Romans 8.28−30

The rest were hardened, as it is written,
  'God gave them a spirit of stupor,
  eyes that should not see and ears that
    should not hear,
  down to this very day.'

Romans 11.7−

It was ordained by angels through an intermediary.

Galatians 3.1

He chose us in him before the foundation of the world, that we should be holy an blameless before him. He destined us in love to be his sons through Jesus Christ, according to the purpose of his will.

Ephesians 1.4—5

We who first hoped in Christ have been destined and appointed to live for the praise of his glory.

Ephesians 1.12

In him you also, who have heard the word of truth, the gospel of your salvation, and have believed in him, were sealed with the promised Holy Spirit, which is the guarantee of our inheritance until we acquire possession of it, to the praise of his glory.

Ephesians 1.13—14

The manifold wisdom of God might now be made known to the principalities and powers in the heavenly places . . . according to the eternal purpose which he has realised in Christ Jesus our Lord.

Ephesians 3.10—11

You know that you were ransomed from the futile ways inherited from your fathers, not with perishable things such as silver or gold, but with the precious blood of Christ, like that of a lamb without blemish or spot. He was destined before the foundation of the world but was made manifest at the end of the times for your sake.

1 Peter 1.18—20

And I saw a beast rising out of the sea, with ten horns and seven heads, with ten diadems upon its horns and a blasphemous name upon its heads . . . and all who dwell on earth will worship it, every one whose name has not been written before the foundation of the world in the book of life of the Lamb that was slain.

Revelation 13.1,8

Pregnancy

He will gather the lambs in his arms, he will carry them in his bosom, and gently lead those that are with young.

Isaiah 40.11

Preparation

But the Lord sits enthroned for ever, he has established his throne for judgment.

Psalms 9.7

Thou preparest a table before me in the presence of my enemies.

Psalms 23.5

Go to the ant, O sluggard; consider her ways, and be wise. Without having any chief, officer or ruler, she prepares her food in summer, and gathers her sustenance in harvest.

Proverbs 6.6—8

Prepare your work outside, get everything ready for you in the field; and after that build your house.

Proverbs 24.27

Set your house in order; for you shall die, you shall not recover.

Isaiah 38.1

In the wilderness prepare the way of the Lord, make straight in the desert a highway for our God.

Isaiah 40.3

Build up, build up, prepare the way, remove every obstruction from my people's way.

Isaiah 57.14

Go through, go through the gates, prepare the way for the people; build up, build up the highway, clear it of stones, lift up an ensign over the peoples.

Isaiah 62.10

Sow for yourselves righteousness, reap the fruit of steadfast love; break up your fallow ground, for it is the time to seek the Lord, that he may come and rain salvation upon you.

Hosea 10.12

Do not lay up for yourselves treasures on earth, where moth and rust consume and where thieves break in and steal, but lay up for yourselves treasure in heaven, where neither moth nor rust consumes and where thieves do not break in and steal. For where your treasure is, there will your heart be also.

Matthew 6.19—21

But of that day and hour no one knows, not even the angels of heaven, nor the Son, but the Father only. As were the days of Noah, so will be the coming of the Son of man. For as in those days before the flood they were eating and drinking, marrying and giving in marriage, until the day when Noah entered the ark, and they did not know until the flood came and swept them all away, so will be the coming of the Son of man. Then two men will be in the field; one is taken and one is left. Two women will be grinding at the mill; one is taken and one is left. Watch therefore, for you do not know on what day your Lord is coming. But know this, that if the householder had known in what part of the night the thief was coming, he would have watched and would not have let his house be broken into. Therefore you also must be ready; for the Son of man is coming at an hour you do not expect.

Matthew 24.36—44

Watch therefore, for you know neither the day nor the hour.

Matthew 25.13

He will go before him in the spirit and
    power of Eli'jah,
to turn the hearts of the fathers to the
    children,
and the disobedient to the wisdom of the
    just,
to make ready for the Lord a people
    prepared.

Luke 1.17

For mine eyes have seen thy salvation
which thou hast prepared in the presence of
    all peoples.

Luke 2.30—31

In my Father's house are many rooms; if it were not so, would I have told you that I go to prepare a place for you? And when I go and prepare a place for you, I will come again and will take you to myself, that where I am you may be also.

John 14.2—3

What no eye has seen, nor ear heard,
nor the heart of man conceived,
what God has prepared for those who love
    him.

1 Corinthians 2.9

Consequently, when Christ came into the
    world, he said,
'Sacrifices and offerings thou hast not
    desired,
but a body hast thou prepared for me.'

Hebrews 10.5

Presence

Then he said, 'Do not come near; put off your shoes from your feet, for the place on which you are standing is holy ground.'

Exodus 3.5

Take heed that you do not go up into the mountain or touch the border of it; whoever touches the mountain shall be put to death; no hand shall touch him, but he shall be stoned or shot; whether beast or man, he shall not live.

Exodus 19.12—13

'You cannot see my face; for man shall not see me and live.' And the Lord said, 'Behold, there is a place by me where you shall stand upon the rock; and while my glory passes by I will put you in a cleft of the rock, and I will cover you with my hand until I have passed by; then I will take away my hand, and you shall see my back; but my face shall not be seen.'

Exodus 33.20—23

Whither shall I go from thy Spirit?
    Or whither shall I flee from thy presence?
If I ascend to heaven, thou art there!
    **If I make my bed in Sheol, thou art
      there!**

If I take the wings of the morning
    and dwell in the uttermost parts of the
        sea,
even there thy hand shall lead me,
    and thy right hand shall hold me.
If I say, 'Let only darkness cover me,
    and the light about me be night,'
even the darkness is not dark to thee,
    the night is bright as the day;
    for darkness is as light with thee.

Psalms 139.7–12

God is with us.

Isaiah 8.10

Yet he is not far from each one of us, for
'In him we live and move and have our
    being.'

Acts 17.27–28

Do not be afraid, but speak and do not be
silent; for I am with you, and no man shall
attack you to harm you.

Acts 18.9–10

Behold, I stand at the door and knock; if
any one hears my voice and opens the door,
I will come in to him and eat with him, and
he with me.

Revelation 3.20

Present

A gift in secret averts anger;
    and a bribe in the bosom, strong wrath.

Proverbs 21.14

Presumption

The man who acts presumptuously, by not
obeying the priest who stands to minister
there before the Lord your God, or the
judge, that man shall die.

Deuteronomy 17.12

The prophet who presumes to speak a
word in my name which I have not commanded him to speak, or who speaks in the
name of other gods, that same prophet
shall die.

Deuteronomy 18.20

How are the mighty fallen!

2 Samuel 1.19

Where were you when I laid the
    foundation of the earth?
    Tell me, if you have understanding.

Job 38.4

Arise, O Lord! Let not man prevail.

Psalms 9.19

Do not boast about tomorrow,
    for you do not know what a day may
        bring forth.

Proverbs 27.1

Woe to those . . . who say: 'Let him make
    haste,
    let him speed his work
    that we may see it;
let the purpose of the Holy One of Israel
    draw near,
    and let it come, that we may know it!'

Isaiah 5.18–19

Shall the axe vaunt itself over him who
    hews with it,
    or the saw magnify itself against him who
        wields it?
As if a rod should wield him who lifts it,
    or as if a staff should lift him who is not
        wood!

Isaiah 10.15

When you are invited by any one to a
marriage feast, do not sit down in a place of
honour.

Luke 14.8

For every one who exalts himself will be
humbled, and he who humbles himself will
be exalted.

Luke 14.11

Do you presume upon the riches of his
kindness and forbearance and patience? Do
you not know that God's kindness is meant
to lead you to repentance?

Romans 2.4

But who are you, a man, to answer back to
God? Will what is moulded say to its moulder, 'Why have you made me thus?'

Romans 9.20

Pretension

Better is a man of humble standing who
works for himself
than one who plays the great man but
lacks bread.

Proverbs 12.9

One man pretends to be rich, yet has
nothing;
another pretends to be poor, yet has
great wealth.

Proverbs 13.7

A wicked man puts on a bold face,
but an upright man considers his ways.

Proverbs 21.29

Pride

See also **Abuse, Arrogance, Insult, Vanity**

How are the mighty fallen!

2 Samuel 1.19

Look on every one that is proud, and bring
him low;
and tread down the wicked where they
stand.

Job 40.12

May the Lord cut off all flattering lips,
the tongue that makes great boasts,
those who say, 'With our tongue we will
prevail,
our lips are with us; who is our master?'

Psalms 12.3–4

Keep back thy servant also from
presumptuous sins;
let them not have dominion over me!
Then I shall be blameless,
and innocent of great transgression.

Psalms 19.13

Pride and arrogance and the way of evil
and perverted speech I hate.

Proverbs 8.13

When pride comes, then comes disgrace.

Proverbs 11.2

The Lord tears down the house of the
proud.

Proverbs 15.25

Pride goes before destruction,
and a haughty spirit before a fall.

Proverbs 16.18

Before destruction a man's heart is
haughty,
but humility goes before honour.

Proverbs 18.12

Haughty eyes and a proud heart,
the lamp of the wicked, are sin.

Proverbs 21.4

A man's pride will bring him low.

Proverbs 29.23

For the Lord of hosts has a day
against all that is proud and lofty,
against all that is lifted up and high.

Isaiah 2.12

The Lord will lay low his pride together
with the skill of his hands.

Isaiah 25.11

Woe to the proud crown.

Isaiah 28.1

Hear and give ear; be not proud,
for the Lord has spoken.

Jeremiah 13.15

Those who walk in pride he is able to
abase.

Daniel 4.37

Behold, I will make you small among the
nations,
you shall be utterly despised.
The pride of your heart has deceived you,
you who live in the clefts of the rock,
whose dwelling is high,
who say in your heart,
'Who will bring me down to the ground?'
Though you soar aloft like the eagle,
though your nest is set among the stars,
thence I will bring you down,
says the Lord.

Obadiah 2–4

Slander, pride, foolishness. All these evil things come from within, and they defile a man.

Mark 7.23

No human being might boast in the presence of God.

1 Corinthians 1.29

None of you may be puffed up in favour of one against another. For who sees anything different in you? What have you that you did not receive? If then you received it, why do you boast as if it were not a gift?

1 Corinthians 4.6—7

Prison

See also **Oppression**

Come, O blessed of my Father, inherit the kingdom prepared for you from the foundation of the world; for . . . I was sick and you visited me, I was in prison and you came to me.

Matthew 25.34,36

Remember those who are in prison, as though in prison with them; and those who are ill-treated, since you also are in the body.

Hebrews 13.3

Procrastination

Do not say to your neighbour, 'Go, and come again,
tomorrow I will give it' — when you have it with you.

Proverbs 3.28

When you vow a vow to God, do not delay paying it; for he has no pleasure in fools. Pay what you vow. It is better that you should not vow than that you should vow and not pay.

Ecclesiastes 5.4—5

Another of the disciples said to him, 'Lord, let me first go and bury my father.' But Jesus said to him, 'Follow me, and leave the dead to bury their own dead.'

Matthew 8.21—22

Jesus said to him, 'No one who puts his hand to the plough and looks back is fit for the kingdom of God.'

Luke 9.62

Strive to enter by the narrow door; for many, I tell you, will seek to enter and will not be able. When once the householder has risen up and shut the door, you will begin to stand outside and to knock at the door, saying, 'Lord, open to us.' He will answer you, 'I do not know where you come from.'

Luke 13.24—25

Progress

See also **Maturity**

But the path of the righteous is like the
light of dawn,
which shines brighter and brighter until
full day.

Proverbs 4.18

And so, from the day we heard of it, we have not ceased to pray for you, asking that you may be filled with the knowledge of his will in all spiritual wisdom and understanding, to lead a life worthy of the Lord, fully pleasing to him, bearing fruit in every good work and increasing in the knowledge of God.

Colossians 1.9—10

Love one another . . . we exhort you, brethren, to do so more and more.

1 Thessalonians 4.10

Let us leave the elementary doctrine of Christ and go on to maturity.

Hebrews 6.1

Prolonging (of Life)

I have heard your prayer, I have seen your tears; behold, I will add fifteen years to your life.

Isaiah 38.5

Which of you by being anxious can add one cubit to his span of life?

Matthew 6.27

Promiscuity

See also **Prostitution**

For the lips of a loose woman drip honey,
and her speech is smoother than oil;
but in the end she is bitter as wormwood,
sharp as a two-edged sword.
Her feet go down to death;
her steps follow the path to Sheol;
she does not take heed to the path of life;
her ways wander, and she does not
know it.

Proverbs 5.3—6

The mouth of a loose woman is a deep pit;
he with whom the Lord is angry will fall
into it.

Proverbs 22.14

For a harlot is a deep pit;
an adventuress is a narrow well.
She lies in wait like a robber
and increases the faithless among men.

Proverbs 23.27—28

Promotion

Thou didst exalt me above my adversaries,
thou didst deliver me from men of
violence.
For this I will extol thee, O Lord, among
the nations.

2 Samuel 22.49—50

He does not keep the wicked alive,
but gives the afflicted their right.
He does not withdraw his eyes from the
righteous,
but with kings upon the throne
he sets them for ever, and they are
exalted.

Job 36.6—7

Wait for the Lord, and keep to his way,
and he will exalt you to possess the land;
you will look on the destruction of the
wicked.

Psalms 37.34

Let thy salvation, O God, set me on high!

Psalms 69.29

But it is God who executes judgment,
putting down one and lifting up another.

Psalms 75.7

He raises the poor from the dust,
and lifts the needy from the ash heap,
to make them sit with princes,
with the princes of his people.

Psalms 113.7—8

The wise will inherit honour,
but fools get disgrace.

Proverbs 3.35

The beginning of wisdom is this:
Get wisdom,
and whatever you get, get insight.
Prize her highly, and she will exalt you;
she will honour you if you embrace her.

Proverbs 4.7—8

Promptitude

When you vow a vow to God, do not
delay paying it; for he has no pleasure in
fools. Pay what you vow. It is better that
you should not vow than that you should
vow and not pay.

Ecclesiastes 5.4—5

Proof

Why do you put the Lord to the proof?

Exodus 17.2

We must not put the Lord to the test.

1 Corinthians 10.9

Property

See also **Possessions**

You shall not covet your neighbour's
house; you shall not covet . . . his ox, or his
ass, or anything that is your neighbour's.

Exodus 20.17

You shall not see your brother's ox or his
sheep go astray, and withhold your help

from them; you shall take them back to your brother.

Deuteronomy 22.1

When you go into your neighbour's standing grain, you may pluck the ears with your hand, but you shall not put a sickle to your neighbour's standing grain.

Deuteronomy 23.25

If you would be perfect, go, sell what you possess and give to the poor, and you will have treasure in heaven.

Matthew 19.21

And all who believed were together and had all things in common; and they sold their possessions and goods and distributed them to all, as any had need.

Acts 2.44–45

If I give away all I have, and if I deliver my body to be burned, but have not love, I gain nothing.

1 Corinthians 13.3

You joyfully accepted the plundering of your property, since you knew that you yourselves had a better possession and an abiding one.

Hebrews 10.34

Prophets

If a prophet arises among you, or a dreamer of dreams, and gives you a sign or a wonder, and the sign or wonder which he tells you comes to pass, and if he says, 'Let us go after other gods,' which you have not known, 'and let us serve them,' you shall not listen to the words of that prophet or to that dreamer of dreams; for the Lord your God is testing you, to know whether you love the Lord your God with all your heart and with all your soul. You shall walk after the Lord your God and fear him, and keep his commandments and obey his voice, and you shall serve him and cleave to him. But that prophet or that dreamer of dreams shall be put to death.

Deuteronomy 13.1–5

Where there is no prophecy the people cast off restraint.

Proverbs 29.18

On that day every prophet will be ashamed of his vision when he prophesies; he will not put on a hairy mantle in order to deceive, but he will say, 'I am no prophet, I am a tiller of the soil; for the land has been my possession since my youth.'

Zechariah 13.4–5

Beware of false prophets, who come to you in sheep's clothing but inwardly are ravenous wolves. You will know them by their fruits.

Matthew 7.15–16

A prophet is not without honour except in his own country and in his own house.

Matthew 13.57

O foolish men, and slow of heart to believe all that the prophets have spoken!

Luke 24.25

Make love your aim, and earnestly desire the spiritual gifts, especially that you may prophesy.

1 Corinthians 14.1

Tongues are a sign not for believers but for unbelievers, while prophecy is not for unbelievers but for believers.

1 Corinthians 14.22

Prosperity

See also **Money, Wealth**

Accept, I pray you, my gift that is brought to you, because God has dealt graciously with me, and because I have enough.

Genesis 33.11

If you are pure and upright,
surely then he will rouse himself for you
and reward you with a rightful habitation.
And though your beginning was small,
your latter days will be very great.

Job 8.6–7

If you return to the Almighty and humble
    yourself,
  if you remove unrighteousness far from
      your tents,
  if you lay gold in the dust,
  and gold of Ophir among the stones of
      the torrent bed,
and if the Almighty is your gold,
  and your precious silver;
then you will delight yourself in the
    Almighty,
  and lift up your face to God.

Job 22.23–26

Blessed is the man
  who walks not in the counsel of the
      wicked . . .
but his delight is in the law of the Lord,
  and on his law he meditates day and
      night.
He is like a tree
  planted by streams of water,
that yields its fruit in its season,
  and its leaf does not wither.
In all that he does, he prospers.

Psalms 1.1–3

Bless the Lord, O my soul,
  and forget not all his benefits . . .
who satisfies you with good as long as
    you live.

Psalms 103.2,5

Unless the Lord builds the house,
  those who build it labour in vain.
Unless the Lord watches over the city,
  the watchman stays awake in vain.
It is in vain that you rise up early and go
    late to rest,
eating the bread of anxious toil;
  for he gives to his beloved sleep.

Psalms 127.1–2

Blessed is every one who fears the Lord,
  who walks in his ways!
You shall eat the fruit of the labour of your
    hands;
  you shall be happy, and it shall be well
    with you.

Psalms 128.1–2

Wealth hastily gotten will dwindle,
  but he who gathers little by little will
    increase it.

Proverbs 13.11

Righteousness exalts a nation.

Proverbs 14.34

In the day of prosperity be joyful, and in
the day of adversity consider; God has
made the one as well as the other, so that
man may not find out anything that will be
after him.

Ecclesiastes 7.14

Prostitution

Do not profane your daughter by making
her a harlot, lest the land fall into harlotry
and the land become full of wickedness.

Leviticus 19.29

You shall not bring the hire of a harlot, or
the wages of a dog, into the house of the
Lord your God in payment for any vow; for
both of these are an abomination to the
Lord your God.

Deuteronomy 23.18

For the lips of a loose woman drip honey,
  and her speech is smoother than oil;
but in the end she is bitter as wormwood,
  sharp as a two-edged sword.
Her feet go down to death;
  her steps follow the path to Sheol.

Proverbs 5.3–5

A harlot may be hired for a loaf of bread,
  but an adulteress stalks a man's very life.

Proverbs 6.26

For at the window of my house
  I have looked out through my lattice,
and I have seen among the simple,
  I have perceived among the youths,
  a young man without sense,
passing along the street near her corner,
  taking the road to her house
in the twilight, in the evening,
  at the time of night and darkness.
And lo, a woman meets him,
  dressed as a harlot, wily of heart.

She is loud and wayward,
   her feet do not stay at home;
now in the street, now in the market,
   and at every corner she lies in wait . . .
With much seductive speech she
     persuades him;
   with her smooth talk she compels him.
All at once he follows her,
   as an ox goes to the slaughter . . .
Let not your heart turn aside to her
    ways,
   do not stray into her paths;
for many a victim has she laid low;
   yea, all her slain are a mighty host.
Her house is the way to Sheol,
going down to the chambers of death.

Proverbs 7.6−12,21−22,25−27

For a harlot is a deep pit;
   an adventuress is a narrow well.
She lies in wait like a robber
   and increases the faithless among men.

Proverbs 23.27−28

One who keeps company with harlots
   squanders his substance.

Proverbs 29.3

If a man offered for love
   all the wealth of his house,
   it would be utterly scorned.

Song of Solomon 8.7

Tax collectors and the harlots go into the kingdom of God before you. For John came to you in the way of righteousness, and you did not believe him, but the tax collectors and the harlots believed him.

Matthew 21.31−32

Do you not know that your bodies are members of Christ? Shall I therefore take the members of Christ and make them members of a prostitute? Never! Do you not know that he who joins himself to a prostitute becomes one body with her? For, as it is written, 'The two shall become one flesh.' But he who is united to the Lord becomes one spirit with him.

1 Corinthians 6.15−17

Be sure of this, that no fornicator or impure man, or one who is covetous (that is, an idolator), has any inheritance in the kingdom of Christ and of God.

Ephesians 5.5

Let marriage be held in honour among all, and let the marriage bed be undefiled; for God will judge the immoral and adulterous.

Hebrews 13.4

Protection

See also **Rescue**

But thou, O Lord, art a shield about me,
   my glory, and the lifter of my head.

Psalms 3.3

My shield is with God,
   who saves the upright in heart.

Psalms 7.10

Keep me as the apple of the eye;
   hide me in the shadow of thy wings.

Psalms 17.8

The Lord is my rock, and my fortress, and
    my deliverer,
   my God, my rock, in whom I take refuge,
   my shield, and the horn of my salvation,
    my stronghold.

Psalms 18.2

The Lord is my light and my salvation;
   whom shall I fear?
The Lord is the stronghold of my life;
   of whom shall I be afraid?

Psalms 27.1

The Lord is my strength and my shield;
   in him my heart trusts;
so I am helped, and my heart exults,
   and with my song I give thanks to him.

Psalms 28.7

The steps of a man are from the Lord.

Psalms 37.23

God is our refuge and strength,
   a very present help in trouble.
Therefore we will not fear though the earth
    should change,

though the mountains shake in the heart
of the sea;
though its waters roar and foam,
though the mountains tremble with its
tumult.

Psalms 46.1–3

Hear my voice, O God, in my complaint;
preserve my life from dread of the
enemy,
hide me from the secret plots of the wicked,
from the scheming of evildoers.

Psalms 64.1–2

For the Lord God is a sun and shield.

Psalms 84.11

The Lord will keep you from all evil;
he will keep your life.
The Lord will keep
your going out and your coming in
from this time forth and for evermore.

Psalms 121.7–8

He is a shield to those who walk in
integrity,
guarding the paths of justice.

Proverbs 2.7–8

For thou hast been a stronghold to the
poor,
a stronghold to the needy in his distress,
a shelter from the storm and a shade
from the heat;
for the blast of the ruthless is like a storm
against a wall,
like heat in a dry place.

Isaiah 25.4–5

He will feed his flock like a shepherd,
he will gather the lambs in his arms,
he will carry them in his bosom,
and gently lead those that are with
young.

Isaiah 40.11

I, I am he that comforts you;
who are you that you are afraid of man
who dies,
of the son of man who is made like grass?

Isaiah 51.12

Behold . . . In those days and at that time
I will cause a righteous Branch to spring
forth for David; and he shall execute justice
and righteousness in the land. In those days
Judah will be saved and Jerusalem will
dwell securely.

Jeremiah 33.14–16

Do not be afraid, but speak and do not be
silent; for I am with you, and no man shall
attack you to harm you.

Acts 18.9–10

For I am sure that neither death, nor life,
nor angels, nor principalities, nor things
present, nor things to come, nor powers,
nor height, nor depth, nor anything else in
all creation, will be able to separate us from
the love of God in Christ Jesus our Lord.

Romans 8.38–39

Provocation

A stone is heavy, and sand is weighty,
but a fool's provocation is heavier than
both.

Proverbs 27.3

Prudence

See also **Care**

For the ear tests words
as the palate tastes food.

Job 34.3

Keep sound wisdom and discretion.

Proverbs 3.21

I, wisdom, dwell in prudence.

Proverbs 8.12

The vexation of a fool is known at once,
but the prudent man ignores an insult.

Proverbs 12.16

Good sense wins favour.

Proverbs 13.15

In everything a prudent man acts with
knowledge.

Proverbs 13.16

The wisdom of a prudent man is to discern his way.

Proverbs 14.8

The simple believes everything,
but the prudent looks where he is going.

Proverbs 14.15

The simple acquire folly,
but the prudent are crowned with knowledge.

Proverbs 14.18

He who heeds admonition is prudent.

Proverbs 15.5

A prudent man sees danger and hides himself;
but the simple go on, and suffer for it.

Proverbs 22.3

Make friends quickly with your accuser, while you are going with him to court, lest your accuser hand you over to the judge, and the judge to the guard, and you be put in prison.

Matthew 5.25

For which of you, desiring to build a tower, does not first sit down and count the cost, whether he has enough to complete it? Otherwise, when he has laid a foundation, and is not able to finish, all who see it begin to mock him, saying, 'This man began to build, and was not able to finish.'

Luke 14.28–30

So do not let your good be spoken of as evil.

Romans 14.16

In him we have redemption through his blood, the forgiveness of our trespasses, according to the riches of his grace which he lavished upon us. For he has made known to us in all wisdom and insight the mystery of his will.

Ephesians 1.7–9

Let every man be quick to hear, slow to speak, slow to anger.

James 1.19

Punishment

See also **Judgment (Last)**

Be assured, an evil man will not go unpunished.

Proverbs 11.21

He who spares the rod hates his son,
but he who loves him is diligent to discipline him.

Proverbs 13.24

To impose a fine on a righteous man is not good.

Proverbs 17.26

A man of great wrath will pay the penalty;
for if you deliver him, you will only have to do it again.

Proverbs 19.19

Blows that wound cleanse away evil;
strokes make clean the innermost parts.

Proverbs 20.30

Because sentence against an evil deed is not executed speedily, the heart of the sons of men is fully set to do evil. Though a sinner does evil a hundred times and prolongs his life, yet I know that it will be well with those who fear God, because they fear before him; but it will not be well with the wicked, neither will he prolong his days like a shadow, because he does not fear before God.

Ecclesiastes 8.11–13

According to their deeds, so will he repay,
wrath to his adversaries, requital to his enemies.

Isaiah 59.18

I will punish you according to the fruit of your doings,
says the Lord.

Jeremiah 21.14

And my eye will not spare you, nor will I have pity; but I will punish you for your ways, while your abominations are in your midst. Then you will know that I am the Lord.

Ezekiel 7.4

For they sow the wind,
  and they shall reap the whirlwind.

Hosea 8.7

The day of their watchmen, of their
    punishment, has come;
  now their confusion is at hand.

Micah 7.4

The Lord is a jealous God and avenging,
  the Lord is avenging and wrathful;
the Lord takes vengeance on his adversaries
  and keeps wrath for his enemies.

Nahum 1.2

And do not fear those who kill the body but cannot kill the soul; rather fear him who can destroy both soul and body in hell.

Matthew 10.28

Beloved, never avenge yourselves, but leave it to the wrath of God.

Romans 12.19

If you do wrong, be afraid, for he does not bear the sword in vain; he is the servant of God to execute his wrath on the wrong-doer.

Romans 13.4

He who sows to his own flesh will from the flesh reap corruption.

Galatians 6.8

For the wrongdoer will be paid back for the wrong he has done, and there is no partiality.

Colossians 3.25

God deems it just to repay with affliction those who afflict you, and to grant rest with us to you who are afflicted, when the Lord Jesus is revealed from heaven with his mighty angels in flaming fire, inflicting vengeance upon those . . . who do not obey the gospel of our Lord Jesus. They shall suffer the punishment of eternal destruction and exclusion from the presence of the Lord and from the glory of his might.

2 Thessalonians 1.6–9

The Lord knows how to rescue the godly from trial, and to keep the unrighteous under punishment until the day of judgment.

2 Peter 2.9

Purity

See also **Cleanliness, Innocence**

The Lord rewarded me according to my
    righteousness;
  according to the cleanness of my hands
    he recompensed me.

2 Samuel 22.21

The promises of the Lord are promises
    that are pure,
  silver refined in a furnace on the ground,
    purified seven times.

Psalms 12.6

Therefore the Lord has recompensed me
    according to my righteousness,
  according to the cleanness of my hands in
    his sight.
With the loyal thou dost show thyself loyal;
  with the blameless man thou dost show
    thyself blameless;
with the pure thou dost show thyself pure.

Psalms 18.24–26

The commandment of the Lord is pure,
  enlightening the eyes.

Psalms 19.8

Who shall ascend the hill of the Lord?
  And who shall stand in his holy place?
He who has clean hands and a pure
    heart . . .
  will receive blessing from the Lord,
  and vindication from the God of his
    salvation.

Psalms 24.3–5

Purge me with hyssop, and I shall be clean;
wash me, and I shall be whiter than snow.

Psalms 51.7

How can a young man keep his way pure?
  By guarding it according to thy word.

Psalms 119.9

All the ways of a man are pure in his own
eyes,
  but the Lord weighs the spirit.

Proverbs 16.2

Even a child makes himself known by his
acts,
  whether what he does is pure and right.

Proverbs 20.11

Every word of God proves true.

Proverbs 30.5

Though your sins are like scarlet,
  they shall be as white as snow;
though they are red like crimson,
  they shall become like wool.

Isaiah 1.18

Many shall purify themselves, and make
themselves white, and be refined.

Daniel 12.10

But who can endure the day of his coming,
and who can stand when he appears?
  For he is like a refiner's fire and like
fullers' soap; he will sit as a refiner and
purifier of silver, and he will purify the sons
of Levi and refine them like gold and silver,
till they present right offerings to the Lord.

Malachi 3.2−3

Blessed are the pure in heart, for they
shall see God.

Matthew 5.8

And it is my prayer that your love may
abound more and more, with knowledge
and all discernment, so that you may
approve what is excellent, and may be pure
and blameless for the day of Christ.

Philippians 1.9−10

Whatever is just, whatever is pure . . .
think about these things.

Philippians 4.8

Do not be hasty in the laying on of hands,
nor participate in another man's sins; keep
yourself pure.

1 Timothy 5.22

So shun youthful passions and aim at
righteousness, faith, love, and peace, along
with those who call upon the Lord from a
pure heart.

2 Timothy 2.22

To the pure all things are pure.

Titus 1.15

The wisdom from above is . . . pure.

James 3.17

If we confess our sins, he is faithful and
just, and will forgive our sins and cleanse us
from all unrighteousness.

1 John 1.9

We shall be like him, for we shall see him
as he is. And every one who thus hopes in
him purifies himself as he is pure.

1 John 3.2−3

Purpose

See also **Predestination**

Plans are established by counsel.

Proverbs 20.18

We know that in everything God works
for good with those who love him, who are
called according to his purpose.

Romans 8.28

For he has made known to us in all wisdom
and insight the mystery of his will, according to his purpose which he set forth in
Christ as a plan for the fulness of time.

Ephesians 1.9−10

God . . . saved us and called us with a
holy calling, not in virtue of our works but
in virtue of his own purpose and the grace
which he gave us in Christ Jesus.

2 Timothy 1.9

As the outcome of your faith you obtain
the salvation of your souls.

1 Peter 1.9

Q

Quarrelling

See also **Argument**

Do not contend with a man for no reason,
when he has done you no harm.

Proverbs 3.30

By insolence the heedless make strife.

Proverbs 13.10

It is an honour for a man to keep aloof
from strife.

Proverbs 20.3

It is better to live in a desert land
than with a contentious and fretful
woman.

Proverbs 21.19

Drive out a scoffer, and strife will go out,
and quarrelling and abuse will cease.

Proverbs 22.10

He who meddles in a quarrel not his own
is like one who takes a passing dog by the
ears.

Proverbs 26.17

As charcoal to hot embers and wood to
fire,
so is a quarrelsome man for kindling
strife.

Proverbs 26.21

If a kingdom is divided against itself, that
kingdom cannot stand. And if a house is
divided against itself, that house will not be
able to stand.

Mark 3.24–25

If possible, so far as it depends upon you,
live peaceably with all.

Romans 12.18

As for the man who is weak in faith,
welcome him, but not for disputes over
opinions.

Romans 14.1

I appeal to you, brethren, to take note of
those who create dissensions and difficulties, in opposition to the doctrine which you
have been taught; avoid them. For such
persons do not serve our Lord Christ, but
their own appetites, and by fair and flattering words they deceive the hearts of the
simple-minded.

Romans 16.17–18

Now the works of the flesh are plain . . .
strife, jealousy, anger . . . those who do
such things shall not inherit the kingdom of
God.

Galatians 5.19–21

Avoid disputing about words, which does
no good, but only ruins the hearers.

2 Timothy 2.14

Have nothing to do with stupid, senseless
controversies; you know that they breed
quarrels. And the Lord's servant must not
be quarrelsome.

2 Timothy 2.23–24

Remind them . . . to speak evil of no one,
to avoid quarrelling.

Titus 3.1

Avoid . . . quarrels over the law, for they
are unprofitable and futile.

Titus 3.9

Questioning

Do all things without grumbling or questioning.

Philippians 2.14

Quietness

See also **Peace**

Then they cried to the Lord in their
    trouble,
  and he delivered them from their distress;
he made the storm be still,
  and the waves of the sea were hushed.
Then they were glad because they had
    quiet,
  and he brought them to their desired
    haven.

Psalms 107.28–30

He who listens to me will dwell secure
  and will be at ease, without dread of evil.

Proverbs 1.33

Better is a dry morsel with quiet
than a house full of feasting with strife.

Proverbs 17.1

Better is a handful of quietness than two
hands full of toil and a striving after wind.

Ecclesiastes 4.6

The words of the wise heard in quiet are
better than the shouting of a ruler among
fools.

Ecclesiastes 9.17

In quietness and in trust shall be your
strength.

Isaiah 30.15

It is good that one should wait quietly
  for the salvation of the Lord.

Lamentations 3.26

Aspire to live quietly, to mind your own
affairs.

1 Thessalonians 4.11

R

Racism

See also **Apartheid, Bigotry**

The man called his wife's name Eve, because she was the mother of all living.

Genesis 3.20

You have trespassed and married foreign women, and so increased the guilt of Israel. Now then make confession to the Lord the God of your fathers, and do his will; separate yourselves from the peoples of the land and from the foreign wives.

Ezra 10.10–11

Have we not all one father? Has not one God created us? Why then are we faithless to one another?

Malachi 2.10

God has shown me that I should not call any man common or unclean.

Acts 10.28

Truly I perceive that God shows no partiality, but in every nation any one who fears him and does what is right is acceptable to him.

Acts 10.34–35

And he made from one every nation of men to live on all the face of the earth.

Acts 17.26

For there is no distinction between Jew and Greek; the same Lord is Lord of all and bestows his riches upon all who call upon him. For, 'every one who calls upon the name of the Lord will be saved.'

Romans 10.12–13

Here there cannot be Greek and Jew, circumcised and uncircumcised, barbarian, Scyth'ian, slave, free man, but Christ is all, and in all.

Colossians 3.11

But if you show partiality, you commit sin.

James 2.9

But he who hates his brother is in the darkness and walks in the darkness, and does not know where he is going, because the darkness has blinded his eyes.

1 John 2.11

Rape

See also **Lust**

But if in the open country a man meets a young woman who is betrothed, and the man seizes her and lies with her, then only the man who lay with her shall die. But to the young woman you shall do nothing; in the young woman there is no offence punishable by death.

Deuteronomy 22.25–26

Readiness

See also **Preparation**

Repent, for the kingdom of heaven is at hand.

Matthew 3.2

Reason

See also **Philosophy**

Can you find out the deep things of God?
Can you find out the limit of the
Almighty?

Job 11.7

Should a wise man answer with windy
  knowledge,
and fill himself with the east wind?
Should he argue in unprofitable talk,
  or in words with which he can do no
  good?

Job 15.2−3

Trust in the Lord with all your heart,
  and do not rely on your own insight.

Proverbs 3.5

There is a way which seems right to a man,
  but its end is the way to death.

Proverbs 14.12

And I applied my mind to seek and to
search out by wisdom all that is done under
heaven; it is an unhappy business that God
has given to the sons of men to be busy
with.

Ecclesiastes 1.13

You shall love the Lord your God with all
your heart, and with all your soul, and with
all your mind.

Matthew 22.37

I see in my members another law at war
with the law of my mind.

Romans 7.23

I will pray with the spirit and I will pray
with the mind also.

1 Corinthians 14.15

Always be prepared to make a defence to
any one who calls you to account for the
hope that is in you.

1 Peter 3.15

But these, like irrational animals . . . reviling in matters of which they are ignorant,
will be destroyed in the same destruction.

2 Peter 2.12

Reasonableness

You shall not hate your brother in your
heart, but you shall reason with your neighbour, lest you bear sin because of him.

Leviticus 19.17

Rebellion

Only, do not rebel against the Lord.

Numbers 14.9

Rebellion is as the sin of divination.

1 Samuel 15.23

There did we rejoice in him,
  who rules by his might for ever,
whose eyes keep watch on the nations —
  let not the rebellious exalt themselves.

Psalms 66.6−7

The rebellious dwell in a parched land.

Psalms 68.6

An evil man seeks only rebellion,
  and a cruel messenger will be sent
    against him.

Proverbs 17.11

If you are willing and obedient,
  you shall eat the good of the land;
but if you refuse and rebel,
  you shall be devoured by the sword;
  for the mouth of the Lord has spoken.

Isaiah 1.19−20

'Woe to the rebellious children,' says the
    Lord,
  'who carry out a plan, but not mine;
and who make a league, but not of my
    spirit,
  that they may add sin to sin.'

Isaiah 30.1

I will purge out the rebels from among you,
and those who transgress against me; I will
bring them out of the land where they
sojourn, but they shall not enter the land of
Israel. Then you will know that I am the
Lord.

Ezekiel 20.38

To us, O Lord, belongs confusion of face
. . . because we have sinned against thee.

Daniel 9.8

For those who are factious and do not
obey the truth, but obey wickedness, there
will be wrath and fury.

Romans 2.8

Therefore he who resists the authorities resists what God has appointed, and those who resist will incur judgment.

Romans 13.2

Be subject for the Lord's sake to every human institution.

1 Peter 2.13

Rebuke

As for those who persist in sin, rebuke them in the presence of all, so that the rest may stand in fear.

1 Timothy 5.20

Receptivity

Receive instruction from his mouth,
 and lay up his words in your heart.

Job 22.22

The wise of heart will heed
 commandments.

Proverbs 10.8

He who gives heed to the word will
 prosper.

Proverbs 16.20

The hearing ear and the seeing eye,
 the Lord has made them both.

Proverbs 20.12

For lack of wood the fire goes out;
 and where there is no whisperer,
  quarrelling ceases.

Proverbs 26.20

He who receives you receives me, and he who receives me receives him who sent me.

Matthew 10.40

Blessed are your eyes, for they see, and your ears, for they hear.

Matthew 13.16

As for what was sown on good soil, this is he who hears the word and understands it; he indeed bears fruit, and yields.

Matthew 13.23

Whoever does not receive the kingdom of God like a child shall not enter it.

Mark 10.15

Reciprocation

See also **Retribution**

When a man causes a disfigurement in his neighbour, as he has done it shall be done to him, fracture for fracture, eye for eye, tooth for tooth.

Leviticus 24.19−20

Those who honour me I will honour, and those who despise me shall be lightly esteemed.

1 Samuel 2.30

The Lord requite the evildoer according to his wickedness!

2 Samuel 3.39

Cast your bread upon the waters,
 for you will find it after many days.

Ecclesiastes 11.1

They sow the wind,
 and they shall reap the whirlwind.

Hosea 8.7

Love your enemies . . . For if you love those who love you, what reward have you? Do not even the tax collectors do the same? And if you salute only your brethren, what more are you doing than others?

Matthew 5.44,46−47

So whatever you wish that men would do to you, do so to them.

Matthew 7.12

All who take the sword will perish by the sword.

Matthew 26.5?

Recognition

My sheep hear my voice, and I know them, and they follow me; and I give them eternal life, and they shall never perish, and no one shall snatch them out of my hand.

John 10.27−28

Reconciliation

Agree with God, and be at peace;
thereby good will come to you.

Job 22.21

And he will turn the hearts of fathers to their children and the hearts of children to their fathers, lest I come and smite the land with a curse.

Malachi 4.6

If you are offering your gift at the altar, and there remember that your brother has something against you, leave your gift there before the altar and go; first be reconciled to your brother, and then come and offer your gift.

Matthew 5.23–24

If your brother sins against you, go and tell him his fault, between you and him alone. If he listens to you, you have gained your brother.

Matthew 18.15

Therefore, since we are justified by faith, we have peace with God through our Lord Jesus Christ.

Romans 5.1

For if while we were enemies we were reconciled to God by the death of his Son, much more, now that we are reconciled, shall we be saved by his life.

Romans 5.10

All this is from God, who through Christ reconciled us to himself and gave us the ministry of reconciliation; that is, in Christ God was reconciling the world to himself, not counting their trespasses against them, and entrusting to us the message of reconciliation.
So we are ambassadors for Christ, God making his appeal through us. We beseech you on behalf of Christ, be reconciled to God. For our sake he made him to be sin who knew no sin, so that in him we might become the righteousness of God.

2 Corinthians 5.18–21

For he is our peace, who has made us both one, and has broken down the dividing wall

of hostility, by abolishing in his flesh the law of commandments and ordinances, that he might create in himself one new man in place of the two, so making peace, and might reconcile us both to God in one body through the cross, thereby bringing the hostility to an end.

Ephesians 2.14–16

And you, who once were estranged and hostile in mind, doing evil deeds, he has now reconciled in his body of flesh by his death.

Colossians 1.21–22

Redemption

See also **Justification, Salvation**

I will redeem you with an outstretched arm and with great acts of judgment, and I will take you for my people, and I will be your God; and you shall know that I am the Lord your God.

Exodus 6.6–7

You shall remember that you were a slave in the land of Egypt, and the Lord your God redeemed you.

Deuteronomy 15.15

For I know that my Redeemer lives.

Job 19.25

Redeem Israel, O God,
out of all his troubles.

Psalms 25.22

But as for me, I walk in my integrity;
redeem me, and be gracious to me.

Psalms 26.11

The Lord redeems the life of his servants;
none of those who take refuge in him will
be condemned.

Psalms 34.22

Rise up, come to our help!
Deliver us for the sake of thy steadfast
love!

Psalms 44.26

Answer me, O Lord, for thy steadfast love
    is good;
  according to thy abundant mercy, turn to
    me.
Hide not thy face from thy servant;
  for I am in distress, make haste to answer
    me.
Draw near to me, redeem me,
  set me free because of my enemies!

Psalms 69.16−18

He has pity on the weak and the needy,
  and saves the lives of the needy.
From oppression and violence he redeems
    their life;
  and precious is their blood in his sight.

Psalms 72.13−14

Bless the Lord, O my soul,
  and forget not all his benefits,
who forgives all your iniquity,
  who heals all your diseases,
who redeems your life from the Pit.

Psalms 103.2−4

O give thanks to the Lord, for he is good;
  for his steadfast love endures for ever!
Let the redeemed of the Lord say so,
  whom he has redeemed from trouble.

Psalms 107.1−2

For with the Lord there is steadfast love,
  and with him is plenteous redemption.

Psalms 130.7

The ransom of a man's life is his wealth,
  but a poor man has no means of
    redemption.

Proverbs 13.8

Our Redeemer — the Lord of hosts is his
    name —
  is the Holy One of Israel.

Isaiah 47.4

And the ransomed of the Lord shall
    return,
  and come to Zion with singing;
everlasting joy shall be upon their heads;
  they shall obtain joy and gladness,
  and sorrow and sighing shall flee away.

Isaiah 51.11

Thou, O Lord, art our Father,
  our Redeemer from of old is thy name.

Isaiah 63.16

I will deliver you out of the hand of the
    wicked,
  and redeem you from the grasp of the
    ruthless.

Jeremiah 15.21

Let our supplication come before you, and
pray to the Lord your God for us, for all
this remnant (for we are left but a few of
many, as your eyes see us), that the Lord
your God may show us the way we should
go, and the thing that we should do.

Jeremiah 42.2−3

Shall I ransom them from the power of
    Sheol?
  Shall I redeem them from Death?
O Death, where are your plagues?
O Sheol, where is your destruction?

Hosea 13.14

For the Son of man also came not to be
served but to serve, and to give his life as a
ransom for many.

Mark 10.45

Blessed be the Lord God of Israel,
  for he has visited and redeemed his people.

Luke 1.68

Look up and raise your heads, because
your redemption is drawing near.

Luke 21.28

Since all have sinned and fall short of the
glory of God, they are justified by his grace
as a gift, through the redemption which is in
Christ Jesus, whom God put forward as an
expiation by his blood, to be received by
faith.

Romans 3.23−2.

We . . . groan inwardly as we wait for
adoption as sons, the redemption of our
bodies.

Romans 8.22−2

Christ redeemed us from the curse of the
law, having become a curse for us — for

is written, 'Cursed be every one who hangs on a tree.'

Galatians 3.13

But when the time had fully come, God sent forth his Son, born of woman, born under the law, to redeem those who were under the law, so that we might receive adoption as sons.

Galatians 4.4–5

Do not grieve the Holy Spirit of God, in whom you were sealed for the day of redemption.

Ephesians 4.30

Our great God and Saviour Jesus Christ . . . gave himself for us to redeem us from all iniquity.

Titus 2.13–14

He entered once for all into the Holy Place, taking not the blood of goats and calves but his own blood, thus securing an eternal redemption.

Hebrews 9.12

You know that you were ransomed from the futile ways inherited from your fathers, not with perishable things such as silver or gold, but with the precious blood of Christ, like that of a lamb without blemish or spot.

1 Peter 1.18–19

For thou wast slain and by thy blood didst ransom men for God.

Revelation 5.9

No one could learn that song except the hundred and forty-four thousand who had been redeemed from the earth.

Revelation 14.3

Refining

But he knows the way that I take;
    when he has tried me, I shall come forth
      as gold.

Job 23.10

I will turn my hand against you
    and will smelt away your dross as with lye
    and remove all your alloy.

Isaiah 1.25

Behold, I have refined you, but not like
    silver;
I have tried you in the furnace of
    affliction.

Isaiah 48.10

Therefore thus says the Lord of hosts:
'Behold, I will refine them and test them,
    for what else can I do, because of my
      people?'

Jeremiah 9.7

Awake, O sword, against my shepherd,
    against the man who stands next to me,
      says the Lord of hosts.
Strike the shepherd, that the sheep may be
      scattered;
    I will turn my hand against the little ones.
In the whole land, says the Lord,
    two thirds shall be cut off and perish,
    and one third shall be left alive.
And I will put this third into the fire,
    and refine them as one refines silver,
    and test them as gold is tested.
They will call on my name,
    and I will answer them.
I will say, 'They are my people';
    and they will say, 'The Lord is my God.'

Zechariah 13.7–9

But who can endure the day of his coming, and who can stand when he appears?

For he is like a refiner's fire and like fullers' soap; he will sit as a refiner and purifier of silver, and he will purify the sons of Levi and refine them like gold and silver, till they present right offerings to the Lord.

Malachi 3.2–3

God is a consuming fire.

Hebrews 12.29

In this you rejoice, though now for a little while you may have to suffer various trials, so that the genuineness of your faith, more precious than gold which though perishable is tested by fire, may redound to praise and glory and honour at the revelation of Jesus Christ.

1 Peter 1.6–7

Reflection

See also **Meditation**

Consider the wondrous works of God.

Job 37.14

A fool takes no pleasure in understanding,
  but only in expressing his opinion.

Proverbs 18.2

It is not good for a man to be without
    knowledge,
  and he who makes haste with his feet
    misses his way.

Proverbs 19.2

Be not rash with your mouth, nor let your
heart be hasty to utter a word before God,
for God is in heaven, and you upon earth.

Ecclesiastes 5.2

Consider the work of God;
  who can make straight what he has made
    crooked?

Ecclesiastes 7.13

Consider how you have fared.

Haggai 1.7

Reform

See also **Repentance**

A rebuke goes deeper into a man of
    understanding
  than a hundred blows into a fool.

Proverbs 17.10

Blows that wound cleanse away evil;
  strokes make clean the innermost parts.

Proverbs 20.30

Wash yourselves; make yourselves clean;
  remove the evil of your doings
  from before my eyes;
cease to do evil,
  learn to do good;
seek justice,
  correct oppression;
defend the fatherless,
  plead for the widow.

Isaiah 1.16–17

Amend your ways and your doings, and I
will let you dwell in this place.

Jeremiah 7.3

Amend your ways and your doings, and
obey the voice of the Lord your God, and
the Lord will repent of the evil which he has
pronounced against you.

Jeremiah 26.13

Let us test and examine our ways,
  and return to the Lord!
Let us lift up our hearts and hands
  to God in heaven:
'We have transgressed and rebelled,
  and thou hast not forgiven.'

Lamentations 3.40–42

Again, when a wicked man turns away
from the wickedness he has committed and
does what is lawful and right, he shall save
his life.

Ezekiel 18.27

Again, though I say to the wicked, 'You
shall surely die,' yet if he turns from his sin
and does what is lawful and right, if the
wicked restores the pledge, gives back what
he has taken by robbery, and walks in the
statutes of life, committing no iniquity; he
shall surely live, he shall not die. None of
the sins that he has committed shall be
remembered against him; he has done what
is lawful and right, he shall surely live.

Ezekiel 33.14–16

Let man and beast be covered with sackcloth, and let them cry mightily to God;
yea, let every one turn from his evil way
and from the violence which is in his hands.

Jonah 3.8

Brethren, if a man is overtaken in any
trespass, you who are spiritual should restore him in a spirit of gentleness.

Galatians 6.1

Let the thief no longer steal, but rather let
him labour, doing honest work with his
hands, so that he may be able to give to
those in need.

Ephesians 4.28

Regeneration

See also **Revival**

Create in me a clean heart, O God,
and put a new and right spirit within me.

Psalms 51.10

They who wait for the Lord shall renew
their strength.

Isaiah 40.31

And I will give them one heart, and put a
new spirit within them; I will take the stony
heart out of their flesh and give them a
heart of flesh, that they may walk in my
statutes and keep my ordinances and obey
them; and they shall be my people, and I
will be their God.

Ezekiel 11.19–20

Cast away from you all the transgressions
which you have committed . . . and get
yourselves a new heart and a new spirit . . .
I have no pleasure in the death of any one,
says the Lord God; so turn, and live.

Ezekiel 18.31–32

Thus says the Lord God to these bones:
Behold, I will cause breath to enter you,
and you shall live. And I will lay sinews
upon you, and will cause flesh to come
upon you, and cover you with skin, and put
breath in you, and you shall live; and you
shall know that I am the Lord.

Ezekiel 37.5–6

The Lord, your God, is in your midst,
a warrior who gives victory;
he will rejoice over you with gladness,
he will renew you in his love.

Zephaniah 3.17

Truly, I say to you, in the new world,
when the Son of man shall sit on his glorious throne, you who have followed me
will also sit on twelve thrones, judging the
twelve tribes of Israel.

Matthew 19.28

Truly, truly, I say to you, unless one is
born anew, he cannot see the kingdom of
God.

John 3.3

Do you not know that all of us who have
been baptized into Christ Jesus were baptized into his death? We were buried therefore with him by baptism into death, so that
as Christ was raised from the dead by the
glory of the Father, we too might walk in
newness of life.

For if we have been united with him in a
death like his, we shall certainly be united
with him in a resurrection like his. We
know that our old self was crucified with
him so that the sinful body might be destroyed, and we might no longer be enslaved
to sin.

Romans 6.3–6

Do not yield your members to sin as
instruments of wickedness, but yield yourselves to God as men who have been
brought from death to life.

Romans 6.13

Now we are discharged from the law, dead
to that which held us captive, so that we
serve not under the old written code but in
the new life of the Spirit.

Romans 7.6

Do not be conformed to this world but be
transformed by the renewal of your mind,
that you may prove what is the will of God,
what is good and acceptable and perfect.

Romans 12.2

Though our outer nature is wasting away,
our inner nature is being renewed every
day.

2 Corinthians 4.16

Therefore, if any one is in Christ, he is a
new creation; the old has passed away,
behold, the new has come.

2 Corinthians 5.17

Put off your old nature which belongs to
your former manner of life and is corrupt
through deceitful lusts, and be renewed in
the spirit of your minds, and put on the new
nature, created after the likeness of God in
true righteousness and holiness.

Ephesians 4.22–24

Do not lie to one another, seeing that you have put off the old nature with its practices and have put on the new nature, which is being renewed in knowledge after the image of its creator.

Colossians 3.9—10

When the goodness and loving kindness of God our Saviour appeared, he saved us, not because of deeds done by us in righteousness, but in virtue of his own mercy, by the washing of regeneration and renewal in the Holy Spirit, which he poured out upon us richly through Jesus Christ our Saviour.

Titus 3.4—6

You have been born anew, not of perishable seed but of imperishable, through the living and abiding word of God.

1 Peter 1.23

Rehabilitation

Let the thief no longer steal, but rather let him labour, doing honest work with his hands, so that he may be able to give to those in need.

Ephesians 4.28

Rejection

For he grew up before him like a young
    plant . . .
He was despised and rejected by men;
    a man of sorrows, and acquainted with
        grief;
and as one from whom men hide their faces
    he was despised, and we esteemed him
        not.

Isaiah 53.2—3

He who hears you hears me, and he who rejects you rejects me, and he who rejects me rejects him who sent me.

Luke 10.16

I ask, then, has God rejected his people? By no means! I myself am an Israelite, a descendant of Abraham, a member of the tribe of Benjamin. God has not rejected his people whom he foreknew.

Romans 11.1

Rejoicing

See also **Joy**

Praise his people, O you nations;
    for he avenges the blood of his servants,
and takes vengeance on his adversaries,
    and makes expiation for the land of his
        people.

Deuteronomy 32.43

Nehemi'ah . . . said . . . 'This day is holy to the Lord your God; do not mourn or weep.' For all the people wept when they heard the words of the law. Then he said to them, 'Go your way, eat the fat and drink sweet wine and send portions to him for whom nothing is prepared; for this day is holy to our Lord; and do not be grieved, for the joy of the Lord is your strength.'

Nehemiah 8.9—10

But I have trusted in thy steadfast love;
    my heart shall rejoice in thy salvation.
I will sing to the Lord,
    because he has dealt bountifully with me.

Psalms 13.5—6

Be glad in the Lord, and rejoice,
        O righteous,
    and shout for joy, all you upright in
        heart!

Psalms 32.11

Then my soul shall rejoice in the Lord,
    exulting in his deliverance.

Psalms 35.9

But may all who seek thee
    rejoice and be glad in thee;
may those who love thy salvation
    say continually, 'Great is the Lord!'

Psalms 40.16

But let the righteous be joyful;
    let them exult before God;
    let them be jubilant with joy!
Sing to God, sing praises to his name;
    lift up a song to him who rides upon the
        clouds;
    his name is the Lord, exult before him!

Psalms 68.3—4

Gladden the soul of thy servant,
for to thee, O Lord, do I lift up my soul.

Psalms 86.4

The Lord reigns; let the earth rejoice;
let the many coastlands be glad!

Psalms 97.1

Then they cried to the Lord in their
trouble,
and he delivered them from their
distress . . .
Let them thank the Lord for his
steadfast love,
for his wonderful works to the sons
of men!
And let them offer sacrifices of
thanksgiving,
and tell of his deeds in songs of joy!

Psalms 107.19,21–22

The father of the righteous will greatly
rejoice;
he who begets a wise son will be glad in
him.

Proverbs 23.24

Do not rejoice when your enemy falls,
and let not your heart be glad when he
stumbles;
lest the Lord see it, and be displeased,
and turn away his anger from him.

Proverbs 24.17–18

When the righteous triumph, there is great
glory.

Proverbs 28.12

Rejoice, O young man, in your youth, and
let your heart cheer you in the days of your
youth.

Ecclesiastes 11.9

For as a young man marries a virgin,
so shall your sons marry you,
and as the bridegroom rejoices over the
bride,
so shall your God rejoice over you.

Isaiah 62.5

For behold, I create new heavens and a
new earth;
and the former things shall not be
remembered

or come into mind.
But be glad and rejoice for ever in that
which I create.

Isaiah 65.17–18

Blessed are you when men hate you, and
when they exclude you and revile you, and
cast out your name as evil, on account of
the Son of man! Rejoice in that day, and
leap for joy, for behold, your reward is
great in heaven.

Luke 6.22–23

Rejoice in the Lord.

Philippians 3.1

Without having seen him you love him;
though you do not now see him you believe
in him and rejoice with unutterable and
exalted joy. As the outcome of your faith
you obtain the salvation of your souls.

1 Peter 1.8–9

Rejuvenation

Bless the Lord, O my soul,
and forget not all his benefits,
who forgives all your iniquity,
who heals all your diseases,
who redeems your life from the Pit,
who crowns you with steadfast love and
mercy,
who satisfies you with good as long as you
live
so that your youth is renewed like the
eagle's.

Psalms 103.2–5

Remembrance

My heart goes out to the commanders of
Israel
who offered themselves willingly among
the people.
Bless the Lord.

Judges 5.9

For of the wise man as of the fool there is
no enduring remembrance, seeing that in
the days to come all will have been long

forgotten. How the wise man dies just like the fool! So I hated life, because what is done under the sun was grievous to me; for all is vanity and a striving after wind.

Ecclesiastes 2.16–17

When he had given thanks, he broke it, and said, 'This is my body which is for you. Do this in remembrance of me.' In the same way also the cup, after supper, saying, 'This cup is the new covenant in my blood. Do this, as often as you drink it, in remembrance of me.' For as often as you eat this bread and drink the cup, you proclaim the Lord's death until he comes.

1 Corinthians 11.24–26

Remorse

See also **Confession, Penitence, Repentance**

O my God, I am ashamed and blush to lift my face to thee, my God, for our iniquities have risen higher than our heads, and our guilt has mounted up to the heavens.

Ezra 9.6

O Lord, rebuke me not in thy anger,
   nor chasten me in thy wrath!
For thy arrows have sunk into me,
   and thy hand has come down on me.
There is no soundness in my flesh
   because of thy indignation;
there is no health in my bones
   because of my sin.
For my iniquities have gone over my head;
   they weigh like a burden too heavy
      for me . . .
For I am ready to fall,
   and my pain is ever with me.
I confess my iniquity,
   I am sorry for my sin.

Psalms 38.1–4,17

Have mercy on me, O God, according to
   thy steadfast love;
   according to thy abundant mercy blot out
      my transgressions.
Wash me thoroughly from my iniquity, and
   cleanse me from my sin!
For I know my transgressions, and my sin is
   ever before me.

Psalms 51.1–3

The sacrifice acceptable to God is a broken
   spirit;
   a broken and contrite heart, O God, thou
      wilt not despise.

Psalms 51.17

For thus says the high and lofty One
   who inhabits eternity, whose name
      is Holy:
'I dwell in the high and holy place,
   and also with him who is of a contrite and
      humble spirit,
to revive the spirit of the humble,
   and to revive the heart of the contrite.'

Isaiah 57.15

Behold, O Lord, for I am in distress,
   my soul is in tumult,
my heart is wrung within me,
   because I have been very rebellious.

Lamentations 1.20

You shall remember your ways and all the doings with which you have polluted yourselves; and you shall loathe yourselves for all the evils that you have committed. And you shall know that I am the Lord.

Ezekiel 20.43–44

Cleanse your hands, you sinners, and purify your hearts, you men of double mind. Be wretched and mourn and weep. Let your laughter be turned to mourning and your joy to dejection. Humble yourselves before the Lord and he will exalt you.

James 4.8–10

Renewal

Do not be conformed to this world but be transformed by the renewal of your mind, that you may prove what is the will of God, what is good and acceptable and perfect.

Romans 12.2

Though our outer nature is wasting away, our inner nature is being renewed every day.

2 Corinthians 4.16

Do not lie to one another, seeing that you have put off the old nature with its practices and have put on the new nature, which

being renewed in knowledge after the
image of its creator.

Colossians 3.9–10

Repentance

See also **Confession, Penitence, Remorse**

If my people who are called by my name
humble themselves, and pray and seek my
face, and turn from their wicked ways, then
I will hear from heaven, and will forgive
their sin and heal their land.

2 Chronicles 7.14

Do not be like your fathers and your
brethren, who were faithless to the Lord
God of their fathers, so that he made them
a desolation, as you see. Do not now be
stiff-necked as your fathers were, but yield
yourselves to the Lord, and come to his
sanctuary, which he has sanctified for ever,
and serve the Lord your God, that his fierce
anger may turn away from you. For if you
return to the Lord, your brethren and your
children will find compassion . . . For the
Lord your God is gracious and merciful,
and will not turn away his face from you.

2 Chronicles 30.7–9

If you return to me and keep my commandments and do them, though your dis-
persed be under the farthest skies, I will
gather them thence and bring them to the
place which I have chosen, to make my
name dwell there.

Nehemiah 1.9

If a man does not repent, God will whet his
sword;
  he has bent and strung his bow;
he has prepared his deadly weapons,
  making his arrows fiery shafts.

Psalms 7.12–13

The sacrifice acceptable to God is a broken
spirit;
  a broken and contrite heart, O God, thou
wilt not despise.

Psalms 51.17

When I think of thy ways,
  I turn my feet to thy testimonies.

Psalms 119.59

Seek the Lord while he may be found,
  call upon him while he is near;
let the wicked forsake his way,
  and the unrighteous man his thoughts;
let him return to the Lord, that he may
    have mercy on him,
  and to our God, for he will abundantly
    pardon.

Isaiah 55.6–7

If that nation, concerning which I have
spoken, turns from its evil, I will repent of
the evil that I intended to do to it.

Jeremiah 18.8

Amend your ways and your doings, and
obey the voice of the Lord your God, and
the Lord will repent of the evil which he has
pronounced against you.

Jeremiah 26.13

Have I any pleasure in the death of the
wicked, says the Lord God, and not rather
that he should turn from his way and live?

Ezekiel 18.23

When a wicked man turns away from the
wickedness he has committed and does
what is lawful and right, he shall save his
life. Because he has considered and turned
away from all transgressions which he had
committed, he shall surely live, he shall not
die.

Ezekiel 18.27–28

Repent and turn from all your transgressions, lest iniquity be your ruin. Cast
away from you all the transgressions which
you have committed against me, and get
yourselves a new heart and a new spirit!

Ezekiel 18.30–31

Turn back, turn back from your evil ways;
for why will you die, O house of Israel?

Ezekiel 33.11

Shall I ransom them from the power
    of Sheol?
  Shall I redeem them from Death?

Hosea 13.14

Return to the Lord, your God,
  for he is gracious and merciful,

slow to anger, and abounding in steadfast
love,
    and repents of evil.

Joel 2.13

Let man and beast be covered with sackcloth, and let them cry mightily to God;
yea, let every one turn from his evil way
and from the violence which is in his hands.

Jonah 3.8

Return to me, and I will return to you,
says the Lord of hosts.

Malachi 3.7

Repent, for the kingdom of heaven is at
hand.

Matthew 3.2

Bear fruit that befits repentance.

Matthew 3.8

The time is fulfilled, and the kingdom of
God is at hand; repent, and believe in the
gospel.

Mark 1.15

And Jesus answered them, 'Those who are
well have no need of a physician, but those
who are sick; I have not come to call the
righteous, but sinners to repentance.'

Luke 5.31–32

Unless you repent you will all likewise
perish.

Luke 13.3

So he told them this parable: 'What man of
you, having a hundred sheep, if he has lost
one of them, does not leave the ninety-nine
in the wilderness, and go after the one
which is lost, until he finds it? And when he
has found it, he lays it on his shoulders,
rejoicing. And when he comes home, he
calls together his friends and his neighbours, saying to them, "Rejoice with me,
for I have found my sheep which was lost."
Just so, I tell you, there will be more joy in
heaven over one sinner who repents than
over ninety-nine righteous persons who
need no repentance.
'Or what woman, having ten silver coins,
if she loses one coin, does not light a lamp
and sweep the house and seek diligently
until she finds it? And when she has found
it, she calls together her friends and neighbours, saying, "Rejoice with me, for I have
found the coin which I had lost." Just so, I
tell you, there is joy before the angels of
God over one sinner who repents.'
And he said, 'There was a man who had
two sons; and the youngest of them said to
his father, "Father, give me the share of
property that falls to me." And he divided
his living between them. Not many days
later, the younger son gathered all he had
and took his journey into a far country, and
there he squandered his property in loose
living. And when he had spent everything,
a great famine arose in that country, and he
began to be in want. So he went and joined
himself to one of the citizens of that country, who sent him into his fields to feed
swine. And he would gladly have fed on the
pods that the swine ate; and no one gave
him anything. But when he came to himself
he said, "How many of my father's hired
servants have bread enough and to spare,
but I perish here with hunger! I will arise
and go to my father, and I will say to him,
'Father, I have sinned against heaven and
before you; I am no longer worthy to be
called your son; treat me as one of your
hired servants.' " And he arose and came to
his father. But while he was yet at a dis-
tance, his father saw him and had compassion, and ran and embraced him and
kissed him. And the son said to him,
"Father, I have sinned against heaven and
before you; I am no longer worthy to be
called your son." But the father said to his
servants, "Bring quickly the best robe, and
put it on him; and put a ring on his hand
and shoes on his feet; and bring the fatted
calf and kill it, and let us eat and make
merry; for this my son was dead, and is
alive again; he was lost, and is found." And
they began to make merry.
'Now his elder son was in the field; and
as he came and drew near to the house, he
heard music and dancing. And he called
one of the servants and asked what this
meant. And he said to him, "Your brother
has come, and your father has killed the
fatted calf, because he has received him
safe and sound." But he was angry an

refused to go in. His father came out and entreated him, but he answered his father, "Lo, these many years I have served you, and I never disobeyed your command; yet you never gave me a kid, that I might make merry with my friends. But when this son of yours came, who has devoured your living with harlots, you killed for him the fatted calf!" And he said to him, "Son, you are always with me, and all that is mine is yours. It was fitting to make merry and be glad, for this your brother was dead, and is alive; he was lost, and is found." '

Luke 15.3—32

Thus it is written . . . that repentance and forgiveness of sins should be preached in his name to all nations.

Luke 24.46—47

Repent, and be baptized every one of you in the name of Jesus Christ for the forgiveness of your sins; and you shall receive the gift of the Holy Spirit.

Acts 2.38

Repent therefore, and turn again, that your sins may be blotted out, that times of refreshing may come from the presence of the Lord.

Acts 3.19

You have neither part nor lot in this matter, for your heart is not right before God. Repent therefore of this wickedness of yours, and pray to the Lord that, if possible, the intent of your heart may be forgiven you.

Acts 8.21—22

The times of ignorance God overlooked, but now he commands all men everywhere to repent, because he has fixed a day on which he will judge the world in righteousness.

Acts 17.30—31

I was not disobedient to the heavenly vision, but declared . . . that they should repent and turn to God and perform deeds worthy of their repentance.

Acts 26.19—20

Do you not know that God's kindness is meant to lead you to repentance?

Romans 2.4

Cleanse your hands, you sinners, and purify your hearts, you men of double mind. Be wretched and mourn and weep. Let your laughter be turned to mourning and your joy to dejection.

James 4.8—9

The Lord is not slow about his promise as some count slowness, but is forbearing toward you, not wishing that any should perish, but that all should reach repentance.

2 Peter 3.9

Reproach

He who forgives an offence seeks love,
　but he who repeats a matter alienates a
　　friend.

Proverbs 17.9

Reputation

The works of his hands are faithful and
　　just;
　all his precepts are trustworthy,
they are established for ever and ever . . .
He sent redemption to his people;
　he has commanded his covenant for ever.
　Holy and terrible is his name!

Psalms 111.7—9

Let not loyalty and faithfulness forsake
　　you;
　bind them about your neck,
　write them on the tablet of your heart.
So you will find favour and good repute
　in the sight of God and man.

Proverbs 3.3—4

The memory of the righteous is a blessing,
　but the name of the wicked will rot.

Proverbs 10.7

A good name is to be chosen rather than
　　great riches,
　and favour is better than silver or gold.

Proverbs 22.1

A good name is better than precious ointment.

Ecclesiastes 7.1

Woe to you, when all men speak well of you, for so their fathers did to the false prophets.

Luke 6.26

Have this mind among yourselves, which is yours in Christ Jesus, who, though he was in the form of God, did not count equality with God a thing to be grasped, but emptied himself, taking the form of a servant, being born in the likeness of men. And being found in human form he humbled himself and became obedient unto death, even death on a cross. Therefore God has highly exalted him and bestowed on him the name which is above every name.

Philippians 2.5—9

Rescue

See also **Redemption**

He sets on high those who are lowly,
  and those who mourn are lifted to safety.
He frustrates the devices of the crafty,
  so that their hands achieve no success.

Job 5.11—12

Deliverance belongs to the Lord;
  thy blessing be upon thy people!

Psalms 3.8

Many are the afflictions of the righteous;
  but the Lord delivers him out of them all.

Psalms 34.19

How long, O Lord, wilt thou look on?
  Rescue me from their ravages,
  my life from the lions!

Psalms 35.17

My vows to thee I must perform, O God;
  I will render thank offerings to thee.
For thou has delivered my soul from death,
  yea, my feet from falling,
that I may walk before God
  in the light of life.

Psalms 56.12—13

Deliver us, and forgive our sins,
  for thy name's sake!

Psalms 79.9

He who dwells in the shelter of the Most High,
  who abides in the shadow of the Almighty,
will say to the Lord, 'My refuge and my fortress;
  my God, in whom I trust.'
For he will deliver you from the snare of the fowler
  and from the deadly pestilence;
he will cover you with his pinions,
  and under his wings you will find refuge.

Psalms 91.1—4

He sent redemption to his people;
  he has commanded his covenant for ever.
  Holy and terrible is his name!

Psalms 111.9

Rescue those who are being taken away to death;
  hold back those who are stumbling to the slaughter.
If you say, 'Behold, we did not know this,'
  does not he who weighs the heart
  perceive it?

Proverbs 24.11—12

He who is bowed down shall speedily be released;
  he shall not die and go down to the Pit,
  neither shall his bread fail.
For I am the Lord your God.

Isaiah 51.14—15

And lead us not into temptation,
  But deliver us from evil.

Matthew 6.13

Who will deliver me from this body of death? Thanks be to God through Jesus Christ our Lord!

Romans 7.24—25

He delivered us from so deadly a peril and he will deliver us; on him we have set our hope that he will deliver us again.

2 Corinthians 1.1

Our Lord Jesus Christ . . . gave himself for our sins to deliver us from the present evil age, according to the will of our God and Father.

Galatians 1.4

The Lord will rescue me from every evil and save me for his heavenly kingdom.

2 Timothy 4.18

My brethren, if any one among you wanders from the truth and some one brings him back, let him know that whoever brings back a sinner from the error of his way will save his soul from death and will cover a multitude of sins.

James 5.19–20

He who saved a people out of the land of Egypt, afterward destroyed those who did not believe.

Jude 5

And convince some, who doubt; save some, by snatching them out of the fire.

Jude 22–23

Resignation

See also **Patience**

Behold, happy is the man whom God
  reproves;
  therefore despise not the chastening of
  the Almighty.

Job 5.17

My son, do not despise the Lord's discipline or be weary of his reproof,
for the Lord reproves him whom he loves.

Proverbs 3.11–12

Who has commanded and it came to pass,
  unless the Lord has ordained it?
Is it not from the mouth of the Most High
  that good and evil come?
Why should a living man complain?

Lamentations 3.37–39

My Father, if it be possible, let this cup
pass from me; nevertheless, not as I will,
but as thou wilt.

Matthew 26.39

Rejoice in your hope, be patient in tribulation, be constant in prayer.

Romans 12.12

Do all things without grumbling or questioning.

Philippians 2.14

Resilience

For the righteous will never be moved;
  he will be remembered for ever.
He is not afraid of evil tidings;
  his heart is firm, trusting in the Lord.
His heart is steady, he will not be afraid,
  until he sees his desire on his adversaries.

Psalms 112.6–8

Respect

See also **Reverence**

Do not come near; put off your shoes from your feet, for the place on which you are standing is holy ground.

Exodus 3.5

Honour your father and your mother, that your days may be long in the land which the Lord your God gives you.

Exodus 20.12

You shall rise up before the hoary head, and honour the face of an old man, and you shall fear your God.

Leviticus 19.32

Have regard for thy covenant.

Psalms 74.20

He who pursues righteousness and kindness will find life and honour.

Proverbs 21.21

Do not put yourself forward in the king's
  presence
  or stand in the place of the great.

Proverbs 25.6

What is exalted among men is an abomination in the sight of God.

Luke 16.15

For Jesus himself testified that a prophet has no honour in his own country.

John 4.44

If any one serves me, the Father will honour him.

John 12.26

God has shown me that I should not call any man common or unclean.

Acts 10.28

Love one another with brotherly affection; outdo one another in showing honour.

Romans 12.10

Pay all of them their dues, taxes to whom taxes are due, revenue to whom revenue is due, respect to whom respect is due, honour to whom honour is due.

Romans 13.7

Do nothing from selfishness or conceit, but in humility count others better than yourselves. Let each of you look not only to his own interests, but also to the interests of others.

Philippians 2.3–4

Those who serve well as deacons gain a good standing for themselves.

1 Timothy 3.13

Do not rebuke an older man but exhort him as you would a father; treat younger men like brothers, older women like mothers, younger women like sisters, in all purity.

1 Timothy 5.1–2

Honour all men. Love the brotherhood. Fear God. Honour the emperor.

1 Peter 2.17

Responsibility

The Lord God took the man and put him in the garden of Eden to till it and keep it.

Genesis 2.15

Then the Lord said to Cain, 'Where is Abel your brother?' He said, 'I do not know; am I my brother's keeper?'

Genesis 4.9

The fathers shall not be put to death for the children, nor shall the children be put to death for the fathers; every man shall be put to death for his own sin.

Deuteronomy 24.16

A righteous man has regard for the life of
 his beast,
 but the mercy of the wicked is cruel.

Proverbs 12.10

The soul that sins shall die. The son shall not suffer for the iniquity of the father, nor the father suffer for the iniquity of the son.

Ezekiel 18.20

On the day of judgment men will render account for every careless word they utter; for by your words you will be justified, and by your words you will be condemned.

Matthew 12.36–37

For it will be as when a man going on a journey called his servants and entrusted to them his property; to one he gave five talents, to another two, to another one, to each according to his ability. Then he went away . . . Now after a long time the master of those servants came and settled accounts with them. And he who had received the five talents came forward, bringing five talents more . . . His master said to him, 'Well done, good and faithful servant; you have been faithful over a little, I will set you over much.'

Matthew 25.14–15,19–21

He who is faithful in a very little is faithful also in much; and he who is dishonest in a very little is dishonest also in much. If then you have not been faithful in the unrighteous mammon, who will entrust to you the true riches? And if you have not been faithful in that which is another's, who will give you that which is your own?

Luke 16.10–12

Having gifts that differ according to the grace given to us, let us use them: if prophecy, in proportion to our faith; if service, in our serving; he who teaches, in his teaching.

Romans 12.6−7

For there is no authority except from God, and those that exist have been instituted by God. Therefore he who resists the authorities resists what God has appointed . . . For rulers are not a terror to good conduct, but to bad.

Romans 13.1−3

We are God's fellow workers; you are God's field, God's building.

1 Corinthians 3.9

This is how one should regard us, as servants of Christ and stewards of the mysteries of God. Moreover it is required of stewards that they be found trustworthy.

1 Corinthians 4.1−2

Each man will have to bear his own load.

Galatians 6.5

If any one does not provide for his relatives, and especially for his own family, he has disowned the faith and is worse than an unbeliever.

1 Timothy 5.8

Guard what has been entrusted to you.

1 Timothy 6.20

As each has received a gift, employ it for one another, as good stewards of God's varied grace.

1 Peter 4.10

Tend the flock of God that is your charge, not by constraint but willingly.

1 Peter 5.2

Rest

see also **Leisure, Sabbath**

Six days shall work be done; but on the seventh day is a sabbath of solemn rest, a holy convocation; you shall do no work.

Leviticus 23.3

For God alone my soul waits in silence.

Psalms 62.1

Better is a handful of quietness than two hands full of toil.

Ecclesiastes 4.6

Give rest to the weary.

Isaiah 28.12

For thus says the Lord God, the Holy One of Israel,
  'In returning and rest you shall be saved.'

Isaiah 30.15

Thus says the Lord:
  'Stand by the roads, and look,
  and ask for the ancient paths,
where the good way is; and walk in it,
  and find rest for your souls.'

Jeremiah 6.16

Come to me, all who labour and are heavy laden, and I will give you rest. Take my yoke upon you, and learn from me; for I am gentle and lowly in heart, and you will find rest for your souls. For my yoke is easy, and my burden is light.

Matthew 11.28−30

So then, there remains a sabbath rest for the people of God; for whoever enters God's rest also ceases from his labours as God did from his. Let us therefore strive to enter that rest.

Hebrews 4.9−11

Blessed are the dead who die in the Lord henceforth. 'Blessed indeed,' says the Spirit, 'that they may rest from their labours, for their deeds follow them!'

Revelation 14.13

Restitution

If a man steals an ox or a sheep, and kills it or sells it, he shall pay five oxen for an ox, and four sheep for a sheep. He shall make restitution; if he has nothing, then he shall be sold for his theft. If the stolen beast is found alive in his possession, whether it is an ox or an ass or a sheep, he shall pay double.

Exodus 22.1–2

Zacchae'us stood and said to the Lord, 'Behold, Lord, the half of my goods I give to the poor; and if I have defrauded any one of anything, I restore it fourfold.'

Luke 19.8–9

Resurrection

For I know that my Redeemer lives,
   and at last he will stand upon the earth;
and after my skin has been thus destroyed,
   then from my flesh I shall see God.

Job 19.25–26

Therefore my heart is glad, and my soul
   rejoices;
   my body also dwells secure.
For thou dost not give me up to Sheol,
   or let thy godly one see the Pit.

Psalms 16.9–10

He will swallow up death for ever.

Isaiah 25.8

Thy dead shall live, their bodies shall rise.
   O dwellers in the dust, awake and sing
      for joy!
For thy dew is a dew of light,
   and on the land of the shades thou wilt
      let it fall.

Isaiah 26.19

Thus says the Lord God to these bones: 'Behold, I will cause breath to enter you, and you shall live. And I will lay sinews upon you . . . and cover you with skin, and put breath in you, and you shall live; and you shall know that I am the Lord.' . . . and the bones came together, bone to its bone. And as I looked, there were sinews on them, and flesh had come upon them . . . and the breath came into them, and they lived, and stood upon their feet . . . Then he said to me, 'Son of man, these bones are the whole house of Israel.'

Ezekiel 37.5–8,10–11

And many of those who sleep in the dust of the earth shall awake, some to everlasting life, and some to shame and everlasting contempt.

Daniel 12.2

But for you who fear my name the sun of righteousness shall rise, with healing in its wings.

Malachi 4.2

But Jesus answered them, 'You are wrong, because you know neither the scriptures nor the power of God. For in the resurrection they neither marry nor are given in marriage, but are like angels in heaven. And as for the resurrection of the dead, have you not read what was said to you by God, "I am the God of Abraham, and the God of Isaac, and the God of Jacob"? He is not God of the dead, but of the living.'

Matthew 22.29–32

The hour is coming when all who are in the tombs will hear his voice and come forth, those who have done good, to the resurrection of life, and those who have done evil, to the resurrection of judgment.

John 5.28–29

Jesus said to her, 'I am the resurrection and the life; he who believes in me, though he die, yet shall he live, and whoever lives and believes in me shall never die.'

John 11.25–26

Yet a little while, and the world will see me no more, but you will see me; because I live, you will live also.

John 14.19

But this I admit to you, that according to the Way, which they call a sect, I worship the God of our fathers, believing everything laid down by the law or written in the prophets, having a hope in God which these themselves accept, that there will be a resurrection of both the just and the unjust.

Acts 24.14–15

Why is is thought incredible by any of you that God raises the dead?

Acts 26.8

For if we have been united with him in a death like his, we shall certainly be united with him in a resurrection like his . . . But if we have died with Christ, we believe that we shall also live with him. For we know that Christ being raised from the dead will never die again; death no longer has dominion over him. The death he died he died to sin, once for all, but the life he lives he lives to God.

Romans 6.5,8−10

He who raised Christ Jesus from the dead will give life to your mortal bodies also through his Spirit which dwells in you.

Romans 8.11

But if there is no resurrection of the dead, then Christ has not been raised; if Christ has not been raised, then our preaching is in vain and your faith is in vain . . .

But in fact Christ has been raised from the dead, the first fruits of those who have fallen asleep. For as by a man came death, by a man has come also the resurrection of the dead. For as in Adam all die, so also in Christ shall all be made alive.

1 Corinthians 15.13−14,20−22

What is sown is perishable, what is raised imperishable. It is sown in dishonour, it is raised in glory. It is sown in weakness, it is raised in power. It is sown a physical body, is raised a spiritual body.

1 Corinthians 15.41−44

The dead will be raised imperishable.

1 Corinthians 15.52

When the perishable puts on the imperishable, and the mortal puts on immortality, then shall come to pass the saying that is written: 'Death is swallowed up in victory.'

1 Corinthians 15.54

God . . . raises the dead.

2 Corinthians 1.10

He who raised the Lord Jesus will raise us so with Jesus.

2 Corinthians 4.14

For he who sows to his own flesh will from the flesh reap corruption; but he who sows to the Spirit will from the Spirit reap eternal life.

Galatians 6.8

And the dead in Christ will rise first; then we who are alive, who are left, shall be caught up together with them in the clouds to meet the Lord in the air.

1 Thessalonians 4.16−17

Christ Jesus . . . abolished death and brought life and immortality to light through the gospel.

2 Timothy 1.10

Blessed be the God and Father of our Lord Jesus Christ! By his great mercy we have been born anew to a living hope through the resurrection of Jesus Christ from the dead, and to an inheritance which is imperishable, undefiled, and unfading, kept in heaven for you.

1 Peter 1.3−4

Reticence

He who belittles his neighbour lacks sense, but a man of understanding remains silent.

Proverbs 11.12

The vexation of a fool is known at once, but the prudent man ignores an insult.

Proverbs 12.16

A prudent man conceals his knowledge, but fools proclaim their folly.

Proverbs 12.23

He who guards his mouth preserves his life; he who opens wide his lips comes to ruin.

Proverbs 13.3

He who restrains his words has knowledge, and he who has a cool spirit is a man of understanding.

Proverbs 17.27

He who keeps his mouth and his tongue
keeps himself out of trouble.

Proverbs 21.23

For lack of wood the fire goes out;
and where there is no whisperer,
quarrelling ceases.

Proverbs 26.20

Be not rash with your mouth, nor let your
heart be hasty to utter a word before God,
for God is in heaven, and you upon earth;
therefore let your words be few.

Ecclesiastes 5.2

Therefore he who is prudent will keep
silent in such a time;
for it is an evil time.

Amos 5.13

Let every man be quick to hear, slow to
speak, slow to anger, for the anger of man
does not work the righteousness of God.

James 1.19–20

Retort

The north wind brings forth rain;
and a backbiting tongue, angry looks.

Proverbs 25.23

Retribution

Your eye shall not pity; it shall be life for
life, eye for eye, tooth for tooth, hand for
hand, foot for foot.

Deuteronomy 19.21

The wrath of God is revealed . . . against
all . . . who by their wickedness suppress
the truth.

Romans 1.18

Revelation

The heavens are telling the glory of God;
and the firmament proclaims his
handiwork.
Day to day pours forth speech,
and night to night declares knowledge.
There is no speech, nor are there words;

their voice is not heard;
yet their voice goes out through all the
earth,
and their words to the end of the world.

Psalms 19.1–4

There is a God in heaven who reveals
mysteries.

Daniel 2.28

Surely the Lord God does nothing,
without revealing his secret.

Amos 3.7

Nothing is covered that will not be revealed, or hidden that will not be known.

Matthew 10.26

The words that I have spoken to you are
spirit and life.

John 6.63

He who has my commandments and keeps
them, he it is who loves me; and he who
loves me will be loved by my Father, and I
will love him and manifest myself to him.

John 14.21

Now to him who is able to strengthen you
according to my gospel and the preaching of
Jesus Christ, according to the revelation of
the mystery which was kept secret for long
ages but is now disclosed and through the
prophetic writings is made known to all
nations, according to the command of the
eternal God, to bring about the obedience
of faith — to the only wise God be glory for
evermore through Jesus Christ!

Romans 16.25–27

Revenge

See also **Vengeance**

You shall not take vengeance.

Leviticus 19.18

When a man causes a disfigurement in his
neighbour, as he has done it shall be done
to him, fracture for fracture, eye for eye,
tooth for tooth; as he has disfigured a man
he shall be disfigured.

Leviticus 24.19–20

Vengeance is mine, and recompense.

Deuteronomy 32.35

Do not say, 'I will repay evil';
  wait for the Lord, and he will help you.

Proverbs 20.22

Do not say, 'I will do to him as he has
      done to me;
  I will pay the man back for what he has
      done.'

Proverbs 24.29

The Lord is a jealous God and avenging,
  the Lord is avenging and wrathful;
the Lord takes vengeance on his adversaries
  and keeps wrath for his enemies.

Nahum 1.2

You have heard that it was said, 'An eye
for an eye and a tooth for a tooth.' But I
say to you, Do not resist one who is evil.
But if any one strikes you on the right
cheek, turn to him the other also.

Matthew 5.38–39

Repay no one evil for evil.

Romans 12.17

Beloved, never avenge yourselves, but
leave it to the wrath of God; for it is
written, 'Vengeance is mine, I will repay,
says the Lord.'

Romans 12.19

See that none of you repays evil for evil,
but always seek to do good to one another
and to all.

1 Thessalonians 5.15

Reverence

See also **Godliness, Respect**

You shall not profane my holy name, but I
will be hallowed among the people of
Israel.

Leviticus 22.32

Gather the people to me, that I may let
them hear my words, so that they may learn
to fear me all the days that they live upon

the earth, and that they may teach their
children so.

Deuteronomy 4.10

Fear the Lord your God, you and your son
and your son's son, by keeping all his
statutes and his commandments, which I
command you, all the days of your life . . .
that your days may be prolonged.

Deuteronomy 6.2

You shall fear the Lord your God; you
shall serve him and cleave to him, and by
his name you shall swear.

Deuteronomy 10.20

Fear the Lord, and serve him in sincerity
and in faithfulness.

Joshua 24.14

Those who honour me I will honour, and
those who despise me shall be lightly
esteemed.

1 Samuel 2.30

Worship the Lord in holy array;
  tremble before him, all the earth.

1 Chronicles 16.29

Behold, the fear of the Lord, that is
      wisdom;
  and to depart from evil is understanding.

Job 28.28

The friendship of the Lord is for those who
      fear him,
  and he makes known to them his
      covenant.

Psalms 25.14

The fear of the Lord is the beginning of
knowledge.

Proverbs 1.7

The fear of the Lord is hatred of evil.

Proverbs 8.13

The fear of the Lord leads to life;
  and he who has it rests satisfied;
  he will not be visited by harm.

Proverbs 19.23

Fear God, and keep his commandments; for this is the whole duty of man.

Ecclesiastes 12.13

I will make with them an everlasting covenant, that I will not turn away from doing good to them; and I will put the fear of me in their hearts, that they may not turn from me.

Jeremiah 32.40

Be silent, all flesh, before the Lord; for he has roused himself from his holy dwelling.

Zechariah 2.13

Let us cleanse ourselves from every defilement of body and spirit, and make holiness perfect in the fear of God.

2 Corinthians 7.1

Work out your own salvation with fear and trembling.

Philippians 2.12

Reversal

How are the mighty fallen!

2 Samuel 1.19

Revival

I dwell in the high and holy place,
and also with him who is of a contrite and
humble spirit,
to revive the spirit of the humble,
and to revive the heart of the contrite.

Isaiah 57.15

Reward

See also **Wages**

Therefore you shall do my statutes, and keep my ordinances and perform them; so you will dwell in the land securely.

Leviticus 25.18

The Lord recompense you for what you have done, and a full reward be given you

by the Lord, the God of Israel, under whose wings you have come to take refuge!

Ruth 2.12

The Lord requite the evildoer according to his wickedness!

2 Samuel 3.39

Take courage! Do not let your hands be weak, for your work shall be rewarded.

2 Chronicles 15.7

As for me, I shall behold thy face in
righteousness;
when I awake, I shall be satisfied with
beholding thy form.

Psalms 17.15

The ordinances of the Lord are true,
and righteous altogether . . .
in keeping them there is great reward.

Psalms 19.9,11

Love the Lord, all you his saints!
The Lord preserves the faithful,
but abundantly requites him who acts
haughtily.

Psalms 31.23

Evil shall slay the wicked;
and those who hate the righteous will be
condemned.
The Lord redeems the life of his servants;
none of those who take refuge in him will
be condemned.

Psalms 34.21–22

I have been young, and now am old;
yet I have not seen the righteous forsaken
or his children begging bread.

Psalms 37.25

The righteous shall be preserved for ever,
but the children of the wicked shall be
cut off.
The righteous shall possess the land,
and dwell upon it for ever.

Psalms 37.28–29

Rise up, O judge of the earth;
render to the proud their deserts!

Psalms 94.2

Lo, sons are a heritage from the Lord,
   the fruit of the womb a reward.

Psalms 127.3

The wage of the righteous leads to life.

Proverbs 10.16

One who sows righteousness gets a sure
reward.

Proverbs 11.18

Misfortune pursues sinners,
   but prosperity rewards the righteous.

Proverbs 13.21

To the eunuchs who keep my sabbaths,
   who choose the things that please me and
      hold fast my covenant,
I will give in my house and within my walls
      a monument and a name
   better than sons and daughters.

Isaiah 56.4–5

Keep your voice from weeping,
   and your eyes from tears;
for your work shall be rewarded.

Jeremiah 31.16

As you have done, it shall be done to you,
   your deeds shall return on your
      own head.

Obadiah 15

Blessed are you when men revile you and
persecute you and utter all kinds of evil
against you falsely on my account. Rejoice
and be glad, for your reward is great in
heaven.

Matthew 5.11–12

For the Son of man is to come with his
angels in the glory of his Father, and then
he will repay every man for what he has
done.

Matthew 16.27

For to every one who has will more be
given, and he will have abundance; but
from him who has not, even what he has
will be taken away.

Matthew 25.29

Go, sell what you have, and give to the
poor, and you will have treasure in heaven.

Mark 10.21

Each shall receive his wages according to
his labour.

1 Corinthians 3.8

Whatever your task, work heartily, as
serving the Lord and not men, knowing that
from the Lord you will receive the inheritance as your reward.

Colossians 3.23–24

Without faith it is impossible to please
him. For whoever would draw near to God
must believe that he exists and that he
rewards those who seek him.

Hebrews 11.6

Jesus the pioneer . . . for the joy that was
set before him endured the cross . . . and is
seated at the right hand of the throne of
God.

Hebrews 12.2

Be the more zealous to confirm your call
and election, for if you do this you will
never fall; so there will be richly provided
for you an entrance into the eternal kingdom of our Lord and Saviour Jesus Christ.

2 Peter 1.10–11

Riches

See also **Money, Possessions, Wealth**

Thine, O Lord, is the greatness . . . Both
riches and honour come from thee, and
thou rulest over all.

1 Chronicles 29.11–12

Better is a little that the righteous has
   than the abundance of many wicked.

Psalms 37.16

Why should I fear in times of trouble,
   when the iniquity of my persecutors
      surrounds me,
men who trust in their wealth
   and boast of the abundance of their
      riches?

Truly no man can ransom himself,
    or give to God the price of his life.

                                Psalms 49.5—7

Why do you boast, O mighty man,
    of mischief done against the godly? . . .
God will break you down for ever;
    he will snatch and tear you from your
        tent;
    he will uproot you from the land of the
        living.
The righteous shall see, and fear, and shall
        laugh at him, saying,
'See the man who would not make God
        his refuge,
    but trusted in the abundance of his
        riches,
    and sought refuge in his wealth!'

                                Psalms 52.1,5—7

If riches increase, set not your heart on
them.

                                Psalms 62.10

Praise the Lord.
    Blessed is the man who fears the Lord,
    who greatly delights in his
        commandments!
His descendants will be mighty in the land;
    the generation of the upright will be
        blessed.
Wealth and riches are in his house;
    and his righteousness endures for ever.

                                Psalms 112.1—3

In the way of thy testimonies I delight
    as much as in all riches.

                                Psalms 119.14

Happy is the man who finds wisdom . . .
Long life is in her right hand;
    in her left hand are riches and honour.

                                Proverbs 3.13,16

The blessing of the Lord makes rich,
    and he adds no sorrow with it.

                                Proverbs 10.22

Riches do not profit in the day of wrath,
    but righteousness delivers from death.

                                Proverbs 11.4

He who trusts in his riches will wither.

                                Proverbs 11.28

One man pretends to be rich, yet has
        nothing;
    another pretends to be poor, yet has
        great wealth.

                                Proverbs 13.7

The reward for humility and fear of the
        Lord
    is riches and honour and life.

                                Proverbs 22.4

By wisdom a house is built,
    and by understanding it is established;
by knowledge the rooms are filled
    with all precious and pleasant riches.

                                Proverbs 24.3—4

Riches do not last for ever.

                                Proverbs 27.24

Every man also to whom God has given
wealth and possessions and power to enjoy
them, and to accept his lot and find enjoyment in his toil — this is the gift of God.

                                Ecclesiastes 5.19

I will give you the treasures of darkness
    and the hoards in secret places,
that you may know that it is I, the Lord.

                                Isaiah 45.3

Like the partridge that gathers a brood
        which she did not hatch,
so is he who gets riches but not by right;
in the midst of his days they will leave him,
    and at his end he will be a fool.

                                Jeremiah 17.11

As for what was sown among thorns, this
is he who hears the word, but the cares of
the world and the delight in riches choke
the word, and it proves unfruitful.

                                Matthew 13.22

Truly, I say to you, it will be hard for a
rich man to enter the kingdom of heaven.
Again I tell you, it is easier for a camel to
go through the eye of a needle than for a
rich man to enter the kingdom of God.

                                Matthew 19.23—24

There was a rich man, who was clothed
in purple and fine linen and who feasted

sumptuously every day. And at his gate lay a poor man named Laz'arus, full of sores, who desired to be fed with what fell from the rich man's table; moreover the dogs came and licked his sores. The poor man died and was carried by the angels to Abraham's bosom. The rich man also died and was buried; and in Hades, being in torment, he lifted up his eyes, and saw Abraham far off and Laz'arus in his bosom. And he called out, 'Father Abraham, have mercy upon me, and send Laz'arus to dip the end of his finger in water and cool my tongue; for I am in anguish in this flame.' But Abraham said, 'Son, remember that you in your lifetime received your good things, and Laz'arus in like manner evil things; but now he is comforted here, and you are in anguish.'

Luke 16.19−25

O the depth of the riches and wisdom and knowledge of God!

Romans 11.33

As for the rich in this world, charge them not to be haughty, nor to set their hopes on uncertain riches but on God who richly furnishes us with everything to enjoy.

1 Timothy 6.17

Come now, you rich, weep and howl for the miseries that are coming upon you. Your riches have rotted and your garments are moth-eaten. Your gold and silver have rusted, and their rust will be evidence against you and will eat your flesh like fire. You have laid up treasure for the last days.

James 5.1−3

Right

See also **Justice, Righteousness**

And you shall do what is right and good in the sight of the Lord, that it may go well with you, and that you may go in and take possession of the good land which the Lord swore to give to your fathers.

Deuteronomy 6.18

All may go well with you and with your children after you, when you do what is right in the sight of the Lord.

Deuteronomy 12.25

We are in your hand: do as it seems good and right in your sight to do to us.

Joshua 9.25

Far be it from me that I should sin against the Lord by ceasing to pray for you; and I will instruct you in the good and the right way.

1 Samuel 12.23

The precepts of the Lord are right.

Psalms 19.8

Every way of a man is right in his own
eyes,
but the Lord weighs the heart.

Proverbs 21.2

The ways of the Lord are right,
and the upright walk in them.

Hosea 14.9

Blessed are those who hunger and thirst for righteousness, for they shall be satisfied.

Matthew 5.6

Do not judge by appearances, but judge with right judgment.

John 7.24

Righteousness

See also **Right**

For the Lord is righteous, he loves
righteous deeds;
the upright shall behold his face.

Psalms 11.7

The righteous flourish like the palm tree,
and grow like a cedar in Lebanon.
They are planted in the house of the Lord,
they flourish in the courts of our God.

Psalms 92.12−13

The Lord has made known his victory,
he has revealed his vindication in the
sight of the nations.

Psalms 98.2

He comes to judge the earth,
He will judge the world with righteousness,
 and the peoples with equity.

Psalms 98.9

The Lord is just in all his ways,
 and kind in all his doings.

Psalms 145.17

The Lord's curse is on the house of the
 wicked,
 but he blesses the abode of the righteous.

Proverbs 3.33

Righteousness delivers from death.

Proverbs 10.2

Righteousness guards him whose way is
 upright,
but sin overthrows the wicked.

Proverbs 13.6

Better is a little with righteousness
 than great revenues with injustice.

Proverbs 16.8

The wicked flee when no one pursues,
 but the righteous are bold as a lion.

Proverbs 28.1

Be not righteous overmuch, and do not
make yourself overwise; why should you
destroy yourself?

Ecclesiastes 7.16

Open the gates,
 that the righteous nation which keeps
 faith
 may enter in.
Thou dost keep him in perfect peace,
 whose mind is stayed on thee,
 because he trusts in thee.

Isaiah 26.2–3

The way of the righteous is level;
 thou dost make smooth the path of the
 righteous.

Isaiah 26.7

It is fitting for us to fulfil all righteousness.

Matthew 3.15

For I tell you, unless your righteousness
exceeds that of the scribes and Pharisees,
you will never enter the kingdom of
heaven.

Matthew 5.20

So also David pronounces a blessing upon
the man to whom God reckons righteousness apart from works.

Romans 4.6

The promise to Abraham and his descendants, that they should inherit the world,
did not come through the law but through
the righteousness of faith.

Romans 4.13

Since, therefore, we are now justified by
his blood, much more shall we be saved by
him from the wrath of God.

Romans 5.9

The Gentiles who did not pursue
righteousness have attained it, that is, righteousness through faith.

Romans 9.30

The kingdom of God is not food and drink
but righteousness and peace and joy in the
Holy Spirit.

Romans 14.17

As servants of God we commend ourselves
. . . with the weapons of righteousness for
the right hand and for the left.

2 Corinthians 6.4,7

For through the Spirit, by faith, we wait
for the hope of righteousness.

Galatians 5.5

I have kept the faith. Henceforth there is
laid up for me the crown of righteousness,
which the Lord, the righteous judge, will
award to me on that Day.

2 Timothy 4.7–8

The anger of man does not work the righteousness of God. Therefore put away all
filthiness and rank growth of wickedness.

James 1.20–21

And the harvest of righteousness is sown in peace by those who make peace.

James 3.18

When he was reviled, he did not revile in return; when he suffered, he did not threaten; but he trusted to him who judges justly.

1 Peter 2.23

To those who have obtained a faith of equal standing with ours in the righteousness of our God and Saviour Jesus Christ.

2 Peter 1.1−2

If you know that he is righteous, you may be sure that every one who does right is born of him.

1 John 2.29

Rights

See also **Justice**

He does not keep the wicked alive,
but gives the afflicted their right.

Job 36.6

Woe to those who decree iniquitous
decrees . . .
to turn aside the needy from justice
and to rob the poor of my people
of their right.

Isaiah 10.1−2

For wicked men are found among
my people . . .
They know no bounds in deeds of
wickedness;
they judge not with justice
the cause of the fatherless, to make it
prosper,
and they do not defend the rights of the
needy.

Jeremiah 5.26,28

To turn aside the right of a man
in the presence of the Most High,
to subvert a man in his cause,
the Lord does not approve.

Lamentations 3.35−36

Then I will draw near to you for judgment; I will be a swift witness against . . . those who oppress the hireling in his wages, the widow and the orphan, against those who thrust aside the sojourner, and do not fear me, says the Lord of hosts.

Malachi 3.5

Blessed are those who wash their robes, that they may have the right to the tree of life and that they may enter the city by the gates.

Revelation 22.14

Risk

Cast your bread upon the waters,
for you will find it after many days.
Give a portion to seven, or even to eight,
for you know not what evil may happen
on earth.

Ecclesiastes 11.1−2

Robbery

Rob no one by violence or by false accusation, and be content with your wages.

Luke 3.14

He said therefore, 'A nobleman went into a far country to receive a kingdom and then return. Calling ten of his servants, he gave them ten pounds, and said to them, "Trade with these till I come." But his citizens hated him . . . saying, "We do not want this man to reign over us." When he returned, having received the kingdom, he commanded these servants, to whom he had given the money, to be called to him, that he might know what they had gained by trading. The first came before him, saying, "Lord, your pound has made ten pounds more." And he said to him, "Well done, good servant! Because you have been faithful in a very little, you shall have authority over ten cities." And the second came, saying, "Lord, your pound has made five pounds." And he said to him, "And you are to be over five cities." Then another came, saying, "Lord, here is your pound, which I kept laid away in a napkin; for I was afraid of you, because you are a severe man; you take up what you did not lay down, and reap what you did not sow." He said to him, "I will condemn you out of your own mouth, you wicked servant! You knew that I was a severe man, taking up what I did not lay down and reaping what I did not sow? Why then did you not put my money into the bank, and at my coming I should have collected it with interest?" And he said to those who stood by, "Take the pound from him, and give it to him who has the ten pounds." '

Luke 19.12–25

S

Sabbath

See also **Rest**

And on the seventh day God finished his work which he had done, and he rested on the seventh day . . . God blessed the seventh day and hallowed it, because on it God rested from all his work which he had done in creation.

Genesis 2.2–3

Remember the sabbath day, to keep it holy. Six days you shall labour, and do all your work; but the seventh day is a sabbath to the Lord your God; in it you shall not do any work, you, or your son, or your daughter, your manservant, or your maidservant, or your cattle, or the sojourner who is within your gates.

Exodus 20.8–10

Six days you shall do your work, but on the seventh day you shall rest; that your ox and your ass may have rest, and the son of your bondmaid, and the alien, may be refreshed.

Exodus 23.12

Six days shall work be done; but on the seventh day is a sabbath of solemn rest, a holy convocation; you shall do no work; it is a sabbath to the Lord in all your dwellings.

Leviticus 23.3

If you turn back your foot from the sabbath,
    from doing your pleasure on my holy day,
and call the sabbath a delight
    and the holy day of the Lord honourable;

if you honour it, not going your own ways,
    or seeking your own pleasure, or talking idly;
then you shall take delight in the Lord.

Isaiah 58.13–14

Moreover I gave them my sabbaths, as a sign between me and them, that they might know that I the Lord sanctify them.

Ezekiel 20.12

The Son of man is lord of the sabbath.

Matthew 12.8

It is lawful to do good on the sabbath.

Matthew 12.12

The sabbath was made for man, not man for the sabbath; so the Son of man is lord even of the sabbath.

Mark 2.27–28

Which of you, having a son or an ox that has fallen into a well will not immediately pull him out on a sabbath day?

Luke 14.5

Now concerning the contribution for the saints . . . On the first day of every week, each of you is to put something aside and store it up.

1 Corinthians 16.1–2

Therefore let no one pass judgment on you in questions of food and drink or with regard to a festival or a new moon or a sabbath. These are only a shadow of what is to come; but the substance belongs to Christ.

Colossians 2.16–17

Sacrifice

Because you have done this, and have not withheld your son, your only son, I will indeed bless you.

Genesis 22.16−17

To obey is better than sacrifice.

1 Samuel 15.22

For thou hast no delight in sacrifice;
    were I to give a burnt offering, thou
        wouldst not be pleased.
The sacrifice acceptable to God is a broken
        spirit;
    a broken and contrite heart, O God, thou
        wilt not despise.

Psalms 51.16−17

The sacrifice of the wicked is an
        abomination to the Lord,
    but the prayer of the upright is his
        delight.

Proverbs 15.8

To do righteousness and justice
    is more acceptable to the Lord than
        sacrifice.

Proverbs 21.3

For I desire steadfast love and not
        sacrifice,
    the knowledge of God, rather than burnt
        offerings.

Hosea 6.6

To love him with all the heart, and with all the understanding, and with all the strength, and to love one's neighbour as oneself, is much more than all whole burnt offerings and sacrifices.

Mark 12.33

I appeal to you therefore, brethren, by the mercies of God, to present your bodies as a living sacrifice, holy and acceptable to God, which is your spiritual worship.

Romans 12.1

Through him then let us continually offer up a sacrifice of praise to God, that is, the fruit of lips that acknowledge his name. Do not neglect to do good and to share what you have, for such sacrifices are pleasing to God.

Hebrews 13.15−16

Sadness

Even in laughter the heart is sad,
    and the end of joy is grief.

Proverbs 14.13

Safety

See also **Protection**

The joy of the Lord is your strength.

Nehemiah 8.10

But let all who take refuge in thee rejoice,
    let them ever sing for joy;
and do thou defend them,
    that those who love thy name may exult
        in thee.

Psalms 5.11

O Lord my God, in thee do I take refuge;
    save me from all my pursuers, and deliver
    me.

Psalms 7.1

Keep me as the apple of the eye;
    hide me in the shadow of thy wings,
from the wicked who despoil me,
    my deadly enemies who surround me.

Psalms 17.8−9

A king is not saved by his great army;
    a warrior is not delivered by his great
        strength.
The war horse is a vain hope for victory,
    and by its great might it cannot save.
Behold, the eye of the Lord is on those who
        fear him,
    on those who hope in his steadfast love.

Psalms 33.16−18

The angel of the Lord encamps
    around those who fear him, and delivers
    them.

Psalms 34.7

How precious is thy steadfast love,
O God!
  The children of men take refuge in the
    shadow of thy wings.

Psalms 36.7

The salvation of the righteous is from the
  Lord;
  he is their refuge in the time of trouble.
The Lord helps them and delivers them;
  he delivers them from the wicked, and
    saves them,
  because they take refuge in him.

Psalms 37.39−40

God is our refuge and strength,
  a very present help in trouble.

Psalms 46.1

For God alone my soul waits in silence;
  from him comes my salvation.
He only is my rock and my salvation,
  my fortress; I shall not be greatly moved.

Psalms 62.1−2

Blessed is the man who fears the
  Lord . . .
For the righteous will never be moved;
  he will be remembered for ever.

Psalms 112.1,6

The Lord preserves all who love him;
  but all the wicked he will destroy.

Psalms 145.20

For wisdom will come into your heart,
  and knowledge will be pleasant to your
    soul;
discretion will watch over you;
  understanding will guard you.

Proverbs 2.10−11

Where there is no guidance, a people falls;
  but in an abundance of counsellors there
    is safety.

Proverbs 11.14

And the first-born of the poor will feed,
  and the needy lie down in safety.

Isaiah 14.30

Woe to him who gets evil gain for his
  house,
to set his nest on high,

to be safe from the reach of harm!
You have devised shame to your house
  by cutting off many peoples;
  you have forfeited your life.
For the stone will cry out from the wall,
  and the beam from the woodwork
    respond.

Habakkuk 2.9−11

Seek righteousness, seek humility;
  perhaps you may be hidden
  on the day of the wrath of the Lord.

Zephaniah 2.3

If any one walks in the day, he does not
stumble, because he sees the light of this
world. But if any one walks in the night, he
stumbles, because the light is not in him.

John 11.9−10

Salvation

See also **Justification, Redemption**

The Lord is my strength and my song,
  and he has become my salvation.

Exodus 15.2

Deliver us, O God of our salvation,
  and gather and save us from among the
    nations,
that we may give thanks to thy holy name,
  and glory in thy praise.

1 Chronicles 16.35

Let thy priests, O Lord God, be clothed
with salvation.

2 Chronicles 6.41

The Lord is my light and my salvation;
  whom shall I fear?

Psalms 27.1

Our God is a God of salvation;
  and to God, the Lord, belongs escape
    from death.

Psalms 68.20

May those who love thy salvation
  say evermore, 'God is great!'

Psalms 70.4

Surely his salvation is at hand for those who fear him.

Psalms 85.9

Sing to the Lord, bless his name;
   tell of his salvation from day to day.

Psalms 96.2

Salvation is far from the wicked,
   for they do not seek thy statutes.

Psalms 119.155

I will abundantly bless her provisions;
   I will satisfy her poor with bread.
Her priests I will clothe with salvation,
   and her saints will shout for joy.

Psalms 132.15–16

Turn to me and be saved,
   all the ends of the earth!

Isaiah 45.22

My deliverance draws near speedily,
   my salvation has gone forth . . .
Lift up your eyes to the heavens,
   and look at the earth beneath;
for the heavens will vanish like smoke,
   the earth will wear out like a garment,
   and they who dwell in it will die
      like gnats;
but my salvation will be for ever,
   and my deliverance will never be ended.

Isaiah 51.5–6

You will go before the Lord to
      prepare his ways,
to give knowledge of salvation to his people
in the forgiveness of their sins,
through the tender mercy of our God.

Luke 1.76–78

All flesh shall see the salvation of God.

Luke 3.6

For the Son of man came to seek and to save the lost.

Luke 19.10

For God sent the Son into the world, not to condemn the world, but that the world might be saved through him.

John 3.17

I am the door; if any one enters by me, he will be saved, and will go in and out and find pasture.

John 10.9

Jesus said to him, 'I am the way, and the truth, and the life; no one comes to the Father, but by me.'

John 14.6

And there is salvation in no one else, for there is no other name under heaven given among men by which we must be saved.

Acts 4.12

We believe that we shall be saved through the grace of the Lord Jesus.

Acts 15.11

Believe in the Lord Jesus, and you will be saved, you and your household.

Acts 16.31

I am not ashamed of the gospel: it is the power of God for salvation to every one who has faith.

Romans 1.16

If you confess with your lips that Jesus is Lord and believe in your heart that God raised him from the dead, you will be saved. For man believes with his heart and so is justified, and he confesses with his lips and so is saved.

Romans 10.9–10

Besides this you know what hour it is, how it is full time now for you to wake from sleep. For salvation is nearer to us now than when we first believed.

Romans 13.11

Behold, now is the acceptable time behold, now is the day of salvation.

2 Corinthians 6.2

For God has not destined us for wrath, but to obtain salvation through our Lord Jesus Christ.

1 Thessalonians 5.9

Christ Jesus came into the world to save sinners.

1 Timothy 1.15

But as for you, continue in what you have learned and have firmly believed, knowing from whom you learned it and how from childhood you have been acquainted with the sacred writings which are able to instruct you for salvation through faith in Christ Jesus.

2 Timothy 3.14−15

And being made perfect he became the source of eternal salvation to all who obey him.

Hebrews 5.9

Christ, having been offered once to bear the sins of many, will appear a second time, not to deal with sin but to save those who are eagerly waiting for him.

Hebrews 9.28

As the outcome of your faith you obtain the salvation of your souls.

1 Peter 1.9

Like newborn babes, long for the pure spiritual milk, that by it you may grow up to salvation.

1 Peter 2.2

If the righteous man is scarcely saved, where will the impious and sinner appear?

1 Peter 4.18

Sanctification

For he delivers the needy when he calls,
  the poor and him who has no helper.
He has pity on the weak and the needy,
  and saves the lives of the needy.
From oppression and violence he redeems
    their life;
  and precious is their blood in his sight.

Psalms 72.12−14

Sanctify them in the truth; thy word is truth.

John 17.17

But now that you have been set free from sin and have become slaves of God, the return you get is sanctification and its end, eternal life.

Romans 6.22

He is the source of your life in Christ Jesus, whom God made our wisdom, our righteousness and sanctification and redemption.

1 Corinthians 1.30

Sanctity (of Life)

Are not two sparrows sold for a penny? And not one of them will fall to the ground without your Father's will. But even the hairs of your head are all numbered. Fear not, therefore; you are of more value than many sparrows.

Matthew 10.29−31

Do you not know that you are God's temple and that God's Spirit dwells in you? If any one destroys God's temple, God will destroy him. For God's temple is holy, and that temple you are.

1 Corinthians 3.16−17

Satiation

If you have found honey, eat only enough
    for you,
  lest you be sated with it and vomit it.

Proverbs 25.16

He who is sated loathes honey,
  but to one who is hungry everything
    bitter is sweet.

Proverbs 27.7

Woe to you that are full now, for you shall hunger.

Luke 6.25

Scorn/Scepticism

See also **Doubt, Mockery**

Why do the wicked live,
  reach old age, and grow mighty in
    power? . . .

They say to God, 'Depart from us!
  We do not desire the knowledge of thy
    ways.
What is the Almighty, that we should serve
    him?
  And what profit do we get if we pray to
    him?'

Job 21.7,14−15

Blessed is the man
  who walks not in the counsel of the
    wicked . . .
  nor sits in the seat of scoffers.

Psalms 1.1

My tears have been my food
  day and night,
while men say to me continually,
  'Where is your God?'

Psalms 42.3

Have mercy upon us, O Lord, have mercy
    upon us,
  for we have had more than enough of
    contempt.
Too long our soul has been sated
  with the scorn of those who are at ease,
  the contempt of the proud.

Psalms 123.3−4

How long, O simple ones, will you love
    being simple?
How long will scoffers delight in their
    scoffing
  and fools hate knowledge?
Give heed to my reproof.

Proverbs 1.22−23

Toward the scorners he is scornful.

Proverbs 3.34

If you are wise, you are wise for yourself;
  if you scoff, you alone will bear it.

Proverbs 9.12

A scoffer does not listen to rebuke.

Proverbs 13.1

A scoffer seeks wisdom in vain,
  but knowledge is easy for a man of
    understanding.

Proverbs 14.6

A scoffer does not like to be reproved;
  he will not go to the wise.

Proverbs 15.12

Strike a scoffer, and the simple will learn
    prudence.

Proverbs 19.25

Condemnation is ready for scoffers,
  and flogging for the back of fools.

Proverbs 19.29

When a scoffer is punished, the simple
    becomes wise.

Proverbs 21.11

'Scoffer' is the name of the proud, haughty
    man
  who acts with arrogant pride.

Proverbs 21.24

Drive out a scoffer, and strife will go out,
  and quarrelling and abuse will cease.

Proverbs 22.10

The scoffer is an abomination to men.

Proverbs 24.9

Therefore hear the word of the Lord, you
    scoffers.

Isaiah 28.14

For the ruthless shall come to naught and
    the scoffer cease,
  and all who watch to do evil shall be cut
    off.

Isaiah 29.20

But you, draw near hither, sons of the
    sorceress,
  offspring of the adulterer and the harlot.
Of whom are you making sport?
  Against whom do you open your mouth
    wide
  and put out your tongue?
Are you not children of transgression, the
    offspring of deceit?

Isaiah 57.3−4

At that time I will search Jerusalem with
    lamps,
  and I will punish the men
who are thickening upon their lees,

those who say in their hearts,
'The Lord will not do good,
    nor will he do ill.'

Zephaniah 1.12

Why do you pass judgment on your brother? Or you, why do you despise your brother?

Romans 14.10

God chose what is low and despised in the world.

1 Corinthians 1.28

For God has not called us for uncleanness, but in holiness. Therefore whoever disregards this, disregards not man but God, who gives his Holy Spirit to you.

1 Thessalonians 4.7−8

A man who has violated the law of Moses dies without mercy at the testimony of two or three witnesses. How much worse punishment do you think will be deserved by the man who has spurned the Son of God?

Hebrews 10.28−29

First of all you must understand this, that scoffers will come in the last days with scoffing, following their own passions and saying, 'Where is the promise of his coming? For ever since the fathers fell asleep, all things have continued as they were from the beginning of creation.' They deliberately ignore this fact, that by the word of God heavens existed long ago, and . . . the heavens and earth that now exist have been stored up for fire, being kept until the day of judgment and destruction of ungodly men.

2 Peter 3.3−5,7

Scripture

All scripture is inspired by God and profitable for teaching, for reproof, for correction, and for training in righteousness, that the man of God may be complete, equipped for every good work.

2 Timothy 3.16−17

Search

If you seek him, he will be found by you; but if you forsake him, he will cast you off forever.

1 Chronicles 28.9

I love those who love me,
    and those who seek me diligently find me.

Proverbs 8.17

The Lord is good to those who wait for him,
    to the soul that seeks him.

Lamentations 3.25

Let us know, let us press on to know the Lord;
    his going forth is sure as the dawn;
he will come to us as the showers,
    as the spring rains that water the earth.

Hosea 6.3

For whoever would draw near to God must believe that he exists and that he rewards those who seek him.

Hebrews 11.6

Seasons

See also **Calendar, Time**

And God said, 'Let there be lights in the firmament of the heavens to separate the day from the night; and let them be for signs and for seasons and for days and years.'

Genesis 1.14

While the earth remains, seedtime and harvest, cold and heat, summer and winter, day and night, shall not cease.

Genesis 8.22

Thou hast made the moon to mark the seasons;
    the sun knows its time for setting.

Psalms 104.19

For everything there is a season, and a time for every matter under heaven:

a time to be born, and a time to die;
a time to plant, and a time to pluck up
    what is planted.

Ecclesiastes 3.1−2

Second Coming

For the Son of man is to come with his angels in the glory of his Father, and then he will repay every man for what he has done. Truly, I say to you, there are some standing here who will not taste death before they see the Son of man coming in his kingdom.

Matthew 16.27−28

For as the lightning comes from the east and shines as far as the west, so will be the coming of the Son of man. Wherever the body is, there the eagles will be gathered together.
    Immediately after the tribulation of those days the sun will be darkened, and the moon will not give its light, and the stars will fall from heaven, and the powers of the heavens will be shaken; then will appear the sign of the Son of man in heaven, and then all the tribes of the earth will mourn, and they will see the Son of man coming on the clouds of heaven with power and great glory; and he will send out his angels with a loud trumpet call, and they will gather his elect from the four winds, from one end of heaven to the other.

Matthew 24.27−31

For the Lord himself will descend from heaven with a cry of command, with the archangel's call, and with the sound of the trumpet of God. And the dead in Christ will rise first; then we who are alive, who are left, shall be caught up together with them in the clouds to meet the Lord in the air; and so we shall always be with the Lord.

1 Thessalonians 4.16−17

And then the lawless one will be revealed, and the Lord Jesus will slay him with the breath of his mouth and destroy him by his appearing and his coming.

2 Thessalonians 2.8

Christ, having been offered once to bear the sins of many, will appear a second time, not to deal with sin but to save those who are eagerly waiting for him.

Hebrews 9.28

Secrecy

He knows the secrets of the heart.

Psalms 44.21

A foolish woman is noisy . . .
    to him who is without sense, she says,
'Stolen water is sweet,
    and bread eaten in secret is pleasant.'

Proverbs 9.13,16−17

Do not disclose another's secret.

Proverbs 25.9

For God will bring every deed into judgment, with every secret thing, whether good or evil.

Ecclesiastes 12.14

Woe to those who hide deep from the
        Lord their counsel,
    whose deeds are in the dark,
    and who say, 'Who sees us?
        Who knows us?'

Isaiah 29.1

Nothing is covered up that will not be revealed, or hidden that will not be known. Therefore whatever you have said in the dark shall be heard in the light, and what you have whispered in private rooms shall be proclaimed upon the housetops.

Luke 12.2−

But we impart a secret and hidden wisdom of God, which God decreed before the ages for our glorification.

1 Corinthians 2

Seduction

See also **Enticement, Temptation**

If a man seduces a virgin who is not betrothed, and lies with her, he shall give the marriage present for her, and make her his wife. If her father utterly refuses to give her to him, he shall pay money equivalent to the marriage present for virgins.

Exodus 22.16–17

If a man meets a virgin who is not betrothed, and seizes her and lies with her, and they are found, then the man who lay with her shall give to the father of the young woman fifty shekels of silver, and she shall be his wife, because he has violated her; he may not put her away all his days.

Deuteronomy 22.28–29

If sinners entice you,
  do not consent.

Proverbs 1.10

The reproofs of discipline are the way of
    life,
  to preserve you from the evil woman,
  from the smooth tongue of the
    adventuress.
Do not desire her beauty in your heart,
  and do not let her capture you with her
    eyelashes.

Proverbs 6.23–25

A righteous man turns away from evil,
  but the way of the wicked leads them
    astray.

Proverbs 12.26

A man of violence entices his neighbour
  and leads him in a way that is not good.

Proverbs 16.29

He who misleads the upright into an evil
    way
  will fall into his own pit.

Proverbs 28.10

False Christs and false prophets will arise
nd show signs and wonders, to lead astray,
  possible, the elect.

Mark 13.22

But I am afraid that as the serpent
ceived Eve by his cunning, your thoughts
ill be led astray from a sincere and pure
votion to Christ.

2 Corinthians 11.3

Now the Spirit expressly says that in later times some will depart from the faith by giving heed to deceitful spirits and doctrines of demons, through the pretensions of liars whose consciences are seared, who forbid marriage and enjoin abstinence from foods which God created to be received with thanksgiving by those who believe and know the truth.

1 Timothy 4.1–3

In the last days there will come times of stress. For men will be lovers of self, lovers of money . . . lovers of pleasure rather than lovers of God, holding the form of religion but denying the power of it. Avoid such people. For among them are those who make their way into households and capture weak women, burdened with sins and swayed by various impulses, who will listen to anybody and can never arrive at a knowledge of the truth . . . but they will not get very far, for their folly will be plain to all.

2 Timothy 3.1–2,4,7–9

Each person is tempted when he is lured and enticed by his own desire.

James 1.14

Bold and wilful, they are not afraid to revile the glorious ones . . . They have eyes full of adultery, insatiable for sin. They entice unsteady souls . . . uttering loud boasts of folly, they entice with licentious passions of the flesh men who have barely escaped from those who live in error.

2 Peter 2.10,14,18

Self-Assessment

Though I am innocent, my own mouth
    would condemn me;
  though I am blameless, he would prove
    me perverse.
I am blameless; I regard not myself;
  I loathe my life.

Job 9.20–21

He who trusts in his own mind is a fool.

Proverbs 28.26

Our transgressions are with us,
   and we know our iniquities.

Isaiah 59.12

Let us test and examine our ways, and return to the Lord!

Lamentations 3.40

For by the grace given to me I bid every one among you not to think of himself more highly than he ought to think, but to think with sober judgment, each according to the measure of faith which God has assigned him.

Romans 12.3

I am not aware of anything against myself, but I am not thereby acquitted. It is the Lord who judges me.

1 Corinthians 4.4

Let a man examine himself, and so eat of the bread and drink of the cup. For any one who eats and drinks without discerning the body eats and drinks judgment upon himself.

1 Corinthians 11.28—29

Let us not love in word or speech but in deed and in truth.
   By this we shall know that we are of the truth, and reassure our hearts before him whenever our hearts condemn us.

1 John 3.18—19

Self-Castigation

You have heard that it was said, 'You shall not commit adultery.' But I say to you that every one who looks at a woman lustfully has already committed adultery with her in his heart. If your right eye causes you to sin, pluck it out and throw it away; it is better that you lose one of your members than that your whole body be thrown into hell. And if your right hand causes you to sin, cut it off and throw it away; it is better that you lose one of your members than that your whole body go into hell.

Matthew 5.27—30

And if your hand or your foot causes you to sin, cut it off and throw it away; it is better for you to enter life maimed or lame than with two hands or two feet to be thrown into the eternal fire.

Matthew 18.8

Self-Control

See also **Discipline, Moderation**

He who belittles his neighbour lacks sense,
   but a man of understanding remains
      silent.

Proverbs 11.12

He who guards his mouth preserves his
      life;
   he who opens wide his lips comes to ruin.

Proverbs 13.3

The wisdom of a prudent man is to discern
      his way.

Proverbs 14.8

He who is slow to anger is better than the
      mighty,
   and he who rules his spirit than he who
      takes a city.

Proverbs 16.32

He who restrains his words has
      knowledge,
   and he who has a cool spirit is a man of
      understanding.

Proverbs 17.27

Even a fool who keeps silent is considered
      wise;
   when he closes his lips, he is deemed
      intelligent.

Proverbs 17.28

It is an honour for a man to keep aloof
      from strife;
   but every fool will be quarrelling.

Proverbs 20.

He who keeps his mouth and his tongue
   keeps himself out of trouble.

Proverbs 21.2

Put a knife to your throat
 if you are a man given to appetite.
>> *Proverbs 23.2*

A man without self-control
 is like a city broken into and left without
  walls.
>> *Proverbs 25.28*

A fool gives full vent to his anger,
 but a wise man quietly holds it back.
>> *Proverbs 29.11*

Let not sin therefore reign in your mortal
bodies, to make you obey their passions.
>> *Romans 6.12*

Every athlete exercises self-control in all
things. They do it to receive a perishable
wreath, but we an imperishable. Well, I do
not run aimlessly, I do not box as one
beating the air; but I pommel my body and
subdue it.
>> *1 Corinthians 9.25–27*

Take every thought captive to obey Christ.
>> *2 Corinthians 10.5*

God did not give us a spirit of timidity but
a spirit of power and love and self-control.
>> *2 Timothy 1.7*

Urge the younger men to control themselves.
>> *Titus 2.6*

Let every man be quick to hear, slow to
speak, slow to anger, for the anger of man
does not work the righteousness of God.
Therefore put away all filthiness and rank
growth of wickedness and receive with
meekness the implanted word, which is able
to save your souls.
>> *James 1.19–21*

If any one thinks he is religious, and does
not bridle his tongue but deceives his heart,
this man's religion is vain.
>> *James 1.26*

Therefore gird up your minds . . . do not
be conformed to the passions of your
former ignorance.
>> *1 Peter 1.13–14*

Self-Defence/Self-Protection

For the protection of wisdom is like the
 protection of money;
 and the advantage of knowledge is that
  wisdom preserves the life of him who
  has it.
>> *Ecclesiastes 7.12*

Do not resist one who is evil.
>> *Matthew 5.39*

Then Pilate said to him 'Do you not hear
how many things they testify against you?'
But he gave him no answer, not even to a
single charge.
>> *Matthew 27.13–14*

Let us then cast off the works of darkness
and put on the armour of light.
>> *Romans 13.12*

But as servants of God we commend ourselves in every way . . . with the weapons
of righteousness for the right hand and for
the left.
>> *2 Corinthians 6.4,7*

Put on the whole armour of God, that you
may be able to stand against the wiles of the
devil.
>> *Ephesians 6.11*

Stand therefore, having girded your loins
with truth, and having put on the breastplate of righteousness, and having shod
your feet with the equipment of the gospel
of peace; besides all these, taking the shield
of faith, with which you can quench all the
flaming darts of the evil one. And take the
helmet of salvation, and the sword of the
Spirit, which is the word of God.
>> *Ephesians 6.14–17*

Self-Delusion

Beware lest there be . . . one who . . .
blesses himself in his heart, saying, 'I shall
be safe, though I walk in the stubbornness
of my heart.' This would lead to the sweep-
ing away of moist and dry alike. The Lord

would not pardon him, but rather the anger of the Lord and his jealousy would smoke against that man, and the curses written in this book would settle upon him, and the Lord would blot out his name from under heaven.

Deuteronomy 29.18–20

Let him not trust in emptiness, deceiving himself;
  for emptiness will be his recompense.

Job 15.31

For the wicked boasts of the desires of his heart,
  and the man greedy for gain curses and renounces the Lord.
In the pride of his countenance the wicked does not seek him;
  all his thoughts are, 'There is no God.'

Psalms 10.3–4

As for me, I said in my prosperity,
  'I shall never be moved.'
By thy favour, O Lord,
  thou hadst established me as a strong mountain;
thou didst hide thy face,
  I was dismayed.

Psalms 30.6–7

He flatters himself in his own eyes
  that his iniquity cannot be found out and hated.

Psalms 36.2

Yea, he shall see that even the wise die,
  the fool and the stupid alike must perish and leave their wealth to others.
Their graves are their homes for ever,
  their dwelling places to all generations,
  though they named lands their own.
Man cannot abide in his pomp,
  he is like the beasts that perish.
This is the fate of those who have foolish confidence,
  the end of those who are pleased with their portion.

Psalms 49.10–13

There is a way which seems right to a man,
  but its end is the way to death.

Proverbs 14.12

All the ways of a man are pure in his own eyes,
  but the Lord weighs the spirit.

Proverbs 16.2

Haughty eyes and a proud heart,
  the lamp of the wicked, are sin.

Proverbs 21.4

Do you see a man who is wise in his own eyes?
  There is more hope for a fool than for him.

Proverbs 26.12

The sluggard is wiser in his own eyes
  than seven men who can answer discreetly.

Proverbs 26.16

A rich man is wise in his own eyes,
  but a poor man who has understanding will find him out.

Proverbs 28.1

There are those who are pure in their own eyes
  but are not cleansed of their filth.

Proverbs 30.1

Woe to those who are wise in their own eyes.

Isaiah 5.2

For they are a rebellious people . . .
who say to the seers, 'See not';
  and to the prophets, 'Prophesy not to us what is right;
speak to us smooth things,
  prophesy illusions.'

Isaiah 30.9–

Now therefore hear this, you lover of pleasures,
  who sit securely,
who say in your heart,
  'I am, and there is no one besides me;
I shall not sit as a widow
  or know the loss of children.'
These two things shall come to you
  in a moment, in one day.

Isaiah 47.8–

They have spoken falsely of the Lord,
  and have said, 'He will do nothing;
no evil will come upon us,
  nor shall we see sword or famine . . .'
Therefore thus says the Lord, the God
      of hosts:
'Because they have spoken this word,
behold, I am making my words in your
      mouth a fire,
  and this people wood, and the fire shall
      devour them.'

Jeremiah 5.12,14

The horror you inspire has deceived you.

Jeremiah 49.16

Because you consider yourself as wise as a
      god,
therefore, behold, I will bring strangers
      upon you,
  the most terrible of the nations;
and they shall draw their swords against the
      beauty of your wisdom
  and defile your splendour.
They shall thrust you down into the Pit,
  and you shall die the death of the slain
  in the heart of the seas.

Ezekiel 28.6–8

All the sinners of my people shall die by
      the sword,
  who say, 'Evil shall not overtake or
      meet us.'

Amos 9.10

The pride of your heart has
      deceived you . . .
who say in your heart,
  'Who will bring me down to the
      ground?'

Obadiah 3

Why do you see the speck that is in your
brother's eye, but do not notice the log that
in your own eye? Or how can you say to
our brother, 'Let me take the speck out of
our eye,' when there is the log in your own
eye? You hypocrite, first take the log out of
your own eye, and then you will see clearly
take the speck out of your brother's eye.

Matthew 7.3–5

He also told this parable to some who
trusted in themselves that they were righteous and despised others: 'Two men went
up into the temple to pray, one a Pharisee
and the other a tax collector. The Pharisee
stood and prayed thus with himself, 'God, I
thank thee that I am not like other men,
extortioners, unjust, adulterers, or even
like this tax collector. I fast twice a week, I
give tithes of all that I get.' But the tax
collector, standing far off, would not even
lift up his eyes to heaven, but beat his
breast, saying, 'God, be merciful to me a
sinner!' I tell you, this man went down to
his house justified rather than the other.

Luke 18.9–14

Let no one deceive himself. If any one
among you thinks that he is wise in this age,
let him become a fool that he may become
wise. For the wisdom of this world is folly
with God.

1 Corinthians 3.18–19

For you yourselves know well that the day
of the Lord will come like a thief in the
night. When people say, 'There is peace
and security,' then sudden destruction will
come upon them as travail comes upon a
woman with child, and there will be no
escape.

1 Thessalonians 5.2–3

Come now, you who say, 'Today or
tomorrow we will go into such and such a
town and spend a year there and trade and
get gain'; whereas you do not know about
tomorrow. What is your life? For you are a
mist that appears for a little time and then
vanishes. Instead you ought to say, 'If the
Lord wills, we shall live and we shall do this
or that.' As it is, you boast in your arrogance. All such boasting is evil.

James 4.13–17

If we say we have no sin, we deceive ourselves, and the truth is not in us.

1 John 1.8

For you say, I am rich, I have prospered,
and I need nothing; not knowing that you
are wretched, pitiable, poor, blind, and
naked.

Revelation 3.17

Self-Denial

See also **Self-Sacrifice**

Remember, O Lord, in David's favour,
    all the hardships he endured;
how he swore to the Lord
    and vowed to the Mighty One of Jacob,
'I will not enter my house
    or get into my bed;
I will not give sleep to my eyes
    or slumber to my eyelids,
until I find a place for the Lord,
    a dwelling place for the Mighty One of
        Jacob.'

Psalms 132.1—5

If your right eye causes you to sin, pluck it out and throw it away; it is better that you lose one of your members than that your whole body be thrown into hell.

Matthew 5.29

Brother will deliver up brother . . . and you will be hated by all for my name's sake. But he who endures to the end will be saved.

Matthew 10.21—22

He who loves father or mother more than me is not worthy of me; and he who loves son or daughter more than me is not worthy of me; and he who does not take his cross and follow me is not worthy of me.

Matthew 10.37—38

He who finds his life will lose it, and he who loses his life for my sake will find it.

Matthew 10.39

Then Jesus told his disciples, 'If any man would come after me, let him deny himself and take up his cross and follow me. For whoever would save his life will lose it, and whoever loses his life for my sake will find it. For what will it profit a man, if he gains the whole world and forfeits his life? Or what shall a man give in return for his life?

Matthew 16.24—26

There are eunuchs who have been made eunuchs by men, and there are eunuchs who have made themselves eunuchs for the sake of the kingdom of heaven.

Matthew 19.12

If you would be perfect, go, sell what you possess and give to the poor, and you will have treasure in heaven; and come, follow me.

Matthew 19.21

For which of you, desiring to build a tower, does not first sit down and count the cost, whether he has enough to complete it? Otherwise, when he has laid a foundation, and is not able to finish, all who see it begin to mock him, saying, 'This man began to build, and was not able to finish.' Or what king, going to encounter another king in war, will not sit down first and take counsel whether he is able with ten thousand to meet him who comes against him with twenty thousand? And if not, while the other is yet a great way off, he sends an embassy and asks terms of peace. So therefore, whoever of you does not renounce all that he has cannot be my disciple.

Luke 14.28—3

He looked up and saw the rich putting their gifts into the treasury; and he saw poor widow put in two copper coins. And he said, 'Truly I tell you, this poor widow has put in more than all of them; for they all contributed out of their abundance, but she out of her poverty put in all the living that she had.'

Luke 21.1—

He who loves his life loses it, and he who hates his life in this world will keep it for eternal life.

John 12..

So then, brethren, we are debtors, not to the flesh, to live according to the flesh for if you live according to the flesh you will die, but if by the Spirit you put to death the deeds of the body you will live.

Romans 8.12—

We who are strong ought to bear with the failings of the weak, and not to please ourselves.

Romans 1

I have been crucified with Christ; it is no longer I who live, but Christ who lives in me.

Galatians 2.20

Indeed I count everything as loss because of the surpassing worth of knowing Christ Jesus my Lord. For his sake I have suffered the loss of all things, and count them as refuse, in order that I may gain Christ.

Philippians 3.8

Abstain from the passions of the flesh that wage war against your soul.

1 Peter 2.11

And they have conquered . . . by the word of their testimony, for they loved not their lives even unto death.

Revelation 12.11

Self-Destruction

Let the wicked together fall into their own nets.

Psalms 141.10

Self-Employment

Better is a man of humble standing who
  works for himself
than one who plays the great man but
  lacks bread.

Proverbs 12.9

Self-Examination

How many are my iniquities and my sins?
  Make me know my transgression and my
  sin.

Job 13.23

Commune with your own hearts on your
  beds, and be silent.

Psalms 4.4

Clear thou me from hidden faults . . .
  Then I shall be blameless.

Psalms 19.12–13

I commune with my heart in the night.

Psalms 77.6

When I think of thy ways,
  I turn my feet to thy testimonies.

Psalms 119.59

The heart is deceitful above all things,
  and desperately corrupt;
who can understand it?

Jeremiah 17.9

Let us test and examine our ways,
  and return to the Lord!

Lamentations 3.40

Thus says the Lord of hosts: Consider how you have fared.

Haggai 1.7

But if we judged ourselves truly, we should not be judged.

1 Corinthians 11.31

Examine yourselves, to see whether you are holding to your faith. Test yourselves. Do you not realise that Jesus Christ is in you? — unless indeed you fail to meet the test!

2 Corinthians 13.5

Let each one test his own work, and then his reason to boast will be in himself alone and not in his neighbour.

Galatians 6.4

Self-Fulfilment

See also **Wholeness**

I cry to God Most High,
  to God who fulfils his purpose for me.

Psalms 57.2

There came a woman of Samar'ia to draw water. Jesus said to her, 'Give me a drink.' For his disciples had gone away into the city to buy food. The Samaritan woman said to him, 'How is it that you, a Jew, ask a drink of me, a woman of Samar'ia?' For Jews have no dealings with Samaritans. Jesus answered her, 'If you knew the gift of God, and who it is that is saying to you, "Give me a drink," you would have asked him, and he would have given you living water.' The woman said to him, 'Sir, you have nothing to draw with, and the well is deep; where do you get that living water? Are you greater than our father Jacob, who gave us the well, and drank from it himself, and his sons, and his cattle?' Jesus said to her, 'Every one who drinks of this water will thirst again, but whoever drinks of the water that I shall give him will never thirst; the water that I shall give him will become in him a spring of water welling up to eternal life.' The woman said to him, 'Sir, give me this water, that I may not thirst, nor come here to draw.'

John 4.7−15

Do not labour for the food which perishes, but for the food which endures to eternal life, which the Son of man will give to you; for on him has God the Father set his seal.

John 6.27

And it is my prayer that your love may abound more and more, with knowledge and all discernment, so that you may approve what is excellent, and may be pure and blameless for the day of Christ.

Philippians 1.9−10

For in him the whole fulness of deity dwells bodily, and you have come to fulness of life in him, who is the head of all rule and authority.

Colossians 2.9−10

Self-Indulgence

See also **Greed, Luxury, Selfishness**

Let us conduct ourselves becomingly as in the day, not in revelling and drunkenness, not in debauchery and licentiousness, not in quarrelling and jealousy. But put on the Lord Jesus Christ, and make no provision for the flesh, to gratify its desires.

Romans 13.13−14

For you were called to freedom, brethren; only do not use your freedom as an opportunity for the flesh.

Galatians 5.13

Walk by the Spirit, and do not gratify the desires of the flesh. For the desires of the flesh are against the Spirit.

Galatians 5.16−17

And those who belong to Christ Jesus have crucified the flesh with its passions and desires.

Galatians 5.24

Selfishness

See also **Self-Indulgence**

The people curse him who holds back grain.

Proverbs 11.26

And do you seek great things for yourself? Seek them not; for, behold, I am bringing evil upon all flesh.

Jeremiah 45.5

As for you, my flock, thus says the Lord God: Behold, I judge between sheep and sheep, rams and he-goats. Is it not enough for you to feed on the good pasture, that you must tread down with your feet the rest of your pasture; and to drink of clear water, that you must foul the rest with your feet? And must my sheep eat what you have trodden with your feet, and drink what you have fouled with your feet?
   Therefore, thus says the Lord God to them: Behold, I, I myself will judge between the fat sheep and the lean sheep.

Ezekiel 34.17−22

Let no one seek his own good, but the good of his neighbour.

1 Corinthians 10.24

And he died for all, that those who live might live no longer for themselves but for him who for their sake died and was raised.

2 Corinthians 5.15

In humility count others better than yourselves. Let each of you look not only to his own interests, but also to the interests of others.

Philippians 2.3−4

They all look after their own interests, not those of Jesus Christ.

Philippians 2.21

Abstain from the passions of the flesh that wage war against your soul.

1 Peter 2.11

If any one has the world's goods and sees his brother in need, yet closes his heart against him, how does God's love abide in him?

1 John 3.17

Self-Knowledge

Clear thou me from hidden faults.

Psalms 19.12

I commune with my heart in the night;
 I meditate and search my spirit.

Psalms 77.6

I bid every one among you not to think of himself more highly than he ought to think, but to think with sober judgment, each according to the measure of faith which God has assigned him.

Romans 12.3

Examine yourselves, to see whether you are holding to your faith. Test yourselves.

2 Corinthians 13.5

Look to yourself.

Galatians 6.1

But let each one test his own work, and then his reason to boast will be in himself alone and not in his neighbour. For each man will have to bear his own load.

Galatians 6.4−5

Self-Love

He who gets wisdom loves himself.

Proverbs 19.8

One of the scribes came up and . . . asked him, 'Which commandment is the first of all?' Jesus answered, 'The first is . . . The Lord our God, the Lord is one . . . The second is . . . You shall love your neighbour as yourself. There is no other commandment greater than these.'

Mark 12.28,31−32

Self-Reliance

See the man who would not make God his refuge,
but trusted in the abundance of his riches.

Psalms 52.7

Self-Righteousness

Do not say in your heart . . . 'It is because of my righteousness that the Lord has brought me in to possess this land.'

Deuteronomy 9.4

For you say, 'My doctrine is pure,
 and I am clean in God's eyes.'
But oh, that God would speak . . .
Know . . . that God exacts of you less
 than your guilt deserves.

Job 11.4−6

Can a man be profitable to God?
 Surely he who is wise is profitable to
 himself.
Is it any pleasure to the Almighty if you are
 righteous,
 or is it gain to him if you make your ways
 blameless?

Job 22.2−3

Do you think this to be just?
 Do you say, 'It is my right before God,'
that you ask, 'What advantage have I?
 How am I better off than if I had sinned?'

Job 35.2−3

The way of a fool is right in his own eyes,
 but a wise man listens to advice.

Proverbs 12.15

He who conceals his transgressions will not
 prosper,
but he who confesses and forsakes them
 will obtain mercy.

Proverbs 28.13

Woe to those who are wise in their own
   eyes,
and shrewd in their own sight!

Isaiah 5.21

How can you say, 'We are wise,
and the law of the Lord is with us'?

Jeremiah 8.8

On that day many will say to me, 'Lord,
Lord, did we not prophesy in your name,
and cast out demons in your name, and do
many mighty works in your name?' And
then will I declare to them, 'I never knew
you; depart from me, you evildoers.'

Matthew 7.22–23

I came not to call the righteous, but
sinners.

Matthew 9.13

And he said to him '. . . If you would
enter life, keep the commandments . . .
You shall not kill, You shall not commit
adultery, You shall not steal, You shall not
bear false witness, Honour your father and
mother, and, You shall love your neighbour
as yourself.' The young man said to him,
'All these I have observed; what do I still
lack?' Jesus said to him, 'If you would be
perfect, go, sell what you possess and give
to the poor, and you will have treasure in
heaven; and come, follow me.' When the
young man heard this he went away sorrowful; for he had great possessions.

Matthew 19.17–22

You are those who justify yourselves
before men, but God knows your hearts;
for what is exalted among men is an abomination in the sight of God.

Luke 16.15

He also told this parable to some who
trusted in themselves that they were righteous and despised others: 'Two men went
up into the temple to pray, one a Pharisee
and the other a tax collector. The Pharisee
stood and prayed thus with himself, "God, I
thank thee that I am not like other men,
extortioners, unjust, adulterers, or even
like this tax collector. I fast twice a week,
I give tithes of all that I get." But the tax
collector, standing far off, would not even
lift up his eyes to heaven, but beat his
breast, saying, "God, be merciful to me a
sinner!" I tell you, this man went down to
his house justified rather than the other; for
every one who exalts himself will be
humbled, but he who humbles himself will
be exalted.

Luke 18.9–14

Let any one who thinks that he stands take
heed lest he fall.

1 Corinthians 10.12

For if any one thinks he is something,
when he is nothing, he deceives himself.

Galatians 6.3

Self-Sacrifice

See also **Self-Denial**

But he was wounded for our
   transgressions,
   he was bruised for our iniquities;
upon him was the chastisement that made
   us whole,
   and with his stripes we are healed.
All we like sheep have gone astray;
   we have turned every one to his own
      way;
and the Lord has laid on him
   the iniquity of us all.

Isaiah 53.5–6

The good shepherd lays down his life for
the sheep.

John 10.11

Greater love has no man than this, that a
man lay down his life for his friends.

John 15.13

In my flesh I complete what is lacking in
Christ's afflictions for the sake of his body
that is, the church.

Colossians 1.24

And every priest stands daily at his
service, offering repeatedly the same sacrifices, which can never take away sins. But
when Christ had offered for all time a single
sacrifice for sins, he sat down at the right
hand of God.

Hebrews 10.11–12

Separation

To the married I give charge, not I but the Lord, that the wife should not separate from her husband.

1 Corinthians 7.10

Service

Know the God of your father, and serve him with a whole heart and with a willing mind; for the Lord searches all hearts, and understands every plan and thought. If you seek him, he will be found by you; but if you forsake him, he will cast you off for ever.

1 Chronicles 28.9

Then Jesus said to him, 'Begone, Satan! for it is written,
  'You shall worship the Lord your God
  and him only shall you serve.'

Matthew 4.10

And there are varieties of service, but the same Lord.

1 Corinthians 12.5

Slaves, be obedient to those who are your earthly masters, with fear and trembling, in singleness of heart, as to Christ; not in the way of eye-service, as men-pleasers, but as servants of Christ, doing the will of God from the heart, rendering service with a good will as to the Lord and not to men.

Ephesians 6.5–7

Servants, be submissive to your masters with all respect, not only to the kind and gentle but also to the overbearing. For one is approved if, mindful of God, he endures pain while suffering unjustly. For what credit is it, if when you do wrong and are beaten for it you take it patiently?

1 Peter 2.18–20

Sex

Be fruitful and multiply.

Genesis 1.28

Sexism

There is neither Jew nor Greek, there is neither slave nor free, there is neither male nor female; for you are all one in Christ Jesus.

Galatians 3.28

Sharing

He who has two coats, let him share with him who has none; and he who has food, let him do likewise.

Luke 3.11

Share what you have, for such sacrifices are pleasing to God.

Hebrews 13.16

Sign

How great are his signs,
  how mighty his wonders!

Daniel 4.3

And I will give portents in the heavens and on the earth, blood and fire and columns of smoke. The sun shall be turned to darkness, and the moon to blood, before the great and terrible day of the Lord comes. And it shall come to pass that all who call upon the name of the Lord shall be delivered; for in Mount Zion and in Jerusalem there shall be those who escape, as the Lord has said, and among the survivors shall be those whom the Lord calls.

Joel 2.30–32

Silence

See also **Quietness**

Even a fool who keeps silent is considered wise;
  when he closes his lips, he is deemed intelligent.

Proverbs 17.28

But the Lord is in his holy temple;
  let all the earth keep silence before him.

Habakkuk 2.20

Be silent before the Lord God!

Zephaniah 1.7

Be silent, all flesh, before the Lord; for he has roused himself from his holy dwelling.

Zechariah 2.13

Sin

See also **Evil, Sinners, Wrong**

All the congregation of the people of Israel moved on from the wilderness of Sin by stages, according to the commandment of the Lord.

Exodus 17.1

Be sure your sin will find you out.

Numbers 32.23

The fathers shall not be put to death for the children, or the children be put to death for the fathers; but every man shall die for his own sin.

2 Chronicles 25.4

How then can man be righteous before God?
  How can he who is born of woman be clean?
Behold, even the moon is not bright
  and the stars are not clean in his sight;
how much less man, who is a maggot,
  and the son of man, who is a worm!

Job 25.4–6

Be angry, but sin not.

Psalms 4.4

Clear thou me from hidden faults.

Psalms 19.12

Blessed is he whose transgression is forgiven,
  whose sin is covered.

Psalms 32.1

He who despises his neighbour is a sinner.

Proverbs 14.21

Righteousness exalts a nation,
  but sin is a reproach to any people.

Proverbs 14.34

Haughty eyes and a proud heart,
  the lamp of the wicked, are sin.

Proverbs 21.4

Though your sins are like scarlet
  they shall be as white as snow.

Isaiah 1.18

Woe to those who draw iniquity with cords of falsehood,
  who draw sin as with cart ropes.

Isaiah 5.18

The soul that sins shall die.

Ezekiel 18.20

She will bear a son, and you shall call his name Jesus, for he will save his people from their sins.

Matthew 1.21

The Son of man has authority on earth to forgive sins.

Matthew 9.6

Truly, truly, I say to you, every one who commits sin is a slave to sin. The slave does not continue in the house for ever; the son continues for ever. So if the Son makes you free, you will be free indeed.

John 8.34–36

Since all have sinned and fall short of the glory of God, they are justified by his grace as a gift, through the redemption which is in Christ Jesus.

Romans 3.23–24

Sin came into the world through one man and death through sin, and so death spread to all men because all men sinned.

Romans 5.12

Where sin increased, grace abounded all the more, so that, as sin reigned in death, grace also might reign through righteousness to eternal life through Jesus Christ our Lord.

Romans 5.20–21

We know that our old self was crucified with him so that the sinful body might be destroyed, and we might no longer be enslaved to sin.

Romans 6.6

The death he died he died to sin, once for all, but the life he lives he lives to God. So you also must consider yourselves dead to sin and alive to God in Christ Jesus. Let no sin therefore reign in your mortal bodies.

Romans 6.10–11

For the wages of sin is death.

Romans 6.23

Now if I do what I do not want, it is no longer I that do it, but sin which dwells within me.

Romans 7.20

So then, I of myself serve the law of God with my mind, but with my flesh I serve the law of sin.

Romans 7.25

God has done what the law, weakened by the flesh, could not do: sending his own Son in the likeness of sinful flesh and for sin, he condemned sin.

Romans 8.3

Whatever does not proceed from faith is sin.

Romans 14.23

Thus, sinning against your brethren and wounding their conscience when it is weak, you sin against Christ.

1 Corinthians 8.12

Christ died for our sins.

1 Corinthians 15.3

Come to your right mind, and sin no more.

1 Corinthians 15.34

The sting of death is sin.

1 Corinthians 15.56

Now the works of the flesh are plain: fornication, impurity, licentiousness, idolatry, sorcery, enmity, strife, jealousy, anger, selfishness, dissension, party spirit, envy, drunkenness, carousing, and the like. I warn you, as I warned you before, that those who do such things shall not inherit the kingdom of God.

Galatians 5.19–21

Christ Jesus came into the world to save sinners. And I am the foremost of sinners.

1 Timothy 1.15

As for those who persist in sin, rebuke them in the presence of all, so that the rest may stand in fear.

1 Timothy 5.20

Do not . . . participate in another man's sins.

1 Timothy 5.22

Every high priest chosen from among men is appointed to act on behalf of men in relation to God, to offer gifts and sacrifices for sins.

Hebrews 5.1

If we sin deliberately after receiving the knowledge of the truth, there no longer remains a sacrifice for sins.

Hebrews 10.26

Each person is tempted when he is lured and enticed by his own desire. Then desire when it has conceived gives birth to sin; and sin when it is full-grown brings forth death.

James 1.14–15

If we say we have no sin, we deceive ourselves, and the truth is not in us. If we confess our sins, he is faithful and just, and will forgive our sins and cleanse us from all unrighteousness. If we say we have not sinned, we make him a liar, and his word is not in us.

1 John 1.8–10

If any one does sin, we have an advocate with the Father, Jesus Christ the righteous; and he is the expiation for our sins, and not for ours only but also for the sins of the whole world.

1 John 2.1–2

Every one who commits sin is guilty of lawlessness; sin is lawlessness. You know that he appeared to take away sins, and in him there is no sin. No one who abides in him sins; no one who sins has either seen him or known him.

1 John 3.4–6

He who commits sin is of the devil; for the devil has sinned from the beginning.

1 John 3.8

If any one sees his brother committing what is not a mortal sin, he will ask, and God will give him life for those whose sin is not mortal. There is sin which is mortal.

1 John 5.16

All wrongdoing is sin, but there is sin which is not mortal.

1 John 5.17

Sincerity

See also **Honesty, Integrity**

Now therefore fear the Lord, and serve him in sincerity and in faithfulness.

Joshua 24.14

Thou hatest all evildoers.
Thou destroyest those who speak lies;
 the Lord abhors bloodthirsty and
  deceitful men . . .
For there is no truth in their mouth;
 their heart is destruction,
their throat is an open sepulchre,
 they flatter with their tongue.

Psalms 5.5−6,9

Blessed is the man to whom the Lord
 imputes no iniquity,
and in whose spirit there is no deceit.

Psalms 32.2

Behold, thou desirest truth in the inward
 being;
 therefore teach me wisdom in my secret
  heart.

Psalms 51.6

Beware of false prophets, who come to you in sheep's clothing but inwardly are ravenous wolves. You will know them by their fruits. Are grapes gathered from thorns, or figs from thistles? So, every sound tree bears good fruit, but the bad tree bears evil fruit.

Matthew 7.15−17

Not every one whose says to me, 'Lord, Lord,' shall enter the kingdom of heaven, but he who does the will of my Father who is in heaven.

Matthew 7.21

And in anger his lord delivered him to the jailers, till he should pay all his debt. So also my heavenly Father will do to every one of you, if you do not forgive your brother from your heart.

Matthew 18.34−35

Let love be genuine; hate what is evil, hold fast to what is good.

Romans 12.9

Let us, therefore, celebrate the festival, not with the old leaven, the leaven of malice and evil, but with the unleavened bread of sincerity and truth.

1 Corinthians 5.8

As men of sincerity, as commissioned by God, in the sight of God we speak in Christ.

2 Corinthians 2.17

Slaves, be obedient to those who are your earthly masters, with fear and trembling, in singleness of heart, as to Christ; not in the way of eye-service, as men-pleasers, but as servants of Christ, doing the will of God.

Ephesians 6.5−6

Whereas the aim of our charge is love that issues from a pure heart and a good conscience and sincere faith.

1 Timothy 1.5

In your teaching show integrity, gravity, and sound speech that cannot be censured.

Titus 2.7−8

Put away all . . . insincerity and . . . slander. Like newborn babes, long for the pure spiritual milk, that by it you may grow up to salvation.

1 Peter 2.1−2

Let us not love in word or speech but in deed and in truth.

1 John 3.18

Sinners

See also **Sin**

Blessed is the man
    who walks not in the counsel of the
        wicked,
nor stands in the way of sinners.

Psalms 1.1

Good and upright is the Lord;
    therefore he instructs sinners in the way.

Psalms 25.8

Restore to me the joy of thy salvation,
    and uphold me with a willing spirit.
Then I will teach transgressors thy ways,
    and sinners will return to thee.

Psalms 51.12–13

Let sinners be consumed from the earth,
    and let the wicked be no more!

Psalms 104.35

If the righteous is requited on earth,
    how much more the wicked and the
        sinner!

Proverbs 11.31

Sin overthrows the wicked.

Proverbs 13.6

Misfortune pursues sinners.

Proverbs 13.21

The sinner's wealth is laid up for the
    righteous.

Proverbs 13.22

Let not your heart envy sinners,
    but continue in the fear of the Lord all
        the day.

Proverbs 23.17

God gives . . . to the sinner . . . the work
of gathering and heaping, only to give to
one who pleases God.

Ecclesiastes 2.26

And I found more bitter than death the
woman whose heart is snares and nets, and
whose hands are fetters; he who pleases
God escapes her, but the sinner is taken by
her.

Ecclesiastes 7.26

I have not come to call the righteous, but
sinners to repentance.

Luke 5.32

God does not listen to sinners, but if any
one is a worshipper of God and does his
will, God listens to him.

John 9.31

God shows his love for us in that while we
were yet sinners Christ died for us.

Romans 5.8

Christ Jesus came into the world to save
sinners.

1 Timothy 1.15

For it was fitting that we should have such
a high priest, holy, blameless, unstained,
separated from sinners.

Hebrews 7.26

Consider him who endured from sinners
such hostility against himself, so that you
may not grow weary or faint-hearted.

Hebrews 12.3

Cleanse your hands, you sinners.

James 4.8

The devil has sinned from the beginning.

1 John 3.8

Skill

Do you see a man skilful in his work?
    he will stand before kings;
    he will not stand before obscure men.

Proverbs 22.29

Then I saw that all toil and all skill in work
come from a man's envy of his neighbour.
This also is vanity and a striving after wind.

Ecclesiastes 4.4

Slander

See also **Criticism, Gossip, Perjury**

You shall not utter a false report.

Exodus 23.1

You shall not go up and down as a slanderer among your people.

Leviticus 19.16

If any man takes a wife, and goes in to her, and then spurns her, and charges her with shameful conduct, and brings an evil name upon her, saying, 'I took this woman, and when I came near her, I did not find in her the tokens of virginity,' then the father of the young woman and her mother shall take and bring out the tokens of her virginity to the elders of the city . . . Then the elders of that city shall take the man and whip him.

Deuteronomy 22.13–15,18

O Lord, who shall sojourn in thy tent?
 Who shall dwell on thy holy hill?
He . . . who does not slander with his
  tongue.

Psalms 15.1–3

To the wicked God says:
'What right have you to recite my statutes,
or take my covenant on your lips? . . .
You give your mouth free rein for evil,
 and your tongue frames deceit.
You sit and speak against your brother;
 you slander your own mother's son . . .
But now I rebuke you, and lay the
  charge before you.'

Psalms 50.16,19–21

Him who slanders his neighbour secretly
 I will destroy.

Psalms 101.5

He who conceals hatred has lying lips,
 and he who utters slander is a fool.

Proverbs 10.18

With his mouth the godless man would
  destroy his neighbour.

Proverbs 11.9

Let every one beware of his neighbour,
 and put no trust in any brother;

for every brother is a supplanter,
 and every neighbour goes about as a
  slanderer.

Jeremiah 9.4

Blessed are you when men revile you and persecute you and utter all kinds of evil against you falsely on my account.

Matthew 5.11

The good man out of the good treasure of his heart produces good, and the evil man out of his evil treasure produces evil; for out of the abundance of the heart his mouth speaks.

Luke 6.45

Gossips, slanderers, haters of God . . . Though they know God's decree that those who do such things deserve to die, they not only do them but approve those who practise them.

Romans 1.29,32

Let all bitterness and wrath and anger and clamour and slander be put away from you with all malice.

Ephesians 4.31

Do not speak evil against one another.

James 4.11

So put away all malice and all guile and insincerity and envy and all slander.

1 Peter 2.1

Always be prepared to make a defence to any one who calls you to account for the hope that is in you, yet do it with gentleness and reverence; and keep your conscience clear, so that, when you are abused, those who revile your good behaviour in Christ may be put to shame.

1 Peter 3.15–16

Sleep

Sweet is the sleep of a labourer, whether he eats little or much; but the surfeit of the rich will not let him sleep.

Ecclesiastes 5.12

Sleepiness

Love not sleep, lest you come to poverty;
  open your eyes, and you will have plenty
    of bread.

Proverbs 20.13

Sleeplessness

Do not enter the path of the wicked,
  and do not walk in the way of evil men.
Avoid it; do not go on it;
  turn away from it and pass on.
For they cannot sleep unless they have done
    wrong;
  they are robbed of sleep unless they have
    made some one stumble.

Proverbs 4.14—16

Snobbery

My brethren, show no partiality as you
hold the faith of our Lord Jesus Christ, the
Lord of glory. For if a man with gold rings
and in fine clothing comes into your assembly, and a poor man in shabby clothing also
comes in, and you pay attention to the one
who wears the fine clothing and say, 'Have
a seat here, please,' while you say to the
poor man, 'Stand there,' or, 'Sit at my feet,'
have you not made distinctions among
yourselves, and become judges with evil
thoughts?

James 2.1—4

Sobriety

See also **Gravity, Moderation**

Think with sober judgment, each according to the measure of faith which God has
assigned him.

Romans 12.3

Let us conduct ourselves becomingly as in
the day, not in revelling and drunkenness,
not in debauchery and licentiousness, not in
quarrelling and jealousy.

Romans 13.13

For you are all sons of light and sons of the
day; we are not of the night or of darkness.
So then let us not sleep, as others do, but
let us keep awake and be sober.

1 Thessalonians 5.5—6

Bid the older women likewise to be reverent in behaviour, not to be slanderers or
slaves to drink.

Titus 2.3

Keep sane and sober for your prayers.

1 Peter 4.8

Solitude

Then the Lord God said, 'It is not good
that the man should be alone.'

Genesis 2.18

He who is estranged seeks pretexts
  to break out against all sound judgment.

Proverbs 18.1

But when you pray, go into your room and
shut the door and pray to your Father who
is in secret; and your Father who sees in
secret will reward you.

Matthew 6.6

Son

Lo, sons are a heritage from the Lord,
  the fruit of the womb a reward.
Like arrows in the hand of a warrior
  are the sons of one's youth.
Happy is the man who has
  his quiver full of them!

Psalms 127.3—5

Hear, O sons, a father's instruction,
  and be attentive, that you may gain
    insight.

Proverbs 4.1

A wise son makes a glad father,
  but a foolish son is a sorrow to his
    mother.

Proverbs 10.1

A foolish son is ruin to his father.

Proverbs 19.13

He who does violence to his father and
  chases away his mother
is a son who causes shame and brings
  reproach.

Proverbs 19.26

Discipline your son, and he will give you
  rest;
he will give delight to your heart.

Proverbs 29.17

Song

See also **Hymn**

Sing to God, sing praises to his name;
  lift up a song to him who rides upon the
    clouds;
  his name is the Lord, exult before him!

Psalms 68.4

Sorrow

See also **Misery, Mourning, Remorse**

Man that is born of a woman is of few
days, and full of trouble.

Job 14.1

For his anger is but for a moment,
  and his favour is for a lifetime.
Weeping may tarry for the night,
  but joy comes with the morning.

Psalms 30.5

But I am afflicted and in pain;
  let thy salvation, O God, set me on high!

Psalms 69.29

May those who sow in tears
  reap with shouts of joy!
He that goes forth weeping,
  bearing the seed for sowing,
shall come home with shouts of joy,
  bringing his sheaves with him.

Psalms 126.5−6

By sorrow of heart the spirit is broken.

Proverbs 15.13

For in much wisdom is much vexation,
and he who increases knowledge increases
  sorrow.

Ecclesiastes 1.18

Sorrow is better than laughter,
  for by sadness of countenance the heart is
    made glad.

Ecclesiastes 7.3

The Lord God will wipe away tears from
all faces, and the reproach of his people he
will take away from all the earth; for the
Lord has spoken.

Isaiah 25.8

And though the Lord give you the bread
of adversity and the water of affliction, yet
your Teacher will not hide himself any
more.

Isaiah 30.20

I will turn their mourning into joy,
  I will comfort them, and give them
    gladness for sorrow.

Jeremiah 31.13

Is it nothing to you, all you who pass by?
  Look and see
if there is any sorrow like my sorrow which
    was brought upon me,
which the Lord inflicted on the day of his
    fierce anger.

Lamentations 1.12

Blessed are you that weep now, for you
    shall laugh . . .
Woe to you that laugh now, for you
    shall mourn and weep.

Luke 6.21,25

Truly, truly, I say to you, you will weep
and lament, but the world will rejoice; you
will be sorrowful, but your sorrow will turn
into joy. When a woman is in travail she
has sorrow, because her hour has come; but
when she is delivered of the child, she no
longer remembers the anguish, for joy that
a child is born into the world. So you have
sorrow now, but I will see you again and
your hearts will rejoice, and no one will
take your joy from you.

John 16.20−22

Rejoice with those who rejoice, weep with those who weep.

Romans 12.15

Blessed be the God and Father of our Lord Jesus Christ, the Father of mercies and God of all comfort, who comforts us in all our affliction, so that we may be able to comfort those who are in any affliction, with the comfort with which we ourselves are comforted by God.

2 Corinthians 1.3−4

Be wretched and mourn and weep. Let your laughter be turned to mourning and your joy to dejection.

James 4.9

Behold, the dwelling of God is with men. He will dwell with them, and they shall be his people, and God himself will be with them; he will wipe away every tear from their eyes, and death shall be no more, neither shall there be mourning nor crying nor pain any more.

Revelation 21.3−4

Speculation

You may charge certain persons not to teach any different doctrine, nor to occupy themselves with myths and endless genealogies which promote speculations rather than the divine training that is in faith; whereas the aim of our charge is love that issues from a pure heart and a good conscience and sincere faith. Certain persons by swerving from these have wandered away into vain discussion, desiring to be teachers of the law, without understanding either what they are saying or the things about which they make assertions.

1 Timothy 1.3−7

Spirit/Spirituality

See also **Mysticism**

And he humbled you and let you hunger and fed you with manna, which you did not know, nor did your fathers know; that he might make you know that man does not live by bread alone, but man lives by everything that proceeds out of the mouth of the Lord.

Deuteronomy 8.3

Into thy hand I commit my spirit;
    thou hast redeemed me, O Lord.

Psalms 31.5

Create in me a clean heart, O God,
    and put a new and right spirit within me.

Psalms 51.10

A downcast spirit dries up the bones.

Proverbs 17.22

The spirit of man is the lamp of the Lord,
    searching all his innermost parts.

Proverbs 20.27

For I will pour water on the thirsty land,
    and streams on the dry ground;
I will pour my Spirit upon your
        descendants,
    and my blessing on your offspring.

Isaiah 44.3

Cast away from you all the transgressions which you have committed against me, and get yourselves a new heart and a new spirit!

Ezekiel 18.31

And it shall come to pass afterward,
    that I will pour out my spirit on all flesh;
your sons and your daughters shall
        prophesy,
    your old men shall dream dreams,
    and your young men shall see visions.
Even upon the menservants and
        maidservants
    in those days, I will pour out my spirit.

Joel 2.28−29

The Lord . . . stretched out the heavens and founded the earth and formed the spirit of man within him.

Zechariah 12.1

The spirit indeed is willing, but the flesh is weak.

Mark 14.38

That which is born of the flesh is flesh, and that which is born of the Spirit is spirit.

John 3.6

But the hour is coming, and now is, when the true worshippers will worship the Father in spirit and truth.

John 4.23

God is spirit, and those who worship him must worship in spirit and truth.

John 4.24

Do not labour for the food which perishes, but for the food which endures to eternal life, which the Son of man will give to you; for on him has God the Father set his seal.

John 6.27

It is the spirit that gives life, the flesh is of no avail; the words that I have spoken to you are spirit and life.

John 6.63

But now we are discharged from the law, dead to that which held us captive, so that we serve not under the old written code but in the new life of the Spirit.

Romans 7.6

For I delight in the law of God, in my inmost self.

Romans 7.22

There is therefore now no condemnation for those who are in Christ Jesus. For the law of the Spirit of life in Christ Jesus has set me free from the law of sin and death.

Romans 8.1–2

Walk not according to the flesh but according to the Spirit.

Romans 8.4

To set the mind on the Spirit is life and peace.

Romans 8.6

But you are not in the flesh, you are in the Spirit, if in fact the Spirit of God dwells in you. Any one who does not have the Spirit of Christ does not belong to him. But if Christ is in you, although your bodies are dead because of sin, your spirits are alive because of righteousness.

Romans 8.9–10

For if you live according to the flesh you will die, but if by the Spirit you put to death the deeds of the body you will live.

Romans 8.13

When we cry, 'Abba! Father!' it is the Spirit himself bearing witness with our spirit that we are children of God.

Romans 8.16

Never flag in zeal, be aglow with the Spirit, serve the Lord.

Romans 12.11

For the Spirit searches everything, even the depths of God.

1 Corinthians 2.10

For what person knows a man's thoughts except the spirit of the man which is in him?

1 Corinthians 2.11

Now we have received not the spirit of the world, but the Spirit which is from God, that we might understand the gifts bestowed on us by God. And we impart this in words not taught by human wisdom but taught by the Spirit . . .

The unspiritual man does not receive the gifts of the Spirit of God, for they are folly to him, and he is not able to understand them because they are spiritually discerned. The spiritual man judges all things, but is himself to be judged by no one.

1 Corinthians 2.12–15

Do you not know that you are God's temple and that God's Spirit dwells in you? If any one destroys God's temple, God will destroy him. For God's temple is holy, and that temple you are.

1 Corinthians 3.16–17

Now there are varieties of gifts, but the same Spirit; and there are varieties of service, but the same Lord; and there are varieties of working, but it is the same God who inspires them all in every one. To each is given the manifestation of the Spirit for the common good.

1 Corinthians 12.4−7

If there is a physical body, there is also a spiritual body. Thus it is written, 'The first man Adam became a living being'; the last Adam became a life-giving spirit. But it is not the spiritual which is first but the physical, and then the spiritual.

1 Corinthians 15.44−46

The Spirit gives life.

2 Corinthians 3.6

Now the Lord is the Spirit, and where the Spirit of the Lord is, there is freedom. And we all, with unveiled face, beholding the glory of the Lord, are being changed into his likeness from one degree of glory to another; for this comes from the Lord who is the Spirit.

2 Corinthians 3.17−18

The fellowship of the Holy Spirit be with you all.

2 Corinthians 13.14

Walk by the Spirit, and do not gratify the desires of the flesh.

Galatians 5.16

But the fruit of the Spirit is love, joy, peace, patience, kindness, goodness, faithfulness, gentleness, self-control.

Galatians 5.22−23

He may grant you to be strengthened with might through his Spirit in the inner man.

Ephesians 3.16

If then you have been raised with Christ, seek the things that are above, where Christ is, seated at the right hand of God. Set your minds on things that are above, not on things that are on earth.

Colossians 3.1−2

For this is why the gospel was preached even to the dead, that though judged in the flesh like men, they might live in the spirit like God.

1 Peter 4.6

Starvation

Behold, I will rain bread from heaven for you.

Exodus 16.4

Steadfastness

Woe to him who builds a town with blood,
and founds a city on iniquity!
Behold, is it not from the Lord of hosts
that peoples labour only for fire,
and nations weary themselves for naught?
For the earth will be filled
with the knowledge of the glory of the
Lord,
as the waters cover the sea.

Habakkuk 2.12−14

Though the fig tree do not blossom,
nor fruit be on the vines,
the produce of the olive fail
and the fields yield no food,
the flock be cut off from the fold
and there be no herd in the stalls,
yet I will rejoice in the Lord,
I will joy in the God of my salvation.

Habakkuk 3.17−18

Therefore, my beloved brethren, be steadfast, immovable, always abounding in the work of the Lord, knowing that in the Lord your labour is not in vain.

1 Corinthians 15.58

So then, brethren, stand firm and hold to the traditions which you were taught by us, either by word of mouth or by letter.

2 Thessalonians 2.15

Count it all joy, my brethren, when you meet various trials, for you know that the testing of your faith produces steadfastness. And let steadfastness have its full effect, that you may be perfect and complete, lacking in nothing.

James 1.2−4

Strangers

Do not neglect to show hospitality to strangers, for thereby some have entertained angels unawares.

Hebrews 13.2

Strength

See also **Ability, Power**

He will guard the feet of his faithful ones;
but the wicked shall be cut off in darkness;
for not by might shall a man prevail.

1 Samuel 2.9

For who is God, but the Lord?
  And who is a rock, except our God?
This God is my strong refuge,
  and has made my way safe.

2 Samuel 22.32–33

Seek the Lord and his strength,
  seek his presence continually!

1 Chronicles 16.11

Thou rulest over all. In thy hand are power
and might.

1 Chronicles 29.12

I love thee, O Lord, my strength.
  The Lord is my rock, and my fortress,
    and my deliverer,
  my God, my rock, in whom I take refuge.

Psalms 18.1–2

Yea, by thee I can crush a troop;
  and by my God I can leap over a wall.

Psalms 18.29

Now I know that the Lord will help his
  anointed;
  he will answer him from his holy heaven
  with mighty victories by his right hand.

Psalms 20.6

Wait for the Lord;
  be strong, and let your heart take
    courage;
  yea, wait for thc Lord!

Psalms 27.14

The Lord is my strength and my shield;
  in him my heart trusts.

Psalms 28.7

The Lord is the strength of his people,
  he is the saving refuge of his anointed.

Psalms 28.8

May the Lord give strength to his people!

Psalms 29.11

Once God has spoken;
  twice have I heard this;
that power belongs to God.

Psalms 62.11

Thou dost cause the grass to grow for the
  cattle,
  and plants for man to cultivate,
that he may bring forth food from
  the earth,
  and wine to gladden the heart of man,
oil to make his face shine,
  and bread to strengthen man's heart.

Psalms 104.14–15

The Lord is a stronghold to him whose way
  is upright.

Proverbs 10.29

The glory of young men is their strength.

Proverbs 20.29

A wise man is mightier than a strong man.

Proverbs 24.5

In quietness and in trust shall be your
  strength.

Isaiah 30.15

Strengthen the weak hands,
  and make firm the feeble knees.
Say to those who are of a fearful heart,
  'Be strong, fear not!
Behold, your God
  will come with vengeance,
with the recompense of God.
  He will come and save you.'

Isaiah 35.3–4

He gives power to the faint,
  and to him who has no might he increases
    strength.
Even youths shall faint and be weary,
  and young men shall fall exahusted;
but they who wait for the Lord shall renew
    their strength.

Isaiah 40.29–31

I am your God;
I will strengthen you, I will help you,
  I will uphold you with my victorious right
    hand.

Isaiah 41.10

Only in the Lord, it shall be said of me,
are righteousness and strength.

Isaiah 45.24

God, the Lord, is my strength;
he makes my feet like hinds' feet,
he makes me tread upon my high places.

Habakkuk 3.19

You shall love the Lord your God with all
your heart, and with all your soul, and with
all your mind, and with all your strength.

Mark 12.30

No distrust made him waver concerning
the promise of God, but he grew strong in
his faith as he gave glory to God.

Romans 4.20

We who are strong ought to bear with the
failings of the weak.

Romans 15.1

Stand firm in your faith, be courageous, be
strong.

1 Corinthians 16.13

For this reason I bow my knees before the
Father, from whom every family in heaven
and earth is named, that according to the
riches of his glory he may grant you to be
strengthened with might through his Spirit
in the inner man.

Ephesians 3.14−16

Be strong in the Lord and in the strength
of his might.

Ephesians 6.10

I can do all things in him who strengthens
me.

Philippians 4.13

May you be strengthened with all power,
according to his glorious might, for all
endurance and patience.

Colossians 1.11

Stubbornness

I have seen this people, and behold, it is a
stiff-necked people; now therefore let me
alone, that my wrath may burn hot against
them and I may consume them.

Exodus 32.9−10

If now I have found favour in thy sight, O
Lord, let the Lord, I pray thee, go in the
midst of us, although it is a stiff-necked
people; and pardon our iniquity and our
sin, and take us for thy inheritance.

Exodus 34.9

If a man does not repent, God will whet his
sword;
he has bent and strung his bow;
he has prepared his deadly weapons,
making his arrows fiery shafts.

Psalms 7.12−13

He who is often reproved,
yet stiffens his neck
will suddenly be broken beyond healing.

Proverbs 29.1

Hearken to me, you stubborn of heart,
you who are far from deliverance:
I bring near my deliverance, it is not far off,
and my salvation will not tarry.

Isaiah 46.12−13

You stiff-necked people, uncircumcised in
heart and ears, you always resist the Holy
Spirit.

Acts 7.51

It hurts you to kick against the goads.

Acts 26.14

But by your hard and impenitent heart
you are storing up wrath for yourself on the
day of wrath when God's righteous judgment will be revealed.

Romans 2.5

So then he has mercy upon whomever he
wills, and he hardens the heart of whomever he wills.

Romans 9.18

Stupidity

Whoever loves discipline loves knowledge,
but he who hates reproof is stupid.

Proverbs 12.1

The way of a fool is right in his own eyes,
but a wise man listens to advice . . .
A prudent man conceals his knowledge,
but fools proclaim their folly.

Proverbs 12.15,23

My people are foolish,
  they know me not;
they are stupid children,
  they have no understanding.
They are skilled in doing evil,
  but how to do good they know not.
Jeremiah 4.22

Subversion

For there are many insubordinate men, empty talkers and deceivers, especially the circumcision party; they must be silenced, since they are upsetting whole families by teaching for base gain what they have no right to teach.
Titus 1.10–11

Take care, brethren, lest there be in any of you an evil, unbelieving heart, leading you to fall away from the living God.
Hebrews 3.12

Success

See also **Promotion**

But remember me, when it is well with you.
Genesis 40.14

Take heed lest you forget the Lord your God, by not keeping his commandments and his ordinances and his statutes, which I command you this day: lest, when you have eaten and are full, and have built goodly houses and live in them, and when your herds and flocks multiply, and your silver and gold is multiplied . . . then your heart be lifted up, and you forget the Lord your God . . . Beware lest you say in your heart, 'My power and the might of my hand have gotten me this wealth.' You shall remember the Lord your God, for it is he who gives you power to get wealth.
Deuteronomy 8.11–14,17–18

Therefore be careful to do the words of this covenant, that you may prosper in all that you do.
Deuteronomy 29.9

This book of the law shall not depart out of your mouth, but you shall meditate on it day and night, that you may be careful to do according to all that is written in it; for then you shall make your way prosperous, and then you shall have good success.
Joshua 1.8

Believe in the Lord your God, and you will be established; believe his prophets, and you will succeed.
2 Chronicles 20.20

O Lord, let thy ear be attentive to the prayer of thy servant, and to the prayer of thy servants who delight to fear thy name; and give success to thy servant today, and grant him mercy in the sight of this man.
Nehemiah 1.11

Honour the Lord with your substance
  and with the first fruits of all your
    produce;
then your barns will be filled with plenty,
  and your vats will be bursting with wine.
Proverbs 3.9–10

When it goes well with the righteous, the
    city rejoices;
and when the wicked perish there are
    shouts of gladness.
Proverbs 11.10

A desire fulfilled is sweet to the soul.
Proverbs 13.19

Did not your father eat and drink
  and do justice and righteousness?
Then it was well with him.
Jeremiah 22.15

Suffering

See also **Distress**

Cursed is the ground because of you;
  in toil you shall eat of it all the days of
    your life;
thorns and thistles it shall bring forth to
    you;
  and your shall eat the plants of the field.
In the sweat of your face
  you shall eat bread

till you return to the ground,
  for out of it you were taken;
you are dust,
  and to dust you shall return.

Genesis 3.17–19

Man that is born of a woman is of few days, and full of trouble.

Job 14.1

How long, O Lord? Wilt thou forget me
  for ever?
How long wilt thou hide thy face from
  me?
How long must I bear pain in my soul,
  and have sorrow in my heart all the day?
How long shall my enemy be exalted over
  me?

Psalms 13.1–2

The heart knows its own bitterness.

Proverbs 14.10

I have refined you, but not like silver;
  I have tried you in the furnace of
    affliction.

Isaiah 48.10

There will be tribulation and distress for every human being who does evil.

Romans 2.9

We rejoice in our sufferings, knowing that suffering produces endurance, and endurance produces character, and character produces hope.

Romans 5.3–4

We are children of God, and if children, then heirs, heirs of God and fellow heirs with Christ, provided we suffer with him in order that we may also be glorified with him.

I consider that the sufferings of this present time are not worth comparing with the glory that is to be revealed to us.

Romans 8.16–18

We know that as you share in our sufferings, you will also share in our comfort.

2 Corinthians 1.7

For godly grief produces a repentance that leads to salvation and brings no regret, but worldly grief produces death.

2 Corinthians 7.10

Stand firm . . . not frightened in anything by your opponents. This is a clear omen to them of their destruction, but of your salvation, and that from God. For it has been granted to you that for the sake of Christ you should not only believe in him but also suffer for his sake.

Philippians 1.27–29

Share in suffering for the gospel in the power of God.

2 Timothy 1.8

For because he himself has suffered and been tempted, he is able to help those who are tempted.

Hebrews 2.18

For one is approved if, mindful of God, he endures pain while suffering unjustly. For what credit is it, if when you do wrong and are beaten for it you take it patiently? But if when you do right and suffer for it you take it patiently, you have God's approval. For to this you have been called, because Christ also suffered for you, leaving you an example, that you should follow in his steps.

1 Peter 2.19–21

Now who is there to harm you if you are zealous for what is right? But even if you do suffer for righteousness' sake, you will be blessed.

1 Peter 3.13–14

Since therefore Christ suffered in the flesh, arm yourselves with the same thought, for whoever has suffered in the flesh has ceased from sin.

1 Peter 4.1

If one suffers as a Christian, let him not be ashamed, but under that name let him glorify God.

1 Peter 4.16

Therefore let those who suffer according to God's will do right and entrust their souls to a faithful Creator.

1 Peter 4.19

And after you have suffered a little while, the God of all grace, who has called you to his eternal glory in Christ, will himself restore, establish, and strengthen you.

1 Peter 5.10

Do not fear what you are about to suffer . . . Be faithful unto death, and I will give you the crown of life.

Revelation 2.10—11

Suicide

He who misses me injures himself;
all who hate me love death.

Proverbs 8.36

Do not harm yourself.

Acts 16.28

If any one destroys God's temple, God will destroy him. For God's temple is holy, and that temple you are.

1 Corinthians 3.17

Superficiality

See also **Appearance**

If you faint in the day of adversity,
your strength is small.

Proverbs 24.10

Your love is like a morning cloud,
like the dew that goes early away.
Therefore I have hewn them by the
prophets,
I have slain them by the words of my
mouth.

Hosea 6.4—5

As for what was sown on rocky ground, this is he who hears the word and immediately receives it with joy; yet he has no root in himself, but endures for a while, and when tribulation or persecution arises on account of the word, immediately he falls away.

Matthew 13.20—21

Woe to you . . . for you tithe mint and dill and cummin, and have neglected the weightier matters of the law, justice and mercy and faith.

Matthew 23.23

Superstition

See also **Magic, Occult**

Charge certain persons not to teach any different doctrine, nor to occupy themselves with myths and endless genealogies which promote speculations rather than the divine training that is in faith.

1 Timothy 1.3—4

Have nothing to do with godless and silly myths.

1 Timothy 4.7

Preach the word, be urgent in season and out of season, convince, rebuke, and exhort, be unfailing in patience and in teaching. For the time is coming when people will not endure sound teaching, but having itching ears they will accumulate for themselves teachers to suit their own likings, and will turn away from listening to the truth and wander into myths.

2 Timothy 4.2—4

For there are many insubordinate men, empty talkers and deceivers . . . they must be silenced, since they are upsetting whole families by teaching for base gain what they have no right to teach . . . Therefore rebuke them sharply, that they may be sound in the faith, instead of giving heed to . . . myths or to commands of men who reject the truth.

Titus 1.10—11,13—14

Support

See also **Help**

Two are better than one, because they have a good reward for their toil. For if they fall, one will lift up his fellow; but woe to him who is alone when he falls and has not another to lift him up. Again, if two lie together, they are warm; but how can one be warm alone? And though a man might prevail against one who is alone, two will withstand him. A threefold cord is not quickly broken.

Ecclesiastes 4.9—12

Survival

See also **Rescue**

Lift up your prayer for the remnant that is left.

2 Kings 19.4

And the surviving remnant of the house of Judah shall again take root downward, and bear fruit upward; for out of Jerusalem shall go forth a remnant, and out of Mount Zion a band of survivors.

2 Kings 19.30−31

O Lord the God of Israel, thou art just, for we are left a remnant that has escaped, as at this day.

Ezra 9.15

For though your people Israel be as the sand of the sea, only a remnant of them will return.

Isaiah 10.22

There shall come forth a shoot from the
     stump of Jesse,
  and a branch shall grow out of his roots.
And the Spirit of the Lord shall rest upon
     him,
  the spirit of wisdom and understanding,
  the spirit of counsel and might,
  the spirit of knowledge and the fear of
     the Lord.
And his delight shall be in the fear of the
     Lord.

Isaiah 11.1−3

And it shall come to pass that all who call upon the name of the Lord shall be delivered; for in Mount Zion and in Jerusalem there shall be those who escape, as the Lord has said, and among the survivors shall be those whom the Lord calls.

Joel 2.32

Hate evil, and love good,
  and establish justice in the gate;
it may be that the Lord, the God of hosts,
  will be gracious to the remnant of Joseph.

Amos 5.15

Suspicion

Saul eyed David from that day on . . . an evil spirit from God rushed upon Saul, and he raved within his house, while David was playing the lyre, as he did day by day. Saul had his spear in his hand and . . . cast the spear, for he thought, 'I will pin David to the wall.' But David evaded him twice. Saul was afraid of David, because the Lord was with him but had departed from Saul.

1 Samuel 18.9−12

Peter said to him, 'Even though they all fall away, I will not.' And Jesus said to him, 'Truly, I say to you . . . before the cock crows twice, you will deny me three times.'

Mark 14.29−30

Swearing

See also **Oaths**

Again you have heard that it was said to the men of old, 'You shall not swear falsely, but shall perform to the Lord what you have sworn.' But I say to you, Do not swear at all, either by heaven, for it is the throne of God, or by the earth, for it is his footstool, or by Jerusalem, for it is the city of the great King. And do not swear by your head, for you cannot make one hair white or black. Let what you say be simply 'Yes' or 'No'; anything more than this comes from evil.

Matthew 5.33−37

But above all . . . do not swear, either by heaven or by earth or with any other oath, but let your yes be yes and your no be no, that you may not fall under condemnation.

James 5.12

Sympathy

See also **Compassion, Pity**

Anxiety in a man's heart weighs him
     down,
  but a good word makes him glad.

Proverbs 12.25

Rejoice with those who rejoice, weep with those who weep.

Romans 12.15

He who prophesies speaks to men for their upbuilding and encouragement and consolation.

1 Corinthians 14.3

So if there is any encouragement in Christ, any incentive of love, any participation in the Spirit, any affection and sympathy, complete my joy by being of the same mind, having the same love.

Philippians 2.1–2

Be at peace among yourselves . . . encourage the fainthearted, help the weak, be patient with them all.

1 Thessalonians 5.13–14

For every high priest chosen from among men . . . can deal gently with the ignorant and wayward, since he himself is beset with weakness.

Hebrews 5.1–2

Let us consider how to stir up one another to love and good works.

Hebrews 10.24

Remember those who are in prison, as though in prison with them; and those who are ill-treated, since you also are in the body.

Hebrews 13.3

Religion that is pure and undefiled before God and the Father is this: to visit orphans and widows in their affliction.

James 1.27

Have unity of spirit, sympathy, love of the brethren, a tender heart and a humble mind.

1 Peter 3.8

T

Tact

Set a guard over my mouth, O Lord,
  keep watch over the door of my lips!

Psalms 141.3

A soft answer turns away wrath,
  but a harsh word stirs up anger.

Proverbs 15.1

A gentle tongue is a tree of life,
  but perverseness in it breaks the spirit.

Proverbs 15.4

To make an apt answer is a joy to a man,
  and a word in season, how good it is!

Proverbs 15.23

The mind of the wise makes his speech
      judicious,
  and adds persuasiveness to his lips.

Proverbs 16.23

A word fitly spoken
  is like apples of gold in a setting of silver.

Proverbs 25.11

With patience a ruler may be persuaded,
  and a soft tongue will break a bone.

Proverbs 25.15

For everything there is a season . . . a
  me to keep silence, and a time to speak.

Ecclesiastes 3.17

f the serpent bites before it is charmed,
  there is no advantage in a charmer.

Ecclesiastes 10.11

Even in your thought, do not curse the
      king,
  nor in your bedchamber curse the rich;

for a bird of the air will carry your voice,
  or some winged creature tell the matter.

Ecclesiastes 10.20

I have become all things to all men, that I
might by all means save some.

1 Corinthians 9.22

Though if I wish to boast, I shall not be a
fool, for I shall be speaking the truth. But I
refrain from it, so that no one may think
more of me than he sees in me or hears
from me.

2 Corinthians 12.6

Talent

See also **Ability, Gifts**

Having gifts that differ according to the
grace given to us, let us use them.

Romans 12.6

I give thanks to God always for you because of the grace of God which was given
you in Christ Jesus, that in every way you
were enriched in him.

1 Corinthians 1.4–5

Each has his own special gift from God,
one of one kind and one of another.

1 Corinthians 7.7

Talkativeness

Wise men lay up knowledge,
  but the babbling of a fool brings ruin
    near.

Proverbs 10.14

When words are many, transgression is
  not lacking,
  but he who restrains his lips is prudent.

Proverbs 10.19

There is one whose rash words are like
  sword thrusts,
  but the tongue of the wise brings healing.

Proverbs 12.18

A prudent man conceals his knowledge,
  but fools proclaim their folly.

Proverbs 12.23

He who guards his mouth preserves his
  life;
  he who opens wide his lips comes to ruin.

Proverbs 13.3

The talk of a fool is a rod for his back,
  but the lips of the wise will preserve
    them.

Proverbs 14.3

The more words, the more vanity, and
what is man the better?

Ecclesiastes 6.11

Avoid such godless chatter, for it will lead
people into more and more ungodliness,
and their talk will eat its way like gangrene.

2 Timothy 2.16–17

No human being can tame the tongue — a
restless evil, full of deadly poison.

James 3.8

Tattoo

You shall not make any cuttings in your
flesh on account of the dead or tattoo any
marks upon you: I am the Lord.

Leviticus 19.28

Tax

Pay taxes, for the authorities are ministers
of God, attending to this very thing. Pay all
of them their dues, taxes to whom taxes are
due, revenue to whom revenue is due,
respect to whom respect is due, honour to
whom honour is due.

Romans 14.6–7

Teaching

See also **Education, Learning**

Only take heed, and keep your soul diligently, lest you forget the things which your
eyes have seen, and lest they depart from
your heart all the days of your life; make
them known to your children and your children's children.

Deuteronomy 4.9

Now this is the commandment, the statutes
and the ordinances which the Lord your
God commanded me to teach you . . . And
these words which I command you this day
shall be upon your heart; and you shall
teach them diligently to your children, and
shall talk of them when you sit in your
house, and when you walk by the way, and
when you lie down, and when you rise.

Deuteronomy 6.1,6–7

You shall therefore lay up these words of
mine in your heart and in your soul; and
you shall bind them as a sign upon your
hand, and they shall be as frontlets between
your eyes. And you shall teach them to
your children, talking of them when you are
sitting in your house, and when you are
walking by the way, and when you lie
down, and when you rise.

Deuteronomy 11.18–19

Far be it from me that I should sin against
the Lord by ceasing to pray for you; and I
will instruct you in the good and the right
way.

1 Samuel 12.23

But ask the beasts, and they will teach
  you;
  the birds of the air, and they will tell you;
or the plants of the earth, and they will
    teach you;
  and the fish of the sea will declare to you.
Who among all these does not know
  that the hand of the Lord has done this?

Job 12.7–

Let days speak,
and many years teach wisdom.

Job 32.7

Behold, God is exalted in his power;
who is a teacher like him?

Job 36.22

Make me to know thy ways, O Lord;
teach me thy paths.

Psalms 25.4

Good and upright is the Lord;
therefore he instructs sinners in the way.
He leads the humble in what is right,
and teaches the humble his way.

Psalms 25.8–9

Who is the man that fears the Lord?
Him will he instruct in the way that he
should choose.

Psalms 25.12

Teach me thy way, O Lord;
and lead me on a level path
because of my enemies.

Psalms 27.11

Give instruction to a wise man, and he will
be still wiser;
teach a righteous man and he will
increase in learning.

Proverbs 9.9

I am the Lord your God,
who teaches you to profit,
who leads you in the way you should go.

Isaiah 48.17

Whoever then relaxes one of the least of
these commandments and teaches men so,
shall be called least in the kingdom
of heaven.

Matthew 5.19

Go therefore and make disciples of all
nations . . . teaching them to observe all
that I have commanded you.

Matthew 28.19–20

And when they bring you before the
synagogues and the rulers and the authorities, do not be anxious how or what you are
to answer or what you are to say; for the
Holy Spirit will teach you in that very hour
what you ought to say.

Luke 12.11–12

But the Counsellor, the Holy Spirit, whom
the Father will send in my name, he will
teach you all things, and bring to your
remembrance all that I have said to you.

John 14.26

Let him who is taught the word share all
good things with him who teaches.

Galatians 6.6

God chose to make known . . . this mystery, which is Christ in you . . . Him we
proclaim, warning every man and teaching
every man in all wisdom, that we may
present every man mature in Christ.

Colossians 1.27–28

What you have heard from me before
many witnesses entrust to faithful men who
will be able to teach others also.

2 Timothy 2.2

All scripture is inspired by God and profitable for teaching, for reproof, for correction, and for training in righteousness, that
the man of God may be complete, equipped
for every good work.

2 Timothy 3.16–17

Bid the older women . . . to teach what is
good, and so train the young women to love
their husbands and children, to be sensible,
chaste, domestic, kind.

Titus 2.3–4

For though by this time you ought to be
teachers, you need some one to teach you
again the first principles of God's word.

Hebrews 5.12

But the anointing which you received from
him abides in you, and you have no need
that any one should teach you; as his
anointing teaches you about everything,
and is true, and is no lie, just as it has
taught you, abide in him.

1 John 2.27

Temperance

See also **Moderation, Self-Control**

If you have found honey, eat only enough
for you,
    lest you be sated with it and vomit it.

Proverbs 25.16

But put on the Lord Jesus Christ, and
make no provision for the flesh, to gratify
its desires.

Romans 13.14

Every athlete exercises self-control in all
things. They do it to receive a perishable
wreath, but we an imperishable. Well, I do
not run aimlessly, I do not box as one
beating the air; but I pommel my body and
subdue it.

1 Corinthians 9.25–27

And those who belong to Christ Jesus
have crucified the flesh with its passions and
desires.

Galatians 5.24

A bishop must be . . . temperate, sensible
. . . and no lover of money.

1 Timothy 3.2–3

No longer drink only water, but use a little
wine for the sake of your stomach.

1 Timothy 5.23

For a bishop, as God's steward, must be
blameless; he must not be . . . a drunkard
. . . but hospitable . . . upright, holy, self-
controlled.

Titus 1.7–8

For the grace of God has appeared for the
salvation of all men, training us to renounce
irreligion and worldly passions, and to live
sober, upright, and godly lives in this world.

Titus 2.11–12

Make every effort to supplement your
faith with virtue, and virtue with knowledge, and knowledge with self-control.

2 Peter 1.5–6

Temptation

See also **Enticement, Seduction**

The serpent said to the woman, 'You will
not die. For God knows that when you eat
of it your eyes will be opened, and you will
be like God, knowing good and evil.' So
when the woman saw that the tree was good
for food, and that it was a delight to the
eyes, and that the tree was to be desired to
make one wise, she took of its fruit and ate.

Genesis 3.4–6

If a prophet arises among you, or a
dreamer of dreams, and gives you a sign or
a wonder, and the sign or wonder which he
tells you comes to pass, and if he says, 'Let
us go after other gods,' which you have not
known, 'and let us serve them,' you shall
not listen to the words of that prophet or to
that dreamer of dreams; for the Lord your
God is testing you, to know whether you
love the Lord your God with all your heart
and with all your soul.

Deuteronomy 13.1–3

My son, if sinners entice you,
    do not consent.

Proverbs 1.10

For the lips of a loose woman drip honey,
    and her speech is smoother than oil;
but in the end she is bitter as wormwood,
    sharp as a two-edged sword.
Her feet go down to death;
    her steps follow the path to Sheol;
she does not take heed to the path of life;
    her ways wander, and she does not
        know it.

Proverbs 5.3–

Why should you be infatuated,
    my son, with a loose woman
and embrace the bosom of an adventuress?

Proverbs 5.2

For the commandment is a lamp and the
        teaching a light,
    and the reproofs of discipline are the
        way of life,
to preserve you from the evil woman,

from the smooth tongue of the
    adventuress.
Do not desire her beauty in your heart,
    and do not let her capture you with her
    eyelashes;
for a harlot may be hired for a loaf of
    bread,
    but an adulteress stalks a man's very life.

Proverbs 6.23–26

All at once he follows her,
    as an ox goes to the slaughter,
or as a stag is caught fast
    till an arrow pierces its entrails;
as a bird rushes into a snare;
    he does not know that it will cost him his
    life.

Proverbs 7.22–23

A foolish woman is noisy;
    she is wanton and knows no shame.
She sits at the door of her house,
    she takes a seat on the high places of the
    town,
calling to those who pass by,
    who are going straight on their way,
'Whoever is simple, let him turn in here!'
    And to him who is without sense she
    says,
'Stolen water is sweet,
    and bread eaten in secret is pleasant.'
But he does not know that the dead are
    there,
    that her guests are in the depths of Sheol.

Proverbs 9.13–18

A man of violence entices his neighbour
    and leads him in a way that is not good.

Proverbs 16.29

The mouth of a loose woman is a deep pit;
    he with whom the Lord is angry will fall
    into it.

Proverbs 22.14

He who misleads the upright into an evil
    way
    will fall into his own pit.

Proverbs 28.10

Woe to the world for temptations to sin!
For it is necessary that temptations come,
but woe to the man by whom the temptation comes! And if your hand or your foot
causes you to sin, cut it off and throw it
away; it is better for you to enter life
maimed or lame than with two hands or two
feet to be thrown into the eternal fire. And
if your eye causes you to sin, pluck it out
and throw it away; it is better for you to
enter life with one eye than with two eyes
to be thrown into the hell of fire.

Matthew 18.7–9

Watch and pray that you may not enter
into temptation; the spirit indeed is willing,
but the flesh is weak.

Mark 14.38

Then let us no more pass judgment on one
another, but rather decide never to put a
stumbling block or hindrance in the way of
a brother.

Romans 14.13

Do not refuse one another [husbands and
wives] except perhaps by agreement for a
season, that you may devote yourselves to
prayer; but then come together again, lest
Satan tempt you through lack of self-
control.

1 Corinthians 7.5

If a man is overtaken in any trespass, you
who are spiritual should restore him in a
spirit of gentleness. Look to yourself, lest
you too be tempted.

Galatians 6.1

But those who desire to be rich fall into
temptation, into a snare, into many senseless and hurtful desires that plunge men
into ruin and destruction.

1 Timothy 6.9

Because he himself has suffered and been
tempted, he is able to help those who are
tempted.

Hebrews 2.18

For we have not a high priest who is
unable to sympathise with our weaknesses,
but one who in every respect has been
tempted as we are, yet without sin.

Hebrews 4.15

Let no one say when he is tempted, 'I am tempted by God'; for God cannot be tempted with evil and he himself tempts no one; but each person is tempted when he is lured and enticed by his own desire.

James 1.13–14

Testifying

See also **Swearing**

You are the light of the world. A city set on a hill cannot be hid. Nor do men light a lamp and put it under a bushel, but on a stand, and it gives light to all in the house. Let your light so shine before men, that they may see your good works and give glory to your Father who is in heaven.

Matthew 5.14–16

Do not be ashamed then of testifying to our Lord.

2 Timothy 1.8

Tests / Trials

Do not fear; for God has come to prove you, and that the fear of him may be before your eyes, that you may not sin.

Exodus 20.20

Vindicate me, O Lord . . .
Prove me, O Lord, and try me;
    test my heart and my mind.

Psalms 26.1–2

For thou, O God, hast tested us;
    thou hast tried us as silver is tried.
Thou didst bring us into the net;
    thou didst lay affliction on our loins;
thou didst let men ride over our heads;
    we went through fire and through water;
yet thou hast brought us forth to a spacious
        place.

Psalms 66.10–12

And I will . . . refine them as one
    refines silver,
    and test them as gold is tested.

They will call on my name,
    and I will answer them.
I will say, 'They are my people';
    and they will say, 'The Lord is my God.'

Zechariah 13.9

Watch and pray that you may not enter into temptation.

Matthew 26.41

Forgive us our sins, for we ourselves forgive every one who is indebted to us; and lead us not into temptation.

Luke 11.3

Each man's work will become manifest; for the Day will disclose it, because it will be revealed with fire, and the fire will test what sort of work each one has done.

1 Corinthians 3.13

Count it all joy, my brethren, when you meet various trials, for you know that the testing of your faith produces steadfastness.

James 1.2–3

Blessed is the man who endures trial, for when he has stood the test he will receive the crown of life.

James 1.12

You . . . by God's power are guarded through faith for a salvation ready to be revealed in the last time. In this you rejoice, though now for a little while you may have to suffer various trials, so that the genuineness of your faith, more precious than gold which though perishable is tested by fire, may redound to praise and glory and honour at the revelation of Jesus Christ . . . and rejoice with unutterable and exalted joy.

1 Peter 1.5–8

Beloved, do not be surprised at the fiery ordeal which comes upon you to prove you, as though something strange were happening to you. But rejoice in so far as you share Christ's sufferings, that you may also rejoice and be glad when his glory is revealed.

1 Peter 4.12–13

Thankfulness

See also **Gratitude**

I bring the first of the fruit of the ground, which thou, O Lord, hast given me.

Deuteronomy 26.10

Offer to God a sacrifice of thanksgiving.

Psalms 50.14

It is good to give thanks to the Lord,
  to sing praises to thy name, O Most
    High;
to declare thy steadfast love in the morning,
  and thy faithfulness by night,
to the music of the lute and the harp,
  to the melody of the lyre.
For thou, O Lord, hast made me glad by
    thy work;
  at the works of thy hands I sing for joy.

Psalms 92.1–4

O give thanks to the Lord, call on his
    name,
  make known his deeds among the
    peoples!

Psalms 105.1

O give thanks to the Lord, for he is good;
  for his steadfast love endures for ever!
Who can utter the mighty doings of the
    Lord,
  or show forth all his praise?

Psalms 106.1–2

Honour the Lord with your substance
  and with the first fruits of all your
    produce.

Proverbs 3.9

They are without excuse; for although they
knew God they did not honour him as God
or give thanks to him.

Romans 1.21

Thanks be to God, who gives us the
victory through our Lord Jesus Christ.

1 Corinthians 15.57

Let there be no filthiness, nor silly talk,
nor levity, which are not fitting; but instead
let there be thanksgiving.

Ephesians 5.4

Be filled with the Spirit . . . always and for
everything giving thanks.

Ephesians 5.18,20

Have no anxiety about anything, but in
everything by prayer and supplication with
thanksgiving let your requests be made
known to God.

Philippians 4.6

May you be strengthened with all power,
according to his glorious might, for all
endurance and patience with joy, giving
thanks to the Father, who has qualified us
to share in the inheritance of the saints in
light.

Colossians 1.11–12

Continue steadfastly in prayer, being
watchful in it with thanksgiving.

Colossians 4.2

Give thanks in all circumstances; for this is
the will of God in Christ Jesus for you.

1 Thessalonians 5.17–18

Everything created by God is good, and
nothing is to be rejected if it is received
with thanksgiving.

1 Timothy 4.4

Let the lowly brother boast in his exalta-
tion, and the rich in his humiliation.

James 1.9

Theft

You shall not steal.

Exodus 20.15

If a man steals an ox or a sheep, and kills it
or sells it, he shall pay five oxen for an ox,
and four sheep for a sheep. He shall make
resitution; if he has nothing, then he shall
be sold for his theft. If the stolen beast is
found alive in his possession, whether it is
an ox or an ass or a sheep, he shall pay
double.
  If a thief is found breaking in, and is
struck so that he dies, there shall be no

bloodguilt for him; but if the sun has risen upon him, there shall be bloodguilt for him.

Exodus 22.1–3

You shall not steal, nor deal falsely, nor lie to one another.

Leviticus 19.11

You shall not oppress your neighbour or rob him.

Leviticus 19.13

When you go into your neighbour's vineyard, you may eat your fill of grapes, as many as you wish, but you shall not put any in your vessel.

Deuteronomy 23.24

Put no confidence in extortion,
  set no vain hopes on robbery.

Psalms 62.10

The getting of treasures by a lying tongue is a fleeting vapour and a snare of death.

Proverbs 21.6

Do not rob the poor, because he is poor.

Proverbs 22.22

He who robs his father or his mother
  and says, 'That is no transgression,'
  is the companion of a man who destroys.

Proverbs 28.24

Every one who steals shall be cut off henceforth.

Zechariah 5.3

Truly, truly, I say to you, he who does not enter the sheepfold by the door but climbs in by another way, that man is a thief and a robber.

John 10.1

You then who teach others, will you not teach yourself? While you preach against stealing, do you steal?

Romans 2.21

Neither the immoral . . . nor robbers will inherit the kingdom of God.

1 Corinthians 6.9–10

Let the thief no longer steal, but rather let him labour, doing honest work with his hands, so that he may be able to give to those in need.

Ephesians 4.28

Thirst

For he satisfies him who is thirsty,
  and the hungry he fills with good things.

Psalms 107.9

Thoughtfulness

The mind of the righteous ponders how to answer.

Proverbs 15.28

Time

See also **Calendar, Seasons**

God said, 'Let there be lights in the firmament of the heavens to separate the day from the night'.

Genesis 1.14

He has described a circle upon the face of
    the waters
  at the boundary between light and
    darkness.

Job 26.10

For everything there is a season, and a time for every matter under heaven.

Ecclesiastes 3.1

Take heed, watch; for you do not know when the time will come.

Mark 13.33

It is not for you to know times or seasons which the Father has fixed by his own authority.

Acts 1.7

We look not to the things that are seen but to the things that are unseen; for the things that are seen are transient, but the things that are unseen are eternal.

2 Corinthians 4.18

For he has made known to us in all wisdom and insight the mystery of his will, according to his purpose which he set forth in Christ as a plan for the fulness of time.

Ephesians 1.9

With the Lord one day is as a thousand years, and a thousand years as one day.

2 Peter 3.8

Tiredness

see also **Weakness**

The Lord is the everlasting God,
  the Creator of the ends of the earth.
He does not faint or grow weary.

Isaiah 40.28

They who wait for the Lord shall renew
    their strength,
  they shall mount up with wings like
    eagles,
they shall run and not be weary,
  they shall walk and not faint.

Isaiah 40.31

The Lord God has given me
  the tongue of those who are taught,
that I may know how to sustain with a word
  him that is weary.

Isaiah 50.4

For I will satisfy the weary soul, and every languishing soul I will replenish.

Jeremiah 31.25

When my soul fainted within me,
  I remembered the Lord.

Jonah 2.7

Come to me, all who labour and are heavy laden, and I will give you rest.

Matthew 11.28

Let us not grow weary in well-doing.

Galatians 6.9

Do not be weary in well-doing.

2 Thessalonians 3.13

Tolerance

He that will hear, let him hear; and he that will refuse to hear, let him refuse.

Ezekiel 3.27

They shall sit every man under his vine and
    under his fig tree,
  and none shall make them afraid;
  for the mouth of the Lord of hosts has
    spoken.

Micah 4.4

Judge not, that you be not judged.

Matthew 7.1

John said to him, 'Teacher, we saw a man casting out demons in your name, and we forbade him, because he was not following us.' But Jesus said, 'Do not forbid him; for no one who does a mighty work in my name will be able soon after to speak evil of me. For he that is not against us is for us.'

Mark 9.38–40

You yourselves know how unlawful it is for a Jew to associate with or to visit any one of another nation; but God has shown me that I should not call any man common or unclean.

Acts 10.28

As for the man who is weak in faith, welcome him, but not for disputes over opinions. One believes he may eat anything, while the weak man eats only vegetables. Let not him who eats despise him who abstains, and let not him who abstains pass judgment on him who eats; for God has welcomed him. Who are you to pass judgment on the servant of another? It is before his own master that he stands or falls.

Romans 14.1–4

Why do you pass judgment on your brother? Or you, why do you despise your brother?

Romans 14.10

We who are strong ought to bear with the failings of the weak.

Romans 15.1

May the God of steadfastness and encouragement grant you to live in . . . harmony with one another.

Romans 15.5

You gladly bear with fools, being wise yourselves! For you bear it if a man makes slaves of you, or preys upon you, or takes advantage of you, or puts on airs, or strikes you in the face.

2 Corinthians 11.19–20

Let all men know your forbearance.

Philippians 4.5

You . . . must forgive.

Colossians 3.13

Toughness

Enter by the narrow gate; for the gate is wide and the way is easy, that leads to destruction, and those who enter by it are many. For the gate is narrow and the way is hard, that leads to life, and those who find it are few.

Matthew 7.13–14

Tradition

See also **Ancestors**

Stand by the roads, and look,
 and ask for the ancient paths,
where the good way is; and walk in it,
 and find rest for your souls.

Jeremiah 6.16

So then, brethren, stand firm and hold to the traditions which you were taught by us, either by word of mouth or by letter.

2 Thessalonians 2.15

Training

Train yourself in godliness; for while bodily training is of some value, godliness is of value in every way, as it holds promise for the present life and also for the life to come.

1 Timothy 4.7–8

Tranquillity

See also **Peace**

A tranquil mind gives life to the flesh,
 but passion makes the bones rot.

Proverbs 14.30

Transcendence

Have you not known? Have you not
 heard?
Has it not been told you from the
 beginning?
Have you not understood from the
 foundations of the earth?
It is he who sits above the circle of the
 earth,
 and its inhabitants are like grasshoppers;
who stretches out the heavens like
 a curtain,
 and spreads them like a tent to dwell in;
who brings princes to naught,
 and makes the rulers of the earth
 as nothing.

Isaiah 40.21–2

For my thoughts are not your thoughts,
 neither are your ways my ways, says
 the Lord.
For as the heavens are higher than the
 earth,
 so are my ways higher than your ways
 and my thoughts than your thoughts.

Isaiah 55.8–

His voice you have never heard, his for
you have never seen; and you do not ha
his word abiding in you, for you do r
believe him whom he has sent. You sear
the scriptures, because you think that
them you have eternal life; and it is th
that bear witness to me; yet you refuse
come to me that you may have life.

John 5.37–

But we have this treasure in earth
vessels, to show that the transcend
power belongs to God and not to us.
are afflicted in every way, but not crush
perplexed, but not driven to despair; per
cuted, but not forsaken; struck down,

not destroyed; always carrying in the body
the death of Jesus, so that the life of Jesus
may also be manifested in our bodies. For
while we live we are always being given up
to death for Jesus' sake, so that the life of
Jesus may be manifested in our mortal
flesh. So death is at work in us, but life in
you.

2 Corinthians 4.7–12

Transformation

And we all, with unveiled face, beholding
the glory of the Lord, are being changed
into his likeness from one degree of glory to
another; for this comes from the Lord who
is the Spirit.

2 Corinthians 3.18

Transience

Man that is born of a woman is of few
days, and full of trouble.
He comes forth like a flower, and withers;
he flees like a shadow, and continues not.

Job 14.1–2

Thou dost sweep men away; they are like a
dream,
like grass which is renewed in the
morning.

Psalms 90.5

For all our days pass away under thy
wrath,
our years come to an end like a sigh.
The years of our life are threescore and ten,
or even by reason of strength fourscore;
yet their span is but toil and trouble;
they are soon gone, and we fly away.

Psalms 90.9–10

Of old thou didst lay the foundation of the
earth,
and the heavens are the work of thy
hands.
They will perish, but thou dost endure;
they will all wear out like a garment.
Thou changest them like raiment,
and they pass away.

Psalms 102.25–26

Transvestism

A woman shall not wear anything that
pertains to a man, nor shall a man put on a
woman's garment; for whoever does these
things is an abomination to the Lord your
God.

Deuteronomy 22.5

Travel

The Lord will keep
your going out and your coming in
from this time forth and for evermore.

Psalms 121.8

Treachery

See also **Betrayal**

The crookedness of the treacherous
destroys them.

Proverbs 11.3

The desire of the treacherous is for
violence.

Proverbs 13.2

Good sense wins favour,
but the way of the faithless is their ruin.

Proverbs 13.15

Tribulation

See also **Suffering, Trouble**

May my life be precious in the sight of the
Lord, and may he deliver me out of all
tribulation.

1 Samuel 26.24

Immediately after the tribulation of those
days the sun will be darkened, and the
moon will not give its light, and the stars
will fall from heaven, and the powers of the
heavens will be shaken.

Matthew 24.29

Through many tribulations we must enter
the kingdom of God.

Acts 14.22

Who shall separate us from the love of Christ? Shall tribulation, or distress, or persecution, or famine, or nakedness, or peril, or sword?

Romans 8.35

God deems it just to repay with affliction those who afflict you, and to grant rest with us to you who are afflicted, when the Lord Jesus is revealed from heaven with his mighty angels in flaming fire.

2 Thessalonians 1.6–7

Triumph

See also **Success, Victory**

But thanks be to God, who in Christ always leads us in triumph, and through us spreads the fragrance of the knowledge of him everywhere.

2 Corinthians 2.14

To him who conquers I will grant to eat of the tree of life, which is in the paradise of God.

Revelation 2.7

He who has an ear, let him hear what the Spirit says to the churches. He who conquers shall not be hurt by the second death.

Revelation 2.11

He who conquers and who keeps my works until the end, I will give him power over the nations, and he shall rule them with a rod of iron, as when earthen pots are broken in pieces, even as I myself have received power from my Father; and I will give him the morning star.

Revelation 2.26–28

He who conquers shall be clad thus in white garments, and I will not blot his name out of the book of life; I will confess his name before my Father and before his angels.

Revelation 3.5

Trouble

See also **Tribulation**

For affliction does not come from the dust,
 nor does trouble sprout from the ground;
but man is born to trouble
 as the sparks fly upward.

Job 5.6–7

The Lord is a stronghold for the
 oppressed,
 a stronghold in times of trouble.

Psalms 9.

The Lord answer you in the day of trouble
Psalms 20.

Thou art a hiding place for me,
 thou preservest me from trouble.

Psalms 32.

This poor man cried, and the Lord heard
 him,
 and saved him out of all his troubles.

Psalms 34.

I will sing aloud of thy steadfast love in the
 morning.
 For thou hast been to me a fortress
and a refuge in the day of my distress.

Psalms 59.

O grant us help against the foe,
 for vain is the help of man!

Psalms 60.

In the day of my trouble I seek the Lord;
 in the night my hand is stretched out
 without wearying;
 my soul refuses to be comforted.

Psalms 77

Though I walk in the midst of trouble,
 thou dost preserve my life.

Psalms 138

The righteous is delivered from trouble,
 and the wicked gets into it instead.

Proverbs 11

He who troubles his household will inherit
wind.

Proverbs 11.

The righteous escapes from trouble.

Proverbs 12.13

The Lord is good,
a stronghold in the day of trouble;
he knows those who take refuge in him.

Nahum 1.7

Let not your hearts be troubled; believe in God, believe also in me.

John 14.1

In the world you have tribulation; but be of good cheer, I have overcome the world.

John 16.33

We are afflicted in every way, but not crushed; perplexed, but not driven to despair.

2 Corinthians 4.8

He who is troubling you will bear his judgment.

Galatians 5.10

Trust

See also **Faith**

The Lord will provide.

Genesis 22.14

Can papyrus grow where there is
no marsh?
Can reeds flourish where there is
no water?
While yet in flower and not cut down,
they wither before any other plant.
Such are the paths of all who forget God;
the hope of the godless man shall perish.
His confidence breaks in sunder,
and his trust is a spider's web.

Job 8.11–14

Let him not trust in emptiness, deceiving
himself;
for emptiness will be his recompense.

Job 15.31

Offer right sacrifices,
and put your trust in the Lord.

Psalms 4.5

Into thy hand I commit my spirit.

Psalms 31.5

Many are the pangs of the wicked;
but steadfast love surrounds him who
trusts in the Lord.

Psalms 32.10

Behold, the eye of the Lord is on those
who fear him,
on those who hope in his steadfast love.

Psalms 33.18

Trust in the Lord, and do good;
so you will dwell in the land, and enjoy
security.

Psalms 37.3

Blessed is the man who makes
the Lord his trust,
who does not turn to the proud,
to those who go astray after false gods!

Psalms 40.4

Why should I fear . . .
men who trust in their wealth
and boast of the abundance of their
riches?

Psalms 49.5–6

Trust in him at all times, O people;
pour out your heart before him;
God is a refuge for us.

Psalms 62.8

He is not afraid of evil tidings;
his heart is firm, trusting in the Lord.

Psalms 112.7

I kept my faith, even when I said,
'I am greatly afflicted.'

Psalms 116.10

It is better to take refuge in the Lord
than to put confidence in man.
It is better to take refuge in the Lord
than to put confidence in princes.

Psalms 118.8–9

Those who trust in the Lord are like
Mount Zion,
which cannot be moved, but abides for
ever.

Psalms 125.1

Put not your trust in princes,
   in a son of man, in whom there is no
   help.

Psalms 146.3

Trust in the Lord with all your heart,
   and do not rely on your own insight.

Proverbs 3.5

He who trusts in his riches will wither.

Proverbs 11.28

He who trusts in the Lord will be
enriched.

Proverbs 28.25

He who trusts in his own mind is a fool.

Proverbs 28.26

The fear of man lays a snare,
   but he who trusts in the Lord is safe.

Proverbs 29.25

A good wife who can find? . . .
The heart of her husband trusts in her.

Proverbs 31.10−11

Behold, God is my salvation;
   I will trust, and will not be afraid.

Isaiah 12.2

Open the gates,
   that the righteous nation which keeps
      faith
   may enter in.
Thou dost keep him in perfect peace,
   whose mind is stayed on thee,
   because he trusts in thee.
Trust in the Lord for ever,
   for the Lord God
   is an everlasting rock.

Isaiah 26.2−4

In returning and rest you shall be saved;
   in quietness and in trust shall be your
      strength.

Isaiah 30.15

From of old no one has heard
   or perceived by the ear,
no eye has seen a God besides thee,
   who works for those who wait for him.

Isaiah 64.4

Cursed is the man who trusts in man
   and makes flesh his arm.

Jeremiah 17.5

You shall have your life as a prize of war,
because you have put your trust in me, says
the Lord.

Jeremiah 39.18

Wait continually for your God.

Hosea 12.6

Put no trust in a neighbour,
   have no confidence in a friend;
guard the doors of your mouth
   from her who lies in your bosom;
for the son treats the father with contempt,
   the daughter rises up against her mother,
the daughter-in-law against her mother-in-
      law;
   a man's enemies are the men of his own
      house.
But as for me, I will look to the Lord,
   I will wait for the God of my salvation;
   my God will hear me.

Micah 7.5−7

Let not your hearts be troubled; believe in
God, believe also in me.

John 14.1

We have our hope set on the living God
who is the Saviour of all men.

1 Timothy 4.10

Set your hope fully upon the grace that i
coming to you at the revelation of Jesu
Christ.

1 Peter 1.13

Trustworthiness

See also **Faithfulness, Loyalty, Trust**

A bad messenger plunges men into
      trouble,
   but a faithful envoy brings healing.

Proverbs 13.17

Like the cold of snow in the time of
   harvest

is a faithful messenger to those who send
   him,
he refreshes the spirit of his masters.

Proverbs 25.13

A faithful man will abound with blessings.

Proverbs 28.20

He who is faithful in a very little is faithful
also in much.

Luke 16.10

If you have not been faithful in that which
is another's, who will give you that which is
your own?

Luke 16.12

It is required of stewards that they be
found trustworthy.

1 Corinthians 4.2

Truth

See also **Honesty**

The word of the Lord in your mouth is
truth.

1 Kings 17.24

O Lord, who shall sojourn in thy tent?
   Who shall dwell on thy holy hill?
He who walks blamelessly, and does what is
      right,
   and speaks truth from his heart.

Psalms 15.1–2

All the paths of the Lord are steadfast love
      and faithfulness,
   for those who keep his covenant and his
      testimonies.

Psalms 25.10

He comes to judge the earth.
He will judge the world with righteousness,
   and the peoples with his truth.

Psalms 96.13

All thy commandments are true.

Psalms 119.151

The sum of thy word is truth.

Psalms 119.160

He who speaks the truth gives honest
evidence.

Proverbs 12.17

Truthful lips endure for ever,
   but a lying tongue is but for a moment.

Proverbs 12.19

Lying lips are an abomination to the Lord,
   but those who act faithfully are his
      delight.

Proverbs 12.22

Buy truth, and do not sell it.

Proverbs 23.23

Behold my servant, whom I uphold . . .
he will faithfully bring forth justice.

Isaiah 42.1,3

So that he who blesses himself in the land
   shall bless himself by the God of truth,
and he who takes an oath in the land
   shall swear by the God of truth.

Isaiah 65.16

Speak the truth to one another, render . . .
judgments that are true.

Zechariah 8.16

He who does what is true comes to the
light, that it may be clearly seen that his
deeds have been wrought in God.

John 3.21

If you continue in my word, you are truly
my disciples, and you will know the truth,
and the truth will make you free.

John 8.31–32

I am the way, and the truth, and the life;
no one comes to the Father, but by me.

John 14.6

When the Counsellor comes, whom I shall
send to you from the Father, even the Spirit
of truth, who proceeds from the Father, he
will bear witness to me.

John 15.26

When the Spirit of truth comes, he will
guide you into all the truth.

John 16.13

For this I was born, and for this I have come into the world, to bear witness to the truth. Every one who is of the truth hears my voice.

John 18.37

Love . . . does not rejoice at wrong, but rejoices in the right.

1 Corinthians 13.6

We cannot do anything against the truth, but only for the truth.

2 Corinthians 13.8

Speaking the truth in love, we are to grow up in every way into him who is the head, into Christ.

Ephesians 4.15

Therefore, putting away falsehood, let every one speak the truth with his neighbour, for we are members one of another.

Ephesians 4.25

Stand therefore, having girded your loins with truth, and having put on the breastplate of righteousness.

Ephesians 6.14

The word of the truth, the gospel . . . has come to you, as indeed in the whole world it is bearing fruit and growing.

Colossians 1.6

God our Saviour . . . desires all men to be saved and to come to the knowledge of the truth.

1 Timothy 2.4

The Spirit is the truth.

1 John 5.7

Tyranny

The wicked man writhes in pain all his days,
  through all the years that are laid up for the ruthless.

Job 15.20

Nay, in your hearts you devise wrongs;
  your hands deal out violence on earth

. . . O God, break the teeth in their mouths;
  tear out the fangs of the young lions, O Lord!
Let them vanish like water that runs away;
  like grass let them be trodden down and wither.

Psalms 58.2,6–7

Rescue me, O my God, from the hand of the wicked,
  from the grasp of the unjust and cruel man.

Psalms 71.4

He has pity on the weak and the needy,
  and saves the lives of the needy.
From oppression and violence he redeems their life.

Psalms 72.13–14

Woe to those who decree iniquitous decrees,
  and the writers who keep writing oppression,
to turn aside the needy from justice
  and to rob the poor of my people of their right.

Isaiah 10.1–2

The Lord has broken the staff of the wicked,
  the sceptre of rulers.

Isaiah 14.5

For the ruthless shall come to naught and the scoffer cease,
  and all who watch to do evil shall be cut off.

Isaiah 29.20

Jesus . . . said to them, 'You know that those who are supposed to rule over the Gentiles lord it over them, and their great men exercise authority over them. But it shall not be so among you; but whoever would be great among you must be your servant, and whoever would be first among you must be slave of all.'

Mark 10.42–44

Masters, treat your slaves justly and fairly, knowing that you also have a Master in heaven.

Colossians 4.1

Tend the flock of God . . . not as domineering over those in your charge but being examples to the flock.

1 Peter 5.2−3

U

Ugliness

Do not look on his appearance or on the height of his stature . . . for the Lord sees not as man sees; man looks on the outward appearance, but the Lord looks on the heart.

1 Samuel 16.7

The north wind brings forth rain;
    and a backbiting tongue, angry looks.

Proverbs 25.23

Who has believed what we have heard?
    And to whom has the arm of the Lord
        been revealed?
For he grew up before him like a young
        plant,
    and like a root out of dry ground;
he had no form or comeliness that we
        should look at him,
    and no beauty that we should desire him.
He was despised and rejected by men . . .
Surely he has borne our griefs
    and carried our sorrows.

Isaiah 53.1−2,4

Unbelief

See also **Doubt**

I will hide my face from them,
    I will see what their end will be,
for they are a perverse generation,
    children in whom is no faithfulness.

Deuteronomy 32.20

Thus says the Lord God . . .
If you will not believe,
    surely you shall not be established.

Isaiah 7.7,9

Look among the nations, and see;
    wonder and be astounded.
For I am doing a work in your days
    that you would not believe if told.

Habakkuk 1.5

This is why I speak to them in parables, because seeing they do not see, and hearing they do not hear, nor do they understand.

Matthew 13.13

Jesus . . . went away from there, and coming to his own country he taught them . . . And they took offence at him. But Jesus said to them, 'A prophet is not without honour except in his own country and in his own house.' And he did not do many mighty works there, because of their unbelief.

Matthew 13.53,54,57−58

He who believes and is baptized will be saved; but he who does not believe will be condemned.

Mark 16.16

You will be silent and unable to speak until the day that these things come to pass, because you did not believe my words, which will be fulfilled in their time.

Luke 1.20

The seed is the word of God. The ones along the path are those who heard; then the devil comes and takes away the word from their hearts, that they may not believe and be saved.

Luke 8.11−12

When the Son of man comes, will he find faith on earth?

Luke 18.8

He who does not believe is condemned already, because he has not believed in the name of the only Son of God.

John 3.18

He who does not obey the Son shall not see life, but the wrath of God rests upon him.

John 3.36

You do not have his word abiding in you, for you do not believe him whom he has sent.

John 5.38

How can you believe, who receive glory from one another and do not seek the glory that comes from the only God?

John 5.44

You will die in your sins unless you believe that I am he.

John 8.24

I did not come to judge the world but to save the world. He who rejects me and does not receive my sayings has a judge; the word that I have spoken will be his judge on the last day.

John 12.47—48

He said to Thomas, 'Put your finger here, and see my hands; and put out your hand, and place it in my side; do not be faithless, but believing.' Thomas answered him, 'My Lord and my God!'

John 20.27—28

How are men to call upon him in whom they have not believed? And how are they to believe in him of whom they have never heard? And how are they to hear without a preacher?

Romans 10.14

They were broken off because of their unbelief, but you stand fast only through faith.

Romans 11.20

The unspiritual man does not receive the gifts of the Spirit of God, for they are folly to him, and he is not able to understand them because they are spiritually discerned.

1 Corinthians 2.14

If any brother has a wife who is an unbeliever, and she consents to live with him, he should not divorce her. If any woman has a husband who is an unbeliever, and he consents to live with her, she should not divorce him. For the unbelieving husband is consecrated through his wife, and the unbelieving wife is consecrated through her husband.

1 Corinthians 7.12—14

Do not be mismated with unbelievers.

2 Corinthians 6.14

Pray . . . that we may be delivered from wicked and evil men; for not all have faith.

2 Thessalonians 3.1—2

To the pure all things are pure, but to the corrupt and unbelieving nothing is pure; their very minds and consciences are corrupted.

Titus 1.15

Take care, brethren, lest there be in any of you an evil, unbelieving heart, leading you to fall away from the living God.

Hebrews 3.12

Without faith it is impossible to please him. For whoever would draw near to God must believe that he exists and that he rewards those who seek him.

Hebrews 11.6

For if they did not escape when they refused him who warned them on earth, much less shall we escape if we reject him who warns from heaven.

Hebrews 12.25

He who does not believe God, has made him a liar, because he has not believed in the testimony that God has borne to his Son.

1 John 5.10

Uncertainty (of Life)

See also **Doubt**

Come now, you who say, 'Today or to-morrow we will go into such and such a town and spend a year there and trade and get gain'; whereas you do not know about tomorrow. What is your life? For you are a mist that appears for a little time and then vanishes. Instead you ought to say, 'If the Lord wills, we shall live and we shall do this or that.'

James 4.13−15

Understanding

See also **Wisdom**

But where shall wisdom be found?
    And where is the place of understanding?
Man does not know the way to it,
    and it is not found in the land of the
        living.

Job 28.12−13

Behold, the fear of the Lord, that is
        wisdom;
    and to depart from evil is understanding.

Job 28.28

Through thy precepts I get understanding.

Psalms 119.104

The wise man also may hear and increase
        in learning,
    and the man of understanding acquire
        skill.

Proverbs 1.5

Yes, if you cry out for insight
    and raise your voice for understanding,
if you seek it like silver
    and search for it as for hidden treasures;
then you will understand the fear of the
        Lord
    and find the knowledge of God.

Proverbs 2.3−5

For the Lord gives wisdom;
    from his mouth come knowledge and
        understanding.

Proverbs 2.6

Happy is the man who finds wisdom,
    and the man who gets understanding.

Proverbs 3.13

The Lord by wisdom founded the earth;
    by understanding he established the
        heavens.

Proverbs 3.19

Leave simpleness, and live,
    and walk in the way of insight.

Proverbs 9.6

It is like sport to a fool to do wrong,
    but wise conduct is pleasure to a man of
        understanding.

Proverbs 10.23

A scoffer seeks wisdom in vain,
    but knowledge is easy for a man of
        understanding.

Proverbs 14.6

Wisdom abides in the mind of a man of
        understanding,
    but it is not known in the heart of fools.

Proverbs 14.33

The mind of him who has understanding
seeks knowledge.

Proverbs 15.14

Wisdom is a fountain of life.

Proverbs 16.22

Evil men do not understand justice, but
those who seek the Lord understand it com-
pletely.

Proverbs 28.5

He has made everything beautiful in its
time; also he has put eternity into man's
mind, yet so that he cannot find out what
God has done from the beginning to the
end.

Ecclesiastes 3.1

He gives wisdom to the wise
    and knowledge to those who have
        understanding.

Daniel 2.2

Seeing they do not see, and hearing they do not hear, nor do they understand.

Matthew 13.13

When any one hears the word of the kingdom and does not understand it, the evil one comes and snatches away what is sown in his heart.

Matthew 13.18–19

As for what was sown on good soil, this is he who hears the word and understands it; he indeed bears fruit, and yields, in one case a hundredfold, in another sixty, and in another thirty.

Matthew 13.23

I have fully preached the gospel of
    Christ . . . as it is written,
'They shall see who have never been
    told of him,
and they shall understand who have
    never heard of him.'

Romans 15.19–21

Now I know in part; then I shall understand fully, even as I have been fully understood.

1 Corinthians 13.12

For one who speaks in a tongue speaks not to men but to God; for no one understands him, but he utters mysteries in the Spirit.

1 Corinthians 14.2

Do not be children in your thinking; be babes in evil, but in thinking be mature.

1 Corinthians 14.20

For this reason I bow my knees before the Father, from whom every family in heaven and on earth is named, that according to the riches of his glory he may grant you to be strengthened with might through his Spirit in the inner man, and that Christ may dwell in your hearts through faith; that you, being rooted and grounded in love, may have power to comprehend with all the saints what is the breadth and length and height and depth, and to know the love of Christ which surpasses knowledge, that you may be filled with all the fulness of God.

Ephesians 3.14–19

We have not ceased to pray for you, asking that you may be filled with the knowledge of his will in all spiritual wisdom and understanding.

Colossians 1.9

The Lord will grant you understanding in everything.

2 Timothy 2.7

By faith we understand that the world was created by the word of God.

Hebrews 11.3

And we know that the Son of God has come and has given us understanding, to know him who is true; and we are in him who is true, in his Son Jesus Christ.

1 John 5.20

Ungodliness

See also **Unbelief**

Should you help the wicked and love those who hate the Lord? Because of this, wrath has gone out against you from the Lord.

2 Chronicles 19.2

Blessed is the man
    who walks not in the counsel of the
      wicked,
nor stands in the way of sinners,
    nor sits in the seat of scoffers.

Psalms 1.1

The wrath of God is revealed from heaven against all ungodliness and wickedness of men who by their wickedness suppress the truth.

Romans 1.18

Christ died for the ungodly.

Romans 5.7

The law is not laid down for the just but for the lawless and disobedient, for the ungodly and sinners, for the unholy and profane.

1 Timothy 1.9

Avoid such godless chatter, for it will lead people into more and more ungodliness.

2 Timothy 2.16

The grace of God has appeared for the salvation of all men, training us to renounce irreligion and wordly passions.

Titus 2.11–12

By turning the cities of Sodom and Gomor'rah to ashes he condemned them to extinction and made them an example to those who were to be ungodly.

2 Peter 2.6

Whoever does not do right is not of God, nor he who does not love his brother.

1 John 3.10

For admission has been secretly gained by some who long ago were designated for this condemnation, ungodly persons who pervert the grace of our God into licentiousness and deny our only Master and Lord, Jesus Christ.

Jude 4

The Lord came . . . to execute judgment on all, and to convict all the ungodly of all their deeds of ungodliness which they have committed in such an ungodly way, and of all the harsh things which ungodly sinners have spoken against him.

Jude 14–15

Uniqueness

If you will obey my voice and keep my covenant, you shall be my own possession among all peoples; for all the earth is mine, and you shall be to me a kingdom of priests and a holy nation.

Exodus 19.5–6

The Lord is God; there is no other besides him.

Deuteronomy 4.35

As in water face answers to face, so the mind of man reflects the man.

Proverbs 27.19

My dove, my perfect one, is only one.

Song of Solomon 6.9

Who can forgive sins but God only?

Luke 5.21

There is one God, and there is one mediator between God and men, the man Christ Jesus.

1 Timothy 2.5

I charge you to keep the commandment unstained and free from reproach until the appearing of our Lord Jesus Christ; and this will be made manifest at the proper time by the blessed and only Sovereign, the King of kings and Lord of lords, who alone has immortality.

1 Timothy 6.14–16

Christ . . . gave himself for us to redeem us from all iniquity and to purify for himself a people of his own.

Titus 2.14

You are a chosen race, a royal priesthood, a holy nation, God's own people, that you may declare the wonderful deeds of him who called you.

1 Peter 2.9

Unity

See also **Peace**

Behold, how good and pleasant it is
when brothers dwell in unity!

Psalms 133.1

Hark, your watchmen lift up their voice,
together they sing for joy;
for eye to eye they see.

Isaiah 52.8

Let us join ourselves to the Lord in an everlasting covenant which will never be forgotten.

Jeremiah 50.5

You have one teacher, and you are all brethren.

Matthew 23.8

All who believed were together and had all things in common.

Acts 2.44

The company of those who believed were of one heart and soul, and no one said that any of the things which he possessed was his own, but they had everything in common.

Acts 4.32

He made from one every nation of men.

Acts 17.26

As in one body we have many members, and all the members do not have the same function, so we, though many, are one body in Christ, and individually members one of another.

Romans 12.4–5

Live in harmony with one another; do not be haughty, but associate with the lowly.

Romans 12.16

May the God of steadfastness and encouragement grant you to live in such harmony with one another, in accord with Christ Jesus, that together you may with one voice glorify the God and Father of our Lord Jesus Christ.

Romans 15.5–6

I appeal to you, brethren, by the name of our Lord Jesus Christ, that all of you agree and that there be no dissensions among you, but that you be united in the same mind and the same judgment.

1 Corinthians 1.10

He who is united to the Lord becomes one spirit with him.

1 Corinthians 6.17

Agree with one another, live in peace, and the God of love and peace will be with you.

2 Corinthians 13.11

Lead a life worthy of the calling to which you have been called . . . eager to maintain the unity of the Spirit in the bond of peace.

Ephesians 4.1,3

We all attain to the unity of the faith and of the knowledge of the Son of God, to mature manhood, to the measure of the stature of the fulness of Christ.

Ephesians 4.13

Speaking the truth in love, we are to grow up in every way into him who is the head, into Christ, from whom the whole body, joined and knit together by every joint with which it is supplied, when each part is working properly, makes bodily growth and upbuilds itself in love.

Ephesians 4.15–16

Complete my joy by being of the same mind, having the same love, being in full accord and of one mind.

Philippians 2.2

All of you, have unity of spirit, sympathy, love of the brethren, a tender heart and a humble mind.

1 Peter 3.8

Universalism

See also **Wholeness**

Abraham shall become a great and mighty nation, and all the nations of the earth shall bless themselves by him.

Genesis 18.18

Clap your hands, all peoples!
  Shout to God with loud songs of joy!
For the Lord, the Most High, is terrible,
  a great king over all the earth.

Psalms 47.1–2

May God be gracious to us and bless us
  and make his face to shine upon us,
that thy way may be known upon earth,
  thy saving power among all nations.

Psalms 67.1–2

Thou art the God, thou alone, of all the kingdoms of the earth.

Isaiah 37.16

Let all the nations gather together,
  and let the peoples assemble.

Isaiah 43.9

Turn to me and be saved,
all the ends of the earth!
For I am God, and there is no other.

Isaiah 45.22

I saw in the night visions, and behold, with
the clouds of heaven
there came one like a son of man,
and he came to the Ancient of Days
and was presented before him.
And to him was given dominion
and glory and kingdom,
that all peoples, nations, and languages
should serve him;
his dominion is an everlasting dominion,
which shall not pass away,
and his kingdom one
that shall not be destroyed.

Daniel 7.13–14

I will pour out my spirit on all flesh.

Joel 2.28

Then every one that survives of all the
nations that have come against Jerusalem
shall go up year after year to worship the
King, the Lord of hosts, and to keep the
feast of booths.

Zechariah 14.16

For mine eyes have seen thy salvation
which thou hast prepared in the presence
of all peoples.

Luke 2.30–31

I have other sheep, that are not of this
fold; I must bring them also, and they will
heed my voice. So there shall be one flock,
one shepherd.

John 10.16

To the Gentiles also God has granted
repentance unto life.

Acts 11.18

The God who made the world and everything in it, being Lord of heaven and earth,
does not live in shrines made by man, nor is
he served by human hands, as though he
needed anything, since he himself gives to
all men life and breath and everything. And
he made from one every nation of men to
live on all the face of the earth, having
determined allotted periods and the boundaries of their habitation, that they should
seek God, in the hope that they might feel
after him and find him. Yet he is not far
from each one of us, for
'In him we live and move and have our
being'.

Acts 17.24,26–28

The free gift is not like the trespass. For if
many died through one man's trespass,
much more have the grace of God and the
free gift in the grace of that one man, Jesus
Christ abounded for many.

Romans 5.15

For there is no distinction between Jew
and Greek; the same Lord is Lord of all
and bestows his riches upon all who call
upon him.

Romans 10.12

God our Saviour . . . desires all men to be
saved and to come to the knowledge of the
truth. For there is one God, and there is
one mediator between God and men, the
man Christ Jesus, who gave himself as a
ransom for all, the testimony to which was
borne at the proper time.

1 Timothy 2.4–6

Jesus Christ the righteous . . . is the expiation . . . for the sins of the whole world.

1 John 2.1–2

After this I looked and behold, a great
multitude which no man could number,
from every nation, from all tribes and
peoples and tongues, standing before the
throne and before the Lamb, clothed in
white robes, with palm branches in their
hands, and crying out with a loud voice,
'Salvation belongs to our God who sits
upon the throne, and to the Lamb!'

Revelation 7.9–10

I saw another angel flying in midheaven,
with an eternal gospel to proclaim to those
who dwell on earth, to every nation and
tribe and tongue and people.

Revelation 14.6

Unobtrusiveness

He will not cry or lift up his voice,
  or make it heard in the street;
a bruised reed he will not break,
  and a dimly burning wick he will not
    quench;
he will faithfully bring forth justice.

Isaiah 42.2—3

Unpopularity

Am I now seeking the favour of men, or of
God? Or am I trying to please men? If I
were still pleasing men, I should not be a
servant of Christ.

Galations 1.10

Unrighteousness

See also **Immorality, Ungodliness**

Let the wicked forsake his way,
  and the unrighteous man his thoughts;
let him return to the Lord, that he may
    have mercy on him.

Isaiah 55.7

Woe to him who builds his house by
    unrightousness,
  and his upper rooms by injustice.

Jeremiah 22.13

He who is faithful in a very little is faithful
also in much; and he who is dishonest in a
very little is dishonest also in much.

Luke 16.10

Since they did not see fit to acknowledge
God, God gave them up to a base mind and
to improper conduct. They were filled with
all manner of wickedness, evil, covetousness, malice. Full of envy, murder, strife,
deceit, malignity.

Romans 1.28—29

For those who are factious and do not
obey the truth, but obey wickedness, there
will be wrath and fury.

Romans 2.8

Do not yield your members to sin as
instruments of wickedness.

Romans 6.13

The unrighteous will not inherit the kingdom of God. Do not be deceived; neither
the immoral, nor idolaters, nor adulterers,
nor sexual perverts, nor thieves, nor the
greedy, nor drunkards, nor revilers, nor
robbers will inherit the kingdom of God.

1 Corinthians 6.9—10

God sends upon them a strong delusion, to
make them believe what is false, so that all
may be condemned who did not believe the
truth but had pleasure in unrighteousness.

2 Thessalonians 2.11—12

I will be merciful toward their iniquities,
  and I will remember their sins no more.

Hebrews 8.12

All wrongdoing is sin, but there is sin
which is not mortal.

1 John 5.17

Urgency

Preach the word, be urgent in season and
out of season, convince, rebuke, and exhort, be unfailing in patience and in
teaching.

2 Timothy 4.2

Usefulness/Utility

See also **Purpose**

Do not turn aside after vain things which
cannot profit or save, for they are vain. For
the Lord will not cast away his people.

1 Samuel 12.21—22

Now, brethren, if I come to you speaking
in tongues, how shall I benefit you unless I
bring you some revelation or knowledge or
prophecy or teaching?

1 Corinthians 14.6

Train yourself in godliness; for while
bodily training is of some value, godliness is

of value in every way, as it holds promise for the present life and also for the life to come.

1 Timothy 4.7–8

I desire you to insist on these things, so that those who have believed in God may be careful to apply themselves to good deeds; these are excellent and profitable to men.

Titus 3.8

Usury

See also **Interest**

If you lend money to any of my people with you who is poor, you shall not be to him as a creditor, and you shall not exact interest from him.

Exodus 22.25

You shall not lend upon interest to your brother, interest on money, interest on victuals, interest on anything that is lent for interest. To a foreigner you may lend upon interest, but to your brother you shall not lend upon interest.

Deuteronomy 23.19–20

O Lord, who shall sojourn in thy tent?
   Who shall dwell on thy holy hill?
He . . . who does not put out his money
   at interest.

Psalms 15.1–2,5

The borrower is the slave of the lender.

Proverbs 22.7

He who augments his wealth by interest
   and increase
gathers it for him who is kind to the poor.

Proverbs 28.8

If a man is righteous and does what is lawful and right . . . he does not . . . lend at interest or take any increase.

Ezekiel 18.5,8

If you do good to those who do good to you, what credit is that to you? For even sinners do the same. And if you lend to those from whom you hope to receive, what credit is that to you? Even sinners lend to sinners, to receive as much again. But love your enemies, and do good, and lend, expecting nothing in return; and your reward will be great.

Luke 6.33–35

V

Vanity

See also **Arrogance, Pride, Self-Righteousness**

He who makes his door high seeks destruction.

Proverbs 17.19

Charm is deceitful, and beauty is vain,
but a woman who fears the Lord is to be
praised.

Proverbs 31.30

The Lord said:
Because the daughters of Zion are haughty
and walk with outstretched necks,
glancing wantonly with their eyes,
mincing along as they go,
tinkling with their feet;
the Lord will smite with a scab
the heads of the daughters of Zion,
and the Lord will lay bare their secret
parts.

Isaiah 3.16–17

Whoever exalts himself will be humbled,
and whoever humbles himself will be
exalted.

Matthew 23.12

I bid every one among you not to think of
himself more highly than he ought to think.

Romans 12.3

It is not the man who commends himself
that is accepted, but the man whom the
Lord commends.

2 Corinthians 10.18

Let us have no self-conceit, no provoking
of one another, no envy of one another.

Galatians 5.26

Let no one disqualify you, insisting on self-
abasement and worship of angels, taking his
stand on visions, puffed up without reason
by his sensuous mind.

Colossians 2.18

Variety

The kingdom of heaven is like a net which
was thrown into the sea and gathered fish of
every kind.

Matthew 13.47

For as in one body we have many members, and all members do not have the same
function, so we, though many, are one body
in Christ, and individually members one of
another. Having gifts that differ according
to the grace given to us, let us use them.

Romans 12.4–6

There are varieties of gifts, but the same
Spirit; and there are varieties of service, but
the same Lord; and there are varieties of
working, but it is the same God who inspires them all in every one.

1 Corinthians 12.4–6

There are doubtless many different languages in the world, and none is without
meaning; but if I do not know the meaning
of the language, I shall be a foreigner to the
speaker and the speaker a foreigner to me.

1 Corinthians 14.10–11

In many and various ways God spoke of
old to our fathers by the prophets.

Hebrews 1.1

Vengeance

See also **Revenge**

Exalted be my God, the rock of
  my salvation,
the God who gave me vengeance
  and brought down peoples under me.

2 Samuel 22.47−48

The righteous will rejoice when he sees the
    vengeance;
  he will bathe his feet in the blood of the
    wicked.
Men will say, 'Surely there is a reward for
    the righteous;
  surely there is a God who judges on
    earth.'

Psalms 58.10−11

O Lord, thou God of vengeance,
  thou God of vengeance, shine forth!
Rise up, O judge of the earth;
  render to the proud their deserts!

Psalms 94.1−2

Let the faithful exult in glory;
  let them sing for joy on their couches.
Let the high praises of God be in their
    throats
  and two-edged swords in their hands,
to wreak vengeance on the nations
  and chastisement on the peoples.

Psalms 149.5−7

Behold, your God
  will come with vengeance,
with the recompense of God.
  He will come and save you.

Isaiah 35.4

In anger and wrath I will execute
    vengeance
  upon the nations that did not obey.

Micah 5.15

The Lord is a jealous God and avenging,
  the Lord is avenging and wrathful;
the Lord takes vengeance on his adversaries
  and keeps wrath for his enemies.
The Lord is slow to anger and of great
    might,
  and the Lord will by no means clear the
    guilty.

Nahum 1.2−3

Never avenge yourselves, but leave it to
the wrath of God; for it is written, 'Vengeance is mine, I will repay, says the Lord.'

Romans 12.19

God deems it just to repay with affliction
those who afflict you.

2 Thessalonians 1.6

Victory

Blessed be God Most High,
  who has delivered your enemies into your
    hand!

Genesis 14.20

May we shout for joy over your victory,
  and in the name of our God set up our
    banners!

Psalms 20.5

Through thee we push down our foes;
  through thy name we tread down our
    assailants.
For not in my bow do I trust,
  nor can my sword save me.
But thou hast saved us from our foes,
  and hast put to confusion those who hate
    us.
In God we have boasted continually,
  and we will give thanks to thy name for
    ever.

Psalms 44.5−8

He will deliver my soul in safety
  from the battle that I wage,
  for many are arrayed against me.
God will give ear, and humble them.

Psalms 55.18−19

O Sing to the Lord a new song,
  for he has done marvellous things!
His right hand and his holy arm
  have gotten him victory.

Psalms 98.1

The horse is made ready for the day of
    battle,
  but the victory belongs to the Lord.

Proverbs 21.31

Behold, my servant whom I have chosen,
  my beloved with whom my soul is well
      pleased . . .
he will not break a bruised reed
  or quench a smouldering wick,
till he brings justice to victory.

Matthew 12.18,20

In the world you have tribulation; but be of
good cheer, I have overcome the world.

John 16.33

We are more than conquerors through him
who loved us.

Romans 8.37

Death is swallowed up in victory.
'O death, where is thy victory?
O death, where is thy sting?'
The sting of death is sin, and the power of
sin is the law. But thanks be to God, who
gives us the victory through our Lord Jesus
Christ.

1 Corinthians 15.54–57

Thanks be to God, who in Christ always
leads us in triumph.

2 Corinthians 2.14

For whatever is born of God overcomes
the world; and this is the victory that overcomes the world, our faith. Who is it that
overcomes the world but he who believes
that Jesus is the Son of God?

1 John 5.4–5

He who conquers, I will grant him to sit
with me on my throne, as I myself conquered and sat down with my Father on his
throne.

Revelation 3.21

I saw what appeared to be a sea of glass
mingled with fire, and those who had conquered the beast and its image and the
number of its name, standing beside the sea
of glass.

Revelation 15.2

To the thirsty I will give from the fountain
of the water of life without payment. He
who conquers shall have this heritage.

Revelation 21.6–7

Vigilance

Watch and pray that you may not enter
into temptation.

Matthew 26.41

Watch therefore — for you do not know
when the master of the house will come, in
the evening, or at midnight, or at cockcrow,
or in the morning — lest he come suddenly
and find you asleep. And what I say to you
I say to all: Watch.

Mark 13.35–37

Be alert.

Acts 20.31

Be watchful, stand firm in your faith, be
courageous, be strong.

1 Corinthians 16.13

Continue steadfastly in prayer, being
watchful in it with thanksgiving.

Colossians 4.2

Let us not sleep, as others do, but let
us keep awake and be sober.

1 Thessalonians 5.6

Be sober, be watchful. Your adversary the
devil prowls around like a roaring lion,
seeking some one to devour.

1 Peter 5.8

Blessed is he who is awake.

Revelation 16.15

Villainy

See also **Unrighteousness, Wickedness**

On every side the wicked prowl,
  as vileness is exalted among the sons of
    men.

Psalms 12.8

The fool will no more be called noble,
  nor the knave said to be honourable . . .
The knaveries of the knave are evil;
  he devises wicked devices
to ruin the poor with lying words,
  even when the plea of the needy is right.

But he who is noble devises noble things,
and by noble things he stands.

Isaiah 32.5,7—8

Violence

See also **Brutality, Cruelty**

Now the earth was corrupt in God's sight,
and the earth was filled with violence . . .
And God said to Noah, 'I have determined
to make an end of all flesh; for the earth is
filled with violence through them; behold, I
will destroy them with the earth.'

Genesis 6.11,13

Cursed be he who slays his neighbour in
secret.

Deuteronomy 27.24

The Lord abhors bloodthirsty and deceitful
men.

Psalms 5.6

His mischief returns upon his own head,
and on his own pate his violence
descends.

Psalms 7.16

The Lord tests the righteous and the
wicked,
and his soul hates him that loves
violence.

Psalms 11.5

Sweep me not away with sinners,
nor my life with bloodthirsty men,
men in whose hands are evil devices.

Psalms 26.9—10

But thou, O God, wilt cast them down
into the lowest pit;
men of blood and treachery
shall not live out half their days.

Psalms 55.23

Let evil hunt down the violent man
speedily!

Psalms 140.11

Such are the ways of all who get gain by
violence;
it takes away the life of its possessors.

Proverbs 1.19

Do not envy a man of violence
and do not choose any of his ways;
for the perverse man is an abomination to
the Lord.

Proverbs 3.31—32

Violent men get riches.

Proverbs 11.16

The desire of the treacherous is for
violence.

Proverbs 13.2

A man of violence entices his neighbour
and leads him in a way that is not good.

Proverbs 16.29

If a man is burdened with the blood of
another,
let him be a fugitive until death.

Proverbs 28.17

Bloodthirsty men hate one who is
blameless.

Proverbs 29.10

Violence shall no more be heard in your
land,
devastation or destruction within your
borders.

Isaiah 60.18

Do no wrong or violence to the alien, the
fatherless, and the widow, nor shed innocent blood in this place.

Jeremiah 22.3

Is it too slight a thing . . . that they should
fill the land with violence, and provoke me
further to anger? . . . Therefore I will deal
in wrath; my eye will not spare, nor will I
have pity.

Ezekiel 8.17—18

If he begets a son who is a robber, a
shedder of blood . . . he shall surely die; his
blood shall be upon himself.

Ezekiel 18.10,13

Because you are guilty of blood, therefore blood shall pursue you.

Ezekiel 35.6

Put away violence and oppression, and execute justice and righteousness.

Ezekiel 45.9

For the violence done to your brother
    Jacob,
    shame shall cover you,
    and you shall be cut off for ever.

Obadiah 10

All who take the sword will perish by the sword.

Matthew 26.52

Soldiers also asked him, 'And we, what shall we do?' And he said to them, 'Rob no one by violence.'

Luke 3.14

And let him who has no sword sell his mantle and buy one.

Luke 22.36

Do not be hasty in the laying on of hands.

1 Timothy 5.22

Virtue

See also **Righteousness**

The Lord knows the way of the righteous.

Psalms 1.6

For thou dost bless the righteous, O Lord;
    thou dost cover him with favour as with a
    shield.

Psalms 5.12

God is with the generation of the
    righteous.

Psalms 14.5

The eyes of the Lord are toward the
    righteous,
    and his ears toward their cry.

Psalms 34.15

Many are the afflictions of the righteous;
    but the Lord delivers him out of them all.

Psalms 34.19

Cast your burden on the Lord,
    and he will sustain you;
he will never permit
    the righteous to be moved.

Psalms 55.22

The Lord loves the righteous . . .
    but the way of the wicked he brings
    to ruin.

Psalms 146.8–9

So you will walk in the way of good men
    and keep to the paths of the righteous.

Proverbs 2.20

A good wife is the crown of her husband,
    but she who brings shame is like
        rottenness in his bones.

Proverbs 12.4

The thoughts of the righteous are just;
    the counsels of the wicked are
        treacherous.

Proverbs 12.5

A righteous man who walks in his
        integrity —
    blessed are his sons after him!

Proverbs 20.7

A good wife who can find?
    She is far more precious than jewels.

Proverbs 31.10

Whatever is true, whatever is honourable, whatever is just, whatever is pure, whatever is lovely, whatever is gracious, if there is any excellence, if there is anything worthy of praise, think about these things.

Philippians 4.8

Show yourself in all respects a model of good deeds.

Titus 2.7

Visions

For God speaks in one way,
and in two, though man does not
perceive it.
In a dream, in a vision of the night,
when deep sleep falls upon men,
while they slumber on their beds,
then he opens the ears of men,
and terrifies them with warnings,
that he may turn man aside from his deed,
and cut off pride from man;
he keeps back his soul from the Pit,
his life from perishing by the sword.

Job 33.14—18

Visiting

Let your foot be seldom in your
neighbour's house,
lest he become weary of you and hate
you.

Proverbs 25.17

Vitality

See also **Energy**

He made my feet like hinds' feet,
and set me secure on the heights.
He trains my hands for war,
so that my arms can bend a bow of
bronze.

2 Samuel 22.34—35

Yea, by thee I can crush a troop;
and by my God I can leap over a wall.

Psalms 18.29

Then shall the lame man leap like a hart,
and the tongue of the dumb sing for joy.

Isaiah 35.6

They who wait for the Lord shall renew
their strength,
they shall mount up with wings like
eagles,
they shall run and not be weary,
they shall walk and not faint.

Isaiah 40.31

The people who know their God shall
stand firm and take action.

Daniel 11.32

Vocation

See also **Calling**

Now you are the body of Christ and
individually members of it. And God has
appointed in the church first apostles,
second prophets, third teachers, then
workers of miracles, then healers, helpers,
administrators, speakers in various kinds of
tongues.

1 Corinthians 12.27—28

Lead a life worthy of the calling to which
you have been called.

Ephesians 4.1

Be the more zealous to confirm your call
and election.

2 Peter 1.10

The Lamb will conquer them . . . and
those with him are called and chosen and
faithful.

Revelation 17.14

Volatility

A man of quick temper acts foolishly,
but a man of discretion is patient.

Proverbs 14.17

He who is slow to anger has great
understanding,
but he who has a hasty temper exalts
folly.

Proverbs 14.29

A hot-tempered man stirs up strife,
but he who is slow to anger quiets
contention.

Proverbs 15.18

Make no friendship with a man given to
anger,
nor go with a wrathful man,
lest you learn his ways
and entangle yourself in a snare.

Proverbs 22.24—25

W

Wages

See also **Reward**

Take this child away, and nurse him for me, and I will give you your wages.

Exodus 2.9

The wages of a hired servant shall not remain with you all night until the morning.

Leviticus 19.13

You shall not oppress a hired servant . . . you shall give him his hire on the day he earns it, before the sun goes down (for he is poor, and sets his heart upon it); lest he cry against you to the Lord, and it be sin in you.

Deuteronomy 24.14–15

The wage of the righteous leads to life,
the gain of the wicked to sin.

Proverbs 10.16

A wicked man earns deceptive wages.

Proverbs 11.18

Woe to him . . .
who makes his neighbour serve him for
nothing,
and does not give him his wages.

Jeremiah 22.13

Consider how you have fared. You have sown much, and harvested little; you eat, but you never have enough; you drink, but you never have your fill; you clothe yourselves, but no one is warm; and he who earns wages earns wages to put them into a bag with holes.

Haggai 1.5–6

I will draw near to you for judgment; I will be a swift witness . . . against those who oppress the hireling in his wages.

Malachi 3.5

Be content with your wages.

Luke 3.14

The labourer deserves his wages.

Luke 10.7

To one who works, his wages are not reckoned as a gift but as his due.

Romans 4.4

For the wages of sin is death.

Romans 6.23

Masters, treat your slaves justly and fairly, knowing that you also have a Master in heaven.

Colossians 4.1

The wages of the labourers who mowed your fields, which you kept back by fraud, cry out; and the cries of the harvesters have reached the ears of the Lord of hosts.

James 5.4

Waiting

See also **Patience**

My soul also is sorely troubled.
But thou, O Lord — how long?

Psalms 6.3

How long, O Lord? Wilt thou forget me
for ever?
How long wilt thou hide thy face from
me?
How long must I bear pain in my soul,
and have sorrow in my heart all the day?

How long shall my enemy be exalted over
   me?

Psalms 13.1–2

Our soul waits for the Lord;
   he is our help and shield.

Psalms 33.20

Be still before the Lord, and wait patiently
for him.

Psalms 37.7

I wait for the Lord, my soul waits,
   and in his word I hope;
my soul waits for the Lord
   more than watchmen for the morning.

Psalms 130.5–6

The Lord waits to be gracious to you;
   therefore he exalts himself to show mercy
     to you.

Isaiah 30.18

It is good that one should wait quietly
   for the salvation of the Lord.

Lamentations 3.26

In this hope we were saved . . . But if we
hope for what we do not see, we wait for it
with patience.

Romans 8.24–25

Waking

Bestir thyself, and awake for my right,
   for my cause, my God and my Lord!

Psalms 35.23

In the path of thy judgments,
   O Lord, we wait for thee;
thy memorial name
   is the desire of our soul.

Isaiah 26.8

Thy dead shall live, their bodies shall rise.
   O dwellers in the dust, awake and sing
     for joy!

Isaiah 26.19

Morning by morning he wakens,
   he wakens my ear

to hear as those who are taught.
The Lord God has opened my ear.

Isaiah 50.4–5

Awake, you drunkards, and weep.

Joel 1.5

Woe to you who desire the day of the
   Lord!
   Why would you have the day of
     the Lord?
It is darkness, and not light.

Amos 5.18

What do you mean, you sleeper? Arise
call upon your god! Perhaps the god wil
give a thought to us, that we do not perish

Jonah 1.6

For still the vision awaits its time;
   it hastens to the end — it will not lie.
If it seem slow, wait for it;
   it will surely come, it will not delay.

Habakkuk 2.

Why do you sleep? Rise and pray tha
you may not enter into temptation.

Luke 22.4

The creation waits with eager longing fo
the revealing of the sons of God.

Romans 8.1

It is full time now for you to wake fro
sleep. For salvation is nearer to us tha
when we first believed.

Romans 13.1

For through the Spirit, by faith, we wa
for the hope of righteousness.

Galatians 5

Awake, O sleeper, and arise from the
   dead,
   and Christ shall give you light.

Ephesians 5.

Walking

No good thing does the Lord withhold
   from those who walk uprightly.

Psalms 84.

He who walks in integrity walks securely,
but he who perverts his ways will be
found out.

Proverbs 10.9

He who walks in uprightness fears the
Lord,
but he who is devious in his ways despises
him.

Proverbs 14.2

He who walks in wisdom will be delivered.

Proverbs 28.26

The wise man has his eyes in his head, but
the fool walks in darkness.

Ecclesiastes 2.14

Come, let us go up to the mountain of the
Lord . . .
that he may teach us his ways
and that we may walk in his paths.

Isaiah 2.3

Come, let us walk
in the light of the Lord.

Isaiah 2.5

Your ears shall hear a word behind you,
saying, 'This is the way, walk in it,' when
you turn to the right or when you turn to
the left.

Isaiah 30.21

Who walks in darkness
and has no light,
yet trusts in the name of the Lord
and relies upon his God?

Isaiah 50.10

All his works are right and his ways are
just; and those who walk in pride he is able
to abase.

Daniel 4.37

Do two walk together,
unless they have made an
appointment? . . .
Surely the Lord God does nothing,
without revealing his secret
to his servants the prophets.

Amos 3.3,7

Walk while you have the light, lest the
darkness overtake you; he who walks in the
darkness does not know where he goes.

John 12.35

Let us hold true to what we have attained.

Philippians 3.16

Want

See also **Need, Poverty**

Because you did not serve the Lord your
God . . . you shall serve your enemies
whom the Lord will send against you, in
hunger and thirst, in nakedness, and in
want of all things.

Deuteronomy 28.47–48

The young lions suffer want and hunger;
but those who seek the Lord lack no
good thing.

Psalms 34.10

The belly of the wicked suffers want.

Proverbs 13.25

The plans of the diligent lead surely to
abundance,
but every one who is hasty comes only to
want.

Proverbs 21.5

Wantonness

Let us conduct ourselves becomingly as in
the day, not in revelling and drunkenness,
not in debauchery and licentiousness.

Romans 13.13

War

See also **Disarmament, Victory**

The Lord is a man of war;
the Lord is his name.

Exodus 15.3

When you go to war in your land against
the adversary who oppresses you, then you
shall sound an alarm with the trumpets, that

you may be remembered before the Lord
your God, and you shall be saved from your
enemies.

Numbers 10.9

When you go forth to war against your
enemies, and see horses and chariots and an
army larger than your own, you shall not be
afraid of them; for the Lord your God is
with you.

Deuteronomy 20.1

I pursued my enemies and destroyed them,
  and did not turn back until they were
    consumed.
I consumed them; I thrust them through,
  so that they did not rise;
  they fell under my feet.
For thou didst gird me with strength for the
    battle;
  thou didst make my assailants sink under
    me.
Thou didst make my enemies turn their
    backs to me,
  those who hated me, and I destroyed
    them.

2 Samuel 22.38–41

Fear not, and be not dismayed at this great
multitude; for the battle is not yours but
God's.

2 Chronicles 20.15

Do not be afraid of them. Remember the
Lord, who is great and terrible, and fight
for your brethren, your sons, your daughters, your wives, and your homes.

Nehemiah 4.14

In famine he will redeem you from death,
  and in war from the power of the sword.

Job 5.20

He trains my hands for war,
  so that my arms can bend a bow of
    bronze.

Psalms 18.34

Thou hast set up a banner for those who
    fear thee,
  to rally to it from the bow.

That thy beloved may be delivered,
  give victory by thy right hand and
    answer us!

Psalms 60.4–5

Plans are established by counsel;
  by wise guidance wage war.

Proverbs 20.18

The horse is made ready for the day of
    battle,
  but the victory belongs to the Lord.

Proverbs 21.31

You shall seek those who contend with
    you,
  but you shall not find them;
those who war against you
  shall be as nothing at all.
For I, the Lord your God,
  hold your right hand.

Isaiah 41.12–13

Prepare war,
  stir up the mighty men.
Let all the men of war draw near,
  let them come up.
Beat your ploughshares into swords,
  and your pruning hooks into spears;
let the weak say, 'I am a warrior.'

Joel 3.9–10

Awake, O sword.

Zechariah 13.7

The end is not yet. For nation will rise
against nation, and kingdom against kingdom; there will be earthquakes in various
places, there will be famines; this is but the
beginning of the birth-pangs.

Mark 13.7–8

The weapons of our warfare are not
worldly but have divine power to destroy
strongholds.

2 Corinthians 10.4

We are not contending against flesh and
blood, but against the principalities, against
the powers, against the world rulers of this
present darkness, against the spiritual hosts
of wickedness in the heavenly places.
Therefore take the whole armour of God

that you may be able to withstand in the evil day, and having done all, to stand.

Ephesians 6.12–13

Stand therefore, having girded your loins with truth, and having put on the breastplate of righteousness, and having shod your feet with the equipment of the gospel of peace; besides all these, taking the shield of faith, with which you can quench all the flaming darts of the evil one. And take the helmet of salvation, and the sword of the Spirit, which is the word of God.

Ephesians 6.14–17

In accordance with the prophetic utterances which pointed to you . . . you may wage the good warfare, holding faith and a good conscience.

1 Timothy 1.18–19

Fight the good fight of the faith.

1 Timothy 6.12

Warning

For God speaks in one way,
   and in two, though man does not
      perceive it.
In a dream, in a vision of the night,
   when deep sleep falls upon men,
   while they slumber on their beds,
then he opens the ears of men,
   and terrifies them with warnings,
that he may turn man aside from his deed,
   and cut off pride from man;
he keeps back his soul from the Pit,
   his life from perishing by the sword.

Job 33.14–18

Cry aloud, spare not,
   lift up your voice like a trumpet;
declare to my people their transgression.

Isaiah 58.1

If you warn the righteous man not to sin,
and he does not sin, he shall surely live,
because he took warning; and you will have
saved your life.

Ezekiel 3.21

If any one who hears the sound of the trumpet does not take warning, and the sword comes and takes him away, his blood shall up upon his own head. He heard the sound of the trumpet, and did not take warning; his blood shall be upon himself. But if he had taken warning, he would have saved his life.

Ezekiel 33.4–5

If you warn the wicked to turn from his way, and he does not turn from his way; he shall die in his iniquity, but you will have saved your life.

Ezekiel 33.9

Admonish the idlers.

1 Thessalonians 5.14

Waste

One who keeps company with harlots
   squanders his substance.

Proverbs 29.3

Why do you spend your money for that
      which is not bread,
   and your labour for that which does not
      satisfy?

Isaiah 55.2

Do not give dogs what is holy; and do not throw your pearls before swine.

Matthew 7.6

Watchfulness

Keep your heart with all vigilance;
   for from it flow the springs of life.

Proverbs 4.23

But of that day or that hour no one knows, not even the angels in heaven, nor the Son, but only the Father. Take heed, watch; for you do not know when the time will come. It is like a man going on a journey, when he leaves home and puts his servants in charge, each with his work, and commands the doorkeeper to be on the watch. Watch therefore — for you do not know when the master of the house will come, in the evening, or at midnight, or at cockcrow, or in the morning — lest he come suddenly and find you asleep. And what I say to you I say to all: Watch.

Mark 13.32—37

Let your loins be girded and your lamps burning.

Luke 12.35

But take heed to yourselves lest your hearts be weighed down with dissipation and drunkenness and cares of this life, and that day come upon you suddenly like a snare; for it will come upon all who dwell upon the face of the whole earth. But watch at all times, praying that you may have strength to escape all these things that will take place, and to stand before the Son of man.

Luke 21.34—36

Way

See, I have set before you this day life and good, death and evil. If you obey the commandments of the Lord your God which I command you this day, by loving the Lord your God, by walking in his ways, and by keeping his commandments and his statutes and his ordinances, then you shall live and multiply.

Deuteronomy 30.15—16

Lead me in the way everlasting!

Psalms 139.24

For the commandment is a lamp and the teaching a light,
 and the reproofs of discipline are the way of life.

Proverbs 6.23

In the path of righteousness is life,
 but the way of error leads to death.

Proverbs 12.28

There is a way which seems right to a man,
 but its end is the way to death.

Proverbs 14.12

And a highway shall be there,
 and it shall be called the Holy Way;
the unclean shall not pass over it,
 and fools shall not err therein.
No lion shall be there,
 nor shall any ravenous beast come up on it;
they shall not be found there,
 but the redeemed shall walk there.
And the ransomed of the Lord shall return,
 and come to Zion with singing;
everlasting joy shall be upon their heads;
 they shall obtain joy and gladness,
and sorrow and sighing shall flee away.

Isaiah 35.8—10

But this I admit to you, that according to the Way, which they call a sect, I worship the God of our fathers, believing everything laid down by the law or written in the prophets, having a hope in God which these themselves accept, that there will be a resurrection of both the just and the unjust.

Acts 24.14—15

Weakness

See also **Illness, Tiredness**

You shall not follow a multitude to do evil, not shall you bear witness in a suit, turning aside after a multitude, so as to pervert justice.

Exodus 23.2

Take courage! Do not let your hands be weak, for your work shall be rewarded.

2 Chronicles 15.7

Be gracious to me, O Lord, for I am languishing;
 O Lord, heal me, for my bones are troubled.

Psalms 6.2

He has pity on the weak and the needy.

Psalms 72.13

Like a muddied spring or a polluted fountain
 is a righteous man who gives way before the wicked.

Proverbs 25.26

Strengthen the weak hands,
and make firm the feeble knees.
Say to those who are of a fearful heart,
'Be strong, fear not!'

Isaiah 35.3—4

He gives power to the faint,
and to him who has no might he increases
strength.

Isaiah 40.29

When my soul fainted within me,
I remembered the Lord;
and my prayer came to thee.

Jonah 2.7

The spirit indeed is willing, but the flesh is
weak.

Matthew 26.41

I have shown you that by so toiling one
must help the weak.

Acts 20.35

I do not understand my own actions. For I
do not do what I want, but I do the very
thing I hate. Now if I do what I do not
want, I agree that the law is good. So then
it is no longer I that do it, but sin which
dwells within me. For I know that nothing
good dwells within me, that is, in my flesh.
I can will what is right, but I cannot do it.
For I do not do the good I want, but the
evil I do not want is what I do. Now if I do
what I do not want, it is no longer I that do
it, but sin which dwells within me.

Romans 7.15—20

I of myself serve the law of God with my
mind, but with my flesh I serve the law of
sin.

Romans 7.25

Likewise the Spirit helps us in our weakness; for we do not know how to pray as we
ought, but the Spirit himself intercedes for
us with sighs too deep for words.

Romans 8.26

As for the man who is weak in faith,
welcome him, but not for disputes over
opinions.

Romans 14.1

The weakness of God is stronger than
men.

1 Corinthians 1.25

Take care lest this liberty of yours somehow become a stumbling block to the weak.

1 Corinthians 8.9

The Lord . . . said to me, 'My grace is
sufficient for you, for my power is made
perfect in weakness.' I will all the more
gladly boast of my weaknesses, that the
power of Christ may rest upon me . . . for
when I am weak, then I am strong.

2 Corinthians 12.8—9

He was crucified in weakness, but lives by
the power of God. For we are weak in him,
but in dealing with you we shall live with
him by the power of God.

2 Corinthians 13.4

Help the weak, be patient with them all.

1 Thessalonians 5.14

We have not a high priest who is unable to
sympathise with our weaknesses.

Hebrews 4.15

Wealth

See also **Money, Possessions, Riches**

You shall remember the Lord your God,
for it is he who gives you power to get
wealth.

Deuteronomy 8.18

Both riches and honour come from thee,
and thou rulest over all.

1 Chronicles 29.12

Surely man goes about as a shadow!
Surely for naught are they in turmoil;
man heaps up, and knows not who will
gather!

Psalms 39.6

Man cannot abide in his pomp,
he is like the beasts that perish.

Psalms 49.20

Blessed is the man who fears the Lord,
who greatly delights in his
commandments! . . .

Wealth and riches are in his house;
  and his righteousness endures for ever.

Psalms 112.1,3

A rich man's wealth is his strong city.

Proverbs 10.15

Wealth hastily gotten will dwindle,
  but he who gathers little by little will
    increase it.

Proverbs 13.11

A good man leaves an inheritance to his
    children's children,
  but the sinner's wealth is laid up for the
    righteous.

Proverbs 13.22

A rich man's worth is his strong city,
  and like a high wall protecting him.

Proverbs 18.11

Wealth brings many new friends.

Proverbs 19.4

He who loves money will not be satisfied
with money; nor he who loves wealth, with
gain: this also is vanity.

Ecclesiastes 5.10

As he came from his mother's womb he
shall go again, naked as he came, and shall
take nothing for his toil, which he may
carry away in his hand. This also is a grievous evil: just as he came, so shall he go;
and what gain has he that he toiled for the
wind, and spent all his days in darkness and
grief, in much vexation and sickness and
resentment?

Ecclesiastes 5.15–17

Every man also to whom God has given
wealth and possessions and power to enjoy
them, and to accept his lot and find enjoyment in his toil — this is the gift of God.

Ecclesiastes 5.19

Woe to you that are rich, for you have
received your consolation.

Luke 6.24

For the sun rises with its scorching heat
and withers the grass; its flower falls, and its

beauty perishes. So will the rich man fade
away in the midst of his pursuits.

James 1.11

Come now, you rich, weep and howl for
the miseries that are coming upon you.
Your riches have rotted and your garments
are moth-eaten. Your gold and silver have
rusted, and their rust will be evidence
against you and will eat your flesh like fire.

James 5.1–3

Welcome

See also **Greeting**

Welcome one another, therefore, as Christ
has welcomed you, for the glory of God.

Romans 15.7

Wholeness

If then your whole body is full of light
having no part dark, it will be wholly
bright, as when a lamp with its rays gives
you light.

Luke 11.36

As the branch cannot bear fruit by itself
unless it abides in the vine, neither can you
unless you abide in me. I am the vine, you
are the branches. He who abides in me, and
I in him, he it is that bears much fruit.

John 15.4–5

We, though many, are one body in Christ
and individually members one of another.

Romans 12.5

He who is united to the Lord becomes one
spirit with him.

1 Corinthians 6.17

No man ever hates his own flesh, but
nourishes and cherishes it, as Christ does
the church, because we are members of his
body.

Ephesians 5.29

By this we know that we abide in him and
he in us, because he has given us of his own
Spirit.

1 John 4.13

Wickedness

See also **Sin, Ungodliness, Unrighteousness**

The Lord requite the evildoer according to
his wickedness!

> *2 Samuel 3.39*

As I have seen, those who plough iniquity
and sow trouble reap the same.

> *Job 4.8*

The tent of the wicked will be no more.

> *Job 8.22*

Yea, the light of the wicked is put out,
and the flame of his fire does not shine.

> *Job 18.5*

The heavens will reveal his iniquity,
and the earth will rise up against him.
The possessions of his house will be carried
away,
dragged off in the day of God's wrath.
This is the wicked man's portion from God,
the heritage decreed for him by God.

> *Job 20.27–29*

The wicked man is spared in the day of
calamity . . .
he is rescued in the day of wrath.

> *Job 21.30*

Therefore the wicked will not stand in the
judgment,
nor sinners in the congregation of the
righteous.

> *Psalms 1.5*

For thou art not a God who delights in
wickedness;
evil may not sojourn with thee.

> *Psalms 5.4*

let the evil of the wicked come to an
end,
but establish thou the righteous.

> *Psalms 7.9*

The Lord has made himself known, he has
executed judgment;
the wicked are snared in the work of their
own hands.

> *Psalms 9.16*

The wicked go astray from the womb,
they err from their birth, speaking lies.
They have venom like the venom of
a serpent,
like the deaf adder that stops its ear,
so that it does not hear the voice of
charmers
or of the cunning enchanter.
O God, break the teeth in their mouths;
tear out the fangs of the young lions,
O Lord!
Let them vanish like water that runs away;
like grass let them be trodden down and
wither.
Let them be like the snail which disolves
into slime,
like the untimely birth that never sees the
sun.
Sooner than your pots can feel the heat of
thorns,
whether green or ablaze, may he sweep
them away!

> *Psalms 58.3–9*

Morning by morning I will destroy
all the wicked in the land,
cutting off all the evildoers
from the city of the Lord.

> *Psalms 101.8*

The desire of the wicked man comes to
naught.

> *Psalms 112.10*

Do not enter the path of the wicked,
and do not walk in the way of evil men.

> *Proverbs 4.14*

The way of the wicked is like deep
darkness;
they do not know over what they
stumble.

> *Proverbs 4.19*

The Lord hates . . . a heart that devises
wicked plans,
feet that make haste to run to evil.

> *Proverbs 6.16,18*

Treasures gained by wickedness do not
profit.

> *Proverbs 10.2*

What the wicked dreads will come upon
him,
but the desire of the righteous will be
granted.

Proverbs 10.24

The fear of the Lord prolongs life,
but the years of the wicked will be short.

Proverbs 10.27

The hope of the righteous ends in
gladness,
but the expectation of the wicked comes
to naught.

Proverbs 10.28

When the wicked dies, his hope perishes,
and the expectation of the godless comes
to naught.

Proverbs 11.7

When it goes well with the righteous, the
city rejoices;
and when the wicked perish there are
shouts of gladness.

Proverbs 11.10

A man is not established by wickedness.

Proverbs 12.3

The words of the wicked lie in wait for
blood.

Proverbs 12.6

Haughty eyes and a proud heart,
the lamp of the wicked, are sin.

Proverbs 21.4

There is no discharge from war, nor will
wickedness deliver those who are given to
it.

Ecclesiastes 8.8

Woe to the wicked! It shall be ill with him,
for what his hands have done shall be
done to him.

Isaiah 3.11

Let the wicked forsake his way,
and the unrighteous man his thoughts;
let him return to the Lord, that he may
have mercy on him,

and to our God, for he will abundantly
pardon.

Isaiah 55.7

But the wicked are like the tossing sea;
for it cannot rest,
and its waters toss up mire and dirt.
There is no peace, says my God, for the
wicked.

Isaiah 57.20–21

We are not contending against flesh and
blood, but against the principalities, against
the powers, against the world rulers of this
present darkness.

Ephesians 6.12

Put away all filthiness and rank growth of
wickedness and receive with meekness the
implanted word, which is able to save your
souls.

James 1.2

We know that we are of God, and the
whole world is in the power of the evil one

1 John 5.1

Widows

See also **Bereavement**

You shall not afflict any widow or orphan.
If you do afflict them, and they cry out to
me, I will surely hear their cry; and my
wrath will burn, and I will kill you with the
sword, and your wives shall become widows
and your children fatherless.

Exodus 22.22–2

The Lord your God is God of gods and
Lord of lords . . . He executes justice for
the fatherless and the widow.

Deuteronomy 10.17–

Father of the fatherless and protector of
widows
is God in his holy habitation.

Psalms 68

The Lord tears down the house of the
  proud,
  but maintains the widow's boundaries.

Proverbs 15.25

Cease to do evil,
  learn to do good;
seek justice . . .
  plead for the widow.

Isaiah 1.16–17

Do no wrong or violence to the alien, the
fatherless, and the widow.

Jeremiah 22.3

Honour widows who are real widows. If a
widow has children or grandchildren, let
them first learn their religious duty to their
own family and make some return to their
parents; for this is acceptable in the sight of
God. She who is a real widow, and is left all
alone, has set her hope on God and continues in supplications and prayers night
and day; whereas she who is self-indulgent
is dead even while she lives.

1 Timothy 5.3–6

If any believing woman has relatives who
are widows, let her assist them; let the
church not be burdened, so that it may
assist those who are real widows.

1 Timothy 5.16

Religion that is pure and undefiled before
God and the Father is this: to visit orphans
and widows in their affliction, and to keep
oneself unstained from the world.

James 1.27

Will

Thy kingdom come,
Thy will be done,
  On earth as it is in heaven.

Matthew 6.10

Not every one who says to me, 'Lord,
Lord,' shall enter the kingdom of heaven,
but he who does the will of my Father who
in heaven.

Matthew 7.21

For whoever does the will of my Father in
heaven is my brother, and sister, and
mother.

Matthew 12.50

I seek not my own will but the will of him
who sent me.

John 5.30

God is at work in you, both to will and to
work for his good pleasure.

Philippians 2.13

The world passes away, and the lust of it;
but he who does the will of God abides for
ever.

1 John 2.17

Wine

See also **Alcohol, Intemperance**

Thou dost cause the grass to grow for the
  cattle,
  and plants for man to cultivate,
that he may bring forth food from the
  earth,
  and wine to gladden the heart of man.

Psalms 104.14–15

Wine is a mocker, strong drink a brawler;
  and whoever is led astray by it is not
  wise.

Proverbs 20.1

He who loves wine and oil will not be rich.

Proverbs 21.17

Be not among winebibbers . . .
for the drunkard and the glutton will
  come to poverty,
  and drowsiness will clothe a man
  with rags.

Proverbs 23.20–21

Who has woe? Who has sorrow?
  Who has strife? Who has complaining?
Who has wounds without cause?
  Who has redness of eyes?
Those who tarry long over wine,
  those who go to try mixed wine.
Do not look at wine when it is red,

when it sparkles in the cup
and goes down smoothly.

Proverbs 23.29–31

Give strong drink to him who is perishing,
and wine to those in bitter distress;
let them drink and forget their poverty,
and remember their misery no more.

Proverbs 31.6–7

Wine gladdens life.

Ecclesiastes 10.19

Wine and new wine
take away the understanding.

Hosea 4.11

Do not get drunk with wine, for that is
debauchery; but be filled with the Spirit.

Ephesians 5.18

Use a little wine for the sake of your
stomach.

1 Timothy 5.23

Winning

Do not be overcome by evil, but overcome
evil with good.

Romans 12.21

Wisdom

See also **Philosophy, Reason, Understanding**

Give thy servant therefore an understanding mind to govern thy people, that I may
discern between good and evil.

1 Kings 3.9

Wisdom is with the aged,
and understanding in length of days.

Job 12.12

But where shall wisdom be found?
And where is the place of understanding?
Man does not know the way to it,
and it is not found in the land of the
living.

Job 28.12–13

The price of wisdom is above pearls.

Job 28.18

It is not the old that are wise,
nor the aged that understand what is
right.

Job 32.9

The mouth of the righteous utters wisdom.

Psalms 37.30

My mouth shall speak wisdom;
the meditation of my heart shall be
understanding.

Psalms 49.3

Behold, thou desirest truth in the inward
being;
therefore teach me wisdom in my secret
heart.

Psalms 51.6

So teach us to number our days
that we may get a heart of wisdom.

Psalms 90.12

O Lord, how manifold are thy works!
In wisdom hast thou made them all.

Psalms 104.24

The fear of the Lord is the beginning of
wisdom.

Psalms 111.10

The wise man also may hear and increase
in learning.

Proverbs 1.5

For the Lord gives wisdom;
from his mouth come knowledge and
understanding.

Proverbs 2.6

For wisdom will come into your heart,
and knowledge will be pleasant to your
soul;
discretion will watch over you;
understanding will guard you;
delivering you from the way of evil,
from men of perverted speech.

Proverbs 2.10–1

The Lord by wisdom founded the earth.

Proverbs 3.1

I, wisdom, dwell in prudence,
and I find knowledge and discretion.

Proverbs 8.12

Wisdom has built her house,
she has set up her seven pillars.
She has slaughtered her beasts,
she has mixed her wine.

Proverbs 9.1–2

The wise of heart will heed commandments.

Proverbs 10.8

The teaching of the wise is a fountain of
life,
that one may avoid the snares of death.

Proverbs 13.14

He who gets wisdom loves himself.

Proverbs 19.8

Apply your mind to instruction
and your ear to words of knowledge.

Proverbs 23.12

He who loves wisdom makes his father
glad.

Proverbs 29.3

For in much wisdom is much vexation,
and he who increases knowledge
increases sorrow.

Ecclesiastes 1.18

The wise man has his eyes in his head, but
the fool walks in darkness; and yet I perceived that one fate comes to all of them.
Then I said to myself, 'What befalls the fool
will befall me also; why then have I been so
very wise?' And I said to myself that this
also is vanity.

Ecclesiastes 2.14–15

Wisdom is good with an inheritance,
an advantage to those who see the sun.
For the protection of wisdom is like the
protection of money;

and the advantage of knowledge is that
wisdom preserves
the life of him who has it.

Ecclesiastes 7.11–12

Wisdom gives strength to the wise man
more than ten rulers that are in a city.

Ecclesiastes 7.19

A man's wisdom makes his face shine.

Ecclesiastes 8.1

Wisdom is better than might, though the
poor man's wisdom is despised, and his
words are not heeded.

Ecclesiastes 9.16

The words of the wise heard in quiet are
better than the shouting of a ruler among
fools.

Ecclesiastes 9.17

Let not the wise man glory in his wisdom
. . . but let him who glories glory in this,
that he understands and knows me, that I
am the Lord.

Jeremiah 9.23–24

Because you consider yourself
as wise as a god,
therefore, behold, I will bring strangers
upon you,
the most terrible of the nations;
and they shall draw their swords against the
beauty of your wisdom
and defile your splendour.
They shall thrust you down into the Pit,
and you shall die the death of the slain
in the heart of the seas.

Ezekiel 28.6–8

Blessed be the name of God for ever and
ever,
to whom belong wisdom and might.

Daniel 2.20

He gives wisdom to the wise
and knowledge to those who have
understanding.

Daniel 2.21

Behold, I send you out as sheep in the
midst of wolves; so be wise as serpents and

innocent as doves . . . he who endures to the end will be saved.

Matthew 10.16,22

The Son of man has come eating and drinking; and you say, 'Behold, a glutton and a drunkard, a friend of tax collectors and sinners!' Yet wisdom is justified by all her children.

Luke 7.34—35

Has not God made foolish the wisdom of the world?

1 Corinthians 1.20

For the foolishness of God is wiser than men, and the weakness of God is stronger than men.

1 Corinthians 1.25

He is the source of your life in Christ Jesus, whom God made our wisdom.

1 Corinthians 1.30

We impart a secret and hidden wisdom of God, which God decreed before the ages for our glorification.

1 Corinthians 2.7

The wisdom of this world is folly with God.

1 Corinthians 3.19

I do not cease . . . in my prayers, that the God of our Lord Jesus Christ, the Father of glory, may give you a spirit of wisdom and of revelation.

Ephesians 1.16—17

If any of you lacks wisdom, let him ask God, who gives to all men generously and without reproaching.

James 1.5

Who is wise and understanding among you? By his good life let him show his works in the meekness of wisdom.

James 3.13

The wisdom from above is first pure, then peaceable, gentle, open to reason, full of mercy and good fruits, without uncertainty or insincerity.

James 3.17

Wit

To make an apt answer is a joy to a man, and a word in season, how good it is!

Proverbs 15.23

Witchcraft

See also Magic, Occult, Superstition

You shall not permit a sorceress to live.

Exodus 22.18

You shall not eat any flesh with the blood in it. You shall not practise augury or witchcraft.

Leviticus 19.26

Do not turn to mediums or wizards; do not seek them out, to be defiled by them.

Leviticus 19.31

There shall not be found among you any one who . . . practises divination, a soothsayer, or an augur, or a sorcerer, or a charmer, or a medium, or a wizard, or a necromancer.

Deuteronomy 18.10—11

Now the works of the flesh are plain . . . idolatry, sorcery . . . those who do such things shall not inherit the kingdom of God.

Galatians 5.19—21

Witnessing

The word is near you, on your lips and in your heart (that is, the word of faith which we preach); because, if you confess with your lips that Jesus is Lord and believe in your heart that God raised him from the dead, you will be saved.

Romans 10.8—

We put no obstacle in any one's way, so that no fault may be found with our ministry, but as servants of God we commend ourselves in every way: through great endurance, in afflictions, hardships, calamities, beatings, imprisonments, tumults labours, watching, hunger; by purity, knowledge, forbearance, kindness, the Holy Spirit, genuine love, truthful speech, and the power of God; with the weapons of righteousness . . . in honour and dishonour, in ill repute and good repute. We are treated as impostors, and yet are true; as unknown, and yet well known; as dying, and behold we live; as punished, and yet not killed; as sorrowful, yet always rejoicing; as poor, yet making many rich; as having nothing, and yet possessing everything.

2 Corinthians 6.3–10

Wives

See also **Betrothal, Marriage**

The Lord God said, 'It is not good that the man should be alone; I will make him a helper fit for him.'

Genesis 2.18

Then the man said,
　'This at last is bone of my bones
　　and flesh of my flesh;
　she shall be called Woman,
　　because she was taken out of Man.'
Therefore a man leaves his father and his mother and cleaves to his wife, and they become one flesh.

Genesis 2.23–24

You shall not covet your neighbour's wife.

Exodus 20.17

Rejoice in the wife of your youth,
　a lovely hind, a graceful doe.
Let her affection fill you at all times with
　　delight,
　be infatuated always with her love.

Proverbs 5.18–19

A good wife is the crown of her husband,
　but she who brings shame is like
　　rottenness in his bones.

Proverbs 12.4

He who finds a wife finds a good thing,
　and obtains favour from the Lord.

Proverbs 18.22

House and wealth are inherited from
　fathers,
　but a prudent wife is from the Lord.

Proverbs 19.14

It is better to live in a corner of the
　housetop
than in a house shared with a contentious
　woman.

Proverbs 25.24

A good wife who can find?
　She is far more precious than jewels.

Proverbs 31.10

Enjoy life with the wife whom you love, all the days of your vain life which he has given you.

Ecclesiastes 9.9

Because of the temptation to immorality, each man should have his own wife and each woman her own husband.

1 Corinthians 7.2

A wife is bound to her husband as long as he lives. If the husband dies, she is free to be married to whom she wishes, only in the Lord.

1 Corinthians 7.39

Wives, be subject to your husbands, as to the Lord. For the husband is the head of the wife as Christ is the head of the church, his body, and is himself its Saviour. As the church is subject to Christ, so let wives also be subject in everything to their husbands.

Ephesians 5.22–24

Husbands should love their wives as their own bodies. He who loves his wife loves himself.

Ephesians 5.28

Wives, be subject to your husbands, as is fitting in the Lord. Husbands, love your wives, and do not be harsh with them.

Colossians 3.18–19

Husbands, live considerately with your wives.

1 Peter 3.7

Women

The Lord God caused a deep sleep to fall upon the man, and while he slept took one of his ribs and closed up its place with flesh; and the rib which the Lord God had taken from the man he made into a woman.

Genesis 2.21–22

To the woman he said,
'I will greatly multiply your pain in
    childbearing;
  in pain you shall bring forth children,
yet your desire shall be for your husband,
  and he shall rule over you.'

Genesis 3.16

Like a gold ring in a swine's snout
  is a beautiful woman without discretion.

Proverbs 11.22

A continual dripping on a rainy day
  and a contentious woman are alike.

Proverbs 27.15

Under three things the earth trembles;
  under four it cannot bear up:
a slave when he becomes king,
  and a fool when he is filled with food;
an unloved woman when she gets a
    husband,
  and a maid when she succeeds her
    mistress.

Proverbs 30.21–23

Charm is deceitful, and beauty is vain,
  but a woman who fears the Lord is to be
    praised.

Proverbs 31.30

Woman is the glory of man. (For man was not made from woman, but woman from man. Neither was man created for woman, but woman for man.)

1 Corinthians 11.8–9

In the Lord woman is not independent of man nor man of woman; for as woman was made from man, so man is now born of woman. And all things are from God.

1 Corinthians 11.11–12

As in all the churches of the saints, the women should keep silence in the churches. For they are not permitted to speak, but should be subordinate, as even the law says. If there is anything they desire to know, let them ask their husbands at home.

1 Corinthians 14.34–35

Women should adorn themselves modestly and sensibly in seemly apparel, not with braided hair or gold or pearls or costly attire but by good deeds, as befits women who profess religion. Let a woman learn in silence with all submissiveness. I permit no woman to teach or to have authority over men; she is to keep silent. For Adam was formed first, then Eve; and Adam was not deceived, but the woman was deceived and became a transgressor. Yet woman will be saved through bearing children, if she continues in faith and love and holiness, with modesty.

1 Timothy 2.9–15

Wonders

Seek the Lord and his strength,
  seek his presence continually!
Remember the wonderful works that he has
    done,
  the wonders he wrought, the judgments
    he uttered.

1 Chronicles 16.11–12

He . . . does great things beyond
    understanding,
  and marvellous things without number.

Job 9.5,10

Stop and consider the wondrous works of
    God.
Do you know how God lays his command
    upon them,
  and causes the lightning of his cloud to
    shine?
Do you know the balancings of the clouds,
  the wondrous works of him who is perfect
    in knowledge.

Job 37.14–16

Thou art the God who workest wonders,
who hast manifested thy might among the
peoples.

Psalms 77.14

Tell of his salvation from day to day.
Declare his glory among the nations,
his marvellous works among all the
peoples!

Psalms 96.2–3

O give thanks to the Lord of lords,
for his steadfast love endures for ever.
to him who alone does great wonders,
for his steadfast love endures for ever.

Psalms 136.3–4

For thou didst form my inward parts,
thou didst knit me together in my
mother's womb.
I praise thee, for thou art fearful and
wonderful.
Wonderful are thy works!

Psalms 139.13–14

Three things are too wonderful for me;
four I do not understand:
the way of an eagle in the sky,
the way of a serpent on a rock,
the way of a ship on the high seas,
and the way of a man with a maiden.

Proverbs 30.18–19

Work

The Lord God took the man and put him
in the garden of Eden to till it and keep it.

Genesis 2.15

In all toil there is profit.

Proverbs 14.23

There is nothing better for a man than that
he should eat and drink, and find enjoyment in his toil. This also, I saw, is from the
hand of God; for apart from him who can
eat or who can have enjoyment?

Ecclesiastes 2.24–25

Then I saw that all toil and all skill in work
come from a man's envy of his neighbour.
This also is vanity and a striving after wind.

Ecclesiastes 4.4

Whatever your hand finds to do, do it with
your might; for there is no work or thought
or knowledge or wisdom in Sheol, to which
you are going.

Ecclesiastes 9.10

The labourer deserves his food.

Matthew 10.11

It is the hard-working farmer who ought to
have the first share of the crops.

2 Timothy 2.6

Worldliness

He has put eternity into man's mind, yet
so that he cannot find out what God has
done from the beginning to the end.

Ecclesiastes 3.11

As for what was sown among thorns, this
is he who hears the word, but the cares of
the world and the delight in riches choke
the word, and it proves unfruitful.

Matthew 13.22

You are from below, I am from above;
you are of this world, I am not of this
world.

John 8.23

My kingship is not of this world.

John 18.36

Do not be conformed to this world but be
transformed by the renewal of your mind,
that you may prove what is the will of God,
what is good and acceptable and perfect.

Romans 12.2

Set your minds on things that are above,
not on things that are on earth.

Colossians 3.2

The grace of God has appeared . . . training us to renounce . . . worldly passions.

Titus 2.11–12

Do you not know that friendship withs the
world is enmity with God?

James 4.4

Do not love the world or the things in the world. If any one loves the world, love for the Father is not in him.

1 John 2.15

They are of the world, therefore what they say is of the world, and the world listens to them. We are of God.

1 John 4.5—6

Worldly Wisdom

He takes the wise in their own craftiness; and the schemes of the wily are brought to a quick end.

Job 5.13

Be not wise in your own eyes.

Proverbs 3.7

A rich man is wise in his own eyes, but a poor man who has understanding will find him out.

Proverbs 28.11

Woe to those who are wise in their own eyes, and shrewd in their own sight!

Isaiah 5.21

Worry

See also **Anxiety, Despair, Doubt**

Cast your burden on the Lord, and he will sustain you.

Psalms 55.22

Trouble befalls the income of the wicked.

Proverbs 15.6

Remove vexation from your mind, and put away pain from your body.

Ecclesiastes 11.10

Do not be anxious about tomorrow, for tomorrow will be anxious for itself. Let the day's own trouble be sufficient for the day.

Matthew 6.34

Worship

See also **Praise**

You shall bow yourselves to him, and to him you shall sacrifice.

2 Kings 17.36

All the ends of the earth shall remember and turn to the Lord; and all the families of the nations shall worship before him.

Psalms 22.27

By day the Lord commands his steadfast love; and at night his song is with me, a prayer to the God of my life.

Psalms 42.8

To thee, O Lord, do I lift up my soul.

Psalms 86.4

O come, let us worship and bow down, let us kneel before the Lord, our Maker! For he is our God.

Psalms 95.6—7

Worship the Lord in holy array; tremble before him, all the earth!

Psalms 96.9

He is exalted over all the peoples. Let them praise thy great and terrible name! Holy is he! Mighty King.

Psalms 99.2—

I was glad when they said to me, 'Let us go to the house of the Lord!'

Psalms 122.

You shall worship the Lord your God and him only shall you serve.

Matthew 4.1

God is spirit, and those who worship him must worship in spirit and truth.

John 4.2

If any one is a worshipper of God and doe his will, God listens to him.

John 9.3

Therefore God has highly exalted him and bestowed on him the name which is above every name, that at the name of Jesus every knee should bow, in heaven and on earth and under the earth, and every tongue confess that Jesus Christ is Lord, to the glory of God the Father.

Philippians 2.9–11

Let all God's angels worship him.

Hebrews 1.6

The twenty-four elders fall down before him who is seated on the throne and worship him who lives for ever and ever; they cast their crowns before the throne.

Revelation 4.10

Fear God and give him glory, for the hour of his judgment has come; and worship him who made heaven and earth, the sea and the fountains of water.

Revelation 14.7

Who shall not fear and glorify thy name,
  O Lord?
For thou alone art holy.

Revelation 15.4

Worth

See also **Merit**

He who does not take his cross and follow me is not worthy of me.

Matthew 10.38

The wedding is ready, but those invited were not worthy. Go therefore to the thoroughfares, and invite to the marriage feast as many as you find.

Matthew 22.8–9

Bear fruits that befit repentance.

Luke 3.8

Lead a life worthy of the Lord, fully pleasing to him, bearing fruit in every good work and increasing in the knowledge of God.

Colossians 1.10

Lead a life worthy of God.

1 Thessalonians 2.12

We always pray for you, that our God may make you worthy of his call.

2 Thessalonians 1.11

Worthy is the Lamb who was slain, to receive power and wealth and wisdom and might and honour and glory and blessing!

Revelation 5.12

Wrong

See also **Sin, Unrighteousness**

Deliver from the hand of the oppressor him who has been robbed.

Jeremiah 22.3

The wrongdoer will be paid back for the wrong he has done.

Colossians 3.25

What credit is it, if when you do wrong and are beaten for it you take it patiently?

1 Peter 2.20

X

Xenophobia

You shall not wrong a stranger or oppress him.

Exodus 22.21

When a stranger sojourns with you in your land, you shall not do him wrong. The stranger who sojourns with you shall be to you as the native among you, and you shall love him as yourself.

Leviticus 19.33−34

You shall have one law for the sojourner and for the native.

Leviticus 24.22

Cursed be he who perverts the justice due to the sojourner.

Deuteronomy 27.19

Y

Yearning

As a hart longs
    for flowing streams,
so longs my soul
    for thee, O God.
My soul thirsts for God,
for the living God.
When shall I come and behold
    the face of God?

Psalms 42.1−2

O that I had wings like a dove!

Psalms 55.6

My soul longs, yea, faints
    for the courts of the Lord.

Psalms 84.2

My soul is consumed with longing
    for thy ordinances at all times.

Psalms 119.20

Out of the depths I cry to thee, O Lord!

Psalms 130.1

My soul yearns for thee in the night,
    my spirit within me earnestly seeks thee.

Isaiah 26.9

Blessed are those who hunger and thirst
for righteousness, for they shall be satisfied.

Matthew 5.6

Jesus said to her, 'Every one who drinks of
his water will thirst again, but whoever
drinks of the water that I shall give him will
never thirst; the water that I shall give him
will become in him a spring of water welling
up to eternal life.' The woman said to him,
'Sir, give me this water, that I may not
thirst, nor come here to draw.'

John 4.13−15

The creation waits with eager longing for
the revealing of the sons of God.

Romans 8.19

Like newborn babes, long for the pure
spiritual milk, that by it you may grow up to
salvation.

1 Peter 2.2

Come, Lord Jesus!

Revelation 22.20

Yield

See also **Harvest**

God said, 'Let the earth put forth vegeta-
tion, plants yielding seed, and fruit trees
bearing fruit in which is their seed, each
according to its kind, upon the earth.'

Genesis 1.11

Yield yourselves to the Lord.

2 Chronicles 30.8

Youth

See also **Children**

Thou, O Lord, art my hope,
    my trust, O Lord, from my youth.
Upon thee I have leaned from my birth;
    thou art he who took me from my
        mother's womb.
My praise is continually of thee.

Psalms 71.5−6

Bless the Lord, O my soul,
    and forget not all his benefits . . .
who satisfies you with good as long as
    you live

so that your youth is renewed like the
    eagle's.

Psalms 103.2,5

The glory of young men is their strength.

Proverbs 20.29

Better is a poor and wise youth than an old
and foolish king, who will no longer take
advice, even though he had gone from
prison to the throne or in his own kingdom
had been born poor.

Ecclesiastes 4.13—14

Rejoice, O young man, in your youth, and
let your heart cheer you in the days of your
youth.

Ecclesiastes 11.9

For youth and the dawn of life are vanity.

Ecclesiastes 11.10

He will feed his flock like a shepherd,
  he will gather the lambs in his arms,
he will carry them in his bosom.

Isaiah 40.11

Do not say, 'I am only a youth';
for to all to whom I send you you shall go,
and whatever I command you you shall
    speak.
Be not afraid of them,
for I am with you to deliver you, says the
    Lord.

Jeremiah 1.7—8

It is good for a man that he bear
  the yoke in his youth.
Let him sit alone in silence
  when he has laid it on him;
let him put his mouth in the dust —
  there may yet be hope.

Lamentations 3.27—29

Let no one despise your youth, but set the
believers an example in speech and
conduct.

1 Timothy 4.12

So shun youthful passions and aim at righteousness, faith, love, and peace, along with
those who call upon the Lord from a pure
heart.

2 Timothy 2.22

Urge the younger men to control themselves.

Titus 2.6

You that are younger be subject to the
elders. Clothe yourselves, all of you, with
humility toward one another, for 'God
opposes the proud.'

1 Peter 5.5

I write to you, fathers, because you know
him who is from the beginning. I write to
you, young men, because you are strong,
and the word of God abides in you, and you
have overcome the evil one.

1 John 2.14

Z

Zeal

Whatever is commanded by the God of heaven, let it be done in full.

Ezra 7.23

Whatever your hand finds to do, do it with your might.

Ecclesiastes 9.10

Never flag in zeal, be aglow with the Spirit, serve the Lord.

Romans 12.11

Whatever your task, work heartily, as serving the Lord and not men.

Colossians 3.23

Now who is there to harm you if you are zealous for what is right?

1 Peter 3.13

So be zealous and repent.

Revelation 3.19